from Peter & Dennis Ashenhurst

The Royal Geographical Society
HISTORY OF
WORLD
EXPLORATION

The Royal Geographical Society
HISTORY OF
WORLD EXPLORATION

General Editor John Keay

GUILD PUBLISHING
LONDON · NEW YORK · SYDNEY · TORONTO

Managing Editor	Trevor Dolby
Project Editor	Alison Leach
Design Editor	Chris Pow
Editor	John Bailie
Designer	Jo Tapper
Picture Research	Judy Todd
Production	Helen Seccombe

The Royal Geographical Society and the publishers
would like to thank the following for their help in the
preparation of this book:
Rufus Bellamy; Peter Clark; Professor Ronald Cooke;
Crispin Day; Peter Derlien; Dr David Drewry (British
Antarctic Survey); Rachel Duncan (RGS Picture
Library); Sylvia Earle; Commander Angus Erskine, RN;
Dr Nick Fleming (Institute of Oceanographic Sciences);
Robin Hanbury-Tenison; Dr Geoffrey Hattersley-Smith;
Robert Headland (Scott Polar Research Institute);
Dr and Mrs Fred Jacka (Mawson Institute for Antarctic
Research, Adelaide); Nicholas McWilliam; Professor
David Quinn; David Wileman; Dr Richard Winton.
Florence Baker's letter to her step-daughter on page
103 is quoted by kind permission of Mrs Anne Baker.

This edition published in 1991 by Guild Publishing by
arrangement with Paul Hamlyn Publishing,
an imprint of Reed International Books,
Michelin House, 81 Fulham Road, London SW3 6RB.

Copyright © Reed International Books Limited 1991.

CN 6516

Typeset by Dorchester Typesetting Group Ltd

Produced by Mandarin Offset
Printed in Hong Kong

Illustration Acknowledgements
The publishers would like to thank all the staff at
the RGS who have helped in researching the illus-
trations for this book, in particular Rachel Duncan
of the Picture Library and David Wileman, Jayne
Dunlop and Edwin Trout of the Library for their
patience and unfailing good humour. Pictures are
from the collections at the RGS with the exception
of those from the following sources:
Bibliothèque Nationale, Paris 43, 169; Bodleian
Library, Oxford 44; Osvaldo Böhm/Museo Correr,
Venice 28; Bridgeman Art Library, London 77
(RGS), 80 bottom (RGS), 188 (Down House,
Downe), 188-9 (Royal College of Surgeons,
London), 190 (Royal Naval College, London); The
British Library, London 39 top, 40, 57, 95, 136-7,
138-9, 180-1, 181; reproduced by courtesy of the
Trustees of the British Museum, London 16, 52,
134, 137, 149 top, 176, 203; O. B., Brown and R.
H. Evans, University of Miami, Rosenstiel School of
Marine and Atmospheric Science 285; Camera
Press, London/Horst Munzig 302 top; Amon
Carter Museum, Fort Worth 163 top (1961.195
'Lewis and Clark on the Lower Columbia' by
Charles M. Russell); Bruce Coleman Limited,
Uxbridge 200 (Nicholas Devore), 245 top
(S. Nielsen); Duchy of Cornwall, London 20; Mary
Evans Picture Library, London 21, 51, 63, 105
bottom, 292; Werner Forman Archive, London 17,
38; Fotomas Index, London 153; Photographie
Giraudon, Paris 46; W. L., Gore & Associates (expe-
dition sponsors) 306 left; Richard Greenhill/Severin
Archive 14, 302 bottom; Sonia Halliday 34 top;
Robin Hanbury-Tenison/RGS 300; John Hillelson
Agency Limited, London/Roland Michaud 33;
Michael Holford 208; R. J. Hopcroft 152; Hulton
Picture Company, London 72, 108, 230; Icewalk
Future Limited, Bedale 304; Institute of Oceano-
graphic Sciences Deacon Laboratory, Godalming
309; International Harvester Company, New York
163; Jet Propulsion Laboratory, Pasadena/Seasat
293 bottom; S. J. Kleinberg 307; Kobe City
Museum 2; Anita McConnell 281 bottom, 284 top
right and bottom left, 286; Mansell Collection,
London 232 bottom; Marconi Company Limited,
Stanmore 294 top; Roger Mear/RGS 303; copyright
© 1979 by The Metropolitan Museum of Art, New
York, Gift of J. Pierpont Morgan 1900 (00.18.2) 166
top; Marion and Tony Morrison/South American
Pictures 164; Musée de l'Homme, Paris 149
bottom; National Archives of Canada, Ottawa 147;
National Art Gallery, Wellington 217 bottom;
National Library of Australia, Canberra/Rex Nan
Kivell Collection 213, 221; National Maritime
Museum, Greenwich 47, 178 bottom, 207, 212, 215,
244, 246; Collection of the National Palace
Museum, Taiwan, Republic of China 27, 42; by
courtesy of the National Portrait Gallery, London
178 top, 248 bottom; National Postal Museum,
London 249 bottom left; Natural Environment
Research Council, Swindon 308; Carlos Navajas 19;
Joseph Needham, *Science and Civilisation in China*,
Vol. 4, Part III (C.U.P., 1971) 45 bottom; Octopus
Publishing Group Ltd 15, 23,25, 34 bottom, 45, 48,
89, 101 top, 154, 202, 220, 245 bottom, 253, 258,
262; Rob Palmer 313, Planet Earth Pictures,
London 128 (Dave Lyons), 236 (Jim Brandenburg),
278 (Peter Scoones), 310 (Flip Schulke); Popperfoto,
London 66; Josephine Powell 32; reproduced by
gracious permission of Her Majesty The Queen
180; Richmond upon Thames Council/RGS 100 left;
Royal Botanic Gardens, Kew 121 top; St Paul
Pioneer Press Dispatch 306 right; reproduced by
permission of the Trustees of the Science Museum,
London 166 bottom, 282 right; Science Photo
Library, London/NASA 305; Scientific Exploration
Society/Mike Christy 312; Scott Polar Research
Institute, Cambridge 251 bottom, 266 right, 272
inset, 294 bottom; Smithsonian Institution, Wash-
ington, Bureau of American Ethnology 160; Society
for Cultural Relations with the USSR, London 254;
Spectrum Colour Library, London 88, 161, 228;
Syndication International, London 233; The Tate
Gallery, London 217 top; Judy Todd 196, 234 right,
235; Transantarctic Expedition 275 bottom; U.S.
Navy 293 top left (Lt. R G. Claypool) and right;
Universitets Oldsaksamling, Oslo 37; Michael
Ward/RGS 50, 59, 85; Bradford Washburn 311
bottom; Weidenfeld & Nicolson Ltd, London 250;
Wellcome Institute for the History of Medicine,
London 109; Whitby Museum/Caedmon of Whitby
242 bottom left; Zisterzienserstift Zwettl Bibliothek
182.

CONTENTS

Chronologies for each chapter researched and written by Shane Winser

John Keay

Mark Greengrass

John Hemming

Selma Huxley Barkham

Anita McConnell

Dorothy Middleton

David Mountfield

Ann Savours

John Ure

Nigel Winser

Shane Winser

About the contributors

John Keay Writer and broadcaster specializing in Asian exploration. Travelled extensively in the Orient researching material for numerous documentary programmes. Author of several books including *When Men and Mountains Meet* and *The Gilgit Game*. Latest work is a history of the East India Company.

Dr Mark Greengrass Senior Lecturer, Department of History, University of Sheffield, and Director of the Hartlib Papers Project, a major research project in the humanities. Associate Editor of *Historical Atlas of World History*.

Dr John Hemming Director and Secretary of the Royal Geographical Society since 1975. Led the RGS Maracá Rainforest Project 1987–8. His many books include *The Conquest of the Incas*, *Red Gold*, *Amazon Frontier*, *Maracá Rainforest Island* and *Roraima: Brazil's northernmost frontier*.

Dr Selma Huxley Barkham Gold Medallist of the Royal Canadian Geographical Society; Order of Canada; Doctor of Letters (*honoris causa*), University of Windsor. Author of

numerous articles in historical and geographical journals in UK, Canada and Spain, and editor of Vol 3 of the Series ITSASOA.

Dr Anita McConnell Member of the Council of the Royal Geographical Society. Formerly a curator at the Science Museum, London, working with the Earth Science collections. Regular contributor to learned journals and magazines including *The Geographical Magazine*, *Annals of Science* and *Notes & Records of the Royal Society*.

Dorothy Middleton Honorary Vice-President of the Royal Geographical Society. Publications include *Victorian Lady Travellers*. Lectured extensively in UK and USA. Member of the Council of the Hakluyt Society.

David Mountfield Fellow of the Royal Geographical Society. Author of numerous books on history, geography and exploration including *History of Polar Exploration* and *History of African Exploration*. Special interest in the early navigators and Polynesian travel.

Ann Savours Worked at Scott Polar Research Institute, Cambridge, before becoming Assistant Keeper of the

National Maritime Museum, London, 1970-87. Editor of *The Discovery Diary of Edward Wilson, 1901-04*, and author of *Scott's Last Voyage*. Hon. Sec., Society for Nautical Research.

Sir John Ure, KCMG, LVO Member of HM Diplomatic Service. Held many overseas posts, most recently as Ambassador to Sweden. While Ambassador to Cuba, 1979-81, and to Brazil, 1984-7, travelled extensively in Central and South America. Author of *Cucumber Sandwiches in the Andes*, *The Quest for Captain Morgan* and *Trespassers on the Amazon*.

Nigel Winser Assistant Director and Expedition Officer of the Royal Geographical Society. Since 1977 responsible for RGS expedition activities, which have included large international multi-disciplinary projects.

Shane Winser Information Officer of the Royal Geographical Society with special responsibility for the Expedition Advisory Centre. Has accompanied her husband, Nigel Winser, on many RGS expeditions. Regular contributor to *The Geographical Magazine*.

ABOUT THE MAPS

Compiled and edited by **Eric Smith**
Cartography **Nick Skelton**

The maps showing explorers' routes in colour have been created especially for this book to illustrate the main journeys discussed in each section. In the vast majority of cases it was possible to locate a required route among the wealth of maps and journals published by the Royal Geographical Society; in these cases the route only had to be adapted to

the projection of the maps for this book. A few routes, however, initially proved to be more elusive but reference for these was found in the Map Room of the British Library. I should particularly like to express my gratitude to Dr Helen Wallis, formerly Map Curator at the British Library, for permission to reproduce a number of tracks that she plotted as part of her D. Phil. thesis entitled *The exploration of the South Sea, 1519 to 1644* (Oxford, 1953). In the case of a very few routes no map seemed to exist, so the track was plotted in accordance with the published

account of the journey in question.

Although the maps show all the important place names and physical features in each area, the limitations of space unfortunately prevented us from including all the names mentioned in each section. Similarly, where a number of people sailed in the same area it is impossible to show each person's route in its entirety. In the case of a very few short journeys – notably in the Antarctic – it was decided that it would be too difficult to attempt to include these but relevant information has been retained in the key. These routes are designated by an asterisk (∗) in the key. **E.S.**

INTRODUCTION

Man is a highly mobile creature, migrating and travelling to every part of the world. In this we are not unique. Migratory birds regularly navigate over amazing distances; whale and sharks roam the oceans; salmon, eels and other fish cross the seas in their breeding cycles; wildebeest, caribou and other animals make great migrations, as do locusts and other plague insects; some families of bat are found in every continent. What sets us apart is the ability to discover. Other creatures share our curiosity; but man alone can communicate his discoveries to his fellows. Our societies acquire a collective awareness of their known world, and the most adventurous have the urge to discover what lies beyond and to return to describe their findings. These brave people are the explorers.

Motives for exploration have changed over the centuries. Prehistoric man performed prodigious feats of discovery and movement, penetrating most of the habitable parts of the world. Our species evolved in East Africa (or possibly in the Indus valley or even in the Orient), and early man naturally settled in warm and fertile valleys such as the Nile or those in Mesopotamia. It must have been the search for game that led pre-agricultural hunters into higher latitudes, to the harsher climate of northern Europe or even the frozen wastes of Siberia.

We do not know what took our ancestors on the most remarkable of all migrations: the colonization of the Americas. This occurred some 20,000 years ago during the late Ice Age, when for many centuries the bed of the shallow Bering Strait between Siberia and Alaska was exposed by the lowered oceans. This land bridge, Beringia, was a forbidding place of frozen mud, lashed by icy winds and sub-zero temperatures. Early man somehow moved eastwards, either on foot across these wastes or along their shores in some form of vessel, and then settled in Alaska before moving south into the uninhabited American continents.

Man's resilience, adaptability and mobility are astonishing. Almost no part of the earth has not felt a human footprint. The Inuit have learned survival in northern Greenland and the naked Yahgan in Tierra del Fuego; the Bedou travel across the waterless Empty Quarter of Arabia, the Tuareg are lords of the western Sahara, and Mongol herdsmen live on the edges of the high Gobi desert; tribal peoples flourish in all the densest tropical forests.

As an example of the speed with which so-called primitive people could move 84 villages of Tupinambua Indians fled from the Portuguese on the coast of Brazil in the 1580s. They migrated with their families, sometimes settling for a time or fighting other tribes. They travelled westwards across South America to the foothills of the Andes until they met Spanish *conquistadores* from Peru. Disillusioned, they turned north-east down the Madeira river and had settled on an island in the Amazon when the first Portuguese arrived there in 1639, amazed to find that these people remembered them from two generations earlier. In that short time, the Tupinamba had covered some 3000 km (1875 miles) of very difficult terrain. They explained that 'with such a multitude of fugitives it was impossible to support them all. They therefore separated over distant trails . . . some peopling one land, some another.'

Australian aborigines know song-line routes right across their vast country; Canadian Indians paddled canoes over immense distances of lakes and rivers; Polynesians navigated to the remotest islands of the Pacific, even managing to settle on Easter Island with their families and domestic animals, although it is thousands of kilometres from any land. So the ability to reach remote places, to travel over great distances in tough conditions, and to understand the lie of the land are by no means the province of sophisticated people. It is rather the written record of their discoveries and adventures that distinguishes our explorers.

Almost all the terrestrial explorers whom we most admire were guided and helped by natives, but their attitudes were often hopelessly Eurocentric. When David Livingstone saw the mighty falls on the Zambezi, he was thrilled by 'the most wonderful sight I have witnessed in Africa' and named them after his Queen Victoria. But to local people they were, and still are, Mosiottatunya, 'The Smoke that Thunders', in the same way that Iguaçu means 'Big Water' in Tupi, and Niagara means 'Thundering Water'.

Until recently, explorers were the men who filled in the blanks on the map – or at least the blanks in our perception, because the places they discovered were home to local people. The essential prerequisite was a basic map that could be improved. There are countless examples of pre-literate societies producing their versions of cartography: drawing on hides, sketching river bends and rapids on a sand bank, carving geographical information on rock outcrops, or simply describing the lie of the land with hand gestures.

No map has survived from Ancient Greece, but we know how it would have looked from the writings on Herodotus or Aeschylus. The great geographer of the 3rd century BC, Eratosthenes of Alexandria, calculated the circumference of the world with remarkable accuracy by measuring the sun's shadow in different locations. But the father of modern geography was Ptolemy (Claudius Ptolemaeus, AD 90–168). It was he who established the convention of placing north at the top of a map, who used a grid of latitude and longitude, who perceived the Earth as a circle and sphere divided into 360 degrees, each of which was subdivided into minutes and seconds, and who devised a way of projecting the spherical Earth on to a flat map.

Ancient Egyptian inscriptions record an expedition in about 3000 BC to the Land of Punt in equatorial Africa, and in the reign of Queen Hatshepsut there was another three-year voyage to Punt that returned in triumph in 1490 BC. Homer's legendary traveller Odysseus (Ulysses to the Romans) lived about seven centuries later. He emerges from the verse of the Odyssey as the archetypal determined explorer. When he allowed one of his frightened men to turn back, Odysseus declared: 'But I shall go on. It is my plain duty.' On another occasion, when his dismasted boat faced shipwreck, he decided not to abandon her: 'As long as the joints of my planks hold, I shall stay where I am. When my boat breaks up, I'll swim for it.' And his men complained to him: 'You are one of those hard men whose spirit never flags and whose body never tires. You must be made of iron.' Greek and Phoenician sailors traded all over the Mediterranean, and a record still exists of a six-year exploration by Pytheas from the Greek colony Massalia (Marseilles), who in 310–304 BC made the first circumnavigation of the British Isles, and discovered the Orkneys and Iceland.

Christian bigotry meant that Europe lost its geographical supremacy during the Middle Ages. Orthodox Christians were made to believe that Jerusalem lay at the centre of a circular world surrounded by places derived from the Old Testament. On one side lay a 'T' of the Mediterranean running from east to west and the Nile and Danube in a straight north-south line at its eastern end. Other religions had similar beliefs. To Hindus, the sacred Mount Meru was 'the centre of the earth', and for the Incas of Peru, their capital city Cuzco was the navel of the world from which projected the four quarters of their empire. In Muslim tradition, Mecca was opposite the centre of the sky and the Ka'bah was the highest point on earth. Although the Chinese had a good knowledge of the geography of their empire from an early age, they tried to locate the capital at a place where a sundial cast no shadow at the summer solstice. Great Christian ecclesiastics such as Saints Augustine and Chrysostom derided the ancient notions of a spherical earth by insisting that the Antipodes (literally 'opposite feet', the southern hemisphere where men's feet pointed upwards) could not possibly exist.

During the centuries when the Church imposed its official amnesia of the discoveries of ancient geographers, ordinary sailors continued to produce accurate descriptions of the coasts of the Mediterranean and surrounding seas. These were either verbal accounts or *portolano* (literally, harbour guide) charts which depicted coasts, uninfluenced by biblical dogma. The Crusades, from the late 11th to the 13th centuries, helped to broaden European horizons and so did the marvellous narratives of the great 13th-century Venetian traveller Marco Polo. It was said of him that 'Messer Marco Polo had knowledge of, or had actually visited, a greater number of the different countries of the World than any other man; the more that he was always giving his mind to get knowledge, and to spy out and enquire into everything in order to have matter to relate to the Lord [the Mongol Emperor Kublai Khan].'

But the finest explorers of Europe's Dark Ages and Middle Ages were the Chinese and Arabs. Chinese cartographers were the equals of their western counterparts. Their maps had graduated divisions or grids and were well able to show topographical features. The Arabs also made fine maps, inspired by the geographer Al-Idrisi. Their equivalent to Marco Polo was the 14th-century traveller Ibn Baṭṭūṭa who described India and most places in the Indian Ocean, all of which he had visited in the dhows that plied those waters. Both he and Marco Polo travelled at times in Chinese ships, for the Chinese had long been trading with the Arab world by sea as well as by overland caravans. Chinese exploration culminated in the expeditions of Zheng Ho, a court eunuch sent to impress the world with the glory of Chinese civilization. He did this in a series of expeditions from 1405 to 1433, visiting every port of the China Sea and Indian Ocean with the largest flotilla that the world had seen: 317 ships crewed by 37,000 men. Luckily for Europe, Chinese policy changed with a new emperor, and that ancient empire withdrew into self-sufficient isolation.

Throughout these centuries, the force that drove exploration was trade in luxury goods. There were a few commodities of high value but relatively small size that inspired sailors and overland traders to take their ships and caravans on dangerous journeys lasting many months; and early travellers joined these fleets or caravans along established trade routes. The goods that justified such effort were jewels and precious metals, aromatic scents, ivory, silk and fine fabrics, and spices to conceal the taste of rotting food in an age before refrigeration.

To us Europeans, the great age of exploration began with the Renaissance. Scholars had rediscovered the works of Greek and Latin geographers, as well as the more fanciful classical legends – which is how the world's largest river came to be named after the mythical Amazons. Christianity was in the ascendant: the Moors were driven out of Spain in the same year that Columbus discovered America.

Portuguese and Spanish *conquistadores* discovered remote lands on the pretext of converting their inhabitants to Christianity. But the true motive for these explorations was financial gain, the hope of bringing back valuable luxuries. The Portuguese made their way down the west coast of Africa and eventually around the Cape of Good Hope in search of a sea route to the spices of India. When four of Vasco da Gama's ships made the first return journey from India to Portugal in 1498, their cargo of pepper, ginger, cinnamon and cloves was worth a fortune.

Such profit inspired Cabral's fleet of 13 ships and 1200 men, that sailed from Lisbon in 1500 and accidentally discovered Brazil on its way to India. Similarly, Columbus set off westwards across the Atlantic in the hope of reaching the rich empires of China and Japan – luckily for him Ptolemy had seriously underestimated the circumference of the globe, so that Columbus assumed that he had reached Japan when he was only in Cuba. In later decades, it was the lure of gold and silver that spurred on Cortés, Pizarro and other conquerors; and the search for a trade route to the Orient took Magellan around the tip of South America.

Columbus located his first settlement in the Americas 'in the best district for gold mines and for every form of trade, both with this continent and with that yonder belonging to the Great Khan'. He promised to bring the Spanish monarchs 'as much gold as they want . . . besides spices and cotton, . . . gum mastic . . . and aloe wood . . . and slaves, as many as they shall order and who will be idolators. And I believe that I have found rhubarb and cinnamon, and I shall find a thousand other things of value.'

All too often, those early explorers were intent only on pillage. Pizarro sent two men ahead under the protection of an Inca general to see the Inca capital Cuzco. They described its magnificent sun temple 'sheathed with gold in large plates on the side where the sun rises . . . The Christians decided to remove the ornament with some copper crowbars, and so they did, as they themselves related . . . They said there was so much gold in all the temples of the city that it was marvellous.' These vandals took as much of this as they could and, in the mausoleum of the dead emperors, 'they went in to see the mummies and stole many rich objects from them.'

When Walter Raleigh in 1596 wrote his famous essay on *The discoverie of the large, rich, and beautiful empire of Guiana*, he tempted adventurers by saying that 'the common soldier shall here fight for golde. . . Those commanders and chieftaines that shoot at honour and abundance, shall finde there more rich and beautifull cities, more temples adorned with golden images . . . than either Cortez found in Mexico or Pizarro in Peru . . . Guiana is a countrey

that hath yet her maydenhead, never sackt, turned, nor wrought, . . . the graves have not bene opened for golde, the mines not broken with sledges, nor their images puld downe out of their temples.'

Trade soon led to permanent trading posts, and these in turn led to colonial occupation. The rare luxuries of the early explorers gave way to bulkier but equally profitable commodities that required forced labour by native peoples: sugar and cotton from plantations; gold, silver, diamonds and emeralds from their respective mines, or pearls brought up by native divers; and later, coffee, cocoa, tea and tobacco. The fleets that brought these goods to Europe unwittingly carried unknown diseases to the Americas; and the resulting depopulation created a demand for slave labour. Explorers were active in all these operations, often pushing beyond the colonial frontier in search of gold, silver, furs or slaves.

It was only in the 17th century that explorers started to venture forth for nobler motives. Some went purely for love of travel, like Fynes Moryson who admitted that 'from my tender youth I had a great desire to see forraine Countries . . . And having once begun this course, I could not see any man without emulation and a kind of vertuous envy, who had seene more Cities, Kingdomes, and Provinces, or more Courts of Princes, Kings and Emperours, then my selfe.' Missionaries went to convert distant peoples, for motives they regarded as elevated even though we may not. The best of them, like the Jesuit St Francis Xavier in Japan, the 13th-century Franciscans who reached Mongolia, or Matteo Ricci who impressed the Emperor of China, were true explorers in the sense of penetrating remote places and reporting their discoveries.

Others started to travel to satisfy scientific curiosity, which is surely the best of all reasons. Captain James Cook, perhaps the greatest explorer of all, returned from his first circumnavigation in 1771. He had observed an eclipse of the sun on Tahiti, made brilliant charts of both islands of New Zealand, explored the fertile east coast of Australia and the Barrier Reef, and brought home a shipload of new botanical and zoological finds, but modestly wrote that 'the discoveries made on this voyage are not great'.

On his second voyage, Cook sailed farther south than any previous explorer and entered the Antarctic pack-ice. He laid to rest the notion of a habitable southern continent.

I have now made the circuit of the Southern Ocean in a high Latitude and traversed it in such a manner as to leave not the least room for the Possibility of there being a continent, unless near the Pole and out of reach of Navigation . . . Thus I flatter my self that the intention of the Voyage has in every respect been fully Answered, the Southern Hemisphere sufficiently explored and a final end put to the searching

9

after a Southern Continent, which has at times ingrossed . . . the Geographers of all ages.

A few years after Captain Cook's death on his third voyage, scientifically curious gentlemen in London established the African Association, which was dedicated to exploring the heart of Africa and which later became the Royal Geographical Society. One of its first explorers was Mungo Park. He set forth into the interior of West Africa well aware of the dangers of disease and hostile natives:

> But this intelligence, instead of deterring me from my purpose, animated me to persist . . . I had a passionate desire to examine into the productions of a country so little known, and to become experimentally acquainted with the modes of life and character of the natives. I knew that I was able to bear fatigue; and I relied on my youth and the strength of my constitution to preserve me from the effects of the climate . . . If I should perish in my journey, I was willing that my hopes and expectations should perish with me; and if I should succeed, [it would render], the geography of Africa more familiar to my countrymen.

Starting with the polymath Baron Alexander von Humboldt, the 19th century was the dawn of scientific exploration. All over the world, scientists tackled virgin fields of discovery. They began to classify plants, animals and insects by the systems devised by the Swedish naturalist Carl Linné, and their investigations led inevitably to the elaboration of the theory of evolution by natural selection. In 1858 the Linnean Society of London published two papers of seminal importance, 'the results of the investigations of two indefatigable naturalists, Mr. Charles Darwin and Mr. Alfred Wallace. These gentlemen having, independently and unknown to one another, conceived the same very ingenious theory to account for the appearance and perpetuation of varieties and of specific forms on our planet, may both fairly claim the merit of being original thinkers in this important line of inquiry.'

Others explored in pursuit of archaeology, geology, anthropology, ethnology, palaeontology or a host of other new natural sciences. The young Heinrich Schliemann discussed the walls of Troy with his father, and declared: '"If such walls existed, they cannot possibly have been completely destroyed: vast ruins of them must still remain, but they are hidden away beneath the dust of ages." . . . We both agreed that I should one day excavate Troy.' Years later, Schliemann stumbled across treasure in the walls of Troy and started to extract it by himself. 'This required great exertion and involved great risk, since the wall of fortification, beneath which I had to dig, threatened every moment to fall down upon me. But the sight of so many objects, every one of which is of inestimable value to archaeology, made me reckless and I never thought of any danger.'

The thrill of scientific discovery spurred on the most adventurous in all the disciplines. Edward Tylor, one of the founders of the study of ethnography, explained that 'to the ethnographer the bow and arrow is a species, the habit of flattening children's skulls is a species, the practice of reckoning numbers by tens is a species. The geographical distribution of these things, and their transmission from region to region, have to be studied as the naturalist studies the geography of his botanical and zoological species.'

Every natural scientist on every expedition experiences the excitement of first seeing unfamiliar nature. Thus, the Yorkshire botanist Richard Spruce wrote:

> At Tauau I first realised my idea of a primeval forest. There were enormous trees, crowned with magnificent foliage, decked with fantastic parasites, and hung over with lianas, which varied in thickness from slender threads to huge python-like masses, were now round, now flattened, and now twisted with the regularity of a cable.

That excitement was, of course, immeasurably heightened when the explorer was sufficiently expert to know that he was making a discovery, finding a genus, a species, a property or a behaviour pattern that was 'new to science'. Such discovery is the noblest form of exploration; and it is happening today at an accelerating rate in every discipline all over the world. We are living in a golden age of scientific discovery, a time when vastly improved means of transport opens every part of the earth, the oceans and even space to man's prying eyes, and when more sophisticated instruments enable us to probe and analyse all the secrets of our planet.

The most famous of the 19th century's explorers were the geographers who 'filled in the blanks on the map', particularly in the mountains of central Asia, the deserts of central Australia, the North-West Passage and the approaches to the Poles, and of course the heart of Africa. Most of these great explorers were disinterested seekers after knowledge, none more so than Dr David Livingstone who travelled so simply and ended his days in a remote African village on another quest for the source of the Nile. But other motives appear. Some explorers were sent by their governments as part of the colonial scramble for Africa and other political vacuums. All too often, carving up by colonial empires was the result of claims based on travels by European explorers.

The Treaty of Madrid of 1750 divided South America between Spain and Portugal, superseding the papal Line of Tordesillas of 1494, and awarded

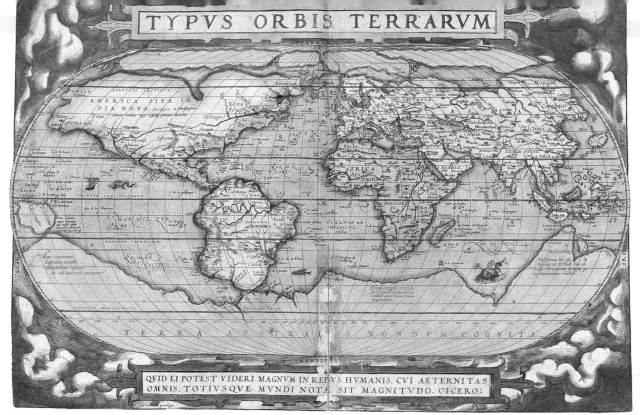

TYPVS ORBIS TERRARVM

QVID EI POTEST VIDERI MAGNVM IN REBVS HVMANIS, CVI AETERNITAS OMNIS, TOTIVSQVE MVNDI NOTA SIT MAGNITVDO. CICERO:

A map of the world by the Flemish geographer Abraham Ortelius from his
Theatrum Orbis Terrarum. *The existence of the Great South Land was not finally disproved until Cook's voyages of 1772–5.*

half the continent to Brazil. In the preamble to the Treaty, its negotiators explained that they based their allocation of territory on discovery or occupation by Europeans – millennia of residence by native tribes were totally ignored. Thus, the reports of slave-raiding thugs or fanatical missionaries who penetrated 'undiscovered' lands assumed great importance; and they still form the basis of any boundary arbitration.

The chaotic frontiers of modern Africa are often the product of incursions by explorers from the different European nations, and they usually moved inland from slave-trading factories or forts on the coasts. The resulting boundaries frequently slice across ethnic territories (as in the case of the Somalis) or lump together incompatible nationalities, thus fuelling civil wars in Nigeria, Chad, Sudan, Uganda, Zaire and other countries. Explorers were thus, unwittingly, responsible for today's bloodshed, famine and flight by refugees. But the colonial scramble that manipulated explorers' accounts was inspired by commerce. Adam Smith wrote in 1776:

> It is not by the importation of gold and silver that the discovery of America has enriched Europe . . . By opening a new and inexhaustible market to all the commodities of Europe, it gave occasion to new divisions of labour and improvements of art . . . The commodities of Europe were almost all new to America, and many of those of America were new to Europe. A new set of exchanges therefore began to take place which had never been thought of before.

Other pioneering adventurers were driven partly by thirst for fame. The most famous explorers became idolized household names, so that the debate between the former travelling companions Richard Burton and John Speke about which man had correctly identified the lake from which the Nile flowed, was to have been a major media event. Henry Stanley was sponsored by an American newspaper and, after the success of his report of finding the missing Dr Livingstone, he had to continue to organize more spectacular expeditions to satisfy the reading public.

Even when there were no colonialist or mercenary trading motives involved, national pride became a motive of exploration. The glory of being the first to reach a remote objective attached to an explorer's country as well as to the man himself. Roald Amundsen turned the first expedition to the South Pole into a race with Captain Robert Scott. He won, by greater efficiency and single-mindedness, and was able to plant the Norwegian flag on the southernmost point on Earth. At that same time, the intrepid Gertrude Bell was visiting Arabian tribes who had never seen a European. They were so impressed by her that they remarked: 'If this is an English woman, what must an English man be like?'

In 1802, Baron Alexander von Humboldt climbed almost to the top of the volcano Chimborazo in Ecuador and was sure that he was ascending the highest mountain in the world. Chimborazo was finally scaled in 1879 by Edward Whymper, the man who in 1865 had been the first to reach the summit of the Matterhorn. This was the start of a marvellous new era of exploration: sporting adventure. In those

11

same closing decades of the 19th century, a new breed of African explorer appeared: big game hunters such as Samuel Baker or Frederick Selous who penetrated remote places in pursuit of animal trophies. Mountaineering developed as a great sport in the early years of the 20th century: Mallory and Irving disappeared near the summit of Mount Everest, and Bill Tilman and Eric Shipton trekked into unknown Himalayan valleys in search of unclimbed peaks. But this and all the other expedition sports – caving, sailing, kayaking, diving, microlight flying, ballooning – have fully blossomed only in the past quarter century.

Remarkable advances in equipment, vastly improved training and techniques, and above all sheer courage have taken explorers to the hidden recesses of our world, to the summits of almost all major mountains, into labyrinths of cave passages and deep submarine holes, down raging white-water rivers, into the canopy of the rainforests, and amid fabulous reefs beneath the oceans.

Bravery and endurance are the hallmarks of all great explorers. These are the qualities that excite our admiration for their achievements, and that make their stories so readable. This book is full of tales of amazing endurance. When Magellan entered the Pacific Ocean, his ship spent almost four months without taking on fresh supplies. 'We ate only old biscuit reduced to powder, which stank from rat droppings, . . . and we drank water that was yellow and stinking. We also ate the ox hides that were under the main yard, . . . and sawdust, and rats each of which cost half a ducat.' Magellan's men suffered so badly from scurvy that their gums swelled too much for them to eat, and many died of starvation.

A few years later, Gonzalo Pizarro's men, deserted by Orellana's boatload on its way down the Amazon, were reduced to eating 'saddle and stirrup leathers, boiled in water and then roasted over ashes . . . The Spaniards were very sick and sore, wan and wretched, in a pitifully afflicted condition . . . They went on, almost dead from hunger, naked and bare-foot, covered in sores, opening a path with their swords. Meanwhile it rained, so that on many days they never saw the sun and could not get dry.'

The great modern explorer Wilfred Thesiger recalled three days without food, during his crossing of the Arabian Empty Quarter:

For the first day my hunger was only a more insistent feeling of familiar emptiness; something which, like a toothache, I could partly overcome by an effort of will. I woke in the grey dawn craving for food, but by lying on my stomach and pressing down I could achieve a semblance of relief . . . [whatever he did next day] a moment's slackness and I was thinking once more of food. I filled myself with water, and the bitter water, which I did not want, made me feel sick . . . The nights were worse than the days. Now I was cold and could not even sleep . . . I was maddened by the thought of some crusts which I had given away in the Urq al Shaiba. I could picture the colour and texture, even the shape, of the fragments which I had left. In the morning I watched Mabkhaut turn the camels out to graze, . . . but I could only think of them as food.

Ernest Giles, who crossed the terrible Gibson Desert in Australia in 1873, lost his companion and was himself about to die when he stumbled upon a dying baby wallaby. 'The instant I saw it, I pounced upon it and ate it, living, raw, dying – fur, skin, bones, skull and all.'

Thesiger and countless other explorers have suffered from thirst. Dervla Murphy recalled, in Pakistan;

The horror of today's trek was really extreme, with heat visibly flowing towards me in malevolent waves off the mountainsides and the dreadful desert stench of burning sand nauseating me; the terrifying dehydration of mouth and nostrils and eyes until my eyelids could barely move and a sort of staring blindness came on, with the ghastly sensation of scorching air filling my lungs . . . and above all the despair of coming round corners and over hilltops time and time again, hoping always to see water – and never seeing it. I have often thought that death by thirst must be grimmer than most deaths and now my surmise has been confirmed.

There are just as many accounts of explorers suffering disease. Baron Georg Langsdorff, who led one of the first scientific expeditions into central Brazil, was struck with violent malaria that eventually drove him mad. He recalled in his journal in 1828: 'As to what happened on the 18th, I know nothing. I fell into a delirium. I was not conscious of what I did.' Days later: 'I did not think that I would endure yesterday . . . Weak in body and soul, I sit here and the only thing that can be said is that I am still alive.' Later that century, the great botanist Richard Spruce lay in his hammock in another part of Amazonia listening to his men discussing how to finish him off and divide his belongings; but he was too weak from malaria to do anything about it.

At the other extreme of climate, Captain Fred Burnaby let his hand be exposed to frost-bite on a Russian sleigh journey:

A feeling of intense pain had seized my extremities; it seemed as if they had been plunged into some corrosive acid which was gradually eating the flesh from the bones. I looked at my finger-nails; they were blue, the fingers and back part of my hands were of the same colour, whilst my wrists and the lower part of the arm were of a waxen hue. . . . The lower portions of the limbs were lost to all sensation, dead to pain, hanging quite listlessly by my side . . . The pain, which had ascended to the glands under my arms, had become more acute than anything I had hitherto experienced . . . All this time the perspiration was pouring down my forehead, my body itself being as if on fire, the pain gradually ascending the parts attacked . There are moments in a man's life when death itself would be a relief.

More even than privation and illness, it is physical danger that makes explorers' tales such gripping reading. Sometimes that danger comes from the people whose land is being invaded. The German Hans Staden was captured by Tupinambua Indians on the coast of Brazil in 1552, stripped naked and taken to a village to be executed and eaten. He was left, tightly bound, 'to the pleasure of the women who gathered around, dancing and singing the songs they usually sing to their own people when they are about to eat them . . . They fell upon me and beat me with their fists, plucking at my beard.' A woman scraped off Staden's eyebrows with a piece of crystal; strings of nut rattles were tied to his legs and a feather ornament was fastened behind his head. 'The women began to sing together and I had to keep time with the rattles on my leg by stamping as they sang. But my wounded leg was so painful that I could hardly stand upright, for my wound had not been dressed.' Staden saved himself by making daring prophesies that came true. Speke and Grant survived a period of house arrest with a dangerously erratic chief in Uganda, and countless other explorers had frightening brushes with suspicious natives. We have the accounts only of those who survived.

Ernest Shackleton saved his shipwrecked men by an epic voyage across the Antarctic Ocean in a 6-metre (20-foot) open boat. One night he was at the tiller when the white crest of an enormous wave bore down on them.

> During twenty-six years' experience of the ocean in all its moods I had not encountered a wave so gigantic. It was a mighty upheaval of the ocean, a thing apart from the big white-capped seas that had been our tireless enemies for many days. I shouted, "For God's sake hold on! It's got us." Then came a moment of suspense that seemed drawn out for hours. White surged the foam of the breaking sea around us. We felt our boat lifted and flung forward like a cork in breaking surf. We were in a seething chaos of tortured water; but somehow the boat lived through it, half full of water, sagging to the dead weight and shuddering under the blow . . .

In 1947, Thor Heyerdahl ended the famous voyage of the raft *Kon-Tiki* when it crashed helplessly on an atoll in the midst of the Pacific Ocean:

> A sea rose straight up under us as we felt the Kon-Tiki being lifted up in the air. The great moment had come; we were riding on the wave-back at breathless speed, our ramshackle craft creaking and groaning as she quivered under us The excitement made one's blood boil . . . A new sea rose high astern of us like a glittering green glass wall; as we sank down it came rolling after us, and in the same second in which I saw it high above me I felt a violent blow and was submerged under floods of water. I felt the suction through my whole body, with such great strength that I had to strain every single muscle in my frame and think of one thing only – hold on, hold on! . . . When the whole mountain of water had rushed on, with an earsplitting roaring and crashing, I saw Knut hanging on beside me, doubled up into a ball . . . The great sea swept just over the ridge of the cabin roof which projected from the water, and there hung the three others . . .

Mountaineering is a highly dangerous sport, and climbers take terrible calculated risks on their way to untrodden peaks. Typical of their hair-raising excitement is Kurt Diemberger's account of his tragic descent of Chogolisa in the Karakoram with the great mountaineer Hermann Buhl. Visibility was bad.

> It was almost impossible to see anything at all. Crack! Something shot through me like a shock. Everything shook and for a second the surface of the snow seemed to shrink. Blindly I jumped sideways to the right – an instantaneous reflex action – two, three great strides, and followed the steep slope downwards a little way, shattered by what I had seen at my feet – the rim of the cornice with little jagged bits breaking away from it. My luck had been in all right. I had been clean out on the cornice . . . Still no Hermann. "Hermann!" I shouted. "For God's sake what's up, Hermann?" I rushed, gasping, up the slope. There it was, the crest . . . and beyond it, smooth snow, and it was empty . . . "Hermann . . . You! . . ." Done for . . . I dragged myself up a little further. I could see his last footmarks in the snow, then the jagged edge of the broken cornice yawning. Then the black depths.

Such are the prices that explorers must pay to break new ground. For 160 years, the Royal Geographical Society has been supporting their endeavours and organizing its own expeditions. Their attitude to danger was summarized by the mediaeval monk Rubruck, who visited the camp of the Tartar Khan Mangu. When that ruler told him 'Fear not', Rubruck responded, 'If I had been afraid, I would never have come.'

EARLY EXPLORATION

THE FIRST CIVILIZATIONS AND EXPLORATION

Around the middle of the fourth millennium before Christ, in the river valleys of the warmer temperate latitudes where agriculture became more intensive, the dispersed human settlements of pastoral nomadism gave way to more complex societies. In the regions of the lower Tigris, the Euphrates valley, the valley of the Nile, the middle regions of the Indus valley and the Yellow River, the transformations took place (for all that is known) independently of each other. The distinguished archaeologist Gordon Childe christened these changes 'the urban revolution'.

The material evidence for the existence of large cities is gradually being uncovered by archaeologists. It is not difficult to imagine the diversity of human labor required to produce the monumental public buildings which make these early civilizations so impressive. The vast zigurrat at Ur, for example, excavated in 1920, is a testimony to the organizing power of Sumerian Mesopotamia.

Such organization implied a concentration of surplus food and the means for its collection and management. It suggested large-scale trade with increased specialization and exchange which made these civilizations look outwards from their metropolitan heartlands. Specialization brought with

At least as long ago as the first century BC dhows left the Red Sea ports to cross to the west coast of India. This was Tim Severin's inspiration to follow the trade route to China in a replica of a medieval Arab sailing ship.

A 15th-century woodcut of Ptolemy who provided a unified picture of a stable universe.

it hierarchical societies with a privileged ruling class. At the heart of each of these early civilizations, of course, lay an imperium, a state organization in which membership was based on residence behind frontiers, rather than upon kinship.

Archaeologists know something about the migration of peoples in these early civilizations. They present the evidence in pottery and metalwork for contact across and beyond the boundaries. Yet of the human endeavour involved in exploration they can say little. For this, the written record is essential and it is only available from much later. The earliest surviving evidence from the pictographic writing of Mesopotamia (from around 3000 BC) or that of China (later still, towards 1500 BC) is silent about exploration. The early clay tablets of Mesopotamia are no more informative apart from an intriguing 'world map' now preserved in the British Library. It is in the hieroglyphs of Egypt that we have the first tantalizing glimpses. And only in the alphabetic literatures which preserve for us the Canaanite language through to the traditions of discovery enshrined in its distant successors, Greek and Latin, can we begin to trace the patterns of ancient exploration.

The directions in which exploration went are not surprising. They were dictated by the dominant geography of their natural surroundings and the resource ecology of their civilizations. What, for example, was more inevitable than Egyptian exploration up the Nile – or, similarly, its voyages following the western coastline of the Red Sea from Suez along the coast of what is now Eritrea and Somalia? The river lay at the heart of a developed hydraulic husbandry upon which Egyptian civilization depended for its survival. At times, the Nile had almost the status of a deity.

It was from the Nubian kingdoms of the upper Nile and the horn of Africa that the high value products

*c.***3200** BC First Egyptian sea voyage recorded in hieroglyphics.
*c.***2300** BC Harkhuf's expeditions up the Nile to Yam (southern Nubia).

*c.***1492** BC An Egyptian voyage by Nehsi to the Land of Punt illustrated the tomb of Queen Hatshepsut who crossed from the Nile to the Red Sea and Lebanon.

*c.***1000** BC Colonization of Polynesia began with settlement by maritime peoples from Taiwan, Philippines and Indonesia.

The earliest surviving world map (5th century BC) comes from Babylon. The city appears at the centre of the map, with the river Euphrates to the south and Armenia to the north.

was no product of individual whim, no romantic quest. It was part of the struggle of a civilization to adapt in order to survive. It was the consequence, generally speaking, of the initiative of strong rulers who knew that knowledge was power, and who recognized that their authority could be extended by controlling supplies of precious commodities.

The Egyptian nobleman Harkhuf, who lived around 2300 BC under the later period of the energetic 6th Egyptian Dynasty, has some claim to be called 'the first known explorer'. He led several expeditions up the Nile beyond the First Cataract to the land of Yam (southern Nubia). Close by Harkhuf's tomb at Elephantine (Aswan) is that of another explorer of the same period, Pyopi-nakht. This 'royal companion, ritual priest, leader of caravans, bringing the products of foreign lands to his lord' also recounted in his funerary inscription his exploits beyond the First Cataract into Nubian territory. In this case, though, he had been sent to pacify or, if necessary, to subdue by force of arms, its dissident tribes and semi-savage people. Another passage hints at the more extensive voyaging which he undertook down the coast of the Red Sea to recover 'the body of his royal companion, the captain of ships, the caravan-leader, Anankht' who had been slain by Nubian tribesmen whilst building a ship for a voyage to Punt.

The Egyptian sources are not specific as to where exactly Punt (var. Pwnt – 'The Sacred') was. It must have been south of the great desert belt which stretches from the Persian Gulf across Arabia and northern Africa. Reputedly fertile, it was where the Egyptians found supplies of the precious myrrh and frankincense, burnt in their temples, used as perfume and as an embalming agent. So Punt should perhaps be equated with somewhere along the southern shore of the Gulf of Aden, or perhaps with the Somali coast of Africa.

in this temple culture came – its incense, ebony, panther skins, gold, ivory and, to a large extent also, its slaves. A civilization like that of Ancient Egypt was vulnerable to attack from without, especially from the Nubian tribes, just as it was susceptible to famine, locusts, the decline in its labour force, and dynastic tensions from within. Egyptian exploration

HARKHUF, THE FIRST KNOWN EXPLORER

Harkhuf's tomb at Elephantine (Aswan) carries an inscription in which he proudly recorded his explorations for posterity. He was sent by the king, he said, 'to explore a road . . .' to Yam. After seven months he returned, 'bringing all kinds of gifts', for which 'he was greatly praised'. From his third expedition, he came back 'with 300 asses, laden with incense, ebony, heknu, grain, panthers, ivory, throw-sticks and every good product. I was more excellent and vigilant than any count, companion, or caravan conductor who had been sent to Yam before.'

On his last expedition, undertaken for the succeeding ruler, King Pyopi, he returned with 'a dancing dwarf of the gods from the land of spirits'. Its appearance created such interest that Harkhuf was instructed to escort the dwarf personally on the 800-km (500-mile) journey down the Nile to Memphis because the king 'desires to see this dwarf more than all the gifts of Sinai and of Punt'.

The African chieftain of Punt and his wife making their first contact with Egyptian civilization.

The second scene records the arrival of the fleet in Punt. It is known from other evidence that the Egyptians had ocean-going ships built of cedarwood, probably from the Lebanon. The fleet is laden with merchandise for trading and the chieftain of Punt is depicted, closely followed by his grossly obese wife (was she suffering from elephantiasis?) and three children, advancing towards the Egyptians. In the background there are huts built on poles among trees. The inscription reads:

The king's emissary in God's country with his army behind him in the presence of the headmen of Punt, doing obeisance with head bent low. These say: Wherefore are you come hither to this land that your people know not? Are you descended from the sky, or are you come by ship that sails upon the sea?

A later scene in the frieze shows the fleet arriving back in Thebes. Some historians have surmised that this scene provides evidence for a Nile–Suez canal; for them, it is difficult to imagine the cargoes (which included myrrh trees in pots) being transported from the Red Sea to the Nile by caravan (a trek of some five days from El Qoseir on the Red Sea to Coptos on the Nile). If this is the case, the frieze is evidence for a Nile–Suez canal built centuries before Darius revived the idea and began its construction in about 500 BC. The bed of such an ancient canal was discovered during the construction of the Suez canal in the 19th century and activated to provide drinking water for the workers.

'TO THE LAND OF PUNT'

Queen Hatshepsut, who reigned between 1501 and 1479 BC, entertained grandiose notions for immortalizing herself and the achievements of her reign. She restored temples and planted vast granite obelisks that had been transported from considerable distances. Her greatest surviving legacy is her huge mortuary temple at Deir el-Bahri, one of the supreme attainments of the Ancient Egyptian architects.

On the walls of the temple were carved reliefs celebrating the queen. In a frieze consisting of 10 pictorial scenes with accompanying hieroglyphic inscriptions, the shipborne expedition to the land of Punt, undertaken at her instigation in around 1492 BC, is recorded in great detail. The expedition would have involved crossing the 250 km (150 miles) of desert from the Nile to the shores of the Red Sea and then rowing and sailing some 2500 km (1500 miles) towards the Arabian sea.

The most remarkable evidence we have for the land of Punt, and for Egyptian exploration in general, comes from the huge mortuary temple for Queen Hatshepsut, the only woman ever to rule the land of the Pharaohs with the full title of queen. The monument still survives at Deir el-Bahri, across the river Nile from the modern city of Luxor. Although sadly defaced by the vengeance of her brother after her death as well as by the ravages of time, the magnificent pictorial frieze on the temple walls was doubtless intended by its patron as the best way to immortalize herself and the achievements of her reign. To us, it is the first dramatic record of exploration as a great human endeavour.

NE PLUS ULTRA

Traditional societies and the challenge of discovery

Exploration was a way by which ancient civilizations adapted in order to survive. But their capacities to adapt should not be overestimated. These traditional, although already complex, societies had certain characteristics which distinguished them from our modern societies. Broadly speaking, they were two-class societies with a tiny elite which was in sharp contrast to a servile majority. Each small elite shared a common high culture, based on its distinctive literacy,

*c.*950 BC King Solomon of Israel used Phoenician sailors to obtain cedarwood from Ophir (possibly the East African coast).
c. 7th century BC Phoenicians, 'people of

purple', searched for new dyes and found them in the Canaries and Madeira.
*c.*650 BC Colaeus discovered Strait of Gibraltar. Much of Mediterranean coast now

known to Greek fishermen and merchants.
*c.*600 BC Pharaoh Necho II's Phoenician fleet searched for a new route from the Red Sea to the Mediterranean and may have

and later often by a common religious inheritance, which together gave it a monopoly upon the transference of knowledge and power. At the same time, the subject majority, whose illiteracy was more or less total, lay imprisoned within a parochial folk culture which separated village from village and region from region along the multiple divides of kinship, dialect and attachment to the soil. Combined,

these elements explain why change (and exploration is *ipso facto* a search for change) was rarely welcomed in traditional societies.

So explorers in traditional societies were not of humble origins. The tyrannies of a fragile self-sufficiency, of family, and of a restricted world view were only overthrown in particular circumstances. Even those within their high cultures must often have regarded exploration with suspicion. The political organization of the classical empires depended on the transport of food and the maintenance of taxation, rentals and the profits of office. It was rare for these necessities to be met by a process of exploration. The politics of the ancient empires were not dominated by relationships with the outside world, but by the constant struggle between rulers and the members of their ruling classes, between autocracy and feudalism. Only occasionally would the 'barbarian' be called in to assist one side against the other in this struggle and, when that happened, the civilization lay vulnerable.

One means by which the elites in traditional societies lessened the perils of dissension in their own ranks was through the influence of universal religions. It is probably not coincidental that nearly all the great religions of the early civilizations trace their origins back to a similar period, around 600 BC. There was a strong, apparently common, movement towards a belief in a single spiritual life-force (of which monotheism was one aspect), a search for a unified ethical system, and a quest for a single overall principle to explain the material world.

This was the period of Confucius and perhaps Lao-tzu in China (with whom the mystical religion of the Tao is associated), of Gautama the Buddha in India, of Zoroaster in Persia, of Isaiah, the greatest of the Hebrew prophets, and of Pythagoras in Greece. These philosophical and religious systems of thought were 'immanentist', accepting the way the world was as part of a wider cosmological symmetry and pattern to which mankind must conform. To that extent, their contribution was to reconcile opposites and limit change rather than promote it. They became the thought systems of great empires, justifying the status quo and reinforcing their mental frontiers. Missionary endeavour, often the spur to exploration in later world history, is notable largely by its absence.

Each of the major civilizations developed profound concepts of its geographical and cultural limits. In linguistic terms, these appeared at an early stage. Ancient Egyptian, Green and Latin senses of the term 'barbarian' were primarily linked in all those

THE PILLARS OF HERCULES

The Strait of Gibraltar, less than 16 km (10 miles) wide, has, to the north, the imposing headland of Gibraltar rock and, to the south, the sentinel rock of Jebel Musa in Morocco. These two guardians of the Atlantic gateway to the Mediterranean are the famous 'Pillars of Hercules' which, according to classical mythology, had been torn asunder by Hercules on one of his adventures in order that the two seas might communicate with each other.

To the Greeks, the twin rocks defined the limits of the Inner Sea, the navigable world, beyond which one could go no further (*ne plus ultra*). Because the Phoenician merchants from Carthage denied passage through the strait to Greek ships from the 5th to the first half of the 3rd centuries BC they were indeed the limits of Greek maritime influence. In the European Renaissance, the emblem of the Pillars was much exploited.

The Holy Roman Emperor Charles V (1500–58) exploited the ancient emblem to indicate how, as ruler of the newly-discovered Americas, he had surpassed the discoveries of the classical civilizations.

circumnavigated Africa.
*c.*515 BC Scylax commissioned to reconnoitre part of the Indus via the Kabul River and went on to explore the shores of

the Arabian and Red Seas.
*c.*470 BC Hanno sailed through the Strait of Gibraltar to found settlements along the north and west coasts of Africa to guard new

trade routes for dyes.
457 BC Herodotus went up the Nile to the first cataract.

civilizations to those who did not share their linguistic traditions. Those who did not speak Chinese were necessarily not members of the 'Middle Kingdom' (*Chung Kuo*) of the Han Dynasty (200 BC-AD 220), the center of the civilized world to Chin culture.

Such linguistic perceptual boundaries in time acquired a geographical formation. For the Egyptians, the First Cataract of the Nile was as important a mental divide between civilization and the unknown as it was a physical barrier. For Darius's empire, just as for the Greek troops of Alexander the Great (356-323 BC), the River Indus formed a great mental as well as natural boundary to his empire. The straits of Gibraltar became, for the Greeks, the Pillars of Hercules, marking the limits of the known and civilized world, beyond which not even Hercules had ventured. For the Chinese empire, the equivalent geographical point was reached at the Jade Gate in the province of Xinjiang, where the Great Wall guarding the celestial kingdom, constructed in its primitive form for the first time by the Ch'in, in *c.*221-206 BC, ended.

Even today, the Chinese talk of those travelling west through the Great Wall as going 'outside the mouth' – or beyond the pale. By the 16th century the Jade Gate had become transformed into the great Ming fortress of Jiayuguan (meaning 'barrier of the Pleasant Valley') where, in the tunnel through its western gate, exiles scratched their poems and messages into the brick as they passed.

On the earliest maps in both China and the West, the hostile humanity outside civilization is often represented in animal-like forms. This zoomorphism

The gatehouse of the 14th-century Jiayuguan Fort, which lay at the furthest point westward of the Great Wall where the famous Silk Road left China towards Dunhuang and the Taklimaken Desert.

is a powerful reminder of the resistance to change in traditional societies. Exploration was regarded with scepticism, even in the pages of our most valuable source, the incomparable historian Herodotus.

HERODOTUS: FATHER OF HISTORY

Herodotus of Halicarnassus (*c.*490/80-429/5 BC) is by far the most important source of reference for ancient exploration. In his *History* he set out to chronicle the wars fought by the Persians, first Darius and then Xerxes, against the Greeks. He presented the conflict as one of world significance, a battle of civilization against the barbarous Asiatic peoples. His sympathies lay with the Athenians, whose rational freedom he contrasted with the irrational despotism of the Persians.

Aristotle called Herodotus a *mythologos*, a weaver of tales, and it is true his dramatic narratives have

much of the rhythm and inevitability of a Greek tragedy to them. But Herodotus was also writing within an older tradition which saw history as ethnography and geography.

This was what led Herodotus to record, with considerable scrupulousness, the accounts which he heard on his own, not inconsiderable, travels. These took him to Athens, Thuria on the gulf of Taras (in southern Italy), and to the island of Samos. He went through the straits into the Euxine (Black Sea), reached the Ister (Danube) and travelled northward across the steppes along the valley of the Don.

He also travelled eastward to the Persian empire, visiting Susa and Babylon. He knew Egypt well, having visited it several times and travelled up the Nile as far as Aswan.

Even where he was sceptical of what he heard (as in the case of Necho's circumnavigation of Africa) he still included the account in his writings. Were it not for Herodotus, nothing would now be known of early circumnavigation of the African continent and nothing of the first Saharan explorers. His scattered and cryptic references have been the starting-point for generations of scholarly investigation.

*c.*410 BC Xenophon took over leadership of Greek army after the death of Cyrus and led the retreat from Baghdad across the Armenian Plateau to the Black Sea.

*c.*401 BC Cyrus with 20,000 mercenaries crossed the Taurus Mountains to the Euphrates in his attempt to overthrow his brother, the king of Persia.

*c.*334-323 BC Alexander the Great extended his empire from the Mediterranean to the Himalayas, travelling over 30,000 km (20,000 miles) in ten years.

THE MEDITERRANEAN COASTAL CIVILIZATIONS

Cross-cultural trade and exploration

The Greek God Hermes was both the god of trade and the god of the boundary-stones which separated one Greek *polis* from another. Merchants were the professional 'boundary-crossers'. At the same time, Hermes was not quite as respectable as other gods. He was a messenger, but also a trickster and a thief, a marginal god for people who were often marginal to established society. In ancient literature, trade was generally despised, to be carried on (if possible) by others, outsiders to the established civilization. In the greatest trading sea of the ancient world, the Mediterranean, the outsiders were the Phoenicians and the Greeks. Their role in exploration was an exceptional one.

Environment and ecology dominated the development of these cross-cultural coastal civilizations. The bare, precipitous and indented shores of the Mediterranean did not require irrigation on a large scale and nor did they permit of easy expansion inland. The coastal inhabitants were compelled to consider

The Isles of Scilly, where Phoenician sailors probably established the furthest outpost of their trading empire to barter for tin. Islands have historically always played a critical role in maritime discovery.

themselves both as independent peoples by their isolation from each other and as inter-dependent by the constant need to exchange men and goods across the sea.

The first Phoenician trading colonies grew outwards from the great Phoenician cities of the ancient world – on the island of Aradus (Raud), the cliff at Byblos, Berytus, Sidon and, above all, the mainland city of Tyre. Tyre was described by the prophet Isaiah, not perhaps without irony, as 'the crowning city, whose merchants are princes, whose traffickers are the honourable of the earth'. It was the Phoenician King of Tyre, Hiram II (969–936 BC) who entered into a usurious contract with King Solomon of Israel to supply him with fir and cedarwood for the great temple at Jerusalem. His sailors played a major part in Solomon's expedition to Ophir, recorded in the First Book of Kings: 'And they came to Ophir, and fetched from thence gold, four hundred and twenty talents and brought it to King Solomon'. The expedition lasted three years and, in addition to gold, the men returned with ivory and apes and peacocks.

The location of Ophir has never been precisely identified; it may have been on the eastern coast of Africa adjacent to the inland kingdoms of the Zambezi, which were rich in gold. It appears that the Phoenicians' navigational skills were again exploited, this time by the Pharaoh Necho II, who despatched a voyage of discovery in *c.*600 BC. Reports of this voyage reached Herodotus 150 years later; whether the Phoenicians really succeeded in circumnavigating the continent of Africa has always been a matter of controversy.

The Assyrians, however, took the Phoenician cities one by one in the 9th century BC and the inhabitants were driven outwards to found coastal colonies, generally where civilized peoples had already settled and where they formed a minority of the population. In Sardinia, Sicily, and along the coasts of Africa and Spain, the Phoenicians became the great merchants of the southern Mediterranean. A technical revolution in the design of ships, with the longer keel strengthened by a rope running fore and aft, enabled the Phoenicians to build strong merchant ships of cedarwood. These were equipped with a single rectangular sail but also propelled by oar. For exploration, however, the Phoenicians and the Greeks used their famous penteconters, small galleys, rowed by 50 men.

They traded the attractions of civilized living in return for raw materials, especially metals. This led them to establish colonies at Massalia (Marseilles) for the overland route for tin from northern Europe,

AROUND AFRICA

It may not have been too difficult for ancient geographers to have conceived of the proposition that the Phoenician explorers could have circumnavigated the continent of Africa. They knew, for example, that salt water poured into the Mediterranean through the Strait of Gibraltar and similarly through the gulf of Aden. They saw no reason why the Earth should not have a vast encircling ocean.

Perhaps they imagined Africa as a symmetrical disc of land whose diameter was roughly the same as the coast of the southern Mediterranean. If so, this possibly explains why, around the year 600 BC, the reigning Pharaoh, Necho, having abandoned his plans for a Nile–Red Sea canal, issued a decree that a fleet should be equipped for such a voyage, using a Phoenician crew and captain. Even so, the fact that the expedition did not apparently turn back when it encountered the immense equatorial and subtropical continent is so surprising that it has long been the subject of critical appraisal by historians of discovery.

We only have Herodotus's sceptical account to go on – and he had heard it from his countrymen on the Nile when he visited Naukratis, the trading centre which Necho's father had set up as a Greek merchant colony.

However one detail, which Herodotus refused to believe, is paradoxically the best attestation as to the story's veracity. 'They told a tale that I personally do not believe . . . how that they had the sun on their right hand as they sailed along the African coast.'

This phenomenon would have been unknown to a Mediterranean sailor but, in the southern hemisphere, for the 800 km (500 miles) westwards from Port Elizabeth to Cape Town and beyond, the sun would certainly have been on the starboard side. Undoubtedly the winds and currents worked in favour of a voyage around Africa from east to west and it is possible to reconstruct something like a detailed itinerary of the voyage.

The circumnavigation of Africa from west to east was a much more difficult proposition. An extraordinary manuscript from the 10th century AD describes in considerable detail the attempted voyage of discovery and colonization of the Phoenician Hanno at some point in the 5th century BC. Precise reconstruction of the voyage is difficult. The exact location of the bay called 'the Horn of the South' where Hanno found an island 'full of savages . . . women with hairy bodies whom our interpreters called "Gorillas"' has never been precisely determined but it may have been somewhere on

Strabo, much respected for having accurately proposed a circumnavigable Africa, portrayed Rome as the centre of a Eurasian world monarchy.

the coast of modern Liberia.

Eudoxus of Cyzicus, a Greek sea captain from the Black Sea, was far less fortunate. The account of his final West African expeditions comes from the Roman geographer Strabo who manages to convey just a hint of scepticism at the magnitude of the task which Eudoxus was attempting using his own resources and without political support. A transformation in sailing techniques would be necessary before the circumnavigation of Africa from west to east could be seriously attempted.

---

at Gades (Cádiz) on the Guadalquivir River in Spain close by rich copper deposits and on the coast of northern Africa – above all at Carthage (Tunis) – for trans-Saharan gold. But, in a pattern to be repeated in the 15th century, it was logical for the Phoenicians to go directly to the source of supply. Hence the voyages of exploration which took Hanno of Carthage down the west coast of Africa and another Carthaginian, Himilco, with instructions 'to explore the further parts of Europe' through the Atlantic.

The Greeks believed that the cross-cultural trading empire of the Phoenicians preceded their own. In fact, they seem to have begun at the same time and developed along similar lines, with the Greeks colonizing from the Aegean outwards along and beyond the northern Mediterranean. They made Miletus on the Aegean shore a rich city, the home-port for expeditions through the Hellespont and Bosphorus to the Black Sea. Greek traders went far across the Black Sea to Georgia and the Caspian, possibly reaching deep into Russia as well.

To the west, the Greeks came up against the Phoenician control at the Strait of Gibraltar. However, seizing the advantage created by a brief collapse in Carthaginian power, Pytheas of Massalia led an expedition on behalf of the trading community there through the strait and northwards beyond the Breton coast to the British Isles and the sources of tin. Sailing round the British Isles, he reached 'Furthest Thule' (*Ultima Thule*) and the contradictory reports of what Pytheas found there, as recorded in a variety of ancient sources, have been a spur to the imagination and curiosity of geographers and explorers ever since.

The Greeks were also not above placing their skills in the service of great foreign rulers. Towards the end of the 6th century BC, Scylax, a Greek from Asia Minor set out at the behest of Darius I, the Persian king, to investigate the course of the Indus. He probably travelled through the Persian empire and reached the Indus by way of the Kabul River, sailing down to its mouth on the Indian Ocean. He then

*c.*330 BC Pytheas circumnavigated the British Isles and went north to Ultima Thule, an unknown northern island, possibly the Faroes or Shetlands.

325 BC Craterus travelled overland by elephant through Baluchistan bringing home the sick of Alexander's army.
325 BC Nearchus, Admiral of Alexander's

fleet, sailed from the Indus through the Strait of Hormuz and into the Persian Gulf to meet the army on the Tigris.
305 BC Megathenes wrote the Indika after

sailed along the bleak Baluchistan coast, across the Gulf of Oman and along the southern coast of Arabia before returning by the Red Sea with good first-hand information about the Indian Ocean and colourful reports of strange one-eyed men to be found in India and men whose ears were fern-shaped and as big as baskets.

No exploration is without danger. The most enterprising and daring of the ancient explorers was Eudoxus of Cyzicus and his endeavours appear to have cost his life and that of his crew. His expeditions are the climax to the commercial possibilities, accumulated navigational skills and geographical knowledge of the Mediterranean cross-cultural communities.

Eudoxus was initially commissioned by Euergetes II, ruler of Egypt in *c.*146 BC, to undertake a voyage to India. Guided by an Indian pilot who had been cast ashore in the Gulf of Aden, he was led to India (whether he followed the monsoon or the coastal route is unclear). He returned with a cargo of spices and precious stones which were promptly seized as treasure trove under Ptolemaic law.

A second expedition took place, this time under the sponsorship of Cleopatra. Returning from India, however, Eudoxus's ship was driven southwards and ashore below Cape Guardafui ('the Cape of Spices'), the most easterly African headland. The native inhabitants treated him well and it was here that he found, floating in the sea, the prow of a wooden ship with a horse carved on it. When he finally returned to Carthage, he learned that this was

identical to the figureheads of ships to be found plying the Atlantic waters off Morocco and Cádiz. The flotsam was conclusive evidence of the sea-route round the coast of Africa.

Eudoxus's last voyage was a rare example of a free-enterprise expedition in the ancient world. He had been forced to surrender his second Indian cargo to Cleopatra and, doubtless intending to explore the sea route, he then built and equipped two expeditions from his own resources (the first ran aground off the coast of Morocco), stocking them with gifts as well as colonizing tools. The second expedition never returned.

Greek science and understanding of the natural world spread more widely than the confines of its political influence. The Mediterranean achievements in maritime exploration and discovery were strongly based on the knowledge of the fundamental principles of physical geography, astronomy and geometry. To an extent, of course, these voyages of discovery were treated as trade secrets. It is not just the ravages of time that make our information at times tantalizingly fragmentary.

The cross-cultural nature of the Mediterranean's trading communities ensured, however, that neither the scientific knowledge of the Greeks nor their geographical discoveries died with the eclipse of Hellenistic civilization. Nor was this rich inheritance exclusive to the Romans or to Christianity. The world of Islam benefited too, and over a millennium later it inspired Europe's maritime reconnaissance in the 15th century.

ULTIMA THULE

Himilcon was probably told to discover the so-called 'Tin Islands' (the Isles of Scilly or St Michael's Mount) where tin was traded. The only surviving account of his voyage is in a geography book known as the *Ora Maritima* of Avienus, written about 800 years later. If that source is to be believed, Himilco took four months to reach the coast of Brittany, finding flat calms, giant 'sea monsters' and great beds of sea-weed on the way.

Massalia (Marseilles) was also the starting-point of a much more impressive and determined maritime expedition. Pytheas was a geographer and accomplished astronomer who

was not afraid of tackling complex problems. He had attempted to work out the position of true north, postulated the alternation of the tides with the phases of the moon and invented an accurate method of determining latitude with a calibrated sundial. Although the report upon his celebrated voyage of reconaissance no longer exists, a considerable amount is known about it from other sources.

He followed the route of Himilco to the west coast of Brittany and then proceeded to find the British Isles. His first view of Albion (Britain) was of Land's End in Cornwall (Belerium). He

found the natives 'hospitable', 'thanks to their trading contacts with foreign traders'. From this point, Pytheas sailed round Britain, noting the customs of the inhabitants. Marvelling at the high seas 'above Britain' he set out on a six-day crossing to reach 'Thule', variously identified with Iceland, the Norwegian coast, the Faeroe Islands and (most plausibly) with the Shetlands. From there, he may have visited Ireland before returning to the continental coast in order to find the 'Amber island' and complete the assignment which he clearly had been given by the Greek trading community of Marseilles.

being Ambassador to northern India.
*c.*300 BC Voyages of Himilco in search of the tin islands (probably the Scilly Isles).
*c.*215 BC Hsu-fu founded colony in Japan.

*c.*146 BC Eudoxus sailed from the Black Sea to West Africa attempting to circumnavigate Africa from west to east.
*c.*138-116 BC Chang Chi'en travelled along

the Silk Road beyond the Jade Gate reaching Fergana and Peshawar. Spent many years imprisoned on the way.

CONQUEST AND EXPLORATION: ALEXANDER THE GREAT

The remarkable mosaic from the Casa del Fauro near Naples evokes the battles of Alexander and Darius. The emperor is depicted in the vigour of his youth.

The empires of the ancient world were gradually pieced together around 500–300 BC. Like all classical empires, they depended upon technical superiority for their survival from nomadic incursions. In the Archaemenid empire of Persia, a prowess in metal technology and horse-breeding provided the basis for a territorial empire in which tribute-paying satraps (provincial governors) administered unified codes of laws, a stable currency and an efficient postal service. Its capital cities at Ecbatana, Nineveh and Persepolis (Hagmatana) were amongst the wonders of the ancient world.

There were similar developments in the Ch'in empire and the kingdom of Magadha in India. But the most outstanding was the territorial empire which transformed the Greek world in the 4th century BC. The extraordinary expeditions of Alexander the Great conquered the Persian empire and opened up the routes to India.

Alexander's father, Philip II of Macedon, had laid the foundations of the Greek territorial empire and first dreamed of overthrowing the Persian king, Darius III. But before he could realize his ambitions, he was assassinated in 336 BC leaving his son, the new Macedonian king, in charge of the combined Greek forces at the age of 20.

Alexander had been Aristotle's pupil and, from him, had acquired an appreciation of the value of knowledge as power. He understood the importance of scientific observation and he was well read in the Homeric legends, whose archaic voyages and conquests he aspired to emulate. Attached to his army were a number of geographers, astronomers, mathematicians, botanists and engineers. *Bematistae*, or human pedometres, counted out the length of the days' marches to assist the geographers in compiling their records.

Although records of his campaigns were carefully

compiled by Aristobulus, Onescritus and his official historian, Callimachus, none has survived. Historians know of them only at second-hand, through the Roman writers, Arrian and Curtius. These sources are testimony to the enduring respect for Alexander as an explorer as well as a military strategist in the Roman world.

His expeditions were concentrated into 11 years of frenetic military campaigning. In the spring of 334 BC he left the Macedonian capital, Pella, with up to 40,000 infantry and 5000 cavalry. In the first year, he marched through Asia Minor (Turkey) subduing local tribes until he laid siege to the island fortress city of Tyre and captured the Persian fleet.

Moving south, he met no further resistance except at Gaza. Instead, he was welcomed at the city of Memphis, where he was crowned Pharaoh in November 332. In the spring of 331 he founded the first of many cities, the sea-port of Alexandria on the island of Pharos in the Nile delta. This had associations for him because it had been mentioned by Homer. It would be a permanent reminder that Alexander had become the master of the Mediterranean.

From there he made the journey to the shrine of Zeus Ammon in the Libyan desert to obtain a recognition of the divine parentage which he had now begun to claim for himself. The difficulties of the eight days' march across the desert may have been exaggerated by historians; but it was good training for what was in store and, when they arrived at the

Persepolis, Darius's capital, became the showpiece city of ancient world empires. It consisted of a maze of columned buildings constructed on a huge stone terrace.

Siwa Oasis, Alexander let it be known that 'he had been told what his heart desired' by the Oracle.

The first expedition beyond the pillars of civilization began with the defeat of the Persian king Darius on the plains of the upper Tigris near Arbela. Darius became a fugitive, and the fabulous cities of the Persian empire lay wide open to Alexander. Babylon and Susa at once surrendered to his armies and Alexander seated himself on Darius's throne. In January 330, he continued his march to Persepolis, crossing the Persian mountains in southern Iran. When he arrived, he put Darius's palace to the torch and seized a vast treasure.

Alexander then chased Darius by forced marches north-westwards into the Iranian mountains, following the caravan trails to Ecbatana (Hamadan), some 1800 metres (6000 ft) above sea-level. By the time Alexander reached there, Darius had already made his way eastwards to the Caspian Gates (now known as the Sirdar Pass), still the route which carries the main road connecting Teheran and Herat.

In the second half of July, Alexander finally caught up with Darius near Hecatompylus (Damghan) only to find him mortally wounded from an attack by a Persian satrap, Bessus, who had promptly declared himself Darius's successor. Alexander waited for the main body of his army to catch up before descending through the dense forests of the north slopes of the Elburz mountains to the shore of the Hircanian (Caspian) Sea.

For the rest of the year, Alexander subdued native tribes and then, skirting the great Asian steppes to the north, followed the water-courses and caravan trails through Arachosia (Kandahar) in pursuit of Darius's successor. In the spring of 329, he took the army up the Panjshir valley and crossed the mountains by the 3475-metre (11,400-ft) Khawak Pass. Up to their waists in snow, suffering from frost-bite and the effects of the high altitude, they lived off terebinth (the 'terpentine tree') and the raw flesh of mules until they reached Kabul and the watershed of the Indus.

With a much depleted force, Alexander moved to the head of the Kabul valley. Beneath the Hindu Kush, he founded another city – Alexandria ad Caucasum (so called because he believed himself to be in the Caucasus). There followed a brutal 17 days' march through the passes north of Kabul into northern Afghanistan and the valley of the Oxus River (Amu Daria). The valley was mostly sandy desert and the river, over 1 km ($^3/_4$ mile) wide at Kelif, almost impossible to bridge. They eventually crossed it on rafts made from their leather tent covers

THE 'OCEAN'

Every great explorer is allowed an obsession. Alexander the Great's was with the 'Ocean'. His tutor Aristotle had taught him that the world was a sphere and that around the land mass flowed a continuous stretch of water which he christened the 'Ocean'. To Alexander, world monarchy was thus dictated by trying to discover where this ocean truly lay.

When he finally arrived at the Caspian Sea, he discovered that it contained no true sea fish and this seemed to disprove the theory of the Ancient Greek geographers that it formed the southernmost tip of the Ocean to the north. However, Craterus, one of Alexander's commanders, found that seals lived in it and this was taken as evidence that it must once have linked up with it.

This obsession guided Alexander's explorations. He did not follow the Oxus into central Asia because he thought that the river merely returned to the Caspian which had been partially dismissed from his quest. He stopped at the Jaxartes for the opposite reason. Ancient geographers had generally regarded that river as directly flowing into the ocean. He knew little about the Indian sub-continent. He seemed to believe that the Indus was part of the headwaters of the Nile and that beyond it would lie the Ocean.

He is supposed to have addressed his exhausted and demoralized troops, having crossed the Indus and reaching the foot of the Himalayas thus: 'If any of you wish to know what limit may be set to this particular campaign, let me tell you that the area of country ahead of us, from here to the Ganges is quite small. You will undoubtedly find that this ocean is connected with the Hyrcanian Sea [Caspian Sea], for the great Stream of Ocean encircles the earth. Moreover I shall prove to you, my friends, that the Indian and Persian Gulfs and the Hyrcanian Sea are all three connected and continuous. Our ships will sail round from the Persian Gulf to Libya as far as the Pillars of Hercules, whence all Libya to the east will soon be ours, and all Asia too, and to this empire there will be no boundaries but what God himself has made for the whole world . . .'

When he finally reached the Indian Ocean, he slaughtered bulls as a sacrifice to Poseidon as a thanksgiving. As it turned out,

Alexander the Great was portrayed with many of the attributes of a deity. On this medallion from Alexandria, the ram's horn of his patron god Ammon is visible on the headdress.

however, it was his commander Nearchus who would discover far more about the Ocean than the land-loving Alexander. But, even at the end of his life, he was still contemplating further explorations to discover the extent of the Ocean – through the Caspian Sea and even, perhaps, around Africa.

stuffed with hay and finally captured Bessus in his native Bactria and despatched him to a singular and gruesome fate.

Alexander then followed what would become the Silk Road to Samarkand and on into the steppes to reach the Jaxartes River (Sir Daria). Here, he founded another city, afterwards known as Alexandria Eschate. Alexander probably believed that this river was the boundary separating Europe from Asia and that it flowed northwards to the 'Ocean'. In the winter of 327, 2000 of his men froze to death as he campaigned in the steppes north of the Hindu Kush.

In the spring, he recrossed the Kush, probably through the 4370-metre (14,340-ft) Kaoshan Pass, arriving in Alexandria ad Caucasum in some ten days (it would take as long as that now). Here he prepared for the assault on India, a subcontinent of which he knew little beyond the Indus. Early in 326, one arm of his army crossed through the Khyber Pass whilst Alexander himself set off with a lighter force via the Kabul river and some of the wildest country in Asia. When he reached the upper Indus, he led an attack on the impregnable fortress Rock of Aornos. The modern observer, looking up the thousands of feet from the river, close to where Alexander built a causeway to bring his siege engines within range of the Pir-Sar ridge, has a measure of Alexander's extraordinary talents.

Advancing now into the 'Land of the Five Rivers' (the Punjab) he crossed the main one, the Hydaspes (Jhelum), when it was in full flood and gave battle to a Punjab rajah in the midst of the monsoon season. Here was where his famous war-horse, Bucephalus, died, the fact recorded in another of the cities Alexander founded – Bucephala. Failing, however, to persuade his army to march beyond the Indus, a contingent of ships was built on the Hydaspes and the remainder of his army sailed down to the Arabian Sea.

One portion of his army returned to the Persian Gulf by sea under the command of Nearchus; the remainder followed Alexander back by land, experiencing aching thirst in the desert of Baluchistan with its sandstorms and quicksands. He reckoned that the 60 days on the Makran coast had cost him the lives of 60,000 people and all their baggage animals. Only when they finally struck inland to Pura, the capital of the province of Gedrosia in the former Persian

AD 54 Diogenes may have discovered the sources of the Nile and Mountains of the Moon on his journey along Ethiopian coast. *c*.AD 60 Periplus of the Erythrean Sea

described the western coast of India from the Indus to Goa.
AD 60 Nero's centurions followed the Nile into the Sudd.

AD 97 Kan Ying attempted to reach Rome but was captured *en route*.
AD 120 Maes Titanius's agents visited Kashgar to obtain information on

empire did they know how far it was back home and that they were safe.

In the course of a decade, Alexander had travelled more than 32,000 km (20,000 miles). He had founded more than 70 cities. He and his commanders had added permanently to the geographical knowledge of the Greeks. They had also collected a vast amount of information about the plant life and the ethnography of the regions. In Bactria, for example, his troops unwittingly constructed an oil well when they set up his tent near the Oxus. In southern Pakistan, they met natives who lived off fish, feeding their flocks off fish meal and living in huts made from whale carcasses.

Alexander died in Babylon on 10 June 323 BC at the age of 32. The story that he was poisoned (and that Aristotle may have prepared the draught) is less likely, however, than that the explorer's experiences (he had contracted dysentery in Bactria, was wounded on the Indus, and his gargantuan appetites were well-attested) had worn him out. The vast empire he left behind him was quickly dismembered by his successors. But his remarkable achievements inspired other men. One of the first was Chandragupta (whom Alexander is supposed to have met on the Indus), who went on to set up the first of the great Indian empires.

THE SILK ROAD

Two thousand years ago, China and the West were held together by a thread. It was known as the Silk Road. Between the stable civilizations of the Mediterranean, India and China – satisfying the exotic tastes of their elites – corals and pearls, amber and glass, woollens and linen were traded eastwards in return for lacquerware, spices (especially cinnamon) and, above all, silk.

The Greeks and Romans knew little of how the silk was made. It was produced, they surmised, by the mysterious 'Seres' (the word derives from the Chinese for silk). Pliny, writing in around AD 70, thought that silk was a pale floss found growing on leaves. Pausanias, a century later, knew that it was spun by insects but this view was not held universally until the eggs of silk worms were transported back to Byzantium from India by monks in the 6th century.

The Silk-Road trade was valuable. In around 100 BC, 12 caravan trains left China for the west each year and the taxes on them provided up to 30 percent of the Chinese Han dynasty's revenues.

Pliny thought that these imports cost the Roman empire a hundred million sesterces per annum.

The Silk Road was the central nervous system to all Asian landed exploration in the period before 1500. From the comparative safety of the Great Wall at Jiayuguan, the caravans started their slow progress through what is now the Chinese province of Xinjiang. To lead a caravan through nomad country would have been dangerous at the best of times. In the centre of Xinjiang, however, lies the Takla Makan desert, some 1000 km (600 miles) east to west and 400 km (250 miles) wide, a wilderness of pure sand, whose dunes reach to 90 metres (300 ft). This wasteland was shunned by explorers for centuries. Marco Polo referred to its 'rumbling sands' whilst a Chinese historian said that 'travellers find nothing to guide them but the bones of men and beasts and the droppings of camels'.

To the north of the desert runs the mountain range of the Tian Shan and, to the south, that of the Kunlun Shan. Both were well-watered so that rivers flowed down towards the Takla Makan from north and south, creating a string of oases along the base of the mountain ranges. These oasis towns provided the stopping points for the vital 1000 km (600 miles) or so of the Silk Road to Kashgar and the outer limits of the Persian empire and its successors.

From Dunhuang, the 'Sand City' of Marco Polo, where the frescoed caves of the underground watercourses are decorated with Hindu figures over 1400 years old, the Bactrian camels were generally led on the northern route to Turfan. There, subterranean

JOURNEY ACROSS CHINA'S BORDERLANDS

It was customary for Chinese travellers to recount the dangers of crossing Tibet, the Karakoram, the Takla Makan and the Pamirs. The geography of China's borderlands certainly did not make landward contact with the rest of Asia easy. It was rendered more difficult by the reputation they acquired amongst native Chinese.

Fu-Hsien describes the treacherous route through the Pamirs in vivid terms: 'Keeping to the range, the party journeyed on . . . for fifteen days over a difficult, precipitous, and dangerous road, the side of a mountain being like a stone wall ten thousand feet in height. On nearing the edge, the eye becomes confused; and wishing to advance, the foot finds no resting place. Below there is a river, named Indus . . .'

caves house some of the earliest and richest sources for Buddhist art. *En route*, dead cities, once oasis towns, still survive in mud ruins of battlements and palaces. At Gaochang, for example, six kilometres (four miles) of ramparts, 9-metres (30-ft) high in places, surround an eerie labyrinth of grid-plan streets and palace compounds. When the steppes to the north were unsettled, there was always the alternative southern route.

The Chinese led the camels but the oasis towns were settled by a succession of nomadic peoples – Uzbeks, Kazaks, Kirgiz and Uighur. They traded in horses, cloth, jade, spices, tea and wood. At Kashgar, the great market town of the Silk Road, Persians, Afghans and Turks bartered their wares. Some went westwards. and others south, across one of the wildest roads imaginable, over the Pamirs to cross the upper waters of the Oxus and into the Indian sub-continent.

Whilst the major civilizations were politically stable and the peoples of the steppes not restless, the possibilities for travel and discovery lay open from both east and west. This was the case particularly from c.150 BC to c.AD 450. In about AD 120 a Greek merchant named Maes Titanius sent out agents to Kashgar to gain information about the Silk Road. This was the source for Ptolemy's fairly accurate descriptions of central Asia. From the east, the Han emperor Wu Ti despatched Chang Ch'ien, an emissary, to Bactria. The Huns, who seized him both on the way there and on the way back, kept him in captivity for over 20 years. In AD 97, a further ambassador named Kan Ying was sent by the Han emperors from China to Rome but he too was captured before he reached his destination.

The Silk Road also provided oases of religious pluralism. Even now, frescoes and vast rock-carved buddhas, pagodas, Persian stupas, islamic minarets and mosques stand in proximity with each other. In the first centuries of the Christian era, Buddhist monks and Nestorian Christians were amongst the most intrepid explorers. Their religion led them to explore very widely in south Asia, taking Buddhism to Burma, Ceylon and down the Malayan peninsula. One Chinese Buddhist monk, Fu-Hsien, known as 'the Manifestation of the Faith', accompanied by three fellow-monks, travelled by the southward side of the Takla Makan in 399. From there, he crossed into India through 'mountains covered with snow both in winter and summer . . . they shelter also dragons which, if once provoked, spit out their poison'.

Using the networks of Buddhist monasteries, Fu-

Merchants on the Silk Road during the period of Mongol hegemony (c.1300) which established peace and security for trans-Asian trade and contact.

Hsien spent 15 years travelling round India in search of Buddhist enlightenment and manuscripts. He returned via Ceylon and Java and ended with a hair-raisingly long voyage back to the Chinese mainland. However, once back in Nanking, he wrote the *Fo-Kwe-Ki* (the *Memoirs of the Buddha Dominions*) which gave details of his routes, the weather, the names and sizes of towns and the customs of the peoples he had encountered.

Two hundred years later, another monk, Hsüan-Tsang, determined to 'travel in the countries of the west in order to question the wise men on the points that were troubling his mind'. Riding an old horse, he

AD 635 A-Lo-Pen, a Nestorian priest from Persia, founded a church in China.

c.AD 800 Norse occupation of the Shetland Islands, Hebrides, Orkneys and Faeroes.

c.AD 850 Soleiman, an Arab Merchant crossed the Indian Ocean to Malacca and reported on Chinese sea routes.

c.AD 860 Ibn Khurdathabah of Baghdad

described the caravan route from western to central Asia.

c.AD 860 Fabled voyages of Naddod, Gardar and St Brendan to North America.

A lodging at a caravanserai, the doorway guarded with chains. There are fires for the travellers whilst their horses stand below the flooring inside the building.

left China in AD 629 and, the following spring, crossed the Tien Shan range by a glacial pass. Travelling extensively in central Asia round its Buddhist monasteries, he then went south to India. Although he lost many manuscripts when he crossed the Indus in around 643 as well as a collection of rare seeds, he eventually returned to Ch'ang-an in the spring of 645 where on the emperor's orders he was given a great welcome after his absence of 15 years. By all accounts, he had brought back with him a chariot drawn by 20 horses and loaded with more than 700 religious manuscripts, statues of the Buddha, prayer-wheels and relics.

Hsüan-Tsang spent the rest of his life compiling the magnificent *Ta-T'ang-Si-Yu-Ki* (or *Memoirs on Western Countries*), an official account issued by the emperor T'ai T'ang. It was the most substantial record of China's neighbours produced under the auspices of its officialdom (many times longer than the Bible) before the 17th century.

ORBIS TERRARUM: THE GEOGRAPHY OF THE ANCIENTS

Mental exploration of the universe by the Greeks and Romans far outstripped their empirical discovery of the Earth's surface. In their search for a full explanation of the world around them, they developed a geography which was integral with their cosmography and which itself drew to the full upon the resources of Greek astronomy, mathematics (especially geometry), physics, astrology and, above all, philosophy.

Symmetry was a basic philosophical premise of Greek scholars. The most symmetrical form was a sphere and therefore, the Greeks argued, the Earth (man's home) must be spherical. Pythagoras (6th century BC) may have been the earliest philosopher to hold this view; at any rate he worked out some of the mathematical laws for the circular motions of celestial bodies, and his pupil Parmenides applied these to observations made from the surface of a round Earth.

Plato, who lived a century after Parmenides, was the first philosopher to announce the concept of a round Earth located in the centre of the universe with the celestial bodies in circular motions around it. Whether this was Plato's original concept, or whether it had been proposed to him by Socrates, cannot now be determined. Aristotle provided crucial additional observations. He pointed out the significance of the fact that, when the shadow of the earth crosses the moon during an eclipse, the edge of the shadow is circular. He also recognized that the height of various stars above the horizon increased as one travelled towards the north, which could only have occurred if the observer were travelling over the curved surface of a sphere. Strangely he never noted the additional support for the concept of a round Earth much more commonly adduced in Europe in later centuries, that of the disappearance of a ship beyond the horizon – hull first.

If the Earth were a circumference, how then was it divided up? Herodotus had thought the Earth's surface must be arranged neatly balanced around the Mediterranean, the Nile to the south matched by the Ister (Danube) to the north and so on. Beyond the known world lay, so he thought, the surrounding 'Ocean'. One of Plato's contemporaries, Eudoxus of Cnidus, developed a more sophisticated theory of zones of climate based on their increasing slope (*klima*) away from the sun on a spherical surface.

This theory was turned by Aristotle into the concept of the varying habitability of the Earth with differences of latitude. Knowing the intense heat experienced in the desert just south of the Mediterranean (the world's record for high temperature is held by a place in Libya) Aristotle concluded that parts of the land-mass close to the equator, the torrid zone, were uninhabitable. The *ekumene*, the inhabited part of the Earth, was in the temperate zones. But much of the Earth was not inhabited because of the

*c.*AD **860** Svavarsson discovered and circumnavigated Iceland.
*c.*AD **862** Rurik and his Viking forces reached Novgorod and Dnieper River.

*c.*AD **865** Floki Vilgerdason attempted to settle in Iceland and named the island.
*c.*AD **870** Norwegian foster brothers Arnarson and Hrodmarsson with their

families settled in Iceland.
AD **875** Viking Ottar reached the White Sea.

CALCULATING THE EARTH'S CIRCUMFERENCE

The difficulties for the Ancients in calculating the Earth's circumference were enormous, the conceptual problems vast. Eratosthenes was the first to put together two separate, dissimilar, and simple observations in order to arrive at an astoundingly accurate result.

The first came from near Syene (Aswan). On an island just below the First Cataract there was a deep well. At the bottom of the well at noon on the summer solstice, the image of the sun was reflected in the water. This was already well-known and, from it, Eratosthenes correctly deduced that the sun must therefore be directly overhead.

The second observation was made outside the Museum in Alexandria (almost due north of Syene) where there was a tall obelisk. Using the obelisk as a gnomon, Eratosthenes measured the length of the shadow at noon on the solstice. He was thus, applying his Greek geometry, able to calculate the angle between the vertical obelisk and the rays of the sun and thereby to arrive at the opposite angle at the centre of the Earth. Eratosthenes measured this as one-fiftieth of the whole Earth's circumference.

It was then only necessary to fill in the distance between Syene and Alexandria which Egyptians already knew to be the equivalent of about 5000 stades (or roughly 800 km/500 miles) and multiply this distance by 50. He thereby concluded that the whole

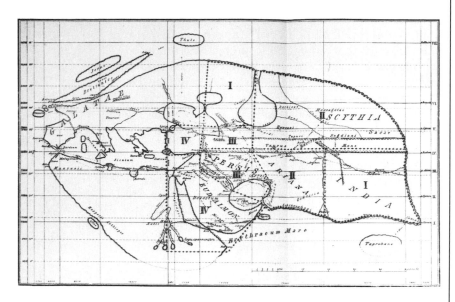

Earth was about 40,250 km (25,000 miles) in circumference (actually, measured through the poles it is 40,008 km/24,860 miles).

The calculation was, to a certain extent, correct only by chance; various inaccuracies had cancelled themselves out. His successor Posidonius was probably not alone in regarding this as an overestimate and recalculated it, using the height of the bright star Canopus above the horizon at Rhodes and Alexandria (which he assumed to be on the same latitude) and calculating the distance between the two places on the basis of the average sailing times for ships. The result was a circumference of

A reconstruction of the world map as envisaged by Eratosthenes. He worked from two axes converging at Rhodes and portrayed the distinctive latitudes of the earth's surface.

29,000 km (18,000 miles).

Overestimating the west-to-east length of Europe and Asia (the *ekumene* was thought to end with India), he therefore reckoned that a ship sailing westward across the Atlantic from western Europe would reach the east coast of India after a voyage of only 11,250 km (7000 miles). This was the basic calculation on which Columbus would rely centuries later.

Ocean. Although there must be a southerly temperate zone, reasoned Aristotle, the Greeks would never reach it because of the intense heat of the torrid zone.

The mapping of the world by the Ancients reached its peak in the remarkable efforts of a generation of scholars in the world's first scientific research institute, the Museum and Library at Alexandria. Eratosthenes, its librarian from 234–192 BC, calculated an astonishingly accurate measurement of the Earth's circumference. He also wrote a book describing the *ekumene*, the inhabited Earth, in which he accepted the major divisions of the Earth's

surface – Europe, Asia, Libya and the five zones (torrid, two temperate, two frigid) – and gave them mathematical boundaries in the form of irregularly spaced lines of longitude and latitude. In addition, he prepared a world map, an *orbis terrarum*, the first known atlas to use a grid pattern, basing his meridian on Alexandria and his prime latitude on a line through the Pillars of Hercules to Rhodes.

Eratosthenes's successor as librarian at Alexandria, Hipparchus, was the first to wrestle with the problem of how the curved surface of a sphere was to be represented on a flat surface. He devised two kinds of projections so that the distortion of the

spherical surface on a map could be carried out mathematically. He explained how to make a stereographic projection by laying out a flat parchment at an imagined tangent to the Earth and then extending the latitude and longitude lines from a point opposite the point of tangency. He also demonstrated the orthographic projection, produced in a similar way only with the lines projected from a point in infinity. Both projections were only capable of producing a hemisphere. On both, either the central portion is too small in relation to the periphery (stereographic) or the central portion is too large (orthographic).

The greatest ancient geographer, however, was Ptolemy (Claudius Ptolemaeus). Nothing is known of his life except that he worked at the library in Alexandria between AD 127 and 150. He was the author of the great work on classical astronomy – the *Almagest* – which long remained the standard reference work on the movements of celestial bodies. His concept of the universe agreed mainly with that of Aristotle. He thought the Earth was a sphere

This woodcut from a 1486 edition of Ptolemy's Geography *indicates the limits of geographical knowledge in Europe, showing a substantial continent joining Africa with south-east Asia and depicting the Indian Ocean as an inland sea.*

LATITUDE AND LONGITUDE

Longitude (east–west relationship) was always much more difficult to determine than latitude (north–south relationship) and especially on board ship. This partly explains why the New World lay for so long undiscovered and why 'East' and 'West' were so long separated by sea.

Discovering latitude is simple, for the circumpolar stars or the altitude of the sun above the horizon provide the crucial facts. At the equator the sun at noon on the equinoxes is directly above or at altitude 90°, while at the North Pole the sun is totally invisible in winter and always visible in summer. In between, the altitude of the sun above the horizon at noon can be noted, and then compared with astronomical tables which, in medieval nautical almanacs, were already so accurate that someone who had properly determined the declination of the sun

could fix his latitude to within half a degree or even less.

For these observations, medieval sailors used a simple cross-staff (or 'Jacob's Staff', known to the Greeks as a *dioptra* and to the Arabs as a *kamal*). The handier backstaff, or English quadrant, which allowed the observer to stand with the sun behind him and avoid being dazzled, was devised in 1595 by an Englishman, John Davis.

Longitude was a different proposition because the navigator had to measure the difference between the time, for example, when the sun was at noon in different places. Sundials and *klepsydra* (literal translation, 'water-thief' – an alabaster or glass vessel with slanting calibrated sides and a small hole at the bottom which functioned as a water-clock) worked only in stable conditions on land, and

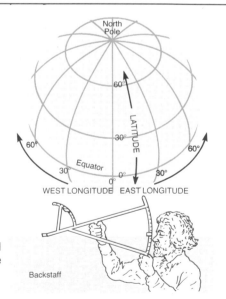

Backstaff

not at sea. The measurement of longitude at sea, out of sight of land, remained a largely insuperable problem until after the European Discoveries.

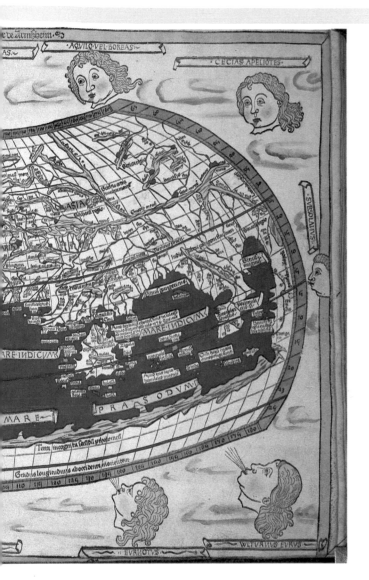

which remained stationary in the centre whilst the celestial bodies moved around it in circular courses. Such was his influence that this became an article of faith in medieval Christendom.

After completing the *Almagest*, Ptolemy undertook to prepare a *Guide to Geography*. The intention was to produce the most accurate and precise *orbis terrarum* that was humanly possible. Adopting a grid of latitude and longitude, his guide went on to detail in six volumes of tables the world's first geographical gazetteer from which to revise the world map. The first and last volumes contained an invaluable discussion of map projections and then, finally, maps of different parts of the world based on the gazetteer.

Accurate measurement of space and time eluded Ptolemy. Latitude could only be determined approximately and there was no way of measuring longitude. So, the further he worked east from his prime meridian (a north-south line through the westernmost islands in the Atlantic, the Canaries or the Madeira islands) the more inaccurate he became. It was not surprising that, on the basis of Ptolemy's calculations and Posidonius's smaller estimate of the Earth's circumference, Columbus estimated that Asia must lie very close to Europe in the west.

The more serious inaccuracy was a perceptual one. Ptolemy indicated on his maps that the Indian

STRABO

Much of what scholars know about these ancient geographers comes from the Roman authority Strabo (*c*.64 BC–AD 20). Most of the written record on geographical ideas in Ancient Greece and Rome has disappeared and has to be pieced together from surviving cross-references. But Strabo's monumental work on geography (the *Geographia*) remains almost intact. It was known in Christian Europe but it was never translated into Arabic. Only at the close of the Middle Ages did its alternative picture of the Indian Ocean as a sea rather than a lake begin to challenge the ascendancy of Ptolemy.

His research was conducted, inevitably, at Alexandria and he drew extensively on his predecessors. He accepted Aristotle's zones of habitability and it was from Aristotle that he had absorbed the existence of

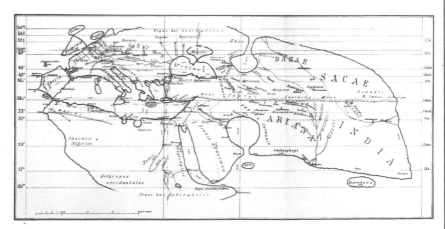

an ocean surrounding the Earth's land mass. He too chose the smaller calculation of the Earth's circumference made by Posidonius.

He provided an inventory of the known world for the administrators of the Roman empire. Although the Romans were not great explorers themselves, they were great empire-builders. Their land-surveys, military

The world according to Strabo's Geographia *which, in contrast to Ptolemy, suggests that the Ocean flowed around the southern tip of Africa.*

maps and coastal charts, to judge from the few surviving examples, were of a high technical proficiency. Upon such skills, future exploration would rely.

*c.*AD **880** King Alfred the Great sent Othere and Wulfstan to examine north cape of Europe. Othere reached Archangel, and Wulfstan explored Prussia and Estonia.

*c.*AD **891** Al-Yaqubi published *Kitab al-Budan*, a first-hand account of routes within the Islamic empire from North Africa to India.

*c.*AD **900** Gunnbjörn discovered Greenland.
*c.*AD **914** Al-Masudi travelled from Baghdad to the Aral Sea and possibly as far as Madagascar and Sind.

Ocean was enclosed by land to the south – in effect he turned it into a lake. This notion had probably originated with one of Hipparchus's projections. This *Terra Australis Incognita* appeared regularly thereafter on Islamic and European world maps. It was only at the end of the Middle Ages that Strabo's influence began to counteract that of Ptolemy.

The discovery of the skies was of vital importance to the discovery of the earth's surface. The Islamic contribution to astronomical knowledge was profound.

THE GOLDEN AGE OF ISLAM

The end of the Ancient World was marked by religious transformation. The religions of the Ancient civilizations had been 'immanentist' – teaching their followers (mainly the literate elite) to accept the way the world was, their place in it, to avoid extremes, and to strive for uniformity and stability within an ordered cosmography. Now, and for complex reasons connected with the failure of those civilizations to encompass more than a limited degree of change, there appeared 'transcendental' religions. Their distinctive features included manifestations of messianism, the preaching of individual salvation, an acceptance of change, instability and discontinuity in the name of religion, and a distinctive religious-based cosmography. God came to earth and changed world time (e.g. AD Christ). These were religions of exploration.

No event in world history between the death of Christ (and, with it, the foundation of the first great 'transcendental' world religion, Christianity) and the European voyages of discovery was more significant than the rise of Islam. The mission of its founder, Mohammed (d. AD 632), was to unite the divided Arab peoples through a new monotheistic religion. His message, obedience to the Almighty power of God, initially aroused the opposition of conservative Arabs. Yet within a century of the prophet's death, it had been carried across the Pyrenees to the west and to the outer confines of India to the East. By AD 750, when the Abbasid Caliphate was founded, Islam was the major civilization west of China.

The Arabs, geographically placed at the crossroads of Eurasia, united for the first time by a common religion, tolerant of other religions and cultures but aware of the fascination which attracted so many to convert to the faith, achieved remarkable prosperity. Islam's heartland lay in the cities such as Baghdad, Cairo, Morocco and Córdoba. Mecca itself became a great city, bazaar and mosque in typically close proximity. It was the place of pilgrimage (Islam, like medieval Christianity, sanctified travel) which all Muslims were enjoined to visit once in their lifetime.

Baghdad was reputed to have been the largest city anywhere in the world before 1600. It is estimated to have had around two million inhabitants in 900 and its surface area was as large as that of Paris at the end of the 19th century. The surviving evidence from the urban villas, commercial ledgers, letters of credit and treatises on arithmetic, law, medicine and cypher, testifies to the wealth of its merchant and

c.AD **920** Ibn Fadlan, as religious adviser to Bulgarians recently converted to Islam, met Viking traders on the Volga River.
c.AD **982** Erik the Red banished from

Iceland, and spent three years exploring the coasts of Greenland.
c.AD **986** Bjarni Herjolfsson discovered lands to the south and west of Greenland, possibly

North America.
c.**1000** Leif Ericsson sailed via Helluland (probably Baffin Island) and Markland (Labrador) to Vinland.

THE MAGNETIC COMPASS

Apart from the directions of the rising and setting sun, which varied with place and season, the only ones which would help a traveler or a sailor orientate himself on the Earth's surface before the compass were those of the winds. By the 1st century BC the Chinese had developed their 24 seasonal winds and used weather vanes and kites to measure them. Ancient Greeks were so accustomed to use the names of the winds to indicate the directions from which they came that for them "wind" signified "direction."

The octagonal Tower of the Winds in Athens (2nd century BC) is a reminder of the vivid symbolism attached to each of their eight winds. The puffed cheeks of the symbolic winds on early maps were not mere decoration but the main direction-markers. The Spanish sailors on Columbus's ships thought of direction not as degrees of compass bearings but as *los vientos*, the winds, and Portuguese sailors continued to call their compass card a *rosa dos ventos*, a "wind rose."

The magnetized needle was first put to nautical use by travelers and

seamen in China around 1000 AD. From there, it was brought back, probably by Arab traders, to the Islamic world. Islam had a peculiar need for a sense of absolute direction because its believers were required to face Mecca in prayer. Only by finding geographical coordinates could they be certain that their mosques were properly orientated toward a distant place. Some of the surviving portable travelers' compasses from Islam are works of art.

Through Islam, the compass reached the west, the first mention of it being in the work of Alexander Neckam (1157–1217), an English monk lecturing at the University of Paris.

The magnetic compass enabled the sailor to find an absolute direction anywhere on the globe without complicated astronomical calculations. But common seamen were often wary of its powers. The prudent sea captain consulted his compass in secret, lest he become accused of consorting with Satan. This helps to explain the origins of the binnacle, the "little house" or box, where the compass was kept away from prying eyes.

The magnetic compass was first discovered in China but became widely used by Muslim pilots in the Indian Ocean and Islamic travelers crossing the desert.

At Sagres, Prince Henry the Navigator would combat such superstitions by accustoming his pilots to the everyday use of the compass. By Columbus's time, the magnetic compass had become indispensable and a captain carried extra magnetized needles. Using his compass, Columbus was able to take his bearings direct for Cipangu and stay on the same latitude, without the aid of celestial navigation.

literate classes, whose prosperity Allah seemed to sanctify, sometimes even to will.

The golden age of Islam was one of commercial prosperity. Its gold and silver coins (*dinar* and *drachma*) circulated widely, the gold recovered from the ore in a new process, the *amalgama* of Islamic alchemists. Demand for silver sent its merchants to Spain, North Africa, Iran and Afghanistan. In the mountains around Kabul at Ma'din Benzihir lay the famous medieval silver mine, operated by up to 10,000 laborers. Similar demand occurred, however, for foodstuffs, horses, wood, other metals and slaves and this led its merchants into contact with the civilizations of medieval Europe, India and China as well as with the nomadic peoples of Sahara and the steppes. Contacts stimulated technical change and adaptation of all kinds.

Techniques of rice cultivation, sugar-cane and citrus fruit production were imported from India to the Middle East. Stirrups, trappings, harnessing

collars, animal medicine and tattooing were all developed in the golden age of Islam. New breeds of camel and horse were achieved by cross-breeding the native animal stocks from North Africa, the Middle East and the steppes. Steel of the kind forged into swords at Damascus and Toledo was imported right across the Arabian world from India – hence its name *al-hindi*. No Islamic city was complete without its slave populations providing the forced labor, supplied via the slave markets of the Sudan and the "Slav" Balkans.

A similar process of adaptation went on in the intellectual world. Greek, Roman, Persian and Indian traditions fed into Islam. This adaptation was helped by the fact that all knowledge (*'ilm*) was sacred and subordinated to the revealed truth, the taste (*dhawq*) for which was transmitted from one generation to another (*al-'ulūm al-naqliyyah*). The mosque was the religious and social center of the Islamic community and its center for learning.

1004 Thorvald Ericsson attempted unsuccessfully to settle in Vinland. Norse attempts at colonization continued to 1013 but failed due to local hostility.

1095-1291 The Crusades in the Holy Land.
*c.***1150** The Jewish medieval traveller, Benjamin of Tudela wrote of his journeys in the western Mediterranean and Levant,

Mesopotamia and Persia.
*c.***1150** Pethahiah of Regensberg visited Jewish communities in Poland, Soviet Central Asia, Syria and Palestine.

The only educational establishments outside the mosques were the hospitals (for medicine) and the observatories (for astronomy, astrology and geography). The observatory as a scientific institution owes its birth to Islamic civilization, its typically domed roof replicating that of a mosque. While in the early Islamic period, the observatory was of a small size and usually associated with a single astronomer, from the 13th century onwards it became a major scientific institution in which numerous scientists gathered to work and teach together. These served as models for those constructed in the 17th century by Tycho Brahe and Kepler.

Islamic cosmology was therefore directly related to the principles of Islamic revelation and the inner teachings of the Prophet. Greek, Persian, and Indian knowledge was selectively drawn on insofar as it supported this revelation. The natural world was 'Islamicized' in much the same way as it was 'Christianized' in the European Middle Ages.

Muslim studies in geography therefore began from a symbolic and sacred geography which viewed the earth as an image of the spiritual world. This did not exclude, however, the most exact mathematical measurement of geographic coordinates. Islamic accuracy was assisted by their systematic use of the compass, an innovation which was imported from India.

Centred most of all on the vast confines of the Islamic world (the *dar al-islam*), and drawing upon Babylonian, Greek, Indian and Persian traditions, its geographies were truly impressive. These were descriptive and mathematical (the most important of which in the Golden Age was *The Figures of the*

Arab dhows carried large payloads with a relatively small crew, as this illustration from a Baghdad manuscript of 1238 suggests. The Golden Age of Islam would have been impossible without them.

Earth (*Ṣurat al-arḍ*) of Muhammad ibn Musa al-Khwarazmi). As Arab and Persian sailors made their way beyond the Indian Ocean to Java and towards China, there were scientific descriptions of their discoveries, such as the *Reports on China* (*Akhbār al-Ṣin*) and the *Reports on India* (*Akhbār al-Hind*) of

AL-IDRISI

Abu 'Abdullah al-Idrisi was a Moroccan geographer who served at the court of Roger II, the Norman king of Sicily. He studied in many mosques throughout the Arab world and had visited Asia Minor when he was only 16 years of age. For his patron he wrote the *Book of Roger* (*Kitāb al-rujāri*) and prepared a world map.

The map of Al-Idrisi corrected Ptolemy's world picture, abandoning an enclosed Indian Ocean and the Caspian Sea as a gulf of the world ocean and correcting the course of numerous rivers.

Based on Hellenistic and earlier Islamic sources, this map was on a vast scale, consisting of 70 sections formed by dividing the Earth north of the Equator into seven climatic zones of equal width (the seven climatic zones of the Greeks had become infused with the mystical mathematical power attributed to that number by Islamic thinkers). Each zone was divided into 10 equal parts along lines of longitude. The large silver planisphere which originally accompanied the maps and text no longer survives.

*c.*1154 Al-Idrisi, Arab traveller and cartographer, confused the Niger with the Nile in *The Book of Roger.* Uncertainty about the relationship of these two rivers persisted to the 19th century.

1170 Madoc, a legendary Welsh Prince, allegedly established a colony in the New World.

1183 Ibn Jubair extended his pilgrimage from Granada to Mecca, to visit Baghdad, Aleppo and Damascus.

IBN BAṬṬŪṬAH

Pity the two Arabs from Qatar, Ihad Amer Chamari and Saled Mohammed Chamari, who set out in February 1987 to retrace on the backs of camels and horses the eight expeditions of Mohammed Ibn Baṭṭūtah who, from 1325 to 1354, visited Timbuktu and Mombasa, saw the Volga River and Samarkand, voyaged to Ceylon and made it to Peking. They have a long way to go.

Ibn Baṭṭūtah (the name means 'Duckling's son') was born in Tangier in 1304. At an early age, he decided to go on pilgrimage by land to Mecca. He turned it into an exploration, praying to a saint here, visiting a mausoleum there, everywhere taking notes of his wanderings. At Damascus, he attended the Koranic teachings in the mosque and was awarded with a 'universal teaching certificate', an Islamic passport to travel.

Then to Arabia, the Holy Land of Muslims, where he made a devout pause in his journey in 1326 for more study and prayer, acquiring the double title of pilgrim and judge (*hadj* and *cadi*), before going eastwards in the company of merchant caravans to the non-Arabic Muslim lands of Asia.

His first long sea-voyages took him to Somalia and what is now Tanzania where he described the difficult relations between the Muslim–Arab traders and the 'pagan' Africans whom they enslaved. Like the modern American tourist, his principle was 'never to follow the same road twice' except to Holy Mecca. So, in 1331–3 he was in Turkey and, fascinated by what he heard of tales of the Golden Horde from travellers on the Silk Road, followed it to India.

Once there, he found himself appointed judge and, the height of his career, sent on embassy to China. It was non-Muslim Asia, but had not the prophet said that dealings with the Infidel 'to gain knowledge' were permitted? In fact he was shipwrecked, pirates taking his valuable notes, and only later did he finally reach Peking, to be saddened by its paganism but admiring of its 'accomplishments and artistic talents'.

Returning to Tangier in 1354 after 29 years' absence, Ibn Baṭṭūtah passed his time until his death in 1370 writing up his notes for the edification of future Muslims, to the thanks of all historians and the admiration of all explorers and travellers.

Suleiman the Merchant and the famous *Wonders of India* (*Ajā'ib al-Hind*) of Buzburg ibn Shahriyar Ramhurmuzi.

The height of Islamic geographical studies is to be found in the great Abu Rayhan al-Biruni, the Islamic master of mathematical, descriptive and cultural geography. His *Determination of the Coordinates of Cities* (*Tahdid nihāyāt al-amākin*) and comparable works of mathematical geography were designed to enable mosque builders to place their buildings upon a precise alignment with Mecca. But they also enabled cartographers such as Abu 'Abdullah al-Idrisi to produce world maps of great detail, accuracy and beauty. As late as the 16th century, the cartographic works of Pir Muhyi al-Din Ra'is, containing maps of Africa and America were to a standard unmatched anywhere in the world and continue to astonish scholars by their accuracy.

By the 12th century Arab cosmographers were producing encyclopedias of their knowledge of the Earth's surface. To this period belongs the incomparable geographical dictionary of Yaqut entitled the *Dictionary of the Lands* (*Mu'jam al-buldān*), which is still an indispensable tool of research for modern scholars. The work incorporated a great deal of local information which had been collected by extensive travel. This was an age of travellers and foremost among them was Ibn Baṭṭūtah, who set out from Tangiers and reached as far east as India and China. In his remarkable book *The Gift of Observers* (*Tuḥfat al-nuẓẓār*), usually known as the *Travels*, he provides extensive geographical and topographical information, not to mention history, religion and ethnography, which made his work one of the outstanding medieval sources in world history.

DARK AGE EUROPE AND THE VIKINGS

Between the founding of the ancient civilizations of Euro-Asia and 1500, Europe's was the only one which became detached from its ancient heritage. During the 3rd century AD, the Roman empire suffered a political and military crisis which almost brought it down. The division of the empire for administrative convenience into a western portion, based on Rome, and an eastern one, based on the new capital at Constantinople (Istanbul), gradually led to a divergence of interests and deprived the vulnerable west of ready access to eastern resources and knowledge. The settlement within the empire of barbarian peoples from beyond the Rhine and the Danube prepared the way for the large-scale barbarian incursions of the 5th century and the subsequent collapse of the western Roman empire. In its place appeared a collection of kingdoms and principalities, some of which, like Britain in the 5th and 6th centuries, were almost closed worlds.

1226-1346 Order of Teutonic Knights conquered and established urban centres in Eastern Europe.
1245-7 Giovanni da Pian del Carpini,

travelled 4750 km (3,000 miles) through Poland and Russia to take a message from the Pope to the Mongol rulers.
1253 Guillaume of Rubruquis sent as

missionary to the tartars by Louis IX of France. Travelled through the Crimea to the Mongol capital in the Karakorams.

The appearance of Christianity as a widespread influence in the Roman empire, contributed to the weakness of the empire and the declining respect accorded to the pagan classical authorities. Knowledge of the classical Greek language declined and Europe tended to rely on abbreviated versions of the classics, often themselves dependent on inferior Latin authors.

Solinus, whose *Collectanea Rerum Memorabilium* won him the name 'Polyhistor' in recognition of the many marvellous things he recounted, delighted in accounts such as that of the Calabrian snakes which sucked milk direct from the cow, of men who turned themselves into wolves, and others who covered themselves with their ears whilst they were asleep. Such authors were widely read in the Christian Middle Ages. In transcendental religions, revelation replaced empirical truth and, in the absence of any opportunity to verify such tales first hand, it was difficult to discriminate between the true and the false.

Christianity did, however, stimulate some aspects of travel and exploration. The practice of pilgrimage was encouraged, if not largely created, by the discovery in Jerusalem in 326 of the relics of the True Cross by the mother of Constantine, the first Christian emperor. Many perhaps followed Antoninus of Placentia who, in 570, carved his name on the very couch (or so they told him on his trip to the Holy Land) used by Christ at the wedding feast of Cana. Like the Welsh saints, David and Caduc (both of whom are said to have visited Jerusalem in the 6th century), he may even have prayed for the gift of tongues to help him on his journey. The idea that Jerusalem was at the centre of the world, which appears in some world maps of the 12th century when the Crusades had served to make the city a focus for everyone's interest, can be traced back much earlier.

Christian conversion provided the spur to some exploration upon the European fringes. The missions to England of St Augustine in 597, and of Theodore and Hadrian in the 7th century, the one from Tarsus in Asia Minor (Turkey) and the other from North Africa, are evidence of a willingness to travel long

THE VINLAND SAGA

Two sagas record the discovery of Vinland and its aftermath. The *Greenlander's Saga* is now thought to date from the latter part of the 12th century and to be the more reliable. *Erik's Saga* was probably compiled in the 13th century and may well have been an edited version to highlight the importance of Erik the Red and his family in the discovery.

According to the *Greenlander's Saga*, Bjarni Herjolfsson, on his way from Iceland to visit his family in Greenland shortly after the first colonizing voyage of 986, was blown off course and reached landfall on the continent of America; various suggestions as to the location have included Sandwich Bay, South Bay and the southern end of Baffin Island. Sailing back to Greenland, Herjolfsson landed by luck where his father had settled and he ended his days a farmer, blissfully unaware of the greatness thrust upon him.

At some date in the 990s, Erik the Red's son, Leif bought Herjolfsson's ship in order to retrace the latter's voyage. There were no sailing

directions and it was a matter of luck, seemingly, that he made his way back to the same place, which Leif now named as Helluland or 'Slabland', a further landing which he called Marklandor 'Forestland'; and finally a third land, mild in climate, ample in fish and vegetation where he overwintered and found grapes and timber, from which Leif named the land Vinland or 'Wineland'.

Leif apparently never returned to his discoveries, but in the following years there were several more voyages from Greenland. His brother Thorvald led the next; they spent the winter in the houses built by Leif in Vinland, explored some of the surrounding country and encountered hostility from the natives, whom the Vikings called 'wretches' (*skraelings*) – possibly American Indians or Eskimos. One of them mortally wounded Thorvald in his armpit with an arrow. He told his men to bury him on a headland that he had thought of as a good site for a settlement. He was followed by his brother Thorstein who failed because of bad weather, and by the second

husband of his sister-in-law, Thorfinn Karlsefni.

The *Greenlander's Saga* also records one more voyage, that of Erik the Red's daughter Freydis, who reached Vinland but later returned to Greenland after murdering her partner in the voyage and killing several of the other womenfolk herself as well.

There have been many attempts to provide archaeological proof of the Viking presence. The site at L'Anse aux Meadows (originally L'Anse au Méduse or 'Jellyfish Creek') in northern Newfoundland, discovered in 1960 by the Norwegian Helge Ingstad, and excavated, is convincing.

The foundations of buildings resembling those in Greenland have been discovered, a few artefacts of Norse origins, and carbon dating confirms the possibility. It is clear that this was a Viking site, and that it was not occupied for long. Nothing, however, conclusively proves that it was the spot inhabited by Leif Ericsson and his successors, convenient though that hypothesis undoubtedly is.

VIKING LONGSHIPS

Ideas of Viking ships are inevitably drawn from the notion of the longship, of which the 9th century Gokstad and Osberg ships are splendid examples. The Atlantic crossing, made in 1893 in as little as 28 days from Bergen to Newfoundland by a replica of the Gokstad ship demonstrated how effective the design was. But the longship (*langskip*) was shallow, intended for coastal passage and very different from the halfship (*hafskip*), shorter, even broader in the beam and much deeper in draught, resistant to high winds and capable of carrying cargo. Ship design was a matter for long evolution, a process to which these voyages probably contributed.

Navigational aids depended on experience rather than equipment. In the absence of a compass, it seems (though the evidence is thin) to have involved observations of the sun and the Pole Star, cloud formations, the flight of birds and the lull and smell that an experienced seaman recognizes as the lee of a distant island. In many respects, Columbus and Vasco da Gama's techniques were not so very different.

Viking longships only give a rough impression of the knorr *or halfships which were guided by a long oar or steerboard (hence 'starboard').*

distances for the faith. Pilgrims continued to visit Jerusalem even after the conquest of the Holy Land by the Arabs in the 630s. A Frankish pilgrim, Arculf, is especially well-known because, on his return in about 680, his ship was blown off course to the remote Scottish island of Iona, where he told his experiences to Adamnan, abbot of the famous Irish monastery there. In 701, his account was given to King Aldfrith of Northumbria, and was later incorporated by Bede into his own works.

The conversion of Ireland itself, begun in the 5th century by Palladius and Patrick, led Irish monks to sail to many of the islands round the British Isles in search of solitude. The voyage literature, known as the *imram*, which became very popular among the Celts, combined pagan notions of an Elysian kingdom somewhere to the west as well as Biblical concepts of a promised land which would be reached by those with faith.

It is in this light that the 9th-century *Life of Brendan* (*Vita Brendani*) and the somewhat later *Navigatio Brendani* (*Voyage of Brendan*) should be interpreted, for (despite the ably presented assertions of some modern commentators to the contrary) there is no proof that St Brendan ever crossed the Atlantic to America. By contrast, the more sober evidence of the Irish scholar Dicuil, who wrote at the court of Emperor Louis the Pious in about 825, confirmed by

Scandinavian sources, strongly suggests that Irish hermits had been in Iceland before the arrival of the Vikings in the middle of the 9th century.

Of all the activities of western European explorers during the Dark Ages, the Scandinavian expansion which began at the end of the 8th century was the most impressive. It was based on the islands off the European continental shelf. The islands around the coasts of Britain and Ireland were the key to wider exploration. Although settlers in the Faeroes and Iceland came from Norway, Norway itself was not the best-placed starting-point for the discovery of islands far out in the Atlantic. Iceland lay 1000 km (600 miles) to the west of Norway and to reach Greenland by the most direct route involved a journey of about 1600 km (1000 miles) from the Faeroes through fierce seas. Such voyages would not have been likely at a first attempt.

Settlement of the Faeroes began early in the 9th century and was followed less than two generations later by that of Iceland. Later sources speak of three separate voyages: of Naddod; of a Swede named Gardar Svavarsson; and of a Norwegian named Floki. They took place between 860 and 870 and were followed by extensive settlement, the first colonization of new territory by Europeans.

The first recorded sighting of Greenland was made around AD 900 by one Gunnbjörn, who had

Thingvellir, the site of the old Icelandic parliament and, according to tradition, an early landfall of the Vikings in Iceland.

apparently been blown off course while on his way from Norway to Iceland. It was, at first, of little use until all the good land in Iceland was used up; the first attempt to settle Greenland in 978 appears to have failed. But in the 980s, Greenland became the home of fugitives from justice as the Viking states of Norway and England began to consolidate.

Erik Thorvaldsson, better known as Erik the Red, and his father, had originally left Norway 'because of some killings' and, in 982, Erik was again exiled for three years from Iceland for a similar offence. He decided to spend the time in exploring the mysterious land found by Gunnbjörn. He found it to be a seemingly endless land mass with high mountains and a great glacier within. Calling it Greenland was a good joke.

The evidence suggests that most of the settlers of Iceland and Greenland came from Norway. The colonists made a remarkably successful job of it, even in Greenland where the climate was more extreme. There were seal and walrus to hunt and grain could be grown because the global climate was favourable to them; the period 1000–1200 is known as 'the Little Climatic Optimum' to historical meteorologists and was several degrees warmer than in the later Middle Ages. The gift of a polar bear to the king of Norway in 1125 induced him to sanction

the appointment of a bishop for Greenland the next year. Viking ships and navigational skills proved easily capable of meeting the demands of ocean voyaging.

One of the most vexatious issues in all exploration literature is the apparent Viking discovery of a small portion of the North American continent. It is a matter where the small amount of potentially useful historical evidence has been clouded by over-enthusiastic commentary on the one hand, and ingenious forgery on the other. Concerning the details, there will never be final agreement and our evidence does not permit of firm conclusions. It is impossible to be sure when the Vikings discovered Vinland, where precisely on the North American coastline they arrived, and what they found when they got there. But, however sceptical one may be as to the details in the sagas, there is no serious doubt but that they represent accounts of genuine voyages to parts of the North American continent.

More intriguing is the question why the existence of Vinland was never more widely known outside Scandinavia. For whatever reason, the Viking exploration had little influence on the second phase of Atlantic exploration which began at the close of the Middle Ages.

MEDIEVAL EUROPE'S DISCOVERY OF ASIA

In 900, Europe chose to know little of the outside world. Even some of the Latin sources had been ostracized through their connections with heresy. Others had been turned into fables or Biblical allegories, such as that India had become the land of demons and giants, or Gog and Magog, who were supposedly prevented from overrunning the Christian world by being contained behind a huge wall built originally by Alexander the Great. *The Etymologies* (*Etymologiae*) of Isidore of Seville (d. 636) became a standard reference work on Asia. This gossamer web of stories – some reflected in the *Mappa Mundi* of Hereford cathedral – was a source for potent Christian legends.

One concerned the apostle St Thomas, who had voyaged to India and converted the natives. The so-called Acts of St Thomas, an apocryphal book composed in the 3rd century AD and translated into Latin, was widely known. King Alfred sent two Englishmen to India to visit his tomb and, in his *Geography of the Known World* (based on Orosius), Alfred mentions India confidently as the land beyond the Don river. With St Thomas in mind, it was not difficult for the

PLAYING WITH THE EVIDENCE

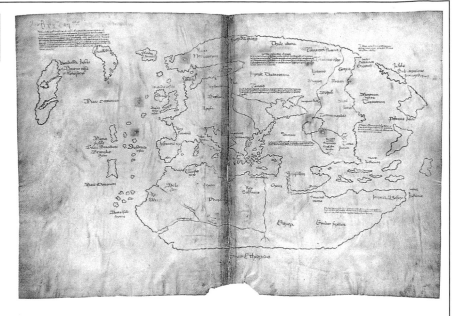

Tales of pre-Columbus contacts with North America abound and their upholders sometimes have ended up treating them almost as articles of faith. They include the possibility that the Irish monk St Brendan sailed across the Atlantic 500 years before the Vikings, a claim that a Welsh prince named Madoc discovered and colonized America soon after 1170, that a Norse expedition of Poul Knudsson to Greenland in 1355 went on to America and explored as far west as Minnesota, that an English Franciscan friar wandered there in the 1360s, and that two Venetians in the 1390s also made their way across the Atlantic.

Of these, only the Irish crossing of St Brendan should be admitted as a likely, but remote, possibility. For the rest, the Madoc legend seems to have derived from 16th-century attempts to glorify the Tudor dynasty. The alleged Knudsson expedition to America originated with the discovery at Kensington in Minnesota in 1898 of a runestone recording the expedition, and rapidly proved a forgery, probably committed by migrant Americans from Scandinavia anxious to prove something in the wake of the 1892 celebrations. The English Franciscan,

Nicholas of Lynn, turns out to have been a Carmelite who worked in, and may never have strayed far from, Oxford. The engaging Venetian narrative is generally held to have been written about the time that it was published, in 1558.

What, in the light of all this, of the famous 'Vinland Map'? Published in 1965, and dated by its editors to the 1440s, it appeared to be solid, if late, evidence for the discovery and continued, settlement of America by Scandinavians. Then the doubts set in, particularly over the ink and parchment. Yet, if it is a forgery, it is

The Vinland Map, whose authenticity is a matter of considerable controversy.

an elaborate one, capable of convincing an impressive team of analytic chemists at the University of California as to its authenticity. Of one thing, there is no doubt; the forthcoming quincentenary in 1992 of Columbus's famous voyage will certainly revive the debate.

Christian world in the era of the Crusades to hope for – ultimately to come to believe in – the existence of a great Christian nation in Asia who would be their ally in the fight against the Saracens. The arrival of an oriental patriarch named John in Rome and his lectures on the East before the Papal Curia seem to have been the origins of its most enduring manifestation, the legend of Prester John.

In another way, Europe came to be unique in the medieval civilizations of Eurasia. It was left comparatively undisturbed by the Mongol invasions. The Mongols were the last, and most violent, assault of nomadic steppe peoples upon the civilized world of Eurasia. The effects in China (invasion, the fall of a dynasty and division), the Middle East (invasion, large-scale displacement of populations and destruction, and the fall of the caliphates) and India (harassment and forays) were profound.

Over 1000 medieval mappae mundi *have survived. Few are as beautiful as the late 13th-century Hereford map. Jerusalem is portrayed at the centre of the world which is a flat disc surrounded by water.*

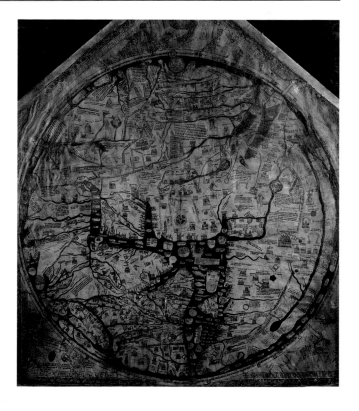

IOANES·PRESBR·MAX·DE·IDIAET·ETHIOPIA·

· FVGE·SVPERBIAN·TER ·
· FVGE·LVXVRIA·DELIGNO ·
· FVGE·GVLAM·DEPLVMBO ·
· FVGE·IRAM·DE·FERRO ·
· FVGE·INVIDIAM·DECVPRO ·
· FVGE·ACIDIAM·DEARGENTO ·
· FVGE·AVARITIAM·DEAVRO ·

PRESTO·GIOVANNI·DE·INDIAETETMIO

PRESTER JOHN

From the second half of the 12th century onwards, Europe's interest in Asia was stimulated by the prospect that somewhere there existed a great Christian priest-king who might once and for all bring about the triumph of Christendom over its enemies. A famous letter, the *Letter of Prester John*, originating around 1165, purported to come from him and was addressed (in the numerous remaining manuscript copies) to the pope.

The authorship of the document has never been finally settled but it was probably a European cleric, possibly German, who was well-grounded in the surviving classical literature of the

The frontispiece to a popular Italian poem, written by Giulano Dati (1445–1524) and entitled 'The Great Magnificence of Prester John, Lord of Greater India and of Ethiopia'.

period and also knew the millenarian and utopian traditions as well. The letter was taken as confirmation of his existence and missions were sent to look for him.

A legend like this found great credence in the eschatological environment of the crusading armies of the 13th century. There were recurring reports that a Prester John figure (sometimes called King David) would destroy the Saracen from the East and they were believed. Pope Honorius III was so convinced that David was on the move westwards that he passed the news on to the bishops of England and France. Prester John acted as a beacon to explorers and it is a sign of Europe's greater knowledge of Asia that, from around the 1330s, the land of Prester John migrated from Asia to Ethiopia or central Africa.

In Europe, although there was a brutal incursion into Poland and Hungary in 1240 when the Mongols sacked Kraków and laid waste Silesia, Moravia and Hungary, the Mongols made no effort to occupy or annex eastern Europe. As a result, Europe's leaders persisted in believing that benefits were to be had in making contact with the Mongol Khans in order to assist Europe against the greater enemy, the Infidel.

After the church council of Lyons in 1245, Innocent IV therefore despatched two ambassadors to the Mongol court. Giovanni da Pian del Carpini (1180?-1252), a Franciscan friar, left with another Franciscan (Benedict of Poland) as his companion and interpreter. He journeyed through Poland and Russia to Mongolia and, two years later, returned to Lyons to write the report of his journey entitled the *History of the Mongols*. Much of the information was later incorporated into the widely read medieval encyclopedia, the *Speculum Historiale* of Vincent of Beauvais. Giovanni was the first European since 900 on record as having travelled east of Baghdad and returned to tell the tale.

Many others followed him in the course of the later 13th century. Among the more notable were André of Longjumeau in France, despatched in 1249, and Guillaume of Rubruquis (Rubruck) in French Flanders, who left in 1253, both sent by that great Crusader, Louis IX of France. A man, claiming to represent the Great Khan had come before the king, then on his way to the Seventh Crusade. The Great Khan, he said, was eager for an alliance

against Islam. The Khan, following the example of his mother, had reputedly converted to Christianity. All the leading Tartars would emulate him.

André of Longjumeau had accompanied Louis IX on the Crusade and knew some Arabic. His task was to be an informal diplomat and missionary for the king, to make an alliance and to assist the conversion of the Mongol people. He failed on both counts. After a remarkable overland journey, André finally reached the court of the Great Khan to find that the Khan had died, that the empire was in the hands of his mother, and that she was certainly no Christian in his eyes. She dismissed him with an insolent missive to his sovereign.

The overland journey back lasted over a year. When André returned, and despite his disappointments, he recounted hopeful reports that the Khan's grandfather had converted to Christianity after a vision in which God promised him dominion over Prester John. He brought cheering news of a Mongol chief, Sartach, son of Batu, whom he reported to be a Christian.

Louis IX was in the Holy Land when he received this optimistic account. With him was Guillaume of Rubruquis, who also knew some Arabic. Louis gave him a Bible, a small sum for expenses and commendatory letters and, in the company of a dipsomaniac friar and two servants, he left Constantinople on 7 May 1253. He went by ship across the Black Sea to the Crimea and then overland across the Don. When they finally reached Sartach, he 'mocked

1254 Nicolò and Maffeo Polo returned from their nine-year journey to the courts of Mongols: Marka and Genghis Khan.
1271-95 Marco Polo's travels through Asia.

1287 Rabban Bar-Sauma sent by the rulers of the Mongol-Persian empire to establish diplomatic relations with the West. Visited Constantinople, Paris and Rome.

1291 Genoese Vivaldi brothers lost their lives in an attempt to establish an all-sea route to India.

the Christians' and so, moving on beyond the Volga, and, suffering from hunger, frost-bite and the bitter winds of the steppes, he finally arrived at the court of the great Khan Mangu on 27 December 1253.

Guillaume stayed at the court until 'the great cold' of winter was over. But he made little progress with the Khan and mistrusted the Nestorian Christians in the court entourage whom he regarded as heretics. But he carried a letter back to Louis IX, returning to Cyprus by mid-June 1255 although by then the king was back in France.

Guillaume of Rubruquis wrote an account of his travels for the king. He described the Don and the Volga, and explained that the Caspian Sea was a lake. He was the first European to observe that Cathay was the same as 'Seres' and showed a keen eye for ethnology. Although his account remained in manuscript until 1600, much of it was embodied in the encyclopedia of his fellow Franciscan, Roger Bacon (c.1220-1292), the notorious 'Doctor Mirabilis' who was suspected of necromancy and magic by his superiors. Through Bacon's *Opus Majus* his discoveries were well-known to Christendom before the more remarkable journeys of Marco Polo.

European merchants in caravan working their way eastwards along the 'Silk Road' – as portrayed in an illustration from the Catalan Atlas of c.1375.

GIOVANNI DA PIAN DEL CARPINI

Giovanni da Pian del Carpini (from near Perugia in Italy) was an excellent choice as Europe's first envoy to the East. He had been one of the early associates of Francis of Assisi. Since 1222, he had played a leading role in the establishment of the Franciscan order. Its vow of strict poverty, coupled with its evangelistic aspirations, made Franciscans (like Buddhist monks) well-suited to the challenges of travel in remote lands.

The reasons for Europe's sudden reconnaissance in the 13th century are not hard to find. Firstly, there was a 12th-century renaissance, a tremendous advance in terms of the acquisition and transmission of knowledge and ideas and the beginnings of Europe's recovery of its classical heritage. This, in turn, was partly a by-product of the assault on Islam and the Spanish Reconquest. Through Christianized Arabs and Jews in Spain, Sicily and the Crusading kingdoms, fresh translations of Greek, Syriac and Arabic manuscripts in Latin became possible, thus transforming every branch of knowledge and science and Europe's perception of the wider world. At the

same time, Europe was transformed by the formation of an urbanized and politically sophisticated society which created a demand for education. For the first time since the Dark Ages, Europe had the beginnings of a literate laity.

Secondly, the Crusades placed Europe directly at the southern end of the old trade routes across central Asia. And Europe was to make this direct contact just as the Mongolian hegemony, the famous *Pax Mongolica*, was at its greatest extent. 1264 was the year that Kublai Khan took up residence at Peking and established his summer retreat at Shantu (Xanadu) in the hills north-west of the capital. Among his first visitors were the Polo brothers, Nicolò and Maffeo, who had left the Crimea in 1260.

MARCO POLO

Marco Polo excelled all the other travellers of medieval Europe in his determination, his writings and his influence. His journey through Asia lasted 24 years. He reached further than any of his predecessors, beyond Mongolia to China. He became a confidant of Kublai Khan and the governor of a great Chinese city. He traversed the whole of China, all the way to the Ocean. And he returned to tell the tale which became, for generations of Europeans, the greatest travelogue of their civilization.

His birthplace, Venice, was the centre for commerce in the Mediterranean and, under the influence of the Crusades, increasingly in the Levant and beyond too. Born in 1254, he was just 15 years old when his father, Nicolò, and his uncle Maffeo returned to Venice from their nine-year journey to the East. The family had trading offices in Constantinople and at Soldaia in the Crimea.

Marco Polo's book opens with an account of these earlier travels which had taken his father to the splendid court of Barka Khan, the son of Ghengis who had bought their entire stock of jewels and made the journey worth their while. On the encouragement of Tartar envoys there, they even journeyed to the court of Kublai Khan, a full year's travelling. He proved a man of broad curiosity, eager to learn everything about Europe and he asked the two brothers to be his envoys to the Pope, requesting 100 missionaries educated in all the seven arts to teach his people about Christianity and Western science. He also wanted some oil from the lamp at the Holy Sepulchre in Jerusalem. When they departed, they carried the Emperor's Golden Tablet, his certificate of safe passage, and returned to Venice late in 1269.

Kublai Khan (d.1294), hunting with part of his entourage near his Chinese summer palace. Dressed in ermine, the emperor is watching an archer shoot birds. A merchant camel convoy is in the background.

In 1271, when they once more set out from Venice on their return journey to Kublai Khan, they took with them Nicolò's 17-year-old son Marco and two Dominicans reluctantly accorded them by Pope Gregory X. Before they left the Mediterranean, the monks returned in panic, but the Polo family went on to Baghdad, Ormuz and then overland through the Persian desert and Hindu Kush to join the old Silk Road.

Kublai Khan received the Venetians with honour. No better account re-creates for us the court of the Khan. The Venetians stayed 17 years, acquiring 'great wealth in jewels and gold'. Eventually they returned as escorts of a Tartar princess. After a dreadful sea voyage through the South China Sea to Sumatra and the Indian Ocean, the Polos returned overland by way of Tabriz, finally reaching Venice in the winter of 1295. Then, three years later, in a sea-battle off the Dalmatian coast with the Genoese, a 'gentleman commander' of one of the Venetian

1294 Giovanni of Monte Cervino established Franciscan missions in China.
1313 Marino Sanudo, a commercial traveller in the Near East, published description and maps of Palestine.
1316-30 Odoric of Pordenone crossed China from south to north and returned by way of Lhasa in his attempt to convert the Chinese to Christianity.
1325-54 Ibn Baṭṭūṭah's eight expeditions covered over 120,000 km (75,000 miles) in North Africa and the Middle East.

galleys, one Marco Polo, was captured and brought back in chains to his prison in Genoa. His fellow prisoner, a writer of romances from Pisa called Rustichello saw the engaging possibilities of a true *Description of the World* and persuaded the Venetian to cooperate.

The account was obviously embellished in places by Rustichello. The scene of his first arrival at the court of Kublai Khan, for example, recalls the reception of young Tristan at Camelot, a familiar scene to a writer of medieval romance – indeed one already treated by Rustichello himself. Yet Marco Polo recalled, before his death, that he had only told half the extraordinary things which had occurred to him in his amazing life on the grounds that, had he recounted the other half, no one would have believed a word of it at all.

CHINA AND THE OUTSIDE WORLD

When Marco Polo arrived in China in the 13th century he was amazed by what he saw. China under the Yuan (Mongol) dynasty was a huge empire whose internal economy dwarfed that of Europe. Iron manufacture was around 125,000 tons a year (a level not reached in Europe before the 18th century). Salt production was on a prodigious scale: 30,000 tons a year in one province alone. Metal casting techniques could make standardized military, agricultural and other equipment. The administrative elite, the mandarins, could see to their delivery anywhere in the empire. A canal-based transportation system linked China's huge cities and markets in a vast internal communication network in which paper money and credit facilities were highly developed. The citizens of Suzhou, Nanjing and Hangzhou could purchase paperback books from market stalls with paper money, eat rice from fine porcelain bowls and wear garments of silk, woven to a standard no European craftsman could match.

This success had been achieved largely without help from outside. If you cross the great plains of China today, you can still trace the economic foundations of its ancient civilization. The great rivers wind down from the mountains in the west and then meander across the huge alluvial plains that make up the country's heartland. Running off from these rivers is the network of canals which carries the rich silt and water that allows the land to support an extraordinary density of population and provides its exceptional internal communication network. Controlling its two great river systems, the Yangtse and the Yellow River, preventing floods and building dykes was the task of the empire and its administrators.

Imperial government in China rested on a relatively small number of scholar-bureaucrats, chosen on the basis of scholastic merit. They ensured that the Chinese emperor ruled with the 'mandate of heaven', in accordance with social, economic and cosmological harmony. The Son of Heaven (the emperor) was the mediator between heaven and the people, protecting them from the destructive energies of nature. He was responsible for seeing that the water systems were in order, that relief was available in times of

MARCO POLO'S IMPRESSIONS OF CHINA

As he passed through the cities of the rich Yangtze valley, even a cosmopolitan Venetian like Marco Polo was astounded. He wrote: 'At the end of three days, you reach the noble and magnificent city of Kin-sai [Hangzhou], a name that signifies 'the Celestial City' and which it merits from its pre-eminence to all others in the world in point of grandeur and beauty, as well as from its abundant delights, which might lead an inhabitant to imagine himself in paradise . . . According to common estimation, this city is an hundred miles in circuit. Its streets and canals are extensive and there are squares, or market places, [these] being necessarily proportionate in size to the prodigious concourse of people.'

Venetian merchants trading bales of cloth for the spices of the Orient – from a 15th-century illustrated manuscript of Marco Polo's Travels.

An illustration from a 15th-century manuscript depicting the departure of Marco Polo from Venice at the start of his journey to the court of Kublai Khan.

famine and that they were adequately forewarned of disasters.

Prediction was based on astrology and astronomy. This is why the department of astronomy and mathematics was an important instrument of state. The imperial calendar, published each year, specified the days around the country in which essential events such as the release of water for irrigation took place and forced labour for the building of dykes was assembled. Armillary spheres and star-maps helped the mandarins to represent their knowledge of the cosmos.

On the ground, and independent of any influence from the west, the Chinese mandarins devised a grid pattern within which to represent the irregular surface of the earth and their vast empire. The Chinese Ptolemy, Phei Hsui, appointed Minister of Works to the emperor in AD 267, completed an 18-sheet map of China on a rectangular grid pattern using graduated divisions established by means of right-angled triangles. The terms he used for his coordinates (*ching* and *wei*) meant also the warp and weft of cloth which suggests that the origins for the grid pattern of Chinese maps lay in the silk on which they were painted.

In AD 801, during the T'ang dynasty (618–907), the emperor's cartographer completed a grid plan of the whole empire on a scale of 2.5 cm (1 in) to 100 *li* (a *li* was a third of a mile). It measured some 9 metres (30 ft) long and 10 metres (33 ft) high. Maps became so popular that they were found even in the imperial bathrooms. These were maps of the 'Middle Kingdom' (China) in which only China's immediate neighbours appeared, if at all. China's links with the outside world had been limited mainly to the small numbers of merchants who traded beyond the Jade Gates and along the Silk Road. Then, under the Sung dynasty (960–1279), foreign trade began to expand outwards.

The pace of technical innovation was considerably increased and China's commercial and industrial development was so great that it seemed on the threshold of a mercantile, even an industrial, revolution. Just as Europe's industrial revolution resulted in the establishment of an overseas mercantile colonialism, so China seemed poised to go in the same direction centuries earlier. The Sung dynasty, faced with military threats from its northern borders (which eventually overwhelmed it), maintained a huge army and was divided. Struggling to find the resources to meet its commitments, it actively stimulated foreign trade by the sale of licences and monopolies.

Whereas under the T'ang, only one port, Guangzhou, had been allowed to trade with foreigners, by the early 11th century, there were seven others. A new emphasis was given to boat-building, in which innovation was rewarded by the administration. The world's first paddle-boat was designed. Huge ocean-going junks designed like fortresses were sent into battle, equipped with cannon, rockets and bombs of all descriptions. Explosive rockets, which would shoot across the surface of the water, were developed along with submarine guns.

To these ports came Muslim merchants and, as the overland silk routes became impassable because of the Mongols, so the sea routes to the Red Sea became increasingly important. By this means, silk, porcelain, tea and spices reached the Arab world and from there Europe. The scale of this trade was considerable; nearly 10,000 pieces of broken Chinese porcelain have recently been found at Fustat near Cairo, one of the factory bases used in this trade; similar sites have been discovered in Oman and along the Red Sea coast.

Not only trade goods reached the west via this route. The transfer of Chinese technology was, in the long run, of greater importance than the flow of luxury goods. Paper, printing and gunpowder technology flowed westwards, as did that of the magnetic compass.

Another innovation, of eventual importance to Europe's overseas discoveries, was the stern-post rudder. Hitherto, European ocean-going ships had depended upon the use of an oar extending from the back of galleys. The stern-post rudder allowed for the construction of much larger vessels whose direction could be more precisely determined.

The Sung dynasty finally fell to the Mongol emperor Yuan (1279–1368) who extended the policies of maritime expansion adopted by the Sung. For the abortive invasion of Japan in 1281, the Great Khan had 4400 junks constructed. The Ming emperors (1368–1644) turned out to be different.

From their background in rural China, they distrusted the cosmopolitanism of their predecessors. Foreigners were suspect, external trade engaged in trifles, and merchants were exploiters. The Ming Emperor Gaozong expressed it all clearly: 'China's territory produces all goods in abundance, so why should we buy useless trifles from abroad?' In 1433, and again in 1449 and 1452, imperial edicts prohibiting overseas trade and travel, often with draconian penalties, were issued. Any merchant caught attempting to engage in foreign trade was a pirate and executed. Even learning foreign languages was forbidden, as was the teaching of Chinese to foreigners.

The swansong of Chinese maritime expansion

One of the giraffes reputedly brought back from Africa as a present to the emperor by the expeditions of Zheng Ho.

ZHENG HO

The last great naval expeditions of the Chinese empire were led by Zheng Ho. He came from Yunnan province in the south of China and from the Muslim minority which had established itself in the trading communities of the Chinese coastal ports. He was a eunuch, a king-maker, a diplomat and a great naval strategist and was popularly known as the 'Three-Jewelled Eunuch'.

As chief court purveyor, it may be presumed with some confidence that his purpose was partly to provide luxuries for the court as well as to collect tribute from Chinese overseas colonies.

His voyages took him along the east coast of Africa, to Mecca, and to the ports of India, Ceylon and Sumatra. He may even have explored the coast of Australia, but most of the accounts of his voyages and charts were lost or, more probably, destroyed.

He returned with pepper, sapanwood, exotic plants and even a giraffe from Africa, as well as a selection of monarchs who had refused to kowtow, notably the King of Ceylon. But the mandarins distrusted king-makers, meddling eunuchs, dissenting Muslims and Zheng Ho had been all three. With his fall from grace in 1433, the Ming navy shrank to insignificance and China withdrew from the world.

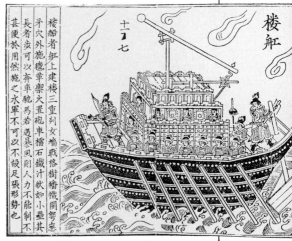

An early 16th-century woodcut of a Chinese warship – similar to the mighty treasure ships which had set out on Zheng Ho's expeditions.

PRINCE HENRY THE NAVIGATOR

Henry the Navigator, son of the Portuguese king, John I, was not a sailor and took no part in any voyages of discovery himself. Yet he has traditionally been seen as the principal driving force behind Portugal's exploration. More recently this has been questioned. The picture of him as a man of great learning has been reassessed – there is little evidence that he read any works of classical geography. He was only known to have been directly involved in sponsoring eight voyages between 1419 and 1460 and more coastline was explored whilst his brother Pedro was regent of Portugal (1440–9).

came in the early 15th century with the expeditions of the Three-Jewelled Eunuch, Admiral Zheng Ho. Between 1405 and 1433 he led seven armadas, consisting of as many as 62 ships carrying up to 40,000 soldiers, across the China Sea and Indian Ocean. His huge treasure ships were five times the size of the Portuguese caravels. Then, suddenly, the Ming emperor banned Chinese merchants from going abroad. The great treasure ships were put out of commission.

In this altarpiece for Lisbon cathedral, St Vincent is surrounded by leading members of the Portuguese royal house including Henry the Navigator wearing a large hat.

One document speaks of the War Office burning the documents relating to the expeditions because they contained 'doubtful exaggerations of bizarre things far removed from the testimony of people's ears and eyes'. When an imperial minister asked for a further search of the archives an official replied: 'The expedition . . . to the Western Ocean wasted tens of myriads of money and grain, and moreover the people who met their deaths on these expeditions may be counted in myriads. Although they returned with wonderful precious things, what benefit was it to the state? This was merely an action of bad government of which ministers should severely disapprove . . .' The minister listened quietly, rose from his seat, and then said: 'Your hidden virtue, Sir, is not small. Surely this seat will soon be yours!' In the next decade, Vasco da Gama arrived in the Indian Ocean.

EUROPE'S RECONNAISSANCE

The 'age of reconnaissance' was launched from one of the smallest of Europe's monarchies, Portugal. The capture in 1415 of the Moorish city of Ceuta in North Africa was followed by three quarters of a century of patient, often difficult, exploration of the West African coast. It was frequently held up by war in the Iberian peninsula, and by Portugal's domestic concerns. At last Bartholomeu Dias triumphantly rounded the Cape of Good Hope in 1487, and in 1498 Vasco da Gama reached India. Europe's first commercial maritime empire was about to be founded.

Unlike Columbus's discovery of America, which would turn out to have been a bold stroke of undreamed-of significance, the Portuguese voyagers undertook a rational, progressive, even systematic, process of exploration. Their reconnaissance involved firm political direction, a sense of objectives, an evaluation of risk and the expectation of reward. It was the prototype for modern exploration.

Portugal, though small, had political advantages over the other larger European states in the early 15th century. It did not experience feudalism in a form which left barons throwing their weight around. It did not suffer the ravages of the Hundred Years War. Its monarchy was well endowed with an inalienable domain and shrewdly played on the sense of national identity among its nobility when it fought the Castilians and undertook a competitive Crusade with them in the early 15th century. Its exploring achievements quickly became the basis for

THE EVOLUTION OF THE PORTUGUESE CARAVEL

Cornelis Anthoniszoon of Amsterdam (1500–54) painted this striking picture of a Portuguese carrack, a monumental wooden vessel, heavily protected by guns.

The caravel was specifically designed to meet explorers' needs. It was manoeuvrable with a small crew before the wind, and yet robust in high seas. It developed from Portuguese *caravos*, ships used by Arabs since ancient times, rigged with 'lateen' slanting and triangular sails, carrying some 30 crew, using a steerboard and constructed with flush planking. There was also a smaller vessel, called the *caravela* which was used on the Douro River in northern Portugal. This had a centre rudder and was clinker-built.

From these two designs, from the medieval traditions of Mediterranean and Atlantic boat design, the Portuguese constructed their ships of exploration. Manned by a small crew of about 20, caravels had a displacement of about 50 tons, were about 21 metres (70 ft) in length and 7.5 metres (25 ft) abeam and carried two or three lateen sails. 'The best ships that sailed the seas,' said Cadamosto.

a 'national' myth. 'This is the story of heroes who, leaving their native Portugal, opened a way to Ceylon, and further, across seas no man ever sailed before' is the opening canto of the famous epic poem *The Lusiads* (*Os Lusiadas*) of Luis de Camões in 1572.

Portuguese exploration was directed by its monarchs and crown princes. 'To discover what lay beyond the Canaries and Cape Bojador; to trade with any Christians who might dwell in the lands beyond; to discover the extent of the Mohammedan dominions; to find a Christian king who would help him to fight the Infidel; to spread the Christian faith; to fulfil the predictions of his horoscope, which bound him to engage in great and noble conquests and attempt the discovery of things that were hidden from other men; to find Guinea.' These, according to Gomes Eanes da Zurara, his official chronicler and author of the *History of Guinea*, were the aims of Prince Henry the Navigator, the most renowned (but not the only member of the royal house) to plan and play a leading part in Portugal's reconnaissance.

Prince Henry's motives were powerful and mixed. At the age of 19, he had been assigned the task of building a fleet and, after two years' preparation, he launched it in the Crusade against Ceuta. Within a day, the Portuguese took the Infidel stronghold and ransacked the caravan freight which they found –

pepper, cinnamon, cloves, ginger, tapestries, rugs, silver and jewels. From the captives he heard tales of the lands from which the treasures had come, and of how the Muslim caravans went southwards from Morocco across the Atlas mountains to arrive after 20 days at the shores of the Senegal River where a 'silent trade' of invisible bartering went on with the native peoples. Prince Henry lived with the sweet smell of that success for the rest of his life. He also lived with the lure of those tales, debating whether that river could be reached by sea.

The technical resources for the organization were gradually assembled. On the desolate and lonely promontory at Sagres, between Cape St Vincent and the bay of Lagos, a small school of navigation was established, with a church, a chapel and a pilotage and the nucleus of a small town with a shipyard. What is left of the great wind-rose that was established there may still be seen by the fortress. Here, and at the nearby port of Lagos, experiments in shipbuilding design produced a new type of ship without which the great seafaring expeditions of the next century would not have been possible, the caravel.

The first rewards from Portuguese discovery came, however, in the form of the Atlantic islands. The Canaries had already been discovered – probably by Genoese sailors – in the 14th century. These, and the Azores and the Madeiras, were colonized from

1435 Eanes explored West African coast almost to the Tropic of Cancer.
1455-60 Cadamosto and Gomes explored the Gambia and Senegal Rivers. May have discovered Cape Verde Islands.
1469-74 Gomes contracted to explore 100 leagues (about 475 km/300 miles) of West African coast per annum. Reached Gulf of Guinea.
1486-90 De Paiva searched for Prester John in Ethiopia.
1487 Covilhã sent by John II of Portugal

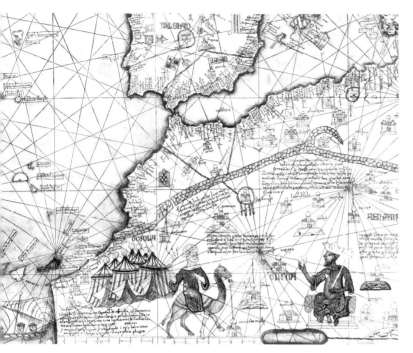

The king of Aragon's cartographer, Abraham Cresques, was probably responsible for compiling (c.1375) the famous mappa mundi *now known as the Catalan Atlas. He endeavoured to include the latest details of travellers from the Spanish peninsula to north-west Africa, even depicting the ruler of Mali, Mansa Musi.*

Portugal in the 1420s and 1430s. When they landed in Madeira (the word means 'wood') they set about clearing the thick vegetation and inadvertently started a fire which raged for seven years. The resulting potash providentially provided a perfect fertilizer for the vineyards planted by the colonists which in turn produced the famous wine.

The great conquest was not, initially, on the ground but in the mind. These islands helped to dispel the prevailing fear of the Atlantic as a desolate and empty place, the 'green sea of darkness'. Even so, Prince Henry sent 15 expeditions southwards between 1424 and 1434 and none of them would go further than Cape Bojador ('Bulging Cape') just south of the Canaries. Their fears may, even today, be understood.

Between Cape Drâa and Cape Bojador, the coast must have seemed dangerous, with heavy swells from the north-west around the Canaries, a stiff current and interminable surfy beaches. In winter there is a lot of fog and in summer the sea can turn red, discoloured by the sand blown offshore from the Sahara. Even Henry's shield-bearer, a noble with crusading pretensions, failed at the first attempt to penetrate further than the Cape. In 1433, however,

he did it and brought back with him from the shoreline a flower, known in Portugal as St Mary's rose, to prove it.

Thereafter, the pace of Portuguese discoveries shifted into a higher gear. In 1441, Antão Gonçalves, Prince Henry's Chamberlain, and Nuno Tristão, also a member of his court, reached Cape Branco (Blanco) – a further 400 km (250 miles) – where they took two natives captive. In 1444, Eanes brought back the first human cargo – 200 Africans to be sold as slaves in the market in Lagos. At the same time, the Portuguese monarchy bestowed on Henry a proportion of the royal profits from the enterprise and sole rights to grant licence to sail beyond Cape Bojador. The possibilities of the voyages became more apparent. Exploration was about to become exploitation.

When Dinís Dias rounded Cape Verde, the western tip of Africa, in 1445, the most barren coastline was past and the prosperous Portuguese trade along the West African coast with the inland kingdom of Timbuktu soon occupied up to 26 caravels a year. By a succession of three Papal decrees (in 1452, 1455 and 1456) the Portuguese king was given permission to enslave all unbelievers, to enjoy a monopoly in all matter and in every place to which the Portuguese conquest had extended and might extend in the future, even as far as the Indies, and to trade with the Infidel.

Thanks to the observant eye of Alvise da Cadamosto, a Venetian trader retained in Prince Henry's service in 1455 who set off in a caravel captained by Vicente Dias, we have a detailed, first-hand report of exploration, the African Gold Coast and its mighty rivers, the inhabitants of the region, its trade and the rapidly developing lore of Portuguese exploration.

In 1460, Prince Henry died. His nephew, Afonso V, in financial difficulties, found a way to make discovery a profitable business. In 1469 he leased the monopoly of the Guinea trade to Fernão Gomes, a wealthy citizen from Lisbon, who committed himself in return to discover at least 100 leagues a year (about 485 km/300 miles) for each of the next five years. The contract resulted in an annual series of African discoveries down a coast which was fever-ridden, subject to violent thunderstorms, offshore winds (the Harmattans) and sudden fogs. By its expiry, the Portuguese had crossed the Equator off the coast of Gabon.

Reinforcing its command over the new-found coastline (harassed by the possibility of Spanish rivalry despite an obsessive secrecy on their part) the

overland to India in search of Prester John.
1487 Dias rounded the Cape of Good Hope.
1492 Columbus sailed across the Atlantic to Hispaniola.

1497 John Cabot became the first European to visit Newfoundland since the Vikings in his attempts to find a North-West Passage to the East.

1498 Vasco da Gama pioneered a new route to India by sailing around the Cape of Good Hope, up the East African coast and across to Calicut.

NAVIGATING IN SOUTHERN LATITUDES

Below the equator it is no longer possible to see the Pole Star. Instead, Cadamosto says, in 1455 they realized the significance of six beautiful stars which they described as the 'Great Bear' of the southern hemisphere. What they had seen was, in fact, the southern cross. To obtain a more accurate reading of latitude, John II collected experts together into a commission headed by two learned Jewish mathematicians. One went on a voyage in 1485 specifically to record the declination of the sun along the whole Guinea coast. The latitude tables which resulted served to guide Portuguese discoverers until well into the next century.

Portuguese built a fortress factory at Elmina and erected a string of stone markers (*padrões*), each surmounted with a cross and the arms of Portugal, a text in Latin or Portuguese and the names of the explorers and discovery date added as necessary. Sailing in southern latitudes posed problems of navigation which also had to be overcome.

When Gomes's contract expired, one was granted to Afonso's son, who became John II in 1481, and this date marks the climax of Portuguese exploration. The establishment of a fortress factory increased Portuguese contacts with native Africans. The Portuguese began to understand more about the existence of inland African kingdoms. This revived the possibilities for the existence of the famous, but still unlocated, Prester John, the leader of a powerful Christian, non-European people. By the 1480s, attention was concentrated on Ethiopia and every new river mouth which they found on the west coast of Africa revived the possibility that this might be a 'western Nile' which would lead to his kingdom. By 1487, John II had organized a two-pronged strategy for searching out the long-sought Christian ally. One expedition would go south-eastward overland, and another by sea around the African coast.

The overland expedition left Santarém on 7 May 1487, a modest affair. It consisted of two men, Pero da Covilhã (1460?–1545?) and Afonso de Paiva. Covilhã was known for his courage, loyalty, linguistic ability and discretion. He had been a secret agent to the king and there was an element of the secret agent to his exploration too. When they reached Aden, the two emissaries separated. Paiva was never heard of again but Covilhã crossed the Indian Ocean, went down the East African coast and back to Cairo. From Cairo he sent a letter to John II which, from his subsequent actions, it seems the king received, telling him all he had learned of Arab seafaring and the commerce of India. Still obedient to the king's commands, Covilhã, continued his mission and, in 1493, after a trip to Mecca in heavy disguise, finally made it to Ethiopia, became the trusted councillor of its king, married an Ethiopian wife and died there many years later.

Meanwhile, the other prong of John II's exploration was a more prestigious affair, carefully planned and organized. The commander was Bartholomeu Dias, a superintendent of the royal warehouses in Lisbon who had already captained a caravel down the Guinea coast. The expedition comprised two caravels of 50 tons each and a store ship (this was the first time the latter had been added). With him went six Africans, well fed and dressed in European clothes to be deposited here and there along the African coast to act as agents for the Portuguese and show the natives the products they wanted.

Landing the last of these mobile salesmen, the ships ran into a gale. They ran before a northerly wind with close-reefed sails in a steep sea for 13 days and were driven away from the coast into open water. The crew, who had suffered heat-stroke at the Equator, gave themselves up for dead and Dias steered east with all sail. For several days he saw no land. Then, turning north for 150 leagues (about 700 km/450 miles), he suddenly viewed high mountains. On 3 February 1488, he anchored in Mossel Bay, about 370 km (230 miles) east of what is now Cape Town. From here they followed the coast, clearly running north-east, another 485 km (300 miles) to the mouth of the Great Fish Bay and into Algoa Bay.

Dias wanted to go on but his crew would have none of it. 'With one voice they began to murmur and demand that they proceed no farther.' Provisions were low and the supply ship had been left behind. Faced with a signed sworn testimony of all the captains to return, Dias agreed. But, as he passed the stone-marker they had set up to record their achievement, Dias wrote that he did so 'with as much sorrow and feeling as though he were taking his last leave of a son condemned to exile forever, recalling with what danger to his own person and to all his men they had come such a long distance with this sole aim, and then God would not grant it him to reach his goal'. When his caravels came sailing into Lisbon harbour in December 1488, Christopher Columbus was among those who saw them arrive.

ASIA

TO THE ORIENT

Asia comprises almost a third of the earth's total land area. It includes the highest mountains (Himalayas), the most extensive forests (in Siberia), ten of the twenty longest rivers and five of the ten largest deserts. An explorer's paradise, one would have thought. Yet for all this, the idea of Asian exploration has always provoked unease. Did Asia, it might be asked, actually need exploring? Wide-eyed accounts by European travellers from Marco Polo onwards confirmed that cities like Delhi, Peking (Beijing) and Edo (Tokyo) far surpassed London or Paris in size and magnificence. In the 14th century Oderic of Pordenone had described Canton (Guangzhou) as being 'as big as three Venices'; and it was still a colossal metropolis when Captain Alexander Hamilton visited it in the 18th century.

Arab, Indian, Chinese and Malay seafarers had been criss-crossing the Indian Ocean and the western Pacific long before Europeans ventured out into the Atlantic, while Asia's internal commerce in furs, silks and spices had spun the most extensive web of overland trade routes in the world. Although both European sea voyages to Asia and transcontinental journeys across it were attended with ample danger, they could not rival similar feats in the New World or the Dark Continent for geographical discoveries.

There were of course vast tracts in Siberia, Arabia and Central Asia which, because they were howling wildernesses, could indeed be considered 'new' or 'dark'. Parts of them would retain their 'unexplored'

The Burhan Budai in the Kunlun range from Xidatan in northern Tibet. The French missionaries Huc and Gabet entered Tibet by this route as did Przhevalsky.

'Wilfrid [Blunt] on the chestnut mare . . . wants nothing but a long lance to make him a complete bedouin.' A reluctant-looking 'bedouin' and the masterful Lady Anne on the road to Ha'il.

tag well into the 19th century and their 'forbidden cities' (Riyadh, Bukhara and Lhasa) would exercise a powerful attraction on the European imagination. But each of these areas constituted a very distinct and local arena of endeavour; and even here exploration had a presumptuous air about it. The antiquity and sophistication of Asia's civilizations, plus their cultural traditions which obstinately located the centre of the world either in China's 'Middle Kingdom', the Hindu-Buddhist Himalayas, or Islam's holy cities, mocked the idea of Europe-based discoveries. To the intense discomfort of the gung-ho explorer, Asia exposed the conceit that underlay the whole notion of exploration.

It also confounded any simple distinction between dedicated explorers and other travellers. If the mystique of exploration was seen to consist largely of describing in a language comprehensible to Europeans some physical feature or some feat of locomotion, then the merchant, the missionary, the soldier and the spy could all aspire to explorer status. In Asia the geographical explorer *per se* is a rarity – and a slightly absurd one at that. With Asia having more to offer in the way of produce, manufactures, antiquities, arts and ideas than any other continent, it was a poor traveller whose mental horizon extended no further than the next contour. Happily the Royal Geographical Society set an admirable example in this respect, frequently supporting and honouring travellers whose purely geographical achievements were secondary if not incidental to their main calling.

Portuguese pioneers

The Portuguese discovery of the sea route to the East really belongs to the story of African exploration. As Vasco da Gama discovered, once round the Cape of Good Hope and through the Mozambique Channel, the battle was won. Arab, Indian and at one time even Chinese vessels traded down to Mombasa and Sofala on the East African coast. The eastern seas and their monsoon winds were common knowledge to a large international community of

Vasco da Gama commanded the first Portuguese fleet to cross the Indian Ocean, thus inaugurating maritime contacts between Europe and Asia.

traders; and it was one of these – variously identified as a Gujarati merchant or possibly the great Arab navigator, Ibn Majid – who piloted da Gama's two ships safely across the Indian Ocean in 1498. It had taken the Portuguese 70 years to feel their way down to and round the Cape; it took just 23 days to cross from Africa to India – and thereafter, comparatively speaking, not much longer to reach the Malay peninsula, China and the Spice Islands.

Da Gama's voyage terminated at Calicut on India's Malabar coast. He was well, if not enthusiastically, received by the Hindu ruler and stayed three months looking for Christians and spices – the main objectives of Portuguese exploration. He found both in abundance. In reality most of the 'Christians' were Hindus and their 'churches' temples. But Portuguese willingness to regard all idols as icons and all non-Muslims as misguided Christians should not be ridiculed; exploration owes a great debt to this bit of wishful thinking.

As for the spices, they were genuine. The Malabar ports were the main outlets for Kerala's large pepper crop as well as important transhipment points on the spice route between Indonesia and the ports of the Red Sea and Persian Gulf. Da Gama's discovery that a hundredweight of pepper, selling for 80 ducats in Venice, could be bought for three in Calicut was to cause a sensation. 'Rejoicing,' as the diarist put it on leaving India, 'in having made so wonderful a discovery,' da Gama sailed back in 1500 to a tumultuous welcome in Lisbon. A second, far bigger fleet was immediately despatched to the Malabar coast under Pedro Álvares Cabral (who discovered Brazil *en route*) and da Gama himself returned in 1502.

Although immensely profitable, both these voyages engendered fierce opposition from Arab traders on the Indian coast. Fresh from contributing to the expulsion of the Moors from Spain, Portugal saw herself as now rolling back the frontiers of Islam in the East. Under Francisco de Almeida and then Afonso de Albuquerque, the newcomers resolutely acquired an *Estado da India* based on command of the sea lanes through a chain of fortified naval bases. Ormuz (Hormuz) at the mouth of the Persian Gulf fell in 1507, Goa in 1510 and Malacca (near the modern Singapore) in 1511. In 1512 a Portuguese fleet, relying again on local (in this case Javanese) navigators, reached the Moluccas and in 1514 the first Portuguese vessel traded on the coast of China. Exploring the trade of the East had taken just 15 years.

This extraordinary achievement was complemented and, to an uncertain extent, assisted by the reconnaissance work of individual travellers. Pedro de Covilhã had been sent by the King of Portugal specifically to assess the feasibility of reaching India from Africa. He had crossed the Mediterranean in 1487, emerged from Cairo disguised as a Muslim merchant in 1488 and, taking ship down the Red Sea to Aden, reached Calicut exactly ten years before Vasco da Gama. Thence he travelled up to Goa, back across to Aden, and on down the African coast as far as Mozambique. By 1490 he was back in Cairo with commercial information of quite inestimable value to his patron. He entrusted it to a Portuguese agent and set off again, ostensibly to look for Prester John's lost slice of Christendom in Ethiopia.

In fact Covilhã preferred first to exhaust the Islamic world, visiting Ormuz, then making pilgrimages to Mecca, Medina and Mount Sinai, before finally landing at Massawa (Mits'iwa) and disappearing into Ethiopia. There, 30 years later, a Portuguese emissary rediscovered him, by then a much respected and comfortably housed patriarch but glad once again to be of service to a fellow-countryman.

route from Europe to the East via the Cape of Good Hope to Calicut in India.
1502-8 Varthema was the first Christian to visit the holy city of Mecca, and first to reach the Molucca Islands.
1553-4 Willoughby and Chancellor searched for North-East Passage via Barents Sea. Chancellor travelled overland to Moscow.
1557 Jenkinson followed Chancellor's route to Moscow, then sailed down the Volga to the Caspian Sea, and eastwards to Bukhara.

He was the first European to record visiting the Arabian mainland since the Roman Empire.

Covilhã's discoveries were deemed far too valuable for publication. Not so those of his unaccredited successor, Lodovico de Varthema, whose popular account of his rather similar itinerary 15 years later constitutes an early example of the travel writing genre. Varthema, 'a gentleman of Rome', offers no explanation for his journey other than an 'ardent desire of knowledge' about 'such parts as here before have not been sufficiently known'. What he supplies is a revealing personal narrative, thin on dates and verifiable observations but rich in anecdote and incident which, however credulous, is never obviously fabricated. It is possible that he withheld hard political and commercial detail for the information of interested parties – such as the Portuguese. But the evidence for this supposition is purely circumstantial in that he, like Covilhã, had an uncanny knack of visiting places that thereafter quickly succumbed to Portuguese attack.

Briefly, he tells us that in 1503, having sweet-talked his way into the ranks of a Mameluke troop, he joined the escort of a Mecca-bound caravan from Damascus. After several pitched battles and a visit to Medina, he reached Mecca (where he found the Ka'bah 'similar to the Colosseum of Rome') and then Jeddah. Thence he took ship to Aden where his disguise as a Muslim was penetrated. He responded by feigning insanity. He killed an ass that would not recite the Muslim profession of faith, sprayed his accusers with urine, and took off all his clothes. The last of these expedients made a great impression on the Yemeni Sultana who, somewhat improbably, fell

THE SPICE ISLANDS

It was to reach Milton's 'Islands of Spicerie' as much as Cathay that Columbus sailed west and da Gama east. Spices for both culinary and medicinal use had epitomized the exotic nature of oriental trade since at least the time of the Roman Empire. High in value, light in weight and easily divided into loads, they were ideal cargoes both for the sea-borne trade from South-East Asia to the Red Sea and Persian Gulf and for the caravan trade thence to the Mediterranean.

When Europeans first reached the East they found the berries of the pepper vine the most readily obtainable. The Portuguese acquired pepper along with cardamom from India's Malabar ports, and the Dutch and English from Sumatra and Java. Cinnamon came mainly from Sri Lanka. But the most prized spices were cloves and nutmegs and these grew only in the Moluccas at the far end of the Indonesian archipelago and on the same longitude as Darwin in Australia. The Moluccas were considered the true 'Spice Islands'.

But even in the Moluccas only certain islands actually produced spices. Cloves, the buds of a dainty willow-size tree, were found in Tidore, Ternate (where Sir Francis Drake obtained a supply), Bacan, Ambon and western Seram. In 1608 David

Middleton of the East India Company's Third Voyage purchased a cargo for under £3000 which sold in London for £36,000.

Nutmeg, the kernel of a peach-like fruit, and mace, the membrane round the stone of the same fruit, were even more specialized, growing only in the miniscule Banda islands. None of these idyllic atolls is much bigger than a golf course. They lie about 160 km (100 miles) south of Ambon clustered round an active volcano whose occasional dusting of the nutmeg

Clove-rich Ternate in the north Moluccas boasts an active volcano. 17th-century engravings tended to exaggerate the elemental setting of the Spice Islands.

groves with volcanic fall-out is considered as vital to a good crop as the moist sea breezes. The clove plantations of Tidore and Ternate also sheltered beneath lively volcanoes – all of which added an elemental mystery to their remote location and inspired some rather fanciful engravings.

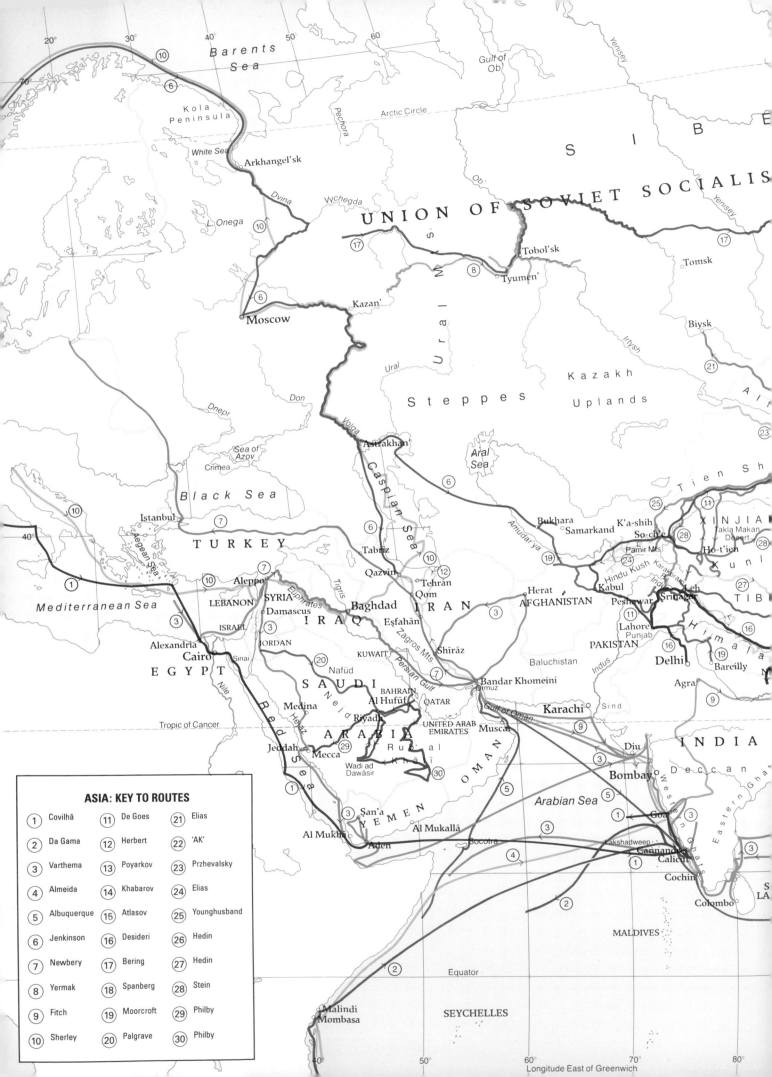

ASIA: KEY TO ROUTES

①	Covilhã	⑪	De Goes	㉑	Elias
②	Da Gama	⑫	Herbert	㉒	'AK'
③	Varthema	⑬	Poyarkov	㉓	Przhevalsky
④	Almeida	⑭	Khabarov	㉔	Elias
⑤	Albuquerque	⑮	Atlasov	㉕	Younghusband
⑥	Jenkinson	⑯	Desideri	㉖	Hedin
⑦	Newbery	⑰	Bering	㉗	Hedin
⑧	Yermak	⑱	Spanberg	㉘	Stein
⑨	Fitch	⑲	Moorcroft	㉙	Philby
⑩	Sherley	⑳	Palgrave	㉚	Philby

Longitude East of Greenwich

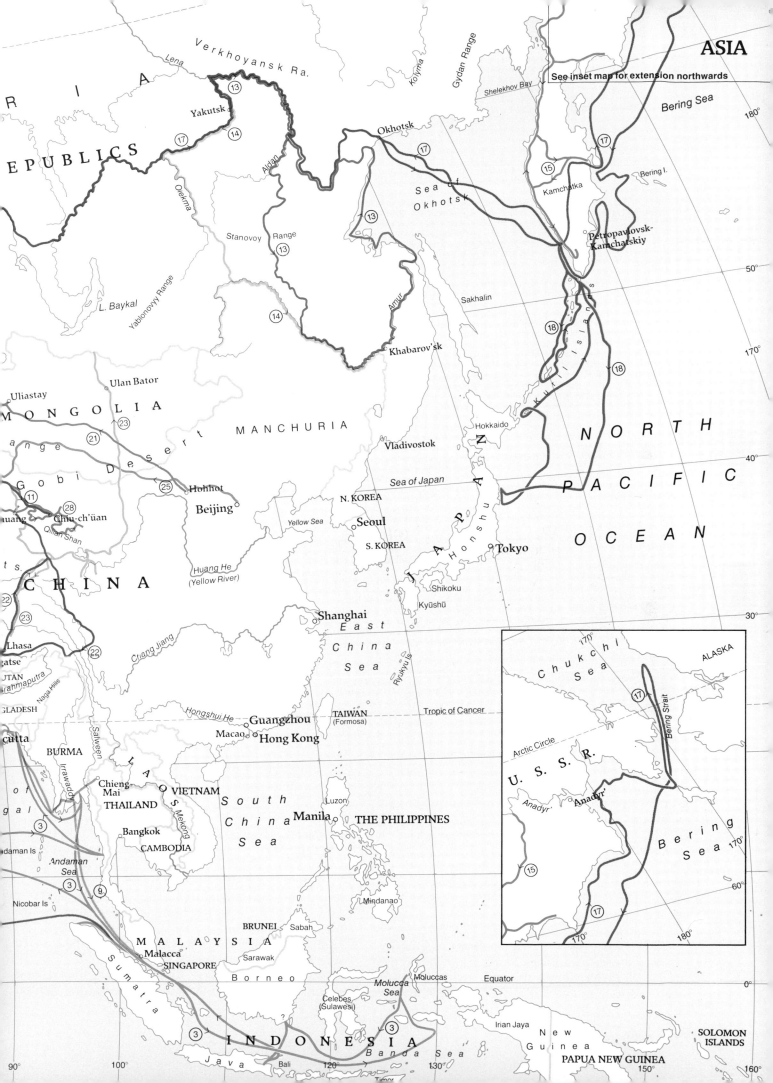

ASIA

See inset map for extension northwards

1561-4 Jenkinson travelled down the western shore of the Caspian Sea to trade with Kasvin, the Persian capital.
1579 Drake reached the Spice Islands.

1581-2 Newbery was the first Englishman to travel down the Euphrates on his journey from Aleppo to Ormuz, and Istanbul.
1581-5 Yermak Timofeyevich and his

Cossacks took control of Siberian capital Iskir.
1583 Newbery and Fitch arrested attempting to make overland trade route from Ormuz to Goa for the Levant Company.

ASIA: KEY TO ROUTES

① **Covilhã** 1487–9. Sailed to Alexandria, crossed to the Red Sea and sailed on to Aden, Cannanore, Calicut and Goa.

② **Da Gama** 1497–9. Sailed from the E African coast to Calicut.

③ **Varthema** 1502–8. Sailed to Egypt, then visited Lebanon, Syria, Arabia, Yemen, India, Persian Gulf, Muscat, Iran, India (Cheo, Cambay Chaul, Bijapur, Bijayanagar), Sri Lanka, Burma, Bangladesh, Malacca, Sumatra, Molucca Islands, Borneo and Java.

④ **Almeida** 1505–9. Sailed from Africa to India and settled in Cochin as Viceroy of India. In 1509 defeated Moorish fleet off Diu.

⑤ **Albuquerque** 1507–11. Sailed from Africa to Socotra, Muscat, Ormuz, Cannanore, Cochin, Goa and Malacca.

⑥ **Jenkinson** 1557–64. Sailed to Archangel'sk; overland to Moscow and Astrakhan', then via the Caspian Sea to Bukhara. In 1561 made the same journey to Astrakhan', thence via the Caspian to Qazvin.

⑦ **Newbery** 1581–2. From Tripoli, Lebanon, to Aleppo, Ormuz, Eşfahãn and through Turkey.

⑧ **Yermak** 1581–2. Crossed the Urals to the western tributaries of the Irtysh.

⑨ **Fitch** (partly with Newbery) 1583–91. From Ormuz to Goa, inland to Fatehpur Sikri, to the Bay of Bengal, Burma and Malacca.

⑩ **Sherley** 1598–1600. Sailed from Venice to Syria then overland to Qazvin and Eşfahãn. Returned to Europe via the Caspian and Archangel'sk.

⑪ **De Goes** 1603–7. From Lahore to Kabul, So-ch'e and Chin-ch'üan.

⑫ **Herbert** 1627–9. Sailed to the S coast of Iran, then overland to Shirãz, Eşfahãn, Tehrãn and Qom, and returned to the coast.

⑬ **Poyarkov** 1643–6. From Yakutsk through the Stanovoy Mts and descended the Amur to the sea. Returned via the Aldan.

⑭ **Khabarov** 1649–51. From Yakutsk ascended Lena and Olekma rivers, then descended the Amur to vicinity of present Khabarov'sk.

⑮ **Atlasov** 1697–9. From the Anadyr' to the Kamchatka peninsula.

⑯ **Desideri** 1714–6. From Delhi to Lahore, Srinagar, Leh and Lhasa.

⑰ **Bering** 1725–30. Crossed Urals and Siberia to Okhotsk; crossed Kamchatka, then sailed to the Chukchi Sea.

⑱ **Spanberg** 1738–9. Sailed from Kamchatka to Kuril Is and in 1739 to Honshu, Japan.

⑲ **Moorcroft** 1819–25. From Bareilly to Leh, Srinagar, Peshawar, Kabul, Bukhara and part-way to Samarkand.

⑳ **Palgrave** 1862. From Ma'an across Arabia to the Persian Gulf.

㉑ **Elias** 1872–3. From Hohhot, China, across Mongolia to Biysk, Siberia.

㉒ **'AK' (Kishen Singh)** 1878–82. From Darjeeling to Lhasa, then crossed the Gobi to Dunhuang. Returned via more easterly route.

㉓ **Przhevalsky** 1879–80. From Kazakhstan to N Tibet, then back across the Gobi to the Russian border.

㉔ **Elias** 1885–6. From Xinjiang crossed the Pamirs to N Afghanistan.

㉕ **Younghusband** 1887–91. From Beijing across the Gobi to Xinjiang then across the Karakorams to Srinagar.

㉖ **Hedin** 1900–1. From Xinjiang travelled in N Tibet and in 1901 from Xinjiang crossed Tibet to Leh.

㉗ **Hedin** 1906–6. From Leh through the Karakorams and Kunlun Mts to Shigatse, then returned to Leh.

㉘ **Stein** 1906–8. From the Hindu Kush he travelled eastwards along the fringe of the Takla Makan Desert and the Kunlun Mts to central China, then westwards to Xinjiang, crossed the Takla Makan twice and finally crossed the Karakorams.

㉙ **Philby** 1917–8. From the Persian Gulf to Riyadh and Jeddah. In 1918 he travelled south from Riyadh along the Jabal Tuwayq to Wadi ad Dawãsir.

㉚ **Philby** 1932. From Al Hufûf to the Rub' al Khãlî, then westwards to Wadi ad Dawãsir.

madly in love with him . 'I held her for two hours,' reports Varthema, 'and she told me I was marvellously strong.' After further assignations and a brief trip to Şan'ã, she kindly arranged his escape aboard a ship heading for India.

The ship called at Diu on the Gujarat coast; Varthema then doubled back to Ormuz in the Persian Gulf; both places would be in Portuguese hands within a couple of years. Back in India, he actually enlisted in the Portuguese forces in the course of a leisurely tour of the west coast. By 1505 he was in Ceylon (Sri Lanka), still heading east but now in the guise of a merchant. Trade took him to Burma, Bengal (Bangladesh) and eventually Malacca (near the modern Singapore), 'the principal port of the main ocean . . . and truly more ships arrive here than in any other place in the world'; within five years they would include Portuguese caravels. Thence, though the itinerary becomes hazier, he seems to have made his way down the Indonesian archipelago to an island 'where nothing grows but nutmegs' – which must be one of the Bandas – and to the 'Monoch' islands where the cloves grew – presumably the Moluccas. It was the end of the line. He turned for home, making his first European port of call Lisbon where he received the Order of Chivalry.

This quite extraordinary journey can be seen as an epic of exploration; Varthema, after all, was the first European to reach the Spice Islands and the

first to describe, albeit perfunctorily, practically everywhere that he visited *en route*. It can also be seen as a rumbustious personal odyssey which probably masked an ingenious piece of espionage. Alternatively, it can be seen simply as vivid testimony to the extent and vitality of the Asian trading world on the eve of European intervention.

The English in Central Asia . . .

A century later the story of English attempts to muscle in on the trade of mainland Asia exhibits the same mix of overland reconnaissance and maritime penetration. It began with high hopes of matching the Portuguese and Spanish by reaching Cathay (China) and the Spice Islands by the northern equivalents of the Cape Horn and Cape of Good Hope routes – the North-West and North-East Passages. As these failed, it culminated with the voyages (1595–1615) of Sir James Lancaster and the infant East India Company which took the Portuguese route round Africa. Commercially and politically, the East India Company's first voyages were of enormous importance, anticipating the shape of the future British empire in the East. But with the possible exception of three disastrous visits to the Red Sea, they made few landfalls at which either the Portuguese or the Dutch were not already established.

It was the other way round with the overland reconnaissances; and in Anthony Jenkinson it is

1584-91 Fitch escaped to go down the Ganges eventually to Bangladesh, explore the Irrawaddy, and visit Malacca.
1587 Foundation of Tobol'sk enabled

Cossacks to move north down the Ob River into Mansiyskiy along the Arctic coast.
1598 Anthony and Robert Sherley crossed the Zagros Mountains from Baghdad to

Isfahan.
1601 Lancaster commanded first East India Company voyage to establish an English trading post on Java.

tempting, if unfashionable, to recognize the first great English explorer. Jenkinson's early travels had taken him to the eastern Mediterranean where in 1553 he had had an audience with the Sultan, Suleiman the Magnificent. But the commercial concessions thus gained evidently came to nothing for four years later he had joined the Muscovy Company and was in command of an expedition which, following the death of Richard Chancellor, was to renew commercial contacts with the Tsar's dominions by way of the White Sea and then to push east overland towards Cathay.

After a typically grim voyage round the top of Scandinavia, Jenkinson and his party landed at the future port of Archangel'sk and reached Moscow in December 1557. There Tsar Ivan IV ('The Terrible') entertained the English at a succession of gargantuan banquets and entered enthusiastically into Jenkinson's plans, providing him with letters of introduction to 'sundry kings and princes'. They included the Khan of Bukhara whose city, once an important centre of Islamic scholarship, was destined to epitomize Central Asian bigotry to future generations of Englishmen. But to Jenkinson its importance was as

a terminus on the ancient Silk Route to Cathay. With high hopes the expedition sailed down the Volga to Kazan' and then to Astrakhan' on the Caspian Sea. At the time this was the limit of the Tsar's conquests in Central Asia and, not without a shudder, Jenkinson reported in detail on the nomadic lifestyle of his Tartar subjects:

> Town or house they have none, but live in the open fields. Corn they sow not, neither do they eat any bread, mocking the Christians for disabling our strengths . . . by eating the top of a weed and drinking a drink made of the same.

At Astrakhan' Jenkinson, an able navigator as well as a merchant, bought a ship, hoisted 'the red cross of St George', and with his two English companions plus 'certain Tartars and Persians', sailed boldly east out of the Volga. Needless to say, he was the first and perhaps the only Englishman ever to command a ship on the Caspian. The voyage across to the

A 19th-century view of Mecca shows a river of haj *pilgrims but scarcely bears out Varthema's description of the Ka'bah.*

ASIA

1601 Ricci established Jesuit mission in Peking.
1603-7 De Goes, travelling from Lahore along the Silk Route, became first European

since Marco Polo to reach China from the west.
1604 Cossack fur traders worked upstream along the Ob River to found Tomsk.

1608 Jourdain was the first Englishman to give an account of the Seychelles and the first Englishman to visit Yemen.
1610 Kurochkin and other Russian traders

Mangyshlak peninsula took two weeks. There they moored the vessel and prepared for the long desert haul through Turkmen territory. Their caravan consisted of a thousand camels and for 20 days they found 'neither town nor habitation . . . [so that] we were driven by necessity to eat one of my camels and a horse'. This was, however, preferable to the exactions and dangers that awaited them along the river Oxus (Amudar'ya). Safe-conducts had to be purchased from each of Khiva's rulers and still the caravan was waylaid by brigands. 'Had it not been for four handguns which I and my company had, and used, we had been overcome and destroyed.' Their assailants demanded the surrender of any non-Muslims in the caravan. Jenkinson's Tartar companions refused to denounce him. 'And so upon the 23rd day of December 1557 we arrived at the city of Bukhara.'

Jenkinson found the city 'very great' and was much taken with its gilded mosques and its 'bath-stoves'. For 'a barbarous king' the Khan was affable enough; 'he devised with me familiarly in his secret chamber.' But trade was at a standstill. Great caravans from Cathay, India, Russia, and Afghanistan did indeed converge on Bukhara but what with the Khan being at war with Persia (Iran) and other wars prevailing in Xinjiang, it was three years since they had materialized. After a stay of ten weeks, the longest by any Englishman of his own volition until the 20th century, Jenkinson began to retrace his steps. With a party of freed Russian slaves, Khivan and Bukharan ambassadors, and 'a cow's tail of Cathay' – all destined for the Tsar – he regained his ship and eventually delivered his charges safely in Moscow. Thence north again to the White Sea and so back to England where he arrived, after a three-and-a-half-year journey 'so miserable, dangerous and chargeable as my pen is not able to express the same', in 1560.

. . . and Persia

Jenkinson reported that the distance from Bukhara to Cathay entailed another nine months' travelling. When they added this to the similar time span needed for the two voyages and the long overland journey just to reach Bukhara, even the incorrigible merchants of Tudor England had to concede defeat. But if the old Silk Route from Cathay was closed, there was still the old Spice Route from India via the Persian Gulf. Bukhara's war with Persia had prevented Jenkinson from investigating the Persian trade but, when his employers mooted the idea, he immediately volunteered. Within nine months of his return he

was sailing round Norway's North Cape once again prior to another amphibious marathon from the Arctic Circle to the deserts of Central Asia.

Some measure of the Muscovy Company's confidence in their new champion may be gathered from their instructions. Besides negotiating exclusive transit arrangements with the Tsar, Jenkinson was to obtain trading privileges from the Sophie (or Shah), to discover a passage for overland commerce with India and, on his return journey, to make a small diversion by way of Novaya Zemlya to resolve the question of the North-East Passage.

Undaunted, Jenkinson followed his old route down to the Caspian and this time sailed south. He landed in the province of Shirvan, then part of Persia, now in Soviet Azerbaijan. The local governor became a firm friend and duly furnished an escort to Kasvin (Qazvīn), then the Persian capital. But here Jenkinson's remarkable diplomatic skills failed him. He delivered to the Shah a letter from Queen Elizabeth which, though written in Latin, Italian *and* Hebrew, Shah Tamasp found incomprehensible. And this led him to suspect Jenkinson's Islamic credentials. The Englishman explained that he was a Christian. What was that? asked the Shah. Jenkinson explained further. '"Oh thou unbeliever," saith he, "we have no need to have friendship with unbelievers".' Whereupon Jenkinson was dismissed and the palace thoroughly dusted with sand by way of disinfection against such heretical sentiments.

An ignominious deportation seemed inevitable but, after further rancorous exchanges, the friendly governor of Shirvan interceded on his behalf and in March 1562 Jenkinson was allowed to withdraw to Russia with dignity. He returned by much the same route, reaching London after a second absence of about three-and-a-half years. Rather surprisingly the venture was deemed a modest success. In Kasvin he had made contact with some Indian merchants who assured him that they could supply unlimited quantities of spices; and from the Shirvan governor he had received an assurance that the province's stocks of raw silk were at his disposal.

In 1565–8 further deputations from the Muscovy Company had some success in selling English woollens to the Azerbaijanis and in buying Persian silk. In the process they reached both Kashan and the southern shores of the Caspian. Jenkinson himself returned to Moscow in 1566 and again in 1567 and 1571. No less than Francis Drake he inaugurated the age of English expansion. But Drake's coup in reaching the Spice Islands by sea (1579), Moscow's growing preoccupation with Siberia (from 1581

sailed down the Yenisey to its mouth.
1612 English started trade in Siam through port of Patani in the Malay peninsula.
1618 Samuel travelled overland from Siam to Burma for the East India Company.
1620-7 Persaert visited Kashmir and north-west India on behalf of the Dutch East India Company.
1623 Penda and other fur hunters reached the Lena from the Yenisey, a round trip of 8000 km (5000 miles), covering much new ground.

The old city of Lhasa is still dominated by the Potala, the palace of the Dalai Lama and the seat of Tibetan government – both now in exile in India.

onwards), and English expectations of new commercial concessions in the Levant (1580) brought to an end the first phase of Anglo-Persian trade.

Overland to India

Like the Muscovy Company in the 1560s, the Levant Company in the 1580s opened a new doorway into Asia through which the enterprising merchant-explorer could, not without risk, venture east. John Newbery, 'citizen and merchant of London', had already made a tour of the Holy Land before setting out in 1580 from Aleppo to Ormuz, the great Portuguese fortress at the mouth of the Persian Gulf. He was the first Englishman to travel down the Euphrates valley, to reach Ormuz and to return over-land through southern Persia to Isfahan (Eṣfahān) and thence to Tabrīz and Istanbul. He claimed simply to be 'desirous to see the world' and he carried no merchandise; but he travelled in disguise and concentrated on commercial reconnaissance.

Three years later he was back in Ormuz, this time with another merchant, Ralph Fitch, two other companions, £400 of trading capital provided by the Levant Company and letters from Queen Elizabeth to both the Moghul Emperor of India and the 'King of China'. It was a serious bid to open an overland trade with the East and the Portuguese authorities in Ormuz duly moved to pre-empt it. Thus it was as

prisoners that Newbery and his companions reached Goa, the Portuguese capital on India's west coast. There they were detained while word was awaited from Lisbon as to their fate.

Fearing the worst, Newbery and Fitch contrived to escape into the neighbouring kingdom of Bijāpur. Thence they made their way north into the Moghul's dominions and on to his capital of Fatehpur Sikri near Agra. Presumably the Queen's letter was delivered to the Emperor Akbar. Then the two split up. Newbery was to hasten back overland to London with news of their journey and then return to India by sea for, according to Fitch, he 'did promise me if it pleased God to meet me in Bengal within two years with a ship out of England'.

Meanwhile Fitch was to continue east. During the winter of 1584–5 he sailed down the Ganges to Patna, then visited the Bhutan frontier, doubled back to the Bay of Bengal and spent the best part of a year in what is now Bangladesh. He was probably waiting for Newbery to keep their rendezvous. If so, he was wasting his time. Like several of his notable successors, Newbery, the leader of the first commercial expedition from England to India, had simply

1626 Andrade travelled through Srinagar across the Mana Pass into western Tibet, establishing a mission at Tsaparang.
1627 British delegation to Persia included

Sherley and Herbert who made extensive journeys there.
1631 Azevedo journeyed from Tsaparang to Leh and opened Rotang Pass.

1639 Russian traders and soldiers reached the Sea of Okhotsk.
1641 Dutch traders explored up the Mekong River in Indochina.

disappeared into the depths of Central Asia never to be heard of again. Fitch, whose description of the expedition – written many years later – is thus the only record, took ship to Burma. He next ventured inland as far as Chiengmai (Chieng-Mai) in northern Siam (Thailand) in search of 'China work'. In 1588 he reached Malacca and collected further details of both the China trade and the spice trade.

Back home it was the year of the Grand Armada. By now Fitch's family had long since given him up for dead; his will was duly read and his estate divided. When in 1591, eight years after his departure, the indomitable traveller came ashore unannounced in the Thames, delight must have been tempered with consternation. But to the Levant Company, many of whose promoters were now turning their attention to the possibility of an East India trade round the Cape, Fitch was a man to be closely questioned. Nine years later he was called in to advise the newly formed East India Company on a suitable cargo for its first voyage to the East.

At the court of the Grand Sophie

The Twelve Voyages (1600–13) which opened the East India Company's trading account suggest a programme of commercial exploration as carefully planned as the space programmes of *Apollo* or *Challenger*. It seemed as if the Company were systematically probing each eastern market in turn with one fleet to Java, another to the Spice Islands, others to Arabia, India, Thailand and Japan. None contributed much in the way of geographical information. But it is to the journals of the Company's commanders that we owe the first detailed descriptions in English of all the more accessible regions of south and south-east Asia. Particularly informative are the accounts of Aden, Mocha (Al Mukhā) and the Yemen by Sir Henry Middleton and John Jourdain, of Moghul India and Agra by William Hawkins and others, of the Bay of Bengal and Siam by Peter Floris, of Japan under the Shoguns by John Saris, and of the Moluccas by Sir Henry Middleton and his brother David.

In this category also fall the travels of a few ambassadorial figures whose missions were designed to dignify the Company's commercial activities. Deputed to India in 1615 Sir Thomas Roe wrote a pained account of his sojourn at the Moghul court where he found due regard for his 'qualitye' conspicuously lacking. He might have fared better in Persia where the great Shah Abbas seemed, if anything, to attach too much importance to English courtiers in general and to two in particular.

These were the flamboyant Sherley brothers, Sir Anthony and Sir Robert, who, arriving out of the blue in Kasvin in 1598, claimed to be representing not just Queen Elizabeth but the whole of Christendom. Protégés of the Earl of Essex, they hoped to persuade Shah Abbas to join the sovereigns of Europe in a concerted attack on the Turks. This would naturally dislocate Persian trade with Europe which passed through the Turkish domains. The Sherleys hoped to re-align it to their own, and possibly England's, benefit either via Jenkinson's Russian route or via the Indian Ocean.

In short the extremely plausible Sherleys were adventurers with no official status. But they had arrived at Kasvin at a particularly propitious moment, the Shah having just routed his Uzbek neighbours. 'Nearly every expedition of the many that Sir Anthony embarked upon was doomed to failure,' writes his biographer. But in a lifetime of bewildering fiascos, this was the one exception. While transferring to his new capital of Isfahan, Shah Abbas took the strangers into his confidence and eventually conferred on Sir Anthony the diplomatic status he affected. He was to return to Europe as Persian ambassador and to promote the anti-Turkish alliance. This obviously precluded travelling via the Turkish Levant; Sherley therefore opted for the Caspian and Jenkinson's route to Archangel.

He was thus the first to traverse the Eurasian land mass from Mesopotamia to the Arctic. Thereafter he toured the courts of Europe, leaving a trail of debtors and never returning either to Persia or England. But his brother, Sir Robert, who had been left in Persia as a hostage and had married a sensationally beautiful Circassian lady, was soon following in his official wake. In 1611 he enjoyed the unusual distinction for an Englishman of being presented to his sovereign as the Persian ambassador. He duly returned to Persia on the East India Company's Twelfth Voyage, accompanied by the first English ambassador to the court of Shah Abbas. Somehow the vessel overshot the Persian coast and landed its distinguished passengers in 'the mouldy land of Baluchistan'. The English ambassador, his wife, and their son all died almost immediately; only Sir Robert and the majestic Lady Sherley regained Isfahan.

Ten years later Sir Robert re-appeared in London. Although the East India Company was highly suspicious of him, King James nominated a new English ambassador to Persia, Sir Dodmore Cotton. Cotton sailed with Sherley in 1627, having in his suite a young man called Thomas Herbert whose

1643-6 Poyarkov crossed the Stanovoy Mountains in winter to explore Daurien and the Amur River.
1648 Dezhnyov sailed from the Kolyma River around the Chukchi peninsula, through what was to become the Bering Strait.
1649-51 Khabarov linked the Olekma River to the Amur. Established Daurien as part of Chinese Manchuria.
1655 Dutch traders, Goyer and Keyser, reached the Yangstse; others reached Peking.

long account of the mission would be the standard work on Persia for the next 200 years.

This is partly explained by the comprehensive itinerary forced on the mission by Shah Abbas. (Herbert thought that the Shah wanted to impress them by demonstrating the extent of his kingdom.) Thus, landing at Gombroon (Bandar Khomeini), the mission had to travel the length of the country to Ashraf (Esref) on the Caspian before being received. Thence they trailed behind the Shah to Kasvin, where both ambassadors (Sherley and Cotton) died within a few days of one another, thus leaving Herbert and his companions to make the best of their way back to Gombroon – a round trip of, in all, some 2900 km (1800 miles).

In the process the English visited Lār, Shīrāz, Isfahan, Teheran (Tehrān), Qum (Qom) and Kāshān. Though Newbery had passed through some of these cities, Herbert was the first to describe them in detail. His enthusiastic account of the ruins of Persepolis no less than his descriptions of the southern shores of the Caspian and of the majestic Elburz Mountains were a revelation to English readers. Where other travellers provide an itinerary interpolated with incident and anecdote, Herbert fills in the detail with vivid word-pictures of the people, buildings and landscapes. Henceforth Persia could no more be portrayed as virgin territory awaiting the intrepid explorer than China or India.

The fathers of Himalayan travel

By the 1620s English commercial endeavours had come to focus on south Asia as the Dutch tightened their hold on the Indonesian archipelago. The Portuguese, assailed throughout their *Estado da India*, hung on to a few scattered enclaves like Goa and Macao. But if Portugal's commerce was in decline, not so its zeal for converts. As of 1601 the Jesuit, Mattheo Ricci, had found high favour with the Chinese emperor and had removed from Macao to Peking where he established a long-lasting Jesuit mission. Thereafter Jesuit priests travelled widely

MAURITIUS AND THE DODO

By chance the East Indiaman in which Thomas Herbert returned from Persia in 1629 called at the Indian Ocean island of Mauritius. Though uninhabited, Herbert considered it a paradise and paid particular attention to its unusual fauna. Francisco de Almeida had been the first to visit the island in 1505 but, finding there 'crosses and other symbols of Christianity', declined to 'esteem himself the first Christian discoverer'. The Dutch took possession in 1598 and named it Mauritius after Prince Maurice; it remained largely uninhabited until occupied by the French in 1664. Renamed Ile de Bourbon, it was France's main naval base in the East during the 18th century and was taken by the British during the Napoleonic Wars. By then its most celebrated denizen was already extinct.

Dodos, according to Herbert, were 'round and fat (which occasions the slow pace) and so great as few of them weigh less than 50 pounds. Meat it is to some but better to the eye than the stomach [and] such as only a strong appetite can vanquish

... It is of a melancholy visage, as sensible of nature's injury in framing so massive a body to be directed by complimentary wings, such indeed as are unable to hoist her from the ground [and] serving only to rank her amongst the birds. Her head is variously dressed, for one half is hooded with down of a dark colour the other half naked and of a white hue; her bill hooks and bends downwards ... Her eyes are round

Thomas Herbert's drawing of the cock and the hen dodo included a 'cacato' (cockatoo) to give some idea of scale.

and bright, and instead of feathers she has a most fine down; her train (like a Chinaman's beard) is no more than three or four short feathers. Her legs are thick and black: her talons great: her stomach fiery, so as she can easily digest stones – in that and shape not a little resembling the ostrich.'

The Sasar Pass, although not the highest of the five great passes on the Karakoram route from Ladakh to Xinjiang, was considered the most dangerous.

within China. When, in the late 17th century, Russia's push into Siberia resulted in a collision with the Chinese empire along the Amur river, it was the Jesuits with their geographical knowledge and their contacts in Europe who negotiated a settlement.

To Ricci there was no question that the Cathay of Marco Polo, Jenkinson and other Central Asian travellers must be identical with the China of south Asian travellers like Varthema and Fitch. But this was not obvious to Ricci's colleagues at the Moghul court in India. In 1595 Brother Bento de Goes, a native of the Azores, accompanied the Moghul emperor on a summer visit to Kashmir. There he met a merchant from Kashgar (K'a-shih) in Xinjiang who regaled him with tales of a mission to Cathay. Apparently Cathay was not only still fabulously rich but also teeming with Christians. This revelation was supported by constant rumours that just beyond the Himalayas lay a thriving monastic society where the smoke of incense mingled with the chant of prayer while the be-robed brethren told their beads. This time, surely, some long lost community was just waiting to be restored to the true faith. De Goes was sent to investigate.

Disguised as an Armenian merchant, he left Lahore with a caravan of other traders in 1603. The normal route from India to Cathay made a wide sweep round the Himalayas through Afghanistan. This was a long way from Tibet but somewhere near the Khyber Pass de Goes was rewarded with a meeting with a man from Kafiristan (Nuristan) who told him of a people who abhorred all Muslims and 'never visited their temples except in black dresses'. They were in fact the Shī'ah Posh Kafirs of the Hindu Kush. From Kabul the caravan pushed through the Hindu Kush and struck Marco Polo's route at Taliq-an about 485 km (300 miles) east of Bukhara.

Like the Polos, de Goes felt the effects of altitude while crossing the Pamirs and his caravan was repeatedly attacked by bandits. From Yarkand (So-ch'e) in Xinjiang he made an excursion to Khotan (Ho-t'ien) before following the northern arm of the old Silk Route via Kucha (Ku-ch'e) and Kara Shahr (Yen-ch'i). There he met a returning caravan, some of whose merchants had stayed in Peking 'at the same hostelry with members of [my] Society'. So that was it. Cathay was indeed China. De Goes continued across the Gobi Desert to Su-chou (Chiu-ch'üan) where he collapsed. After some delay Ricci heard of his arrival and in 1607 sent a Chinese convert to his rescue. The man arrived just as Brother Benedict was about to breathe his last. 'Seeking Cathay, he found Heaven,' notes the Jesuits' annalist. He had also resolved a long-standing geographical mystery; and, taken in conjunction with the travels of Jenkinson and Sir Anthony Sherley, his journey virtually completed the reconstruction of the Polos's overland route.

*c.*1687 English sailor Pitts, in slavery to Barbary pirates, visited Mecca.
1689 Treaty of Nerchinsk ensured Russians withdrew from Amur, which was returned to

Chinese Manchurian possession.
1691 De la Loubère provided one of the best early accounts of Siam.
1714-6 Desideri traversed Tibet from Ladakh

to Lhasa, where he lived for five years.
1720-7 Prussian naturalist Messerschmidt explored from the Urals to Mongolia.

It remained only to investigate those rumours of Christian fervour in the Himalayas. In 1626 Father Antônio Andrade joined a party of Hindu pilgrims heading for the source of the Ganges. Striking out on his own, he crossed the Mana Pass in deep snow and saw ahead 'an awful desert'. Undeterred, he descended into the fantastical canyons of the upper Sutlej. At Tsaparang (Tse-pu-lung) and Toling (T'o-lin), the ancient capitals of western Tibet, he was generously welcomed and permitted to establish a mission whence much information about Tibet found its way into the Jesuit archives.

The mission lasted only four years but the possibility of reviving it provided a pretext for several later journeys across the Himalayas. In 1631 Father Francisco Azevedo retraced Andrade's route to Tsaparang and continued north-west to Leh in Ladakh and thence back through the mountains to India. Thirty years later Fathers d'Orville and Grueber set off from China via Lake Koko Nor (Ching Hai Hu) to Lhasa and on to Nepal. They were probably the first Europeans to visit the Tibetan capital and Grueber brought back the first news of the Potala, the Dalai Lama's towering palace.

Finally, in 1714–6, the Italian Jesuit, Ippolito Desideri, linked all these journeys with a magnificent traverse of Tibet from Ladakh to Lhasa followed by a five-year residence in and around Lhasa. Desideri compiled an exhaustive account of the country and is now rightly regarded as the first of the great Tibetan explorers. But his account remained unpublished and almost unread until its rediscovery in 1904. Thus, unaware of Desideri's achievement and conveniently ignoring the sketchy reports of his predecessors, the 19th-century explorer could, and did, regard Tibet as an unknown land.

SIBERIA

Reversing the normal procedure, the exploration of Siberia begins with overland journeys across the heart of the continent and ends with voyages of discovery round it. The North Asian land mass – unlike, say, Africa or Australia – was explored from the interior outwards. The reasons are obvious. While most of the coast is ice-bound for most of the year, inland several vast river systems combine to provide a nearly linked chain of waterways stretching from the Ural mountains (the same longitude as Tehrān) to the Sea of Okhotsk (the same longitude as Tokyo). Unusually, Siberia's 770 million hectares (1900 million acres) of forest thus proved more

navigable than its off-shore waters; and locating the source of a river often preceded the discovery of its mouth.

In the absence of lofty mountains, lost cities or a mysterious hydrography, this vast wilderness posed few of the geographical challenges beloved of explorers. Its main obstacles – intolerable climate and interminable distances – were overcome by the predatory exploits of troops and traders during the early 17th century. Their surprisingly rapid penetration of the land mass was more about economic exploitation and political assimilation than scientific enquiry.

Yermak's conquests

The process began in the year 1581. A resurgent Moscow under the rule of Ivan IV ('The Terrible') confronted a remnant of the now fragmented Golden Horde across the Urals in the shape of the Khanate of Sibir (Siberia) under Kuchum, a descendant of Genghiz Khan. Although in the extreme north Russian traders had already crossed the Urals towards the mouth of the Ob, Kuchum's domains on the Ob's Irtysh, Tobol and Tura tributaries effectively blocked expansion to the east. Sibir had entered into a vassal relationship with Moscow in 1555 and the Tsar had farmed out concessionary rights on the far side of the Urals in 1574. But thereafter the initiative rested solely with the concessionaires, the wealthy Stroganov family, and with their military allies, a band of Volga Cossacks under Yermak Timofeyevich.

Yermak's river-borne advance into Siberia mirrored that of the conquistadores *in South America, combining Christian fervour and European firepower.*

ASIA

1733-6 Gmelin explored steppe regions on both sides of the Caspian Sea and in northern Persia.
1741 Bering's Great Northern Expedition

confirmed Asia and North America to be separate land masses.
1761 The first scientific expedition to explore Arabia. Niebuhr survived to give an

excellent description of Yemen Tihamāh.
1763-82 Rennell's surveys of Bengal.
1768-74 Pallas explored a large tract of country between southern Russia and the

It was Yermak with his 600 free-booting followers who forced the gates of Siberia in 1581.

Of Yermak's origins little is known for certain. The term 'Cossack' denoted no more than a free frontiersman. Some were Russian, some Tartar (Yermak was probably the former); some were *banditti,* some irregular militia (Yermak had been both). Combining the crusading zeal of *conquistadores* with the frontier spirit of the American West, the Cossacks were both a menace and an asset to Moscow. As Yermak pushed across the watershed of the Urals and then down the River Tura, it was unclear whether he was assisting the Stroganovs or pre-empting them. Resistance from Kuchum's vassals was met with a well-directed fire and punitive reprisals. Belying their popular image, it was the Cossacks who enjoyed the advantage of firearms and who travelled by boat, the enemy who relied on bows and arrows and rode on horseback.

The freezing of the River Tura brought the advance to a halt. Yermak occupied a ruined Tartar town on the site of what is now Tyumen' and set up winter quarters. Kuchum used the winter months to gather his disparate forces. By May 1582 the river was again navigable and the Cossacks resumed their eastwards advance to the River Tobol. Encouraged by a variety of strange portents, plus a vision of the heavenly host, they inflicted two defeats on the enemy, neither of which was decisive, and survived a number of ambushes from the shore. Kuchum seemed to be saving his crack troops in the hopes that exhaustion and exposure would effect what bows and arrows could not. Yermak's men just kept on coming. By October they had reached the junction of the Tobol and the Irtysh, upstream of which stood the capital of Iskir (later Tobol'sk).

Here, over four days, the decisive battle was fought. Yermak needed safe quarters and adequate provisions for the winter months; but Kuchum had barred his further progress with a barrage across the Irtysh. The Cossacks had either to retreat downstream to a grim winter in a makeshift camp, or come ashore and contest Iskir with the Khan's forces, described as 'more numerous than the forests and countless as the sands'. Against them, according to the illustrated *Remezov Chronicle*, Yermak could now field just 45 men – a figure which, though the Cossacks were certainly dwindling, may safely be multiplied by ten. On the night before the battle God signified his intentions by revealing to the Cossacks the vision of a city with its church bells ringing atop a pillar of fire. 'God wished to glorify this site,' explains the chronicler.

Though at first powder and flint repaid spears and arrows with interest, the battle degenerated into sword-to-sword, then hand-to-hand, struggles. The Cossacks fought with the desperation of men who had nowhere to go. The Khan's motley horde merely 'lamented, fought unwillingly, and died'; by the fourth day Kuchum's Tartars, Ostyaks and Voguls were melting back into the forests. Yermak was master of Iskir and so of Siberia.

It was not of course the Siberia of the atlases, merely an indefinite and marginal extremity of it. And with his troops decimated yet again and with no immediate prospect of reinforcements, Yermak was as much its prisoner as its victor. For the next two years it was all he could do to hold out. While the Tsar celebrated the Cossack victories and the Stroganovs rejoiced at their commercial prospects – and while legend lavishly embroidered the whole saga – Yermak suffered the pangs of every Russian invader. His foraging parties were surprised and massacred; his last powder was spent in a desperate defence of Iskir.

On 4 August 1584, a band of Cossacks under Yermak's command, while trying to protect a trading caravan from Xinjiang, camped for the night on an island in the Irtysh. Heavy rain lulled them to sleep. They knew nothing of Kuchum's attack until swords slashed through the canvas. The *Remezov Chronicle* has Yermak attempting to swim to the boats but drowning under the weight of a double suit of chain mail gifted to him by the Tsar. This may represent a veiled criticism of Tsarist ambivalence. With the 'Conqueror of Siberia' conveniently out of the way, there could be no question of the erstwhile Khanate becoming a Cossack or Stroganov preserve; it belonged to Russia.

Already the first detachment of Muscovite troops had reached Iskir. On Yermak's death, they and the few remaining Cossacks fell back to the Urals. But within a year a steady stream of troops, traders and officials from the west had retaken Iskir and were pushing forward unopposed into the immensity beyond. In disposing of the Khanate of Kuchum, the one major obstacle, Yermak had opened up the largest wilderness on earth, an achievement nearly as momentous as that of Columbus.

The great Russian advance

After Yermak's exploits the penetration of Siberia makes up for its lack of well-documented drama by its sensational rapidity. From Tobol'sk, founded in 1587 near the site of Iskir, the first advance was northwards, down the Ob to the fur-rich land of Mansiyskiy. A string of *ostrogs* (forts-cum-trading posts) marked its progress – Pelym (1592), Beresovo (1594) and Obdursk (1595) on the Arctic Ocean. Russia had acquired her first, albeit frozen, stretch of Asian coastline.

Eastwards fur traders with their Cossack escorts followed the Ob upstream to Tomsk which in 1629 became a provincial capital. East again and the shortest of portages enabled the pioneers to transfer from the eastern tributaries of the Ob to the western streams of the Yenisey. Another vast river system beckoned, another vast slice of territory became accessible.

Meanwhile in 1620 Cossacks from Mansiyskiy had pushed down from the north to a tributary of the Lena, the third of Siberia's great rivers. Vasily Bugor reached the Lena itself in 1628 and four years later another Cossack, Peter Beketov, founded the *ostrog* of Yakutsk. Here the advance split into three prongs. One continued east reaching the Sea of Okhotsk in 1639. Thus in less than two generations the Russian advance had reached Pacific waters, 4750 km (3000 miles) from Yermak's starting point west of the Urals. Very roughly, it represented a rate of expansion of 13,000 sq km (5000 sq miles) a year.

From the new *ostrog* of Okhotsk came word of the Amur. Though well to the south of the Russian line of advance, this east-flowing river system reputedly supported a settled population who grew corn, a scarce commodity in Siberia. According to the Siberian Yakuts, who may have originally migrated from the Amur, the land was called Daurien, home of the Daur. To investigate what, by Siberian standards, sounded like a veritable Arcadia, the Yakutsk governor despatched a man too bloodthirsty even for the Cossacks. With a cannon and a hundred soldiers, Vasily Poyarkov forced a passage through the frozen Stanovoy Mountains in the winter of 1643–4 and descended on Daurien.

When the Daur's supplies failed to materialize, Poyarkov left his men to feed on the Daurs. Fifty corpses were eaten. Preceded by his gruesome reputation, and apparently unaware that the Amur was also the Heilong-jiang and the Daurs Chinese subjects, Poyarkov tricked and tortured his way downstream to the mouth of the river. Now minus most of his followers he spent a winter waiting to sail north towards Okhotsk and another winter in its vicinity before finally striking inland to Yakutsk.

Although Poyarkov's considerable feat had been horribly prejudiced by his conduct, equally ruthless expedients were adopted by his more celebrated

Finding the shores of the Amur River a veritable Arcadia compared to Siberia, Russian explorers were loath to recognize Chinese claims to the area.

successor. Yerofey Pavlovich Khabarov was a man of substance, a native Russian who had already made good in Siberia. His two expeditions to the Amur, although liberally provided with cannon and troops, were largely private ventures. The first (1649–51), by way of reconnaissance, pioneered a new route up the Olekma tributary of the Lena and established that Daurien was indeed part of Chinese Manchuria.

Undeterred, Khabarov merely returned to the fray with more guns. Albasin (now named in his honour Yerofey-Pavlovich) was fortified as a Russian base and another bloody advance downstream began. 'With God's help . . . we burned them, we knocked them on the head, and counting adults and children we killed 661'; 350 women and children and a like number of horses and cattle were simply appropriated; the Russian loss was 4 dead and 45 wounded – and that was just the first of several engagements.

In Russia Khabarov was hailed as a second Yermak. From Yakutsk and Lake Baykal (first reached in 1643) a rabble of adventurers and renegades headed for his Promised Land of abundant harvests and plentiful women. But word of his excesses had also reached Peking. A Chinese army slowly mobilized and in 1652, somewhere in the vicinity of the future Kharabov'sk, the first of those interminable Sino-Russian border clashes along the Amur resulted in a Russian victory. Khabarov's triumph, however, was short-lived. His force disintegrated into roving bands of robbers, he

THE FUR TRADE

It was by exacting tribute from the indigenous peoples in the form of furs, and then sending to Moscow 2400 sable skins, that Yermak Timofeyevich signified his conquest of Sibir. Siberia's well-wooded habitat made it one vast game park. Its scanty population of scarcely one human to every 260 sq km (100 sq miles) meant that the wildlife was exceptionally tame; and its severity of climate meant that every species of this teeming fauna, from small rodents to large bears, was endowed with the finest of pelts. By throwing open the gates of Siberia to fur traders and firearms, Yermak inaugurated the greatest slaughter in history.

As the gold rush was to the westward advance in North America so the fur rush was to the eastward advance in northern Asia. Fur fuelled the Russian economy, inspired the move into Siberia, financed its conquest and administration and, as returns from existing hunting grounds declined, ensured a speedy progression to ever remoter regions in the north and east. On the Arctic and North Pacific coasts walrus tusks, seal skins and above all sea-otters

replaced the sables. In pursuit of the sea-otter the Russian advance continued across the Bering Strait and down the coasts of Alaska and British Columbia.

Until the 19th century furs were also the currency of Siberia. A tin kettle woudl be sold for as many sables as it could accommodate; the choicest skins were sometimes exchanged for as many bars of silver as could be stuffed inside them. Collecting revenue – in Siberia as elsewhere the sole purpose and sum total of early colonial administration – meant levying tribute on such natives as could be found. The tribute took the form of *yassack,* an assessment in terms of animal skins.

Thus in 1675 the Yakutsk district, comprising a wilderness about the size of western Europe, was credited with a population of just 10,680 who were to yield an annual *yassack* of 18,450 sables, 6284 red foxes, 11 black foxes, 2 brown foxes, 1 red-brown fox, and 1 fox coat.

Yet this official levy was but the tip, as it were, of the sable's tail. Every official provided for his own enrichment by an additional

Sables, a small species of marten (here hanging from the trapper's belt), and foxes were the stock-in-trade of Siberia's fur-crazed pioneers.

assessment in furs; every military commander funded his exploits by a booty in furs; and every trader demanded for his stocks of vodka and tobacco payment in furs.

himself was superseded in 1653, and in the following year the Chinese began to roll back the Russian advance. In 1689 the Treaty of Nerchinsk at last reasserted Chinese rights to the whole Amur valley. Not until the 19th century would the Russians return to the Amur.

Land's end?

Checked in the east by the sea and in the south-east by the Celestial Empire, Siberia's explorers yet faced their stiffest challenge in the north-east. From Yakutsk to the Bering Strait is another 3250 km (2000 miles) of increasingly mountainous terrain and sub-zero temperatures. Together with the 1300-km (800-mile) long Kamchatka peninsula, this region constitutes a veritable sub-continent nearly as big as India.

As early as 1630 the first fur traders had reached the mouth of the Lena and begun working east along the Arctic coast. They were rewarded with frost-bite and the best black sables in Siberia. In addition the north yielded ivory in the form of both walrus and mammoth tusks (the latter, some 2000 in all, dug from mastodons deep-frozen in the permafrost). It also posed a particularly horny

geographical problem. Where did this seemingly endless land mass stop? Did it join on to the American continent or on to some Arctic continent? Or could you in fact sail out of the Arctic Ocean and into the Pacific as proponents of the North-East Passage had always maintained?

Curiously this conundrum had been solved almost as soon as it was posed. In 1648 Semyon Ivanovich Dezhnyov, a dogged government *yassack* collector, and Fedot Alexeyev, the representative of a Moscow merchant, sailed east from the Kolyma River on the Arctic coast and rounded the Chukchi peninsula into the Pacific. A storm then separated their puny vessels and deposited Dezhnyov somewhere south of the Anadyr' River and Alexeyev somewhere even further south on the Kamchatkan coast. Alexeyev never resurfaced and Dezhnyov, though he wrote a report of his voyage, failed to grasp the significance that would come to attach to it. The report thus disappeared into the Yakutsk archives where its discovery 87 years later looked uncommonly like a piece of Russian propaganda, and duly elicited ruthless scrutiny from non-Russian scholars.

There was nothing inherently suspect about Dezhnyov's achievement. No doubt, before

1806-15 Seetzen travelled through much of the Middle East and was the first to journey around the Dead Sea.
1810 Pottinger and Christie explored eastern Persia and western Afghanistan dressed as horse dealers.
1811 Manning became the first Englishman to enter Lhasa.
1812 Moorcroft and Hearsey crossed the central Himalayas to explore the interior of Tibet.

Dezhnyov, many local Chukchis had rounded their own peninsula without colliding with Alaska. But the rules of exploration demand that the explorer register his claim and have it ratified. Dezhnyov satisfied the first requirement but was pipped on the second. For by the time his report was unearthed by a member of the Great Northern Expedition in the 1730s, that expedition's outstanding figure, Vitus Bering, had just repeated the feat by sailing through what is now the Bering Strait (and thus passing what is now Cape Dezhneva).

East to Alaska

The last years of the 17th century had witnessed the exploration of Kamchatka (and the ruthless suppression of the Kamchadales) by Vladimir Atlasov. A port to link the new peninsula with Okhotsk was established at Bol'sheretsk and by 1700 maps of the region were showing yet another tongue of land even further east. Whether this was an island, another Siberian peninsula, or a bit of America was unknown. But it was obviously the next challenge both for expansionist Russia and for her fur-hungry pioneers. It also aroused much scientific speculation, to assuage which in 1725 Peter the Great despatched Captain Vitus Bering, a Dane serving in the Russian navy, to build a ship in Kamchatka and sail north for as far as was necessary to establish whether and where Asia became America.

What with first having to cross the entire breadth of Siberia, then the Sea of Okhotsk and then Kamchatka, Bering's voyages entailed vastly more overland travel than sailing. It took him and his men three years just to reach the starting line and construct their ship, the *Saint Gabriel*. In 1728 they sailed north, 40 men with provisions for a year, and passing Cape Chukotski reached 67´18° on 8 August. This was further north than any known latitude on the adjacent coast and it was thus rightly presumed that they had passed from the Pacific to the Arctic Ocean. Content to have established the eastern extremity of the Eurasian land mass, Bering was back in Kamchatka in under two months.

But there remained the question of the unseen land to the east. Did it exist? Was it America? Could there in fact be a continental land-bridge still further to the north? For five years of endeavour (he regained St Petersburg in 1730), Bering's six weeks at sea begged more questions than they answered. A new expedition was promptly suggested and speedily approved. It

GEORG WILHELM STELLER

Steller (1709–46) was both the most brilliant and the most controversial of the many German scientists who contributed to Siberian exploration. A graduate of – amongst others – Halle University, he shared with Ludwig Leichhardt, a later alumnus and the explorer of northern Australia, an incorrigible belief in his own genius which was not without foundation.

Reaching St Petersburg (Leningrad) as a naval doctor, he secured an appointment as botanist with the Great Northern Expedition and made extensive forays in Kamchatka, Yakutsk and the Kuril Islands. He worked round the clock, travelled light, lived off the land, and generally shamed his more comfort-conscious colleagues to whom he was both a trial and an inspiration.

Adversity only made him more obnoxious and more brilliant. Joining the second Bering voyage in Kamchatka, he alienated the entire crew of the *St Peter* with his criticisms of their navigation yet was usually right in his own predictions, founded on a study of seaweeds and wave shapes, about the proximity of land. He alone took full advantage of the ten hours spent on Kayak Island, collecting no less than 150 varieties of plants. On Bering Island it was his example of living ashore in burrows and making the most of what the island offered in the way of meat, roots and herbs that largely contributed to the expedition's survival.

His account of the island's abundant fauna – Arctic foxes, seals, sea-otters, sea-lions and sea-cows – is a curious mixture of detailed scientific observation and nauseating culinary tips. Particularly interesting, because no other scientist would see one before they were hunted to extinction, is his description of the sea-cow, or manatee, an endearing creature which grazed on sea-weed

G.W. Steller measures the now extinct Steller's sea cow. To these inoffensive monsters grazing the seaweed of Bering Island, the expedition largely owed its survival.

and could grow to 10 metres (35 ft) long. Steller recommended hanging the meat until it crawled with worms and then boiling it for half an hour. The fat was 'of such exceptionally good flavour that we drank it by the cupful'.

THE BLUE FOX

Of four-footed land animals there occur on Bering Island only the stone or Arctic Fox (Lagopus). I had opportunity during our unfortunate sojourn on this island to become acquainted only too closely with the nature of this animal which far surpasses the common fox in impudence, cunning and roguishness.

They crowded into our dwellings by day and by night, and stole everything that they could carry away. They knew in such an unbelievably cunning way how to roll off a weight from our provision casks that at first we could hardly ascribe it to them. At night when we camped in the open they pulled the nightcaps and the gloves from under our heads and the sea-otter skins from under our bodies.

When we sat down by the wayside they came so near that they began to gnaw the straps on our home-made shoes and even the shoes themselves. If we lay down to sleep they sniffed our nostrils to see whether we were dead or alive; if one held one's breath they even nipped our noses and were about to bite. When we first arrived they bit off the noses, fingers and toes of our dead while their graves were being dug. They also attacked the weak and ill so that we could hardly hold them off. One night when a sailor on his knees wanted to urinate out of the door of the hut, a fox snapped at the exposed part and, in spite of his cries, did not soon let go. No one could relieve himself without a stick in his hand. . . .

In as much as they left us no rest by day or by night we killed young and old, did them all possible harm and, whenever we could, tortured them most cruelly. I personally may have been responsible during my sojourn on the island for having killed over 200. The third day after my arrival I killed with an axe within three hours over 70 from whose skins the root of our hut was made. . . .

From G.W. Steller's *Topographical and Physical Description of Bering Island* in *Bering's Voyages*, ed. by F.A. Golder, New York, 1925.

was to incorporate exploration of both the Arctic and Pacific coasts; to locate Japan as well as America; to accommodate a vast array of distinguished scientists; and to build at least four ships. But the scale of the enterprise was nearly its undoing. This time it took Bering five years of travel and acrimony to assemble his veritable army of shipwrights, sailors and scientists on what was almost the other side of the world from St Petersburg (Leningrad) and another two years to construct the *St Peter* and *St Paul* for the voyage east from Petropavlosk.

'Kapitan-Komandor' Bering, now 60, admitted that he no longer had the energy for the task in hand; only a strong sense of duty and the almost universal regard of his men sustained him. Sailing circuitously to the south-east, the two ships lost touch in a storm, leaving Chirikov in the *St Paul* to make a landfall near Prince of Wales Island on 15 July 1741. On the same day Bering's *St Peter* sighted Mount St Elias to the east of what is now Valdez.

When it became apparent from the extent of the mountains and the very different flora that this must indeed be America, the Komandor merely shrugged his shoulders. As if forewarned of disaster, his only concern was for a speedy return to Kamchatka. Just one day was spent on Kayak Island loading fresh water before the vessel sailed west; no attempt was made to explore the new land nor to claim it. 'Ten years were devoted to the preparation for this great enterprise,' wrote a disgusted Georg Steller, the

expedition's naturalist, 'and ten hours were devoted to its main purpose.'

By the end of August they were off the tip of the Alaskan peninsula on the return leg and already succumbing to scurvy. September brought storms and more scurvy. Bering, now bed-ridden, handed over command. But so few were fit to man the sails that the St Peter 'drifted along at the mercy of the winds' like a ghost ship. In early November they sighted land. The crew clung to the idea that it must be Kamchatka. Bering and Steller knew otherwise and, when the ship ran helplessly aground, were duly proved right.

In honour of the Komandor, who died of frost-bite and scurvy soon after being landed, it was named Bering Island. Here, for nine desperate snow-bound months, the crew of the St Peter were marooned. They sheltered in caves, burrows, and makeshift huts; they lived off seal meat and they died of exposure. Only 46 out of 77 survived to put back to sea the following August. Ironically they found they were only four days' sailing from Kamchatka and safety.

Scientists and eccentrics

The Great Expedition, of which Bering's Second Voyage was part, included the first voyage from Kamchatka to Japan in 1738–9 of Martin Spanberg (who explored the Kuril Islands *en route*) and further endeavours along the Arctic coastline. Naturalists

and then travelled to Kamchatka.
1829 Humboldt crossed the Altai
Mountains, returning down the Volga and
Caspian Sea to Moscow.

1831 Jacquemont travelled in the Kashmir
Valley and Baltistan for Paris Botanic Garden.
1834-6 Wellsted and Whitelock explored
inland from the south Arabian coast to the

edge of the Rub' al Khālī.
1835 Chesney's Euphrates River expedition
mapped the Euphrates and Tigris in an
attempt to find shipping route to India.

like Steller and J.G. Gmelin, antiquarians like G.F. Muller (the discoverer of Dezhnyov's reports), and ethnographers like S.P. Krasheninikov (the authority on Kamchatka) brought Siberia within the purview of science.

Previously the only scientific work had been that carried out by a gifted but neglected doctor, D.G. Messerschmidt, who for seven years (1720–7) wandered penniless and despised from the Urals to Mongolia making notes on natural history. Now science led the way and the Great Expedition was followed by a second multi-disciplinary assault on Siberia's mysteries led by another German doctor, P.S. Pallas, in the early 1770s. Pallas recommended further exploration of the Chukchi peninsula but another Bering-type expedition under the Englishman Joseph Billings (1785–93) failed to connect explorations in the Bering Strait and off Alaska with the Russian settlements on the Arctic coast at the mouth of the Kolyma.

Billings had previously served with Captain Cook on his last voyage (1776–9) to Alaska and Kamchatka. So had the American, John Ledyard who with the support of Pallas and of that great impresario of exploration, Sir Joseph Banks, set out in 1786 to cross Eurasia and America from west to east. He failed, being arrested in Yakutsk and escorted back to the Polish border. But his example fired a number of eccentric Britons. There was John Dundas Cochrane, 'the pedestrian traveller', who abandoned a rather promising attempt to walk round the world when in Kamchatka he fell helplessly in love with a 13-year-old Kamchadale beauty; there was James Holman, 'the blind traveller' who, in spite of his infirmity, managed to reach Irkutsk and get himself deported as a spy; and somewhat later there was Kate Marsden, one of the first women to be elected a Fellow of the Royal Geographical Society, who travelled extensively in the Yakutsk district looking for lepers.

Meanwhile more attempts were being made to complete the map of Siberia's long and gruesome Arctic coast. In the 1820s Cochrane had found an expedition under Baron Wrangel endeavouring once again to explore the north coast of the Chukchi peninsula. Wrangel concluded that there was more land to the north-east and in 1849, while looking for Sir John Franklin, Captain H. Kellett sighted and named it – Wrangel Island. But it was not the long sought land-bridge between Asia and America and this idea was now abandoned.

Clearly a North-East Passage from Europe to the Pacific did indeed exist. It remained only for the Englishman, Joseph Wiggins, and the Finn, A.E. Nordenskiöld, to demonstrate that steam had made its navigation possible. While Wiggins opened trade between Dundee and Siberia by way of the Kara Sea and the Yenisey, Nordenskiöld left Tromsø in Norway in 1878 heading for the Bering Strait. After wintering just a hundred miles short of the strait, the *Vega* rounded Cape Dezhneva into the Pacific. It was 325 years since Willoughby and Chancellor had first attempted the passage and 230 years since Dezhnyov had demonstrated its feasibility.

ARABIA

Though easily accessible from the Mediterranean, the Arabian peninsula retained its mystery for a long time. As late as 1852 Richard Burton secured the support of the Royal Geographical Society for an expedition to remove what he called 'that opprobrium to modern adventure, the huge white blot in our maps which still notes the Eastern and Central Regions of Arabia'. Yet even the insufferable Burton, something of an 'opprobrium to modern adventure' himself, failed to get further than Mecca. Much of the peninsula was still unexplored at the beginning of the 20th century.

Petra, the Nabataean city in Jordan, was discovered by Burckhardt in 1812. Its 'Convent of El Deir' was painted by David Roberts 27 years later.

It was partly the appalling nature of the terrain and partly the fanatically anti-Christian sentiments of its population. Additionally, there were no political incentives to explore the interior until the 19th century and no commercial incentives until the discovery of oil. Arabian explorers are thus more disingenuous than most about their motives. Not a few, in their heart of hearts, would have agreed with St John Philby who declared simply, 'My ambition is fame.' They did as much, went as far, as was necessary to assure it. Most were burdened, even tortured by their own egos; many eventually committed suicide. If Siberia encouraged the acquisitive, and if the Himalayas humbled the ambitious, then the desert nurtured the disorientated.

When the modern age of exploration dawned, only the Hejaz, the area bordering the Red Sea, had been visited by Europeans. A few, following Covilhā and Varthema, had reached Mecca and Medina, most of them converts to Islam like the Devon-born Joseph Pitts who had been enslaved by Barbary pirates and taken on *haj* (pilgrimage) by his master (*c.*1687). Further south, in the Yemen, representatives of the Dutch and English East India Companies had

'Harry' St John Philby and his Saudi-supplied escort reach Jeddah in late 1917, thus completing what was then the most southerly traverse of the Arabian peninsula.

occasionally been summoned, and more often abducted, from their trading stations at Mocha and Aden and marched to Ṣan‘a, the Yemeni capital two weeks into the mountains.

The rest of the peninsula's 3.25 million sq km (1¼ million sq miles) of desert, from the Nafūd in the north to the Rub‘ al Khali (the Empty Quarter) in the south, was unknown. It presented a worthy challenge to science, and it was a scientific expedition which inaugurated the new age. Like Bering's last expedition (1741), this Arabian initiative (1762) involved a galaxy of German and Scandinavian savants and was intended to confer intellectual prestige on its sponsor (in this case the King of Denmark). Disappointingly its explorations extended no further than the already familiar triangle of the Yemen. Yet Carsten Niebuhr, its surveyor and sole survivor, has been credited with the 'intelligence and courage which first opened Arabia to Europe' (W.G. Palgrave).

From observation and careful enquiry Niebuhr gained a clearer idea of the country's geography than any of his predecessors and, taking issue with accepted notions of the desert Arabs as skulking *banditti,* he portrayed its inhabitants as a pure and noble people of great antiquity and simplicity 'like the patriarchs of old'. One of the first Orientalists, Niebuhr contributed to the rehabilitation of Arabist studies and, by highlighting Arab ideas of hospitality and liberty, whetted the appetites of more romantic travellers.

Mecca and Medina

Niebuhr also drew attention to a wave of religious and political revivalism that was sweeping through the interior under the leadership of Muḥammad Ibn Sa‘ūd and inspired by the teachings of ‘Abd al-Wahhāb. The fanatical Wahhābīyah had contrived something of a revolution in Nejd and by the turn of the century were pushing rapidly into Syria and Mesopotamia and were about to strike at Mecca. But Niebuhr had also ventured that 'an European might travel in safety even through this remote part [Nejd] of Arabia'. Sensitive – as ever – to the threat of Islamic revivalism, the European powers were on the look-out for agents who would do just that.

In 1806 Badia y Leblich, a Spaniard in the employ of Napoleon Bonaparte, made the *haj* and in 1809 Ulrich Jasper Seetzen followed him on behalf of the Tsar. Five years later Johann Ludwig Burckhardt while waiting to proceed with the African Association's quest for the Niger – and not without first alerting the British government – triplicated the feat.

and excavated Nineveh in Iraq.
1848 Hooker described the plants of Nepal and Sikkim.
1851 Semenov led the first of the Russian

expeditions into Chinese Turkestan which were to map here for the next 50 years.
1853-6 Maksimovich studied natural history of the trans-Baikal country.

1854-62 Naturalist Wallace travelled in the Malay Archipelago.
1854 East Siberian expedition of the Imperial Geographical Society under Schwarz.

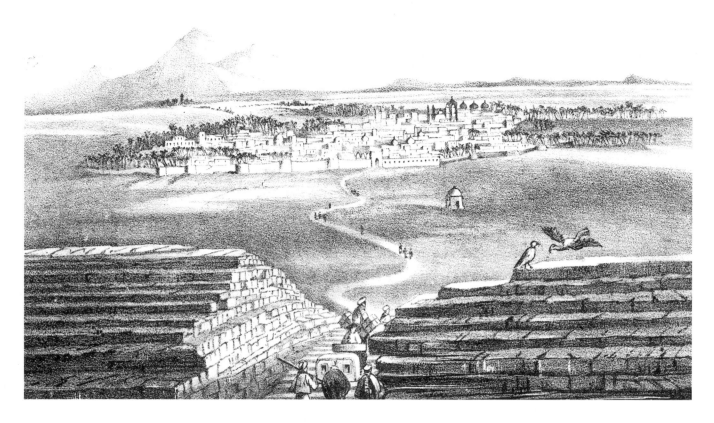

In Medina, where the Prophet formed his first community and where He was buried, Richard Burton joined a haj *caravan for the onward journey to Mecca.*

All these men travelled in disguise and none more convincingly than the methodical Burckhardt, an Anglophile Swiss who had spent seven years preparing himself physically and culturally for exploration in Islamic lands. His Arabic studies had been completed with a translation of *Robinson Crusoe* and in 1812, while heading south from Syria to Cairo, he had contrived to discover the rock-cut ruins of Petra, the ancient Nabataean city in Jordan. An excursion up the Nile followed; then he made his Arabian debut as Sheikh Ibrahim, 'a reduced Egyptian gentleman' who arrived by sea at Jeddah in 1814.

The Wahhābīyah had recently been expelled from the Holy Cities by the Egyptians and it was thus under Egyptian patronage that Burckhardt made his way first to Taif (Aṭ Ṭa'if) and then to Mecca. There he stayed four months and 'never enjoyed such perfect ease' as he compiled a minute description of the city and an account of the Wahhābī war that still raged in the surrounding countryside. Eventually he proceeded up the coast to Medina, the Prophet's burial place, and there too compiled an exhaustive dossier, in spite of being stricken with malaria. He returned to Egypt by sea from Yanbu and died two

years later. Several weighty volumes, published posthumously, could be said to have exhausted once and for all the Holy Cities of the Hejaz.

This, however, did not deter Richard Burton in 1853 from making an almost identical journey in reverse – except that more settled conditions enabled his caravan to take the usual inland route between the two cities. Reasoning that 'what might be perilous to other travellers would be safe to me', Burton, then a Lieutenant in the East India Company's forces, had first proposed to cross the whole of Arabia from the Hejaz to Muscat. The Company had objected and authorized just a year's Arabic study. Had Burton found that 'removing the huge white blot' was as easy (for him) as he had implied, he certainly would have attempted it.

In the event he discovered nothing that Burckhardt had not already described in painful detail. For this lack of novelty Burton compensated by lacing his narrative with gratuitous pornography, erudite digressions and suspect heroics – all of which naturally made it a best-seller. He also succeeded where Burckhardt and others had failed in conveying the romance of the desert, 'a haggard land infested with wild beasts and wilder men, a region whose very fountains murmur the warning words "Drink and away!" What can be more exciting? What more sublime.'

71

Trans Arabia

Somewhat inconveniently the first crossing of the Arabian peninsula, which should in all conscience have been reserved, if not for Burton, then for one of the other lions of Arabian exploration, had already been made by a reluctant Captain in HM's 47th Foot regiment. Sent from India to congratulate the Egyptians on their defeat of the Wahhābīyah and to arrange for joint action against the pirates of Muscat, Captain George Sadlier had landed in the Gulf in 1819. Thence he set off inland to find Ibrahim Pasha, the Egyptian commander. Ibrahim was not at Hufhuf (Al Hufūf) so the Captain continued east to Diriyyah (Ad Dir'iyah). The Pasha was not there either, nor was he at Rass (Ar-Rass); Sadlier and his Egyptian escort just kept going. Not till the suburbs of Medina did he run his quarry to ground and thence the only way home was down to Yanbu on the Red Sea. Throughout this three-month journey, Captain Sadlier never pretended to be anyone other than himself, never wore Arab clothes, found nothing remotely 'sublime' or 'exciting' about the desert, and cordially detested both the brutal Egyptian soldiery and their cringing Bedouin foes. No wonder the Arabists give him such short shrift.

Their preferred candidate is the brilliant if elusive William Gifford Palgrave who in 1862 left Ma'an in southern Jordan to make the first west-east crossing. Palgrave, an Oxford scholar and Bombay infantryman, adopted the guise of Mahmoud el-Eys, a Syrian doctor. In fact at the time this man of many incarnations and more aliases was also both a Jesuit missionary, specially blessed by the Pope to survey central Arabia's potential for missionaries, and an agent of Louis Napoleon, in search of allies who might consolidate the political advantages anticipated from the construction of the Suez canal.

Untroubled by these conflicting and compromising loyalties, Palgrave and his companion, also a priest, sped 'stealthily but rapidly' across 'a dreary land of death' to the oases of Jauf (Al Jawf) on the edge of the great sandy desert of Nafūd. There they secured the services of a wizened and 'half-cracked' Bedou, who closely resembled a locust but who, hailing from Hā'il on the other side, undertook to conduct them across the Nafūd. It was mid-summer; the Nafūd's 300 km (200 miles) of soft red sand lay licked into 'a vast sea of fire' between whose towering dunes 'the traveller finds himself imprisoned in a suffocating sand-pit, hemmed in by burning walls'. Halting for just three hours in every 24, they sighted the sheer cliffs of the Nejd on the fourth hellish day.

William Gifford Palgrave, scholar, soldier, priest, spy, diplomat and, as Mahmoud el-Eys, Syrian doctor and doyen of Arabian explorers. 'Much, how much! is left untold.'

Hā'il was the power base of Talal Ibn Rashid, a rival to the Wahhābī Saudis for supremacy of the Nejd and so the obvious candidate for French and Catholic overtures. Like George Wallin, a Finn in Egyptian employ who had been in Hā'il 15 years earlier, Palgrave was profoundly impressed both by Talal and his model government. He stayed three weeks, practising medicine, conferring with Talal and making copious notes. Thence on to Riyadh, the new capital of the house of Saud and the stronghold of the fanatical Wahhābīyah. Sadleir had passed it but without investigating what was then a place of little significance; Wallin had turned back from Hā'il. Palgrave was thus the first European to spy what he called 'the lion's den'.

It fully lived up to expectations. During a stay of nearly six weeks in Riyadh the Fathers were in constant fear for their lives and only survived thanks to a timely escape engineered by Abu Isa, a Syrian caravan leader of commanding personality who had become Palgrave's mentor. The three then made a dash across the wastes of the Dahna to Hufhuf and reached the Gulf opposite Bahrain at the end of 1862, six months after leaving Ma'an.

In due course Palgrave published a classic account of his journey which ended with the enigmatic

'Much, how much! is left untold'. Presumably this referred to his undercover work, news of which was reserved for Louis Napoleon. Acting on it, another French agent reached Hā'il in 1864. Italian by birth and a horse breeder by profession, Carlo Guarmani fully confirmed Palgrave's opinion of Talal. In search of Arab thoroughbreds he also travelled extensively in Nejd from Buraida and Anaisha in the east to Khaibar and Naima in the west.

This was much the same ground as that covered, admittedly in more desperate circumstances, by Charles Doughty twelve years later. Doughty's magnificent *Arabia Deserta* therefore made only a minimal contribution to knowledge of the area. It was as he would have wished. He wanted the book read not for information but for the way it was written, for how 'the seeing of a hungry man and the telling of a most weary man' might constitute literature.

While a dishevelled Doughty bartered and begged for his daily crust on the fringes of Bedou society, two of his compatriots were experiencing the peculiar satisfaction of being 'persons of distinction in search of other persons of distinction'. This was how Lady Anne Blunt proposed to explain the uninvited arrival of herself and her husband, Wilfrid, to the Rashidi ruler of Hā'il. Wealthy aristocrats as well as literary figures, the Blunts also travelled for pleasure and edification. As they plunged, using an approach route similar to Palgrave's, into the dreaded Nafūd, 'charming . . . interesting' were the adjectives which gushed from Lady Anne's pen.

In Arabia as elsewhere the traveller sees what he, or she, wants. Queen Victoria was being proclaimed Empress of India; a British expedition was about to march into Afghanistan. The Blunts's well-stocked caravan swept into Nejd in 1879 on a wave of late Victorian certainties. Bedou or British, the world consisted of gentlemen, players and scoundrels. Each recognized its own. To the Blunts, who made no secret of their identity, Sheikhs and Emirs were invariably courteous, not at all like 'those disagreeable ones described by Mr Palgrave'. And if Hā'il, like Riyadh, was now a 'lion's den', it was all right – 'we were friends with the lion.'

Thoroughly delighted with the Rashidi capital and with its political arrangements, the Blunts left for

CHARLES MONTAGU DOUGHTY

A large red-haired recluse with a bad stammer and an obsession about the English language, Doughty (1843 1926) was an improbable candidate for Arabian laurels. He was also tactless and uncompromising, refusing either to conceal his Christianity or to affect any sympathy for Islam ('the most dangerous grown confederacy and secret conspiracy, surely, in the whole world', he called it). Not surprisingly his travels became a succession of trials and humiliations. The wonder is that he survived at all.

Travelling on a scholar's budget, he had learned Arabic in Damascus and in 1876 joined the *haj* caravan as far as Madá'in Sālih where he spent three months studying Nabataean tombs and inscriptions. For reasons unexplained he then attached himself to a family of Bedou graziers, and subsequently other nomadic groups, in whose company he travelled and on whose hospitality he depended. Although seldom welcome and often robbed and abandoned, he also experienced great kindness, especially

from the women, and came to appreciate the harsh realities of life for the over-romanticized Bedouin.

He was twice expelled by the Rashidis of Hā'il, once by the Turks of Khaybar, and seemed condemned to wander the intervening wastes indefinitely until in 1878 he managed to reach 'Unåyzah. There, besides the usual stone-throwing mob, he found friends who secreted him in a garden outside the city and arranged for his departure with a caravan heading for Mecca.

On entering the Hejaz he was again robbed, made prisoner and all but murdered. 'I passed one good day in Arabia; and all the rest were evil because of the people's fanaticism.' Penniless and wretched he reached the safety of Jeddah after a two-year odyssey.

Of *Travels in Arabia Deserta*, published ten years later, Doughty would insist that the style was far more important than the content. A passionate admirer of Chaucer and Spenser, he recognized in Bedouin

dialogue and manners a fitting subject for an eccentric prose style combining Elizabethan structures with Chaucerian language. The result, 'a bible of its kind' according to T.E. Lawrence, is regarded by many as a classic of travel literature.

OMAN AND THE HADHRAMAWT

Cut off from the rest of the peninsula by the Empty Quarter, Oman and the Hadhramawt were first penetrated from the sea. In the mid-1830s Lieutenants Whitelock and Wellsted of the *Palinurus,* a survey ship from Bombay, secured the support of the Sultan of Muscat for two journeys into the mountainous interior. From Bilād Banī Bū Ali they made a wide arc to Sīb and then attempted to reach Nejd but were turned back near Ibrī. The verdant valleys came as a revelation but it was another 40 years before Colonel C.B. Miles extended and corrected these early surveys.

The same officers explored the coast of neighbouring Dhufar, whence Bertram Thomas would launch himself into the Empty Quarter. They also investigated the island of Socotra, much visited by Portuguese and English shipping in the 17th century and whose scenery, according to James Wellsted, 'yields to none in wildness and romantic grandeur'.

They did not, however, penetrate to the Hadhramawt, the populous valley between Dhufar and Aden. Baron Adolf von Wrede, a Bavarian soldier who landed at Al Mukallā in 1843, seems to have been the first European visitor to enter this unique corner of the peninsula whose fabled cities and great wealth date back to biblical times and the trade in incense and myrrh. Von Wrede was pleasantly surprised by the cosmopolitan character of its sheikhs, one of whom lent him a copy of Scott's *Life of Napoleon Bonaparte*. But he also fell foul of their fanaticism and was forced to flee minus his baggage and papers.

The same hostility dogged Theodore and Mabel Bent when in 1893 they explored and photographed the Hadhramawt during a tour of southern Arabia that also included Socotra, Dhufar and Oman. They were succeeded, in the 1930s, by two German expeditions which found the Hadhramawt rent by tribal strife. Peace,

The high-rise architecture of Shibam in the Hadhramawt (Yemen) is of considerable antiquity and a convincing proof of the region's commercial prosperity.

courtesy of the millionaire Saiyyid Bubakr and the British representative, Harold Ingrams (accompanied by his formidable wife Doreen), came in 1936 after an extended mission by the Ingrams and the construction of a road from Al Mukallā.

Meshed Ali and Mesopotamia. Lady Anne, the first European woman to reach Nejd, wrote up their travels in a lively and eventually disarming narrative which includes homely insights into harem life and gourmet verdicts on antelope, hyena and locust. For Wilfrid Blunt the journey proved a turning point. Much of his life was subsequently devoted to the cause of Arab independence and to the dismantling of British imperialism.

Similar causes would be taken up by Harry St John Bridger Philby, though in Philby's case inspired by reverence for the house of Saud (Riyadh) rather than that of Rashid (Hā'il). Philby's epitaph describes him as 'The Greatest of Arabian Explorers'. The RGS awarded him its Founders Medal in 1920 and his marathons by camel (1917, 1918, 1932) and later by car may be said to have completed the exploration of the peninsula. All, though, were undertaken under more favourable circumstances than those of Palgrave, Guarmani and Doughty.

In the years preceding the First World War a steady trickle of British advisers and adventurers – William Shakspear, Gerald Leachman, Gertrude Bell – had demonstrated that disguise was not essential to survival in Nejd. This was not the case in Mecca and Medina, where Burton's exploits had set a precedent imitated by Arthur Wavell in 1908 and by numerous subalterns and undergraduates in more recent years; but in the Hejaz as a whole the

construction of a railway from Damascus and a permanent British presence in Jeddah brought the region firmly within the ambit of Middle East politics and foreshadowed the exploits of T.E. Lawrence and the Arab League.

The other major development concerned the Saudis. Under Abdul Aziz ibn Saud their fortunes had revived dramatically and it was to persuade them to attack the now pro-Turkish Rashidis that Philby and others were sent to Riyadh in 1917. The mission approached from the Gulf via Hufhuf. Another mission was expected from the Hejaz but failed to materialize because the Hejaz authorities claimed that its safety could not be guaranteed. Ibn Saud, whose territory was now supposedly contiguous with the Hejaz, took exception to this.

Thus when Philby, already mightily taken by the Saudi, suggested that he should prove the point by continuing from Riyadh right across to Jeddah, the King eagerly agreed. With camels, escort and emissaries to the intervening tribes all provided by the King, Philby set forth on 9 December. Midwinter found central Arabia at its greenest; game was abundant, water plentiful. By Christmas Day Philby was in Taif and the most southerly crossing yet of the peninsula ended in Jeddah a few days later.

In 1918 he was back in Riyadh and, with the encouragement and support of his Saudi patron, made another pioneering foray, this time to the

1865 Johnson traversed the Aksai Chin Plateau and crossed the Kun Lun to Khotan.
1866 French Mekong River expedition attempt to find navigable route to Chinese

Yunnan was abandoned near Laos/Cambodia border.
1868 Sladen's expedition established a steamer service to Bhamo on the Irrawaddy.

1868 Radlov studied the people of the Altai region.
1868 Shaw crossed the Aksai Chin to become the first Englishman to enter

south. Although it was May, one of the hottest months, Philby determined to combine the journey with a survey. Long detours for triangulation purposes brought his escort to the brink of mutiny. But he pushed south for some 485 km (300 miles) along the wholly unknown Jabal Tuwayq as far as As Sulayyil and Dam before turning back. Both these places lie on the northern fringe of the Rub' al Khālī – the Empty Quarter. It was all that remained of 'the huge white blot'. It was also, by 1920, practically the only huge white blot left. Not unreasonably Philby thought it should be his.

The Empty Quarter

In 1924 and again in 1926 Philby was ready to go; Ibn Saud put him off. In 1930 he embraced Islam not without an eye to the effect this might have on his prospects; still the King prevaricated. In 1931 Bertram Thomas emerged from the sands at Doha. Two months earlier he had struck north from Salālah in Dhufar; he had thus crossed the Empty Quarter. Philby shut himself away for a whole week. 'Damn and blast Thomas . . .' he wrote.

'The final and greatest prize of Arabian exploration' (Wilfrid Thesiger) had been snatched by a scholarly and unassuming political officer in the service of the Sultan of Muscat. Thomas had prepared the ground with a number of reconnaissances and he had the support of the Sultan. But he had failed to contact Riyadh and could expect no favours from the fanatical Murra Bedouin of the interior. Winning their confidence by patient negotiation was his greatest achievement according to Thesiger. A scholar of wide interests, he also contributed much to an understanding of the ethnology and zoology of the region.

Philby derived some satisfaction from repeatedly pointing out that Thomas had taken the easiest, shortest, fastest route possible. In no sense had he explored the Empty Quarter. 'I have sworn a great oath,' wrote Philby, 'not to go home until I have crossed the RK twice! and left nothing in it for future travellers.' In fact he did neither; but in January 1932, with the permission and support of King Saud at last forthcoming, he set off from Hufhuf on the most gruelling of all Arabian journeys.

It took him to Nayfah deep in the Empty Quarter and then due west across virgin desert for 2000 km (1250 miles) to Mecca. In these western sands he rode for 650 km (400 miles) between one well and the next; his escort baulked in spite of the dire punishment that they could expect in Riyadh; water had to be dribbled into the camels' nostrils. In any comparison with Thomas's achievement 'the discerning will regard it as the greater of the two'. This was Wilfrid Thesiger's verdict.

Invited to investigate the supposed breeding grounds of the locust, Thesiger crossed the Empty Quarter to the east of Thomas's route in 1946 and again, from the Hadhramawt, in 1947–8. Like so

The first crossing of the Empty Quarter was achieved by Bertram Thomas in 1930–1. He is photographed here entering the Rub' al Khālī at Wadi Muqshin.

Wilfrid Thesiger (1910–) 'craved for adventures in savage lands' from childhood. He turned to the Empty Quarter as 'the final challenge of desert exploration'.

Yarkand.
1868 Hayward explored the valleys between the Kunlun and Karakoram Mountains, and north of Gilgit where he was murdered.

1868-9 Elias traced course of the Huang Ho.
1868-72 Richthofen's seven expeditions explored southern Manchuria, crossed from Canton to Peking, and went into Szechwan.

1870-85 Przhevalsky made four attempts to enter Tibet and made first survey of Altyn Tagh Mountains.
1871 Hari Ram completed a circuit of the

many of his illustrious predecessors, his first object was 'to win distinction as a traveller'. He succeeded like no other living explorer. But he also hoped to find in the empty wastes 'the peace that comes from solitude and, among the Bedou, comradeship in a hostile world'. If *Arabian Sands* stands comparison with the classic narratives of Burton, Palgrave and Doughty, it is precisely for these human insights. No doubt there are still corners of Arabia to be explored. 'The huge white blot' was never just a hole in the map; it was – is – a hunger of the soul.

CENTRAL ASIA AND THE HIMALAYAS

Judging by the gold medals awarded by the Royal Geographical Society, the heart of Asia between the Caspian Sea and the Great Wall of China represented the 19th century's most important arena of exploration. Here the highest mountains in the world plus the sources of all the main rivers of central, south and south-east Asia are locked into an incredibly complex system of mountain ranges flanked by high plateaux and vast deserts. As if these geographical attractions were not enough, commercially the region was both the crossroads of the continent and a source of gold, carpets and shawls; and culturally it embraced forgotten cities, lost tribes, and the most other-worldly civilization imaginable.

But of even greater importance, in the 19th century Central Asia and the Himalayas became a scene of intense political rivalry. It was, as the title of one stirring narrative had it, *Where Three Empires Meet*. Two of these, the British and Russian (the third was China), seemed destined not just to meet but to collide. Hence the high priority given to exploring the lands that intervened between them and hence the clandestine and military nature of so much of that exploration.

William Moorcroft

All these interests first surface in the voluminous writings, left scattered across Asia as if for a paper chase, by that most endearing of explorers, William Moorcroft. Because Moorcroft's obsessions so faithfully anticipated those of his successors, and because his travels so nearly embraced the entire region, he may be regarded as the father of exploration in the Himalayas and Central Asia.

A vet by profession but a man of many other near-manic enthusiasms, Moorcroft had arrived in India late in life as Superintendent of the East India Company's stud farm; and it was to find breeding stock for the Company's cavalry that he started

travelling. But his first journey outside India in 1812 was a wholly unauthorized foray across the Himalayas in search of Tibetan goats. The goats produced the wool from which Kashmir's famous shawls were woven. The idea was to bring some of these goats back to India and so establish a shawl industry. Moorcroft was very keen on agricultural improvement. He was also exceedingly curious about the mountains that ringed India's northern frontiers, about the rivers that emerged from them, and about the commercial possibilities of the lands that lay beyond them – indeed anything which offered a pretext for exploration.

The 1812 journey was made with Hyder Young Hearsey, an Anglo-Indian adventurer. Both men disguised themselves as wealthy Hindu pilgrims and with the help of two brothers, Bhutias from Kumaun whose descendants were to do more for trans-Himalayan exploration than anyone, they secured yaks, porters and guides to cross the 5070-metre (16,630-ft) Niti Pass (west of the present day frontier of Nepal). From the pass 'the prospect was awfully grand', according to Hearsey. Before them stretched the bleak Tibetan plateau intersected by the canyons of the Sutlej with the peaks of the Kailas range 'tipt with snow' on the horizon. Moorcroft, who was suffering from both dysentery and altitude sickness, failed to note that they were the first Englishmen ever to cross the central Himalayas and the first Europeans since the Portuguese Jesuits.

At Daba, near the Jesuits's now abandoned Tsaparang (Tse-pu-lung), they were referred to the provincial authorities in Gartok (Ka-erh-ya-sha). There Moorcroft correctly identified the north-west flowing river as the infant Indus and there he obtained both goats and sheep. The return journey – more of a drove – was made by way of Lake Manasarowar (Ma-fa-mu-ts'o Hu), reputedly the source of the Indus, Sutlej, Ganges and Tsang-po (Brahmaputra) and so a place of pilgrimage for Hindus and an enduring conundrum to geographers. Moorcroft's rough survey seemed to establish that the lake had no outlets whatsoever; but the adjoining lake of Rakas Tal (Lan-chia Ts'o) he correctly identified as the source of the Sutlej.

Back on the right side of the Himalayas, both men were taken prisoner by the Gurkhas (Nepalis). Although British pressure eventually secured their release, the repercussions of this affair overshadowed their achievement and did nothing to endear either Moorcroft or his obsessive schemes to his employers. It was thus six years before, with a grudging permission to continue his search for bloodstock, Moorcroft left

Bareilly in north India on what must be one of the longest odysseys (1819–25) in 19th-century exploration. He never returned; neither did either of his European companions; and so circuitous and leisurely was his progress, so copious his observations, and so various his activities that one doubts whether he ever intended to return.

Now well into his 50s – and so positively antique by British Indian standards – Moorcroft left British India by crossing the lower Sutlej River (on inflated buffalo skins), wintered in the Punjab hills, and crossed the Great Himalaya into Ladakh. There, during nearly two years while he waited for authorization to cross the Karakorams into Chinese Turkestan (Xinjiang), he mapped the passes and valleys of this extremity of the Tibetan plateau, grew desperately fond of the people, and became hopelessly embroiled in political intrigues to thwart supposed Russian overtures.

Rebuffed by the Chinese in Xinjiang and reprimanded by the British in India, he eventually descended into the valley of Kashmir. After another long halt during which he studied the shawl industry, Kashmiri bee-keeping and horticulture, he headed determinedly east for Afghanistan. The Hindu Kush was crossed by the Hajigak Pass to Bamiyan; near the Oxus the whole party was detained by an Uzbek chief. But the goal was in sight. On 25 February 1825, 'after a long and laborious pilgrimage of more than five years', Moorcroft and his companions sighted the domes and minarets of Bukhara. Not since Jenkinson's visit had an Englishman been there; never had the journey from India been made by a non-Asian.

What happened thereafter remains a mystery. The evidence suggests that Moorcroft and both his English companions died either from fever or poison within a few weeks of one another. Twenty years later, though, two French missionaries insisted that Moorcroft had subsequently spent 12 years in Lhasa. Whatever the truth, the legend of Moorcroft haunted the Himalayas and Central Asia for the rest of the century. His name was found scratched beside one of the great rock sculptures of Bamiyan; a Ladakhi continued to tend his garden in Leh and a shepherd in the Great Himalaya claimed the sheep he was grazing were Moorcroft's; his papers and possessions were still being discovered 15 years later.

Afghanistan and beyond

Because of the expedition's untimely end, it was not till 1841 that a narrative of Moorcroft's great journey was published. Distilled from the journals then available, the book was both exceedingly boring and hopelessly out of date, others by then having

The winter camp of the Afghan boundary commission. It surveyed the Pamirs and Hindu Kush mountains to help establish the Afghan frontiers.

THE GREAT GAME

At the beginning of the 19th century British India and Tsarist Russia were separated by some 3000 km (1875 miles); by the end of the century their respective territories almost touched. The process of exploration and annexation by which the intervening lands were gobbled up is known as the 'Great Game', a phrase popularized by Rudyard Kipling in the novel *Kim*. It was 'great' because the two imperial superpowers so nearly collided in an Asian armageddon, and it was a 'game' because, like Grandmother's Footsteps, the contestants pretended not to be advancing at all.

Nearly every journey made into Central Asia was seen as a forward move in this game. Geographical enquiry became a euphemism for strategic espionage, commercial activity for political intrigue. But since both governments habitually disowned their players, it is difficult to tell the professional agent from the amateur. Moorcroft was certainly a freelance, although by recruiting native surveyors and agents he invented one of the most typical ploys. Burnes, Christie, Pottinger, Elias and Younghusband were all professionals. So of course were the Survey of India's employees. But of Vigne, Shaw, Hayward, and even Kawaguchi it is impossible to be certain.

The overwhelming consideration from a British point of view was the

George Hayward posing as a Chitrali chief with trophies, including a mullah. *The photograph was evidently taken in Kashmir, probably in 1870.*

security of its Indian empire. As once in Siberia so now in Central Asia, Russia appeared to be expanding at a phenomenal rate. In the 1860s it was put at 143 sq km (55 sq miles) a day. In the north, Tibet and the Himalayas seemed to provide India with a natural barrier until at the turn of the century a Russian emissary was reported in Lhasa. Further west, in Kashmir, the problem of deciding which mountain range offered the more defensible frontier prompted the meticulous examination of every pass undertaken by Lockhart, Younghusband and Elias. It was here, with a bit of boundary engineering, that the 32-km (20-mile) wide Wakhan corridor was created to

keep the two empires apart.

Still further west, where the Hindu Kush sinks into the deserts of Afghanistan, there was no obvious frontier at all. British policy veered erratically – and disastrously through three Afghan Wars – between withdrawing to the Indus and pushing forward to the Oxus. The final compromise running through the Khyber Pass has since become the frontier between Pakistan and Afghanistan.

already followed in Moorcroft's footsteps. Of these the most successful was Lt Alexander Burnes who with Dr James Gerard duplicated Moorcroft's journey to Bukhara in 1832.

Burnes, a brilliant linguist and canny political officer, represented the new thinking in British India which endorsed Moorcroft's anxieties about Russian expansionism. The first major alarm had come some 20 years earlier when Russian advances in the Caucasus had brought British missions from both London and India to offer support to the Shah of Persia. Simultaneously two Indian Army officers, Captain Charles Christie and Lt Henry Pottinger, had been sent into Persia overland to gauge the vulnerability of India from an attack through Persia. Setting out from Sind in 1810 disguised as Tartar horse dealers, Christie had reached Herat and then Mashhad while Pottinger crossed the deserts of Baluchistan to Kerman. So successfully did they

blend into their surroundings that, when they met again three months later in Eṣfahān, neither recognized the other.

Much valuable intelligence had been gathered by Christie and Pottinger but it soon became apparent that in thwarting Russian moves into Persia, the British had merely deflected them. In 1819 Nikolai Muraviev, retracing Jenkinson's route from the Caspian Sea, spied out the defences of Khiva and in 1820 a Russian 'commercial' mission was well received in Bukhara. The Great Game had begun in earnest.

Burnes's task was to assess the strategic and political potential of northern Afghanistan and to pay particular attention to the feasibility of a Russian advance up the Oxus river. Although little of this could be divulged to the general public, Burnes made the most of the cloak and dagger aspect of Central Asian travel. Beneath his flowing

1878-82 Kishen Singh sent to Tibet to survey the route to Chinese Turkestan. Reached the western end of the Gobi Desert.
1878-9 Wilfrid and Anne Blunt travelled

through the Middle East to buy horses in the Nejd.
1879 Nordenskiöld navigated the North-East Passage.

1879 Parvie Mission mapped 673,000 sq km (260,000 sq miles) of Siam, Cambodia, Laos and Vietnam. Scientific results in 11 volumes.

Afghan robes he tied a bank draft to one arm, letters of introduction to the other, and a bag of gold coins round his waist. Although refused an audience with Bukhara's ruler, he made a great impression in Kabul and, returning directly to London, caused a sensation in Europe.

His three-volume narrative won him one of the RGS's first gold medals, a similar award from the Paris Geographical Society and an audience with the King. 'Bokhara Burnes' was feted as no other traveller of his day, and by 1837 he was back in Afghanistan, ostensibly on a mission to open the Indus River for trade. His party included a naval officer, Lt John Wood, who, while Burnes intrigued in Kabul, travelled north to Kunduz and from there made a remarkable foray to the source of the Oxus.

Legend, partly relayed by Marco Polo, had the Oxus rising from a vast lake which, like Manasarowar in Tibet, was also the source of other rivers and which lay in the heart of the unknown Pamirs. Wood knew and loved his Marco Polo and so thought nothing of the misfortune that meant he would be entering this icy region in the dead of winter; nor does he seem to have bothered about the irony of a naval officer being the first to penetrate to the very heart of Asia.

As he rode east through Badakhshan his thermometer dropped to $-22°C$ ($-7°F$), its lowest marking; it stayed there and he was still at only 1800 metres (5900 ft). In Jurm he was delayed by blizzards for six weeks; only when the river froze over was he able to move on. He met travellers coming the other way who had lost whole limbs with frost-bite; rounded uplands deep in snow, the Pamirs were somewhere between a plateau and a mountain range. At last, on 19 February 1838, 'we stood, to use a native expression, upon the *Bam-i-Duniah* or Roof of the World, while before us lay stretched a noble but frozen sheet of water, from whose western end issued the infant river of the Oxus.' Wood reckoned the altitude at 4725 metres (15,500 ft); the depth of the lake, ascertained after much hard work with a pick-axe, proved to be just 3 metres (10 ft).

Sixty years later Lord Curzon, the future Viceroy of India, would take issue with Wood. From an exhaustive study of all the evidence Curzon concluded that the lake, Zorkul' (also known as Victoria in spite of Wood's express wish that it should retain its old name) was not in fact the main source of the river. Somewhere in that icy wilderness, according to Curzon, Wood had followed the wrong tributary; the highest and remotest source was a glacier further east. Such quibbling would not have impressed Wood. A

man of 'extremely retiring disposition', he had even failed to collect the medal awarded him by the RGS.

Kashmir and the Western Himalayas

In the Western Himalayas as in Central Asia the laurels that might have been Moorcroft's went to others. Commissioned by the Jardin des Plantes in Paris, Victor Jacquemont, the first of many distinguished Himalayan botanists, visited the Kashmir valley in 1831. He was followed in 1832 by Joseph Wolff, the most phenomenal traveller of the century, and then in 1835 by both Baron Carl von Hugel, an Austrian botanist who also won an RGS medal, and Godfrey Thomas Vigne, sportsman and artist. Vigne also reached Ladakh and during a number of journeys to the north of the Kashmir valley explored Baltistan. He was the first to describe the great massif which is Nanga Parbat (although he underestimated its height by some 2400 metres/ 8000 ft) and he was the first to confirm the existence of the Karakorams barring further progress from Baltistan towards Xinjiang. His descriptions of the mightiest glacial system outside the polar regions provoked considerable scepticism, glaciers being thought improbable in such warm latitudes.

Officially all these places were out of bounds to travellers from British India. Special permission was given only when it suited British policy or when the applicant had exceptional credentials. The Sikh Wars of the 1840s changed this. Kashmir came under the rule of a British feudatory and in 1847–8 an attempt was made to demarcate the frontier between the new state (including Ladakh) and Tibet. Tibetan representatives failed to turn up; but the British boundary commissioners, Alexander Cunningham, Thomas Thomson and Henry Strachey, explored the whole of Ladakh and some adjacent areas of western Tibet. Cunningham, the father figure of Indian archaeology, produced a standard work on Ladakh; Thomson, a geologist and botanist, published an account of the first journey through Zaskar; and Strachey, the party's geographer and surveyor, compiled a physical geography of western Tibet. Both Thomson and Strachey won RGS gold medals.

Although their instructions were secret, the boundary commissioners, like every other visitor to Kashmir since Moorcroft, attempted to push north through the mountains to Yarkand – and failed. Thanks to the hearsay reports of Moorcroft, Burnes and others, Yarkand (So-ch'e) and Kashgar (Ka-Shih), the twin cities of Xinjiang, now enjoyed a 'forbidden' reputation that made them as irresistible as Lhasa itself. The Chinese refused all communications from

Ladakh; a gigantic wall painting of a European warned Yarkandis of what to look out for; and when in 1857 Adolph von Schlagintweit duly reached Kashgar, he paid the penalty and was publicly executed.

Apart from the political complications, it was now clearly understood that although both Baltistan and Ladakh lay on the other side of the Great Himalaya, an even more formidable range (the Karakorams) still lay ahead and, beyond that, possibly another (the Kunlun). Vigne had showed that the former was uncrossable from Baltistan; the only possible route was that from Ladakh where a calvary marked by the bones of dead pack animals, open for only four months in the year, and involving five passes of 5–6000 metres (about 16,500–19,500 ft), snaked towards the heavens.

Firmer evidence of the challenge posed by the Karakorams was provided by the surveyors who now made their first appearance in Kashmir. In 1856

Colonel H.H. Godwin-Austen's topographical surveys in the Karakorams led to suggestions that K2, the second highest mountain, be named after him.

Herman and Robert von Schlagintweit (brothers of the unfortunate Adolph), while engaged on a magnetic survey, crossed the 6000-metre (19,500-ft) Karakoram Pass and then veered east towards Khotan. In the same year the Great Trigonometrical Survey moved north from the Kashmir valley. T.G. Montgomerie and H.H. Godwin-Austen, both of whom were awarded RGS medals, penetrated but failed to cross the Baltistan Karakorams, while in 1865 W.H. Johnson circumvented the Ladakh Karakorams by way of the Aksai Chin plateau, crossed the Kun Lun, and reached Khotan (Ho-t'ien). Johnson then came within two days' march of Yarkand before his nerve failed him; but he did return to Ladakh by the classic Karakoram route of the five great passes.

He also brought word of a revolution in Xinjiang. Chinese rule was being overthrown by the indigenous Uighurs under an ambitious adventurer called Yakub Beg; and Yakub Beg, anxious for new allies and new trading partners, was about to turn to Russia. Suddenly the British authorities were less hostile to attempts to reach the 'forbidden' cities. Thus in 1868 two quite separate expeditions collided in the bleak and featureless wastes of the Aksai Chin. Robert Shaw, a tea-planter from India, considered himself first in the field and demanded his rival's withdrawal; George Hayward, supported by Sir

Colonel H.H. Godwin-Austen's watercolour of the Panmah glacier shows his survey party in camp amidst the greatest glacier complex outside the polar regions.

THE GREAT TRIGONOMETRICAL SURVEY

Arguably the most ambitious scientific project undertaken in the 19th century was the mapping of the Indian subcontinent. It began in 1800 when William Lambton was authorized to commence a trigonometrical survey of the extreme south of the peninsula; and it ended, 70 years and 3250 km (2000 miles) later, when the survey probed through the Himalayas into Tibet and Chinese Xinjiang.

Trigonometrical surveys aim to provide a framework of vantage points whose relative positions have been established with such unimpeachable accuracy that they can be used by topographical surveyors to fill in the detail of a map and by geodesists and cartographers to place this work in a global context. The survey is extended by a process of triangulation whose accuracy depends heavily on that of the base line from which operations commence.

Lambton started by measuring two base lines, at Bangalore and Madras, both of about 11 km (7 miles) long. Using a 30-metre (100-ft) steel chain, supported on tripods, housed in 6-metre (20-ft) coffins to reduce heat expansion, and tensioned by capstans, this operation was carried out by a carefully drilled squad who would have had to dismantle and reassemble the whole contraption about 500 times.

Confident that 'no error exceeding 8 or 10 inches' (20–25 cm) could arise over the full 11 km (7 miles), Lambton next used a massive zenith sector, which required 14 porters, to take astronomical observations for latitude at either end. Then with the Great Theodolite – half a ton of brass, glass and gun metal – he measured the angle between the base line and the line to a third pre-selected vantage point on which flagmen had already erected a pole. By doing this at both ends of the base line, the position of the third point could be precisely calculated and one of the lines to it used, without the need for further measurement on the ground, as the base for the next triangle.

So much for the theory. But this was India. Tigers terrorized the flagmen who sometimes disappeared into trackless jungle for weeks before their signal was at last sighted from some distant eminence. South of Madras, hills were few and a sea of waving palms obscured the line of vision. Winching the great theodolite to the top of the Tanjore temple, a guy rope broke and the carefully calibrated scales buckled as forged steel clattered against 1000-year-old sandstone sculptures.

Nothing if not determined, by 1805 Lambton had reached the west coast and discovered that the peninsula was 65 km (40 miles) narrower than the maps showed. By 1810 he had reached Cape Comorin, and in 1818 the Government officially endorsed the idea of extending what was now called the Great Trigonometrical Survey throughout India.

For the advance through central India's jungles he was joined by George Everest, an artillery officer with a foul temper, chronic dysentery and the determination of a steam roller. When Lambton died, aged 70 and only 65 km (40 miles) short of Nagpur, Everest took over, eventually completing the longest meridional (north-south) arc yet measured when he reached the Himalayas at Dehra Dun.

From Dehra Dun, the headquarters of the Survey of India, a longitudinal (east-west) series of triangles was begun along the fever-ridden Nepalese border and so skirting the central Himalayas. The casualties, mainly from malaria, were reckoned worse than those sustained in recent Indian campaigns. Nevertheless the series provided a set of trig stations from which 79 of the giant peaks could at last be correctly measured. They were each given a roman numeral and after computation Sir Andrew Waugh, Everest's successor as Surveyor General, declared peak XV at 8840 metres (29,002 ft) the highest then known to science. It was named in honour of George Everest. Whether it was the highest in the

In completing the south-north triangulation of India, Sir George Everest also completed the longest arc of the meridian yet measured.

world was not at the time (1856) certain. For in the same year reports were coming in from the new Kashmir series of 'two fine peaks standing high above the general range' of the Karakorams. Captain T.G. Montgomerie, in charge in Kashmir, called them K1 and K2 but not until 1858 were the heights ascertained and K2 declared second only to Everest.

With a mountain barrier 485 km (300 miles) wide to surmount, the Kashmir series meant coming to grips with the peaks. Many of the trig stations were at over 5200 metres (17,000 ft) where just erecting a shelter was a formidable task, never mind dragging the instruments up to it and then waiting, sometimes for weeks, for a break in the cloud.

W.H. Johnson of the GTS held the world altitude record for many years with ascents of 5800–6700 metres (19–22,000 ft) in the Kunlun; Colonel H.H. Godwin-Austen of the simultaneous topographical survey was the first to explore the Karakoram glaciers, to stand on the Baltoro Glacier amidst the greatest assemblage of peaks in the world, and to glimpse at close quarters 'the great peak K2'. The suggestion that it should be named after him was never officially adopted.

Henry Rawlinson and the RGS, considered himself the professional explorer and refused more than a ten days' headstart. This slight advantage was lost when Shaw was detained at the frontier outpost of Shahidulla, regained when he was permitted to proceed while Hayward remained in detention, and lost again when Hayward broke out of captivity. But Hayward then disappeared on a breakneck reconnaissance of the wild valleys between the Karakoram and Kunlun.

ASIA

1890 Isabella Bird rode 1000 km (600 miles) from Baghdad to Tehran, and later traveled in Kurdistan and the Hakkiari Mountains. **1891** Bower and Thorold crossed the Chang

Thang from Leh, through western Tibet to Atma Ram. **1891-7** Hedin explored the Kun Lun and Takla Makan Desert, unearthing buried

cities along the old Silk Route. **1892** Conway in the Karakoram Mountains. **1893** Theodore and Mabel Bent entered the Wadi Hadhramawt on an expedition inland

In December 1868 Shaw thus became the first Englishman to enter Yarkand. Hayward reappeared a few weeks later and both men were sent on to Kashgar. There during three months' detention they were reminded of Schlagintweit's fate and of the long capitivity and eventual execution of two British officers who had followed Burnes to Bukhara. But Yakub Beg at last relented and, still eyeing one another with intense suspicion, both men returned to Kashmir.

For Hayward it was just the beginning of a frantic and fatal rampage through the mountains. His goal was the Pamirs, the "Roof of the World" unvisited since Wood's foray up the Oxus. But he never got there and there is good reason to suppose that his brief was as much about assessing the viability of the passes that led to it. Traveling rough and at incredible speed he was the first to explore north of Gilgit; there, near the Darkot Pass in Yasin during a second visit to the area in 1870, he was savagely attacked and murdered. The tragic loss of such a remorseless explorer made a deep impression and was immortalized in Sir Henry Newbolt's poem *He Fell Among Thieves*. But Hayward had had a strong presentiment of disaster and the motive was certainly not robbery. The "thieves" were acting on orders; whose and why has never been established.

Meanwhile Shaw was returning to Xinjiang with the first of two official missions led by Sir Douglas Forsyth (1870 and 1873). The second which included military strategists, Survey of India officers, and various scientists, succeeded in Hayward's objective of exploring the southern Pamirs and reported that

The Mongolian plateau barred access to Tibet from the north. Nikolai Przhevalsky crossed it four times in the 1870s.

they posed no obstacle to forces coming from the north. This information caused great alarm at a time when the Russian advance in Central Asia was at its height. Over the next 20 years it prompted a succession of journeys and missions to examine the passes on the Indian side – by John Biddulph at Gilgit, William MacNair in Chitral (who was the first since Bento de Goes to visit the Shi'ah Posh tribe, supposedly descendants of Alexander the Great's forces), and by Colonel William Lockhart in the valleys in between.

Simultaneously two of the greatest explorers of the day were probing the passes from the north. Ney Elias had already surveyed the mouth of the Huang Ho in China (1869), made a sensational solo crossing of the Gobi Desert and Mongolia from Sining (Hsi-ning) to Biysk on the Siberian Ob (1872), and had twice climbed the passes into Xinjiang from Ladakh (1879 and 1880). In 1885 he returned to Xinjiang a third time and then turned west to make the first crossing of the Pamirs by an Englishman. By now Russian surveyors and agents had already scrambled over the "Roof of the World." Elias was to check on their activities and to propose a possible partition of the area. In the process he discovered the 7546-meter (24,758-ft) peak of Muztagh Ata (previously confused with the neighboring Kungur) and reconnoitered more than a dozen passes of over 4000 meters (about 13,000 ft). It was his recommendation that a finger of Afghan territory – the Wakhan corridor – could legitimately be interposed between the British presence in Kashmir and Gilgit and the Russian claims on the Pamirs.

Returning from his epic across the Pamirs in a state of collapse, the enigmatic Elias was succeeded in his role as frontier patrol by one of the few men who appreciated his dedication. This was the young

Francis Younghusband, a nephew of Robert Shaw, the first Englishman to reach Yarkand. Like Elias, Younghusband had made his name with a journey from China. In 1887 after crossing the Gobi by the main post route to Xinjiang, he had headed south for Kashmir across the central Karakorams. The Muztagh Pass into Baltistan had previously defeated even Godwin-Austen, but in what Sven Hedin called 'the most difficult and dangerous achievement in these mountains so far', Younghusband somehow got across using turbans for ropes and a pick-axe to cut steps.

There followed assignments in the rugged no-man's land between the Karakorams and the Kunlun first visited in 1889 by Hayward, then in the idyllic kingdom of Hunza in 1890 and finally in Xinjiang and the Pamirs in 1891. The comparatively minor geographical discoveries were overshadowed by two polite but dramatic encounters with Russian agents which encapsulated the final phase of the Great Game. No less significant was the profound effect which the mountains exercised on Younghusband's psyche. In the majesty of the high peaks and the purity of an untrodden world he experienced an emancipation which amounted to spiritual revelation. No one better expresses that sense of privileged communion, felt by all his predecessors in the mountains and elevated to the status of an inner quest by many of his successors.

The race for Lhasa

With the globe's unexplored white spaces shrinking rapidly, the late 19th-century adventurer was inclined to exaggerate such mysteries as remained. Certainly Tibet was mysterious. Where else did a God-King preside, in a land of surreal perspectives, over a medieval society that seemed as spiritually aloof as it

The Passu glacier in the Hunza valley ever threatens to block the main route from Gilgit to Xinjiang. Hereabouts Francis Younghusband played hide and seek with Russian spies in the 1890s.

was physically inaccessible? Yet geographically Tibet was not, and never had been, a complete mystery. Desideri's traverse of the country in 1713 was followed by the first approaches from British India as George Bogle in 1772 and then Samuel Turner in 1783 visited Tashilunpo (near Shigatse) to explore the country's commercial prospects.

In 1811 an Englishman actually reached Lhasa. Thomas Manning, an eccentric genius but a wretched traveller, was endeavouring with his Chinese servant named Sid to reach Peking by the back door. He failed to get further than Lhasa but 33 years later the route he would have taken was negotiated in reverse by two intrepid French missionaries, Regis-Evariste Huc and Joseph Gabet. Huc's narrative, full of delightful descriptions like that of the Fathers sliding down a pass on their bottoms, also contains the first descriptions of Kham, the eastern province of Tibet through which they were escorted back to China.

Twenty years later the systematic exploration of the country was carried out by Indian 'Pundits' recruited by the Survey of India. From 1865–85 their routes criss-crossed the Tibetan plateau from Nepal to Mongolia. They left a few white spaces most notably in the great wilderness of the north-west,

1904-5 Younghusband led the military expedition which invaded Lhasa.
1906-8 Hedin explored southern Tibet around Lake Manasarowar and the sources of the Indus and Brahmaputra.
1907-14 Dutch administration used 800 people to map the interior of New Guinea.
1908 Wavell used the Hejaz railway to visit Mecca disguised as a Zanzibari.
1909 Abruzzi's photogrammetric survey of K2.
1911 Gertrude Bell crossed the Syrian desert from 'Amurath to Amurath'.

THE PUNDITS

Following invasions from Nepal in 1792 and from Punjab in 1841, Tibet pursued a policy of rigorously excluding all foreigners. Few managed to evade this ban and by the 1860s the ignorance about India's vast and strategically important neighbour prompted Captain T.G. Montgomerie of the Survey of India to develop the idea, first tried by Moorcroft, of training and equipping native surveyors to undertake the exploration of Tibet.

The men thus recruited were known as 'Pundits' (ie teachers, which had indeed been the profession of several). Many were descendants of the Kumaun Bhutias (men of Tibetan stock) who had befriended Moorcroft and Hearsey. For reasons of secrecy they operated under code names and were forbidden to publish their exploits.

Yet emphatically they were not simple hill-men programmed to quarter Tibet like a fleet of robots but men of substance and scholarship,

The Pundit Kishen Singh in 1904, the year when the Younghusband Expedition entered Lhasa. Thirty years earlier he had conducted a four-year survey of Tibet.

not to mention daring, the accuracy of whose marathon route surveys transcended the limitations of the necessarily basic instruments which they carried. Typically these included a boiling point thermometer concealed in the Pundit's hollowed out walking stick, a sextant packed in the false bottom of his trunk, a compass built into his prayer wheel, and a specially made rosary on which he could keep count of his previously measured strides.

The programme opened in 1865 when 'No I', otherwise Nain Singh, slipped out of Kathmandu and across the Himalayas with a Ladakh-bound caravan. At Tradom (Cha-tung) on the upper Tsangpo he switched to a Lhasa caravan and became the first British Indian employee to enter the Tibetan capital. Returning via the Tsangpo valley and Manasarowar, he reached India after 18 months, 2000 km (1250 miles), and some 2.5 million carefully counted paces. He had connected the observations of Moorcroft in western Tibet with those of Bogle round Shigatse, had tracked the Tsangpo to its glacial source east of Manasarowar, and had obtained the first accurate bearings for the location of Lhasa.

A second journey took Nain Singh to the region between Manasarowar and the upper Indus, and a third (1874) from Ladakh to Lhasa across the Chang Thang. At an average altitude of over 5000 metres (16,500 ft) the hardships of the dreaded Chang Thang lived up to expectations. On the other hand he reported that the terrain, though unfrequented and devoid of supplies, was not difficult.

He also confirmed the existence of another towering mountain chain, with peaks up to 7625 metres (25,000 ft), between his route and the Tsangpo 250 km (150 miles) to the south. He conjectured that this range was the watershed between the rivers of central and south Asia and nearby he discovered the lake region of Tengri Nor (Tangra Tso). Sven Hedin, who would make these discoveries his own, considered this journey the greatest of all those undertaken by the Pundits.

It was, though, overshadowed by at least two other marathons. In 1878 'AK', otherwise Kishen Singh, another

Kumaun Bhutia, headed due north for Mongolia. After a long delay in Lhasa he was robbed in the Chang Thang, recouped his losses by working as a herdsman, and then continued on across the Gobi. There followed seven-months' detention in Dunhuang before he made his way back through Ching-hai and across the rugged country of Kham as a lama's servant. Reaching the Tsangpo east of Lhasa he was again arrested, this time as a thief.

In 1882, four years since his departure and two since he had been given up for lost, AK eventually regained India having conducted a continuous survey over some 4750 km (3000 miles) of territory most of which was unknown to his employers. It was quite simply 'one of the greatest feats of exploration ever undertaken' (Sir Eric Teichman).

Both Singhs had vainly attempted to track the Tsangpo east to the point at which it supposedly became the Brahmaputra. The mystery of how and where the river cut through the Great Himalaya and abruptly dropped 1500 metres (5000 ft) greatly intrigued Lt H. Harman of the Survey who in 1880 sent a Mongolian lama to cut, tag, and launch 500 logs of a prescribed size from wherever the Tsangpo disappeared into the mountains; on the other side Harman would be waiting by the upper Brahmaputra to identify them. Unfortunately the lama preferred to squander the Survey's funds and then sell into slavery the Sikkimese porter Harman had provided.

The lama was never heard of again; but the porter, Kinthup, eventually escaped, headed for the Tsangpo gorges and was promptly rearrested. It was another four months before he was able to cut his logs, another three before he was able to reach Lhasa and find a letter-writer to communicate his plan to India, and another nine before he regained the gorges and released his logs. They duly bobbed down through the cataracts and, unobserved, on down the Brahmaputra to the Bay of Bengal.

Kinthup's message had never reached the Survey; Harman had died in Europe some months before. Greater dedication can seldom have been so poorly rewarded.

but emphatically not in the vicinity of Lhasa nor of the routes from India. If all their findings were slow to appear on the maps, this was more because of the secrecy that surrounded them than because of any reservations about their accuracy. Notwithstanding their anonymity, the RGS rightly recognized the Pundits' achievements with at least two awards.

So what was left? For the serious explorer there was the vast Chang Thang, the Kunlun and Altyn Tagh (King Ata Tagh), and the finer points of hydrography in the Manasarowar region and of orography north of the Tsangpo. There was also the challenge of being the first outsider for 50 years to reach Lhasa. The latter made the headlines; a few thousand miles of featureless plain and nameless rock did not.

Thus Nikolai Przhevalsky, the greatest of Russia's explorers whose journeys (1867–85) extending from the Siberian Amur to Mongolia, the Gobi, Tibet and Xinjiang, dwarf even Elias's contemporary travels in the same region, is remembered not for his work in the Altyn Tagh and Tsaidam but for two abortive and incidental attempts (1873 and 1879) to reach Lhasa. Similarly the French explorer Gabriel Bonvalot (1890), the British agent Hamilton Bower (1891) and the delightful Mr and Mrs St George Littledale (who in 1896 came within 80 km/50 miles of the city, the nearest yet) had all previously made important journeys in the Pamirs and Kunlun. They stand apart from the missionaries and publicity-seekers whose often rash attempts to gatecrash Tibet's isolation did little to further the cause of exploration.

And then there was Sven Hedin, most ambitious of all Asian travellers. In the 1890s Hedin resumed the task, begun by Przhevalsky, of exploring the Kunlun and the Takla Makan desert. In the process he unearthed the first sand-buried cities of the old Silk Route and very nearly died of dehydration. Thence in 1900–1 he made two attempts to reach Lhasa. Both relied on surprise and speed and both were frustrated by the vigilance of the Tibetans. They were also superfluous. In the same year a remarkable Japanese scholar, Ekai Kawaguchi, had already won the 'race for Lhasa'. As a genuine Buddhist monk Kawaguchi enjoyed certain advantages over the European explorer, but he was woefully unprepared in such basics as lighting a camp fire and was no less an object of suspicion for being Japanese. In all probability he was also relaying information to the British Indian authorities.

Three years later, suspecting Russian intrigues with Lhasa, Lord Curzon as Viceroy ended Tibet's isolation by despatching the Younghusband Expedition

Yamdrok Tso, the sacred lake beside the main route from Sikkim and Bhutan to Lhasa. In 1811 Thomas Manning was the first European to describe it.

(1904–5) which, though planned as a diplomatic offensive, ended as a military invasion. Briefly Lhasa swarmed with British troops and correspondents; to Sven Hedin Lord Curzon apologized for 'destroying the virginity of the bride to which you aspired, viz Lhasa'. But amends were made by reimposing the embargo on Tibetan travel thus guaranteeing maximum acclaim for Hedin's unauthorized but exhaustive journeys of 1906–8. In the course of them he explored what he called the 'Transhimalaya', the mountain system discovered by Nain Singh and which Hedin chose to regard as 'the most striking of the world's geographical mysteries'. 'Unknown, the Transhimalaya had waited millions of years for my coming,' he wrote, 'I love it as my own possession.'

In similar spirit Hedin re-explored the Manasarowar region reaching the source of the Indus and what he claimed to be the source of the Brahmaputra. Like Wood on the Oxus, he was possibly wrong about the latter; determining the principal feeder amongst contending rills whose discharge fluctuates hourly with the snow-melt and whose length and altitude may be blurred by glaciation is a notoriously arcane science. Happily Tibetan exploration ended neither with the sterile debate which resulted nor with the obsessive Hedin. There was still the snow-wrapped world of the high Himalayas.

1926 Kingdon Ward made botanical expeditions at the source of the Irrawaddy.
1930 Thomas crossed the Empty Quarter of Arabia from south to north.

1930 Freya Stark looked for evidence of early Persian civilizations in the Valley of the Assassins in the Elburz Mountains.
1931 Kamet, the first peak over 7625 metres

(25,000 ft) in the Himalayas, was climbed by Smythe.
1932 Philby crossed Rub' al Khālī via a westerly route to Wadi ad Dawāsir.

LOST CITIES

Historical sites provided a strong incentive to exploration in many parts of Asia. Herbert's description of Persepolis is echoed in the almost disbelieving account by Henri Mouhot (1859) of the cyclopean halls and galleries of Cambodia's Angkor temples. Similarly Burckhardt's discovery of Petra can be matched by the travels in western Iran of Henry Layard which culminated with his identification and excavation of Nineveh (1845–7) in Iraq.

In India travellers and surveyors were also richly rewarded. In 1824 a sportsman tracked a tiger into the caves of Ajanta in Maharashtra, thus discovering the greatest gallery of frescoes in the subcontinent. Fourteen years later a young lieutenant stumbled upon the majestic temples of Khajrāho, then choked by jungle.

Assisted by translations of the 5th and 7th century travels of Fu-Hsien and Hsüan-Tsang, Alexander Cunningham of the 1847 Tibet Boundary Commission would spend the rest of his life locating and exploring the Buddhist sites of northern India and the western Himalayas. The same texts, plus Marco Polo's account, directed attention to the old Silk Route and to the garrison towns and monastic centers which once dotted its course round the Takla Makan and Gobi. Both these deserts had clearly advanced since Polo's day but the

Sven Hedin bestrides a camel in Xinjiang. His later flirtation with Nazism scandalized his many British admirers.

rumors of buried treasure, and the artefacts which were offered for sale to European travellers in Kashgar and Yarkand, suggested that the advancing sands might have preserved the ancient settlements.

In the 1890s Sven Hedin proved that this was indeed the case when he discovered numerous sites including Lou-Lan in what Polo had called the desert of Lop. Taking his cue from Hedin, Aurel Stein, a Hungarian-born teacher in British India, began a series of archaeological journeys which starting with the discovery of paintings and manuscripts in the lost cities east

of Khotan eventually extended right across the deserts to Dunhuang. Here Prżhevalsky had visited the famous Caves of a Thousand Buddhas in 1879; but the Russian was more interested in natural history.

Stein was the first to trace a section of the Great Wall in the vicinity and so identify the place as the site of the Jade Gate, the beginning of the Silk Route. It was also here that he made his most famous find, 140 cu metres (500 cu ft) of manuscripts and paintings which had been walled up in a cave since about AD 1000. They included the world's oldest printed book. Stein's discovery was compared to that of the Dead Sea Scrolls but his acquisition of part of this collection has been bitterly resented by successive Chinese governments.

To the top of the world

After the conquest of the polar regions the Himalayan peaks came to be regarded as the last great challenge in terrestrial exploration. Everest in particular seemed to mock man's claim to be master of his environment. It had to be climbed 'because it was there', the most obvious physical challenge on humanity's horizon. Mountaineers had begun to make their appearance in the Himalayas towards the end of the 19th century; but expeditions, like that of Sir Martin Conway in the Karakorams (1892), were concerned more with reconnaissance than ascents and this continued to be the case until the outbreak of the First World War.

Much had to be learned about the configuration and approach to each mountain, and about acclimatizing to high altitude. Alpine climbing techniques, typified by a host of Swiss guides recruited for the early expeditions, had to be adapted to the Himalayas; a reserve of experienced Gurkhas and eventually Sherpas from the Everest region had to be created; and so did the bureaucracy necessary for obtaining funds and permits to enter sensitive frontier regions. Hence the foundation in 1920 of the Everest Committee, a joint venture by the RGS and the Alpine Club under the chairmanship of Sir Francis Younghusband, and in 1927 of the India-based Himalayan Club comprising all the then luminaries of Himalayan mountaineering – C.G. Bruce,

T.G. Longstaff, Douglas Freshfield, Norman Collie, Conway and Younghusband.

The British government also lent its support and, as the days of empire were seen to be limited, the ascent of Everest came to represent something of national priority. Yet this cut, so to speak, no ice with the Nepalese authorities and during the inter-war years it was only from Tibet – and when the Dalai Lama's blessing was forthcoming – that attempts were possible. The first full-scale reconnaissance was made in 1921; and in the following year the first assault, though marred by the loss of six Sherpas in an avalanche, produced encouraging results with two climbers getting within 600 metres (2000 ft) of the summit. A second assault in 1924 ended in another disaster when George Mallory and Andrew Irvine made a bid for the summit and were never seen again. It is possible, but unlikely, that before presumably falling to their deaths they did in fact reach it.

No further attempts were made until 1933 but in the interim Kamet, beside Moorcroft's Niti Pass in the Kumaun Himalaya, became the first peak of over 7625 metres (25,000 ft) to be conquered. Fresh from this triumph, Eric Shipton and Frank Smythe were amongst the galaxy of climbers assembled for the 1933 assault on Everest. They came within 300 metres (1000 ft) of the summit before bad weather aborted the expedition. Shipton was back for a further reconnaissance in 1935 when he climbed 26 peaks of over 6000 metres (19,500 ft). His achievement seemed to suggest that the elaborate commissariat, the hundreds of porters and tons of equipment that had become associated with Everest expeditions were unnecessary and possibly a hindrance.

The 1936 expedition, organized on a massive scale, seemed to prove the point when it too was defeated by the weather. H.W. Tilman shared Shipton's reservations and following a successful assault on Nanda Devi in 1936, Tilman led a small party, including Shipton and Smythe, for the 1938 assault on Everest. In driving blizzards and temperatures of −34°C (−30°F) the party fought its way to 8290 metres (27,200 ft) before thigh-deep snow prevented any further progress.

The Second World War brought great technical advances in oxygen apparatus and camping equipment plus a new political scenario. The Cold War saw the Chinese returning to Tibet in 1950; in the same year Nepal opened its doors to an American expedition which included Tilman. The following year Shipton and others, including the New Zealander Edmund Hillary, reconnoitred the Nepalese approaches to the mountain from the Khumbu glacier and reached the Western Cwm. Thence a possible route led to the South Col and the summit. Given careful planning, reasonable weather, and good luck, the ascent was on. But the 1952 climbing season had been pre-booked by the Swiss.

The British assault was thus reserved for 1953, allowing ample time for preparation – and for acrimony when leadership of the expedition passed from Shipton to John Hunt. Happily this did not affect the outcome. At 11.30 on 29 May 1953 Hillary and Tenzing Norgay stood on the top of the world. Rightly the expedition was seen as a triumph for team spirit in which the endeavours of those who over 30 years had carried and climbed, dared and died, were also remembered.

Edmund Hillary on the successful 1953 Everest expedition. Acknowledging his debt to Nepal, he subsequently devoted himself to social projects amongst the Sherpas. Tenzing Norgay on Chukhung peak in 1953. Six weeks later, wearing protective clothing and oxygen mask, he would adopt a similar pose on the summit of Everest.

AFRICA

EARLY EXPLORERS

The systematic exploration of Africa began in real earnest with the foundation in 1788 of the Association for Promoting the Discovery of the Interior Parts of Africa, but that does not mean nothing was known of the continent in earlier times. There it lies, on Europe's doorstep, a great squat triangle, embracing one-fifth of the world's land mass, seamed with rivers which cascade from wide table-lands to flow east into the Indian Ocean, west into the Atlantic, pitted with great lakes, and with snow mountains standing on the Equator at the continent's very heart. The fact that Africa contains Egypt, one of the world's oldest civilizations, ensured that the continent was known to Europe a long way back in history.

The Egyptians seem to have discovered both the main stream of the Nile as far south as Khartoum and the Blue Nile which joins it there from its source in Lake Tana in Ethiopia. The Greeks were probably the first to take an abstract interest in the Nile sources. The historian Herodotus of Halicarnassus visited the ancient kingdom of Merowe in the southern Sudan in the year 460 BC and brought back stories of four fountains which gave birth to the river much further south. In AD 150 Ptolemy, the Greek-Egyptian geographer of Alexandria, incorporated in a map the legend of a merchant called Diogenes who had made his way inland from the east coast of Africa and found two great lakes at the foot of the 'Mountains of the Moon', from which the Nile was said to spring. The Romans also explored the Nile; the Emperor Nero sent an expedition into Nubia in about AD 66.

The Victoria Falls: 'No one can imagine the beauty of the view,' wrote Livingstone. 'It had never been seen by European eye, but scenes so lovely must have been gazed upon by angels in their flight.'

A warrior of the Sheikh of Bornu.

Arab invasions, from the 7th to the 12th centuries, were to provide opportunities for a remarkable series of scholars and travellers, such as Ibn Hawqal who was in Egypt, the Maghreb and other parts of Africa between AD 943 and 973, and al-Idrisi, whose *Book of Roger* (written in c.1154 for the King of Sicily) contains 70 maps. The peripatetic Ibn Battutah visited North and East Africa at intervals between 1325 and 1353, and in the early 16th century Leo Africanus wrote *Descrittione dell'Africa* which was translated into English by Hakluyt's friend, John Pory, and published in 1600.

THE PORTUGUESE VOYAGES

The Portuguese voyages of the 15th century along the African coast did much to establish the shape and extent of the continent. The capture of Ceuta in 1415 had given Portugal access to the African mainland, revealed something of the geography of the north-west and suggested possibilities of trade, especially in the gold which had been coming for centuries across the Sahara from the West African coast.

Prince Henry of Portugal was quick to see commercial possibilities as well as the extension of Christian influence into the world of Islam. It was he who initiated the voyages which were to give him the name of 'the Navigator', he who inspired the design of the caravels with their lateen sails which were to carry his countrymen round the furthest tip of Africa and on to India. The first aim of these voyages was to find a point on the west African coast where the source of gold might be tapped.

By Henry's death in 1460 Portuguese seamen had rounded Cape Bojador, hitherto their furthest point from home, and a further series of voyages went far enough to sight the coast of Sierra Leone. In the 1470s the Portuguese were in the Gulf of Guinea and in contact with what came to be called the Gold Coast, where, in 1482, John II of Portugal ordered

A F R I C A

1348-53 Ibn-Baṭṭūtah crossed the Atlas Mountains and Sahara to the Niger.
1482 Cão discovered mouth of the Congo/Zaire River and travelled 160 km

(100 miles) upstream.
1488 Dias sailed along the West African coast and round the Cape of Good Hope.
1498 da Gama sailed up East African coast

to Mombasa *en route* to India.
1520 Lopes de Sequeira made first complete circumnavigation of Africa.
1613 Paez saw Lake Tana, the source of the

the building of a fortress and trading post at São Jorge da Mina (later called Elmina). The King, who had inherited something of his great-uncle Henry's vision, then urged his captains to sally further and ever further south in search of a sea route to India, leaving stone pillars engraved with the royal arms of Portugal and the date at suitable landfalls.

Remains of such pillars have been found at the mouth of the Congo/Zaire, entered by Diogo Cão in 1482, and further down the coast, while Bartholomeu Dias left one after rounding the Cape of Good Hope some six years later. He lacked the resources to continue on his way, and the route to India was finally established by Vasco da Gama who sailed as far north as Mombasa in 1498 and then across the Indian Ocean to Calicut on the Malabar coast.

As the route to India became established there were landings on the eastern mainland. In 1605 a settlement was founded at Sofala and two years later a firm foothold was gained in Mozambique. By the middle of the 17th century an avenue for trade was being pursued up the Zambezi as far as Tete; Jesuit

The course of the Nile according to Ptolemy of Alexandria from a manuscript copy of his Geography.

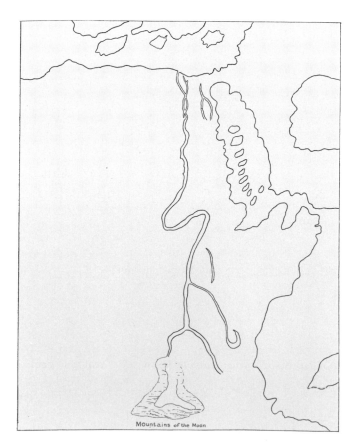

Mountains of the Moon

missionaries and peaceful traders began to find their way inland as far as the borders of present day Zimbabwe. On the west coast, at least one important geographical discovery had been made when Diogo Cão recognized as a great river the water pouring into the Atlantic Ocean from what was, in fact, the mouth of the Congo/Zaire. He called it the Zaire, the name to which it has now reverted. Cão sailed up the river to where Matadi stands today and carved his name on a rock face above the river. He could go no further, stopped by the falls in which the Zaire cascades down from Stanley Pool (Malebo) to flow the last 160 km (100 miles) to the sea. These were the falls named 'Livingstone' by Stanley which caused him such dismay and loss in 1877.

JAMES BRUCE AND ABYSSINIA

In planning the African voyages Henry the Navigator and his successors had more in mind than the extension of commerce. They sought also the extension of Christendom and the overthrow of Islam; King John's stone pillars bore the sign of the Cross. They hoped by travelling east to find the Empire of Prester John, the priest-king, who was a potent legend in medieval and early modern times. He was said to preside, somewhere in Asia or Africa, over a kingdom where wealth and virtue were universal and where he himself enjoyed eternal youth. By the time the Portuguese voyages were on their way, the legend had begun to shrink into reality and to be equated with the remote but not unknown Christian realm of Abyssinia (as Ethiopia was generally called at that time).

The Portuguese began to make contact with Abyssinia following da Gama's voyage to India and in 1520 despatched an embassy which was to make the country better known through the writings of its chaplain, Francisco Alvarez. During the following century Jesuit missionaries came to Abyssinia intent on converting the Emperor and his subjects from their practice of Coptic rites to those of Rome. The mission was expelled in 1633 but not before some of its members had to a certain extent explored the land and were later to record their experiences. Among them were Pedro Paez who visited the source of the Blue Nile at Gojam in 1613 and Jerônimo Lobo who followed him a few years later.

Abyssinia had, however, to wait another century before the fashion for exploration, inspired by the spirit of the Age of Enlightenment, began to take hold in the West, and a true explorer was ready to

Blue Nile in Ethiopia.
1628 Lobo followed Blue Nile from Lake Tana to the Tisisat Falls.
1652 Dutch East India Company

established settlement at Cape Town.
1770-3 Bruce followed Blue Nile from its source to the sea at Cairo.
1777-9 Gordon discovered the Orange

River. Then explored South African coast.
1788 The African Association was founded.
1788 Ledyard died in Cairo before his attempt to reach the Niger River.

Right   *James Bruce of Kinnaird (1730–94) in disillusioned old age, but with his finger firmly placed on the Nile.*

Far right   *Sir Joseph Banks (1743–1820), naturalist and traveller, President of the Royal Society, 1778–1820. He was created a baronet in 1781 and in 1795 made a Companion of the Bath, an honour he valued above all other.*

brave the unknown in Africa. James Bruce (1730–94) of Kinnaird was the son of an old Scottish family. He acquired a taste for travel when in Spain and Portugal on business and in 1768 he set forth to seek the source of the Nile. Conceiving this to be in Abyssinia, he made his way to Massawa on the Red Sea coast (in modern Eritrea) and some time in 1770 arrived in Gondar and settled himself, with remarkable success, in the Imperial Court. He was accompanied – though he never mentions the fact in his subsequent book – by Luigi Balugani, the talented Italian draughtsman who was to accompany him throughout his subsequent travels, dying in Abyssinia.

Bruce spent three years at the court, making himself useful as a doctor and popular as a sportsman, but hampered from pursuing his quest by the civil war then raging. The young Emperor was under the dominance of one of Abyssinia's war lords, Ras Michael, who was engaged in a ferocious power struggle with his rival Fasi. Bruce managed to hold his own in a dangerous atmosphere by virtue of several advantages: he was a big man of powerful physique, he spoke Arabic, he was a fine rider, a good shot and something of a swordsman. Fortune played into his hands when he found on his arrival that a smallpox epidemic was raging. By his confident bearing he succeeded in calming the fears of three important ladies at the court – the Iteghe (or dowager empress) and her daughters, the Ozoro Altash and the Ozoro Esther, the latter being the wife of Ras Michael. Bruce fumigated the palace chambers 'with incense and myrrh . . . washed them with warm water and vinegar, and adhered strictly to the rules which my worthy and skilful friend,

Doctor Russel, had given me in Aleppo', adding 'the more scrupulous and particular, the more the confidence of the ladies increased.' Fortunately for Bruce, Ozoro Esther's son by Ras Michael survived.

Homeward bound: a prophet without honour

At last Bruce was allowed to join Ras Michael's troop in a campaign which brought him within reach of his goal and in November 1770 he found himself at the spring south of Lake Tana from which the Blue Nile rises. For the rest of his life, his attainment of what he always regarded as the source of the main Nile was to remain his finest hour, though it is hardly to Bruce's credit that he dismissed the Jesuits who had preceded him as 'Liars'. He came next to Sennar in the Sudan where he was asked to attend the King's harem, an alarming experience described by Bruce in a passage which might have come out of *Gulliver's Travels*. 'Although all acquaintance with the fair sex has hitherto been much to my advantage' he did not enjoy being forced to strip (albeit only to the waist) in order that his white skin might be marvelled at. Moving on from Sennar near the site of ancient Merowe, he travelled to Cairo and thence home.

He was not as warmly received as he had expected; his awkward manner and confused way of telling stories did not go down well in society. Fanny Burney was chiefly impressed by his bulk – she thought him 'the tallest man you ever saw – *gratis*'. Dr Johnson, the translator of Le Grand's French version of Lobo's *Travels*, passed the ambiguous judgment that Bruce was 'neither abounding nor deficient in sense; I did not perceive any superiority of understanding.'

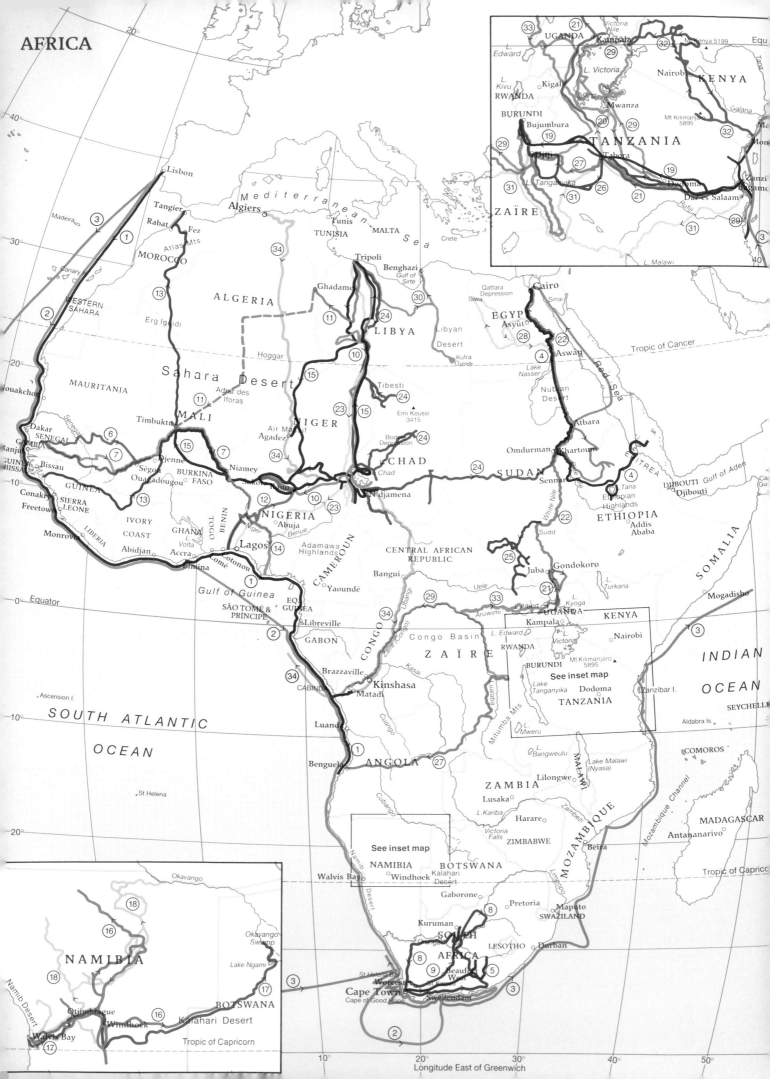

AFRICA

1788 Lucas failed to reach the Niger from Tripoli.
1790 Houghton followed the Gambian route eastwards to the Niger but was murdered on his return journey.
1796 Park explored the course of the Senegal and Gambia rivers. Discovered true orientation of the Niger River.
1798 Lacerda followed the Zambezi River, then travelled north between Lake Nyasa and Lake Bangweolu where he died.

When an account of his travels was published in 1790, the handsome five-volume work with Balugani's illustrations was greeted with incredulity, although time has proved it to be a very fair and well observed account of the people and customs of Ethiopia, not only then but in some respects today. James Bruce died in retirement at Kinnaird.

THE MYSTERY OF THE NIGER

The founder of the Association for Promoting the Discovery of the Interior Parts of Africa, Sir Joseph Banks corresponded with Bruce on plans to sponsor individual travellers. With the founding of the Association, scientific and humanitarian motives came into play, in line with the spirit of the Age of Enlightenment. On 18 June 1788 twelve members of the comfortable Saturday Club met for dinner and sketched out their plans. There was plenty to 'discover' in the interior of Africa, plenty of blanks on the map, but it was debatable which of these should first receive attention.

Records of the Association note that 'the southern extremity of the African peninsula may perhaps be justly considered as explored', and eastern Africa had been pretty fully reported on by Bruce. North and west seemed therefore to offer a more promising field for investigation so Banks and his friends looked to the Sahara and beyond for the solution of the mystery of the Niger.

The Niger was known by hearsay in its middle reaches where Timbuktu stood, a magnet for the romantic explorer just as El Dorado had been in the past and as Lhasa would be in the future, its legend linked with the gold trade of the Moors across the Sahara. It was not known where the river rose, which way it flowed (Leo Africanus some 200 years earlier thought westwards) or how it ended.

Some geographers tried to link it with the Nile, some with Lake Chad, some even with the Congo/Zaire. Captain J.K. Tuckey, leading a naval expedition in 1816, was instructed to make his way up the Congo/Zaire to ascertain whether it was connected with the Niger; like Diogo Cão in 1482, he was stopped by the great falls a hundred miles upstream.

The Association's first ventures to put the Niger on the map were abortive. Simon Lucas, instructed to take the southern route from Tripoli, found his way barred by warring tribes. John Ledyard, a widely travelled American who had sailed with Cook on the third Pacific voyage, died in Cairo while preparing for a journey westward. Daniel Houghton took off from the Gambia and reached the Niger only to die on his way back in 1790.

AFRICA: KEY TO ROUTES

(1) **Cão** 1482–4. From Lisbon sailed to Elmina, up the Congo R. to Matadi, then S to Cabo de Santa Maria in modern Angola.

(2) **Dias** 1487–8. From Lisbon sailed beyond Cão's furthest point and reached Great Fish River area.

(3) **Da Gama** 1497–8. Landed in St Helena Bay, rounded the Cape, called at Seal Bay, Quelimane R., Mozambique I., Mombasa and Malindi, and left for India.

(4) **Bruce** 1769–73. Landed at Mits'iwa (Massawa), modern Eritrea, travelled to L. Tana and source of Blue Nile. Continued to Aswan and sailed to Cairo.

(5) **Gordon** 1777–8. From Cape Town to Swellendam, to modern Aberdeen, and to Zeekoe R. and Orange R. near modern Bethulie.

(6) **Park** 1795–7. From Karantaba, Gambia R. to Silla on Niger R., returning via Ségou and Bamako.

(7) **Park** 1805–6. From Kaiai, Gambia R. to Bamako; descended the Niger to Bussa Rapids.

(8) **Campbell** 1813. From Cape Town crossed the Orange R. and returned to Cape Town.

(9) **Moffat** 1820. From Cape Town to Griekwastad and Kuruman.

(10) **Clapperton, Denham and Oudney** 1822–5. From Benioleed, near Tripoli, to Lake Chad, Kano and Sokoto.

(11) **Laing** 1825–6. From Tripoli to Timbuktu. Killed near by at Sahab.

(12) **Clapperton and Richard Lander** 1825–7. From Badagry, near Lagos, to Bussa, Kano and Sokoto.

(13) **Caillié** 1827–8. From the coast of modern Guinea to Djenné and down river to Timbuktu, then N to Fez, Rabat and Tangier.

(14) **The Lander Brothers** 1830. From Badagry to Bussa; sailed down the Niger R. to the sea.

(15) **Barth** 1850–5. From Tripoli to Kano, Lake Chad, Yola, Timbuktu, Lake Chad and back to Tripoli.

(16) **Galton and Andersson** 1850–2. From Walvis Bay through Namaqualand to Rehoboth, Damaraland and Ovamboland.

(17) **Andersson** 1853–4. From Walvis Bay to Lake Ngami, exploring part of Taoghe R.

(18) **Andersson** 1857–8. From Walvis Bay NE to the Okavango R.

(19) **Burton and Speke** 1857–8. From Bagamoyo to Tabora and Lake Tanganyika.

(20) **Speke** 1858. From Tabora to Lake Victoria.

(21) **Speke and Grant** 1860–3. From Bagamoyo to Tabora, Lake Victoria, Gondokoro, then down the Nile to Cairo.

(22) **Baker** 1861–5. From Cairo to the Nile tributaries of Ethiopia, then further up the Nile to Lake Albert.

(23) **Rohlfs** 1865–7. From Tripoli to Lake Chad, the Benue and Niger rivers, and Lagos.

(24) **Nachtigal** 1869–74. From Tripoli to Lake Chad area, then E to Omdurman on the Nile.

(25) **Schweinfurth** 1869–71. Travelled among the affluents of the Bahr el Gazal tributary of the Nile to the Uele R. in modern Zaïre.

(26) **Stanley** 1871–2. From Bagamoyo to Ujiji and N end of Lake Tanganyika.

(27) **Cameron** 1873–5. From Bagamoyo to survey Lake Tanganyika, then to W coast at Benguela.

(28) **Rohlfs** 1873–4. From Asyūt to oases at Farafra, Dachel and Siwa. Returned to Nile.

(29) **Stanley** 1874–7. From Zanzibar to Lakes Victoria and Tanganyika, then down Congo R. to sea.

(30) **Rohlfs** 1878–9. From Tripoli to the Kufra Oases and Benghazi.

(31) **Thomson** 1879–80. From Dar es Salaam to Lakes Malawi and Tanganyika.

(32) **Thomson** 1883–4. From Mombasa to Kilimanjaro region, Mt Kenya and Lake Victoria.

(33) **Stanley** 1887–9. Up the Congo and Aruwimi rivers to Lake Edward and Zanzibar.

(34) **Foureau** 1898–1900. From Algiers to Lake Chad and the Ubangi and Congo rivers.

Livingstone's routes are shown on p. 107.

The Swiss Johann Ludwig Burchardt (1784–1817) was thwarted by illness. He was the most scholarly of the travellers to be employed by the Association, spending three years in Syria learning Arabic before

taking the road. He arrived in Cairo, visiting Petra on the way, in 1812, to find that no caravan in the direction of Timbuktu was expected. Unwilling to remain idle, Burchardt turned south into Nubia where he was the first in modern times to see Abu Simbel; then, disguised as a pilgrim, he travelled to Mecca. Back in Cairo, he fell ill and died of dysentery before he could embark on his journey into the desert. His records of what he had experienced in five years of travel were published by the Association in five volumes between 1819 and 1830.

The great name not only in the Association's history but also the annals of African exploration is that of Mungo Park, the Scottish doctor. He had been a ship's surgeon, with a taste for travel; his interest in botany had brought him to the notice of Sir Joseph Banks. In 1796 he set out from Karantaba

Mungo Park (1771–1806), the Scots doctor and African traveller who lost his life in his exploration of the Niger.

Park's camp at Kamalia, in modern Mali, where he was delayed for seven months on his way back from the Niger in 1797.

Calabar and Rouger from Morocco. The entire plan failed.
1816 Tuckey tried to prove the connection of the Congo/Zaire to the Niger. He

ascended the Congo/Zaire. Stopped by the Livingstone Falls.
1817 Political upheavals led to the despatch of Jones and Bowditch to Ashanti. Bowditch

visited the Gabon region.
1818 Mollieu discovered the sources of the Gambia, Corubal and Senegal rivers.

on the Gambia river with the Association's instructions in his pocket; his equipment was 'a few changes of linen, an umbrella, a pocket sextant, a magnetic compass and a thermometer; two fowling pieces and two pairs of pistols'. He wore a large hat in which he kept his papers.

Park was travelling through the country ruled by successive chiefs in the conglomeration of states bordering the Niger. To the north, the Muslim Moors operated the trade routes and these people were uniformly aggressive and obstructive, especially the Tuareg, the famous 'veiled men of the desert' who were to put up such continuous and fierce opposition to strangers attempting to enter their territory. The pagan negroes in the southerly part of Park's route were more kindly, especially the women who fed and sheltered him; he records that some of them composed a song of which the refrain was 'Oh, pity the white man, no mother has he!'

After terrible hardships and robbed of nearly all he possessed, he reached the Niger at Ségou in modern Mali on 20 July 1796 where he 'saw with infinite pleasure the great object of my mission: the long sought-for and majestic Niger, glistening in the morning sun, as broad as the Thames at Westminster, and floating slowly *to the eastward*.' He was obliged then to return, having run out of provisions. In 1805 the British Government, taking up the running from Banks and the Association, sent Park back to the Niger in command of a quasi-military expedition made up to a total of 45, with a rabble of ill-disciplined soldiery. The venture was a disaster, the death toll almost total. With great difficulty Park secured a boat downstream from Timbuktu in which to navigate the river but lost his life in the Bussa Rapids, either by drowning or in a fight with unfriendly tribesmen on the bank.

The Lander brothers

The Government persevered, however, and despatched an expedition, officered, not very harmoniously, by Hugh Clapperton, Dixon Denham and Walter Oudney, which left Tripoli in 1822. This venture was concerned as much with the pioneering of commercial openings as with exploration, but Lake Chad was located and useful information brought back from the states of Sokoto and Bornu in modern northern Nigeria. The results were promising enough from the trading point of view for Clapperton to be sent back to Africa in 1825, accompanied by his man-servant Richard Lander.

Explorers are on the whole an unlikeable lot, jealous of their own fame, ruthless in overcoming

The Lander brothers at Badagry on their way to the Niger in 1830, wearing the 'unusual' garments which so amused the local populace.

obstacles material and human. Lander is one of the most engaging travellers ever to set foot upon the continent. The almost illiterate son of a Cornish inn-keeper, he was cheerful and affectionate, and had a mania for travel. He carried a bugle with him on which he played appropriate homely airs – 'Over the hills and far away' as he and Clapperton set off for Sokoto on their second mission. As Clapperton lay dying at the furthest point of their journey, he recited to cheer him a 'little poem "My native Highland home"' (Clapperton was a Scot), and when the end came, 'I flung myself on the bed of death and prayed Heaven would in mercy take my life.' Fortunately Heaven turned a deaf ear and Lander returned to England with his master's papers and his own pertinent comments.

He was sent back to Africa in 1830, accompanied by his brother John (to whom His Majesty's Government paid no salary), with rather casual instructions from the Colonial Office to follow the Niger. They landed at Badagry, an evil haunt of slave dealers near modern Lagos, dressed strangely in scarlet tunics, full Turkish trousers and enormous straw hats bigger than umbrellas, causing much amusement to the local people. 'So unusual a dress might well cause the people to laugh heartily . . . but the more modest of the females, unwilling to give us any uneasiness, turned aside to conceal the titter from which they were quite unable to refrain.'

The simple Cornish brothers were to succeed where the more sophisticated Mungo Park had failed. In the face of every possible setback, they sailed down the Niger from Bussa, south of Timbuktu, noting as they went the great confluence of the Benue with the major river, which occurs not far beyond where Park lost his life. Finally they emerged at the delta, thus establishing the course of the river.

They were shabbily treated by the Government on their return, Richard receiving £100 reward, John nothing; private enterprise did better in that John Murray paid £1000 for their book (mostly in John's words). Richard was the first traveller to be honoured by the newly founded (later Royal) Geographical Society of London and received the Society's premium of 50 guineas. He died on a subsequent expedition designed to open up trade in the Niger delta and upstream, launched as a result of his and his brother's earlier success.

The Landers' epic journey proved the Niger to be navigable into the interior of Africa at a time when the abolition of the slave trade was encouraging the pursuit of legitimate trade and of Christian missions. Expeditions, both privately and officially sponsored, followed the emergence of Richard and John Lander at the river delta, but the death toll from fever on what came to be known as the 'white man's grave', was so heavy that progress came to a halt. Eventually, with improvements in medical knowledge and better observance of hygiene, it became possible to pursue the Niger adventure.

Much was due to Dr William Baikie who first sailed up the river in 1854 and from 1857 to 1864 was in charge of a Government trading settlement at Lokoja at the confluence of the Niger and Benue. Baikie was a true pioneer, proving the efficacy of quinine against malaria and moreover adjusting himself to local conditions and mastering local tongues. He translated the Book of Genesis into Hausa and compiled a grammar of the Fuldi language. He adopted the comfortable local dress of a long cotton shirt and baggy trousers, and lived with a black mistress who bore him several children. It is sad to relate that although he avoided the deadly local fever by dosing himself regularly with quinine, he died of dysentery.

Heinrich Barth: a scholarly explorer

Neither the commercial nor the anti-slavery lobbies were to remain satisfied with a foothold on the Niger at Lokoja. What Clapperton had reported of the states lying along the north bank of the river, of Bornu and Sokoto, suggested a promising field for trade, while the philanthropists felt that penetration of these lands would provide a chance to destroy the slave trade at one of its sources. An expedition was officially sanctioned by the British Government in 1849 to be led by James Richardson of the Anti-Slavery Society accompanied by a geographer and a geologist to study the lie of the land.

The geographer chosen was Heinrich Barth, a well recommended young German from Berlin, who was to prove himself one of Africa's most successful explorers. Barth was a master of Arabic and had all the painstaking, if not to say pedantic, thoroughness associated with German scholarship. The expedition's route was south from Tripoli across the Sahara to Lake Chad. Richardson, and later Overweg the geologist, died at an early stage but Barth was not dismayed; he travelled on alone, covering a distance of some 16,000 km (10,000 miles) over a period of five years, with pitifully little cash from a parsimonious British Government and often in danger as a Christian in a Muslim country.

Barth thoroughly examined Lake Chad and, striking south, explored the upper waters of the Benue which he proved to have no connection with the lake. Later he travelled west to Timbuktu, before returning to England in 1855. His meticulous observations were incorporated in five volumes packed with information, though not written in the lively style expected by Victorian readers, who turned gratefully to Livingstone's *Missionary Travels* published at about the same time, and offering more spirited reading. Barth received the Patron's Medal from the RGS and various other honours but died, however, feeling that his achievements had never been fully recognized.

THE NILE QUEST

Snow mountains and vast lakes

The work of Park and the Landers, of Clapperton and of Barth, had gone far to dissipate the mystery which had cloaked the Niger for so long. Travellers began to look for another legendary goal, to the source or sources of the Nile, to those four fountains of Herodotus and to Ptolemy's map. Much more recently the French had stimulated interest in Egypt when scholars and archaeologists had accompanied Napoleon's invasion and recorded the glories of ancient Egypt.

The Richardson expedition to the Sudan: frontispiece to August Petermann's account, published in 1855, showing the routes. Clockwise from top left: Richardson, Overweg, Vogel, Barth.

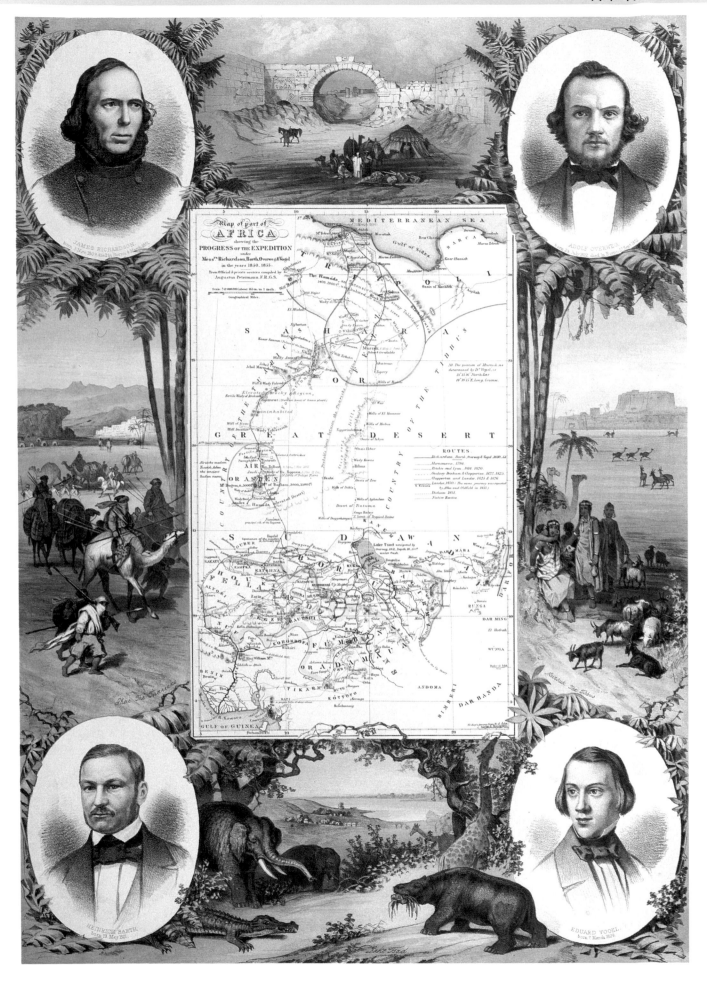

1827-8 Caillié became the first man to visit Timbuktu and survive to tell the tale.
1830 Richard and John Lander sailed down the Niger from Bussa mapping its course.

1830 Royal Geographical Society founded.
1831 Ruppell spent two years working to north and east of Lake Tana.
1834 Start of the Boer trek and the

foundation of the Cape of Good Hope Association for exploring Central Africa.
1836-8 Alexander's South African safari through Cape Province and Namibia.

Following the French withdrawal, the Viceroy of Egypt Mehemet Ali had had dreams of economic expansion southward into the Sudan. He launched two important expeditions in 1839 and 1841 which reached the navigable head of the Nile at a place called Gondokoro in the vicinity of modern Juba. It was thus proved that sailing boats could penetrate the *sudd*, the floating vegetation which varies from year to year in density, sometimes blocking all progress between Khartoum and Gondokoro. By mid-century only the rapids south of Gondokoro remained between the traveller and the Nile sources.

Mehemet Ali was not interested, however, in geographical exploration, and neither were the adventurers and traders who then began to penetrate south into the Sudan. They raided the southlands for ivory and slaves, but in their detestable way contributed to geographical knowledge by blazing trails through unknown country and from time to time allowing explorers to tag along with them and to share their protection.

The Royal Geographical Society, founded in 1830, was to play a leading part in what came to be known as 'The Nile Quest'. It inherited a special interest in Africa from the African Association which it absorbed in 1831. During its first 20 years or so the Society was preoccupied, so far as Africa was concerned, mostly with the west and with the course of the Niger. Into the 1840s, it was collecting information from travellers in Ethiopia; the German naturalist Ruppell, the French surveyors the brothers d'Abbadie, and the learned Kentish doctor Charles Beke among them.

The traders' path

A new direction was given to the search in the 1840s, however, by missionaries working inland from the east coast on behalf of the Church Missionary Society. Ludwig Krapf, Johann Rebmann and Johann Erhardt not only made some important journeys but collected information from the Arab traders operating inland from the east coast. From them they heard of just the same natural phenomena in the interior as the merchant Diogenes had recounted nearly 2000 years ago and which Ptolemy had placed on his map. There were it seemed great lakes and huge mountains. These latter Krapf and his companions thought they had seen for themselves, covered with snow. Snow mountains on the Equator!

The Paris Geographical Society awarded the men a medal, but the English geographers lagged behind, ridiculing the idea at first. The mountains were, in fact, Mounts Kilimanjaro and Kenya, snow

mountains on the Equator indeed, and although these do not form part of the Nile system, it was the report of their existence that set men thinking of the possibility of an approach to the Nile from the east coast. Erhardt made a map, which Speke was to study at the RGS before he embarked on his first journey in 1856. It showed one huge piece of water which was to resolve itself eventually into Lakes Victoria, Albert and Tanganyika.

Burton and Speke: explorers at odds

In 1854 two men whose names will always be associated with the Nile first came together: Richard Burton and John Hanning Speke. Burton had recently accomplished his spectacular journey to Mecca and was keen to travel in Africa. Speke, like Burton an Indian Army officer, was anxious to try his luck big game hunting; this was his first enthusiasm, his preoccupation with finding the source of the Nile was to grow on him later. In 1856 the RGS invited Burton to lead an expedition in search of the Nile sources from the east coast of Africa. Instructions were based largely on the reports of the Mombasa missionaries and reference made to Erhardt's rather fanciful map of a vast inland sea – jokingly called the 'slug map' as this was the shape given in the drawing to the reported sheet of water.

Burton and Speke collected their supplies and hired their porters in Zanzibar, starting point for so many African travellers, the Sultan being the nominal overlord of the mainland. Zanzibar was the base of the Arab ivory and slave traders, where the Indian bankers had their depots and where porters congregated for hire. From points on the east coast the trading routes ran inland, most importantly to Tabora (which Burton and Speke called Kazé), some 800 km (500 miles) inland. This was about two-thirds of the way between the coast and the lake later named Tanganyika, where the Arabs were to develop Ujiji as a centre from which to extend their operations into the Congo.

They set off on 16 June 1857 from Bagamoyo. They did not know at this stage whether they were likely to find one lake, or two, or three. The RGS told them to explore first 'the Nyasa' (the Swahili word for lake) and then turn north to investigate possible mountains which might give rise to the White Nile. The Arab traders they met at Tabora told them of a lake due north (in fact, the Victoria) which Speke would have liked to visit immediately. But Burton disagreed, and they made their way west to Lake Tanganyika which ranks as Burton's 'discovery'.

GORILLAS

Travellers in Africa revealed to the Western world not only geographical features but hitherto unknown wonders of the animal kingdom. The reading public was interested but not always thrilled by the latter: Thomson's gazelle looked much like any other gazelle to the armchair geographer, and there was nothing to set the pulses racing in Burchell's 'white' rhino, or in the fact that the zebra called after the same naturalist was striped brown and white, rather than black and white.

What really caused a thrill and a certain amount of incredulity was the gorilla. The young American of French extraction, Paul du Chaillu (1831–1903), exploring up the Ogowé river in the Gabon in the 1850s, was the first outsider to encounter these great apes – now alas an endangered species. He described them in truly purple prose. 'The fierce untameable gorilla which approaches nearest, in physical conformation and in certain habits to man, and whose unconquerable ferocity has made it the terror of the bravest native hunters . . .' (He wrote in somewhat similar terms of the local tribespeople, allegedly cannibal.) And when he actually came on the tracks of a band of gorillas, 'My heart beat till I feared its loud pulsations would alarm the gorilla, and my feelings were really excited to a painful degree.'

Mary Kingsley, however, working her way through the same region some forty years later, had a great regard for du Chaillu, calling him 'the inaugurator of geographical knowledge in this region' and considering he had truthfully described all that he saw there. Paul du Chaillu knew the Gabon well. His father had a factory there and the young man had lived long enough in the country to learn the language and become familiar with the local people.

Paul du Chaillu enjoys the unenviable distinction of having been the first European to kill a gorilla, here shown in a pose of 'unconquerable ferocity'.

They arrived there too ill and with stores too depleted to pursue their exploration of the lake. Burton's legs were paralysed. Speke was almost blind from ophthalmia and he had gone deaf owing to a beetle penetrating his ear. It was impossible to hire a boat to take them to the north end of the lake where a river was reported as running either *out of* or *into* the lake. In the first case it might be the Nile, in the second case it could not be. That this was left in doubt prolonged the argument about the Nile sources until Livingstone and Stanley visited the northern tip of Lake Tanganyika in 1872 and established without doubt that the Ruzizi was an inflowing stream.

Back at Tabora, both somewhat recovered, Speke took an opportunity to visit the lake to the north, of which he had heard from the Arabs. His immediate claim that here was the source of the Nile was no more than an inspired guess and it was to be many years before it was confirmed by further exploration. However, he had no hesitation in naming it 'Victoria', though Burton (according to Speke) 'snubbed' him 'most unpleasantly'. This was the beginning of the famous quarrel between Burton and Speke which

1842 Beke's North Abyssinian expedition explored Blue Nile.
1847 Magyar travelled in Kalahari desert.
1848 Rebmann saw Mount Kilimanjaro.

1849 Magyar began his exploration of the upper Zambezi and Congo/Zaire basin.
1849 Rebmann and Krapf saw Mount Kenya.

1849 Livingstone and Oswell crossed the Kalahari desert to Lake Ngami.
1850-5 Barth travelled over 16,000 km (10,000 miles) in the Sahara reaching Lake

Above   *Sir Richard Burton (1821–90) traveller, anthropologist, oriental scholar; enfant terrible, who delighted in baiting the Victorian Establishment.*
Right   *John Hanning Speke (1827–64), Army officer, big game hunter, whose claim to have located the source of the Nile was proved correct after years of dispute.*

continues to interest people to this day – a film on the subject was being shown in America as recently as 1989.

The upshot of the argument over whether Tanganyika or Victoria was the Nile source could only be resolved by the collection of more information. In 1860 the RGS sent Speke back to Africa, with James Augustus Grant, a more congenial companion than the brilliant, eccentric Burton. The two men worked their way up the western shore of Lake Victoria into the kingdom of Buganda which they were the first Europeans to visit and of which Speke has left historians an interesting account. His description of how he measured the vital statistics of some of the royal ladies sent a delicious shiver of horror down Victorian spines.

They spent five months in Buganda subject to the whims of the Kabaka Mtesa, but at last Speke was allowed to make a quick dash to the northern end of the lake where he identified the Nile flowing over what he called the Ripon Falls. He went alone –

unwisely as it turned out; Grant had become very lame and marched slowly so was sent on ahead on the last lap of the journey. Together they then followed the river downstream into Bunyoro, but since time was pressing and supplies running short they had to cut across country to Gondokoro where they hoped to find boats to take them down the Nile to Khartoum. Here, to their amazement, they encountered an old friend, Samuel Baker, accompanied by a lovely young woman; Grant was to write rather priggishly to his brother on the subject.

Samuel White Baker was a wealthy sportsman who had spent a roving life, having no necessity to earn a regular living. He and his brother founded and for a time managed a farm in the highlands of Ceylon, a ploy which left them plenty of time for big game hunting. On their return to England Sam's wife died, leaving him temporarily at a loss with four little daughters to care for. Entrusting the children to a sister, he left England and went off to the Balkans to hunt wild boar. Idly wandering one

Chad, visiting Timbuktu, and went on down the Niger.

1850-2 Galton and Andersson attempted to reach Lake Ngami. Reached just beyond the Etosha Pan.

1851 Livingstone and Oswell reached the source of the Upper Zambezi River.

1853-4 Andersson reached Lake Ngami and journeyed north for 100 km (60 miles).

1853-6 Livingstone made first west-east crossing of the continent via the Zambezi. Discovered Victoria Falls.

day into the market place at the Turkish garrison town of Vidin (in modern Bulgaria) he found an auction of slaves in progress and on impulse bid for a beautiful girl who was one of a crowd of Hungarian refugees being put up for sale. Together Sam and Florence went off to Africa where he had conceived the idea of searching for the Nile source.

'When I gazed on the map of Africa,' he wrote later, 'I had a wild hope mingled with humility, that, even as the insignificant worm boring through the hardest oak, I might by perseverance reach the heart of Africa.' They started off up the Nile from Cairo in April 1861, disembarking at Korosko where the river takes its great bend to the west, and here they mounted camels for an exhausting ride across the Nubian desert. At Berber Baker made his plans to study what he called 'the great drains of Abyssinia' – the Atbara, Setit, Royan, Salam, Angareb, Rahad and Dinder rivers, and the Blue Nile itself, pouring down from the highlands to swell the yearly flood of the White Nile.

The Bakers made a pretty thorough survey of the rivers in these foothills of Ethiopia. They had learned Arabic and could converse with the local people, and made several interesting visits to chiefs; Baker had good sport pursuing big game with the locals. A year to the day from when they had set off from Berber, the Bakers arrived in Khartoum, ready to begin the real expedition up the main course of the White Nile. Making their way upstream, their arrival at Gondokoro coincided with Speke's marching in from the south with Grant. Baker was at first a little downcast to hear that Speke had 'discovered' the source of the Nile in Lake Victoria. 'Does not one leaf of the laurel remain for me?' he asked. Speke was quick to reassure him that indeed there was; though he had virtually settled that the Victoria was the main source, there was another lake to the west which probably formed part of the Nile system, and which the Bakers would do well to make for. Speke wrote out some instructions, and Grant gave them a map drawn by himself of the probable location of this lake.

The Bakers set off across country, with a following of porters likely to mutiny and under the doubtful protection of one of the bands of ivory and slave traders operating out of Gondokoro. The distance

James Augustus Grant (1827–92). Speke's companion on the Nile Quest and life-long pillar of the geographical Establishment.

Below   *Grant's map, which guided the Bakers to Lake Albert.*

from Gondokoro to the northern end of Lake Albert is no more than 290 km (180 miles) in a straight line, but it was by no means a straight line the Bakers were able to take, travelling at the whim of Kurshid Agha the trader, hampered by lack of porters, afflicted by fever and obliged to ride on oxen when the horses died. Sam and Florence, however, made the best of things, making friends with the local people and even, on one protracted stay, planting vegetables to vary their diet.

Baker is one of the few African explorers who made jokes and could bring a comic scene to life. At a rather desperate stage of the journey he was unpacking one of the loads, lugged painfully by mutinous porters into the centre of Africa, and took out 'a full dress Highland suit . . . I was quickly attired in kilt, sporran and Glengarry bonnet . . . A general shout of exclamation arose from the assembled crowd, and taking my seat upon an *angarep*, and attended by ten of my people as escort, I was carried towards the camp of the great Kamrasi'. On another occasion he had a tweed suit ready so as to accentuate his likeness to Speke and so inspire confidence in the locals.

All difficulties at last overcome, they reached the lake on 4 March 1864. 'The glory of our prize burst suddenly upon me!' wrote Baker, 'there like a sea of quicksilver, lay far beneath the grand expanse of water . . . I felt too serious to vent my feelings in vain cheers for victory and I sincerely thanked God for having guided and supported us through all dangers to the good end . . . I called this great lake "the Albert Nyanza".'

To reach the lake they had crossed Speke's Nile west of its exit from Lake Victoria, and had come to Lake Albert near the southern end. Owing to the mist which for most of the year hangs over the Ruwenzori range, it seemed to Baker that a huge lake stretched far to the south, and he saw no mountains. They skirted the eastern shore of Lake Albert by boat and at the northern end found a river flowing into the lake, and almost immediately south out of it. The inflowing current they assumed (rightly) to be the Nile, which they had already crossed higher up on its way from east to west, but Florence insisted that they should make their way up this river to make sure.

They were stopped by the great falls which Baker named Murchison, today a National Park and a popular tourist resort. The Bakers then landed on the north bank and made their way back to Gondokoro, thence to Khartoum and Cairo. A stretch of the Nile between the two lakes was left

Mary Henrietta Kingsley who inherited a passion for travel and an unquenchable vitality from her father George Kingsley, brother of the novelist Charles.

May French Sheldon, alias Bébé Bwana or 'Lady Boss', dressed to kill, on ceremonial visits to local chiefs.

WOMEN IN AFRICA

Any mention of women in Africa evokes the austere and somewhat freakish figure of Mary Kingsley (1862–1900), forerunner of those anthropologists, many of them women, who have studied and recorded African life and customs in the 20th century. Her interests were primarily scientific and after the death of her parents, she decided to visit West Africa to study nature in all its forms; she called it a quest for 'fish and fetish', returning with rare specimens of the former and valuable information about the latter.

Unwilling to 'go about Africa in things you would be ashamed of at home', she travelled through bush and swamp in a long, tight-waisted skirt and high-necked blouse, armed with an umbrella, paying her way as a trader. Her goods consisted of cloth, tobacco and fish-hooks to be exchanged mostly for rubber. Once even her own blouses were accepted as currency. Pledged not to undercut local traders she sometimes struck an even harder bargain than the professionals. Mary's travels in 1895 among the unpredictable Fang tribe in the interior of present day Gabon were as noteworthy as her prowess as a navigator in the tangled creeks of the Niger delta. She died sadly young, nursing Boer prisoners during the South African war.

In sharp contrast was May French Sheldon (1848–1936) nicknamed 'Bébé Bwana' or 'Lady Boss', who in 1891 conducted a Stanley-style safari with a full complement of porters and

Bébé Bwana's personal luggage. At the end of each day's march 'the dainty cloth was spread' and she sat down to supper in a silk gown.

luggage, to Kilimanjaro. She took with her a ball dress and a long blonde wig in which to visit local chiefs, as described in her lively book *Sultan to Sultan*. She only turned back on the borders of Masai territory because her porters, not she, feared to go further. She was carried back in a Palanquin with a collection of local artefacts, and was one of the first women to be elected to the Royal Geographical Society. Later, she visited the Belgian Congo and Liberia, and lived out a long life in a London flat, surrounded by mementoes of her travels.

Mary Kingsley went to Africa out of scientific curiosity and love of adventure; May French Sheldon in a burst of feminist exhibitionism. Florence Baker went because she owed everything to Sam and would have followed him over the rim of the world. 'Possessing a share of *sangfroid* admirably adapted for African travel, Mrs Baker was not a *screamer*,' he wrote, and later declared that he owed 'my success and my life' to her. She first comes into focus at Baker's camp on the borders of Abyssinia in 1862 which was decorated with 'many charms and indescribable little comforts that could only be affected by a lady's hand'. It was rougher going up the Nile at Gondokoro, rendezvous of the ivory and slave traders who were devastating the countryside. There Florence helped to quell an incipient mutiny among their own men, and to persuade the least hostile of the traders to let them accompany him into the interior.

Perhaps her star turn after that was when the Bunyoro chief, on whom they depended for transport to the lake which they hoped to prove a source of the Nile, offered to swap wives. 'My wife, naturally indignant . . . made a little speech in Arabic . . . with a countenance as amiable as the head of Medusa . . .' and the offer was quickly withdrawn. Surviving heat stroke and a virulent fever, Florence was then able to reach Lake Albert and, with her Sam, drink of the waters of the Nile.

On a second Sudan expedition she acted as 'my good little officer', and so cleverly managed the commissariat that there was food for all on the perilous retreat from Masindi in June

Florence Baker in middle age, once the girl who enchanted the Nile folk by washing her long golden hair in their river, (below) Sam Baker in the hunting suit his wife designed and made for him.

1872. She carried not only spare ammunition but 'two bottles of brandy, two drinking cups and two umbrellas and my pistol in my belt, and a heap of little things'. As she was to write to her stepdaughter Agnes, 'I was always *so* dreadfully afraid that something would happen to dear Papa.' 'God shall give her long life!' cried the men when they found she had saved enough food to keep them on the march. They reached safety in a region where the people called her 'the Morning Star' in recognition of her beauty and kindliness. It is good to record that both as Mrs and later as Lady Baker, Florence enjoyed a long and happy married life.

1855 Burton led expedition to Abyssinia, the first European to reach Harar.
1855-9 Du Chaillu travelled on the Gabon River. First description of gorillas.

1856 Moffat surveyed the Orange River.
1857-8 Burton and Speke travelled inland from Zanzibar and discovered Lake Tanganyika.

1858 On the return journey Speke discovered the Victoria Nyanza claiming it to be the source of the Nile.
1858 Livingstone attempted to navigate the

The Bakers with their monkey Wallady, valued by Sam as 'a guarantee of my peaceful intentions, for no one intending hostilities would travel about with a monkey'.

unexplored, and the dimensions of Lake Albert in doubt when they returned to Cairo in the summer of 1865.

The Nile sources in dispute

Meanwhile Speke and Grant sailed away down the river with the 18 porters who had stood by them all the way from Zanzibar – some 6500 km (4000 miles)! 'Speke's Faithfuls', they came to be called with Manua Sera and Bombay in the lead. Speke cabled home 'The Nile is settled', and he and Grant returned to a hero's welcome in London. But the Nile was not settled. There were the inevitable gaps in Speke's account and the fact that he had gone alone to the source told against him. Burton was hostile as ever, but the dispute could have been kept within bounds if Speke had been more tactful, and if Burton had not been the sort of man who enjoyed a quarrel.

The row spread, and in the interests of geographical truth Burton and Speke were invited to address the British Association for the Advancement of Science at Bath in September 1864. But on the day the debate was to have taken place, Speke died in a shooting accident, the news of which was brought to the hall where a large company was assembled to hear the two men discuss their differences. The gap in the programme was hastily filled by a talk from Burton on the customs of Dahomey, and one from Livingstone who had just returned from his Zambezi

expedition. It was an obvious move to ask the country's foremost African explorer to undertake a further expedition to locate the Nile source.

DAVID LIVINGSTONE

David Livingstone (1813–73) had originally come to the notice of the RGS in 1849 when he had been the first European to cross the Kalahari and to stand on the shore of Lake Ngami. He was born in Blantyre, near Glasgow, into a family of straitened means, strict living and religious fervour. Largely self-educated, he qualified as a doctor and was accepted for service with the London Missionary Society, a Protestant, interdenominational body with interests in southern Africa. He arrived at the Cape in 1841 on the way to Kuruman (in Bechuanaland) some 1600 km (1000 miles) to the north, the station built and run by the veteran missionary Robert Moffat whose daughter Mary was to marry Livingstone in 1845. The young couple were perpetually on the move, building three successive mission stations in an effort to establish themselves beyond territory constantly in dispute between Boer farmers and the local people, with the missionary in the unenviable role of pig-in-the-middle.

In 1849 David undertook his first Lake Ngami expedition in company with William Cotton Oswell, a wealthy big game hunter who paid all expenses and was to become a life-long friend. In 1850, Livingstone again visited Ngami taking his wife and four children with him. In 1851, the same party reached the Chobe and Zambezi rivers beyond which lay a 'blank on the map' which would have intrigued the African Association. Here spring the headwaters of the Zambezi flowing south and east to the Indian Ocean and those of the Congo/Zaire flowing north and west to the Atlantic. The region contains a vast watershed abounding in streams, swamps, rivers and seasonal floods.

It is Livingstone's understanding of the nature of the ground he was to traverse, his careful notes and well designed maps that have placed him in the front rank of geographers. In his steady foot-slog across Africa he studied the lie of the land as it unfolded before him, fitting its features into the great jigsaw which was to become the map of Africa. It is often claimed that others – the Hungarian László Magyar, for instance, and the Portuguese Candido – reached the source of the Zambezi and crossed the Continent before him, but it was Livingstone who recorded the geography and gave it

Zambezi. Ascended the Shire River and discovered Lake Chilwa and Lake Nyasa.
1858 Andersson reached the Okovango.

1859-61 Duveyrier explored the Algerian Sahara. First ethnology of the Tuareg.
1860 Speke and Grant reached Lake Victoria and discovered its outlet the Ripon

Falls, the primary source of the Nile.
1861 Chapman and Baines pioneered route to Victoria Falls to establish a trade route with the Zambezi.

David Livingstone on his return from the Zambezi in 1864 with his younger daughter Anna Mary.
Livingstone on safari: 'Waggon travelling is a prolonged system of picknicking,' he wrote, 'excellent for the health and agreeable to those ... who delight on being in the open air.'

to the world. What he saw on his 1851 journey convinced him that only by prospecting further north could he find sites for mission stations out of the range of Boer harassment. This was a task beyond the capacity of women and children; he sent his wife and family off to England and prepared himself for his great adventure.

Across Africa

Collecting supplies in Cape Town, Livingstone set out alone for the homelands of Sekeletu, chief of the Makololo, between the Chobe and the Zambezi rivers. Here he hoped to establish a mission out of the reach of land-hungry Boers. From Sekeletu's capital of Linyanti he travelled west with a hand-picked group of Makololo – companions, not hired porters – to prospect an avenue of trade with the coast which might be the means of combating the slave trade that was beginning to penetrate inland. It was in Angola that he first met this scourge of Africa, and coming back disappointed to Linyanti, he made his way down the Zambezi. As he went he visited the great falls of 'Mosi-oa-tunya', or 'the smoke that thunders', which Livingstone called 'Victoria'.

Conditions in Mozambique were even worse than in Angola, and Livingstone reached England in 1856

AMERICANS IN AFRICA

Colonel Charles Chaillé-Long, American soldier, diplomat and explorer. He was honoured in his own country and also commended by the RGS for his work on the Nile.

English, Scottish, Welsh, Dutch, German – they all travelled the Nile, but it fell to a citizen of the USA to drop into place one of the last pieces of the puzzle. Charles Chaillé-Long (1842–1917), Gold Medallist of the American Geographical Society, was one of a group of army officers (from both sides of the conflict), at a loose end at the conclusion of the American Civil War, who found employment abroad. Chaillé-Long and his fellow colonels, Mason and Prout, took service in the Egyptian army and were posted to the staff of General Charles Gordon, the Governor of Equatoria in the southern Sudan in the 1870s.

Chaillé-Long, an ambitious, flamboyant young man, was sent on several missions by his chief in which he decidedly distinguished himself. On his return from one to the Kingdom of Buganda the American covered over 160 km (100 miles) of hitherto unexplored Nile waterway, proving irrefutably that Speke's Nile flowing out of Lake Victoria was the same river as Baker's Nile flowing into and out of Lake Albert. En route he became the first traveller to come upon Lake Kioga which he called Lake Ibrahim after the son of the then Khedive of Egypt –

very angry he was when a later British survey gave it its present name.

Chaillé-Long's next adventure was into the Azande country of the Nile–Congo/Zaire watershed. No geographical discovery was made there, but a trophy was brought back in the person of a pygmy woman purchased with a red handkerchief (no improper relationship is suggested). Ticki-Ticki spent the rest of her life in Cairo, apart from a rather surprising jaunt to Vienna, the first pygmy to visit Europe.

Chaillé-Long resigned from the Egyptian service in 1876 and though the rest of his career was full of incident, it was no longer connected with Africa. His colleagues Mason and Prout served Egypt and Gordon well though with less *éclat*. Mason accompanied Gordon's second-in-command, the distinguished Italian Romolo Gessi, on the first circumnavigation and survey of Lake Albert. 'What a pity you are not English!' Gordon is said to have remarked when Gessi reported to him; at which the Italian flung his uniform cap on the ground and resigned.

convinced that his purpose in life must be to fight the slave trade. He received the Royal Geographical Society's Patron's Medal for 1855 for his great enlargement of geographical knowledge, and spent most of his time stirring up the British public against the trade in humans which was destroying Africa.

The Zambezi

Livingstone was back in Africa in 1858 as the leader of an expedition sponsored by the British Government and by the RGS, dedicated to opening up the Zambezi as a highway into the interior. Circumstances were as unfavourable to his solitary genius as can well be imagined. He was to have six colleagues all wanting directions and encouragement; there were relations to be established with the Portuguese authorities who controlled the Zambezi some way beyond Tete. Livingstone had neither the gift for handling colleagues and subordinates (nor the wish to acquire it) and he detested the Portuguese. Moreover the whole project was ill-conceived from a practical point of view.

The extent to which the idea of navigating the Zambezi had taken hold of Livingstone's imagination can be measured by the extent to which it upset his geographical judgment. He allowed himself to assume that the river was navigable as far upstream as the Victoria Falls, although on his way downstream in 1856 he had cut across country between Zumbo and Tete and so had never reconnoitred the part of the river which contains the steep fall of the Kebrabasa (Cabora Bassa) gorge; the river was impassable at this point and the energies of the expedition were diverted to the ascent of the Shire river into Lake Nyasa (present day Malawi).

Many things went wrong: the steam launch from which much was expected, the *Ma Robert* (called after the African name for Mrs Livingstone), gave endless trouble; the Universities Mission which was one *raison d'être* of the expedition failed to establish itself on the Shire; Mary Livingstone died of fever. Not even the ascent of the Shire and the geographical information gained on the lake could redeem the Zambezi Expedition which was recalled in 1864, in time for the fatal meeting of the British Association.

1861 Burton, as Consul of Fernando Po, explored mountains of Cameroon.
1861-2 Von de Decker explored the region around Kilimanjaro.

1863-6 German botanist Schweinfurth explored Red Sea coast, Abyssinia and up the Nile to Khartoum.
1863 Tinné travelled down the Nile and

penetrated the Bahr el Ghazal.
1864 Baker discovered Lake Albert, a secondary feeder of the White Nile, and the Murchison Falls.

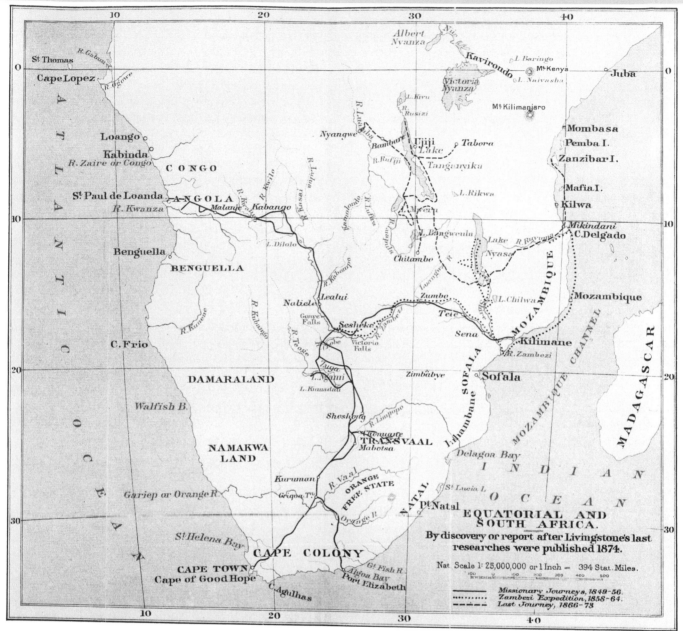

EQUATORIAL AND SOUTH AFRICA.
By discovery or report after Livingstone's last researches were published 1874.

Nat. Scale 1: 25,000,000 or 1 Inch = 394 Stat. Miles.

- - - - - Missionary Journeys, 1849-56.
· · · · · · Zambezi Expedition, 1858-64.
– · – · – Last Journey, 1866-73

The last journey

Sir Roderick Murchison, President of the RGS, was one of Livingstone's few close friends and between them they worked out a scheme for finding the Nile sources, centring on Lake Tanganyika (Burton's choice) as being the most likely origin of the river. Livingstone liked the idea of working Tanganyika into the Nile system, lying as it did within reach of country he knew. He was to make his way by the Rovuma river which was not in Portuguese territory and might turn out to be that highway into the interior (this was one of Livingstone's fixed ideas) – in fact it proved as impracticable as the Zambezi. He was then to make his way to his own Lake Nyasa and so north to Lake Tanganyika.

He left in 1867. The expedition was modestly equipped, but it was not thought that an experienced traveller like Livingstone, on partly familiar ground, need be away long. In the event, he spent six years on his last journey, drifting here and there in the wake of the Arab caravans which traded round Ujiji on Lake Tanganyika, isolated in an Africa ever more demoralized by the slave trade and swept by disease. His powers, moral and physical, began to fail him, supplies ran out, communications with Zanzibar were cut, his porters mutinied.

Dr Livingstone, I presume

When Stanley broke through from Zanzibar to Ujiji in late 1871 with supplies and home news, he found a tired and broken man. Livingstone revived in

1865-70 Grandidier gave comprehensive geographical account of Madagascar.
1865-7 Rohlfs crossed the Sahara from the Mediterranean to the Gulf of Guinea.

1867-71 Livingstone explored for sources of the Nile around Lake Tanganyika and the headwaters of the Congo/Zaire.
1868 Erskine reached the Olifants River and

continued to the mouth of the Limpopo.
1869-71 Schweinfurth investigated the hydrology of the Bahr el Ghazal and the forests of the Nile-Congo/Zaire divide.

Stanley's bracing company and together they visited the northern end of Lake Tanganyika and ascertained that the Ruzizi flowed into and not out of the lake, which could not therefore be connected with the Nile. Livingstone became ever more convinced that the Lualaba to the west of Tanganyika was a headwater of the Nile, and that somewhere at its source were the four fountains from which Herodotus claimed the great river rose. Yet, he doubted.

'I am oppressed,' he wrote, 'by the apprehension that it may, after all, turn out that I have been following the Congo, and who would risk being put into a cannibal pot and converted into a black man for it?' His last journals are full of such self-communication, and while obstinacy hardened, confidence ebbed. He would not take Stanley's advice to return to England to restore his health. He was determined to trudge on until he found the Nile fountains.

Jacob Wainwright guards his master's coffin. 'The youth evinced remarkable quickness and intelligence,' reported The Times, *'and his devotion to Livingstone appears to have been almost romantic.'*

On the shores of Lake Bangweulu, a whole 10°S of the Equator (where the Nile sources lie), following the Lualaba, which is in truth the Congo/Zaire, Livingstone died early in May 1873. Before carrying his body back to the coast, one of his followers had the elementary medical knowledge to remove the heart and internal organs. These were buried beside a tree on which were carved his name and the date. The outer bark with the inscription is now preserved at the Royal Geographical Society. The body was identified by its broken arm and brought home to be greeted as a hero's and buried like a king's in Westminster Abbey.

VERNEY LOVETT CAMERON: THE EMPIRE BUILDER

Stanley's successful relief of Livingstone in 1871 was not well received by the mandarins of the geographical establishment in London. This Yankee journalist was, it was felt, trespassing on their ground, an impression painfully reinforced by the interloper's return to Zanzibar at the precise moment that an official Livingstone Search Expedition arrived from

The so-called 'Congo medicine chest', designed by Stanley and widely used by travellers in the 1870s and onwards.

MEDICAL SUPPLIES

Fever was the travellers' greatest enemy. They called it malaria ('bad air'), supposing it to be caused by unhealthy vapours rising from swampy ground; it was not until the end of the 19th century that Sir Ronald Ross identified the mosquito as the carrier of the disease. Treatment was hit or miss, prevention hardly thought of, though William Baikie survived the deadly climate of the Niger for years owing to the regular use of quinine. 'After taking my morning dose (2–4 grains) I feel fit for any kind of duty,' he wrote in an official report which seems to have been totally ignored by his superiors in London. Baikie only defeated the fever, however, to die of dysentery, another ill to which travellers were prone and which hastened the death of Livingstone, the greatest of them all, despite his strict adherence to his own tenets – to keep going, and to maintain a good supply of the fearsome home-made pills which were known as 'Livingstone's rousers'.

Francis Galton, who had had some medical training, saw no advantage in carrying a large supply of drugs; emetics, purgatives, quinine for ague (another name for malaria), Condy's fluid and a few other homely remedies should suffice. The traveller should be prepared to improvise – a charge of gunpowder in warm water 'makes an effective emetic' is one of the throw-away lines in Galton's *Art of Travel*. An improvisation not thought of by this inventive man was devised by Louis-Gustave Binger surveying in the French Ivory Coast in 1887; he eased the pain of a rupture by strapping an opened sardine tin over the painful spot.

It was left to Stanley on his return from finding Livingstone in 1871 to take things more seriously with his medicine chest designed in consultation with the pharmaceutical firm of Burroughs and Wellcome containing 'all the medicines required for my black men as well as for my white men, beautifully prepared and arranged in most elegant fashion'. A far cry from the Landers navigating the unknown Niger forty years before with Epsom salts as a purgative, carbonate of soda against dysentery and calomel as their preferred remedy for fever. But Richard Lander was glad he carried a strong emetic when ill-disposed slave traders tried to poison him on his return from his first journey.

The two great problems in designing these chests were bulk and the preservation of the contents for long periods. The chests were originally made of japanned sheet iron, but later of the much lighter aluminium. Some of them contained a first aid manual, and all included the current purgative, emetic and disinfectant. An outdated remedy was opium (with or without lead), and all the chests contained quinine although its correct use and purpose was not fully understood. The medicines were packed in neat glass phials, tightly screwed down to prevent deterioration. Galton would have preferred tin ones so that the contents could be stamped on the bottom as well as on the lid and so confusion avoided when several phials were opened. The men seemed to have used both these and earlier remedies as often as not to astonish the locals by making seidlitz powder fizz in water.

Women on safari took the matter more seriously; many of them took courses in first aid and nursing before leaving England for all parts of the world. A classic example, but not the only one, of the women's care for the indigenous people is Mary Kingsley's account of the thorough treatment given to a chief's wife in the depth of the African bush.

'I opened the abscess at once, and then the old lady frightened me out of my wits by gently subsiding, I thought dying, but soon found out merely going to sleep. I then washed the abscess well out, and having a lot of baked plaintains, I made a big poultice of them, mixed with boiling water and more Condy in the tub, and laid her arm right in this . . . I left her to her nap.' Put to sleep after a strong purgative, the old lady recovered pretty well. 'Her son was very anxious to have some pills too; so I gave him some, with firm injunctions only to take one at the first time. I knew that that one would teach him not to take more than one for ever after . . . Then all the afflicted of Egaja turned up for medical advice.'

England. The would-be searchers, who included Livingstone's son Oswell, melted away in discomfiture making way for one of the most vigorous and successful of the Victorian explorers.

Verney Lovett Cameron was an officer in the Royal Navy who had developed a hearty loathing of the slave trade during service in the anti-slavery squadron off the East African coast; he was also a dedicated explorer. He persuaded the RGS that it was still worthwhile sending into the interior, to see if Livingstone was still in need, and on 28 March 1873 Cameron set off from Bagamoyo on the old trade route to Tabora. There he met Susi and Chuma and their companions with their master's body; Cameron however resolved to go on to Ujiji to rescue such of Livingstone's possessions and papers that might have been left there.

Having arrived at the explorer's old camp, he decided to continue westward to the Lualaba and perhaps the Congo/Zaire. He first made a thorough survey of Lake Tanganyika, identifying 96 in-flowing streams as well as the only outlet from the lake – a channel leading to the Lukuga river and thence to the Lualaba. Marching on from the lake Cameron became convinced by the general lie of the land that the Lualaba could have no connection with the Nile, but probably flowed on to become the Congo/Zaire. Unable to secure river transport at the Arab camp of Nyangwe, he abandoned any further search in that direction and turned south to arrive on 7 November 1875 at Catumbela north of Benguela in Angola on the Atlantic coast, becoming the first European to make an east-west crossing of Africa.

Cameron seems to have regarded geographical discovery as primarily serving the need to develop Africa commercially, and in such development Britain, he insisted, should play a dominant part. There was nothing new, of course, in the idea that the explorer should blaze a trail for the trader. What was new was the plea to Great Britain to move into Africa and to administer chosen regions on the pattern of British rule in India. Cameron looked forward to seeing 'the Union Jack flying permanently in the centre of Africa, and not merely passing through it as when I carried it there'. The 'Scramble for Africa' is thus foreshadowed.

HENRY MORTON STANLEY: CONGO OR NILE?

H.M. Stanley (1841–1904) was equally keen to exploit Africa's resources, not only for the sake of the entrepreneurs of Europe, but for the good of the local people. Stanley never became popular with the Establishment, but he came to be accepted and even admired for his drive and efficiency. His origins were obscure and somewhat shady, his manner abrasive, and an American newspaperman was a kind of animal hitherto unknown in scientific circles.

His own account of his early life contains much fantasy, but certain facts remain. He was born at Denbigh in North Wales, the illegitimate son of John Rowlands and Elizabeth Parry, but registered as John Rowlands. At the age of five he was consigned

Henry Morton Stanley, the workhouse boy who made good as explorer and Empire builder. Married in 1890, elected to Parliament in 1895 and knighted in 1899.

to the St Asaph Workhouse where he seems to have received a fair education; he wrote a good hand and was a voracious reader. He ran away to sea and led a roving life in America, eventually finding his true vocation as a reporter, on campaigns against the Indians in the American West. He changed his name to Henry Stanley after a New Orleans merchant who had befriended him, later adding 'Morton'. He worked as a war correspondent for the *New York Herald* and was commissioned by them to 'find Livingstone'; thus he appears on the exploration scene.

Stanley's relief of Livingstone changed his life; he conceived a devotion for the older man and at the same time learned the rudiments of exploration techniques. On hearing of his hero's death in 1873 he decided to follow up Livingstone's researches on the Congo/Zaire and Nile systems and at the same time to examine the findings of Speke, Burton and Baker. It was a grandiose project, funded by the *New York Herald* and London's *Daily Telegraph*. On 17 November 1874 a well-equipped caravan marched out of Bagamoyo, over 350 strong including some women and children. Led by the experienced Manua Sera as chief captain and with Stanley and his three European companions bringing up the rear, it made a brave show with drums beating, horns blowing and flags flying. Among the loads carried were the sections making up a novel item of equipment – the boat named the *Lady Alice* after Miss Alice Pike of New York to whom Stanley was engaged (but who married someone else in his absence).

The route was by Lake Victoria where Stanley was the first European to visit the Kingdom of Buganda since Speke and Grant were there in 1862. The *Lady Alice* was launched and the lake explored, confirming Speke's estimate of its extent and importance. There were some rough encounters with the lake people for which Stanley was to be severely criticized, especially at Bumbireh where casualties were inflicted on the local population. Owing to the tribal unrest between Buganda and Bunyoro it proved impossible to visit Lake Albert, and the column turned south for Lake Tanganyika, noting Lake Edward on the way. Stanley's circumnavigation of Tanganyika finally proved that it had no connection

with the Nile, the lake's only outlet (as Cameron had observed) being the Lukuga which in turn drains into the Lualaba.

Stanley then set himself to examine Livingstone's theories on the Lualaba and made for Nyangwe, the Arab trading post on the river which had been Livingstone's and Cameron's furthest point north. There in October 1876 Stanley found Tippu Tib the famous Arab trader, well-supplied and with an armed guard. Stanley persuaded him to join forces on a further exploration of the Lualaba, but the menace of the untravelled forest region was too much for the Arabs who turned back after 300 km (200 miles) of difficult and dangerous going under constant attack by local tribes. The two parties first celebrated Christmas with feasting and dancing, and a foot race in which Tippu Tib beat Frank Pocock, Stanley's only surviving European companion.

The desperate situation of Zaidi in the Stanley Falls and his rescue: 'Uledi and his friend Murzouk stepped into the canoe with the air of gladiators.'

1876-7 Stanley circumnavigated Lake Tanganyika. Followed the Lualaba into the Congo/Zaire River.
1878 Rohlfs led scientific exploration of the

Libyan desert reaching the Al Kufrah oasis.
1878 Thomson explored unknown land between Lake Nyasa and Lake Tanganyika.
1879-80 Johnston and Thomson surveyed

drainage of Central Africa between Lakes Nyasa and Tanganyika.
1879-86 Junker's exploration of Uele River showed it to be part of Congo/Zaire system.

AFRICAN FOLLOWERS

Africa could never have been explored without the aid of the continent's own people, especially in East Africa where the prevalence of the tsetse fly prevented the use of pack animals. A work force of 350 or more could be needed for an expedition, as when Stanley crossed the continent in 1874–7. The point of departure from the east coast was Zanzibar where a British Consul (the influential Sir John Kirk) had the ear of the Sultan and so could help forward the plans of would-be explorers.

Porters were recruited (in competition with Arab ivory and slave traders), in Zanzibar itself, on the mainland from communities of freed slaves and from the Nyamwezi people south of Lake Victoria who made a speciality of portering. These were the rank and file; captains and headmen had to be selected with more care. Such were Livingstone's Chuma and Susi, Speke's Bombay, Stanley's coxswain Uledi and his captain Manua Sera. An old-fashioned 'master and man' relationship often developed, as between Speke and Bombay, the latter long cherishing a wish, never achieved, to visit his old leader's grave in England. An instance of such mutual commitment was the decision of Chuma and Susi and their companions to carry Livingstone's body and his precious journals back 2250 km (1400 miles) to the coast so that he might rest among his own people. Women sometimes accompanied their menfolk on the white man's safaris; Livingstone's cook Halima was among those following his body – a journey which took nine months.

The first duty of the captain and his subordinate headmen was to organize the caravan and here 'Chuma was in his element,' noted Joseph Thomson preparing to march his 150 men out of Dar es Salaam in 1879: 'He danced about with indignation, seizing this man by the ear, and that by the throat, while he volleyed out his threats, or lashed them with his satire.' The men were paid in Maria Theresa dollars, equivalent to about four English shillings; when Stanley set out to find

Livingstone in 1871 the going rate was two and a half dollars a month, but three years later it had doubled in some cases. Experienced men with responsibilities of course received more; Lovett Cameron paid Bombay 12 dollars as captain on the trans-continental journey of 1874.

Arms and ammunition, camping equipment and scientific instruments, as well as personal belongings had to be carried, all in addition to goods for barter and as gifts for chiefs. Cloth for this purpose – the popular American unbleached cotton (or *merikani*) – was made up into rolls which could weigh 35 kg (70 lb), the maximum weight for one man, and beads in long bags weighing 25 kg (50 lb). Once assembled the send-off was a lively affair, drums beating, horns blowing, the leaders conspicuous in red robes, the scarlet flag of Zanzibar flying over all. When they were well launched, the day's march would begin as early as 4 a.m. and by midday the heat would compel a halt. It was 'wonderful', mused Speke, that by the evening the men had spirits and energy enough for

dancing and 'stamping with their arms and legs flying about like the wings of a semaphore', to the steady beat of the drums.

The leaders could also be useful in negotiations with local chiefs. Most of these interpreters spoke Swahili and mission education had taught them some English. Freed slaves whose homes had been in the interior might find themselves once more on home ground, where the language was familiar, as happened to Chuma when travelling in Yao country with Bishop Steere in 1872. An instance of the efficacy of mission teaching occurred when Dallington Maftaa proved capable of translating passages from the Bible into Swahili which were then rendered into Ganda by a scribe at the Buganda court for the edification of the Kabaka. Dualla Idris, who accompanied Teleki to Lake Turkana in 1886, could handle Somali, Arabic, English and Swahili, as well as a smattering of other tongues.

Inevitably there were troubles on the way in the course of a journey which could take three years – mutinies,

1879-84 Stanley returned to the Congo for Leopold II of Belgium.
1879 De Brazza established French territorial claim to part of the Congo.

1880 Flatters sent to survey a rail route from Algeria to Niger. Murdered by Tuareg.
1880-6 Wissman made three major journeys in the Congo.

1882 Foureau led French military expedition into the Central Sahara.
1882 Fischer reached Kilimanjaro, Great Rift Valley and Lake Naivasha.

Thomas Baines and James Chapman breaking camp in the Zambezi country on their way from Walvis Bay to the Victoria Falls in 1862.

desertions, thefts and quarrels. Punishment was prompt and brutal: a mutineer could be lucky to escape hanging and severe flogging was the lot of the thief.

Survivors of the great exploring years – such as Speke's 'Faithfuls' – could receive pensions or gifts of land, rewards much preferred to the medals and commemorative rings sometimes distributed. A number of old hands carried on working in a new era of commercial and imperial expansion; Dualla Idris, for example, travelled with Lugard who took an expedition into Buganda in 1890 on behalf of the Imperial British East Africa Company. The need for manpower declined, however, with the coming of the railways in the 1880s, and though it revived temporarily during the First World War, it became eventually a mere matter of memory and at last of historical record.

Stanley had managed to secure *en route* 22 canoes which with the *Lady Alice*, were to provide transport on the river for all his men, so he was the less sorry to see the Arabs go. He then embarked on one of the worst journeys in the history of exploration, one that was to prove that the Lualaba (which Stanley called the Livingstone) was in truth the Congo/Zaire, flowing north and then west and south-west in a great arc across the Equator and down impassable cataracts to the sea. Initially, he was faced with the turbulent white water of the Stanley (Boyoma) Falls where the boats had to be constantly pulled out of the water and carried along the bank. By the time they reached the foot of the Falls, Stanley and his men had fought 24 battles against the hostile forest people, and there were eight more to come against warriors in war canoes.

The Falls behind them, they were in blessedly smooth water, embarked on the 1600 km (1000 miles) of the Upper Congo/Zaire waterway, but the worst hazard was to come – the 350 km (220 miles) of the Livingstone Falls with its 32 murderous cataracts where Frank Pocock was drowned. This was the barrier which had halted Diogo Cão in 1482 and Tuckey in 1816. The river was abandoned, the *Lady Alice* left to rot on the bank above the Isangila cataract. The exhausted band staggered on, managing to send a message to Boma at the mouth of the river which brought blessed relief in the form of a band of four friendly European traders and plentiful refreshment.

Only 114 remained out of the 350 who had marched so bravely out of Bagamoyo three years before, the Pocock brothers and Frank Barker were dead and Stanley's hair was white. But some gallant souls survived, among them the captain Manua Sera and Uledi, coxswain of the *Lady Alice*, who in the course of the journey had saved 13 men from drowning. As they made their way into Boma they sang a song made up by one of their number:

Then sing, O friends, sing the journey is ended;
Sing aloud, O friends, sing to the great sea.

Back to the Nile

Yes, they had reached the sea, proving once and for all that there was no connection between the Nile and the rivers of the south which Livingstone had explored so desperately. The separation between the two systems was even then being confirmed by the discovery of the Nile–Congo/Zaire watershed, that sprawl of great streams in the heart of equatorial Africa, flowing west and south into the Congo/Zaire, north and east into the Nile. To reach the Nile the waters funnel into the swamps of the Bahr el Ghazal and Lake No, sluggish and fever-ridden, from where comes much of the rotting vegetation, or *sudd*, which chokes the Nile south of Khartoum.

It was into this dangerous and unhealthy channel that the adventurous young Dutchwoman, Alexine Tinné, determined to penetrate when cruising up the Nile in the 1860s. She was accompanied by her mother and aunt and a domestic staff which included lady's maids. They were well provisioned in the only steamer available for hire at Khartoum, arousing the envy of Sam Baker and shocking his sense of propriety – 'A young lady alone among the Dinka tribe! . . . They are naked as the day they were born!'

The Tinné party was serious, however, penetrating a long way up the Bahr el Ghazal in 1863 into deso late country where several of them died, including Alexine's mother. Alexine herself was to meet an even sadder fate, for she was murdered in an expedition across the Sahara in 1869.

Some years later the Bahr el Ghazal with its many affluents was more thoroughly explored by the genial German botanist Georg Schweinfurth (1836–1929). He was primarily in search of plants and other natural specimens, but he was able to bring back useful geographical information. He made his way on foot into the Azande country and was the first European to meet with the pygmies who inhabit these dense Congo/Zaire forests. He was the first European, too, to stand on the bank of the Uele river. He realized that it formed no part of the Nile system and he was inclined to link it with the Shari and Lake Chad but in fact it belongs to the Congo/Zaire system.

ENTER LEOPOLD

Joseph Thomson: who goes slowly, goes safely

Stanley emerged from the Congo/Zaire to find a change going on in the field of exploration. A new phase was beginning during which missionaries and traders were being attracted to the lands where there were opportunities for saving souls and making money. After them were to come the imperialists claiming spheres of influence in what was to become known as the 'Scramble for Africa'. This was foreshadowed when in 1876 King Leopold II convened a conference in Brussels to discuss the future of Africa and the part Europe might (and should) play in the development of its resources. Leopold was a big fish in the small pool of newly independent Belgium and had long dreamed of wider horizons, increasingly of founding an Empire.

The calling of the Brussels Conference constituted him initially the patron of African exploration, ultimately the biggest imperialist of them all, one who would be followed eagerly by the nations of Europe carving out colonies for themselves in the 'Scramble'. Great Britain was well represented at Brussels: the RGS sent the President, Sir Rutherford Alcock; the explorers James Grant and Verney Lovett Cameron, were also there. France's chief delegate was the distinguished Saharan traveller Henri Duveyrier. Germany sent her notable explorers Gustav Nachtigal, Gerhard Rohlfs and Georg Schweinfurth. The outcome of the conference was to set up the short-lived International African Association, in which the nations of Europe were to cooperate in establishing cultural centres along routes into the interior to accommodate missionaries, teachers and other men of goodwill who would – it was hoped – bring spiritual enlightenment and material prosperity to the local people.

The RGS however soon withdrew its support from the Association because it was clearly going to promote aims outside the bounds of scientific geography. The Society launched its own scheme – the African Exploration Fund – the object being to follow up routes to the Central Lakes of Africa which its own explorers had already traversed. Nevertheless, the fact that such further exploration would pave the way for trade and missionary endeavour, for roads, railways and telegraph lines, shows the RGS was moving with the times into a new phase of African involvement.

The expedition sent out in 1878 was led by the cartographer Keith Johnston on a route from Dar es Salaam to Lakes Nyasa (Malawi) and Tanganyika. Johnston died at an early stage of the journey and his second-in-command, Joseph Thomson (1858–95), young and inexperienced, felt keenly his inadequacy to take over. Should he simply turn back, he asked himself. No! 'I felt I must go forward, whatever might be my destiny. Was I not the countryman of Bruce, Park, Clapperton, Grant, Livingstone and Cameron?' For Thomson was a Scot, a nation which has contributed much to the history of exploration.

Joseph Thomson is one of the most attractive of African explorers. Informal and full of fun, he was a prudent traveller taking as his motto 'He who goes slowly, goes safely; he who goes safely goes far'. Where other travellers challenged an unfriendly crowd with guns, Thomson charmed them with parlour tricks – removing and replacing his two false

GREAT MOMENTS

Joseph Thomson was instructed by the Royal Geographical Society to pioneer a route from the east coast to Lake Victoria through Masai country. Encamped briefly at the approaches to Mount Kilimanjaro in May 1883, he has left us a picture of the country before the hunters and poachers came.

There, towards the base of Kilimanjaro, are three great herds of buffalo slowly and leisurely moving up from the lower grazing-grounds to the shelter of the forest for their daily snooze and rumination in its gloomy depths. Farther out on the plains enormous numbers of the harmless but fierce-looking wildebeest continue their grazing, some erratic members of the herd gambolling and galloping about with waving tail and strange, uncouth movements. Mixed with these are to be seen companies of that loveliest of all game, the zebra, conspicuous in their beautiful striped skin, here marching with stately step, with heads down bent, there enjoying themselves by kicking their heels in mid-air or running open-mouthed in mimic fight, anon standing as if transfixed, with heads erect and projecting ears, watching the caravan pass. But these are not all. Look! Down in that grassy bottom there are several specimens of the great, unwieldy rhinoceros, with horns stuck on their noses in a most offensive and pugnacious manner. Over that ridge a troop of ostriches are scudding away out of reach of danger, defying pursuit, and too wary for the stalker. See how numerous are the herds of hartebeest, and notice the graceful pallah springing into mid-air with great bounds as if in pure enjoyment of existence. There also among the tall reeds near the marsh you perceive the dignified waterbuck, in twos and threes, leisurely cropping the dewy grass. The wart-hog, disturbed at his morning's feast, clears off in a bee-line with tail erect, and with a steady military trot truly comical. These do not exhaust the list, for there are many other species of game. Turn in whatever direction you please, they are to be seen in astonishing numbers, and so rarely hunted, that unconcernedly they stand and stare at us, within gunshot. The news of our arrival soon spread. The Masai men and women began to crowd into camp, and we mutually surveyed each other with equal interest. Obviously they felt that they were a superior race, and that all others were but as slaves before them.

Through Masai Land, Joseph Thomson. 3rd Edition, 1885.

teeth with magical words and gestures, or frothing fruit salts in water. He prided himself on accomplishing notable journeys with no bloodshed. He was on good terms with his men, for his confident leadership and unfailing cheerful humour. He declared early on that there would be no corporal punishment and all misdemeanours would be paid for by fines. This, however, did not please the porters who much preferred swift, painful chastisement to loss of pay (which, Thomson surmises in his humorous way, they assumed he would pocket himself).

He led his safari successfully to the north end of Lake Nyasa (Malawi) and achieved a useful exploration of Lake Tanganyika. In 1883–4 he was put in command of a more ambitious journey through modern Kenya from Mombasa to the northern end of Lake Victoria, through the territory of the reputedly hostile Masai. It was an area well-known to ivory traders and had been skirted by the Mombasa missionaries in the 1840s but not penetrated to any purpose by explorers. Thomson took a route from the coast to Mount Kilimanjaro where he paused to take breath before striking north along the line of the Rift Valley, that geological phenomenon which runs from Lake Malawi in the south right the way up to the Dead Sea. He was the first traveller from the outside world to assess the nature and importance of this impressive feature.

His outward route crossed today's Amboselli National Park and thence he made a diversion to Mount Kenya, 'discovering' Thomson's Falls (now the Nyapuhura) and catching the first sight of the gazelle called 'Thomson's' in his honour. Eventually he turned west past Lake Baringo and to the shore

1885 Royal Niger Company's expedition to Sokoto.	Traced river linking Lake Edward to Lake Albert.	**1891** May French Sheldon explored Lake Chala in a copper pontoon.
1887-9 Stanley led Emin Pasha Relief Expedition. Saw Ruwenzori mountains.	**1887-90** Binger explored region contained in the bend of the Niger River.	**1892** Binger determined boundary between Gold Coast and the Ivory Coast.

Joseph Thomson (1858–95) with Chuma ('full of anecdote, fun and jollity') and Makatubu ('a capital fellow, full of life and energy').

THE DESERT

Timbuktu

It was mainly British explorers who were to cut a swathe through the rain forests, rivers and swamps of Central Africa. Between them, Burton, Speke and Grant, Baker, Livingstone and Stanley unveiled the secrets of the Nile, the Zambezi and the Congo/Zaire, and placed on the map Lakes Tanganyika, Victoria, Albert and Malawi (which they called Nyasa); only the 'Mountains of the Moon' remained hidden. The Niger had been traced by Park and the Landers. In the desert country north of the Niger and its border states very different physical conditions had to be faced. Here French and German names predominate, especially the former in view of France's expansion into North Africa following her acquisition of Algeria in 1830.

The French may, perhaps, be allowed a prior claim on the Sahara since it was a Frenchman who succeeded in being the first to reach Timbuktu and to survive. In 1824 the Geographical Society of Paris offered a prize of 10,000 francs to the first traveller to accomplish this feat, and in 1827 a young Frenchman set out on a lone journey. René Caillié (1799–1838) was the son of a French baker, orphaned in childhood and with little or no education; like his contemporary Richard Lander, he let neither this nor lack of resources stand in the way of his determination to explore Africa. For some years he worked in France and in Sierra Leone at menial jobs, saving 2000 francs from his wages. 'This treasure,' he thought, 'seemed to be sufficient to carry me all over the world' – but he did not want the world, only Timbuktu.

The usual approach to the forbidden city was from Tripoli where an old established route ran south-west to the oasis of Ghudāmis, a favourite rendezvous for the Saharan trading caravans. Caillié, however, chose to make his way from country familiar to him in the west, and in April 1827, he set off from the neighbourhood of the Konkoure river on the coast of modern Guinea. He travelled disguised as a Muslim, his cover story being that he was an Egyptian Arab taken as a slave to Europe in childhood, and now returning home – hence his poor Arabic. He kept his notes folded into a Koran which he carried ostentatiously, logging his journey while pretending to study Holy Writ. Half-way in his progress at Tiéme in the Ivory Coast, he collapsed with an attack of scurvy so severe that the skin

of Lake Victoria just south of the present Kenya–Uganda border; he came home across today's Tsavo National Park. Thomson received the Founder's Medal at the hands of the RGS, at that date the youngest explorer to do so. Later he worked for Cecil Rhodes in opening up tracts of present-day Zambia for trade and settlement. He also travelled in North and West Africa. He came home to Scotland to die, at an early age, from injuries received during his travels. His last words are said to have been: 'If I were strong enough to put on my clothes and walk 100 yards, I would go back to Africa yet.'

peeled off his palate. He was nursed back to health by kindly African women who gave him rice water to drink, and concoctions of local herbs.

In January 1828 he was on his feet again and, reaching the Niger, his journey continued downstream for the rest of the way, wrapped in a rug to conceal his pallid European face. He reached Timbuktu in April 1828. Though he 'experienced an indescribable satisfaction' on attaining his goal, he was disappointed to find a city composed of 'ill-looking houses built of mud', and no gold roofs or pavements. He chose not to return by the route he had come but to make the hazardous 1600-km (1000-mile) desert journey north through Morocco with a caravan bound for Fez. So spent and ragged was he when at last he reached Rabat that the French Consul refused to let him into the Consulate and he was obliged to stagger on to Tangier from where officials saw him home to France. He reported his success to the Society in Paris, received his prize and was made a *Chevalier* of the *Légion d'honneur*.

Caillié, alone and with no backing, was lucky; Alexander Gordon Laing (1794–1826), a British Army officer and experienced traveller, Government-sponsored, was consistently unlucky. He was certainly the first European to enter Timbuktu, but not only was he murdered on the return stage, but his journals were lost. On the way out he arrived in Tripoli in May 1825 ready to start, but found himself caught up in the toils of local bureaucracy and frustrated by the wily Bashaw from whom permission had to be obtained before he could start on his journey. He was in the hands of the British Consul, Colonel

Sandstorm experienced by J. S. Lyon in Libya (1820) and by desert travellers elsewhere. James Bruce recommended lying flat on one's face until the gale had blown itself out.

A F R I C A

1898 Foureau-Lamy French military mission to the Southern Sahara ended in disgrace. **1899** Mackinder made first ascent of Mount Kenya.

1902 Destenave's survey of Lake Chad. **1902-3** Anglo-French Niger and Chad Boundary Commission fixed the Northern Boundary of Nigeria.

1903 Beazley surveyed 39,000 sq km (15,000 sq miles) of British Somaliland. **1904** Lenfant ascended the Benne River showing Lake Chad could be reached from

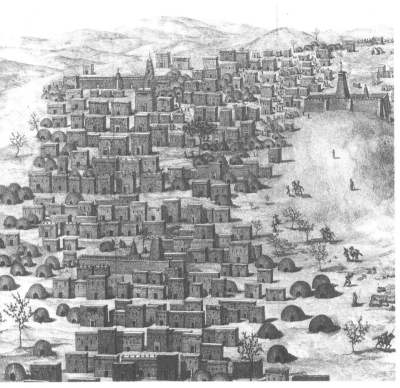

René Caillié's impression of Timbuktu. 'With what gratitude did I return thanks to Heaven,' he wrote, 'for the happy result which attended my enterprise.'

Hanmer Warrington, a blustering windbag of a man, with whose daughter, Emma, Laing fell in love. Her father agreed to marry them, but only on condition that the marriage was not consummated until Laing's return.

At last he set off, on 15 July 1825, accompanied by his West Indian servant 'honest Jack le Bore' and two West African boat builders – he was hoping to leave Timbuktu by river. The party was attacked on the way, Laing left severely wounded and his three companions killed by Tuareg tribesmen. A man of outstanding courage and determination, Laing struggled on to Timbuktu, but he was murdered on his way home by fanatical Muslims; his journals were never recovered. Emma waited two years for the news of his death to filter through; one hopes she secured a brief spell of happiness in her second marriage which only lasted six months before her early death.

The Sahara and beyond

The travels of Heinrich Barth in the 1850s proved an inspiration to a younger generation of would-be travellers, not least to Henri Duveyrier (1840–92) who was to gain a reputation as an expert on the Tuareg tribespeople of the Sahara. Duveyrier was born in Paris into a family devoted to the principles of Charles Henri de Rouvry Saint-Simon, founder of a cult much in vogue among intellectuals in the early years of the 19th century. Saint-Simonism was a complex philosophy sometimes defined as an early kind of socialism; one of its tenets was to advocate friendly cooperation between nations.

Young Duveyrier, inspired by Barth, saw opportunities for a rapprochement on Saint-Simonian principles with the peoples of North Africa. He was convinced, on the evidence of a short Algerian visit in 1857, that the vigorous and aggressive Tuareg would be ideal trading partners for the French. In 1859, when only 19 years of age, he felt ready for the journey among the Tuareg of northern Algeria on which his fame rests. Despite official disapproval of the idealistic teenager let loose in what was regarded as an area of delicate equilibrium, the young man accomplished important research and was rewarded by the *Légion d'honneur* in 1862 and a Gold Medal from the Geographical Society of Paris two years later.

Duveyrier's dream of a utopian future with French and Tuareg in partnership within the French empire was shattered in later years when the official policy of armed expeditions to prospect the way for railways and other aspects of so-called civilization culminated in the massacre in 1889 of Colonel Paul Flatters's survey team and military escort into Tuareg country. The rest of his life was clouded, and he died by his own hand in 1892.

Three German geographers were to make their mark in Barth's wake, notably Georg Schweinfurth, whose travels covered a wide range. Best known, perhaps, for his journey in the watery wastes of the Bahr el Ghazal and into the forests of the Nile Zaire/Congo divide in 1869, he also made his way into the arid expanse of the Sahara. Accompanying Gerhard Rohlfs he covered a wide sweep of unexplored parts of the Libyan desert. Schweinfurth lived to the age of 90, a record for an African explorer at a time when the hardships of travel through the 'dark continent' carried off so many in their prime.

Gerhard Rohlfs (1831–96) took the hard way on to the African scene by enlisting in the Foreign Legion as a young man, thus acquiring a knowledge of Arabic and becoming familiar with desert conditions at their most harsh. He was a sturdy walker, making numerous excursions into the North African desert during the 1860s. The most important of these was accomplished during 1865–7 when he made a traverse from Tripoli to Lagos by way of Bornu and the

Niger. In 1873 he led an expedition on a 36-day march to Siwa Oasis, and in 1878–9 penetrated as far as the Oases of Kufra. By the time of his death, Rohlfs had achieved an unassailable position as an authority on North Africa.

Gustav Nachtigal (1854–85) seems to have been something of a contrast to his rugged compatriot. The son of a Protestant pastor, he was trained as a doctor and served for some years as military surgeon in Algiers and Tunis. Alexine Tinné met him in the course of her fatal bid to cross the Sahara in 1869, and described him in a letter to her brother as 'discreet, unassuming and honest'. Nachtigal's introduction to serious Saharan travel came with his appointment by the King of Prussia to lead a mission to the Sultan of Bornu in 1869.

The task accomplished, he continued on a trek eastward which was to take him on one of the outstanding journeys of the time. He passed through Darfur and Kordofan arriving on the Nile just south of Khartoum five years later. Much of the way had been through territory not only unexplored, but hostile. The English traveller Boyd Alexander took this route in 1909–10 but lost his life in circumstances never explained; one suggestion was that he trespassed, in search of bird life, on a hill held sacred by the local people. Nachtigal was luckier, or more circumspect.

The coming of the colonial period accelerated the work of explorers in the Sahara, and it is significant that in the year 1899 the RGS nominated French travellers in that area for both the Founder's and the Patron's medals. Louis-Gustave Binger (1856–1937) came first to West Africa on military duty but proved himself more than a simple pioneer in the interests of his country. A French reference book describes him as 'infatigable et pacifique, le anti-Stanley, savant scrupuleux et curieux de tout'. He was a great natural explorer and in 1887 embarked on the three-year journey on which he did more than any traveller of his time to open up the country in the great bend of the Niger. In 1892 he undertook the delimitations of the boundary between the British Gold Coast and the French Ivory Coast, of which latter territory he became Governor in 1893.

The commanding position which France achieved in the great expansionist years in North Africa was undoubtedly thanks to Fernand Foureau (1850–1914). Despite sustained opposition from the powerful Tuareg he managed to carry out surveys deep into the desert and finally succeeded in overcoming local opposition. The journey on which this was achieved was undertaken with a military escort commanded by Major Lamy which advanced into the modern Republic of Chad, returning by way of the Congo/Zaire. Foureau's Patron's Medal was presented in recognition of 'continuous exploration of the Sahara'.

An altogether different note from all these brave and, it may be admitted, aggressive, pioneers was struck by the Vicomte de Foucauld (1838–1916) whose posting to Morocco in the French army changed his life. While there he travelled, disguised as a Jewish Rabbi, into dangerous country and his *Reconnaissance au Maroc* established him as a Saharan authority. More important, it brought him under that spell which the desert sometimes casts on travellers, and led him to the religious life. He became a priest of the Trappist order and lived the rest of his life in hermit-like seclusion among the Tuareg of the Hoggar in Algeria. He was murdered in 1916 leaving behind him a reputation not only for outstanding saintliness but of penetrating scholarship.

SOUTHERN AFRICA

Exploration in southern Africa took a rather different form, and had a rather different flavour from elsewhere. Here were no geographical riddles to be solved as on the Niger or the Nile, and no such towering figure as Livingstone or Mungo Park dominates the scene. Here was wide open country, briefly penetrated here and there by the Portuguese from Mozambique, but for the most part awaiting the occupation which was to spread from the Cape. The settlement founded there by the Dutch East India Company in 1652 under the leadership of Jan van Riebeck developed rapidly from a mere victualling station for the East Indies fleets into a thriving colony in need of more land. Hence the early journeys into the interior were by farmers trekking north and east in search of pasture for their flocks; the 'Great Trek' of 1834 was neither the first nor the last of such journeys. At the same time official expeditions were launched from the colony to buy cattle from the Hottentot people, pastoral farmers of mixed Bushman and Hamitic descent, and to investigate rumours of gold and copper in the interior. The Orange River was reached in 1777 by Colonel R.J. Gordon, a Hollander of Scottish extraction in the Netherlands service, who travelled independently in southern Africa. He named the river in honour of the Stadtholder.

The big game of Southern Africa had not only the white hunters to fear: Thomas Baines's impression of local bushmen in hot pursuit.

The naturalists

Among the first visitors from outside were the naturalists, in search of the abounding beauty of southern Africa's plant and animal life. Among the earliest was the Swede Carl Thunberg, 'Father of Cape Botany', a pupil of Linnaeus, who went plant-hunting with his compatriot Anders Sparrman; they swam rivers together (Sparrman clad in nothing but his wig) and slid down precipitous rocks in search of rare specimens. Later Thunberg teamed up with Francis Masson, the first man to be sent abroad to collect plants for the Royal Gardens at Kew. The work of Sparrman and of the English botanist William Paterson was given by the African Association as one reason why 'the southern extremity of the African peninsula may be justly considered to be explored'. William Burchell's is another famous name in the South African story. During his travels there in 1811–2 he made more than 500 drawings and sketches of men, animals, birds, plants and scenery, as well as making a large collection of natural history specimens; he carried some 50 volumes in his wagon, to help in identifications.

The missionaries

Missionaries were not far behind. By the end of the 18th century the London Missionary Society had established itself in south Africa; in 1799 the Reverend William Anderson made the first recorded crossing of the Orange river (other than at the seaward end). In 1813 the Reverend John Campbell travelled as far north as Bechuanaland to look for possible mission sites and 1821 saw established at Kuruman the famous missionary Robert Moffat (himself a doughty traveller) and his wife Mary, under whose auspices Livingstone was to begin his career.

The hunters

A less sympathetic group than either of these was soon to arrive – the big game hunters, crazy for sport and for trophies. It was only incidentally that Cornwallis Harris, Roualeyn Gordon Cumming and their like made known great tracts of land in their pursuit of elephants, rhinoceros and of anything else that moved or was beautiful – or both. The one member of the fraternity who deserves to enter the

FLOWERS, FISH AND SAND

Current comment on African exploration tends to concentrate on its political aspect, to see it as the inspiration and prelude to colonialism. Its scientific side, which in Joseph Banks's day mattered much more, and still persists, is often neglected. Take Francis Masson (1714–1805) for instance, an under-gardener at Kew, whom Banks advised George III to send to South Africa to collect plants for the Royal Gardens. Masson's three journeys between 1772 and 1774 were so successful that he was sent again to the Cape in 1786 when he collected a further 117 plants and bulbs and identified rare specimens of *erica* and *protea*. Linnaeus named the genus Massonia after him. One hundred years later Marianne North visited South Africa on her self-imposed task of painting the world's tropical flora, and was able to add an African section to the North Gallery at Kew.

The botanist Georg Schweinfurth was handsomely funded by the Humboldt-Stiflung in Berlin to study the vegetation of the Bahr el Ghazal region west of the Nile. He travelled mostly on foot rejoicing in the 'variety of hue – green, red, yellow!' and finding in one stretch of the Nile a 'wildly romantic' resemblance to the Bingerloch of the Rhine.

Mary Kingsley approached the famous ichthyologist Dr A.C. Gunther at the British Museum (Natural History) with a rather haphazard collection of fish caught in West Africa on her first voyage, in 1893. He was impressed, had her equipped with a proper outfit, and applauded her return in 1895 with 65 varieties of fish, of which three were named after her as being new to science – she also brought back 18 reptiles. She caught the fish mostly in a stockade trap, but sometimes by rod and line while drifting in a canoe. This gave rise to typical Kingsley accidents such as when a huge catfish caused the boat to capsize and to precipitate them all into the water.

Scientists and travellers continue to cooperate. As colonialism recedes into history, there is a resurgence of interest in the ecology of Africa. In March 1944 Brigadier R.A. Bagnold (1896–1990) was elected a Fellow of the Royal Society for his journeys in Libya when he 'formulated a theory on the motions of blown sand. He also developed navigational and other equipment for desert travel when in command of the Long Range Desert Group in 1940–41.'

Above   *'We can all work hard at what we like best,' declared Marianne North (1830-90): a South African view, with Cabbage Plant.*
Below   *Emin Pasha, Governor of Equatoria, beleagured by hostile forces, continues to collect natural specimens while waiting for Stanley's rescue expedition.*

explorers' hall of fame was William Cotton Oswell who, though sometimes described as the 'Nimrod of Africa', took an intelligent interest in the country. He it was who financed Livingstone's early journeys and to a large extent managed them.

The traders

As the land opened up, the traders came in to vie with the sporting gentlemen in shooting elephants, not for fun but because the ivory provided capital for businesses being built up in the interior. One of the most enterprising of these was James Chapman (1831–72) whose ambition to carry trade to the Zambezi resulted in his pioneering what was to become a regular road to the Victoria Falls. By the 1850s southern Africa had become a land of opportunity for settlers, traders, missionaries alike, often at odds with each other and with the local people. Cape Colony, annexed by the British from the Dutch in 1806, was bounded on the north by the Orange river, and beyond that lay everyman's land. Certain names, however, do stand out from the crowd.

Francis Galton and Charles Andersson

In August 1850 there landed at Walvis Bay on the coast of south-west Africa a true explorer with nothing to gain but a season's amusement and

perhaps a little fame. Francis Galton was a wealthy young man who was to make his name as an amateur scientist and inventor in that heyday of Victorian intellectual life which saw so much vigorous work on the part of the learned societies in Britain; Galton served for many years as Honorary Secretary to the Royal Geographical. He had in mind to follow Livingstone's trail to Lake Ngami but finding the road north from the Cape blocked by disputes between Boer settlers and the local Bantu, he decided on an approach from the west across what is now Namibia. His assistant Charles John Andersson, an Anglo-Swedish naturalist, was to become an expert on the birds of southern Africa.

They journeyed from the coast up the Swakop river, planning to base themselves on a string of German missions which lived under constant threat from the hostile Hottentot tribes south of the river and sometimes from the unpredictable negroid Damaras to the north. Galton arrived at Otjimbingwe to hear that the Hottentots were on the warpath, raiding missions and stealing cattle. There was no hope of successful exploration while

Galton in camp in northern Namibia: note conical tent and neatly accoutred riding ox, as recommended in Art of Travel.

HOW THEY TRAVELLED

To Lake Tanganyika in a Bath Chair is the intriguing title of a book describing how Annie Hore travelled to join her missionary husband on the Lake in the late 1880s. The wheels proved impracticable on the rough tracks of the African bush, and so she was carried as in a litter in the footsteps of Burton and Speke, baby Jack on her knee.

May French Sheldon had an equally odd device in which to travel when she tired of walking on her safari from Mombasa to Kilimanjaro in 1891 – a Palanquin (always written with a capital P). Sometimes she slept in it, with alarming results as when 'I became aware that a cold, clammy, moving object was above me, in truth on the top of my Palanquin . . . it was an enormous python, about fifteen feet long'.

Florence Baker simply rode an ox, like the men. In the tsetse-infected country in East Africa, the explorers often took horses, mules and donkeys, all of which succumbed sooner or later, as did the oxen eventually. Baker had three oxen called Beef, Steak and Suet but was obliged to re-name the first 'Bones' when the fly had done its horrid work.

Galton in south-west Africa was not afflicted with this particular plague and was entirely dependent on oxen. He

Ordeal by python! May French Sheldon was 'not ashamed to confess it was the supreme fear of my life and almost paralyzed me'.

was rather fond of his 'Ceylon' and claimed, 'Oxen are quite good leapers if you give them time.'

As Africa opened up to King Leopold's territorial ambitions, some truly fanciful ideas for transport were mooted (including the use of balloonists), but the only one put into practice was the import of four Indian elephants by a Belgian expedition to Lake Tanganyika in 1879. It was claimed that these beasts were 'easier to feed, more docile, more attentive, more sober than negroes'. Their

'docility', compared with the formidable aspect of the African elephant, certainly caused great wonder, but alas only one survived the 1300 km (800 miles) to the Lake and died there. The problem was not solved until the coming of the railways at the end of the 19th century.

such disturbance was going on in their rear, and Galton determined to tackle the powerful Hottentot chief Jan Jonker Afrikaner and force him to desist.

Like Baker in Central Africa some years later, Galton had come equipped with a fancy dress in which to astonish the locals: 'I had packed my red hunting coat, jackboots, and cords and rode in my hunting cap; it was a costume unknown in these parts and would, I expected, aid in producing the effect I desired . . . even Ceylon (my ox) caught the excitement and snuffled like a warhorse.' They charged right up to Jonker sitting at the door of his hut – pulled up short and – as Galton puts it – 'Conceive the effect!' Conference with Jonker and other chiefs followed and, by dint of threats of vengeance on the part of the Cape Colony government (and partly no doubt owing to Galton's strong personality and extraordinary appearance), Jonker and his marauding friends were induced to promise to keep the peace – an undertaking which lasted out Galton's time.

They did not achieve Lake Ngami after all. Instead they made their way north into hitherto unknown Ovamboland but were thwarted through lack of a guide from reaching the Cunene river and perhaps crossing into Angola. They travelled in the traditional south African style, in two ox wagons accompanied by herds of sheep to supply meat, and a number of oxen both as alternative teams and for slaughter. Much of the experience Galton acquired on the journey was incorporated in his *Art of Travel*, the handbook for explorers which ran into eight editions before the end of the 19th century.

Galton returned to England in January 1852 but Andersson stayed on to make a career for himself in Africa as a trader, traveller and naturalist. He became a well-known figure based on Otjimbingwe where he set up a store and became deeply involved in the tribal politics of the region, as champion of the Damara people. In 1853 he succeeded in reaching Lake Ngami after a trek through Bechuanaland to the western end near where the Taoghe River enters what was then open water. He worked his way along the northern coast to the entry of the Taoghe and would have liked to press on in search of the Okavango but was prevented by local difficulties. He was to reach the Okavango on a later expedition with his eye on the even further goal of the Cunene. He died on 4 July 1867 on his last attempt to reach the Cunene. Andersson's exhaustive *Birds of Damaraland* was published after his death; unfortunately it was found too expensive to have it illustrated by Thomas Baines's magnificent coloured plates.

Thomas Baines

Thomas Baines (1820–75), the artist from King's Lynn, Norfolk, was a close friend of Andersson's and of other pioneers of the time. He came to Africa first in 1848, working for a time as a joiner. He soon developed his painting skills and is perhaps our chief witness of what southern Africa looked like in the busy middle years of the 19th century. His appointment to Livingstone's Zambezi Expedition in 1858 was a disaster since he was treated most unjustly by the great man, who never withdrew false charges made against the artist. However, Baines survived as did the splendid pictures which were the best things to come out of a mismanaged expedition. His fine painting of the Victoria Falls was done on a later visit to the Zambezi with James Chapman in 1861.

No summary of exploration in southern Africa would be complete without reference to Frederick Selous (1851–1917), listed in reference books as 'hunter, trader, explorer, naturalist, collector, pioneer, guide, settler', and awarded the RGS Founder's Medal in 1893 'in recognition of twenty years' exploration and surveys in South Africa'. He came to the country in 1871 intent on elephants, but his interests and actions extended far beyond this simple aim, to make him one of the chief agents in the creation of the Rhodesias. Selous belongs however to the age of Empire rather than to that of geographical discovery: an age dominated not by Sir Joseph Banks but by Cecil Rhodes.

THE AFTERMATH

Stanley and the Congo/Zaire

Stanley emerged from the Congo/Zaire eager to interest the British Government in the development of this huge and fertile region through which he had struggled so painfully. Rebuffed by the cautious Conservative administration of the Marquis of

Salisbury, he was more than ready to respond to the advances of King Leopold who had been quick to see in the Congo/Zaire basin the empire he sought. The International African Association had faded, but Leopold was only too glad to go it alone in Africa. In July 1879 Stanley was back at the river mouth in the service of the Belgian king, with instructions to build a railway up the side of the Falls and to launch steamers on Stanley Pool (Malebo) from where the river was navigable for 1600 km (1000 miles) upstream. Here Stanley drove his engineers and workmen at a gruelling pace for the next five years, earning his nickname of Bula Mutari, 'Breaker of Rocks'.

Leopold was only just in time, barely ahead of France in the person of Count Pierre Savorgnan de

Buffalo stampeding to the brink of the Victoria Falls; incident witnessed and recorded by Thomas Baines.

Congo, stands therefore on one side of the Pool with Kinshasa (Léopoldville) on the other.

Emin Pasha Relief Expedition

Stanley was to return to the Congo on the Emin Pasha Relief Expedition (1887–9). Egypt's short-lived empire in the southern Sudan, dreamed up by the Khedive Ismail and governed first by Sir Samuel Baker from 1869 to 1874 and then by General Gordon until 1879, had been destroyed by the Madhist uprising of 1881; Gordon was killed in Khartoum in an attempt to salvage something from the wreck and the officers he had appointed to provincial posts were all either slain or taken captive. All, that is, except the German botanist Dr Emin, who survived at Wadelai on Lake Albert and was appealing for rescue.

Stanley was chosen to lead the rescue bid and, for reasons never fully explained, chose to do so up the Congo/Zaire from the west coast rather than by the better known and shorter road from the east. The way led, after they left the river at the Aruwimi confluence, through dense, dangerous and unexplored forest in which they struggled for five months to reach open upland country which brought them at last to the western shore of Lake Albert. The difficulties and frustrations they met with there do not belong to the history of exploration; the only addition to geographical knowledge achieved was that on the homeward lap, eastward to the coast, they saw, for the first time by any traveller, the full expanse of the Ruwenzori mountains, round which they traced their way up the Semliki river to Lake Edward from where the water flows into Lake Albert.

Thus was the whole geography of the Nile sources at last laid down on the map.

EPILOGUE

The Berlin Conference, called by Bismarck and in session from November 1884 to February 1885, may be taken as marking the end of the primary exploration of Africa. Its purpose was chiefly to regulate and even to check the speed with which Europe was laying claim to Africa, but the movement had gone too far to be halted and by the end of the century journeys were being taken increasingly for political rather than geographical reasons. King Leopold on Stanley Pool, on the left bank of the Congo/Zaire, and France in the person of de Brazza on the right had set the pattern for the 'Scramble'.

Brazza, an officer in the French Navy who was, in the opinion of Mary Kingsley who covered some of the same ground, 'the greatest of all West African explorers'. De Brazza had in fact come through French Gabon and up the Ogooué in 1878 while Stanley was circumnavigating Lake Victoria, and could, by branching into the Alima river, have reached the Congo/Zaire and claimed it all for France: but when later he found his way that one stage further and came out on the right bank of the Congo/Zaire in Stanley Pool, the other man was in control of the region. Brazzaville, capital of today's

125

The ambitions and rivalries of the powers did, however, sometimes give rise to heroic exploits of the old pattern, as when France attempted to forestall Britain on the upper Nile – an episode known in history as the 'Fashoda Incident'. Captain Jean-Baptiste Marchand's traverse of the virtually unknown country of the Congo/Zaire–Nile watershed, from Libreville in the west to Fashoda on the Nile 650 km (400 miles) south of Khartoum, has the authentic epic quality. The steamer *Faidherbe* was carried in sections for part of the way, her boiler rolled along behind with the kegs of wine indispensable to a French expedition, all to be reassembled and launched on the hopeless swamp waters of the Bahr el Ghazal and Lake No. And at the end, the exhausted party was recalled in face of British opposition. Nevertheless the chief complaint of the expedition doctor seems to have been the occasional serving of '*le corned beef*' for dinner.

For the most part, however, the new drive into Africa was undertaken by the Chartered Companies. It was in the service of the African Lakes, the Imperial British East Africa, the Royal Niger and the British West Charterland Companies, that Lord Lugard (1858–1945) laid the foundations of his reputation as an African explorer and administrator.

Something of the old exploring spirit persisted; for instance, in a scientific expedition to Mount Kilimanjaro in 1884 led by Sir Harry Johnston (1858–1927), explorer, administrator and artist; and 1899 saw the first ascent of Mount Kenya, achieved by the notable academic geographer Halford Mackinder (1861–1947). During 1926–9 Colonel Robert Cheesman (1878–1962) made valuable surveys of stretches of the Blue Nile in Ethiopia, and in 1933 Wilfred Thesiger was cutting his explorer's teeth on a daring lone excursion into the Danakil territory of the same country.

An interesting feature of African travel today is the fascination that the old routes still hold. In 1968 Colonel Blashford-Snell led an ambitious venture, manned and equipped by the armed services, on the descent of the Blue Nile, which Cheesman had only surveyed on foot. The same leader with similar backing in 1974–5 followed Stanley on his passage of the Congo/Zaire on which the specially designed boats and trained crews encountered the same difficulties as had the locally built canoes manned by a hundred Zanzibari porters. In 1975 Christina Dodwell and a friend canoed down the Congo/Zaire from Bangui to Brazzaville, and as recently as 1985 the old heroes were being followed when Lorenzo and Mirella Ricciardi crossed Africa by boat in the wake of Livingstone and Stanley. A bizarre note is struck in an advertisement published in the USA in 1990 for the 'Stanley Expedition', offering to conduct 'experienced hikers' on Stanley's route to Ujiji in 1871 at a cost of $3000 plus air fare.

The deserts of northern Africa have exercised an even more potent spell than the waterways which span the continent, and exploration history is rich in the names of those who have studied this arid region or who have sought personal adventures there. The French have been closely engaged, of course, in what was until recently the site of their colonial empire; Théodore Monod received the RGS Patron's Medal for 1960 in recognition of 'the great breadth of his interests . . . geography, geology, biology, history, archaeology and mapping', and in 1955 he established what was then a record, travelling in desert conditions for 1300 km (800 miles) without water. Another name is that of Henri Lhote who uncovered the rock paintings of Tassili n'Ajjer in the 1950s. Robert Capot-Rey's *Le Sahara français* published in 1953 was one of the many studies made by him in the post-war years.

Nationalities other than the French have also found a workroom and a playground in the Sahara. Francis Rennell (later Lord Rennell of Rodd) received the Founder's Medal of the RGS in 1929 largely for his studies of the Tuareg among whom he had travelled during the 1920s; within this same decade Ahmed Hassanein Bey made a notable journey to the Kufra Oases and beyond into Darfur, and the spirited Rosita Forbes also travelled in North Africa and into the Atlas Mountains.

Today the emphasis is on scientific geography with no political axes to grind, but with less interest than in the past with 'discovery' of mountains and the courses of rivers. Geographers now are concerned with what Mary Kingsley called 'choice spots' as distinct from the 'greatness of length of the red line route of the explorer'. The fashion and the need are for the kind of expedition (or rather 'project' as such are now called) carried out by multi-disciplinary teams in cooperation with local governments and organizations.

A typical project was the one sponsored by the Royal Geographical Society during 1968–70 to a region lying within the Rift Valley in Kenya, to the south and south-west of Lake Turkana – the lake which the Hungarians Teleki von Szek and Hohnel called Rudolf for their royal patron when they foot-slogged their way there in 1887. Under the leadership of Dr Michael Gwynn, 34 scientists plus a number of university students worked for three

Lake Turkana.
1969 Geographical Magazine Trans-African Hovercraft Expedition carried out scientific survey of Lake Chad.

1974-5 Blashford-Snell's Zaire River Expedition.
1975 Dodwell travelled through North and East Africa and down Congo/Zaire by canoe.

1983 RGS Kora Research Project in northern Kenya.
1985 Ricciardi African Rainbow Equatorial Expedition crossed Africa mostly by boat.

seasons on various aspects of this little known semi-arid region. The South Turkana was the first RGS project to use a light aircraft to survey the area before the team's arrival.

The Kora Research Project, led by Dr Malcolm Coe and Richard Leakey (son of Dr L.S.B. Leakey), RGS Patron's Medallist for 1989, took place in 1983; it was concerned with providing an ecological description of the Kora National Reserve for the Wildlife Conservation and Management Department of the Kenya Government, and was a joint venture with the National Museums of Kenya.

So many names, so many projects, and still 'there are some who have no memorial', but all have contributed something to the map of Africa we know today.

WHO PAYS?

The cost of exploration has always been high and has had to be met from various sources – the sponsoring body, the Government concerned and private individuals. The African Association met the needs of modestly equipped, single travellers from its membership fees of five guineas a year – Mungo Park, for instance, was paid 7s 6d a day when in England, 10s when in Africa, while Burckhardt received 10s and £1 respectively. In its 43 years of existence the Association spent some £9000 out of an income of £13,000 on exploration.

The Royal Geographical Society, which took over in 1831, allotted a round sum to each project – a system which depended on the conscientious budgeting of each traveller. It took £3000 wheedled out of the Treasury to settle the £11,000 spent by Verney Lovett Cameron on his transit of Africa

in 1873–5, in the course of which he left a trail of IOUs behind him and on arriving at the coast, bought a quite unnecessary boat.

On the other hand, the Society could underestimate as in the case of Burton and Speke in 1856–8 who were obliged to meet a shortfall out of their own pockets. The Society was fairly safe in giving only £500 towards the Zambezi expedition in view of the Government's £5000. A new element was introduced by Stanley when he persuaded the London *Daily Telegraph* to match the *New York Herald*'s £6000 to finance his expedition of 1874–7 – the first time the British press had supported such a venture.

Today each of the large research projects raises its own funds, from companies interested in the particular

part of the world or from appropriate government-funded research councils or private charities. One of the largest sponsors of the Kora Research Project was the Otis Elevator Company and the British armed forces also gave much logistical help. Companies such as Shell, RTZ, Barclays Bank, Rothschilds, Tate & Lyle and others lodge funds each year for the Society to award to deserving smaller expeditions. In 1988, 42 expeditions, nine of them to Africa, received grants ranging from £50 to £750, not large sums but carrying the valuable guarantee of RGS approval.

Nor must private benevolence be forgotten, of which two instances are the £1000 given by James Young (originator of the paraffin industry) to Livingstone in 1865, and the generous backing of the South Turkana project by Sir Malin and Lady Sorsbie in 1968–70.

Excerpts from 19th-century accounts in the RGS archives – note how a porter on Cameron's expedition was penalized for misdemeanours.

EUROPEAN EXPANSION INTO EASTERN NORTH AMERICA

Apart from the men who led the Norse voyages, all official early European explorers of the North American coastline had one goal: the discovery of a route to China and the Indies. It mattered little whether the leader of an expedition was Columbus, Cabot, Verrazzano, Gómez, Cartier or Frobisher, it was the land of the Great Khan, or the Spice Islands or Cipangu (Japan), which beckoned and glistened like the Holy Grail. The geographical reality of a huge new land mass which blocked the way westward was an unpleasant fact that only began to be acceptable when the gold and silver of the Aztec and Inca civilizations became recognized as commercially viable alternatives to the silks and spices of the East. But it soon became apparent that there were no large quantities of gold or silver in the northeastern parts of North America.

During the decade following the invasion of Mexico by Cortés when adventurers flocked to Central America, there were only dismissive notes on maps or in descriptions of the northern shores of the continent, to the effect that 'Nothing of profit has been found here except for the fishery of cod, which is of little esteem'. Of little esteem the Newfoundland fisheries may have been to explorers and adventurers who had more exotic commerce in

A desire to reach the west coast and to find new areas for the fur trade spurred on most explorers. La Vérendrye's trader sons were the first non-Indians to see the Rocky Mountains.

La Salle went south to the Mississippi rather than west but his trading ships helped pay for his exploration.

mind, but those fisheries were an immediate magnet to men from the underendowed coasts of Europe, particularly from the smaller ports of Brittany and Portugal. A seemingly endless supply of free food awaited fishermen in Newfoundland waters, and by the 1540s profitable companies were marketing cured cod in cities as far apart as Toulouse and Seville, while green (uncured and salted) cod sold well in Rouen and Paris.

Although European dominion had been achieved over wide areas of the New World before 1600, this pattern did not apply everywhere. For instance, by the end of the first century of European contact with what is now Maritime Canada, while nearly every cove and creek of the Atlantic coast and the Gulf of St Lawrence had become known to fishermen who made annual transatlantic crossings, there had still been no successful colonization. Various commercial ventures were flourishing without any benefit from conquest or settlement. And if explorers are those who find and name 'new' places, the exploration of northeastern North America was to a great extent carried out by unsponsored fishermen and undisciplined *coureurs de bois* (trappers). Their efforts have to be recognized just as much as those of La Vérendrye, Hearne and MacKenzie, or Jolliet and La Salle.

THE FIRST HUNDRED YEARS

The first documented transatlantic voyage to have provided posterity with the name of a ship and an approximate date of the ship's arrival on the northeastern coast of North America is quite definitely that of John Cabot's *Matthew*. Exactly where Cabot landed, towards the end of June 1497, is uncertain, but according to a letter written by an English

THE SPANIARDS IN THE SOUTH-WEST AND ON THE PACIFIC COAST

Although the earliest known Spanish land expeditions on the continent of North America started from Florida (which had been discovered in 1513 during the coastal exploration of Juan Ponce de León), the most effective Spanish exploration of the continental hinterland was based on journeys north-westwards from Mexico.

In March 1539, the first viceroy of New Spain, Antonio de Mendoza, sent a French friar, Marcos de Niza, and another Franciscan, called Friar Honoratus, with a small party of mainly Indians and slaves, including a Negro named Esteban, on the earliest official exploratory mission to penetrate beyond the Gila River and the Rio Grande. Esteban was a survivor from a previous overland expedition that had started from Florida in 1528 with several hundred men under Pánfilo de Narváez, and had ended eight years later in Mexico City (via Chihuahua, Sonora and Sinaloa) with only four men, led by Alvar Núñez Cabeza de Vaca. Because of his previous experience, Esteban was sent on ahead by Fray Marcos after they had passed the Mayo River, to the north of Culiacán, and having crossed the pass between the Sonora and the San Pedro rivers, they came eventually to the country of the Zuñi Indians where Esteban was killed.

Although Fray Marcos did not stay long in the Zuñi country, he brought back to Mexico reports of the seven *pueblos* with many-storeyed houses, which seemed to confirm the exciting rumours of a rich kingdom to the north – rumours that Cabeza de Vaca's expedition had started. Mendoza and the governor of Nueva Galicia, Francisco Vásquez de Coronado, along with other keen *conquistadores*, were so intrigued by these reports, that a whole series of expeditions were spawned during the years 1539–43, some by land and some by sea.

The results of most of these exploratory journeys were already visible in 1543 on the maps of a Genoese cartographer, Battista Agnese, who was working in Venice. In 1539 and 1540, two expeditions led respectively by Francisco de Ulloa and Hernando de Alarcón had both sailed up to the head of the Gulf of California, and established the peninsularity of Baja California. Even though some later cartographers show the peninsula as an island, it is clear that Agnese understood the shape of the Gulf, which was often known as the Vermilion Sea. Familiarity not only with the Gulf but also with the Pacific coast of California grew apace with voyages of men such as Juan Rodríguez Cabrillo and Francisco de Bolaños, although it is not certain how far north these voyages went. From 1565 onwards, however, several of the Manila galleons sighted parts of the California coast on their return from the Philippines, certainly as far north as Cape Mendocino at nearly 41°.

When Cabrillo came in contact with natives on the coast at San Diego, Santa Catalina Island and Ventura, they made it clear through sign language that they were already aware that other white men were exploring the interior. It is probable that they were referring to the expedition of Coronado, who had started on his exploration of what is now New Mexico in 1540, with a band of 250 cavalrymen and several hundred Indians and servants. The expedition became dispersed, but one group, under García López de Cárdenas, reached a point on the Colorado River at the Grand Canyon (though they were quite unable to cross that barrier), while Coronado with another group wandered westwards probably as far as Kansas, encountering huge herds of bison and tribes of nomadic Indians. Coronado had opened up an enormous expanse of the south-west, and yet his expedition was considered by many to have been a failure, and it was not until Juan de Oñate, in 1598, led a very large colonizing party across the Rio Grande near El Paso that settlement began to occur in that region. By 1609, a mission and a settlement had been founded at Santa Fe which has ever since been almost continuously occupied, and for a long time it represented the northernmost area of Spanish colonization.

Unlike the fur-trading explorers in the northern half of the continent, the Spaniards who opened up the south-west during the 17th and 18th centuries were aiming at conquest and settlement, with the exception of the Franciscan friars and Jesuit fathers who had at heart the founding of missions to the Indians. Perhaps only on the west coast, among the men who led Spanish naval expeditions northwards, was there a highly professional sense of the need for exploration and mapping. There was, however, a very long gap between the early expeditions and late 18th-century exploration. More than 170 years went by before the discovery and naming of Monterey Bay which took place during Sebastián Vizcaíno's expedition (1602–3), and the naming of Cabo Blanco by Martín de Aguilar and Antonio Flores in the same year at nearly 43°, was surpassed by the much more northerly voyages of Juan Pérez in 1774, and Bruno de Heceta and Juan de la Bodega y Cuadra in 1775.

Heceta found the mouth of the Columbia River after sailing along the coast to about 49°, while Bodega y Cuadra reached the coast of Alaska at about 58°, and landed twice to take possession of the country. Although they had found no sign of Russian fur-trading stations (one of the main political reasons for these long and expensive Spanish voyages, which invariably lost many men from scurvy), nevertheless the journals, maps, and descriptions of the coastal Indians that resulted from the voyages were of considerable scientific interest. In 1779 the year after Cook had penetrated through the Bering Strait, Bodega y Cuadra in the *Favorita* and Ignacio de Arteaga in the *Princesa* also reached Alaska and possibly the Bering Sea, but the Spanish journeys of greatest interest from a scientific point of view were those of 1791 and

Paintings of remarkable totems, houses and canoes of west coast Indians, brought back by expeditions such as Malaspina's, deeply impressed Europeans.

1792, the voyage of Alessandro Malaspina and the last voyage of Bodega y Cuadra to Nootka Sound, where he and George Vancouver met and engaged in a delightful correspondence. (Vancouver had been sent to claim Nootka Sound for Britain.)

These Spanish expeditions not only brought back large catalogues and descriptions of plants and animals, but the human appeal of the scientific studies of the west coast was also enormously enhanced through brilliant sets of drawings by artists such as José Cardero and Tomás de Suría, drawings which gave a remarkably accurate idea of the life and culture of the coastal Indians. By 1792 an unfortunate side-effect of Cook's voyage, which had put the sea-otter trade into the limelight, was beginning to be felt on the coast. The Indians whom Alexander Mackenzie met in 1793 were no longer the untouched tribes that Pérez had met in canoes in 1774. However, the excellent relations of the Spanish explorers with the coastal Indians enabled a great deal of anthropological and linguistic work to be accomplished in a short period which scholars have found useful ever since, irreplaceable work that dates from the first two decades of contact with Europeans.

merchant, John Day, a few months after Cabot's return, he appears to have explored mainly between the Strait of Belle Isle, or the northern tip of Newfoundland, and the Strait of Canso, or the southern coast of Cape Breton Island.

This portion of the Atlantic seaboard of North America, a sailing distance of about 1000–1150 km (600–700 miles) which the *Matthew* covered in about a month, was the eastern rim of the region known throughout most of the 16th century as 'Terranova' or 'Les Terres Neuves'. Cabot was, of course, convinced that he had found the land of the Great Khan. However, whether or not his New Land really was part of the Great Khan's empire or part of the coast that led towards Cipangu, or whether it was simply the 'Island of Brasil' or the 'Island of the Seven Cities', a sufficiently convincing picture of the new 'londe and Iles' emerged from the various accounts of his 1497 voyage for Henry VII to believe that the New Land existed, and to reward Cabot accordingly.

Even though Cabot had brought back no spices or precious stones on his first voyage, he had seen tall trees suitable for masts and signs of human habitation such as animal snares, a hearth and a needle. Above all he and his crew had been deeply impressed by an incredible quantity of fish of the sort called stockfish, that 'in Iceland are dried in the open'. Cabot's description of these fish, so plentiful that they could be brought up in baskets weighted with a stone, soon reached Spain and Italy, and within a few years Terranova cod was having a sensational effect on the lives of many European fishermen.

Whatever illusions Cabot may have had, it is clear that practical fishermen can hardly have thought they were fishing off the shores of China or Japan. In Spain and Portugal part of the New Land was known in the early years of the 16th century as the 'Tierra de los bacallaos' and was placed on maps just to the south-west of the 'Tierra del Labrador'. It is also clear that a voyage to these new fishing grounds was not considered much more adventurous than a voyage to Ireland for Iberian mariners or a voyage to Iceland for English merchants. The extra distance of the voyage to the Codfish Land was more than compensated for by the greater profitability.

It was not long before Cabot's successful expedition had encouraged further exploratory travels particularly by inhabitants of the Azores. These voyages, some under the patronage of Henry VII and some under Portuguese auspices, gradually gave cartographers a set of place-names for the

NORTH AMERICA

Longitude West of Greenwich

coasts of the north-west Atlantic. Within a dozen years of Cabot's first voyage, the names of Gaspar and Miguel Corte Real, and that of Johan Fernandez, known as the 'Labrador' or Azorean landowner, were commemorated on maps as 'Terra Corte Regalis' or 'Tiera Nova de Cortereal', while Cabot's contribution had been almost forgotten.

It is not possible to distinguish accurately which of the Portuguese names that became part of the nomenclature of the Newfoundland coast were given, for instance, by the Corte Real brothers and which were names that became permanently attached to capes, islands and harbours because of fishermen's usage. Nevertheless, it is quite probable that religious names such as the Eleven Thousand Virgins, St Pedro, or St Iria were given by explorers, whereas the small harbours on the Avalon Peninsula between Cape Spear (Cabo de Espera) and Cape Race (Cabo Raso) were almost certainly named by Portuguese fishermen. As they found it necessary to recognize and remember the most outstanding physical characteristics of a place, such as sandy beaches, waterfalls visible from the sea, or distinctive promontories, the same names were often repeated.

Many historians, for reasons best known to themselves, have talked about the cod fishery on the Grand Banks as if it predated the onshore industry; however, the reverse is true. Discovery of a new

geographical location does not always result in immediate exploitation of the area, and even though mariners who made the North Atlantic crossing were fully aware of the Banks, this did not mean that they wanted to fish in the open Atlantic far away from supplies of wood and fresh water. Nearly all the earliest documentation for the Newfoundland fisheries refers to events that took place at fishing establishments on the coasts of Newfoundland and Labrador, and that is why there are clusters of place-names on early maps reflecting the nationalities of the fishermen. For example, the contrast between the Portuguese place-names on the east coast of the Avalon Peninsula and the Breton place-names along the north shore of the Strait of Belle Isle is certainly indicative of the role of fishermen on each of these stretches of coast.

From about 1502 to 1524 it can be said that all effective exploring and naming of the Atlantic coasts of Canada were accomplished by fishermen, but then a series of men, with royal approbation and support, started to fill in areas of the map which were still blank. Giovanni da Verrazzano, in 1524, and Esteban Gómez, in 1525, under French and Spanish auspices respectively, provided a long stretch of eastern America from Florida to Cape Breton with place-names and a reasonably accurate coastline. Both men were seeking a strait or waterway that

NORTH AMERICA: KEY TO ROUTES

(1) **John Cabot** 1497 (*approximate*). Probably sailed along the E coast of Newfoundland and Cape Breton I.

(2) **Gaspar Corte Real** 1500 (*approximate*). Probably sailed along the E coast of Newfoundland.

(3) **Miguel Corte Real** 1501 and 1502 (*approximate*). Sailed towards Greenland and down the Labrador coast and on to Nova Scotia.

(4) **Ponce de León** 1513. Sailed along the E coast of Florida to a little N of St Augustine, then doubled the southern tip of Florida and continued northwards to approximately Tampa Bay.

(5) **Verrazzano** 1524. From landfall at Cape Fear sailed N along the coast to Newfoundland.

(6) **Gómez** 1524–5. From Cuba sailed northwards along the eastern seaboard to Cape Breton I. and southern Newfoundland.

(7) **Rut** 1527. From Labrador coast landfall he sailed S, called at St John's and went on to Santo Domingo.

(8) **Narváez/De Vaca expedition** 1527–36 (*approximate*). Sailed from Santo Domingo and landed in area of Tampa Bay. Travelled overland to St Andrew Bay, sailed to the Mississippi delta area where Narváez was lost. De Vaca sailed on to Galveston Bay and travelled overland to W Mexico and Mexico City.

(9) **Cartier** 1534. Sailed to E coast of Newfoundland and explored Gulf of St Lawrence.

(10) **Cartier** 1535–6. Sailed to Gulf of St Lawrence and up St Lawrence R. to Hochelaga (Montreal).

(11) **De Soto/Moscoso expedition** 1538–43 (*approximate*). Sailed from Cuba to Tampa Bay area and wandered inland to the N and NW. After death of De Soto, Moscoso made unsuccessful attempt to reach Mexico overland but succeeded by sea via the Mississippi.

(12) **Fray Marcos and Esteban** 1539 (*approximate*). From Culiacán northwards and Esteban is said to have reached the Zuñi villages.

(13) **Ulloa** 1539–40. Sailed from Acapulco, followed coast of the Gulf of California to the Pacific Ocean and explored part of the coast of Lower California.

(14) **Coronado/Cárdenas expedition** 1540–2 (*approximate*). From Compostela to Zuñi and modern Kansas. Cárdenas reached the Grand Canyon.

(15) **Cabrillo** 1542–3. From Navidad sailed up the Californian coast to about 37°N.

(16) **Oñate** 1598–1605 (*approximate*). From Mexico City to New Mexico, Zuñi and Kansas. Crossed Arizona and descended the Colorado to the sea.

(17) **Vizcaino** 1602–3. From Acapulco sailed along the Californian coast to about 42°N.

(18) **Champlain** 1604–7. Explored and mapped coast of Nova Scotia, Bay of Fundy and mainland coast to S of Cape Cod.

(19) **Champlain** 1608–16. Made journey S from the St Lawrence to Lake Champlain, then via Ottawa R. to Lakes Huron and Ontario.

(20) **Hudson** 1609. Sailed to Manhattan and up the Hudson R.

(21) **Hudson** 1610–11. Sailed through Hudson Strait to Hudson Bay and James Bay.

(22) **James** 1631–2. Sailed through Hudson Strait and along SW coast of Hudson Bay to James Bay.

(23) **Nicollet** 1634–5. Travelled by canoe from L. Huron to L. Michigan and beyond Green Bay.

(24) **Allouez** 1665–7. Travelled by canoe from L. Huron to L. Superior and L. Nipigon.

(25) **Albanel** 1671–2. From St Lawrence R. to Lake Mistassini and James Bay.

(26) **Jolliet** 1672–3. From Lake Michigan to the Mississippi, down river nearly to confluence with the Arkansas and return via the Illinois.

(27) **La Salle** 1679–82. Sailed from L. Erie to L. Michigan, then descended the Illinois and the Mississippi to the sea.

(28) **La Salla** 1684–7. Sailed from Cuba to Gulf of Mexico, landed on Texas coast; travelled inland.

(29) **Jolliet** 1694. From Strait of Belle Isle sailed along part of Labrador coast.

(30) **La Vérendrye and his sons** 1731–43. From L. Superior to the Missouri R., Saskatchewan R. and the Dakotas.

(31) **Hearne** 1770–2. From Fort Prince of Wales to Dubawnt Lake area, Coppermine R. and return via Great Slave Lake.

(32) **Pérez** 1774. Sailed to Queen Charlotte Is and discovered Nootka Sound, Vancouver Island.

(33) **Heceta/Bodega y Cuadra expedition** 1775. Bodega y Cuadra sailed to Alaskan coast and Heceta discovered the Columbia R.

(34) **Arteaga/Bodega y Cuadra expedition** 1779. Sailed along the coast of the Gulf of Alaska.

(35) **Mackenzie** 1789 and 1792–3. From Lake Athabasca to Mackenzie R. and the Arctic Ocean; later from Lake Athabasca via the Peace R. to Queen Charlotte Sound.

(36) **Lewis and Clark** 1804–6. From St Louis ascended Missouri R. and crossed the Rocky Mts to descend Columbia R. to the sea.

(37) **Thompson** 1807–11. From N Saskatchewan R. explored extensively in Rocky Mts and descended the Columbia.

would lead to the western ocean, and Verrazzano, in hopeful mood, thought that ocean could at least be seen, probably in the region of Pamlico and Albemarle Sound in North Carolina, where a large expanse of water was sighted on the far side of a long barrier of sandbanks and islands. However, by the time they had finished their voyages, neither explorer thought there was any real break in the coastline and most navigators had begun to feel that the only hope of a passage through to the western ocean or Sea of China would be in the higher latitudes of the northern hemisphere, just as Magellan had found his strait in the higher latitudes of the southern hemisphere.

A Baffin Island mother and child (the infant is just visible beneath the mother's hood), apparently drawn by John White on Martin Frobisher's 1577 voyage.

In 1527, John Rut started out with two ships belonging to Henry VIII, the *Mary Guildford* and the *Samson*, and made a voyage which eventually took him from a point off the Labrador coast, at 53°, south to the island of Santo Domingo in the Caribbean. According to one of the Spanish witnesses who saw Rut's ship in the West Indies this English expedition, like the less documented voyage of Sebastian Cabot in 1508-9, had attempted to find a strait through to Tartary, or the kingdom of the Great Khan, by following the northern fringes of the American continent, but 'great islands of ice' had blocked their passage.

The importance of Rut's voyage lay not so much in his exploration as in the information he provided for posterity about the number of ships fishing in Newfoundland. In the 'Haven of St John' on 3 August 1527, he wrote to Henry VIII that he had found 14 ships (eleven Normans, one Breton and two Portuguese) using the harbour, while a Spanish witness reported that Rut had seen a total of about 50 Spanish, French and Portuguese ships along the coast of 'Bacallaos'. It is worth noting that no other English ships were mentioned as fishing that year; at this period they appear to have been more often engaged in capturing French ships coming back up the Channel with their cargoes of cod. Only later did English fishermen develop a strong commercial interest in the Newfoundland fisheries.

From the 1520s onwards the names are known of many French and Spanish fishing ships and of their owners and masters, as well, in several cases, as their exact destination on the coasts of the New Land. Before 1520 the majority of the 'Terranova' fishermen were Portuguese, Bretons and Normans, but gradually more and more ships from the French and Spanish Basque ports were crossing the Atlantic in the third and fourth decades of the century, and not all these ships were doing so for the same reasons. Most fishermen were bound for the cod-fishing and normally searched out harbours with wide gravel beaches where the fish could be cured and dried, but a few ships from the Basque ports were not primarily cod-fishing . . . instead they went whaling. These large Basque ships (sometimes partially financed by merchants from cities outside the Basque provinces such as Bordeaux and Burgos) were bound for the Grand Bay through which immense numbers of right whales (*Eubalaena glacialis*) and bowheads (*Balaena mysticetis*) migrated annually.

The Strait of Belle Isle had become known as the Grand Bay by 1534 when Jacques Cartier, from St

Malo in Brittany, sailed through the strait and into what is now known as the Gulf of the St Lawrence. He was the first recorded explorer to leave an account of this area but he was definitely not the first man to name the harbours in the Grand Bay. On the southern shore of Labrador, between Chateau Bay and the St Paul River, he mentions eight names which were already in existence when he arrived. His great contribution to the geographical understanding of the North American continent did not begin until he was just to the west of the fishing station at the mouth of the St Paul River, then known as Brest.

At least three of the southern Labrador names were transferred toponyms from the west coast of Brittany: Brest, Blanc Sablon and Crozon (which later became Gradun and is now called Middle Bay). Names from other parts of Brittany, familiar to fishermen, were also given to islands on the northern approaches to the incredible waterway which would allow transatlantic ships to sail nearly 1450 km (900 miles) south-westwards into the land that Cartier called New France. However, in the 1530s and 1540s, neither cod-fishermen nor whalers had any desire to penetrate far up this waterway since their best fishing grounds were close to the east coast. Cartier's names given to locations on the St Lawrence River and the Gulf, therefore remained unchallenged for over 40 years, until fishermen and traders became interested in the new regions.

At the time of Cartier's second voyage, in 1535, no other explorer in North or South America had followed a waterway so far into the interior of a continental land mass. His Spanish contemporaries – men like Alvar Núñez Cabeza de Vaca and Hernando de Soto – were making valiant attempts to penetrate into what is now the southern part of the United States, but the usefulness of the Mississippi as a waterway was not appreciated as rapidly as that of the St Lawrence (or the River of Canada as it was then called). Francisco de Orellana's epic journey in 1540–1, following the Amazon from its headwaters to its mouth, was the next geographically brilliant exploit that revolutionized cartography in a similar manner to Cartier's voyages, but in neither case did the cartographic revolution immediately encourage European usage of the newly revealed areas.

In 1542, the same year that Cartier returned to France after his last voyage, Jean Rotz had already depicted on one of the plates of his atlas, the great gulf that Cartier had circumnavigated, and in the atlas of Guillaume Brouscon the following year both a powerful St Lawrence River and a clear-cut

The French colony in northern Florida under Jean Ribault and René de Laudonnière came to a tragic end in 1565, destroyed by the Spaniards.

Saguenay can be seen. But there was no serious development on maps of this region until, in the 1580s, Cartier's place-names began to disappear. The island of Natiscot (now Anticosti), for example, took the place of Cartier's 'l'isle de l'Assomption', and Gaspé replaced Cartier's 'Honguedo'. By the end of the 16th century very few of Cartier's place-names remained in use, simply because the fishermen and traders who started moving into the Gulf and estuary of the St Lawrence in the 1580s had never heard of his names, and had begun to use either those they learned from the indigenous inhabitants or their own new names. In most cases those are the names that are still in use today.

Along the north shore of the Gulf of St Lawrence a new type of exploration was taking place during the last two decades of the century: a search for suitable places for new whaling establishments and the setting up of fur trading contacts with various groups of Indians. Although there are references to trade between fishermen and Indians as early as the 1530s, the most prosperous industry in that region through the middle years of the century was without question the whale oil industry.

That the Basques concentrated their major whaling activities, from about 1545 to 1585, on the stretch of Labrador coast between Cape Charles and the St Paul River is evident from the many lawsuits and notarial documents concerning this enterprise. These show that the fishermen's exploratory movements west into the Gulf do not appear to have taken place until after three events had occurred: the

1583 Gilbert took possession of Newfoundland for Elizabeth I.
1584 Raleigh unsuccessfully tried to establish colony, which was named Virginia

by Elizabeth I.
1596-1605 Spaniard Oñate colonized New Mexico.
1602 Gosnold's arrival in Massachusetts Bay

marked the beginning of English exploration on the east coast.
1602-3 Vizcaíno discovered harbour of Monterey and mapped coast to about 42°N.

taking possession of Newfoundland in the name of Elizabeth I by Sir Humphrey Gilbert in 1583; the fur trading journeys up the St Lawrence River of Cartier's nephews, particularly Jacques Noël who reawakened interest in the area; and the discovery of the lucrative walrus hunt on the Magdalen Islands.

Even though Sir Humphrey Gilbert did not, in fact, carry out any exploration himself, he was one of the fervent promulgators of a more active attitude towards the search for a north-west passage as his *Discourse of a discoverie for a new passage to Cataia* shows. He was also extraordinarily keen on doing as much damage as possible to Spanish shipping, particularly to Basque fishing ships, as reports of the enormous financial success of the whaling voyages had provoked considerable jealousy among English merchants.

John Rotz drew Newfoundland as a fanciful archipelago, but his 1542 map reflects Cartier's 1534 and 1535 voyages, showing the southern entrance to the Gulf.

After some rather unsuccessful attempts at transatlantic expeditions, Gilbert's 1583 voyage was a triumph insofar as he definitely established English sovereignty over a part of the east coast of Newfoundland, and laid the foundations for the English colonies there in the early 17th century. His claims also gave a form of legitimacy to English pirates who not only made life difficult for Portuguese and Basque fishermen but sometimes molested other English ships. It is not surprising that many French and Spanish Basque fishermen at this point began to explore the possibilities of the Gulf, which offered an escape from continuous aggression.

It was more than coincidence that the 1590s saw the opening up of the combined fishing and fur trade at Gaspé in the western part of the Gulf and, following the lead of Jacques Noël, many fishermen were trading upriver at Tadoussac by the turn of the century. Some Basque whalers were moving westwards along the north shore to Mingan and Sept Îles,

1603 Champlain voyaged up the St Lawrence River.
1604-5 Oñate crossed Arizona and followed Colorado River to its mouth.

1604-7 Champlain examined the coast of Nova Scotia, the Bay of Fundy and the mainland coast beyond Cape Cod.
1607 Smith founded Jamestown, Virginia.

1608-9 Champlain travelled the St Lawrence again. Founded city of Quebec. Explored Richelieu River to Lake Champlain.

where the cold Labrador current was still strong enough to attract large whales, while others were even whaling as far up as the mouth of the Saguenay, and a few men like François Gravé du Pont were occasionally trading well to the west of Quebec. It was with Gravé du Pont, on board the *Bonne-Renommée*, a trading ship, that Samuel de Champlain arrived at Tadoussac on 24 May 1603, an event which launched one of the most important periods of exploration in the history of North America. It was an era of private enterprise, which, unlike Cartier's voyages, received very little support from the Crown.

FROM CHAMPLAIN TO LA SALLE, 1603-82

Between the moment that Champlain stepped ashore at Tadoussac and the moment 80 years later when La Salle's expedition reached the mouth of the Mississippi, nearly all the waterways draining

During Raleigh's Virginia voyages John White drew many maps and scenes of Indian life, including this palisaded village.

northwards into Hudson Bay, south-westwards into the Mississippi or eastwards from Lake Superior had become known and named through a precarious form of collaboration established mainly by merchants and missionaries with men whom they called 'Savages'. Many priests and traders died at the hands of the men whose territory was being explored, but the mortality rate soon soared among the indigenous people most closely affected by the commercial rivalries and epidemic diseases that the Europeans had brought with them. The damage to Indian culture was inevitable, and yet some Europeans admired the 'Savages' and made genuine attempts at friendship with them.

One of the many remarkable aspects of Champlain's character was the fact that he seems to have been quite unafraid of committing himself to long journeys with his Algonquin or Huron allies, either alone or with only one or two French companions. At a slightly later date there was no shortage of missionaries or *coureurs de bois* who followed his example, but in 1603 and in 1608–9, during his second visit to the St Lawrence Valley, this type of trust and friendship between Indians and Europeans was still unusual. Although his first visit in 1603 did no more than consolidate and slightly enlarge the previous explorations of Cartier and a few fur traders up the St Lawrence to the Lachine Rapids, or

WINTERINGS

Apart from the Norse voyagers at l'Anse-aux-Meadows (at the south-eastern end of the Strait of Belle Isle), Jacques Cartier and his men are the first Europeans known to have wintered in the northern part of the continent, where ice and snow grip the land for the better part of five months. Champlain, in fact, declared that 'there are *six months* of winter in this country', and both he and Cartier saw many of their men die during that lengthy period. However, the main cause of death among wintering parties was not the extreme cold, but a lack of vitamin C in the diet which resulted in scurvy.

After Cartier had already lost 25 out of 110 men to scurvy on his 1535–6 voyage, and only three or four of the crew were still healthy, he learned from the Indians near his fort at Quebec of a miraculous cure: a drink made from the bark of an evergreen tree which had an almost instantaneous effect on the sick men. Unfortunately the effectiveness of this cure did not become widely known among 16th-century sailors or explorers, and scurvy continued to be a curse even when men like Champlain understood the causes of the disease and blamed it on salted provisions, or when the Jesuit Father, Pierre Biard, noted that if men did not mope in their cabins but spent their time hunting or in other outdoor occupations, they were better able to resist the disease.

Between Cartier's last wintering in Canada in 1541–2 and Champlain's first in 1604–5 on the Sainte Croix River near the Bay of Fundy, the very few other recorded winterings are nearly all for Basque whalers in southern Labrador. Although cod-fishermen did not remain on the coast late enough in the season for their ships to become iced into harbours, the whalers often stayed in the Strait of Belle Isle until January, and if they were locked in by the ice they suffered dire consequences. Of the two earliest known wills written in Canada, one was written for a dying Basque on Christmas Eve 1584, by the ship's surgeon, Joan de Arriaga, who reported that he himself arrived back in Spain after that voyage in very ill condition, while the first mention of a mutiny on a Basque whaling ship was in 1577 when the men refused to stay for the late whaling season, as the mortality rate had been unusually high the previous winter.

The Basques appear to have lived mainly in their ships during the winter, although a few may have slept in the cooper's workshops which had solid, tiled roofs. Explorers and fur traders, however, nearly all built log or wooden houses to shelter themselves before the onset of winter. These not only kept out the worst of the cold but also afforded, in theory, a little protection against marauding Indians. The ironic side of the first wintering at Tadoussac, 1600–1, must, however, be pointed out. When the fur trader, Captain Pierre Chauvin de Tonnetuit left 16 men in a newly built wooden house (7.25 x 6 metres/24 x 18ft), surrounded by a ditch and a protective screen of hurdles, the wintering party soon ran out of food, and half-way through the winter left their house and went to live with the Indians, who very kindly fed and looked after them. The men were so ill-adjusted to coping with Canadian winters that it is amazing any survived; as Champlain said, they had learned the difference between 'La France et Tadoussac'.

Perhaps one of the most successful winterings was that of Captain Thomas James because, in spite of severe hardships, he only lost two of his crew through scurvy. Since his story is typical of the difficulties encountered by many explorers, it is worth looking at his account of how he spent the winter at Charlton Island in James Bay:

When I first resolved to build a house, I chose the most warmest and convenientest place, and the neerest the Ship withall. It was amongst a tuft of thicke trees, vnder a South banke, about a flight-shote from the Seas side. True it is that at that time we could not digge into the ground to make vs a hole or Cave in the earth . . . because we found water within 2 foote digging; and, therefore, that project fail'd. It was a white light sand, so that we could by no meanes make vp a mud-wall. As for stones, there were none neere vs, which, moreover, were all now covered with snow. We had no boords for such a purpose, and, therefore, we must doe the best we could with such materials as we had about vs.

The house was square, about 20 foote every way; as much, namely, as our maynecourse [mainsail] could well cover. First, we drove strong stakes into the earth round about, which we wattled with boughes, as thick as might be, beating them down very close. This, our first worke, was six foote high on both sides, but, at the ends, almost vp to the very top. There we left two holes for the light to come in at; and the same way the smoke did vent out also . . . We left a little low doore to creepe into, and a portall before that, made with piles of wood, that the wind might not blow into it.

They made bedsteads, which they filled with boughs, and 'Canopies and Curtaines' with the small sails and canvas coverings, and they insulated the outside of their house with a 2-metre (6-ft) depth of trees and bushes. Long before Christmas their house was almost entirely covered with snow. Icicles hung on the inner walls and their beds were covered with hoar frost. The casks of vinegar, oil and wine were all frozen solid and the cook had an incredible problem with soaking and rinsing the salt meat. As James said of their brass cauldron, the 'side which was next the fire was very warme, and the other side an

André Thevet wrote unreliable descriptions of Canada between 1558 and 1586. Above Indians on peculiar snowshoes attack a displaced boar.

inch frozen'. But somehow they went out every day for food and water and other necessities, and survived through the careful ministrations of the ship's surgeon until May, when two men died – but others recovered slowly by eating the vetches and scurvy grass that began 'to appeare out of the ground'.

Then to their astonishment, as the much longed for warm weather finally arrived, a new plague came upon them, the plague that tortured so many Canadian explorers: the blackflies. James tore an old flag into pieces and his crew made bags of it to protect their heads, but as James said there was no fortification against the flies:

They would find wayes and means to sting us, that our faces were swolne hard out in pumples, which would so itch and smart that we must needs rubbe and teare them. And these flyes, indeed, were more tormenting to vs than all the cold we had heretofore endured.

The northern part of North America was not an easy region to explore.

down the Richelieu towards the lake that he would find and name 'Lake Champlain' in 1609, it set the tone for his future explorations when information gathered from the Indians led him on to an extraordinary understanding of the general shape of eastern North America.

By 24 August 1603, when Champlain set out for France, he had already learned of the existence of two of the Great Lakes (Lake Ontario and Lake Erie with Niagara Falls between them) and a third which with a little optimism might really have been the 'South Sea', the name the Spaniards had given the Pacific. He had also been correctly informed that the Richelieu led southwards via Lake Champlain and Lake George towards the Hudson River and the coast of Florida, while from a description of the Saguenay basin he had deduced the existence of Hudson's still undiscovered bay. Within a dozen years almost all these geographic suppositions had been confirmed, and Champlain had himself explored up the Ottawa River and, via Lake Nipissing, had arrived at Georgian Bay on the north-eastern side of Lake Huron by the end of July 1615. He found, of course, that Lake Huron was not the salt sea. He named it 'La Mer Douce', and was perfectly aware that there was another Great Lake still further to the north-west (Lake Superior) which flowed into 'La Mer Douce' through what he called the 'Sault de Gaston', but which was soon better known as Sault Ste Marie.

Champlain's drawing shows Pierre Chauvin's house at Tadoussac where the first European wintering on the Saguenay took place in 1600.

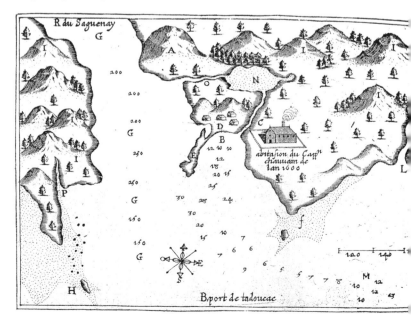

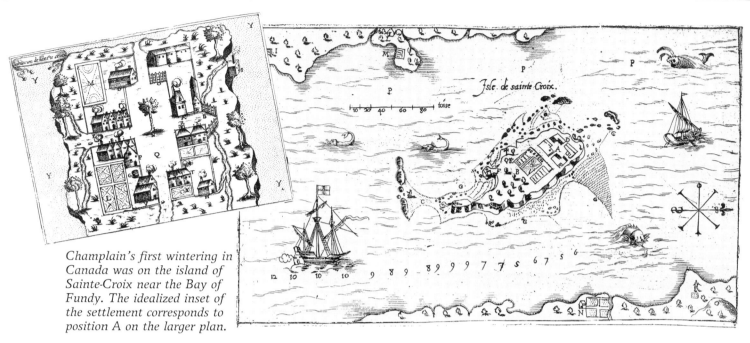

Champlain's first wintering in Canada was on the island of Sainte-Croix near the Bay of Fundy. The idealized inset of the settlement corresponds to position A on the larger plan.

Although Champlain's maps of 1616 and 1632 are not perfect by 20th-century standards (they reduce, for instance, Lake Erie to a waterway with two small connected lakes), nevertheless they would have given anyone who wanted to find his way overland to Hudson Bay, or southwards to the Susquehanna, some idea of possible routes and distances which no other cartographer at that time was capable of providing. During the first third of the 17th century most additions and changes to the cartography of north-eastern America were made through coastal exploration, and Champlain was the only explorer to alter the mapping of the interior radically as well as adding to European knowledge of the Atlantic coast. From 1604 to 1607, while living for three winters on the 'Baye Françoise' (Bay of Fundy), first on the island of Sainte-Croix and later at Port-Royal, he explored and then mapped with careful detail the whole of the coast from Cape Breton to just south of Cape Cod, a distance of at least 600 km (375 miles).

While Verrazzano and Gómez had, as a result of their voyages, been able to give cartographers a general overview of what was to become known as the New England coast, and important features such as Cape Cod and the Penobscot River were depicted on many maps during the second half of the 16th century, no explorer before Champlain had drawn large-scale maps of specific harbours either on that coast or on the coasts of Nova Scotia and New Brunswick. Further south, however, both the disastrous French colony in Florida and the first Virginia colony had inspired considerable exploration and mapping. From 1607 onwards the

founding of new English colonies (beginning with Jamestown near the mouth of Chesapeake Bay and the short-lived Maine colony at the mouth of the Kennebec) stimulated more and more interest in the hinterland among English settlers, many of whom still believed that the other side of the continent was not too far away.

It was not only the English and the French, however, who were immensely desirous of finding a new route or a new strait that would lead to the 'South Sea' and Cathay. The Dutch had been searching for a route to Cathay through a north-east passage, to the north of Norway, and in 1609 the Dutch East India Company employed an experienced English navigator, Henry Hudson, to continue a search in a north-easterly direction. But Hudson's small ship, the *Half Moon*, met with so much ice that the crew threatened to mutiny unless Hudson changed the direction of his search. Thus with a total change of plan, but a similar objective, Hudson found himself on 11 September 1609, alongside the island of Manhattan, which would soon become the first Dutch fur-trading post in North America, and eventually the site of New York City.

In the late summer of 1609 Hudson and Champlain could have almost met. Champlain with his Huron and Algonquin allies was engaged in an attack on an Iroquois encampment near the headwaters of the Hudson River, while a few weeks later Hudson had sailed up the same river far enough to realize that it was not the desired strait leading to Cathay. Both explorers were no doubt unaware that their discoveries were helping to fuel the intense rivalries that arose

the upper Colorado River amongst the
Jumano Indians.
1634-5 Nicollet, the first European to
explore the American Mid-West, travelled

from Lake Huron to Lake Michigan.
1659-60 Groseilliers and Radisson explored
Lake Michigan, Lake Superior and
Wisconsin. Sighted Missouri.

1665-85 Father Allouez travelled over
4750 km (3000 miles) in Wisconsin and the
Great Lakes region as a missionary.

from the fur trade, and which in turn led to the
appalling decimation of many of the Indian tribes
who provided the furs for European markets. But
both men could have realized that the commercial
appeal of fur would handsomely compensate for
their inability to find a waterway across the continent.

Hudson made one more fatal attempt in 1610 to
look for a waterway that would lead westwards from
the strait that John Davis had found 35 years earlier.
But although Hudson, in his *Discovery*, opened up –
as Cartier had done – a vast interior sea which, with
its tributary rivers, would take traders from Europe
half-way across the continent, his lack of leadership
qualities led to a tragic ending for the expedition.
During the wintering in James Bay, Hudson demoted
Robert Bylot who was his second-in-command and
the only other man aboard apart from Hudson with
the capacity to navigate the ship safely on the return
journey. This ill-considered act played directly into
the hands of the mutinous members of the crew.
They persuaded Bylot to remain on their side when
the decision was made to abandon Hudson in a
small boat, with the sick and with the loyal members
of the ship's company.

It was Bylot who not only brought back the eight
survivors but also took part in the subsequent
expeditions of Sir Thomas Button (1612-3), of
William Gibbons (1614), and of William Baffin
(1615 and 1616). These voyages received their main
financial support from the 'Company of the
Merchants of London, Discoverers of the North-West
Passage' (or North-West Company), which was given
a royal charter in 1612. None of these expeditions
nor those sponsored by Christian IV of Denmark,
between 1605 (under the Scottish captain, John
Cunningham, with two other English captains,
James Hall and John Knight) and 1619–20 (when
Jens Munk wintered in the estuary of the Churchill
River), resulted in the discovery of any North-West
Passage either at the head of Baffin Bay or out of
Hudson Bay. And yet the hope lingered on in the
minds of other navigators such as Luke Foxe (1631)
and Thomas James (1631–2) that somewhere a
passage existed, in spite of the facetious remark that
Foxe said he had made to James when they met in
the south-west corner of Hudson Bay: 'You are out of
the way to Japon, for this is not it.'

After the appalling winter that James and his crew
spent on Charlton Island near the mouth of the
Rupert River and after his return to England, the
journal of his voyage was published – *The Dangerous
Voyage of Capt. Thomas James, In his intended
Discovery of a North West Passage into the South Sea.*

In it he had come to the very sensible conclusion
that even if there were a North-West Passage, it
would have to be at a latitude of at least 66°, and
that as 'there is much Land to the Westward . . .
this Streight must be very long and the Weather so
cold, that it will not be durable.' Moreover, in
August and September the wind is inclined to be
contrary so progress would be slow – 'neither can any
great Ships, which are fit for carrying of Merchandize
endure the Ice, and other Inconveniencies, without
extraordinary Danger.' James insisted that it would
be quicker to sail a 1000 leagues (about 4750 km,
3000 miles) southwards and round the Cape of Good
Hope than to attempt 100 leagues (about 475 km,
300 miles) in Arctic seas, and that 'in Navigation,
the farthest Way about' was often the safest and the
best.

The negative reports of Foxe and James as to the
feasibility of a North-West Passage so discouraged the

*At the south-eastern end of Hudson Bay, James Bay was
named after this valiant captain who brought most of his
crew safely through a hard wintering.*

An imaginative view of Quebec City, attacked but not captured by William Phips in 1690.

London and Bristol merchants who had backed these expeditions that no more funds were forthcoming for three decades. Then, the next series of Hudson Bay voyages had an entirely different purpose, the fur trade.

Champlain arrived back in New France in 1633, the year that James published his book, after an enforced absence of four years, because of the capture of Quebec by the Kirke brothers. When Champlain had founded Quebec in 1608, there had been very little competition for the fur trade from merchants who were not of French origin, but at the time when the Kirke brothers had to return Quebec to the French, there was not only considerable interest on the part of English merchants and colonists but also a growing rivalry on the part of the Dutch. Champlain and his associates recognized the importance of keeping the northern routes free from interference so that the fur did not get diverted to New England or 'New Netherland', and for the next century and a half the history of exploration in North America was, to a great degree, inextricably entangled with the history of the fur trade.

Champlain had always employed young men like Etienne Brûlé, Nicolas Marsolet de Saint-Aignan and Jean Nicollet de Belleborne as interpreters after they had spent several years living with Algonquin or Huron tribes, and these tough, capable *coureurs de bois* helped to spread the French trading network over an ever-growing area. In 1634 Nicollet was sent on a voyage of exploration to the region south and west of Lake Huron, far beyond Champlain's own most westward point, in order to make peace among the warring tribes on the western shores of Lake Michigan and to persuade them to be allies of New France. Passing near the future site of Fort Michilimackinac, he explored southwards to the end of Green Bay ('Baye de Puants') and along the Fox River in the hope of finding a water route to the sea. Even though he failed to reach the Wisconsin or the Mississippi, he learned of their existence and could certainly claim to have been the first European to penetrate what is now the American Mid-West.

With an imaginatively theatrical touch, Nicollet had taken on this arduous voyage a long robe made of Chinese damask, embroidered with flowers and multi-coloured birds. When he appeared among the Winnebagoes in this extraordinary attire, it is not surprising that they were alarmed. Apparently taking him for a god, they willingly promised to hold a meeting of four or five thousand men from the surrounding tribes, a meeting which concluded in a peaceful agreement.

Champlain died on Christmas Day 1635, a few months after Nicollet's return to Quebec. The dream of finding a route to 'La Chine' had not been fulfilled in his lifetime but it must have given the old explorer immense satisfaction to know that a new generation was travelling and living with the Indians as he had done.

The *coureurs de bois*, however, were not the only Frenchmen who were in close touch with the Indians and who had made a major contribution to the exploration of the continent. Missionaries were also gradually fulfilling the aims to which Champlain had always been dedicated. The work of the Recollet fathers (a branch of the Franciscan order), four of whom had arrived in Canada in 1615, started with the founding of a mission to the Hurons at Carhagouha, on the south-eastern side of Georgian Bay. There the first mass in central Canada was celebrated by Father Joseph Le Caron, who, apart from exploring locally, also accompanied Champlain on a visit to the Petun Indians in 1616.

It is evident that evangelization would have been unsuccessful without an eloquent command of one

1673 Needham and Arthur discovered the Tennessee. Arthur travelled with Indians to West Florida and South Carolina.
1679-82 La Salle sailed down the Mississippi to Gulf of Mexico. Took possession of Louisiana for France.
1687-1706 Kino made 50 or more overland expeditions to establish missions in Arizona.
1691-2 Kelsey explored the Canadian Plains to the west of Hudson Bay. No one else did so for another 60 years.

or more Indian languages, and most of the missionaries acquired remarkable proficiency wherever they were sent. It was, for instance, the Fathers Le Caron and Nicholas Viel who first compiled a dictionary of the Huron language, while the Fathers Gabriel Sagard and Christien Le Clercq wrote in great detail about the customs and behaviour of the Indians. Le Clercq's major work was among the Micmac of the Gaspé region and the area that is now New Brunswick, as his *Nouvelle Relation de la Gaspésie* reveals. Similarly the title of Sagard's first book, published in Paris in 1632, shows where his main interest lay: *Le grand voyage au pays des Hurons, situé en l'Amérique vers la Mer douce, ès derniers confins de la Nouvelle-France, dite Canada . . . Avec un dictionnaire de la langue huronne, pour la commodité de ceux qui ont à voyager dans le pays, et n'ont l'intelligence d'icelle langue.*

Sagard's books cover the first period of exploration and evangelization by the Recollets in central Canada, from 1615 to 1629, while Le Clercq's volumes belong to the period when the Recollets returned to Canada after 1669. During the major part of those four decades, when the Recollets were absent, it was the Jesuits who bore the brunt of both Indian reaction to the devastation caused by epidemics and the Iroquois destruction of the Huron confederation. The epidemics had affected the Hurons to a much greater extent than the Iroquois because the former were in considerably closer contact with their French trading partners and with the missions than were the latter with the English and Dutch colonists. It is ironic that it was precisely this close relationship that the French had built up which led the Hurons to blame the epidemics on the missions and allowed their shamans to foment a fierce distrust of the new religion.

Evangelization, exploration and trade all suffered from 1649, as missionaries and Hurons alike had to flee from the Iroquois massacres in Huronia, until about 1660 when the situation began to change. However, during the latter half of that decade the exploits of Médard Chouart des Groseilliers and his brother-in-law, Pierre-Esprit Radisson, opened up new trade routes out of range of Iroquois attacks. Between the autumn of 1659 and the summer of 1660 these two redoubtable men explored along the southern shore of Lake Superior, spending the winter at a small lake just beyond the western extremity of Lake Superior, and then six weeks in early spring with the Sioux Indians. Radisson claimed that he had also made a rapid journey from the northern shore of Lake Superior up to James Bay, but he may have made this claim in order to persuade either James II or some London merchants to provide finance for a trading expedition to Hudson Bay by sea.

When Groseilliers and Radisson arrived at Montreal in canoes laden with furs, it was obvious to local merchants that the western voyage was financially viable again, but it was the Jesuits who were perhaps most delighted with the information they received from the *voyageurs*. That very autumn Father René Ménard joined a group of Ottawa Indians who were returning to the west with five French traders. He was the first known priest to visit the Lake Superior Indians, and he founded a mission half-way along the southern shore at a place that he called Chassahamigan (Keweenaw Bay, Michigan). Unfortunately he was lost in the woods in August of the following year, and it was not until 1665 that Father Claude Allouez was able to continue the work that Ménard had begun.

The mission that Allouez started was even further west at Chequamegon Bay, and from there he not only established other missionary posts in the interior of what is now the state of Wisconsin but also voyaged across Lake Superior and up-river to Lake Nipigon. During his 24 years as a missionary he is said to have covered more than 4750 km (3000 miles) of the Great Lakes region and to have been in contact with 23 different Indian nations. On 4 June 1671, when Simon-François Daumont de Saint-Lusson took possession at Sault Ste Marie of all the territory that lay between the North, West and South Seas in the name of Louis XIV, it was Father Allouez who made the official harangue to the members of the 14 nations gathered for the ceremony.

The Intendant of New France, Jean Talon, had sent Saint-Lusson to take possession of the western territories mainly because there had been a sudden surge in commercial competition on the part of English merchants. Groseilliers and Radisson had been so enraged by the behaviour of the governor, Pierre Voyer d'Argenson, who had embargoed their furs when they returned from their voyage in 1660, that over the next few years they had encouraged merchants in New England and in London to take part in joint fur-trading ventures by sea to Hudson Bay. In 1688 the first English post was established at Fort Charles, and on 2 May 1670 the Hudson's Bay Company received its charter.

Until the founding of the Hudson's Bay Company it can be said that nearly all exploration in New France had been undertaken as private enterprise by traders or missionaries, without any official backing

THE GUN, IRON IMPLEMENTS AND THE STEELTRAP

There is no doubt that the history of European exploration in North America would have been very different if Europeans had not had guns at their disposal. Indeed one of the reasons that the Norse settlements were not maintained may well have been that, without superior fire-power, neither the Skraelings nor any other unwelcome visitors could be kept at bay. But although guns gave Europeans an initial advantage, once guns and ammunition had become items of trade, and after French, English and Dutch traders had encouraged Indians to use fire-arms against their rivals, the situation changed fairly rapidly.

The shock of a first encounter with bullets and gunpowder was devastating for any native of the American continents. The earliest known event of this kind in Canada took place on the northern shore of the Baie des Chaleurs. In July 1534, Cartier and his men felt so threatened by the over-enthusiastic approach of 40 or 50 Indian canoes, some of which had surrounded one of Cartier's long boats, that two small cannon were fired from his vessel to scare off the canoes. Since the shots were fired over their heads no Indians were hurt, but 'they made a marvellously loud noise' as they retreated, and when two more missiles were fired at the more persistent canoes whose owners had returned to investigate the men responsible for the new phenomena, the Indians were 'so astonished that they took to flight'.

It was Champlain, however, in 1609 and 1610, who vividly described the effect that three or four Europeans with guns could have on a group of 200 or so Indians when those guns were put to serious use. When his Montagnais and Huron allies went on an expedition against the Iroquois who lived to the south of Lake Champlain in the present states of New York and Vermont, Champlain and two other Frenchmen were used like a secret weapon. After a night of singing and dancing, the Iroquois advanced slowly on the allies 'with gravity and assurance', led by three plumed chiefs. As the allied ranks opened to reveal Champlain and his arquebus, the Iroquois halted to gaze at him, and he at them, but before they could draw their bows the arquebus had been fired and two of the plumed chiefs lay dead while a third man was mortally wounded. The arquebus had been loaded with four pieces of shot, and during the reloading one of Champlain's companions fired another shot from within the woods which so unnerved the Iroquois that they fled.

Champlain's arquebus winning the battle against the Iroquois. The canoes in the foreground are barely more accurate than the palm trees in the background.

The entire population of a beaver lodge being destroyed by Indians with guns, an eloquent example of ecologically unsound practices.

A similar event happened the following year when the allies attacked an Iroquois fort, but it was just a question of time before the Iroquois themselves had acquired guns and were using them to full advantage. Thereafter, it was only the most distant tribes, out of reach of the normal fur trade network, who were unaware of the power of the gun, and Samuel Hearne gives a heart-rending account of a Chipewyan Indian attack in 1772 on the Copper Eskimo who may have been some of the last North Americans to be quite ignorant of the damage that a gun could do.

After the butchering of an entire Inuit encampment on one side of the Coppermine River, the Chipewyans turned their attention to another unfortunate camp, as Hearne relates:

The poor Esquimaux on the opposite shore . . . did not attempt to abandon their tents; and they were so unacquainted with the nature of fire arms, that when the bullets struck the ground, they ran in crowds to see what was sent them, and seemed anxious to examine all the pieces of lead which they found flattened against the rocks. At length one of the Esquimaux men was shot in the calf of the leg, which put them in great confusion. They all immediately embarked in their little canoes, and paddled to a shoal in the middle of the river, which being somewhat more than a gunshot from any part of the shore, put them out of reach of our barbarians.

Guns were not, however, the only arms the fur trade was able to provide. Stone- and flint-tipped weapons were cheerfully cast aside when iron items became available. Since ammunition for guns was not always in regular supply, some of the western tribes, such as the Mandans who lived along the banks of the Missouri in what is now North Dakota, 'appear to have adopted the Spear as a favourite weapon'. When David Thompson was surveying in that region he noted that 'Guns were few in proportion to the number of Men'; so the Mandans made spears, each with 'a handle of about eight feet in length, headed with a flat iron bayonet of nine to ten inches in length . . . from the point regularly enlarging to four inches in width, both

sides sharp edged . . . a formidable weapon in the hands of a resolute man'.

As well as spears, iron arrow heads, axes and knives were all much in demand, because, as Thompson remarked: 'Without iron man is weak, very weak, but armed with Iron, he becomes the Lord of the Earth,' and he then goes on to explain that iron and guns also turn a man into the Destroyer. 'Thus armed the houses of the Beavers were pierced through, the Dams cut through, and the water of the ponds lowered, or wholly run off, and the houses of the Beaver and their Burrows laid dry, by which means they became an easy prey to the Hunter.' Already, by the 1790s Thompson was thoroughly aware of the effect that European arms and implements were having on the ecology of the continent, and in particular on the widespread beaver population whose pelts had been a

major stimulus in the opening up of the country. He laid special blame on the use of the steel trap:

The Nepissings, the Algonquins and Iroquois Indians having exhausted their own countries, now spread themselves . . . and as they destroyed the Beaver, moved forwards to the northward and westward . . . [Then] the Chippaways and other tribes made use of Traps of steel . . . For several years all these Indians were rich . . . The Canoes of the Furr Traders were loaded with packs of Beaver, the abundance of the article lowered the London prices. Every intelligent Man saw the poverty that would follow the destruction of the Beaver . . . A worn out field may be manured, and again made fertile; but the Beaver once destroyed cannot be replaced: they were the gold coin of the country, with which the necessaries of life were purchased.

1698 D'Iberville identified mouth of Mississippi from Gulf of Mexico and established French colony.
1700 Khun explored north of the Colorado

River; produced first map of lower California peninsula.
1714 Saint-Denis, French trader, explored Mississippi and Red Rivers and went

overland to San Juan on the Rio Grande.
1738-43 La Vérendrye and his sons travelled through North and South Dakota.
1739 French traders, Pierre and Paul

from the government. Even when Saint-Lusson had been officially commissioned by Talon to search for the copper mines on the shores of Lake Superior in 1670, this did not imply that any financial support for the voyage would be forthcoming, and this was equally true of the official voyages of Louis Jolliet and René Robert Cavelier de La Salle. However, those post-1670 voyages officially sanctioned by the Intendant or Governor usually had one advantage over other expeditions: the leader was normally rewarded either with the post of commandant of a fort or trading establishment, or with a seigneurie.

Aware that it was vital to prevent English traders from gaining control of western trade routes, Talon, with the full approval of the governor, Louis de Buade de Frontenac, commissioned Jolliet to lead an expedition south-westwards from Lake Michigan. The existence of the Mississippi River had been known ever since the explorations of Jean Nicollet in 1634, but there was no knowledge of where this river discharged into the ocean. Having promised Frontenac that he would find the mouth of the 'Great River', Jolliet had first to draw up an agreement for a trading company with several Quebec merchants to defray the cost of the voyage, before setting out in the autumn of 1672 for Michilimackinac where he was to pick up his remarkable travelling companion, Father Jacques Marquette.

Jolliet delivered a letter to Marquette from the superior of the Jesuits in New France ordering him to join the expedition, an order which fitted perfectly with Marquette's plans: 'to seek out new nations that are unknown to us so that they shall be made to know our great God'. The three powerful motivating forces that lay behind the astonishing expansion of New France were thus united in the seven men who set off in two canoes in mid-May 1673. Political, commercial and religious motives were all equally well represented on this journey which was to open up as important a waterway as those that Cartier and Hudson had found, and to frustrate the expansion of the English colonies westwards for nearly a century.

Jolliet and Marquette did not, in fact, reach the mouth of the Mississippi (which Jolliet had named the River Buade in honour of Frontenac). After passing two impressive tributaries, the Missouri and the Ohio, when they were close to the confluence of the Arkansas and the Mississippi they decided that they had gone as far as it was wise. Although Marquette could speak at least six Indian languages, he was quite unable to communicate with tribes as far to the south as the Arkansas Indians. Moreover,

these were people who traded with the Spaniards and into whose hands it would be undesirable to fall. So having discovered that the Mississippi definitely flowed into the Gulf of Mexico, the expedition turned round and paddled back against the current well over 1600 km (1000 miles) upstream, returning to Lake Michigan via the Illinois River and the portage across to Chicago. Jolliet named a mountain after himself somewhere to the south of Chicago and a large town nearby also now bears his name.

During the winter of 1673–4, Jolliet stayed at the Sault Ste Marie mission, making copies of his journal and map. Leaving these duplicates in the hands of the Jesuits, he set off for Quebec in the spring but with an appalling piece of bad luck his canoe was overturned at Sault St Louis. He was the sole survivor of the accident, and the copies of the map and journals that he had with him were irretrievably lost. To compound this misfortune, the copies he had left at Sault Ste Marie were destroyed in a fire and the journal of Marquette has never been found. Maps do exist that purport to be Jolliet's work, or copies of his work, but posterity has been deprived of a day-to-day account of the first voyage down the Mississippi.

With or without maps and journals, Jolliet had built up a sound reputation as an explorer by 1679 and in that year he was commissioned to survey or inspect 'all the nations and lands in the King's Domain'. This commission really meant that he was to sound out the extent to which the native population of the Hudson Bay basin had come under the influence of English traders. However, another ostensible reason for this northern voyage was to establish a mission and trading post at Nemiskaw, on the Rupert River. The expedition in this case was not covering entirely new ground, since the Jesuit Father Charles Albanel, in 1671–2, had left the mission at Tadoussac and with Montagnais guides, had made his way up to Lake Mistassini, across to Nemiskaw and down the Rupert to the sea. There he had found an English vessel and two deserted houses, but no Europeans since they were apparently all off hunting.

It had been an exhausting voyage – 800 leagues (about 4000 km/2400 miles) to and from the Bay – and the worst winter, Albanel said, of the ten that he had spent in the woods with the 'Savages'. But no sooner had he returned to Quebec than a new voyage was planned by Frontenac whose report of the 13 November 1673 shows the extent to which missionary zeal was made use of by the government of New France:

I have availed myself of the zeal shown by Father Albanel, Jesuit, to set off on a mission to those quarters in order to try to deflect the Savages . . . from taking this route for the English commerce. The said Father Albanel must sound out Des Groseilliers if he meets him and try to see whether he can make him take up our interests again.

Armed with a polite letter from Frontenac, Albanel made another onerous journey overland to the Rupert River, a journey with 200 portages which for a man of over 50 proved a terrible trial. When he arrived in August 1674 at the English fort at the mouth of the Rupert, he found that he was far from welcome. Charles Bayly, the first resident governor of the Hudson's Bay Company, suspected the motives of this French envoy. Since the conversions of Father Albanel, both spiritual and commercial on his last visit had already succeeded in deflecting some of the English trade southwards, the missionary was put firmly aboard a ship to England with new clothes and a little money.

It is interesting that when Jolliet and his companions made the same voyage in 1679 (which Jolliet estimated at 343 leagues (about 1600 km/1000 miles) one way), Governor Bayly received him with the utmost civility as he had apparently heard of Jolliet's explorations down the Mississippi. It would seem that he was trying to persuade the Canadian to change sides as Radisson and Groseilliers had done, offering him well-remunerated service with the English and saying that in England explorers who made discoveries were greatly admired. But the loyalties of Jolliet and Albanel never wavered, and in neither case were their voyaging days finished.

Albanel arrived back at Quebec in July 1676 when his enforced sojourn in England and France was over, and after three days he was already *en route* for 'le pays d'en haut' as the Upper Great Lakes region was then called. He had been immediately appointed superior of the St François-Xavier mission (now De Pere, Wisconsin), and he ended his days at Sault Ste Marie, at the age of 80, a remarkable age for someone who had been described as 'a little old man' and when he was barely 50 had already looked worn out from voyaging.

A 19th-century view of the desolate shores near York Factory, from where the Hudson's Bay Company shipped massive quantities of furs to England and traders journeyed westwards to Lake Winnipeg.

Only by studying maps of the northern continent, or better still by flying over it in a small plane, can the immense courage of priests like Albanel or traders like Jolliet be properly appreciated. The incredible distances travelled by these men with their canoes – from Hudson Bay and the Saguenay to Montreal or Trois-Rivières and then to the 'pays d'en haut' and the western missions – were considered fairly normal at the time, and yet nowadays very few Canadians even drive from Lake Mistassini to Lake Nipigon and on to Lake Michigan on an ordinary business trip. In New France these exploratory journeys were only considered unusual and worthy of note when a man put an entirely new area on the map and claimed it for the Crown. This René Robert Cavelier de La Salle certainly did.

LA SALLE TO HEARNE AND MACKENZIE

Although most contemporaries of Jolliet and La Salle gave full honour for the discovery of the Mississippi to Jolliet, the glory of having followed the great river to its mouth, and of being the founder of 'La Louisiane', put La Salle's explorations into a specially dramatic category. Unfortunately La Salle's own exaggerated sense of drama led in the long run to his downfall. During most of his first 15 years in the colony he had received considerable support in his

A bison or wood buffalo from Hennepin's New Discovery. The animal provided a way of life for nomadic tribes until Buffalo Bill appeared.

trading activities from the authoritarian Governor, Frontenac.

After Frontenac had thoroughly annoyed Montreal merchants by building a fort at the present site of Kingston, Ontario, in 1673, the fort was then ceded to La Salle who promptly changed its name from Fort Cataracoui to Fort Frontenac, and used the post (as Frontenac had intended) as an *entrepôt* to which furs from 'le pays d'en haut' that normally went to Montreal could be diverted. When the Sulpician missionary, François de Salignac de la Mothe-Fénelon, made references in an Easter sermon to the fact that those in authority should not abuse their power, La Salle sprang to his feet and drew the attention of the congregation to the accusing words that appeared to be an attack on Frontenac.

This passionate adherence to the Frontenac camp made many enemies for La Salle, and has resulted in some very biased versions of both his life and the value of his contribution towards the exploration of North America. It is incontestable that he built various forts at strategic places which acted as staging posts in his expedition down and up the Mississippi. However, to what extent he did or did not discover the Ohio River, for instance, is a matter still under discussion by historians. That he was arrogant and self-glorifying there is no doubt. A point which distinguished La Salle from explorers such as Jolliet and Father Albanel, is that instead of voyaging quietly with just two or three Indian guides and one or two other companions, his major expedition started with well over 30 men, several of whom made notable contributions to the journey, particularly in the early stages.

The expedition began with Dominique La Motte de Lucière and Father Louis Hennepin being sent ahead to the eastern end of Lake Erie to choose a site for a fort on the Niagara River, and a suitable place above the falls for the building of a ship. The construction of *Le Griffon*, the first ship, to sail the Great Lakes, was certainly La Salle's idea but he had little to do with the execution of the project that began in mid-winter and was completed in August 1679. Other business kept La Salle at Fort Frontenac until just before the launching of *Le Griffon*, a vessel of about 60 tons with seven cannon . . . an impressive sight.

It soon transpired that the ship had not been built simply to carry the members of La Salle's expedition up to Michilimackinac and on to Green Bay. In total contravention of the King's orders that there was to be 'no commerce with the Savages called the Ottawas or others who bring their beaver and other

THE CANOE, THE HORSE AND OTHER MEANS OF TRANSPORT

From the moment of Champlain's arrival at Tadoussac, the Indian canoe became the most common way of travel for explorers throughout most of North America. There were canoes of all shapes and sizes, but a description of the birchbark canoe used by Alexander Mackenzie on his journey to the Pacific in 1793 will give an idea of the shape and capacity of some of the canoes used for the fur trade:

Her dimensions were twenty-five feet long within, exclusive of the curves of stem and stern, twenty-six inches hold, and four feet nine inches beam. At the same time she was so light, that two men could carry her on a good road three or four miles without resting. In this slender vessel, we shipped provisions, goods for presents, arms, ammunition and baggage, to the weight of 3000 lbs, and an equipage of ten people; viz. Alexander Mackay, Joseph Landry, Charles Ducette, François Beaulieux, Baptist Bisson, François Courtois, and Jacques Beauchamp, with two Indians as hunters and interpreters.

Six of the men who paddled the canoe were French Canadian *voyageurs*, men who were just as expert at negotiating rapids and handling and repairing a canoe as any Indian. And one of the great advantages of travel by canoe was the fact that the materials for making and repairing canoes were available nearly everywhere – birchbark, resin or gum to make the seams watertight, and split 'roots of the spruce-fir' with which 'different parts of the bark canoes are also sewed together'. As soon as the lakes and rivers were free of ice the water routes clearly offered the best way to cross the continent. Travelling on snowshoes in winter, with a 45-kg (90-lb) pack plus a gun and ammunition, was not a rapid means of locomotion, but Europeans needed to adopt this Indian invention for the winter months just as much as they needed the canoe for the rest of the year.

Dogs were used for transport – with and without sleds – by some Indian tribes, but the animal that revolutionized Indian life in the western half of the continent was the horse. A Piegan Indian, Saukamappee, described to David Thompson the first time he came across a horse:

We were anxious to see a horse of which we had heard so much. At last, as the leaves were falling we heard that one was killed by an arrow shot into his belly, but the Snake Indian that rode him, got away; numbers of us went to see him, and we all admired him, he put us in mind of a Stag that had lost his horns; and we did not know what name to give him. But as he was a slave to Man, like the dog, which carried our things; he was named the Big Dog.

John White's painting of Virginia Indians with fish spears and a dug-out canoe. A weir and fish trap are visible in the background.

By the beginning of the 18th century the use of horses among Indian tribes had spread from the Spanish settlements in the south-west northwards as far as the headwaters of the South Saskatchewan and Columbia river systems.

Though herds of wild horses were thereafter a common sight in the western mountains, initially they must well have seemed as surprising an animal to the Indians of the region as the bison was to the Spaniards who first met that impressive beast on the Great Plains in the 1530s and 1540s. The early Spanish explorers described the bison as having 'a hump like a camel' and when it shed the hair on the rear half of its body, it looked 'exactly like a lion' . . . about as accurate a description of a bison as that of the horse as 'a Stag that had lost his horns'.

This Indian petroglyph of a mounted horseman surrounded by warriors with guns illustrates the assimilation of some European imports into native culture.

1787 Michaux explored the Carolina mountains.
1789 Mackenzie followed the Mackenzie River via Great Slave Lake to the Arctic

Ocean – a round trip of 4750 km (3000 miles).
1792-3 Mackenzie completed first crossing of North America.

1793 Michaux explored Kentucky, and went on to study forests of America for the French government.
1799 Russian-American Company sent

Father Louis Hennepin was the first European to publish a picture of the spectacular falls at Niagara.

(Left) René Robert Cavelier de La Salle. His expedition down the Mississippi brought him fame but his life ended tragically.

furs to Montreal', La Salle loaded *Le Griffon* with a cargo of furs and sent it back from Lake Michigan to the fort at Niagara, but, to La Salle's despair, it never arrived.

Considering that exploratory expeditions had to be self-sustaining and received no financial support from the Crown, La Salle could perhaps be forgiven for contravening orders. He was heavily in debt by 1680. Not only had he lost *Le Griffon*, but another ship bringing him 20,000 francs' worth of merchandise for trade had been lost in the St Lawrence. Other men might well have given up at this point, and further calamities were to follow. During a first attempt at descending the Illinois River at the beginning of 1680, La Salle had established a fort which he had suitably called 'Crevecoeur' or Fort Heartbreak. While he was away in Montreal, trying to arrange his financial affairs, some of the men he had left at the fort mutinied and the place was destroyed.

A final attempt was made in January 1682 to complete the Mississippi project, which was now into its fourth year. With his faithful lieutenant, Henri de Tonti, plus 23 Frenchmen and 18 'Savages', La Salle made his way from Fort Crevecoeur to the junction of the Illinois and the

Mississippi. There, the melting of the ice in the middle of February allowed the expedition to use canoes for the rest of the journey, which went extraordinarily well apart from one contretemps. Since that mishap shows the more admirable side of La Salle's controversial character, it is worth recounting.

South of the Ohio River, near the present city of Memphis, the expedition had to call a halt and wait for about ten days while searching for a lost man. Pierre Prudhomme, the son of a Montreal brewer, had gone astray while out hunting, and eventually turned up, starved and exhausted, floating down-river on a piece of wood. Many leaders of expeditions would have been infuriated by the wasted time, but La Salle had employed some of his men in building another fort during the search period and celebrated the return of the stray man by naming the establishment 'Fort Prudhomme'.

Relations with the Indians who lived on either side of the lower Mississippi were excellent. After a brief moment of menacing drums and war cries, the Arkansas Indians decided to smoke a pipe of peace with the newcomers, and plied them with welcome provisions. La Salle with due protocol took possession of their territory for the crown of France, and

agents into the interior of Alaska. Glasanov and Malakov opened Yukon Valley to fur traders.
1804-6 Lewis and Clark's epic trans-

continental journey followed length of the Missouri, crossed the Rockies at their widest and reached Pacific Ocean.
1805 Fraser crossed the Rockies and

followed the course of the Fraser River.
1805-6 Pike explored headwaters of Arkansas and Red Rivers. Wrongly reported valleys to be wastelands.

similar ceremonies took place further down-river with the Taensas and the Coroas. Tonti wrote glowingly of the impressive dignity and beauty of the Taensas, and the generosity of most of the tribes almost overwhelmed the explorers.

The expedition's goal was attained at last when they arrived in view of the sea, but the high point of La Salle's career came three days later when, dressed in a scarlet coat, and to the sound of solemn hymns, he took possession of Louisiana, 'In the name of Louis XIV, King of France and of Navarre, the 9th of April, 1682'.

La Salle had attached to the crown, without a blow, a stretch of territory that almost doubled the size of New France. According to the 'Carte de La Louisiane' of 1684, by Jean Baptiste Louis Franquelin, the new territory ran from the Appalachians, in the east, south-westwards to the Spanish territories, and included the Mexican coast as far south as Tampico; the Rio Grande having been rebaptized after Colbert's son, the 'Rivière Seignelay' (La Salle had already renamed the Mississippi the 'Rivière Colbert').

But Louis XIV was not at all pleased by La Salle's tremendous efforts. He seems to have feared that the frontiers of New France had become over-extended. Far from being flattered by the gift of the enormous territory which had just received his name, he wrote to the recently appointed governor of New France, Joseph Antoine Lefebvre de La Barre, that '*La découverte du sieur de La Salle est fort inutile*', and that in future such useless enterprises must be stopped. For some time official government policy had been to discourage the drift to the woods by so many young 'coureurs de bois', as it was considered much safer for the colony to have resident able-bodied men engaged in agriculture and industries near the chief towns, following the example of the flourishing English colonies. Official policy did not, however, suit the spirit of the young 'Canadiens', or of men like La Salle.

Arriving at La Rochelle just before Christmas 1683, under a cloud of disapproval, La Salle immediately got in touch with men who he hoped would support his new project for a French colony in the region of the Taensas, the Indians who had welcomed his expedition with such warmth and civility. Fortunately the *Relation de la décoverte de l'embouchure de la rivière Mississipi dans le golfe du Mexique, faite par le Sieur De La Salle, l'année passée 1682*, written by Father Zénobe Membré who had accompanied La Salle, had already reached France. La Salle's plan had become embedded in a much more complicated plan and was presented to Colbert by l'abbé Claude Bernou and other men with influence at court.

Suddenly La Salle was back in favour with the king. His forts in Canada that had been confiscated were restored to him, and he was put in charge of a grandiose project to which the king contributed two ships with their crews and 100 soldiers with their officers. A merchant of La Rochelle and the Intendant of Rochfort helped with the provisioning of two more ships. The convoy carried over 320 people, including a few women and children.

If all had gone well, this chapter of La Salle's life could have been put into the category of colonization rather than exploration, but all did not go well. One of the important instigators of this expedition had been a Spaniard, Count Diego de Peñalosa, ex-governor of New Mexico, who, after falling out with the Inquisition, had offered his services to France. Part of his plan was to establish a French colony at the mouth of the Rio Grande (or Rio Bravo del Norte) which would be a strategic post for the conquest of Mexico. Whether on purpose or by accident, La Salle miscalculated the location of the Mississippi's mouth and headed westwards along the northern shore of the Gulf of Mexico, relying on inadequate maps. After various misadventures the major part of the expedition found itself in Matagorda Bay.

On Lavaca, one of the rivers which flow into the bay, La Salle erected his last fort, and established the little colony there in May 1685. The next two years were spent in fruitless exploration: the search for the Mississippi. Finally, after several unsuccessful journeys from the base at Fort St Louis, La Salle decided in January 1687, to try to fetch help from his fort on the Illinois River. Leaving 25 men, women and children, the remnants of the colony at Fort St Louis, La Salle and 16 men started north-eastwards, but on 19 March, near the Trinity, a river which flows south from Dallas to the Gulf, La Salle and three of his men were killed by some of the angry and disillusioned members of the expedition.

To what extent La Salle's journeyings through what is now the state of Texas can be called exploration is a moot point. His wanderings certainly made his compatriots more aware of the space between Florida and Mexico, although it was Pierre Le Moyne d'Iberville, who really 'discovered' by sea or rediscovered, the mouth of the Mississippi in 1698 and over the next few years planted a successful colony there. But very little of the French exploration of regions immediately to the north of the Gulf of

1807-11 Thompson completed his outstanding surveys of western America by following the length of the Columbia River. **1811** Hunt led an overland journey from the

Mississippi across the Blue Mountains to Astoria. Became the Oregon trail. **1819** Long's Yellowstone Scientific expedition used a steamer on the Missouri.

Established myth which persisted for 30 years of barren Great Plains. **1819-22** Franklin explored a new route from the Great Slave Lake to the mouth of the

Mexico led to genuinely new discoveries. Spanish expeditions nearly a century and a half earlier had already crossed the Mississippi on journeys westwards from Florida. It can be said, however, that rediscoveries normally have a more important effect on the development of an area than the original discovery, and that is not only true for the Mississippi but for many other parts of North America.

The rediscovery of Cartier's gulf and 'the River of Canada' in the 1580s, by his nephew and by Basque fishermen and other traders, has already been mentioned, but the rediscovery of the southern and eastern shores of Labrador has not yet been discussed. It was the same energetic Canadian, Louis Jolliet, who as a young man had discovered the upper reaches of the Mississippi and had made his way overland to Hudson Bay, in 1694 mapped and described in detail the Atlantic coast of Labrador for 106 leagues (about 500 km/320 miles) north of the eastern end of the Strait of Belle Isle. He has left for posterity his *Journal de Loüis Jolliet, allant à la descouverte de Labrador, pais des Esquimaux, 1694.*

Born in Quebec in 1645, Jolliet appears to have had the exploration of his country and the well-being of the colony more closely at heart than most of the officials sent over from France. As a merchant he also had a strong interest in the fur trade, and when Colbert refused his request to establish a post in the Illinois region, Jolliet joined forces with his father-in-law and other Quebec merchants and formed a company for trading along the north coast of the St Lawrence. He was conceded a seigneurie that finally included the whole of the north shore up to the western end of the Strait of Belle Isle, where the Basques had formerly exploited their whaling establishments.

The Basques seem to have always enjoyed good relations with the Montagnais Indians along the southern Labrador coast, but trading with the 'Eskimaos' was another matter. There was some trade, apparently in sealskins, but the exchanges were carried on with extreme caution and very little trust on either side. This is why Jolliet's journal of his exploration up the Labrador coast as far as latitude 56°1'11" is of particular interest. He and his companions do not appear to have had a moment of fear during the whole month that their small ship was on the coast. They were invited into Eskimo houses and the Inuit women entertained them with

The Moravian Mission at Makkovik was one of several settlements founded by the United Brethren that brought hospitals and schools to the Labrador coast.

singing and dancing, while the Recollet father who accompanied Jolliet repaid this kindness by intoning hymns which apparently delighted their Inuit hosts.

Jolliet's journey up the Labrador coast, and his comfortable relationship with the Eskimos, was all the more remarkable when compared to descriptions of fierce Inuit attacks on European fishermen in the Strait of Belle Isle throughout the first half of the 18th century, often brought on by the fishermen's over-reaction to Eskimo pilfering. It was only in 1764, when the first of the Moravian missionaries, Jens Haven, was in the Quirpon area at the south-eastern end of the Strait (simultaneously with Captain James Cook), and the following year when four of the Moravians landed at Chateau Bay, that a peaceful atmosphere was again restored between Eskimos and Europeans.

The Moravians were able to talk with the Labrador Eskimos because they had first learned to communicate with the Greenlanders whose language was practically identical. The Labrador Eskimos were so impressed by these men of peace with whom they could converse, and who even wore Eskimo clothing on some occasions, that they allowed them to set up missions, first at Nain and later at Okkak and Hopedale. Whatever is now written about their negative effect on indigenous cultures, there is no doubt that it was often the missions, whether Recollet, Jesuit, Sulpician or Moravian, that protected the 'Savages' from either the worst forms of exploitation or wholesale slaughter by fishermen and settlers who had decided that the best Indian was a dead Indian.

As the Governor of Newfoundland, Hugh Palliser, said when recommending that the Moravians be given all possible assistance, 'Hitherto . . . the Esquimaux have been considered in no other light than as thieves and murderers', while reciprocally the Inuit considered most Europeans to be evil men. The necessity for referees in this long drawn-out conflict is clearly seen in an account of the life of a young boy whose father had been killed by traders and who was taken to England by the Moravians in 1769. During the interval between Jens Haven's first visit and the founding of the missions in the 1770s, 'The old quarrels between the natives and the English traders were renewed; and as no one was present who could act as interpreter and explain the mutual grounds of difference the affair was terminated in bloodshed. Nearly twenty of the natives were killed . . .' In other parts of North America the death toll would have probably been worse.

An ability to speak the languages of the areas through which traders or missionaries were moving

In spite of their guns, several of Frobisher's men were killed during Eskimo attacks. John White apparently witnessed this incident in 1577.

was undoubtedly the main key to successful exploration. Equally, an ability to eat the same food as the 'Savages' and to show an unflinching attitude to walking or canoeing great distances in often prolonged discomfort was naturally a prerequisite for explorers of North America. But another quality was also needed: a suppression of certain European moral and cultural attitudes which even missionaries had to develop. The more sensitive of the European explorers had to learn to hide any disgust they might feel at actions on the part of their hosts which appeared cruel and inhuman, while at the same time finding a way to avoid participation in an event which they abhorred, without looking squeamish. There are several examples of such occurrences in the writings of Samuel de Champlain, and in the *Relations* of the Jesuits, but one particular event has to be mentioned in connection with the first trader to reach the Arctic Ocean overland from Hudson Bay.

By 1769 the Hudson's Bay Company had been in existence for just on a century, but it had not earned a reputation for discovery or the opening up of new territory. It had in fact been criticized for lack of initiative in this matter and to remedy the situation it was proposed that Samuel Hearne should be sent on 'an inland journey, far to the north of Churchill to promote an extension of our trade, as well as for the discovery of a North-West passage, copper mines, etc.' A few of the Company's traders had gone westwards as far as the North and South Saskatchewan rivers, but no one had yet gone far northwards towards the river which according to Indian reports led to the country of the copper mines.

Samuel Hearne had been sent out to Fort Prince of Wales, at the mouth of the Churchill River, as a young man of about 20 and was not more than 24 when he was entrusted with this important mission. He had had considerable experience trading with Eskimos on the north-west coasts of Hudson Bay, and his ability to get on well with them makes the following part of his instructions seem rather unnecessary: 'It is sincerely recommended to you and your companions to treat the natives with civility, so as not to give them any room for complaint or disgust'.

As matters turned out, it was not Hearne who gave his travelling companions any cause for

Indian life on the Alaskan Coast at 58° 36', claimed in 1787 by La Pérouse for France. He had previously captured British forts in Hudson Bay.

discontent, but, particularly during his first attempt at the journey, it was the Indians themselves who broke their agreement to accompany him, deserting him 'nearly 200 miles [320 km] from Prince of Wales' Fort', and stealing most of his supplies. Considering that this first attempt was during the months of November and December, and there was not a plentiful supply of game, it is not too surprising that the Indians, as Hearne said, 'had not the prosperity of the undertaking at heart'. With admirable tenacity of purpose, Hearne set out once more in February with a smaller and more faithful troop, and this time managed about 800 km (500 miles) before an unfortunate occurrence made him retrace his steps to the Churchill again. His quadrant had been blown over and broken, and Hearne felt there was no point in continuing the journey if he were unable to continue with his mapping.

The third attempt began in December 1770, in the company of a distinguished leader of men, called Matonabee. It was a complete success in an exploratory and geographic sense; however, humanly, from Hearne's point of view, there were moments of appalling disaster. At Lake Clowey – not far from the Great Slave Lake – what appeared to be hundreds of Indians joined Hearne's and Matonabee's party, and it suddenly became evident that the exploratory expedition had turned into a military one, with the over-riding purpose of making surprise attacks on any unsuspecting Eskimos whom they happened to find.

Matonabee had promised Hearne that he would take him to the mouth of Coppermine River, but he had not mentioned that his own motivation for the journey was the prospect of collecting as many copper implements as possible from the Eskimos who inhabited that region. Hearne had unwittingly become involved in a traditional raiding party, and was an unwilling witness to the barbaric slaughter and mutilation of a group of men, women and children who were fast asleep in their tents. He ends his description of the attack by saying: 'My situation and the terror of my mind at beholding this butchery, cannot easily be conceived . . . though I summed up all the fortitude I was master of on the occasion, it was with difficulty that I could refrain from tears.'

When the Eskimo tents had been plundered and destroyed, and any escaping Eskimos had been killed, Hearne pursued his survey to the mouth of the river, where as the tide was out 'the water in the river was still perfectly fresh', but he was certain 'of it being the sea, or some branch of it, by the quantity of whalebone and seal-skins which the Eskimaux had

A man from Kodiak in Alaska, and an 'Ishutski' woman, drawn during Captain Billings' Russian expedition in 1790.

at their tents'. And later on he observed, 'For the sake of form . . . after having had some consultation with the Indians, I erected a mark, and took possession of the coast, on behalf of the Hudson's Bay Company.'

Fifty years later, Sir John Franklin, accompanied by Sir John Richardson and Sir George Back, surveyed the lower part of the Coppermine River, and found, exactly as Hearne had described, the Bloody Falls where the massacre had taken place with skulls and bones 'strewed about the ground near the encampment'. It was at a latitude of 67°42'35", and Hearne had unquestionably found the Arctic Ocean at a point just opposite the island that was later to be called Victoria Island. He had also left for future generations an account which can be seen as an interesting comparison to events that were taking place almost simultaneously in Labrador. If Hearne had witnessed the killing of some 20 Labrador Eskimos by European fishermen or traders, he might or might not have condemned that incident so roundly, but he could not have failed to notice, as he implied in his description of

the Coppermine attack, that it was European guns and bullets that allowed one race to dominate the other.

THE LAST HALF OF THE CONTINENT

While the English from Hudson Bay and the French from the Great Lakes had been gradually pushing westwards across the continent, Spanish naval expeditions from Mexico had been slowly exploring northwards up the coast of California, and Russian fur trading expeditions had begun to move southwards from Alaska. The illusion that the Strait of Juan de Fuca or the legendary Strait of Anian crossed the northern part of the continent had been dispelled by the journeys of Samuel Hearne on the one hand, and on the other by the 1778 voyage of Captain Cook up the west coast of Canada to Alaska and the Bering Strait. Although by this time a realistic estimate of the shape and immense size of the continent had been obtained, it had not yet been crossed from coast to coast by any European, nor is it likely that any indigenous North American had traversed from Hudson Bay or the St Lawrence over the Rocky Mountains to the Pacific. Both feats were to be achieved during the next two decades.

A painting of canoe travel on one of the Canadian Arctic expeditions by the RGS medal winner George Black.

The explorations of well-known fur traders such as Hearne and Alexander Mackenzie or David Thompson have been recognized because they left journals describing their expeditions, but the contributions of other equally intrepid men have often been ignored because they left no published accounts. It is clear, however, from the records of the better known 18th-century traders that their most spectacular journeys depended to a large extent on the network of trading establishments that had gradually been set up by previous traders. Moreover, the Scotsmen and Englishmen of the post-conquest period often relied on 'Métis' guides, the sons or daughters of French traders and their Indian wives, who were well adapted to life in the outposts. David Thompson, for instance, married an Indian girl who went with him on many of his journeys, and with whom he had 13 children.

In the case of Meriwether Lewis and William Clark, the American explorers who led an expedition from St Louis to the Pacific Coast (1804–6), it was a Shoshoni Indian girl named Sacajawea, married to a French Canadian trader, Toussaint Charbonneau, who served as guide and interpreter for the expedition. Lewis and Clark met her in one of the Mandan villages, in the present state of North Dakota, and, in spite of the fact that she had a newborn baby to carry with her, she and her husband agreed to accompany the expedition over the Rocky Mountains to the mouth of the Columbia River.

When Mackenzie made his voyage to the Arctic Ocean in 1789, he had with him four French Canadians, two of them with their Indian wives, and an Indian chief with two of his wives. For part of the journey Mackenzie was also accompanied by another French trader called Laurent Leroux who had set up the first trading post on the Great Slave Lake. The expedition started out from Fort Chipewyan on Lake Athabasca, and though this fort had been built by Alexander's cousin, Roderick Mackenzie, in 1788, the first known trader in the Athabasca district was actually Peter Pond, who had been born in Milford, Connecticut, but who by the end of the 1770s knew more about the north-west than any of his contemporaries. He was aware, for instance, that the Peace River flowed east from the Rocky Mountains. Unfortunately, he had also come to the conclusion that the great river that flowed

1846 Emory carried out a reconnaisance from Santa Fe to the west coast at San Diego.
1848 Frémont and Benton attempted to

recce a rail route from Colorado across the San Juan Mountains but were turned back by winter storms.
1851 Sitgreaves crossed the Great Colorado

Plateau between Zuñi River and San Francisco Mountains to Colorado River.

westwards out of Great Slave Lake had its outlet in the Pacific Ocean, even though the Indians had correctly informed him that it flowed north.

It was Pond's information that led Mackenzie to believe that by following this great river, which was eventually to be called the Mackenzie, the expedition would emerge at a point on the West Coast coinciding with the mouth of a large river that had been seen by Captain Cook. That his valiant expedition finally discovered not the Western Ocean but a new part of the Northern Ocean was a matter of considerable disappointment to Mackenzie, but three years later he started, undaunted, on another journey which would attain his desired goal, via the Peace River, and a section of the Fraser River to Bella Coola.

Mackenzie both started and ended his journey to the Pacific at much higher latitudes than any other man attempted to do during the 18th or early 19th century. He set out on his expedition on 10 October 1792, from Fort Chipewyan at a latitude of nearly 59° and finally arrived on a branch of the sea leading to Queen Charlotte Sound, at 52°20'48",

according to his own reckoning 'by the natural horizon'. There on a rock, near Elcho Harbour, he 'mixed up some vermilion in melted grease, and inscribed, in large characters . . . this brief memorial: Alexander Mackenzie, from Canada, by land, the twenty-second of July, one thousand seven hundred and ninety-three.' He could have added the names of the six French Canadians, two Indians and his second-in-command, Alexander Mackay, who made the journey with him, but perhaps there was no room on the rock face.

While it is true that the earliest pioneering journeys over the Rocky Mountains were led by Scotsmen, first Mackenzie and then Simon Fraser, or by the Welshman, David Thompson, or by the Americans, Lewis and Clark, these were by no means the only white men who had crossed the mountains by 1811, nor were they, with the exception of David Thompson, men who had spent years exploring the north-western approaches to the Rockies. During the period 1730 to 1783 (when the North West Company was founded), a network of forts had been established by

SMALLPOX

From the earliest days of contact with Europeans, white-man's diseases had a devastating effect on Indian tribes. Writing about the Plains Indians just to the east of the Rocky Mountains, and other Indians of the north-west, David Thompson, gave several descriptions of the effect of smallpox on native communities in his *Narrative*:

When Hudson Bay was discovered, and the first trading settlement made, the Natives were far more numerous than at present. In the year 1782, the small pox from Canada extended to them, and more than one half of them died.

He then quotes a description by a Piegan Indian, Saukamappee, of an attack on a camp where the Piegans thought their enemies were hiding:

At the dawn of day, we attacked the Tents, and with our sharp flat daggers and knives, cut through the tents and entered for the fight; but our war whoop instantly stopt, our eyes were appalled with terror; there was no one

to fight with but the dead and the dying, each a mass of corruption. We did not touch them, but left the tents, and held a council on what was to be done . . . The second day after this dreadful disease broke out in our camp, and spread from one tent to another as if the Bad Spirit carried it. We had no belief that one Man could give it to another, any more than a wounded Man could give his wound to another . . . about one third of us died, but in some of the other camps there were tents in which every one died. When at length it left us, and we moved about to find our people, it was no longer with the song and the dance; but with tears, shrieks and howlings of despair for those who would never return to us.

Later on Thompson repeats the account by an old fur trader, Mitchell Oman, a native of Stromness in the Orkney Islands, of his first encounter with natives suffering from the disease near the Eagle Hills:

We saw the first camp and some of

the people sitting on the beach to cool themselves, when we came to them, to our surprise they had marks of the small pox, were weak and just recovering . . . None of us had the least idea of the desolation this dreadful disease had done, until we went up the bank to the camp and looked into the tents in many of which they were all dead . . . Those that remained had pitched their tents about 200 yards from them and were too weak to move away entirely . . . they were in such a state of despair and despondence that they could hardly converse with us, a few of them had gained strength to hunt which kept them alive. From what we could learn, three fifths of them had died . . . From the best information this disease was caught by the Chipaways (the forest Indians) and the Sieux (of the Plains) about the same time, in the year 1780 . . . From the Chipaways it extended all over the Indians of the forest to it's northward extremity, and by the Sieux over the Indians of the Plains and crossed the Rocky Mountains.

traders from Montreal between Lake Superior and the Rocky Mountains, and their work was sometimes overlapped by a chain of trading posts set up at a later date by Hudson's Bay Company employees working out of Churchill and York Factory towards Cumberland House and then further westwards from Lake Winnipeg.

There is no doubt that the original exploration into the North West was by French Canadian traders. When men like Pond and Thompson explored or surveyed, for instance, stretches of the North and South Saskatchewan Rivers they were merely following in the footsteps of Pierre Gaultier de la Vérendrye and his four sons, or their contemporaries such as Boucher de Niverville, who founded Fort La Jonquière at the present site of Calgary, within view of the Rockies. Although the expansion of French Canadian traders westwards from Lake Superior was primarily due to the necessity

of finding new, unexploited areas of beaver and other fur-bearing animals, it was also spurred on to a marked degree by the efforts of La Vérendrye and his sons to find the river that the Indians said would lead to the Western Sea. The first stage in this westward process was via a chain of lakes and rivers, past Lake of the Woods to Lake Winnipeg and Lake Winnipegosis and then on to the Assiniboine and Saskatchewan Rivers.

A remarkable map, drawn by the Indian, Ochagach, for La Vérendrye in 1728, shows the extent to which Indian knowledge and cooperation was still vital for explorers, just as it had been in the days of Champlain. Indeed this was still true for explorers in the early 19th century. There are, for

Indian routes from Lake Superior to Lake Winnipeg traced by Ochagach were added to Buache's map, but the Western Sea is still shown too close to Hudson Bay.

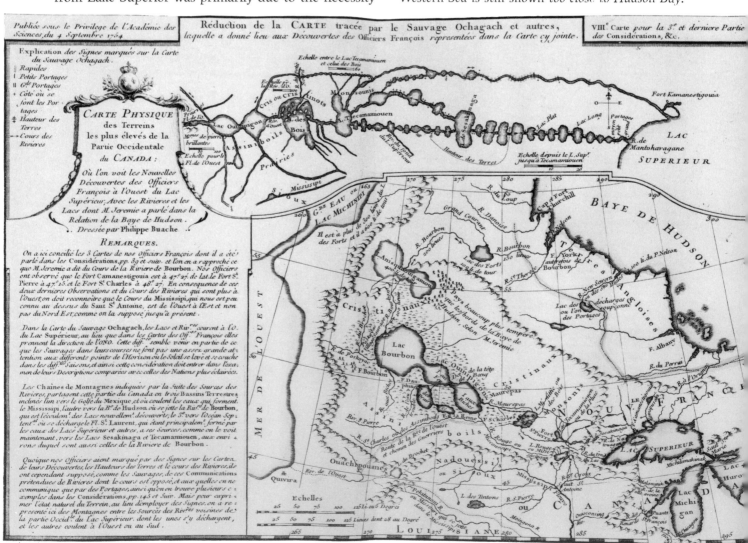

example, two maps redrawn by Peter Fidler, a Hudson's Bay Company trader, from sketches prepared by Blackfoot Indians at Chesterfield House on the South Saskatchewan River in 1801 and 1802. They show the relationship of western rivers such as the Missouri, the Milk and the Bow to the Rocky Mountains, and in one case the rivers flowing from the Rockies to the Pacific with the names of many of the tribes living on both sides of the mountains. In a third case Fidler redrew a map by a Chipewyan, Cotawney yaz-zah, which showed the canoe routes between the Churchill River and Lake Athabasca.

During this period of exploration in the North West the opening up of new routes was quite definitely a joint venture, with Indian experience of how to make the maximum use of favourable currents, and of where to make the best portages, clearly an essential element in the rapid expansion across the continent. Unlike the situation that obtained when La Salle was wandering around in Texas, northern exploration had an efficiency and a sense of purpose that was mutually understandable to both traders and Indians: the former needed furs and the latter needed guns and other manufactured articles. Occasionally there were individual disasters, as when Jean Baptiste de la Vérendrye was killed by a band of Sioux Indians, and his head was sent back to his father, but on the whole the only major disputes arose when one Indian nation wanted to prevent another from receiving arms and ammunition.

An example of a nearly fatal encounter occurred when David Thompson was attempting to make a final push through from the headwaters of the North Saskatchewan to the upper reaches of the Columbia River. The Piegan Indians, with whom Thompson had been trading for several years, became profoundly disturbed at the thought of guns being obtained by tribes on the western side of the Rockies. As Thompson said, 'The Peeagans watched us to prevent our crossing the Mountains and arming the Natives on that side.' While he and his men were building the log-hut settlement called Kootenay House, delegates from the Piegans arrived to check on his activities. Thompson showed them the strength of the stockades and bastions, and told them, 'I know you are come as Spies and intend to destroy us, but many of you will die before you do so; go back to your country and tell them so.' This they apparently did, and Thompson noted in his *Narrative*, 'We remained quiet for the winter.'

In the spring, however, they had a more serious visit from the Piegans. About 40 men were sent by the tribal council to besiege the trading post:

La Pérouse (right) captured Hearne (above) at Fort Prince of Wales in 1782, and insisted that Hearne should publish his travels.

They came and pitched their Tents close before the Gate, which was well barred. I had six men with me, and ten guns, well loaded, the House was perforated with large augur holes, as well as the Bastions, thus they remained for three weeks without daring to attack us.

In the end Thompson sent large quantities of tobacco to the Piegan chiefs, 'with a fine pipe of red porphyry and an ornamented Pipe Stem', which prompted one chief to declare that he was not prepared to go and fight 'Logs of Wood that a ball cannot go through, and with people we cannot see . . .' and the danger was temporarily averted. But Thompson had to change his plans and find a way to the Columbia via the Athabasca, in order to avoid Piegan attacks on his canoes, and he had many more misadventures before eventually reaching the mouth of the Columbia on 14 July 1811.

A few months prior to Thompson's arrival, a trading post called Fort Astoria had been set up at the mouth of the Columbia by agents of John Jacob

An Indian woman in mourning stands wailing before two symbolic features representing the sun and moon with a burial ground in the distance.

Franchère remarked that Thompson travelled 'more like a geographer than a fur trader'. At other moments he referred to him as 'the Astronomer', while some of the Indians apparently called him 'the Star Man'. This epithet was, of course, due to the incessant number of observations Thompson took for ascertaining the latitude and longitude of points on his journeys. Although he may have been criticized for arriving too late to set up the first trading post at the mouth of the Columbia, he had actually set up the first known trading post on the headwaters of the Columbia four years before the establishment of Fort Astoria, and meanwhile had done a brilliant job of surveying the whole length of the Columbia, and many of its tributaries. As he stood on the shores of the Pacific, he could look back with satisfaction on what he had accomplished since he had been put ashore as a boy of 14 at Churchill in Hudson Bay. He concluded his last chapter on the journey to the Pacific with a brief summary of his work:

> Thus I have fully completed the survey of this part of North America from sea to sea, and by almost innumerable astronomical Observations have determined the positions of the Mountains, Lakes, and Rivers, and other remarkable places of the northern part of this Continent; the Maps of all of which have been drawn, and laid down in geographical position, being now the work of twenty seven years.

Thompson's work represents, at the end of the 18th and the beginning of the 19th century, the final phases of a long tradition which would seem to have begun with Champlain. This tradition of individual effort expended in exploration westwards, under often dangerous and appalling conditions, can be seen reflected in the lives not only of fur traders but also of missionaries. However, during Thompson's lifetime many new factors were starting to effect changes in the manner that North America was explored and exploited. Official surveying expeditions with government support became more and more common as political motivations came to the fore.

The Lewis and Clark expedition was an example of this new trend in exploration. Sponsored by the President, Thomas Jefferson, the 45 men who set out from St Louis in May 1804, were led by two military officers and, although ostensibly they were conducting a scientific expedition, Congress had provided funds 'for the purpose of extending the external commerce of the United States'. Even before France had transferred the Louisiana Territory to the United States, Jefferson had announced in a secret message

Astor 'of the City of New York'. The men at the fort had endured a long voyage round Cape Horn, and arriving 'in the rainy season without sufficient shelter from Tents, had suffered from Ague and low Fever'. It must have been a considerable surprise for these men, some of whom were in fact Canadians (ex-clerks of the North West Company) when Thompson's party appeared in sprightly condition after their overland trek, and dramatic journey by canoe (the canoe they had built on the western side of the mountains). One of Astor's employees, Gabriel Franchère, described the arrival:

> Toward midday we saw a large canoe with a flag displayed at her stern, rounding the point which we called Tongue Point. The flag she bore was the British, and her crew was composed of eight Canadian boatmen or voyageurs. A well-dressed man, who appeared to be the commander, was the first to leap ashore.

Thompson had certainly not made the journey in any more comfort than his companions but

1892-4 Tyrrell travelled from Prince Albert on the Saskatchewan to survey the area of Lake Athabasca, and north-east to Chesterfield Inlet and Hudson Bay.

1899 Harriman Alaska Expedition in Aleutian and Pribilof Islands.
1907 Keale explored country between Yukon and Mackenzie Basins.

1914-6 Canadian Arctic expeditions re-surveyed from Kent Peninsula to the Alaska boundary.

to Congress in January 1803, his plans to explore the trans-Mississippi west. His desire to prevent Spanish, British or Russian explorers from claiming the whole of the west coast had no doubt been a great incentive.

By this time the limits of the continent were almost entirely understood except for the High Arctic. But a certain amount of exploration was still required in the surveying of boundary lines, whether the immense length of the Canada–US border (in which Thompson was employed after his retirement from the fur trade), or the slightly lesser distances of the Canadian provinces and the American states. Land grants, timber rights, administrative areas that were a concomitant of the gradual expansion of settlement, plus the laying out of roads and railways, all gave employment to a new generation of surveyors and map makers.

In hardly more than a century the gold-rush phenomena in California and the Klondike, the coralling of Indians into reserves, the wholesale felling of trees, the killing of the buffalo, and the development of agriculture and livestock grazing on a massive scale were some of the factors that transformed North America from a slowly explored wilderness into the mapped and organized part of the world that it is today. But, if it is any consolation to those who would like to have seen the continent as Cartier and Champlain first saw it, there are still extensive areas of Canada's Northland which are as yet untouched by highways, and only marginally affected by other modern development such as low-flying military aircraft. The Rockies, too, can still provide large tracts of spectacular forests and wilderness where mountains have prevented the penetration of roads; however a constant effort will be needed if even a vestige of the untrammelled world of the early explorers is to be preserved.

Sheltered by the eastern slopes of the Rockies, the Valley of the Ten Peaks in Alberta is still a region of remarkable unspoilt natural beauty.

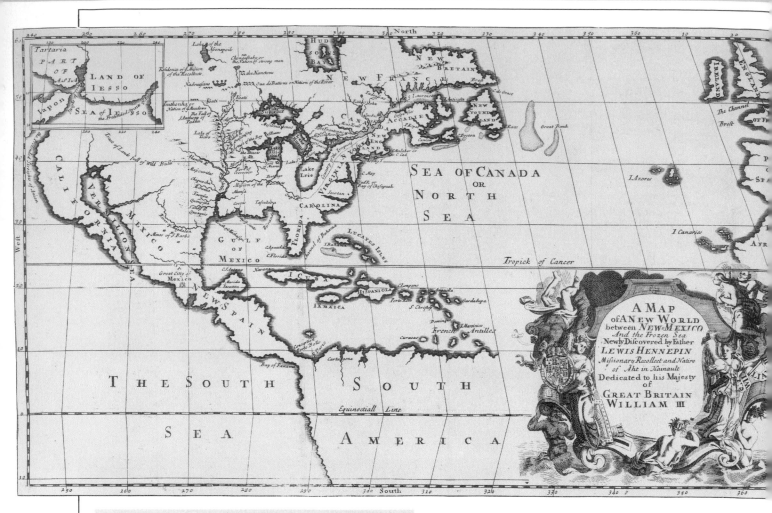

EXPLORATION OF EASTERN NORTH AMERICA

Before the east coast of North America could be explored, its outline and its credibility as a continental land mass had to be established. To the north John Cabot explored some 1000 km (600 miles) in 1497, and his successors at least several hundred more, while Sebastian Cabot not only got as far north as 60° but as far south as about 35°, covering nearly 3250 km (2000 miles) in all.

Meanwhile Spanish explorers had exposed the coast of the Gulf of Mexico by 1519 while Ponce de Léon and Ayllón defined the south-east as far north as Cape Fear (1513-25). To confirm the extent of the continental shoreline and determine if there were passage through to the Pacific, France sent Verrazzano in 1524 and Spain Gómez in 1525 to do this. Their coastal profiles remained standard for much of the 16th century, with the French getting the idea that America narrowed towards the south and with the Spanish assuming that the Penobscot might well lead through the

continent. Neither power – or the British or Portuguese either – were able to do much more in the 16th century.

From Cartier onwards, the French were in the lead and kept it by the accurate definition of the New England and Maritime coast by Champlain between 1604 and 1607, while the British in Virginia from 1607 explored the river estuaries and Chesapeake Bay, but John Smith found each river ceased to be navigable along an inland Fall Line that marked the Piedmont plateau.

For a long period both the British and Dutch were to be checked by this type of obstruction so that only the coastal plain could be effectively exploited. The idea of a narrow America continued to find believers until mid-century at least.

In 1670 John Lederer found and defined the Blue Ridge of the Appalachian chain and worked some hundreds of miles south along the Piedmont. The following year the

Virginians, at last, under Abraham Wood, discovered the Roanoke River valley through the mountains and also the Great Virginia Valley which lay behind the principal mountain chain. From these explorers and traders made many forays westward.

It was not until 1748 that Thomas Walker found the Cumberland Gap in the Appalachians to the south, and opened another channel for explorers and traders into what became Kentucky. From Charleston (1670) explorers and slavers made many thrusts to the south and south-west, making hostile contact with both the Spanish and French. Thomas Welch, indeed, crossed the Mississippi as early as 1698.

The area between these southern colonies and the Mississippi gradually became known to their pioneer explorers and traders. Farther north the British acquisition of New York in 1674 allowed them to use the Hudson River to explore to the north-west and gradually extend their knowledge of the area to the south of Lakes Ontario and Erie by 1750.

The founding of Pennsylvania in 1680, the first inland colony, opened

Left *A vast area in the west of the North American continent is simply annotated 'Tract of Lands full of Wild Bulls' on this 18th-century map.*

Right *President Jefferson instigated the transcontinental expedition led by Lewis and Clark, seen meeting a party of friendly Chinook Indians in the Columbia estuary.*

up the great river systems, first of the Delaware and then the Susquehanna, to explorers. It is reckoned that a series of explorations before 1750 had opened up some 800 km (500 miles) of territory from Philadelphia westwards.

During this process the discovery of the Ohio River diverted much attention to the south-west. James le Tort was trading on the river by 1727, and this led the Virginians, especially, to concentrate on its exploration and exploitation. The Ohio River Company of 1750 first brought George Washington forward as leader in this process.

From 1753 to 1763 French efforts to block the British held up pure exploration, but the transfer of French rights as far west as the Mississippi in 1763 led to further exploration in detail of this vast area in spite of British attempts to seal off white penetration in the interest of Indian trade.

Forays were now being made far to the west, Christopher Post reaching the Wyoming River by 1758. The treaties of 1783 and 1794 opened the area freely to the Americans which they exploited fully by many expeditions.

Finally, the trans-Mississippi west was acquired from France and the great expeditions westwards began, Zebulon Pike travelling north-west in 1805-6 to try to find the source of the Mississippi and in the same year the great transcontinental expedition of Meriwether Lewis and William Clark confirming the unstoppable American exploration to the West, consolidated when the Pacific section of Spanish territory was acquired in 1849 and the mass rush to the West began.

David Quinn
Emeritus Professor of Modern History
University of Liverpool

This romantic view of the early pioneers setting off on their great adventure remains an abiding myth in the folklore of North America.

CENTRAL AND SOUTH AMERICA

SHAFTS OF LIGHT

The history of the exploration of Latin America is in many respects a grim tale dominated in its early years by greed, cruelty and perfidy. The *conquistadores* were convinced of the truth of Columbus's words that 'gold is the most exquisite of all things . . . whoever possesses gold can acquire all that he desires in this world'. The scramble for gold led to torture and enslavement of the Indians, and all too often to harassment or corruption of those missionaries sent to instil a different set of values.

The other grim and recurring theme is the hostility of both the elements and the wild life of so much of South America. Frequently explorers' accounts are dominated by the horrors of tropical diseases, impenetrable jungles, repulsive reptiles and cannibal tribes; further south the emphasis is on frozen wastes, predatory condors and perilous storm-swept waters.

While therefore much of the narrative that follows makes disturbing reading, there are also shafts of light. The sheer courage and self-confidence of the Spanish *conquistadores* was one such shaft. Among the early explorers were men like Father Fritz who dedicated their lives to the service of others; and as time progressed the emphasis of exploration largely changed from the pursuit of gold to the pursuit of knowledge. But common to almost all these explorers, whether they were lusting after gold or earnestly seeking for truth, was their sheer physical courage and mental toughness. These qualities were shared

The Río Camisea snakes its way through the jungle cordillera of eastern Peru. Rivers such as this have provided the only highway for explorers of the primary rain forests of the Amazon basin from the 16th to the 20th centuries.

by men as diverse as Francisco Pizarro, Charles Darwin and Teddy Roosevelt and serve to inspire those who come after them.

COLUMBUS AND THE NEW WORLD

Nordic explorers did indeed reach the New World long before the 15th century (as the Norse site at L'Anse-aux-Meadows discovered by Helge Ingstad in 1960 substantiates) but it was in the northern part of the continent that they made their landfall. The credit for the discovery of the West Indies and Central America, as well as for opening up the New World to Europe, rests squarely with Christopher Columbus, or Cristóbal Colón as the Spanish called him. So too does the credit for persisting with a venture, in the face of hostility and ridicule, until he found a patron who would sponsor and finance him.

Born in the Italian port of Genoa in 1451, Columbus was aware of the excitements and possibilities of maritime exploration from an early age. He developed a knowledge of navigation and cartography and sailed on a number of expeditions. Being convinced (as were most of his more educated contemporaries) that the world was round, he became increasingly intrigued by the idea of sailing into the Atlantic beyond the Azores to reach the fabled lands described by Marco Polo – Cipangu (Japan) and Cathay (China). Any idea of the size of the oceans or of the existence of an American continent between Europe and eastern Asia was not yet conceived.

The natural sponsor for such an expedition appeared to be the Portuguese crown. It was from Portugal that the main thrust of exploration round the African coast had been launched, ever since the days of Prince Henry the Navigator in the early 15th

1498 Christopher Columbus landed on the South American mainland during his third voyage to search for a westward route to the Orient.

1499-1501 Ojeda and Vespucci explored the northern coasts of South America. Ojeda named area little Venice (Venezuela) after seeing houses on stilts.

1500 Pinzón sailed along the coast of Guiana. Discovered Brazil and the mouth of the Amazon River.
1500 Cabral blown off-course whilst

While no portrait of Columbus is fully authenticated, this painting by Sebastiano del Piombo from the early 16th century is believed to portray the discoverer of America.

COLUMBUS'S FLAGSHIP: THE *SANTA MARIA*

This model from the Science Museum in London represents a merchantman as built in one of the Atlantic ports of Spain and Portugal during the 15th century, and is as near as is known to the dimensions of Columbus's ship. The crew numbered around 40 and slept on the decks, as hammocks were a native American invention only introduced to Europe after Columbus's voyage. The overall length of the ship would have been 30 metres (100 ft), and cooking would have been done over a firebox on deck.

century; and it was in a Portuguese ship that Columbus had already made a voyage to Guinea. But Columbus failed to convince the Portuguese crown that his scheme was viable; next he tried France and then Henry VII's England for support. Finally he turned to Spain where, after the capture of Granada from the Moors, the unified monarchs of Aragón and Castile – Ferdinand and Isabella – agreed to put up the money for an expedition of three ships and 120 men and also agreed that Columbus should be hereditary viceroy of any lands he discovered.

He sailed in August 1492, his flagship being the *Santa María*, and put in first at the Canary Islands to replenish stores. He then sailed due west for 33 days without sighting land; at moments his little flotilla was nearly brought to a standstill by the entangled weed of the Sargasso Sea; at other times morale sank so low among the crew that he had to keep a second – false – log book, recording less progress than had been made so that his sailors did not know how far they were from home. But at last they were encouraged by floating weed that could only have come from land, and by shore-loving Bosun birds.

When eventually they made their landfall it was in the Bahamas, and from there they went on to Cuba and Hispaniola (now the Dominican Republic and Haiti) where they managed to barter for a few gold trinkets – such as nose-plugs – from the friendly natives. Having had the misfortune to ground and wreck his flagship on the coast of Hispaniola, Columbus decided to leave some of his crew behind to look for further gold while he returned to Spain to report to Ferdinand and Isabella. So uncertain was he of completing his return voyage safely that he wrote a brief account of his discoveries and put it overboard in a corked bottle, in the hope that if his ship went down, at least the bottle might reach Spain with news of his achievement.

Columbus made three more voyages to the West Indies, but always remained under the impression that he had reached the East Indies and was on the off-shore islands of Cathay. He even despatched a mission to the Great Khan of the Moguls, because when the natives of Cuba talked of gold at 'Cubanacan' (in the interior of Cuba), he thought they were referring to 'Kublai Khan'.

Not everyone shared his geographical convictions, and it has been suggested that the alternative name of Antilles for his newly discovered islands may have indicated that some link was seen with the fabled Atlantic island of Atlantis. Be that as it might, the

following the African coast, was carried by strong currents across the Atlantic to Brazil which he claimed for Portugal.
1501 Vespucci examined the east coast of

South America, finally establishing it to be of continental proportions and not a large island off Asia.
1507 Waldseemüller published Amerigo

Vespucci's letters and map with the name 'America' given for the new continent.
1510 Ojeda and Nicuesa founded Spanish settlement in Darién.

Spanish determined on rapid colonization, although Columbus himself proved less able as an administrator than as an explorer.

The difficulty about colonization was that a title to the newly discovered lands had to be established. Only the Pope could authorize missionary work among the heathen and this activity was the necessary justification for further exploration and settlement. Fortunately for Ferdinand and Isabella, Pope Alexander VI was himself a Spaniard and heavily indebted to them for military and political services elsewhere. The Pope therefore obliged by promulgating a series of bulls − notably the famous *Inter Caetera* − which postulated an imaginary north-south line in the Atlantic 300 leagues (about 1450 km/900 miles) west of the Azores. The world was divided between the Iberian kingdoms, with Spain taking the hemisphere to the west and Portugal the lands to the east. Later, after representations from the King of Portugal, this line was moved further into the Atlantic − to 370 leagues (about 1775 km/1100 miles) west of the Cape Verde Islands − and consolidated into the Treaty of Tordesillas in 1494.

With this mandate secured, the Spanish extended their explorations from the West Indies to the mainland. In Columbus's third expedition of 1498 he went as far down the coast as the mouth of the Orinoco − the largest river to have been discovered by any European at that date − and the following year one of his captains, Vicente Yáñez Pinzón, sailed even further to the coasts of what is now Guiana and the extreme north of Brazil.

The same year, Amerigo Vespucci, another Italian who had come to the New World via Seville, sailed with an expedition that reached the gulf of Venezuela. For a considerable time Amerigo Vespucci was indeed given the credit for discovering this newly found continental land mass and, by dint of his letters to the Medici family and the numerous maps and charts he made of the New World, this whole continent was given his name in perpetuity.

THE PORTUGUESE DISCOVERY OF BRAZIL

It was not only from Spain that intrepid sea captains were setting out across the Atlantic. The Portuguese had been persistently exploring the sea routes round the African coast in order to bring back valuable spices from India. Bartholomeu Dias had rounded the Cape of Good Hope in 1486 and he and his successors had found that, to take advantage of the

The first portrayal of Brazilian Indians, in this woodcut of 1505, shows them as cannibals gnawing at human flesh − see the man on the extreme left.

currents in the south Atlantic, it was best to sail far westwards before turning back to the African coast. It was while practising this manoeuvre that Pedro Alvares Cabral struck land far out into the south Atlantic in 1500. He had in fact reached the coast of Brazil at a point a little south of the present city of Salvador.

Cabral celebrated Easter in this new land and claimed it for King Manuel of Portugal. He had every right to do so: the land fell to the Portuguese side of the dividing line between Spain and Portugal sanctified by the Treaty of Tordesillas six years earlier. Indeed there has always been some speculation as to whether the Portuguese anxiety to move the line further westward was not evidence that they already had some inkling of the existence of Brazil − or at least of some land mass jutting out into the south Atlantic. Be that as it may, Cabral sent home a ship with a valuable report and a few parrots − as an exotic and much prized gift − and continued his journey back across the Atlantic towards the Cape of Good Hope and other eastern discoveries.

Indeed the Portuguese remained preoccupied with the possibilities of lucrative trade with the East (Vasco da Gama had reached India in 1498) and with finding gold in West Africa (the Gold Coast as it became known) rather than with exploiting or developing their South American discovery − 'the Land of the True Cross', as Cabral had named it. Soon however the qualities of the red dye-wood which

grew so plentifully along this coast were found to be useful and profitable, and the country was renamed after this tree – Brazil. The natives also proved attractive and Pedro Vaz de Caminha wrote to King Manuel:

> It is certain that this people is good and of pure simplicity, and there can easily be stamped upon them whatever belief we wish to give them. And furthermore Our Lord gave them fine bodies and good faces . . .

> . . . one of the girls was all painted from head to foot with paint, and she was so well built and so rounded, and her lack of shame so charming, that many women of our own land seeing such attractions, would be ashamed that theirs were not like hers.

Settlement followed discovery. Soon sugar was found to be a more profitable crop than timber, but sugar needed cheap labour and the cheapest sort of labour was slave labour. The American Indians – Amerindians – did not take kindly to toiling all day in the fields for white settlers; they were hunters by inclination, not labourers. Some Amerindians were captured or sold by warring tribes into slavery; but these were outnumbered by those who died (often of European diseases such as smallpox) or escaped.

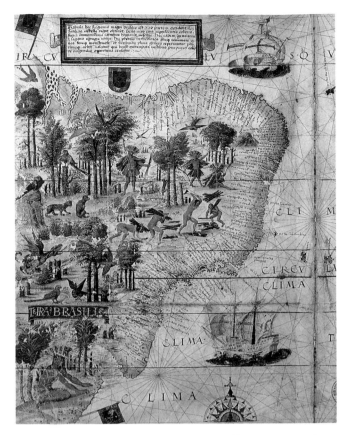

Lopo Homen's lively map of Brazil (1519) illustrates the rich flora and fauna as well as documenting the Portuguese claim with national flags.

The obvious answer seemed to the Portuguese settlers to be the importation of black slaves from their West African trading stations. The settlers also took mistresses among the natives. The mixed racial

CENTRAL AND SOUTH AMERICA: KEY TO ROUTES

(1) **Columbus** 1492–3. Sailed through N West Indies to Cuba and Hispaniola.

(2) **Columbus** 1493–6. Sailed to Dominica, Puerto Rico, Hispaniola, Cuba, Jamaica, Cuba again, Jamaica again and Hispaniola.

(3) **Columbus** 1498. Landfall was Orinoco delta, then NW to Hispaniola.

(4) **Columbus** 1502–4. From Martinique to Hispaniola, Jamaica, Gulf of Honduras, Gulf of Darién, Cuba and Jamaica again.

(5) **Vespucci** 1499–1500. Landfall was Cape Orange in modern Brazil. Visited Amazon and Pará estuaries, Bay of Turiaçu, Curaçao, Gulf of Venezuela and Hispaniola.

(6) **Pinzón** 1499–1500. He sighted land near modern Recife, then explored the Amazon estuary. Proceeded to Grenada, Guadeloupe, Puerto Rico, Hispaniola and the Bahamas.

(7) **Cabral** 1500. Landfall was Monte Pascoal, Brazil. Sailed N to find safer anchorage. Proceeded to Cape of Good Hope.

(8) **Cortés** 1519–21. Sailed from modern Santiago de Cuba to modern Frontera, Mexico, then on to Veracruz. Overland route is shown on p. 172.

(9) **Magellan** 1519–21. Sailed along E coast, explored the River Plate and wintered at San Julián. From Strait of Magellan entered the Pacific in November 1520.

(10) **Sebastian Cabot** 1526. He sailed S along the E coast to the River Plate, then the Paraná and Paraguay rivers.

(11) **Almagro** 1535–7. From Cuzco travelled through Andes to the Salta valley. He crossed the Andes to modern Copiapó. Went S and probably reached Maule R. Returned to Cuzco by coastal route.

(12) **Orellana** 1540. Marched E from Quito and descended Napo R., partly overland, then by barque. Continued on down the Amazon.

(13) **Gonzalo Pizarro** 1540–2. Led party E from Quito to Napo R. Awaited Orellana's return. Continued to confluence with the Amazon, then returned to Quito.

(14) **Valdivia** 1541–7. Travelled S from Cuzco to Chile. Founded La Serena, Santiago, Concepción, La Imperial, Villarrica and Valdivia.

(15) **Anson** 1740–4. Sailed along E coast, passed through Strait of Le Maire and continued N to Mexico.

(16) **Cook** 1768–9. Sailed along the E coast, calling at Rio. Passed through Strait of Le Maire, then proceeded NW across the Pacific.

(17) **Malaspina** 1789–94. Called at River Plate, then continued S, rounding Staten Island and Cape Horn. Sailed N to Mexico.

(18) **Humboldt** 1799–1803. Travelled in modern Venezuela, visited Cuba, and explored in Colombia, Ecuador and Peru. Sailed for Mexico.

(19) **Snow** 1951–2. Travelled from Lake Lauricocha, Peru, to Iquitos on foot and by mule, horse, bus, lorry, raft and canoe; then by riverboat to Belém.

(20) **Hanbury-Tenison** 1958. Made an E-W crossing by jeep from Recife, Brazil, to Lima, Peru.

(21) **Hanbury-Tenison** 1964–5. From Orinoco R. travelled by dinghy across Amazon basin, then overland to sail down the Paraguay R. and River Plate.

Other journeys: Francisco Pizarro, p. 174; Raleigh p. 179; Father Fritz, p. 183; La Condamine, p. 185; Mme Godin, p. 186; Darwin, p. 189; Byron, p. 190; Roosevelt and Rondon, p. 195; and Fawcett, p. 199.

1513 Balboa crossed the Isthmus of Panama, sighted the Pacific and claimed it for Spain, opening the way for the exploration of the west coast of South America.

1520 Magellan sailed along the Patagonian coast and into the Pacific by way of the Strait of Magellan, so pioneering the south-west route to Asia.

1519-21 Cortés travelled from Cuba to Mexico in search of gold. Established a base at Veracruz and occupied the Aztec capital of Tenochtitlán. Many Indians died in the

pattern of Brazil had begun in the earliest years of European settlement. But it was only along the coast that these settlements clustered; progress inland was daunting and difficult, not least because many of the major rivers (unlike those of West Africa) were attended by rapids and waterfalls relatively near the coast. The interior of South America remained a closed world.

MAGELLAN AND THE SOUTH-WEST PASSAGE

Just as Christopher Columbus had offered his services first to the crown of Portugal, so Ferdinand Magellan – himself a Portuguese who had served his country well in India and Morocco – first sought preferment in Lisbon. But when King Manuel declined to approve his advancement in the nobility as a recognition of past services, he too turned to the Spanish crown. He offered to lead a maritime expedition to the Spice Islands – the East Indies – round the south of the American continent 'without touching any sea or land of the King of Portugal'.

The Spanish fitted out five ships for this venture, all of them 'very old and patched up' according to the jaundiced reporting of the Portuguese envoy in Seville. Magellan set sail in September 1519 and by

The use of a sea chart and various contemporary navigational instruments are depicted on the title page from a Dutch edition of The Mariner's Guide *of 1592.*

the end of that year was sailing down the east coast of South America towards Patagonia. The inhabitants of that region appeared to them as giants and they decided to kidnap some Patagonians to take home as curiosities. Being somewhat frightened of them, they set about it in a thoroughly devious way.

Magellan's navigator – Antonio Pigafetta – describes how they loaded two of them with gifts and then, when their hands were full, suggested that they might like to wear large iron bracelets on their ankles:

> These giants took pleasure in seeing the irons, but they did not know where to put them, and it grieved them that they could not take them with their hands, because they were hindered by the other things which they held in them . . . immediately the captain had the irons put on the feet of both of them.

It was the work of a moment to rivet them into their fetters. Having thus dramatically demonstrated their bad faith, they sailed on.

The crews' treachery was not confined to their dealings with the natives: they also persistently plotted against each other. The first mutiny was at San Julián in Patagonia. Magellan had the offending officers' heads cut off and their bodies quartered; others were marooned on the Patagonian coast. Severe as these measures were, they were not to deter others later.

The little fleet was now approaching Tierra del Fuego and it entered the labyrinth of channels between the islands north of Cape Horn. Having penetrated deep into one channel – which they named after the day of the Eleven Thousand Virgins – the sailors became convinced that there was no exit into another sea. Magellan persuaded them to press on by claiming that:

> there was another straight [strait] going out, and said he knew it well, because he had seen it by a marine chart of the King of Portugal, which map had been made by a great pilot and mariner named Martin of Bohemia.

This was sheer invention on Magellan's part. No European had navigated the straits before and Martin Behaim's globe, which had been made in 1492, did not depict any American continent, let alone any specific straits around its southern extremity. But the encouragement was enough and when the leading ships took refuge from a storm around a further headland, they found it did indeed lead on to further navigable waterways. The rest of the fleet

ensuing battles and siege.
1522 Andagoya led coastal survey south from Panama and brought back earliest reports of Inca gold in Peru.

1524-6 Alvarado, chief lieutenant to Cortés, conquered Guatemala and El Salvador.
1527 Cabot sailed up the Rivers Plate, Paraná and Paraguay searching for a route

to the Pacific.
1532-5 Pizarro and his *conquistadores* decimated the Inca empire. Cuzco captured, and new capital established at Lima.

MARINER'S ASTROLABE

Developed by the Greeks and Arabs in medieval Europe, the astrolabe was already in well-established use by the time Magellan sailed around South America in 1519–20. As shown in the woodcut illustration (from Pedro de

Medina's *Regimento de navegación*, published in Seville in 1563) the mariner would calculate latitude by measuring the angle of the sun or the pole star above the horizon. The solid brass face of the astrolabe would be pierced to reduce wind resistance when it was hung on deck for use.

ORIZONTE

ocean had fresh hazards, the chief among which was its sheer size. He headed on a north-westerly bearing for well over 100 days without any opportunity to take on fresh provisions. Pigafetta graphically described the hardships:

> We ate old biscuit, reduced to powder and full of grubs, and stinking from the dirt which the rats had made on it when eating the good biscuit, and we drank water that was yellow and stinking . . . we also ate wood sawdust and rats which cost half-a-crown each . . . the gums of most of our men swelled so much [from scurvy] they could not eat.

As a result of these privations 19 men died and a further 35 'fell ill of divers sicknesses'. When eventually they reached the Philippines in March 1521, Magellan himself was killed in a skirmish with the natives. The only ship of the five to survive was the *Victoria* which returned to Seville, having circumnavigated the globe, three years after it set out; only 18 of the original crews of 243 reached home to tell the tale. The New World had proved, after all, to provide a sea route to the East Indies: a south-west passage was less intractable than a north-west one.

had given them up for lost before they returned, firing off their guns in celebration and giving thanks to the Virgin Mary.

Magellan spent some time exploring among the intricate channels and while he was doing so another of his ships – the *San Antonio* – mutinied and, deserting Magellan's fleet, made off for home. The Patagonian 'giant' whom the mutineers had on board died of heatstroke when the ship reached warmer climes. Meanwhile the other Patagonian kidnap victim with Magellan was faring much better, showing signs of conversion to Christianity and being christened Paul by his captors. The sailing and charting was continued by Magellan and his remaining ships; they were able to work for long hours as even in October the night is only dark at that latitude for three hours – a fact which astonished the crew.

Finally Magellan and his ship broke out of the channels into the ocean beyond on 20 November 1520; their first impression had been of a smooth and sunny ocean which they consequently named the Pacific. (Balboa, when he had first spied this ocean on crossing the isthmus of Panama seven years before, had named it the Southern Ocean because the isthmus ran east-west where he crossed it.) All too soon Magellan was to discover that his new

CORTES CONQUERS MEXICO

Having consolidated their hold on the Isthmus of Panama and the Greater Antilles, the Spanish cast around for further fields to conquer. In the first years of the 16th century rumours were already filtering through to Cuba and Hispaniola of a more developed and richer indigenous civilization to the west of these islands and to the north of the Isthmus.

These rumours were confirmed by reports from the modest expeditions that nosed along the coasts of Yucatán and the Gulf of Mexico in 1517 and 1518. The following year, the Spanish Governor of Cuba – Diego Velázquez – fitted out a more ambitious expedition to Mexico and appointed his secretary, Hernán Cortés (1485–1547), who was also a shareholder in the enterprise, as its commander. The Spanish lust for gold and adventure was as great as ever, and Cortés had little difficulty in attracting 600 volunteers to sail with him.

Cortés was the son of a noble Spanish family from Extremadura, one of the poorest and climatically harshest regions of Spain; after studying at Salamanca university, he had decided to seek his fortune in the New World. Soon after he had left Cuba on his

171

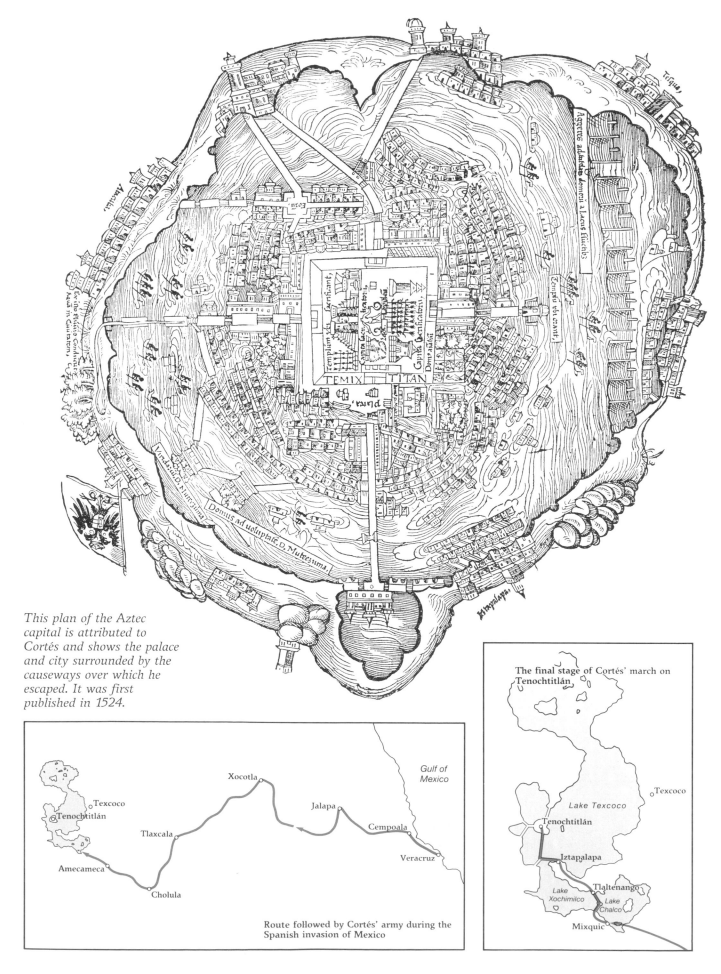

This plan of the Aztec
capital is attributed to
Cortés and shows the palace
and city surrounded by the
causeways over which he
escaped. It was first
published in 1524.

The final stage of Cortés' march on
Tenochtitlán

Texcoco

Lake Texcoco

Tenochtitlán

Iztapalapa

Tlaltenango

Lake
Xochimilco

Lake
Chalco

Mixquic

Gulf of
Mexico

Texcoco

Tenochtitlán

Tlaxcala

Amecameca

Cholula

Xocotla

Jalapa

Cempoala

Veracruz

Route followed by Cortés' army during the
Spanish invasion of Mexico

172

expedition to Mexico he renounced the Governor's sway and determined to make the expedition, and whatever conquests it might achieve, wholly his own.

He landed first at Tabasco and on the strength of information he gleaned there, he sailed on to the port that is now Veracruz. There he spent four months preparing to march inland and confront the power of the Aztec empire; so that there should be no turning back, he burnt his boats on the shore – all except for one, which he despatched back to Spain to explain why he had declared direct allegiance to the Crown rather than to Velázquez.

When all his preparations were completed, Cortés led his band of soldiers-of-fortune on the rough, steep route from the tropical coastal forests of Veracruz to the high plateau of central Mexico. He chose his route to maximize his chances of gaining supporters and in doing so, was obliged to cross some of the most difficult mountain passes in the country. This policy paid off: after some initial resistance, the independent city state of Tlaxcala – which had been regularly subjected to slaving raids by the Aztecs – formed an alliance with Cortés. It was then clear that the Aztec capital of Tenochtitlán in the high valley called Mexico, the centre of Aztec power and the treasure house of the empire, must be Cortés's objective.

At this point Cortés received an embassy from Montezuma, the Aztec king, who wished to dissuade him from advancing further into the kingdom; to this end Montezuma sent him valuable gifts. But these had the opposite effect from that intended: far from buying off the Spaniards from a further advance, they incited them to press on in the expectation of more such golden artefacts. Cortés also deployed some of the gifts to good effect by sending them back to the King of Spain – then the formidable Emperor Charles V – to persuade him to endorse Cortés's own independent command.

Undeterred by threats or gifts, Cortés continued his march on Tenochtitlán. He convinced Montezuma that his purposes were friendly, and the Aztec army escorted the Spanish force across the causeway into their cherished capital of Tenochtitlán and lodged them in a palace in the very centre of this city standing in a lake. The fearless demeanour of the *conquistadores*, their dazzling armour and their awe-inspiring horses all combined to bemuse Montezuma and his subjects. Cortés's native allies remained on the shores of the lake outside the city, and Montezuma himself occupied an equivocal position as part guest and part hostage of the Spaniards. For a while an uneasy calm prevailed.

It was unfortunate that Cortés had to leave his little army at this moment. The reason was that the Governor of Cuba, learning of Cortés's repudiation of his control, had sent another Spanish captain, Narváez, to arrest him and bring him back to Cuba. Cortés decided to confront Narváez at the coast; he did this so successfully that Narváez's men decided to join with Cortés and return with him to Tenochtitlán. It was only just in time.

In his absence the fragile relationship between the *conquistadores* and the Aztecs had become strained to breaking point: his lieutenant, Pedro de Alvarado, had allowed the Spaniards to indulge in some looting and destruction, and sporadic fighting had broken out. Cortés was enabled to re-enter Tenochtitlán but, having done so, found himself and his whole force trapped within the palace. The Aztecs had rejected the authority of Montezuma, whom they considered now to be a tool of the *conquistadores*, and when at Cortés's insistence he tried to reason with his own people, they stoned him and he was mortally wounded. The Spaniards no longer had any effective hostage. The position of the *conquistadores*, isolated in the midst of the Aztec horde, had become desperate.

It was then that Cortés showed his mettle. Gathering his band around him, he fought his way out of the palace and the city across the broken causeways by night; a third of his men fell in the fighting and almost all the treasure, baggage and spare weapons were lost. But Cortés was re-united with his allies from Tlaxcala and determined on a counter offensive. He returned to besiege the Aztecs in Tenochtitlán; he cut off the food and fresh water; he built boats from which to bombard the island fortress; he threw up new causeways; and he waited while the diseases which the Aztecs had contracted from the Spaniards – notably smallpox – took their toll. By 1521 the city had surrendered and the Kingdom of Mexico was at the feet of Cortés.

The looting then started in earnest. The Spaniards combed the fallen city for gold, and tortured prisoners to reveal where more was hidden. They turned on each other, and even on Cortés himself, with accusations of secreting treasure for personal gain. When the haul of gold proved disappointing, Cortés tried to console his followers with grants of land. As soon as he could, he turned his energies once more to exploration; he led expeditions to the Pacific coast of Mexico and even despatched ships into that ocean; he sent other commanders into the Mayan region of Guatemala. As so often happened with the Spaniards, rival commanders fell out with each other; at one point – in 1524 – one of Cortés's commanders moving southward clashed with one of the Spanish commanders from the Isthmus moving northwards; once more, Cortés's presence restored good order and unity.

Eventually he himself returned to Spain to give an account of his conquests and his administration to Charles V. The emperor received him affably enough, and created him Marquis of Oaxaca (in Mexico); but Charles V did not feel comfortable with his over-mighty subject and he gave Cortés no real authority. The greatest of the *conquistadores* retired to die as a private citizen in his native Spain.

PIZARRO AND HIS CAPTAINS: PERU AND CHILE

The success of Cortés in Mexico was to inspire the discovery and conquest of another ancient civilization in the New World – that of the Incas of Peru. After Vasco Núñez de Balboa had reached the Pacific ocean, and claimed 'this unknown sea and all that it contained for the King of Castile', he went on to set up a city on the Pacific seaboard: Panama (a few miles from the site of the present city). From this port expeditions started to sail in both directions along the Pacific coast. One of the main objectives was to find whether there was any channel through the isthmus, linking the Atlantic and Pacific. But the expeditions southwards soon took on an even more urgent purpose.

In 1511, while Balboa had been weighing some gold brought in by the Indians, a young native chief had boasted of a realm to the south of Panama where 'the inhabitants eat and drink out of golden vessels and gold is as cheap as iron'. Rumours persisted that a kingdom of immense wealth lay further down the coast. Among those who heeded the rumours was Francisco Pizarro, an ageing soldier of fortune who had come to the New World – as had Cortés – for adventure and to escape the hard life of the Extremadura region of Spain. The Governor of Panama authorized Pizarro to take an expedition in search of this unknown kingdom, and he made two unsuccessful attempts to reach the empire of the Incas, before finally in 1532 he landed at Tumbes in northern Peru.

Pizarro marched inland and was soon encouraged by encountering friendly envoys from the ruling Inca and further confirmation of the mineral riches of the country. Even so, there were some murmurs of discontent among his followers and Pizarro boldly

This woodcut, from an early Peruvian codex in the royal library at Copenhagen, shows Pizarro and Almagro setting out for the Indies.

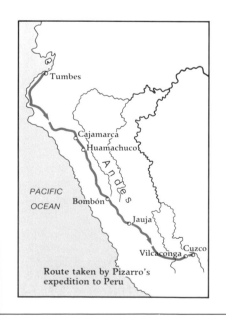

Route taken by Pizarro's expedition to Peru

The same codex depicts the conquistadores *beheading the Inca Atahualpa: other accounts report that he was garrotted. Whatever the form of his execution, it was deplored by the Emperor Charles V.*

For the Spaniards in Peru, exploration was synonymous with conquest. The turning point of Pizarro's campaign was his seizure of Atahualpa, the Inca, in the heart of his own kingdom – an act of daring, deceit and cruelty which permanently stained the honour of the *conquistadores*.

Pizarro had landed at Tumbes in the north of Peru in 1532 with 177 men, of whom 67 were cavalry. With this minuscule force he had marched into the interior, exchanged friendly messages with the ruling Inca, and pressed on to cross the Andes and arrive at Cajamarca where the Inca was awaiting them. The vast size and sophistication of the Inca's army and court at first overawed the Spaniards who realized how rash they had been to venture so far into his power.

Nothing daunted, Pizarro devised a plot to kidnap the Inca himself and hold him as a hostage for their safety. He enticed Atahualpa to pay a visit to him in the main square of Cajamarca where the Spanish force was concealed. Long low buildings lined three sides of the square and each of these had some 20 openings on to the open space in the middle; the cavalry were therefore able to sit mounted and concealed ready to charge out at the signal through the openings. There were delays and doubts as to whether the Inca might not bring a large armed force with him. The Spaniards, despite themselves, were highly jittery and one of them reported seeing others 'urinate out of pure terror'.

The Inca finally arrived in great state, but with his retinue unarmed. On entering the square, he was approached by the Dominican friar who was Pizarro's chaplain and who made a fairly peremptory attempt to explain Christianity to the Inca; when the latter – not surprisingly – declined to be instantly converted and rejected the proferred Bible, the friar returned to Pizarro calling 'I absolve you'.

Pizarro and his men did not hesitate. With cries of 'Santiago' they sprang from their places of hiding into the square and set about slaughtering the Inca's retinue to the accompaniment of artillery and musket fire. Total panic ensued: it was a massacre, not a battle. The Inca's personal bodyguard of nobles stood by him, supporting his litter on their

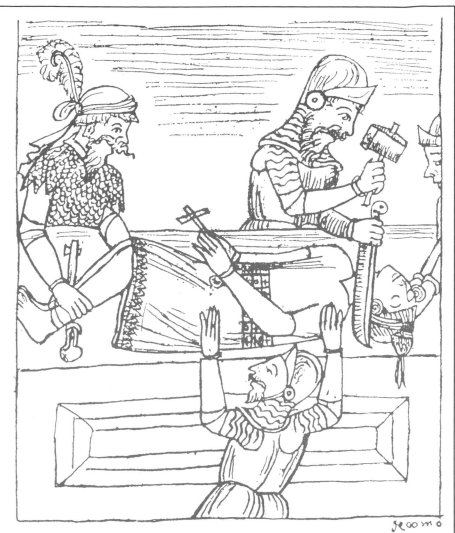

shoulders even when their arms had been cut off. Estimates of the number of the Inca's retainers cut down varied from 2000 to 10,000, and indeed it was only by his physically shielding the Inca that Pizarro (who in the process suffered the only wound of the day on the Spanish side) managed to save Atahualpa from being cut down with the rest.

Once the Inca was taken prisoner, his remaining army and supporters were without a leader and Pizarro was able to consolidate his hold on Cajamarca. Since spreading the gospel of Christ had always been a subsidiary objective to acquiring treasure for themselves, the *conquistadores* soon realized that Atahualpa as a prisoner was not only a useful hostage but that he had a high ransom value. The Inca offered to fill a whole room – 6.70 x 5.20 metres (22 x 17 ft) in dimensions – with gold and silver up to a height of 2.75 metres (9 ft) from the floor as the price of his release. Precious artefacts started pouring in from all over his kingdom to fulfil the condition of his release.

Not satisfied with this tribute to their greed, the Spaniards began to be apprehensive about the Inca's supporters launching a surprise attack on them. Rumours spread that the Inca was using the messengers who brought in the gold to rally military support for his rescue. Pizarro decided that Atahualpa alive was no longer an asset; he set up a hasty parody of a trial, in which the charges against Atahualpa included that 'he was guilty of idolatry and adulterous practices, indulging openly in plurality of wives'. He was predictably condemned to be burnt at the stake and the only mercy Pizarro showed to him was commuting the sentence to being garrotted. The Spanish Emperor Charles V strongly disapproved when he heard of the Inca's judicial murder.

But the treasure the Spaniards had tricked out of the Inca and the terror they inspired by their brutal treatment of him provided both the motive and the means to further conquest and exploration of the rest of Peru in the decade that followed.

1541-6 Valdivia founded the city of Santiago in Chile, and explored south the Río Bío-Bío.
1561 Cavallón and Coronado colonized Costa Rica for Spain.

1577 Drake, blown southward from Strait of Magellan, discovered Drake's Passage. Plundered Spanish galleons off Chile, Peru and Ecuador.

1582-90 Berrío explored the Orinoco valley in search of El Dorado, but was subsequently captured by Sir Walter Raleigh.

invited all those who had any qualms about pressing on further into unknown territory to return to garrison the little colony of San Miguel; out of the 177 Spaniards under his command, only nine opted to turn back.

With this all-volunteer force, Pizarro then faced the crossing of the Andes to meet the Inca Atahualpa. The horses and men shivered and slithered on the precarious mountain ledges along which their route lay. It was the first European experience of this mighty mountain range and of the vicuña, alpaca and condors which inhabited it. True to his protestations of friendship, the Inca had not defended the passes, although some of these had man-made fortifications at strategic points.

Having crossed the *cordillera*, the Spaniards advanced directly on Cajamarca where the Inca and his army were waiting to receive them. They then wondered whether they had not, after all, walked into a trap. They were surrounded by a vastly superior force, in the heart of a country they had come to raid, with no possibility of retreat or reinforcement. In these circumstances Pizarro devised a plot to seize the Inca himself. The massacre which ensued was a prelude to the collection of a vast horde of golden Inca artefacts for the Inca's ransom; but before it was completed, Pizarro had trumped up charges of conspiracy against the Inca and brutally executed him.

The Spaniards marched on to Cuzco, the Inca capital, where yet more treasure swelled their coffers, and then founded their own capital on the coast at Lima. The climate on the coastal plain was (and is) unhealthy and foggy in marked contrast to the sparkling air of Cuzco, and it is still believed by some Peruvians that the Incas may have encouraged Pizarro to choose such an unsuitable site for a capital as a covert act of retaliation.

After their acts of perfidy against the Incas, the Spanish *conquistadores* turned to quarrelling among themselves. But despite their squabbles and internal dissensions, other notable acts of discovery were made. Diego de Almagro, one of Pizarro's companions, set out in 1535 with a group of the *conquistadores* to explore further south: after more terrible experiences in the Andes he arrived in Chile – the first European to do so. The extremes of cold endured in the Andes were to be followed by extremes of heat in the Atacama Desert. He returned from his explorations to find himself fighting Pizarro whose brother eventually had him strangled in prison.

This discovery of Chile was to be consolidated by Pedro de Valdivia who in 1541 founded the city of Santiago in one of the most beautiful and fertile valleys of South America; his capital was an infinitely more agreeable place to live than Lima, and a Spanish community prospered there on farming – and later on vineyards – instead of basing itself solely on the pursuit of gold and precious stones. But further south – and particularly across the Bío-Bío river – colonization was harder: this was the homeland of the Araucanian Indians, who were described by López Vaz as 'the most valiant and furious people in all America'. Valdivia had various encounters with them, but prudently did not press his conquests too far south.

Nor did Valdivia go eastwards across the Andes into what is now Argentina. This area of Patagonia had been explored two decades earlier, in part by Sebastian Cabot who (despite his Venetian birth) was also operating with a Spanish commission. Cabot explored the River Plate (named after the silver he found there), and the Paraná and Paraguay rivers.

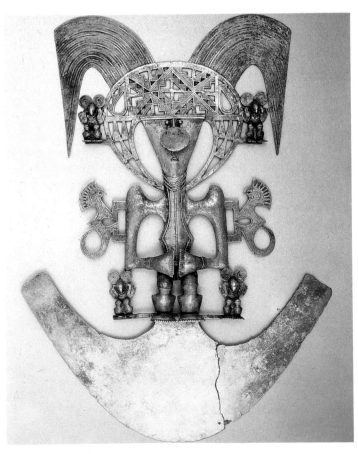

Golden artefacts, such as this pectoral figure with headdress, were collected from all over Peru as a ransom for the Inca Atahualpa: greed for such gold lured the conquistadores *on.*

Indeed, had Cabot penetrated further north up the river system he discovered, he might have reached the empire of the Incas before Pizarro. But he did not, and the glory and shame of the conquest of Peru will forever be attributed to Pizarro.

ORELLANA NAVIGATES THE AMAZON

Another of the Spanish captains, Francisco de Orellana, made an even more remarkable discovery – and made it by accident. In 1540, the *conquistadores* had marched from Quito in modern Ecuador eastwards, out of the land of the Incas and into the cinnamon forests, when they came on a wide river with roaring waterfalls: the Napo. As their rations were exhausted – they had already eaten their horses, pigs and hunting dogs – Gonzalo Pizarro (the brother of Francisco Pizarro) sent Orellana ahead down the river, in a brigantine which it had taken them many weeks to construct, to find food and return to re-provision the whole expedition.

Orellana's brigantine travelled fast on the current in the centre of the stream, and after three days he reached an even wider river. There was still no food to be had and the natives were hostile, so he pressed on. By the time he had found supplies, the prospect of returning to Pizarro's main party, against the strong current, seemed virtually impossible: or at least it seemed easier and more exciting to go on downstream on a mighty and unknown river which he realized must eventually reach the Atlantic and hence the sea route to home.

Fighting off the hostile Indians on the shore, Orellana made his way some 4750 km (3000 miles) down the world's mightiest river that he named Amazon after the ancient legend of warrior women. He sailed up to the West Indies and eventually took passage for Spain where his discoveries were considered sufficiently remarkable to outweigh the dubious ethics of his having abandoned his comrades. He was granted a commission by the king to conquer and colonize the region he had discovered. But he died on the return journey to the Amazon. The river was not to be colonized – in so far as it was ever colonized – by him, but by the Portuguese into whose domain Brazil was to fall.

As for Gonzalo Pizarro and his men, who had been stranded on the banks of the Napo, they waited for weeks for Orellana's return with news and – more important – food. When he failed to come back, they reluctantly followed the river bank to look for him; it took them two months of weary

Araucanian Indians from southern Chile were described by López Vaz as 'the most valiant and furious people in all America', though here they look peaceful enough.

and hungry struggle through the forests to reach the junction with the larger river to which Orellana had been borne by the swift current in less than three days. There they found the half-demented figure of one of their comrades who had been abandoned to his fate by Orellana when he objected to the plan to press on down the river.

They then knew the worst: there was nothing they could do but try to retrace their steps to Quito, living off the jungle and anything they could seize from Indian settlements. They ate insects, snakes and their own leather belts. Many fell by the wayside and themselves provided food for jaguars and alligators. When they regained Quito in June 1542 – two years after they had set out – they had shrunk from a party of 350 Spaniards to a mere 80 survivors: the losses among their Indian porters had been even heavier. The river Amazon had been found, but at a terrible price.

THE SEARCH FOR EL DORADO

Although much harm had been done by the early *conquistadores* to the Amerindians, this had not been the intention of the Spanish crown. Indeed, as early as 1503 Queen Isabella had issued an order forbidding cruel treatment of the Amerindians – but with the important exception of 'a certain people called Cannibals'. The royal decree went on to say that

> If the said Cannibals continue to resist, and do not wish to admit and receive to their lands the Captains and men who may be on such voyages by my orders, nor to hear them in order to be taught our Sacred Catholic Faith . . . they may be captured and taken to be sold.

The region inland from Cartagena was designated 'Cannibal country' in this decree, and therefore there were no inhibitions on the Spanish *conquistadores* who first entered the territory which is now Colombia. Settlements were established on the coast in the first decades of the 16th century, largely to facilitate raiding parties opening up the interior.

Vasco Núñez de Balboa (it was he who had first claimed the Pacific for the Spanish crown) led one such expedition in 1512; his particular objective was to contact an Indian chief called Dabeiba who seemed to be a collecting agent for gold in the region. Indeed, the precious metal was so plentiful that the whole mainland was then officially designated Castilla del Oro.

Encouraged by the examples of Cortés and Pizarro, gold fever reached its height in the 1530s, with three separate expeditions – under Jiménez de Quesada, Federmann (a German) and Benalcázar – meeting together to establish a settlement on the site of the present city of Bogotá and then to explore and exploit the surrounding countryside. These commanders – unlike their contemporaries further south in Peru – avoided falling out between themselves and concentrated on despoiling the natives.

As they collected more and more gold, and captured increasing numbers of Indians, one story began to recur: it concerned a gilded man – 'El Dorado' – and the curious rites which took place at an inland lake near Bogotá called Guatavita. These revolved around the initiation of a new ruler, who would be floated out on to the water on a raft of rushes, with his principal subject chiefs and a great pile of gold and emeralds. The prince himself was then, according to Juan Rodríguez Freyle writing much later in 1636:

MARINER'S COMPASS

This late 16th-century compass from the National Maritime Museum in London was probably made in Italy and is possibly the oldest surviving compass in Europe. The needle is of magnetized iron; the bowl is of ivory and the whole is mounted in two brass gimbals. The needle required recharging with magnetism periodically with a lodestone (a form of magnetite). Elizabethan sea captains such as Sir Walter Raleigh would have used just such compasses on their voyages to the West Indies.

SIR WALTER RALEIGH AND THE ORINOCO

The sight of Spanish coffers filling with gold from the New World was a continual provocation to the sea captains of Elizabethan England. In 1595 Sir Walter Raleigh, with the backing of the Queen and her courtiers, set sail for Guiana to attempt to find El Dorado – this time seeking the fabled golden city in the forests beyond the Orinoco river.

Raleigh lost two of his ships on the Atlantic crossing but eventually landed in Trinidad. His first act was to attack the Spanish settlement at San José (Port of Spain) and capture its governor Antonio de Berrío, who warned him against the hazards of the Orinoco. Undeterred and escorted by Indian guides alienated from the Spaniards by Berrío's cruelty, he and his depleted crew canoed up river for some 800 km (500 miles), continually losing themselves in the maze of interlocking streams. When the rains came, Raleigh recorded 'our hearts were cold to behold the great rage and increase of the Orinoco' and conditions forced him to turn back.

Raleigh had collected samples of what he imagined were gold-bearing ore and rocks which 'exceeded any

diamond in beauty'; but he had not accumulated any substantial treasure in bullion or precious stones. Instead, he came back with an ecstatic account of the beauties of the flora and fauna of the tropical rain forests; he wrote a glowing account of 'a country that hath still her maidenhood'. Elizabeth I, who had backed the voyage financially as well as morally in the hope of rich gains, was unimpressed and declined to allow Raleigh to colonize the region.

Raleigh nonetheless maintained his enchantment with Guiana even during his years in disgrace and imprisonment under James I. In 1617 he sailed there again, having been released from the Tower to make a last desperate attempt to find his El Dorado. The King was so fearful of offending the Spaniards, who claimed sovereignty over the whole region, that he gave details of Raleigh's plans to the Spanish ambassador. Not surprisingly, Raleigh was ambushed and his son Wat killed; he returned disgraced to face the wrath of the King and ultimately execution. He had escaped the dangers of Guiana to no avail.

Raleigh's journeys to Guiana in 1595 and 1617

Left Sir Walter Raleigh with his son Wat who was later killed by the Spaniards on his father's last expedition of exploration up the Orinoco.

The title page of Sir Walter Raleigh's own rapturous account of the beauties of Guiana, written after his first expedition up the Orinoco in 1595. The natives are portrayed

sympathetically in the accompanying woodcut.

THE
DISCOVERIE
OF THE LARGE,
RICH AND BEWTIFVL
EMPIRE OF Gviana, WITH
a relation of the Great and Golden City
of Manoa (which the *spaniards* call El
Dorado) And the prouinces of *Emeria,*
Arromaia, Amapaia and other Coun-
ties, with their riuers, ad-
ioyning.

Performed in the yeare 1595. by Sir
W. *Ralegh,* Knight, Captaine of her
Maiesties Guard, Lo. *Warden*
of the Stanneries, and her High-
neffe Lieutenant generall
of the Countie of
Cornewall.

Imprinted at London by Robert Robinson
1596.

stripped to his skin, and anointed with a sticky earth on which they placed gold dust so that he was completedly covered with this metal . . . when they reached the centre of the lagoon . . . the gilded Indian made his offering, throwing out all the pile of gold into the middle of the lake, and the chiefs who accompanied him did the same.

This is one version of the origin of the El Dorado legend, although the term was later to be attached to a mythical city of gold rather than to a man. The practical point that emerged from the story of the Indian prince and his raft was that the floor of the Lake Guatavita was lined with golden artefacts and precious stones accumulated over a long period: some sources even told the Spaniards of caravans of 40 Indians all laden with gold destined for the lagoon. As corroboration, some gold ornaments were washed up on the fringes of the lake.

Charles V, Holy Roman Emperor and King of Spain. He welcomes the bullion from the New World while being appalled by some of the conquistadores' *brutalities.*

Minds immediately turned towards draining the lagoon. First one of Quesada's captains, and then his brother, attempted the task. The latter waited until the dry season of 1545 and then organized a chain-gang with gourds instead of buckets; they lowered the level of the water by 3 metres (10 ft) and salvaged some 4000 gold coins.

Forty years later a rich Spanish merchant – Antonio de Sepúlveda – employed some 8000 Indians to cut a V-shaped notch in the rim of the lake through which the water drained out; this time the level of the water was lowered by 20 metres (65ft) before the cut fell in, killing many of the Indians and causing the scheme to be abandoned. Twelve thousand pesos had been salvaged and 'Sepúlveda's cut', as it was known, is visible to this day.

Numerous other attempts followed: at the beginning of the 19th century, one of Simón Bolívar's friends developed a plan to syphon the water out of the lake; at the end of the same century a public company was floated with the objective of draining out the water through a tunnel. This last plan had an initial success: the bed of the lake was finally exposed, but it revealed a surface of mud and slime several feet deep which could not be walked upon; by the following day the sun had baked the mud so

Mounted Guaicura warriors such as these were among the hazards facing the bandeirantes *on the pampas when they penetrated inland from São Paulo.*

hard that it could not be penetrated by picks or shovels; by the time that drilling equipment had been procured, the baked mud had blocked the tunnel and the lagoon had refilled with water. A few items were found and later sold at Christie's in London. The secret gold hoard of the Indians (if it ever existed) eluded the Spanish *conquistadores* and still eludes treasure seekers today.

MISSIONARIES AND *BANDEIRANTES*: EXPLORERS IN CONFLICT

In the 16th century, the overriding motivation for the exploration of south and central America had been the greed for gold; the spread of the Gospel had often been little more than a pretext, and the hunt for slaves little more than a means of providing labour for mining precious metals. But by the 17th and 18th centuries, the main thrust of exploration had been taken over by missionaries genuinely intent on converting and protecting the Indians, and in

Brazil by *bandeirantes* (armed marauders collected into bands known as *bandeiras*) equally intent on rounding up Indians as slave labour not only for mines but for plantations and farms along the continental eastern coast line. Inevitably these two groups came into conflict – a conflict as violent as that between the competing groups of *conquistadores* in the 16th century.

Enslaving of Indians had from the earliest days of European settlement been prohibited in South America, both by the Pope and by the crowns of Spain and Portugal. But there were loop-holes in this prohibition: Indians captured in a righteous war could be retained as slave labour, as could Indians captured by one tribe from another and sold to

THE CODEX KÖLER

Hieronymous Köler left an eyewitness account of the way in which Federmann's expedition to conquer the interior of Venezuela in the 1530s was organized in Seville before its departure from Spain. This illustration from his Codex shows the *conquistadores*, having collected their weapons and listened to a special mass, marching in procession to the port, accompanied by drummers and by the red-and-white banner of the German banking family of Welser who had been given a concession to finance the colonization of this part of Spanish America.

Spanish and Portuguese troops marching to occupy a reducción *in Paraguay which had sheltered the Indians before the expulsion of the Jesuits.*

European settlers as an alternative to being massacred (or eaten).

These provisions were wide open to abuse: any raiding party – even one whose sole objective was capturing Indians – could claim to be involved in a 'righteous war'; and the prospect of purchasing slaves from a victorious tribe was an incentive to stir up hostilities between the tribes. The Spanish crown was fairly fastidious about trying to keep its settlers to the rules; but the Portuguese crown, which had a less tight grip on the administration of its overseas possessions, was less so. Cases of settlers being excommunicated and handed over for punishment to the Inquisition – officially, the penalty for slave trading in American Indians – were almost unknown.

The greatest centre for the *bandeirantes* was São Paulo in southern Brazil. From here bands several hundred strong would set out into the interior of Paraguay or of Goiás for expeditions which might last for a year or two. There would frequently be heavy casualties among the *bandeirantes*, some killed in skirmishes, some succumbing to disease and hunger; sometimes whole expeditions disappeared without trace either because they had attempted to cross too arduous a natural obstacle or because

they had tackled an Indian tribe stronger than themselves.

They were frequently accompanied by priests or friars, but these would confine their activities to consoling the dying *bandeirantes* rather than enforcing the papal edicts against enslaving the natives. The *bandeirantes* seldom systematically mapped the terrain they traversed, and as they were not interested in exploration for its own sake, they equally seldom recorded their discoveries accurately. But the interior of the continent was effectively opened up by these 'inland buccaneers' (as Robin Furneaux has described them).

The most effective force ranged against them was the Society of Jesus – the Jesuits. The first Jesuits had landed in Brazil as early as 1549, and while other religious orders had concentrated on tending to the needs of the settlers, the Jesuits concentrated on converting the heathen. They penetrated deep into the forests and swamps, into the savannahs and mountains. At first their efforts appeared to help the settlers: they preached peace and made cannibalistic and belligerent tribes more docile. But when the Jesuits realized that even the Indians whom they had converted to Christianity were not immune from the attentions of the slave raiders, they began to collect their converts into communities which could be protected by the authority of the Church and – if need be – by organized self-defence.

These communities were known (particularly in Paraguay where the Spanish Jesuits were strongest) as *reducciones*. The earliest was established in 1608 and it was among the Tupi-speaking Guarani tribes that the fastest progress was made. Huge stone mission churches were constructed; crops were cultivated and equitably distributed; the Indians were clothed and educated in the scriptures; local dances and traditions were converted into more seemly Christian rituals; arts and handicrafts – particularly those with a religious connotation – were taught and encouraged; everywhere in the *reducciones* discipline tempered with paternalism was the order of the day.

Solid and secure as these Spanish *reducciones* might seem, they were not always safe from predatory attacks by the Portuguese *bandeirantes*. In 1629, bands from São Paulo sacked five such *reducciones* in Paraguay, burning churches and Indians indiscriminately and driving off huge numbers for a march to the slave markets on the coast – a journey that claimed as many fatalities as any slave ship bringing negro slaves from Africa. Thirty thousand Indian souls were calculated to have been lost to the

1650 Missionaries opened up a route to Quito via the Marañón and the Napo. Franciscans explored parts of the upper Amazon.

1674 Dias Paes explored Minas Gerais in search of the legendary silver mountain.
1686 Jesuit Father Fritz began work among the Omagua and Yurimagua Indians of the

Solimões and spent 37 years amongst various Indian groups of the upper Amazon. Drew the first map of the Amazon indicating the different gradients.

Jesuits in this way in the following years, and a massive exodus of one outlying group (not unlike the original biblical exodus in some ways) was organized by Father Montoya and Father Macedo to lead 12,000 surviving Indian converts down the Paraná river to safer havens. Their rafts were smashed in the rapids but they continued on foot through the forests — singing hymns to keep their spirits up — until they finally returned to the Jesuit heartland in Paraguay, southern Brazil and an area of Argentina still today called Misiones.

Further north in the mouth of the Amazon the huge island of Marajó — approximately the same size as Switzerland — defied all incursions by settlers. The 'Nheengaiba' tribes employed the same tactic in the creeks and swamps of Marajó as the Saxon hero Hereward the Wake had employed in the fens of East Anglia in the 11th century: they simply disappeared into their marshes and harassed any intruder with a withering fire of arrows.

The Portuguese despaired of penetrating this fastness (which is to this day a remote region of buffalo ranches) until in 1658 the Jesuit Father Antonio Vieira sent Indian converts there to spread his message of peace; 40,000 Indians promptly accepted both the emissaries and the Faith. Father Vieira's achievements also spread far into the interior.

But the most memorable of all the Jesuit missionaries was a Bohemian — Father Samuel Fritz — who began his work in the forests around the headwaters of the Amazon in 1686. He ranged alone by canoe over a region of some 1600 km (1000 miles) of river and established over 50 Christian settlements of Omagua and Yurimagua Indians. Inevitably he succumbed to exhaustion and fever: he recorded (in a document known as the Évora manuscript and only discovered in 1902) how he had lain sick in a Yurimagua village while the flood waters rose all around him but he was too immobile to be able to quench his thirst, enduring not only sleeplessness but

> the grunting of the crocodiles that were roving around the village, beasts of horrible deformity . . . the rats made their way into my dwelling place, and so hungry, that they gnawed even my spoon and my plate and the haft of my knife.

One alligator even got into the canoe pulled up inside his hut: it was little wonder his fever worsened. Eventually he was evacuated by other missionaries to Pará (now Belém) at the mouth of the Amazon, but there he encountered difficulties of a different kind. Because he had been proselytizing in territory

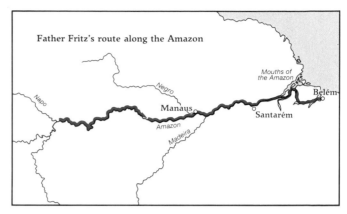

Father Fritz's route along the Amazon

disputed between the Spanish and the Portuguese, the latter viewed him with suspicion and kept him under house arrest for 18 months while they consulted Lisbon about what they should do with him.

When he was finally allowed to go back to his own domain, several thousands of miles upstream, Fritz took the opportunity to chart the course of the river as best he could with the primitive instruments available to him. (When La Condamine, with much improved navigational gear, passed that way half a century later he was impressed by Fritz's efforts.)

The later years of Fritz's life — and he did not die until the age of 70 in 1723 — were spent protecting his protégés against the incursions of slave raiders; like his colleagues further south, he had to organize an exodus — this time to the Andean watershed. When his body was stripped for burial, he was found to be unusually afflicted by bites, and it was revealed that this gentle priest who had combatted for so long the violence of the Portuguese had never killed an insect.

The Jesuits were not the only religious order to perform notable work of exploration in the 17th and 18th centuries; the Carmelites, the Mercedarians, the Franciscans and others had all been active. But it was the Jesuit order who were the most effective and powerful and — as in Europe — the order who attracted the most jealousy and hostility.

When the Marquis of Pombal, the effective ruler of Portugal in the middle of the 18th century, embarked on a campaign of persecution against the Jesuits in Portugal, he therefore had little hesitation about extending his persecution to the New World; in 1756 he stripped the order of its temporal powers and two years later ordered their expulsion from Brazil. The command was carried out by the colonial administrators with alacrity and brutality: one of the great forces for exploring as well as for civilizing the continent was lost.

SELKIRK ON ROBINSON CRUSOE'S ISLAND

Alexander Selkirk was born in 1676, the son of a shoemaker at Largo in Fife, but early left home for a roving life at sea. In 1703 he joined William Dampier, who had made a reputation for himself as one of the most daring buccaneers in the West Indies, on a privateering expedition to the South Seas. The two men did not get on: Selkirk fell foul of Dampier and most of the crew. There are various accounts of the reason for the quarrel, including a version that Selkirk's homosexual advances to other crew members alienated his shipmates.

Dampier knew what to do with recalcitrant seafarers; he had been one himself on a voyage in the Indian Ocean in 1688, and had been put ashore on one of the Nicobar islands in the Bay of Bengal and left to fend for himself, eventually getting safely away. He resolved to maroon Selkirk on one of the tiny uninhabited islands of the Juan Fernández group 485 km (300 miles) off the coast of Chile.

Selkirk remained alone on the semi-tropical island for over four years. He had been provided with a musket and ammunition and did not resist being abandoned. He explored the island in great detail, found ample game, rounded up some wild goats and lived well on the local lobsters (which today provide a livelihood for a few fishing families). He made clothes out of skins and established a look-out point on the island's forest-clad mountain. Eventually he attracted the attention of a passing ship and obtained a passage home to England and thereafter – undaunted by his experience – continued his life at sea.

Among the many who listened with fascination to his tale of improvisation and endurance was the novelist and political pamphleteer Daniel Defoe, who embroidered on his story – and greatly extended the duration of his enforced stay on the island – to produce his most famous book *Robinson Crusoe*. A statue of Selkirk, dressed as Crusoe, stands at his birthplace in Scotland.

The title page of the original edition of Robinson Crusoe, *Defoe's fictional account of how Selkirk was marooned on an island in the Juan Fernández group.*

A FRENCH ACADEMICIAN ON THE AMAZON

Until the 18th century the discovery of South America had mostly been carried out by Italians, Spanish and Portuguese, with some major contributions by Englishmen such as Sir Walter Raleigh and Germans such as Father Fritz; now it was the turn of a Frenchman.

In the early years of the century a great debate was under way in the French Academy of Sciences about the precise shape of the world. Isaac Newton had maintained that the world was not a perfect sphere, but bulged at the equator and was flattened towards the Poles; the accepted wisdom in the French scientific world was that the contrary was the position: the globe was elongated at the Poles and attenuated in the middle.

The Academy decided that the only satisfactory way of resolving the controversy was to send one

expedition to the equator and another to the polar regions, each to measure the precise length of a degree of latitude. The scholar chosen to lead the equatorial expedition to Quito was an aristocrat called Charles-Marie de la Condamine, a former soldier who had turned mathematician, cartographer and naturalist.

La Condamine set out in 1735 accompanied by a small group of French companions. The Spanish crown only agreed to this unprecedented foreign intrusion on its preserve as a favour to Louis XV of France, who had given Philip V of Spain military assistance in Europe in the War of the Spanish Succession. But even then, the Frenchmen were treated with grave suspicion: careful measurements and the use of scientific instruments suggested gold prospecting to the local authorities.

La Condamine had to waste eight months on a special journey to Lima to get the Spanish viceroy's support for his researches. And there were more personal difficulties: one of the French party – a

1740-4 Anson sailed round most of South America, during his circumnavigation.
1749 Godin des Odonais, a member of Condamine's party, returned via the Amazon. His wife was stranded in the forests of the Amazon basin for 20 days until Indians helped her to safety, and she sailed down the Amazon to join her husband.
1759 Jesuits expelled from Brazil by Portuguese.
1766 Byron took possession of the Falkland Islands for Britain and surveyed Tierra del Fuego.

Dr Senièrgues – was lynched by a hostile crowd in the bull-ring; another went mad after the botanical specimens representing five years' sweltering work were destroyed by a careless servant; another died of fever; the expedition's draughtsman was killed in a fall from a ladder. To cap it all, they heard that the polar expedition had returned from Lapland with conclusive evidence that Newton's theory was correct and the French one wrong. After seven frustrating years it was time to move on.

But La Condamine's scientific curiosity was not yet satisfied. He decided to reject offers of a direct passage home and instead to make the crossing of the Andes and the descent to the Amazon basin, and then to follow the whole length of the river to the Atlantic, as Orellana had done just two centuries earlier. What made La Condamine's voyage remarkable was that this was the first time that a trained scientist, equipped with instruments for observation and charting, had navigated these tortuous waters. Some of the higher tributaries were particularly arduous: he had to cross and recross the Chuchunga river more than twenty times in a single day. Further downstream, a balsa-wood raft proved the best conveyance.

In the Pongo de Manseriche gorge La Condamine concluded:

> A canoe on such an occasion would be dashed into a thousand pieces . . . but the beams of the raft being neither nailed nor dovetailed together, the flexibility of the lianas, by which they are fastened, have the effect of a spring.

While negotiating these hazards, La Condamine was continually gathering information. He plumbed the depth of the river regularly and measured its width. He kept compass and watch always to hand in daylight hours and charted twists in the river. He corrected Father Fritz's more primitive findings. He gauged the force of the stream. He recorded details of the flora and fauna of the river, being particularly intrigued by encounters with electric eels, which he recorded could give such a severe shock when touched even with a stick that they inflicted 'a painful numbness in the arm' and could 'lay one prostrate'. He was also the first to codify in a systematic way the miraculous qualities of latex. Indeed it was La Condamine's subsequent display of bottles and syringes of latex in Paris which made Europe aware for the first time of the potential of rubber.

Owing to the devastation of disease and slavers, which had denuded the main Amazon, the Indians were far less of a danger to La Condamine than they

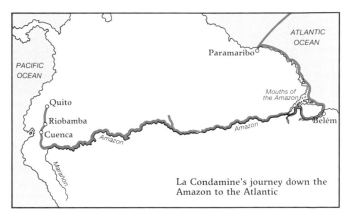

La Condamine's journey down the Amazon to the Atlantic

had been to Orellana; but nonetheless he formed a poor opinion of the Indians, describing them as:

> Voracious gluttons . . . pusillanimous and timid in the extreme, unless transported by drunkenness . . . notwithstanding there are at present no man eaters along the banks of the Marañón, there yet exist inland tribes of Americans who eat their prisoners.

He was also intrigued by the traditional accounts of a tribe of Amazonian women, and reported that:

> In the course of our navigation, we enquired of the people of the various nations if they had any knowledge of those warlike women which Orellana claimed to have encountered . . . we were consistently assured that they had heard their fathers speak of such things.

He concluded that 'a republic of women' had existed but that they had withdrawn further into the interior, beyond the Rio Negro. When he called at mission stations along his route, La Condamine told the missionaries that one of his surviving colleagues – a Monsieur Godin accompanied by his wife – would shortly be following him down the river; he was not to know the tribulations that they would have.

Eventually La Condamine reached the city of Pará (now Belém) at the mouth of the Amazon and from there took ship to French Guiana where he had to wait a further five months for a passage to France. When he regained Paris in February 1745 he had been on his South American travels for 10 years.

Some of the information he had gleaned, for instance about the shape of the earth, had been partially overtaken; other information, for instance that there were no poisonous snakes on the Amazon, was plainly erroneous. But these misconceptions were far outweighed by the massive contribution he had made to Europe's knowledge of the world beyond its own frontiers. His work was to contribute

AN AMAZON SURVIVOR'S TALE

Mme Isabella Godin, though not a voluntary explorer herself, is rightly remembered as one of the great survivors of the Amazon.

Her husband, Jean Godin des Odonais was one of the scientific colleagues of Charles-Marie de la Condamine on his celebrated expedition to Quito in the 1730s to determine the precise shape of the Earth. When La Condamine returned home down the length of the Amazon, the Godins resolved to do the same – but later, because Mme Godin was so frequently pregnant that it was hard to find a good moment for so arduous a journey.

Eventually her husband went ahead and it was not until 1769 that Mme Godin heard that a Portuguese boat was waiting to take her to rejoin her husband. She set off accompanied by her two brothers, a young nephew, three Frenchmen including a doctor, three maid servants, a negro slave and 31 Indian paddlers and porters. This substantial expedition safely reached Canelos where a well-stocked canoe was expected. But Canelos was deserted, following a smallpox epidemic, and all Mme Godin's Indians fled into the forests.

A crucial decision then had to be made: should they press on or turn back? Mme Godin, calculating that it was only 12 days downstream to her rendezvous, got a light canoe built and the depleted party drifted down river. Their only skilled paddler was drowned and eventually the frail craft upset and the remnants of the party swam ashore with what they could

Isabella Godin who was abandoned in the Amazon forests when her companions either deserted her or died, and who struggled on alone to become a legendary survivor.

salvage of their food. The able-bodied men righted the canoe and decided to sail, unencumbered by passengers, to fetch help.

Mme Godin and her family waited 25 days on the river bank. When no help came they tried to make a raft; when that collapsed they set out on foot. It proved impossible to follow the tangled river bank, so they tried to cut out the curves by striking through the jungle. They soon lost their way in the dank forests.

Starving and tired, one by one they died, till only Mme Godin was left. Leaving seven bodies behind her, she stumbled on alone, her clothes torn off her by the undergrowth and eating insects and roots where she could. After nine dazed days she refound the river and two Indians in a canoe picked her up. She survived to be reunited with her husband and to become a legendary warning to Amazonian travellers.

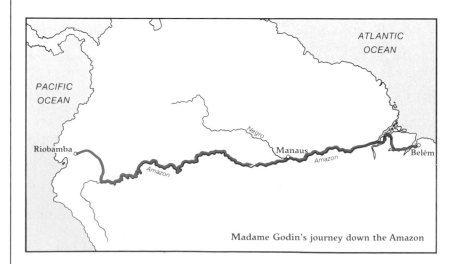

Madame Godin's journey down the Amazon

to the establishment of the metre – originally defined as one ten-millionth of the distance from the Pole to the equator – as the the world's most generally used unit of measuring length. La Condamine had paved the way for the scientific explorers of the following century.

TIRELESS CURIOSITY OF BARON VON HUMBOLDT

More than 50 years divided the travels of Charles-Marie de la Condamine from those of Baron Alexander von Humboldt and during that period scientific knowledge in Europe had made great advances. This was one reason why in five years of intensive travels in South America Humboldt contributed more to the sum of human knowledge than La Condamine had done in ten; but perhaps an even more powerful reason was to be found in Humboldt's own personality, for seldom has any man combined such intellectual curiosity about every aspect of life – geography, anthropology, zoology and medicine among others – with such a tough physique and such an adventurous spirit. In a lifetime which extended from an acquaintance with Frederick the Great of Prussia to a friendship with Sir Walter Scott, he was rightly considered the last truly Renaissance Man.

Humboldt arrived in Venezuela in 1799. In the course of the next five years he explored the Casiquiare river linking the Orinoco and Amazon waterways; he visited Cuba; he sailed up the Magdalena as far as Bogotá; he made an overland trek from Bogotá to Quito, and then from Quito to Lima; he sailed up to Guayaquil, Panama and Mexico; he also climbed numerous Andean peaks including making a memorable assault on the 6250 metre (20,500 ft) summit of Chimborazo. To describe his travels chronologically would be beyond the scope of this work, but it is worth considering some of his more notable achievements.

Together with his invariable companion Aimée Bonpland, he traversed the watershed between the Orinoco and Amazon river systems by means of the unique Casiquiare river (often referred to as a canal) which he found to be a fast-flowing branch of the Orinoco as broad as the Rhine and discharging into the Rio Negro and thence into the Amazon. The myth of 'a river that flowed both ways' was exploded. But in the process of seeking the truth, Humboldt had nearly lost his life on more than one occasion on swamped canoes in turbulent and alligator-infested waters.

The rapids at São Gabriel on the Rio Negro were only one of the perils faced by the 19th-century scientists who mapped and explored the upper Amazon

Humboldt's curiosity led him into other dangers. He experimented with curare, the poison which the Indians used on their arrows, drinking it to prove that it was only lethal when injected into the bloodstream. He also drank the juice of the cow tree, which had an alarming resemblance to latex, until one of companions started vomiting rubber balls.

He persuaded the unfortunate Bonpland to hold one end of an electric eel while he held the other and they received alternate shocks of anything up to 600 volts. He was distressed to find that his dog – a sizeable mastiff – had been eaten by a jaguar. He calmly measured the atmospherical electricity during an earthquake that sent everyone else scurrying for safety. All these and many other painful experiences were dispassionately recorded and analyzed for the benefit of his successors.

But it was when he got into the mountains around Quito that Humboldt took the greatest risks. He climbed various volcanoes and then determined to tackle Chimborazo under the impression that it was the highest mountain in the world. The conditions were against him; at the snow line his guides deserted him; a little higher a mist descended making it impossible for them to see either the way forward or back; he suffered acutely from mountain sickness – nosebleeds and nausea; the track narrowed into a knife-edge with a 300-metre (1000-ft) precipice on one side and an ice-slope of over 30 degrees on the

other; to cap it all, a hail storm hit them. It was only with the greatest reluctance and at a height of over 5800 metres (19,000 ft) – the highest ever to have been reached by any man at that date – that Humboldt turned back. (It was to be left to the alpinist Edward Whymper finally to scale the peak nearly 80 years later).

Humboldt was not only a recorder of scientific data and an adventurer, he was also a philosopher. His observations on the problems of the region have stood the test of time. He denounced slavery and forced labour wherever he encountered them, objecting to humans being used as pack animals and 'described in the same terms as would be employed in speaking of a horse or mule'. He was – more predictably – revolted by cannibalistic practices, but understanding towards a missionary who had found himself unable to punish 'an Indian who, a few years before, had eaten one of his wives, after having taken her to his *canuco* (hut), and fattened her by good feeding'.

He wrote rationally about 'the warlike republic of women without husbands' which had given the name to the river Amazon. He gave credit where credit was due to the mission stations for their compassionate work among the Indians, but he deplored the excessive discipline of some establishments.

On his return to Europe, via the United States, Humboldt was lionized as no explorer/scientist has been before or since. He was compared with Napoleon, whom he met, as one of the great figures of an heroic age; and with Goethe, whom he also met, as one of the great thinkers of his time. Now, when he is remembered in South America at all, it is principally on account of the cold current running up the west coast which bears his name; it was characteristic of him that he recognized the connection between the coldness of the water, the warmth of the air, and the lack of rain on the coastline of the Atacama desert.

Humboldt was always making connections and drawing conclusions, but the greatest connection of all, and the most startling conclusion from any South American journey was not to be his: that was reserved for an Englishman 40 years his junior – Charles Darwin.

NAVIGATORS AND NATURALISTS

Throughout the second half of the 18th century the coastline of South America was being systematically charted and surveyed. The British navy played a

CHARLES DARWIN: A VOYAGE LEADS TO AN IDEA

When Captain Robert Fitzroy set off for South America in 1831 in HMS *Beagle* on a surveying voyage for the British Admiralty, he took with him a young naturalist who was full of enthusiasm to explore the Andes, the pampas and the virtually unknown offshore islands: the Falklands, Tierra del Fuego and the Galápagos. Charles Darwin was 22; he had never been abroad before and he was never to go again.

Darwin's explorations on land (for it had been agreed with Fitzroy before they left that he should be able to leave the ship for lengthy periods) included many adventures. He climbed Corcovado at Rio de Janeiro; he explored in small boats and on land among the channels of Tierra del Fuego, nearly getting stranded on one occasion; he set off with *gauchos* on horseback across the Argentine pampas and made contact with the fearsome General Rosas who was exterminating the Indians of the plains; he hunted ostriches in Patagonia and he shot a condor in Chile; he traversed the Andes suffering mountain sickness in the high passes between Portillo and Mendoza; he rode a giant tortoise in the Galápagos and 'found it a very wobbly seat'.

While participating in all these innocent and indeed boyish adventures, Darwin was keenly observing and note-taking all the time. His studies at Cambridge had extended to geology and entomology as well as natural history. He amassed a large collection of insects in Rio, and an even larger collection of fossils in Patagonia; indeed he commented that 'we may conclude that the whole area of the pampas is one wide sepulchre of . . . extinct giant quadrupeds'. He became convinced the Andes had been below the waters of the ocean and had been thrust upwards – a conclusion that owed much to the sea fossils he found high in the mountains, and to noting the frailty of the Earth's shell during a particularly severe earthquake at Concepción in Chile.

But it was in the Galápagos Islands that he experienced the first inklings of his later theories about the process of natural selection and of the common origin of the species. He noticed how nature improved on herself as different types of life developed and adapted themselves to changing conditions. Even the shapes of the beaks of the finches on the different Galápagos Islands were adapted to cater for the different types of food: nuts that required cracking, insects that required snapping up, fruit that required gouging out. The primeval appearance of so many of the reptiles forced his mind back to a prehistoric period when the world was inhabited by species now extinct.

All this collecting and theorizing placed a considerable strain on Captain Fitzroy, whose cabin Darwin shared. The decks of the *Beagle* became littered with bones, rocks, plants, skins of birds and even rotting fish and fungi. But worse than the disconcerting clutter was the disconcerting talk. Fitzroy was a devout Christian and a fundamentalist: he sincerely believed every word of the Bible to be the literal truth.

Darwin had himself been intended for a career in the church; but now he was beginning to doubt whether the creation could possibly have taken place as late as 4004 BC (the date confidently expounded by the church), whether the flood could really have covered the Earth and Noah's Ark rescued all the surviving species, and whether the heavens and the Earth and all that therein dwelt could conceivably have been created in seven days. Fitzroy, who was already deeply disappointed at his inability to implant a missionary in Tierra del Fuego, then began to feel he was harbouring a religious subversive in the person of Darwin.

It took many years for Darwin to digest and record all the results of what turned out to be a five-year voyage. When eventually he published his *On the Origin of Species by Means of Natural Selection* in 1859 it was followed the next year by a public debate in Oxford in which Darwin's supporters argued the issues with Dr Wilberforce and other leading clerics. The meeting was interrupted by an elderly grey-haired man who denounced Darwin and all his works: he was Vice-Admiral Robert Fitzroy, late of HMS *Beagle*.

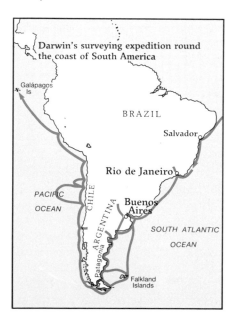

Charles Darwin (left) *who as a young man accompanied HMS* Beagle *on her voyage around the world. Darwin's many excursions ashore – particularly into the Andes and on the Galápagos Islands – led him to develop his theory of the evolution of the species.*

Darwin's surveying expedition round the coast of South America.

189

1801 Azara completed his compilation of topographical information on the Paraguay-Paraná Basin after 13 years.
1803 Humboldt travelled in Mexico, crossing from Acapulco to Veracruz.
1812-24 Waterton's wanderings in the Guianas.
1817-20 Spix and Martius journeyed from Minas Gerais to Belém collecting biological specimens and observing the geology and ethnology, and were then the first non-Portuguese scientists allowed up the Amazon and Negro rivers.

large part in the process. Commodore George Anson had made his celebrated voyage around South America – and on around the world – in 1740–4. He had lost four of his seven ships by the time he put in to the uninhabited islands of the Juan Fernández group (where Selkirk had been marooned 40 years earlier) for refitting, and the crew of one of those lost – the *Wager* – had been shipwrecked among the islands off the southern Chilean coast; John Byron's account of their explorations and adventures is one of the classics of seafarers' tales (and was used by his grandson, Lord Byron, in his description of the storm and wreck in *Don Juan*). Undeterred by his experiences, John Byron made a later voyage, in 1765, to the Falkland Islands and to parts of Tierra del Fuego.

At the end of the same decade Captain James Cook, spurning the shelter of the Strait of Magellan, rounded Cape Horn in the *Endeavour* before going on to Australia and New Zealand. Cook, as well as being an outstanding navigator, had a wider scientific curiosity and enlisted for his voyage the services of two astronomers and the distinguished botanist Joseph Banks. But in terms of comprehensively surveying the South American coast, Cook was surpassed by Alessandro Malaspina, an Italian nobleman who entered the service of Spain and sailed around these coasts between 1789 and 1794, collecting both scientific information and secret political intelligence for the Spanish government. Unfortunately for him, his political views were so

Captain Fitzroy who commanded HMS Beagle *on the voyage with Darwin. Thirty years later, as an elderly admiral, he hotly contested Darwin's findings.*

radical that he was imprisoned on return and only released after the intervention of Napoleon.

The British navy continued its preoccupation with charting South American waters well into the 19th century. HMS *Adventure* and HMS *Beagle* sailed in 1826, their captains being instructed that 'You are to avail yourself of every opportunity of collecting and preserving specimens of such objects of natural history as may be new, rare or interesting.' After the captain of the *Beagle* succumbed to depression and killed himself, his command was taken over by Lieutenant Robert Fitzroy, who himself commanded the *Beagle*'s subsequent – and even more ambitious – survey voyage between 1831 and 1836.

Doubtless impressed by the benefits Cook had derived from taking Banks with him, Fitzroy also recruited a young naturalist in the person of Charles Darwin, whose deductions from the voyage were to make it one of the most memorable in the annals of discovery. Nor were the activities of British naval officers confined to the high seas. Some of the most daring journeys and most graphic accounts of travel in the High Andes were the work of officers such as Captain Basil Hall (1820–2) and Lieutenant Charles Brand (1827).

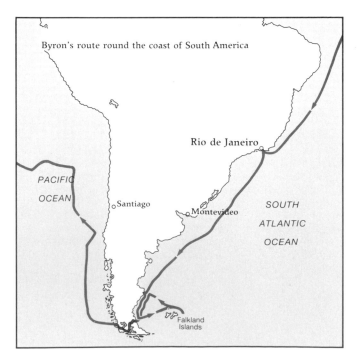

Byron's route round the coast of South America

Rio de Janeiro

PACIFIC OCEAN

Santiago

Montevideo

SOUTH ATLANTIC OCEAN

Falkland Islands

1826-33 French zoologist and ethnologist Orbigny in Brazil, Uruguay, Argentina, Patagonia and west of the Andes.
1831-6 Fitzroy in the *Beagle*, with Darwin as naturalist, charted coasts of Patagonia and Chile, visited Falkland and Galápagos Islands.
1833-44 Schomburgk travelled in British Guiana and northern Brazil. Explored the Rivers Courtantyne, Berbice and Essequibo and its watershed, made first crossing from Uraicoera to the upper Orinoco, then returned via Casiquiare, Negro and Branco rivers.

As the 19th century progressed, so the emphasis was increasingly on scientific expeditions on land. Two Bavarians, the zoologist Johann Baptist von Spix and the botanist Philip von Martius, had managed to attach themselves to the suite of the Archduchess Leopoldina when she came to Brazil in 1817 to marry the future emperor Dom Pedro. Both had comprehensive briefs: Spix was to study the aboriginal inhabitants and the climate as well as the fauna, while Martius was to study the climate and soil as well as the flora. Having explored the rich gold-mining valleys around Ouro Preto in the south of Brazil, they then moved up to the Amazon basin where Martius nearly lost his life in a canoe capsize. By the time they returned to Bavaria in 1820 they had sent home 85 species of mammals, 350 of birds, 130 of amphibians, 116 of fish, 2700 of insects and no less than 6500 species of plants.

A much less scientific and reliable observer was that flamboyant English naturalist Charles Waterton who wandered in the Guianas between 1812 and 1824. He fished for alligators with shark hooks; he rode on the back of a giant cayman, seizing its front legs 'as a bridle'; he wrestled with a boa constrictor and secured its jaws with his braces. Nothing – one feels – was lost in the telling.

Scarcely more modest was the American William H. Edwards who spent eight months on the Amazon in 1846, a region which he dramatically described as one where

> the mightiest of rivers rolls majestically through primeval forests of boundless extent . . . where gold has tempted, and Amazonian women repulsed, the unprincipled adventurer; and where Jesuit missionaries, and luckless traders, have fallen victims to cannibal Indians and epicurean anacondas.

But Edwards's purple prose caught the attention of two far more serious naturalists – Alfred Russell Wallace and Henry Walter Bates – who set off together for the Amazon in 1848.

Wallace and Bates were soon joined by another British naturalist – Richard Spruce. These three men between them spent 32 years on the Amazon and its tributaries. Wallace – like Darwin – developed ideas on evolution. Bates alone collected over 14,000 different species of insects of which 8000 were new

Encounters with alligators or giant cayman such as this lost nothing in the telling in the vivid accounts of such early 19th-century travellers as Charles Waterton.

1834 Smith and Lowe sponsored by the Peruvian government crossed the continent from Lima via the Huallaga, Ucayali and finally the Amazon rivers.

1843-7 Castelnau's French-sponsored expedition into the Brazilian interior.
1848 Wallace and Bates travelled up the Amazon to Manaus, before continuing

separately. Wallace went on up the Negro and across to the Orinoco, returning after six years with a large natural history collection. Bates spent 11 years collecting

to science. Spruce sent back over 30,000 plant specimens to most of the leading natural history museums and universities of Europe; he also mapped much of the 16,000 km (10,000 miles) of river and stream which he navigated by *coberta* (a covered canoe); additionally – and as a hobby – he classified 21 vocabularies of Amazonian Indian languages.

While collecting all this material, the naturalists survived repeated bouts of malaria and dysentery, and had frequent narrow escapes from the more aggressive varieties of natives and wild life: Bates's canoe was attacked one night by an anaconda which hammered a hole in the chicken coop on board with its head and then ate a couple of hens; Wallace almost stumbled over a black jaguar on one occasion, and Spruce awoke in his hammock with a fever to hear his bearers plotting to kill him and make off with his 'trade goods' – the stock of mirrors, beads and trinkets which he took for barter purposes.

All these hazards they accepted as part of the day's work and did not allow them to interfere with the regular routine of field research and the maintenance of Victorian standards of dress and

self-discipline: they drank their 'sundowners' of *cachaça* at dusk, while the Indians washed their 'forest suits' and laid out their butterfly nets and ammonia bottles.

At the same time they were also struggling financially. Bates's agent gave him fourpence a specimen and took 20 per cent commission on the deal; his total profit for 20 months of work was £27. Spruce saw the whole of his meagre savings after 12 years' work disappear when the Guayaquil bank with whom he had deposited it failed. Wallace lost all his collections, from six years' effort, when the ship in which he was returning to England caught fire and sank. Sometimes their funds from home did not arrive and they were reduced to borrowing to survive at all. Their subsequent books give a vivid picture of those practical difficulties of life as well as of the dramatic risks.

Nineteenth-century naturalists such as Bates, Wallace and Spruce spent many years of their lives exploring the upper tributaries of the Amazon by canoe with native paddlers.

On their return to England they were recognized for the work they had done: Bates became the first paid secretary of the Royal Geographical Society in London as well as a fellow of the Royal Society, and Wallace went on to work in south-east Asia, whence he corresponded with Darwin about his own independent ideas about evolution.

WHYMPER SCALES THE HIGH ANDES

When in 1865 Edward Whymper finally reached the summit of the Matterhorn in Switzerland he was undoubtedly the most celebrated alpinist in Europe. He then turned his mind to more distant peaks: as political difficulties ruled out the Himalayas, he decided to explore the Andes. In particular, he wanted to investigate theories about mountain sickness which appeared to afflict mountaineers worse in South America than at comparable heights in Europe.

He arrived at Guayaquil in Ecuador in 1879 and set out directly for Chimborazo – the peak which had so narrowly defeated Humboldt. It was an unsettled country through which to travel and Whymper subsequently wrote in his *Travels Amongst the Great Andes of the Equator* that he believed in

> adopting a policy of non-intervention in all that did not concern us . . . trusting more to our wits than to our credentials, and believing that a jest may conquer where force will fail, that a *bon-mot* is often better than a passport.

By the time Whymper had reached his second camp on the mountain, he and his companions were feverish and suffering severe headaches and thirst; the altitude was indeed affecting them far worse than it had in the Alps.

However they pressed on with their ascent and having first scaled the western summit, they were disappointed to find that it was lower than the eastern one. By the time they had crossed the intervening plateau and conquered the true summit of Chimborazo, they had little more than an hour of daylight left to return to camp; when they finally reached it, it was in pitch darkness at 21.00.

Whymper next turned his attention to the volcano of Cotopaxi. As they ascended the slope, Whymper and his party found that volcanic ash was penetrating their clothing, ears, eyes and nostrils. They camped as near the steaming mouth of the volcano as they dared, and were disconcerted to find that the rubber

THE BEDROOM   THE KITCHEN

Whymper at a mountain camp in the Andes at the equator. He whimsically captioned the illustration as his 'bedroom' and his 'kitchen'.

sheet of their tent floor was melting on lava at a temperature of 43°C (110°F). Undeterred by this, Whymper crawled to the rim of the volcano at night and looked over the edge at the glowing molten mass below.

He went on to scale most of the other outstanding peaks of Ecuador; he discovered unknown glaciers; he took measurements of heights; he collected rare mountain plants, butterflies and even earthworms. But for him the most important achievement was in the area of his original interest – mountain sickness. He established that this was related to atmospheric pressure (the barometer had dropped to 14 inches on the summit of Chimborazo) and was able to make recommendations that would help future climbers not only in the Andes.

HIRAM BINGHAM AND MACHU PICCHU

Pizarro's conquest of the Incas has already been described, and in view of its brutal nature it is hardly surprising that Manco, the puppet ruler whom the Spaniards had set up, should have felt himself insecure. After an unsuccessful rising against the Spaniards in 1537 he fled from Cuzco down the valley of the Urubamba river with some of his troops, three of his sons and all of his favourite wives. The region which he chose as his refuge was the high western watershed of the upper Urubamba; here he was relatively safe from pursuit as canyons, torrential rivers and high passes lay between him and his enemies.

Manco established a capital at Vilcabamba, which the Spanish missionaries who heard about it declared to be 'the chief town and the one in which was the university of idolatry, the professors of witchcraft and teachers of abominations'. Not surprisingly, Manco declined to receive any Spaniards there; but his sons, when they ascended the throne of the Incas, did receive missionaries and others at another impressive site called Vitcos.

Eventually the Spaniards succeeded in invading Vilcabamba and Manco's youngest and only surviving son Tupac Amaru (whose name was centuries later to be adopted by the Tupamaro guerillas) was carried off to Cuzco where he was beheaded. The Inca civilization was finally at an end.

All this was known to a young American lecturer in Latin American history at Yale University in 1908 called Hiram Bingham. After attending a conference in Chile that year, he and a friend decided to explore the Inca fastnesses on muleback. In particular they aspired to find the hidden cities of Vilcabamba and Vitcos. They rode their mules for four days from Cuzco and then, Bingham wrote:

> At times the trail was so steep that it was easier to go on all fours than attempt to walk erect. Occasionally we crossed streams in front of waterfalls on slippery logs or treacherous little foot-bridges. Roughly constructed ladders led us over steep cliffs.

They cut through dense undergrowth and bamboo thickets, and eventually they found an impressive Inca ruin – but not Vilcabamba or Vitcos.

Undeterred, Bingham returned in 1911 at the head of a larger expedition from Yale. While camping in the Urubamba valley, between jungle-clad mountains, the occupant of a nearby hut approached them and –

Rope bridges such as this have always been a feature of Andean travel. Hiram Bingham describes traversing several such in the course of his hunt for the lost cities of the Incas.

on hearing that they were looking for Inca remains – offered to guide them to some ruins at the top of one of the neighbouring mountains. Bingham accompanied him the next day and after a steep climb was rewarded with

> an unexpected sight, a great flight of beautifully constructed stone-faced terraces, perhaps a hundred of them, each hundreds of feet long and ten feet high . . . suddenly I found myself confronted with the walls of ruined houses built of the finest quality of Inca stone work . . . hiding in bamboo thickets and tangled vines, appeared here and there walls of white granite ashlars carefully cut and exquisitely fitted together.

The ruins were overshadowed by a towering sugar-loaf

AN AMERICAN PRESIDENT TURNS EXPLORER

Roosevelt's scientific expedition to Brazil

When Theodore (Teddy) Roosevelt retired from the presidency of the United States and finally from politics in 1912, he was 54 years of age and had a remarkably active and daring career behind him. But he was yearning for one final adventure, and this he found on the headwaters of the Amazon in Brazil.

His arrival in that country coincided with the discovery by Colonel Candido Rondon (the great Brazilian explorer and champion of the Indians after whom the state of Rondônia is named) of the headwater of a totally unknown river which Rondon had christened the Rio da Dúvida – river of doubt. It was suggested to Roosevelt by the Brazilian foreign minister that he and Rondon together should follow the river from near its source to its ultimate and unknown destination – probably in the Amazon.

They set off in March 1914 in a flotilla of canoes with a few American and Brazilian companions and a team of paddlers and porters. Disasters soon overtook them. The river turned out to be a series of rapids. Several of the canoes were swamped and sank, and with them one of the native paddlers. Rondon's dog was shot by unseen and hostile Indians.

Worse was to follow: one of the paddlers went berserk, stole a rifle, shot one of the others and ran away into the forest. Roosevelt decided he should be abandoned and left to his fate in the jungle; but Rondon declared that – as there was no capital punishment in Brazil – he should be found and arrested; eventually it proved impossible to find him. Meanwhile rations ran low and Roosevelt, having got an infected leg and a fever, suggested that he should be left behind to fend for himself. But in the event the party stuck together and pressed on.

After seven weeks they emerged on the river Aripuanã which in turn joined the Madeira – one of the largest tributaries of the Amazon. They had charted 1525 km (950 miles) of a waterway whose very existence had been hitherto unknown. It was no longer the river of doubt but was rechristened the Rio Roosevelt. But the ex-president's health never fully recovered and he died five years later.

Colonel Theodore Roosevelt (left) *was an inveterate hunter during his exploratory navigation of the Madeira river in 1914 with Colonel Rondon of Brazil* (right).

peak called by the locals Huayna Picchu, and the name Machu Picchu was promptly given to the ruins themselves. Bingham was convinced that he had found the lost Inca capital of Vilcabamba.

He was determined to complete his triumph by additionally finding Vitcos, which had been originally described as having close by it 'a temple of the sun and inside it a white stone above a spring of water'. He inquired diligently for such a rock; he was taken to see sites with smaller white rocks and sites with larger non-white rocks; he offered rewards to local residents; he was taken to other rocks that overlooked caves rather than springs; it seemed that the whole Urubamba valley was riddled with Inca sites.

Bingham persevered. He knew that Vitcos was reputed to have wonderful views and ornate buildings. Eventually on a high ridge he found just such a set of Inca ruins with 'the lintels of the doors being of marble and elaborately cut'. The place was called Rosaspata and he was at once convinced that it was Vitcos. When, on the following day, his Indian guides led him to a gigantic white granite boulder

Machu Picchu, most impressive of all the lost Inca cities of the Andes, was a lucky discovery by Hiram Bingham in 1911.

set above a dark mysterious pool and ornamented with Inca carvings amid the ruins of a temple, Bingham was sure that this was the sacred spot which he sought. Its position so close to Vitcos confirmed the identity of the latter.

Bingham returned to the Urubamba valley the following year and his associates cleared the vegetation from the terraces of Machu Picchu while he himself continued to explore for fresh sites. He never again repeated his extraordinary luck of the previous year, but he did go on to find other Inca remains – notably at Espíritu Pampa. It was left to another American explorer – Gene Savoy – to return to this site in 1964 and 1965 and to reveal that it was far more extensive than Bingham had realized.

Gradually it dawned on Savoy and others that it was Espíritu Pampa, and not Machu Picchu, which must have been the last, lost capital of the Incas.

Brazilian, Bolivian-Paraguayan and Bolivian-Peruvian boundary commissions.
1908 Bingham, an American archaeologist, searched for the lost Inca cities of Vilcabamba

and Vitcos, and discovered Machu Picchu in 1911 and Espíritu Pampa in 1912.
1914 Roosevelt-Rondon Scientific Expedition explored Río da Dúvida into the Aripuanã

and Madeira rivers. The former President then travelled down the Amazon to Manaus.
1920 Dyott air-route reconnaissance from the Pacific to the Amazon.

The location was right; it was at the right altitude – much lower and warmer than Machu Picchu; the ruined buildings fitted more closely to contemporary descriptions; its sheer size suggested a capital; and lastly – and most macabrely – its position close to a navigable stretch of the river would have made it possible for Pizarro to have floated down it a sinister message in 1539 (as he was reputed to have done) – the body of Manco's murdered wife Cura Ocllo in a basket.

The last capital of the Incas had been found, but exploration in the forests and gulleys around the Urubamba still continues, and the hazards that beset Bingham and his predecessors still persist. When John Hemming was visiting Choqquequirau in the 1960s he found

> the bridge crossed by Bingham has long since been washed away, but there are now some strands of telegraph wire. I tied myself to a curved piece of wood that slid along these wires, with my feet dangling above the swirling grey waters, and hauled myself across with my arms for 250 feet along the swaying wires.

The remaining mysteries of the Incas are not to be revealed to the faint-hearted.

CONTEMPORARY EXPLORERS

Since the Second World War, South America has attracted many young explorers drawn to one of the last regions of the world which could still provide access to the unknown: a region which – as Sir Walter Raleigh had said three centuries before – 'has still her maidenhood'.

In 1950, a young Englishman called Sebastian Snow decided to travel from a point which he confidently claimed to be the source of the Amazon in the Peruvian Andes to its mouth at Belém some 5500 km (3500 miles) away. As early as 1541, Francisco de Orellana had pursued the course of the river to the Atlantic Ocean; what made Snow's trip remarkable was that he started so high up the river and intended to keep to the actual valley of the Marañón (the Amazon's principal source) for 800 km (500 miles) before the river was reckoned to become navigable.

The first 2000 km (1250 miles) of the journey took him over nine months to accomplish, either struggling along a trackless river bank or encountering repeated setbacks in canoes and rafts while negotiating the cataracts. (Snow was a non-swimmer, and so

particularly vulnerable to capsizes.) Eventually he reached Belém, weakened by dysentery and malnutrition. But his spirit was to inspire followers.

Later in the 1950s, two Oxford undergraduates – Richard Mason and Robin Hanbury-Tenison – decided to take a jeep across South America at its widest point, from Recife on the Atlantic coast of Brazil to Lima on the Pacific coast of Peru. They knew there were few roads in the interior of Mato Grosso, but reckoned that they might find tracks between native villages. In this they were over-optimistic: having floated their jeep on a raft of their own making across the Araguaya river to the world's largest inland island of Bananal, they lurched through rough scrub country until the jeep's chassis broke decisively. Hanbury-Tenison then set off alone, through the country of the uncertain-tempered Karajá Indians, to find help; Mason remained behind to guard the remnants of the jeep and their provisions.

After days of lonely travel on foot, swimming the rivers he encountered, Hanbury-Tenison returned with help. In the mended jeep they pressed on through the territory of the warrior Xavante tribe, passing the starting point of Colonel Fawcett's last journey, skirted the swamps of the Pantanal, had their jeep towed by oxen through the Banadoz of Izozog in Bolivia and eventually reached their destination and were rewarded by the recognition of the Royal Geographical Society. Neither of them had had a surfeit of South American travel.

Richard Mason was the first back. Like Theodore Roosevelt half a century earlier, he had heard of an unexplored river: the Iriri in the heart of Mato Grosso. He and another Oxford friend – John Hemming (later to become director of the RGS) – established a base camp at a small airstrip at Posto Cachimbo and started assembling supplies and constructing canoes. One day Mason was walking alone by a forest track between the camp and the river when he was ambushed by Indians who shot eight arrows through his body, broke his skull with clubs and left him dead by the track. The assailants were a tribe hitherto uncontacted by any *civilizados* – the dreaded Kreen-Akrore; it was the work of several years by patient and daring anthropologists to locate and establish a peaceful relationship with them.

Undeterred by Mason's death, Snow and Hanbury-Tenison returned yet again to South America in the 1960s to journey from the mouth of the Orinoco river in Venezuela by water, through the Amazon river system, to the mouth of the River Plate 9750 km (6000 miles) away in Argentina.

197

1925 Fawcett and two companions disappeared near the Xingu River whilst searching for a lost city. Search expeditions by Dyott in 1928 and Fleming in 1932 concluded they were murdered by local Indians.
1935 Jimmy Angel discovered Angel Falls, the highest waterfall in South America.
1943 Leonardo, Orlando and Cláudio Villas Boas joined the Roncador-Xingu expedition to central Brazil and subsequently devoted their life to the protection of Indians of the Upper Xingu.

Colonel Fawcett at camp in Mato Grosso. The horses had to be sent back at the outset of his final and fatal journey.

COLONEL FAWCETT'S DISAPPEARANCE IN MATO GROSSO

Colonel Percy Fawcett was a life-long explorer of the Mato Grosso region of Brazil and the tributaries of the Amazon who is best remembered for having disappeared there without trace in 1925. But his life, as well as his death, was shrouded in mystery.

As a young army officer, before the First World War, Fawcett – with support and encouragement from the Royal Geographical Society – had undertaken mapping and frontier surveys on the Brazilian–Bolivian border. After the war, in which he had distinguished himself, winning the DSO for bravery, he returned to Brazil and became intrigued with the possibility of finding a ruined city of El Dorado in the Amazon jungle.

He had read an 18th-century manuscript which was unearthed from the archives of Rio de Janeiro and which described in detail a city of romantic riches – gold and silver artefacts, 'great arches, so high that none could read the inscriptions on them', columns and statues – all awaiting discovery. The document may have been spurious, or a deliberate forgery, but Fawcett believed it absolutely and was determined to take up its challenge.

The forests of Mato Grosso held a fatal fascination for Fawcett. Despite having lost companions who had been strangled by boa-constrictors or eaten by piranhas on previous expeditions, he decided to set out in April 1925 for an exploration which was to take him through the untravelled forests between the centre of Brazil and the east coast. He could not follow the course of any river, and the terrain was too dense to take pack animals, so his equipment was restricted to what he and his two companions – his 22-year-old son and his son's friend – could carry.

Not everyone believed he was really looking for his El Dorado; the Brazilian authorities suspected him of prospecting for oil on behalf of an international company (which would have accounted for his obsessive secrecy about his precise route), and others who knew that he was a mystic and scientist thought that he was seeking for hidden sources of solar energy. No one was quite sure what he was up to.

A few messages were sent back at first, and then total silence descended. No one worried at first; after all, he had said he might be away for a year or two. But eventually, in 1928, an American press syndicate financed a rescue operation. This came back with some trinkets that might have belonged to Fawcett and with reports that he and his companions had probably been killed by Indians on or near the Kuluene river. Other reports trickled in of people who had seen a white man held captive by Indians in other parts of the Amazon jungle. A Swiss trapper reported meeting an English colonel in the depths of Mato Grosso. An American missionary found a white child allegedly fathered by Fawcett's son.

A celebrated Brazilian anthropologist living with the Kalapalo tribe was regaled by a story – 25 years after the event – of how this tribe had been provoked by Fawcett and had clubbed him to death; they even dug up some bones which they confessed were Fawcett's. The bones were brought back to England, handed over to the family, examined by experts, and found not to be those of Fawcett — nor even of a European at all.

One positive result at least emerged from all this uncertainty. Peter Fleming was among those who joined a very amateur expedition to search for traces of Fawcett. They canoed up the Araguaya river in 1932 and then struck overland into the region in which Fawcett was thought to have been last seen. Internal dissension and failing rations forced them to turn back. But the book that resulted — *Brazilian Adventure* — is one of the most amusing accounts of exploration ever to have been published: all the awe in which previous travellers had held the 'horrors' of the Amazon jungle are exploded in a riot of bravado and good humour.

But for Colonel Fawcett the Amazon jungle had never been a laughing matter. He perished there, somehow and somewhere, taking his mysterious objectives with him.

1950 Snow followed Amazon from supposed source to sea on balsa-wood rafts and river steamers.
1957 Mason and Hanbury-Tenison crossed South America at its widest point by jeep from Recife to Lima.
1961 Mason and Hemming with Brazilian surveyors mapped the upper Iriri River in central Brazil. Mason killed by Kreen-Akrore Indians.
1962-3 Shipton climbed in Patagonia.

1964 Hanbury-Tenison crossed the continent by boat from the Caribbean to the Atlantic via the Orinoco, Amazon and Paraguay river systems.
1964-5 Savoy cleared the Inca site of Espíritu Pampa, first discovered by Bingham, to establish it as the lost Inca capital, Vilcabamba.
1967-9 Royal Society/Royal Geographical Society Mato Grosso Expedition to Brazil carried out an ecological survey of primary forest made accessible by construction of a new highway.
1968 The Geographical Magazine Hovercraft expedition followed the Amazon up the Negro through the Casiquiare Canal and down the Orinoco.
1987-8 Royal Geographical Society Maracá Rainforest Project carried out an ecological survey of the riverine island of Maracá in Roraima for the Brazilian Secretariat of the Environment.

They set off together in an inflatable rubber dinghy, with two powerful outboard motors, and made the link up with only three brief portages – one watershed and two sets of rapids – on the whole journey. But perhaps the most remarkable feature of the expedition was that it ended up as a solo one: Snow became ill soon after the start and had to go home, leaving Hanbury-Tenison to complete an eight-month journey on his own. He arrived at Buenos Aires to be hailed as 'El Intrépido'.

A less young explorer of a very specialized type was Margaret Mee. From the mid-1950s to the late 1980s Mrs Mee – who only began her Amazonian travels at the age of 47 – undertook a series of canoe journeys up the more remote tributaries of the Amazon: the Arinos, the Içana, the Tefé, the Maués, the Araçá and many others. Always she had her sketch book and her easel with her, and always she was recording in exquisite water-colours the exotic flowers of the rain forests.

ead Horse
Camp
Xingu
São Francisco
Salvador
Mato
Grosso
ATLANTIC
OCEAN
Paraná
Rio de Janeiro
10 FAWCETT
Fawcett's known route and projected route

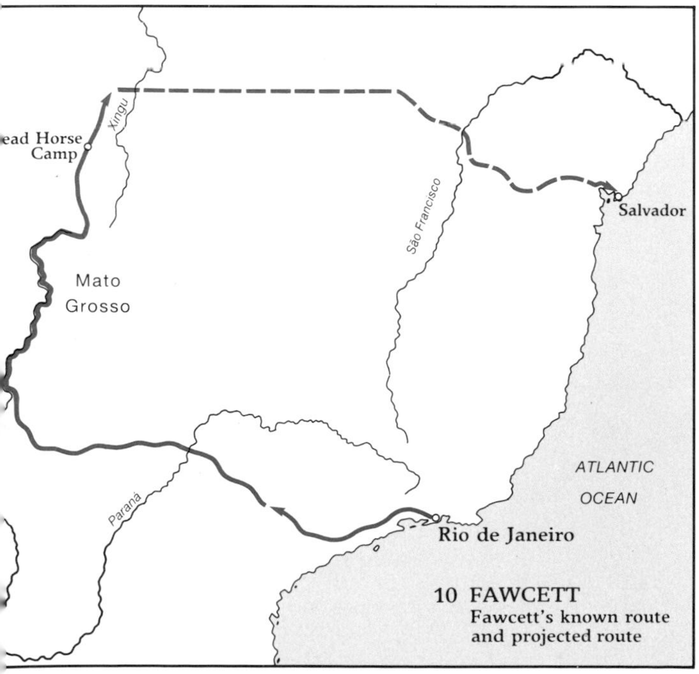

Her collection of paintings is now preserved at Kew Gardens in England and forms a permanent witness to the beauties of those forests whose conservation is now the concern of so many; they also form a memorial to a lady traveller, botanist and explorer who – though frail in form and advanced in years – was a worthy disciple of Bates, Wallace and Spruce.

The adventuring continues. Nicholas Guppy, Francis Huxley, Robin Furneaux and many other young explorers and anthropologists have made memorable journeys, some of them writing equally memorable books thereafter. Frequently the Royal Geographical Society has sponsored or encouraged such undertakings, and in 1987 it launched its own large-scale and year-long scientific expedition on Maracá Island (another inland island – this time in the northern Amazon region). From a base camp deep in the forests and run by the RGS team, entomologists and ornithologists, primatologists and anthropologists, and many varieties of zoologists and naturalists all set out on their own personal quests of discovery.

No longer is the main thrust of exploration motivated by the desire to spread the Gospels (although mission stations are still active in many parts of South America), nor the pursuit of gold and precious materials (although private prospectors and international oil companies are still active too), nor the discovery of 'new' tribes or rivers (although even now such discoveries can be made) but it is motivated by the pursuit of knowledge in all its forms. Humboldt and Darwin rather than Pizarro and Fawcett have proved to be the progenitors of today's explorers.

THE PACIFIC,
AUSTRALIA
AND NEW ZEALAND

THE SOUTH SEA

Although the Pacific Ocean is the globe's largest geographical entity (about one-third of the total surface), it was the last, apart from the polar regions, to be described by European explorers – a natural result of its comparative inaccessibility from European ports. The numerous inhabitants of its lands and islands were completely unknown in Europe in 1500. Even the old civilizations which lined its western shores were shrouded in mystery, the subject of much rumour but little knowledge.

Sharing the ancient maritime traditions of the Chinese – and not even the most Eurocentric historians speak of the 'discovery' of China – the Pacific islands were also inhabited by seagoing peoples capable of making long voyages who naturally knew a great deal more about their environment than their earliest European visitors. Their ancestors had certainly travelled thousands of miles to reach what became their homelands; even transoceanic voyages, no doubt inadvertent, may have been possible (as demonstrated by Thor Heyerdahl). They were the true 'discoverers' of the lands their descendants inhabited, but this knowledge was confined to

The Pacific Ocean offered a fearsome challenge to maritime explorers. After the months of sailing across an ocean that seemed to have no end, they might, when exhausted, sick and starving, be confronted with no welcoming harbour but hidden reefs.

The remarkable feats of navigation by Pacific islanders were not comprehended by early European sailors.

themselves and therefore does not form part of the history of exploration. If the Polynesians had been in a position to print and publish four fat quarto volumes complete with maps, things would have been different.

The span between Magellan and Cook is roughly 250 years, so the exploration of the Pacific cannot be said to have been completed quickly. It was far from complete even in the late 18th century – for instance, Antarctica had not yet been sighted – but the general picture was fairly clear. However, the Pacific presented formidable problems. The most obvious is its sheer size – some 181,300,000 sq km (70 million sq miles). Then, although its islands are numerous, most of them are very small, especially in comparison with the area of the ocean around them. The Solomon Islands, which occupy about 39,000 sq km (15,000 sq miles) and are visible over a considerably larger area, were first discovered in 1567 but, having been inaccurately located, were not seen again by European sailors for another 200 years.

The conditions, particularly the winds and currents, presented a further problem. For a sailing ship, the shortest distance between two points is seldom a straight line, and often it is impossible to follow such a course anyway. For example, contrary winds and currents made it virtually impossible to continue on a westward course after entering the Pacific via the Strait of Magellan, not that many sailors wished to continue in that desolate latitude. The Spaniards had comparatively little trouble establishing the route of the treasure galleon from Acapulco to Manila, but it took them some time to find the best one on the more hazardous return trip.

THE PACIFIC BEFORE MAGELLAN

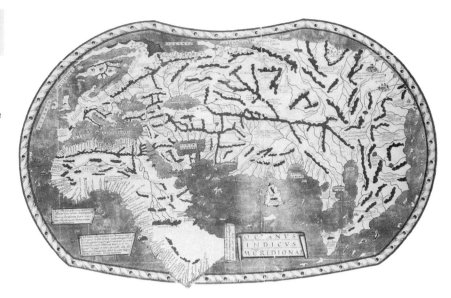

The chief geographic authority in Renaissance Europe was Ptolemy, the Alexandrian scholar of the 2nd century AD whose work, though known to the Arabs for centuries, had been recovered fairly recently. Not unnaturally, Ptolemy laboured under some sizeable misconceptions, which were to have significant results in the dawning age of discovery. In the first place, he underestimated the circumference of the globe by nearly 20 per cent. In the second place, he overestimated the extent of the Eurasian land mass by a large though indefinite amount, not less than 40°. The effect of this was to make the eastern coasts of Asia very roughly where the eastern coasts of North America actually are, thus accounting for Columbus's conviction that the Caribbean islands were the (East) Indies.

It soon became apparent that Columbus's discoveries were part of a New World and that it would be necessary to travel farther west in order to reach the fabled lands of the Orient; but it was not clear how far. It was widely assumed, still on the basis of Ptolemy, that they were quite close, and that a strait would be found through the American obstacle, giving easy access. The search for this strait, by sea and on land, was the motive for innumerable explorations up to the 19th century.

Another feature of Ptolemy's world map, which was to have even longer-lasting effects, was the existence of a vast mass of *terra incognita* to the south, which joined up Africa and eastern Asia, making the Indian Ocean a lake. By the time of Magellan's famous voyage, however, the Portuguese had blown a significant hole in this conception by sailing around the Cape of Good Hope to India. The formidable Albuquerque took Malacca in 1511 (with one Fernão de Magalhães, or Magellan, among his forces) and from there despatched exploratory voyages to the east. One of his captains, Francisco Serrão, established himself in Ternate in the Moluccas – the Spice Islands, chief objective of the Portuguese venture – and this Serrão was a close friend of Magellan.

Meanwhile, in 1513, the first European eyes had alighted upon the Pacific on the other side of the globe,

The 15th-century view of the world, based largely on Ptolemy; the studiously drawn co-ordinates created a misleading impression of cartographical accuracy.

from 'a peak in Darien'. The eyes were not those of 'stout Cortez', as Keats thought, but of Balboa (1475–1517), one of the more attractive (or less unattractive) of the *conquistadores*, who had arrived in Darién in a biscuit barrel with his pet dog after stowing away in Hispaniola (now the Dominican Republic and Haiti). A couple of days later, in the Gulf of Miguel, Balboa waded up to his armpits in the South Sea (its common name until much later; seen from Darién, it was 'south') and, waving a Spanish banner, claimed the ocean and all lands therein on behalf of the Spanish Crown.

MAGELLAN'S VOYAGE

Since the Portuguese had already reached the Spice Islands by the eastern route, they were not interested in finding a western one. In fact such a route was against their interests. The reason why Magellan (c. 1480–1521) forsook the service of his king in order to serve Spain was more personal. He had, at least in his own opinion, been badly treated by the king of Portugal, and he was not the kind of man to accept a slight, even from the king, with equanimity. Such changes of allegiance were not rare, and had Magellan's voyage not been such a striking success, Portuguese complaints would have been less vociferous.

Not all the unanswered questions raised by Magellan's assertion that he could lead the Spaniards to the Spice Islands by sailing west were geographical. There was a political problem. The Treaty of Tordesillas (1494) had delineated Portuguese and Spanish spheres by drawing a line through the Atlantic (Brazil protruded over it, which is why Brazil became Portuguese rather than Spanish). At the time, the line had applied only to the Atlantic, not to the unknown opposite hemisphere, but if it were assumed that the line continued around the globe, the question arose whether the Moluccas were in the Portuguese half or the Spanish half. To be on the safe side, the Portuguese had obtained a papal bull in 1514 which gave Portugal rights to all lands reached by sailing east, but this did not answer the question.

Magellan himself was apparently convinced that the Moluccas were in the Spanish zone. To find his strait, Magellan knew he would have to go a long

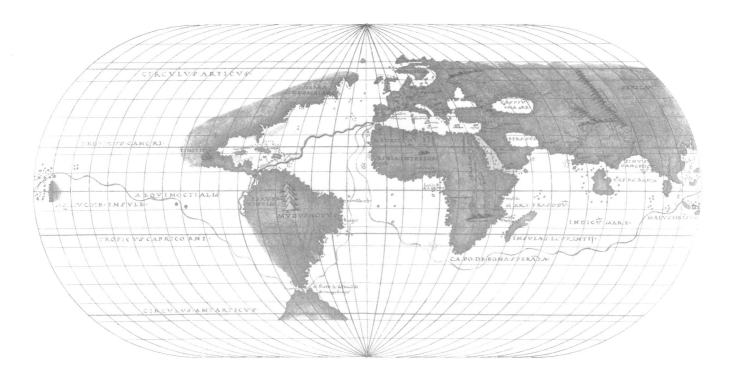

This map, showing Magellan's ship's route around the world, was drawn by Battista Agnese in Venice in 1536 and manifests, uncommonly, a commendable reluctance to speculate.

way south. The River Plate, a promising inlet, had already been investigated and found wanting. Once he had found the strait, the rest ought to have been relatively straightforward, allowing for the underestimation of the size of the Pacific. But it is not clear what Magellan intended to do once he had attained his objective. It seems unlikely that he planned to sail round the world since that would take him through Portuguese territory where he would be unwelcome.

Magellan set sail in August 1519. He had five ships and a somewhat motley crew; trade goods included 20,000 small brass bells. Apart from a spell of nasty weather and predictable trouble with jealous Spanish captains, the Atlantic was crossed without serious incident. There was trade for fresh food with the inhabitants of what is now Rio de Janeiro, and within five months the fleet was in the Plate estuary. Having confirmed that it was a river, they sailed on and decided to winter at the port of San Julián, where the simmering conflicts came to a head and what was to become a frequent problem on such voyages – mutiny – broke out. At one point, three of the five ships were controlled by the mutinous Spanish officers, but a timely assassination recovered one of the ships and the others soon surrendered. One man was beheaded, another marooned – effectively a death sentence.

One ship was lost on a reconnaissance during the winter, though the crew survived, and the remaining four resumed the voyage in October. Within a few days they found a promising inlet and Magellan sent two ships in to investigate. They were gone so long – about a week – that he thought they were lost, when

they reappeared with flags waving and guns firing convinced (correctly) that they had found the Strait of Magellan. Passage of the strait took 38 days, a remarkably short time (as later captains would ruefully confirm) considering the many channels that had to be investigated and the delay in searching for the store-ship, which had in fact deserted. Supplies were an anxiety, and there was talk of turning back, but Magellan insisted they should continue even if they had to eat the leather on the ship's yards, which, had he known it, was an accurate description of their future diet.

The immensity of the Pacific – 'a sea so vast that the human mind can hardly comprehend it' – was then revealed. For 98 days they saw no land except for two small uninhabited islands which offered no sustenance. Finally they reached the Marianas, which Magellan named the Ladrones ('Thieves'), for obvious reasons. In order to regain possession of a ship's boat, he burned a village and killed half a dozen people. This was but a small and insignificant episode in the long and terrible list of crimes against the local inhabitants as the Europeans strived to conquer the world; Magellan was not a particularly brutal man.

Other islanders were more agreeable, and the crews were able to recover from the rigours of the voyage before, on local advice, sailing on to Cebu in the Philippines. The ruler of that land, having heard

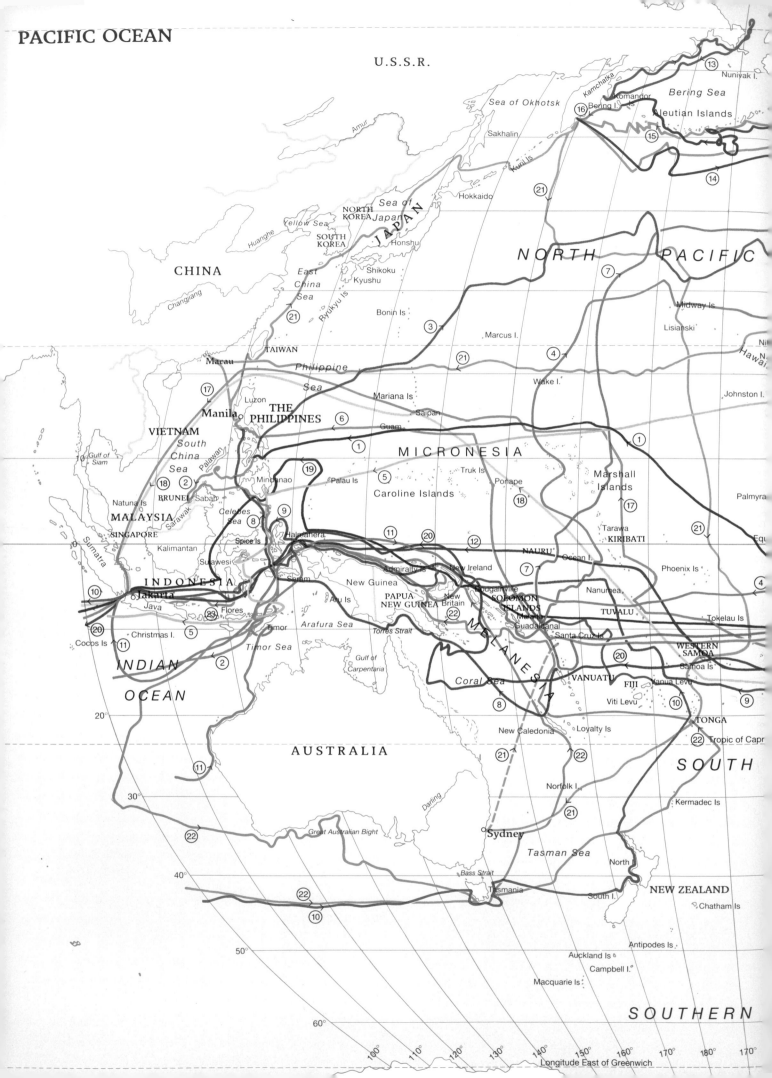

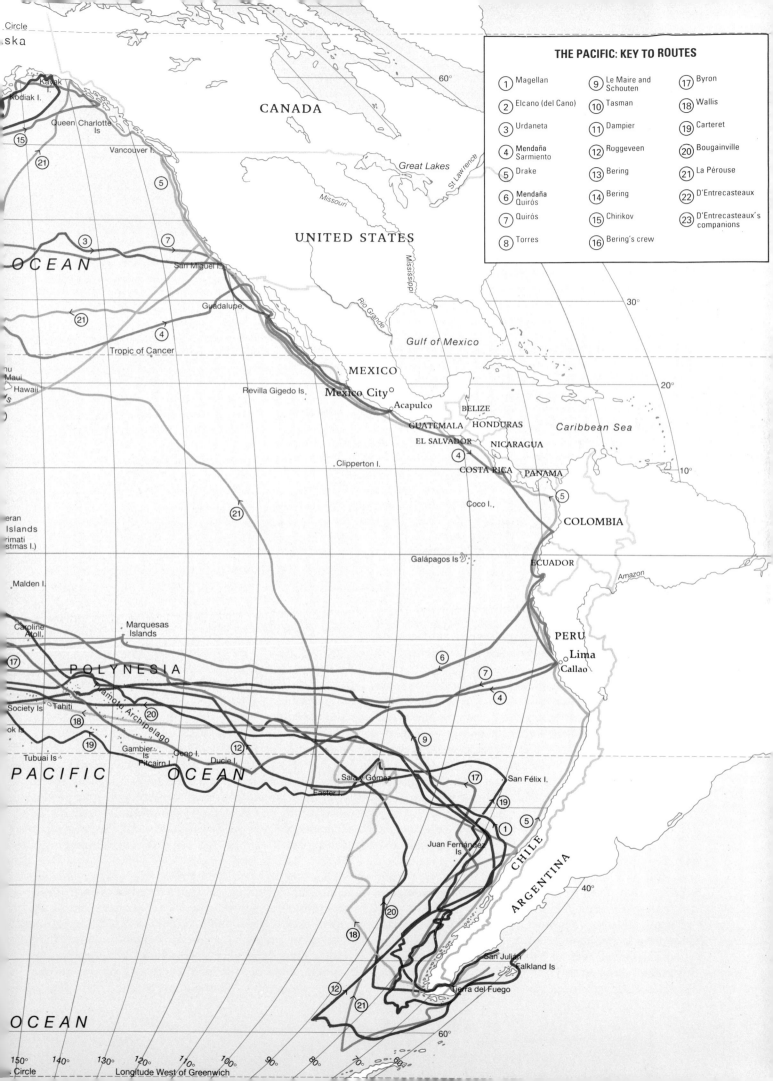

THE PACIFIC: KEY TO ROUTES

1	Magellan	9	Le Maire and Schouten	17	Byron
2	Elcano (del Cano)	10	Tasman	18	Wallis
3	Urdaneta	11	Dampier	19	Carteret
4	Mendaña Sarmiento	12	Roggeveen	20	Bougainville
5	Drake	13	Bering	21	La Pérouse
6	Mendaña Quirós	14	Bering	22	D'Entrecasteaux
7	Quirós	15	Chirikov	23	D'Entrecasteaux's companions
8	Torres	16	Bering's crew		

Circle

ska

Kayak I.

Kodiak I.

15

21

Queen Charlotte Is

Vancouver I.

CANADA

Great Lakes

Missouri

St Lawrence

60°

OCEAN

3

7

San Miguel I.

UNITED STATES

Mississippi

21

Guadalupe

4

Tropic of Cancer

30°

Gulf of Mexico

Maui

Hawaii

MEXICO

Revilla Gigedo Is

Mexico City

Acapulco

BELIZE

20°

eran

Islands

rimati

stmas I.)

Clipperton I.

GUATEMALA   HONDURAS

EL SALVADOR   NICARAGUA

4

COSTA RICA   PANAMA

Caribbean Sea

Coco I.

5

10°

Malden I.

Galápagos Is

ECUADOR

COLOMBIA

Amazon

21

Caroline Atoll

Marquesas Islands

POLYNESIA

PERU

Lima

Callao

6

7

4

17

ok Is

Society Is   Tahiti

amotu Archipelago

20

18

19

Gambier Is

Oeno I.

Pitcairn I.

Ducie I.

12

Sala y Gómez

Easter I.

San Félix I.

17

19

Tubuai Is

PACIFIC   OCEAN

9

1

5

Juan Fernández Is

CHILE

ARGENTINA

40°

20

18

San Julián

Falkland Is

12

Tierra del Fuego

21

OCEAN

60°

150°   140°   130°   120°   110°   100°   90°   80°   70°

Circle   Longitude West of Greenwich

PACIFIC OCEAN AND ISLANDS
1511 Albuquerque took control of Malacca for the Portuguese. Despatched exploratory voyages east to the Spice Islands.

1513 First European sighting of the Pacific by Balboa in Panama. He called it the 'South Sea'.
1519-21 Magellan found strait into the Pacific north of Tierra del Fuego, pioneering

a westward route to the East Indies.
1565 Urdaneta's west-east crossing of the Pacific established a new route from the Philippines to Mexico.

THE PACIFIC: KEY TO ROUTES

(1) **Magellan** 1519–21. Sailed from the Strait of Magellan to Puka Puka in the Tuamotu Archipelago, to Caroline Atoll and from Guam to the Philippines. Killed at Mactán.

(2) **del Cano (Elcano)** 1521–2. Called at Mindanao, Palawan, Brunei, at Tidore in the Spice Is, at Timor, then crossed the Indian Ocean.

(3) **Urdaneta** 1565. Set off from Cebu, Philippines. Next landfall was San Miguel I., off California. Put in at Acapulco.

(4) **Mendaña and Sarmiento** 1567–9. Sailed from Callao, Peru, to the Solomon Is. Returned to Callao.

(5) **Drake** 1577–80. Sailed through Strait of Magellan. Visited Valparaíso, Arica and Callao. May have sailed to 48°N. Returned to San Francisco area, crossed Pacific to Palau Is, Mindanao, the Moluccas, Sulawesi and Java.

(6) **Mendaña and Quiros** 1595–6. Sailed from Callao to the Marquesas Is and Santa Cruz Is. After Mendaña's death Quiros sailed to the Caroline Is, Guam and Manila.

(7) **Quiros** 1605–6. Sailed from Callao. Sighted Ducie and other islands. To Espíritu Santo in Vanuatu. To Acapulco (blown N by wind).

(8) **Torres** 1606–7. After disappearance of Quiros sailed to 21°S in search of 'southern continent'. To New Guinea, passing through Torres Strait, and on to Manila.

(9) **Le Maire and Schouten** 1615–17. Passed through Le Maire Strait, sailed to Tuamotus, Tongan group, Horne Is, New Ireland, N New Guinea and on to Jakarta.

(10) **Tasman** 1642–3. Sailed from Mauritius to Tasmania, New Zealand, Tonga, Fiji, N New Guinea and Jakarta.

(11) **Dampier** 1699–1700. Sailed along part of NW coast of Australia, then to New Ireland, along N coast of New Guinea and on to Jakarta.

(12) **Roggeveen** 1721–2. Entered Pacific via Le Maire Strait. Sailed to Juan Fernández Is, Easter I., the Tuamotus, the Samoa Is and Jakarta.

(13) **Bering** 1728. From Kamchatka sailed to 67°N but did not see the Alaskan coast.

(14) **Bering** 1741. Sailed from Kamchatka and sighted Kayak I., off Alaska. Died on Bering I.

(15) **Chirikov** 1741. Set out with Bering in another ship. Sailed to the vicinity of Sitka, Alaska.

(16) Survivors from Bering's ship 1742. Wintered on Bering I. and returned to Kamchatka.

(17) **Byron** 1764–6. From Strait of Magellan sailed to Tuamotus, Kiribati and Mariana Is, rounding the Philippines to reach Jakarta.

(18) **Wallis** 1766–8. Sailed to Tuamotus, Tahiti, Mariana Is, rounding the Philippines to reach Jakarta.

(19) **Carteret** 1766–9. Sailed to Juan Fernández Is, Pitcairn I., Santa Cruz Is, New Britain, Admiralty Is, Mindanao, Sulawesi and Jakarta.

(20) **Bougainville** 1766–9. From Strait of Magellan through the Tuamotus, to Tahiti, Samoa Is, Vanuatu, Great Barrier Reef, Solomon Is, New Ireland, Admiralty Is and on to Jakarta.

(21) **La Pérouse** 1785–8. From Le Maire Strait sailed to Chile, Easter I., Hawaiian Is, Alaska, California, Macau, Manila, Sakhalin, Kamchatka, Samoa Is, Tonga and Port Jackson (Sydney). Reached Santa Cruz Is by an unknown route where his ship was wrecked on Vanikoro.

(22) **D'Entrecasteaux** 1791–3. Sailed to Tasmania, New Caledonia, New Ireland, Timor, Australia, Tasmania again, Tonga, New Caledonia again, Santa Cruz Is, Solomon Is and New Guinea. He died to NW of Admiralty Is.

(23) **D'Entrecasteaux**'s companions 1793. Sailed along N coast of New Guinea to Surabaya, Java.

The routes of Cook's voyages are shown on pp. 216–7.

---

something of European guns, was quick to embrace Spanish overlordship and the Christian religion, but some of his subjects were not so obliging. In the ensuing conflict, Magellan deemed it wise to support his puppet with arms, but he underestimated the opposition and, in a typically bold rearguard action, the leader of perhaps the greatest maritime exploit in history was killed.

Compelled by their depleted numbers to abandon one ship, the survivors sailed on, via Brunei where there was more trouble with the local inhabitants, until they finally reached their destination, Tidore, an island in the Moluccas, in November 1521. After taking on a cargo of cloves and arranging trade and 'protection' agreements, they set out for home. Though the Portuguese were not yet in control, a fleet was out looking for the Spaniards. The *Trinidad* was in need of complete overhaul, and it was decided that, when repairs were completed, she should return to the east, making for Darién which was still thought to be within easy reach. Forced back by the contrary Trades, the *Trinidad* fell into unsympathetic Portuguese hands.

Meanwhile the *Victoria*, under Juan Sebastián del Cano, made her laboured way around the Cape of Good Hope and back to Spain, arriving at Seville in September 1522 with just 18 men. A few from the *Trinidad* later got back too. The world had been

encompassed, though at a heavy cost. The chief chronicler of the voyage supposed that men would never make such a voyage again, but he was wrong.

PLANTING THE CROSS

The Spaniards failed to dislodge the Portuguese from the Spice Islands, and it was not until 1565 that Manila was settled. Meanwhile, discoveries were few, and the ships that went to Manila followed the established routes, ignorant of what lay to the south or north. In Peru, familiarly, there were legends of lands rich in gold far away in the west, and this, combined with the persistent European belief in a great southern continent – one of the most stubborn fictions in the whole history of exploration – provided the motive for the voyage of Alvaro de Mendaña and Pedro de Sarmiento in 1567.

They set out from Lima in two ships, carrying about 150, including several Franciscan friars. They were gone for almost two years, in the course of which they sailed about 11,500 km (7000 miles), often with only the vaguest notion of where they were. They were charged with 'converting the heathen', but in spite of the protests of the devout and well-meaning Mendaña, they found it easier to shoot them. A perennial source of conflict in Pacific voyaging was the naive supposition of the Europeans that a delicately balanced island economy was capable of providing food for large numbers of hungry sailors and soldiers on demand, without causing conflict.

The chief discovery of the voyage was the Solomon Islands, at first thought to be a spur of the 'southern continent'. In spite of the sufferings of the voyage, Mendaña became fired with the ambition to found a Christian colony in the lands he had discovered. This was the objective of his second great voyage, planned in Spain in 1576 though, owing apparently to Mendaña falling out of favour, not begun until 1595.

In the meantime Drake had made the second circumnavigation of the globe (1577–80), having failed to find a strait in northern California which would lead him back to the Atlantic. Discovery was not the main purpose of Drake's voyage (precisely *what* the main purpose was is a matter of argument) and the only discovery of real importance was that Tierra del Fuego is an island, suspected by Magellan, though others thought it was part of the 'southern continent', below which the Atlantic and Pacific 'meete in a most large and free scope'.

Mendaña, leaving Callao, the port of Lima, in April 1595, had the advantage this time of a first-rate pilot and second-in-command, the Portuguese Pedro Fernandez de Quiros. (The Crowns of Spain and Portugal had been temporarily united in 1580, although this by no means ended Portuguese–Spanish competition abroad.) Nevertheless, the voyage was an almost total disaster, a grisly tale of pain and horror, as recorded by Quiros who, not unnaturally, emerges as the hero among a crowd of selfish and quarrelsome Spaniards.

Mendaña was unable to find the Solomons again (nor could anyone else for nearly two centuries) and, having discovered the Marquesas, at first took *them* to be the Solomons, though they are half an ocean away – a good example of contemporary difficulties in measuring longitude. He was unable to establish a colony there, or in the Santa Cruz Islands, which he stumbled upon next, because the unruly soldiers and intended colonists had killed so many of the inhabitants in both groups that they were in a state of open warfare. Mendaña himself died, along with many others, and Quiros managed to get what was left of the expedition to the Philippines, a considerable feat considering the state of men and ships and his ignorance of the region.

Quiros, who shared both Mendaña's religious zeal

A reconstruction, painted by Gregory Robinson, of Drake's Golden Hind *(formerly the* Pelican*), which completed the second circumnavigation of the world under Drake.*

and the common belief in a 'southern continent', gained support for another voyage in 1605. His three small ships carried nearly 300 men, and his first objective was Santa Cruz. The usual problems arose – incipient mutiny, storms that threw them off course, desperate shortage of water and food – and these were exacerbated by Quiros's poor health and inability to enforce discipline. Several new islands were discovered (their identity now uncertain), but Quiros became increasingly vague about their destination: 'God will guide [the ships],' he said.

They discovered Espíritu Santo in the New Hebrides (Vanuatu) just in time to avert a mutiny. The islands were rich, though the inevitable battle had to be fought to establish Christian ascendancy, and it may have been this which turned Quiros's mind: he began to display signs of a kind of religious megalomania (in later life he regarded himself as another Columbus, if not Julius Caesar). Then, one day, in the course of some local exploration, Quiros's ship was blown out of sight of land. She never reappeared in the area but eventually made the long voyage back to Mexico, reaching it in November 1606. Some mystery surrounds this – involuntary? – defection.

Meanwhile, command of the expedition fell to Luis Vaez de Torres, a more resolute leader and as good a navigator. He continued, according to the orders of the Viceroy of Peru, to look for the 'southern continent' to the south, in spite of vociferous resistance by one and all, who wished to make for Manila right away. Having reached 21°S without sighting land, Torres turned north, meaning

A Japanese view of the early European merchants, characteristically exaggerating aspects that seemed strange such as their breeches; from a painted screen.

to sail along the known northern coast of New Guinea to the Philippines.

Unable to weather the east point, he coasted westward along the south coast, thus solving one of the biggest unanswered questions of the region by proving that New Guinea is an island. Like a number of other momentous discoveries in the history of exploration, the existence of Torres Strait was registered – and ignored (the Spaniards, of course, kept their discoveries secret). History too, unfortunately, must ignore Torres from the moment he finally reached port (with only one man lost): no word of him is heard thereafter.

THE DUTCH

By this time, Spain's golden age was ending. The Dutch were in the process of displacing the Portuguese in the East Indies, and their base at Batavia (Jakarta), commanding the Sunda Strait, was established in 1619, replacing an older factory. The agent of expansion was the Dutch East India Company, then a more formidable organization – practically an arm of the government – than its English counterpart. The interest of the Company was in profit, not exploration, but in the circumstances adventitious discoveries were inevitable, especially as the Dutch adopted a more southerly and much faster route from the Cape of Good Hope: the haziness about longitude ensured that some ships would be carried on to the shores of Australia.

There were some more deliberate probes, and the Dutch soon knew the Australian coast north as far as Cape York Peninsula, west and south as far as the Great Australian Bight. They were not impressed. The inhabitants they regarded as 'wild, cruel savages' (they had the cheek to defend themselves), and the country appeared to lack valuable natural resources, even water.

The one genuine voyage of discovery between Torres and Tasman was that of Le Maire and Schouten in 1615. Isaac le Maire was a maverick Dutch merchant, at odds with the Company of which he had once been a director, who set up a company to trade in the Far East. He aimed to circumvent the East India Company's monopoly of trade via the Strait of Magellan and the Cape by finding another passage in the south-west. The plan worked perfectly when the ship, commanded by his son Jacob with Schouten, an experienced navigator, as second-in-command, discovered Le Maire Strait and became the first to pass Cape Hoorn, so named after Schouten's home town.

By April 1616, they were among the Tuamotus. The inevitable clashes occurred with the islanders, both there and in the northern islets of the Tongan group. Soon afterwards came another important discovery, Horne Islands, between Fiji and Samoa, where the people were friendly, though never more so than when they observed the signs of the Dutchmen's imminent departure.

1567-9 Mendaña commanded the first Spanish exploratory voyage in the South Pacific. Discovered the Solomon Islands.
1577-80 Drake completed the first British

circumnavigation via Drake Passage across the Pacific to East Indies.
1595-6 Mendaña and Quiros discovered the Marquesas, the first important group of

Polynesian islands.
1602 Dutch East India Company given exclusive rights to trade using Cape of Good Hope and Magellan Strait routes.

Le Maire then wanted to head west in search of the Solomons and Quiros's 'southern continent', but the more cautious Schouten, fearing embayment in New Guinea (the Dutch knew nothing of Torres Strait), insisted on a more northerly course. They coasted the north of New Ireland, thinking it was New Guinea, and eventually found someone who could speak Malay and a little Spanish. By the end of October they were at Batavia, having lost only three men on the whole, excellently conducted voyage.

They had a poor welcome. Jan Coen, the East India Company's governor-general and somewhat like a Dutch version of Albuquerque, impounded ships and cargo and sent them home in a Company ship. Le Maire died on the voyage home ('of a broken heart') but his father, who had 21 other children, was not the man to tolerate such treatment. He embarked on a legal vendetta against the Company which ended in full restoration of the confiscated property with interest.

The chief discoveries of the Dutch were due to another dynamic governor at Batavia, Anthonio van Diemen, the major ones occurring during the expedition he despatched in 1642. This was commanded by Abel Janszoon Tasman, an experienced skipper, accompanied by Frans Jacobszoon Visscher, a pilot with a fertile geographical brain. The plan was to search for the 'Southland' by sailing east in a latitude of 52 or 54° (from the staging post of Mauritius); if no land were found before the longitude of New Guinea was reached, the ships should either sail north to New Guinea or continue

east to the supposed longitude of the Solomons, discover them, and then return via the north of New Guinea.

Van Diemen's instructions also contained the command that in any contact with strange people they should 'be patient and long-suffering, no ways quick to fly out'. For once this admonition was observed; Tasman's voyage was unusual in that more casualties through violence were suffered by the explorers than the explored.

They were unable to keep to as southerly a track as planned, and in fact sailed between about 50 and 42°, a course which brought them to the land named after Van Diemen by Tasman but now bearing his own name. In cursory exploration they saw no individual of the aboriginal race later to be the subject of a totally successful exercise in genocide, but Tasman thought they were giants (a favourite Dutch supposition).

They followed the coast until it bore away northwest, into the wind, then turned east again. Within a few days they discovered more new land (New Zealand) and, anchoring in a bay, were approached by canoes. The men seemed friendly at first, but suddenly attacked a longboat, killing four Dutchmen. Tasman left 'Murderers' Bay' (Golden Bay) hastily; it was a sad first contact between Europeans and Maoris.

They coasted north, wondering if this were part of Le Maire's Staten Land (the island east of the tip of South America, proved to be such by another Dutch captain the next year) and looked for a strait that would provide a passage to Chile. They had entered

---

SCURVY

Scurvy is a disease caused by Vitamin C deficiency, resulting from a lack of fresh fruit and vegetables. It was probably the biggest menace to crews on Pacific voyages until the 19th century as, although scurvy took a long time to kill them, it made them weak and was thus responsible for accidents, including shipwreck. There were cases of ships that, reaching home waters after months at sea, were unable to make port because there was no one on board strong enough to haul a rope.

The symptoms were various, the

first usually being swelling of the gums and loosening of the teeth; as the disease worsened, it induced profound lethargy. Men living exclusively on salted provisions sometimes developed the symptoms within six weeks.

Though vitamins were not discovered until the 20th century, a British naval surgeon, James Lind, proved in 1753 by experiments with diet that oranges and lemons were effective against scurvy. A mere 42 years later lemon juice (later, lime, but lemon is better) was made compulsory

for RN crews. The dilatoriness of the Royal Navy is the more remarkable in light of the fact that seamen had been well aware of the efficacy of citrus fruit since the 16th century.

Richard Hawkins found that oranges and lemons are 'a certain remedie for this infirmitie' on his voyage of 1593. Le Maire and Schouten purchased 25,000 lemons in Sierra Leone before crossing the Atlantic in 1615. The problem was that fresh fruit could not be kept long enough. Cook, who was strict about diet and had little trouble with scurvy among his crew, introduced raisins and sauerkraut with good effect, as well as orange and lemon juice, and he never missed an opportunity to take on fresh fruit and vegetables.

1605-6 Torres sailed between New Guinea and Australia's Cape York peninsula proving New Guinea to be an island.
1615-7 Schouten and Le Maire pioneered

new route into Pacific to avoid Dutch East India Company-controlled waters.
1700 Dampier travelled through the Dampier Strait, to the west of New Guinea.

1721-3 Roggeveen searched for great Southern Continent. Discovered Easter Island.
1741 Bering and Chirikov in the North Pacific.

Cook Strait but did not recognize its nature. More 'giants' were visible on distant hills on Three Kings' Island, where they would have sailed east again but were forced north-east by the wind. Following Le Maire, they found the Friendly Isles, as Cook was aptly to call Tonga (though Tasman, less aptly, named various islands after Dutch cities), and got into a terrible tangle amid reefs and rocks in the Fiji group. After failing to find Torres Strait, still unknown outside Spain, they coasted northern New Guinea and reached Batavia ten months after they had set out.

Celebrations were muted. Tasman was criticized for not investigating the lands he had discovered more closely, and in any case the directors of the Company were not greatly interested in Van Diemen's schemes. 'We do not expect great things from the continuation of such explorations,' they informed him frostily. They already had more commercial opportunities than they could cope with, and feared that promising new discoveries would merely be exploited by others, such as the English. In the words of J.H. Parry, 'Trade, which in the 16th century had been a prime stimulus to exploration, became its enemy in the 17th century.'

It is therefore not surprising that the progress of discovery hardly advanced in the remainder of the century, nor that the only other really important Dutch voyage of exploration was carried out by a non-Company man.

Jacob Roggeveen, following, rather late in life (he was 62), an idea of his father for new sources of

trade in the South Sea, was backed by the West India Company, much less grand an institution. In pursuit of the great Southland, he entered the Pacific in 1721 via Le Maire Strait, took a look at Robinson Crusoe's island, in the Juan Fernández group, which he considered a promising base, and searched for a coast, reported by a buccaneer captain, in 27°.

He found no continent, but did find, on Easter Day, a small island whose inhabitants are said to have believed their nearest neighbours were on the Moon. Most astonishing were the giant carved figures, the significance of which Roggeveen was unable to determine (nor has anyone else). After a week they sailed on, still failing to find the continent but wandering for over a month among the Tuamotus. Having lost one ship and a number of his men, Roggeveen then decided to cut his losses and head for Batavia, touching on the pleasant Samoan group on the way.

THE ENGLISH AND THE FRENCH

From Dampier's time onward, there was intense interest in the Pacific in England and France. One example of this was the foundation of the South Sea Company, though it never did any business in the South Sea. For the time being, however, this interest was largely confined to talk, to volumes of *Voyages* and learned (or not so learned) discussions among geographers. Belief in the 'southern continent' was still fervent, though its dimensions had shrunk a

---

DAMPIER AND THE BUCCANEERS

In the 17th century the buccaneers became a considerable force in the Caribbean and, following the example of Henry Morgan, took to raiding on the other side of the Isthmus. A number of notable voyages took place, but neither exploration nor trade, in the usual sense of the term, figured high among the buccaneers' ambitions. However, some unusual characters were to be found among the buccaneers. The most controversial of them was William Dampier (1652–1715), who in the course of his haphazard career sailed around the world three times, on one occasion taking eight years.

By nature Dampier was a rolling stone, but he also had a strong sense of scientific curiosity. What made him famous was his book, *A New Voyage Round the World* (1697), a mass of fascinating observations, which gained him access to the Establishment, helped to inspire books like *Robinson Crusoe* and *Gulliver's Travels*, and, so to speak, put the Pacific on the map of England.

The Admiralty commissioned him to undertake a voyage of discovery to find the 'southern continent', of which Dampier promised much. He was given a rotten ship and a poor crew, and the voyage cannot be accounted

a great success, although Dampier Strait, between the Bismarck Sea and the Solomon Sea, was discovered. The voyage also resulted in Dampier's court martial (since he had lost his ship), but did not destroy his reputation, for he was soon employed again to lead a privateering expedition. This was an even greater disaster: the gift of command was not one of Dampier's assets.

Dampier made one more voyage, this time sailing as the pilot in the privateering voyage (1708–11) of Captain Woodes Rogers, one of the best conducted voyages of its kind. They even captured a Manila galleon.

The headpieces of the mysterious Easter Island statues were still in place when La Pérouse arrived there 64 years after Roggeveen's discovery.

little. It was then thought to consist of New Guinea and Australia, from which New Zealand was divided by a strait, plus a large part of the South Pacific.

Pamphleteers demanded to know why Britain, a country that lived by trade, was not doing something to exploit the rich opportunities there. The French were equally keen. Not uncharacteristically, they claimed priority as discoverers in the Pacific on the basis of a voyage undertaken some years before Magellan which had produced reports of a land called 'South India' (probably Madagascar). They were perhaps more concerned with glory and science than

with vulgar trade, but after the Seven Years' War the discovery of the Pacific became a part of the world-wide commercial-colonial rivalry of the two great maritime nations of the era.

Before that time, comparatively little had been achieved. The Frenchman Bouvet thought he had found the 'southern continent' for a moment, but alas he had discovered only the tiny and insignificant island now named after him. Anson led a British naval expedition around the world, an epic of endurance, but made no important new discoveries.

After the war ended in 1763, the opportunity arose to employ idle ships and men on more interesting, if hardly less dangerous, work, and the 'golden age' of Pacific exploration opened with a little flurry of circumnavigations. First off was Commodore the

A RECIPE FROM THE BATAN ISLANDS

'The Paunches of the Goats would make them an excellent Dish; they drest it in this manner. They would turn out all the chopt Grass and Crudites found in the Maw into their Pots, and set it over the Fire, and stir it about often: This would Smoak and Puff, and heave up as it was Boyling; wind breaking out of the Ferment, and making a very savory Stink. While this was doing, if they had any Fish, and commonly they had 2 or 3 small Fish, these they would make very clean (as hating Nastiness belike) and cut the Flesh from the Bone, and then mince the Flesh as small as possibly they could, and when that in the Pot was well boiled, they would take it up, and strewing a little Salt into it, they would eat it, mixt with their raw minced Flesh. The Dung in the Maw would look like so much boil'd Herbs minc'd very small; and they took up their Mess with their Fingers, as the Moors do their Pillaw, using no Spoons.' (William Dampier, *Dampier's Voyages* (ed. Masefield), 1906, Vol 1, page 424)

1766 Wallis discovered Tahiti, Moorea and a number of the Society Islands.
1767-9 Carteret in the unseaworthy *Swallow* discovered Pitcairn and islands in the

Tuamotos, Solomons and Carolines.
1767 Bougainville became the first Frenchman to sail around the world and claimed seven archipelagos for France.

1769-71 Cook observed the transit of Venus from Tahiti. Discovered and circumnavigated New Zealand. Claimed New South Wales for Britain.

Hon. John ('Foul-weather Jack') Byron, grandfather of the poet. He had few outstanding qualifications for leading a search for the 'southern continent', though he had sailed with Anson and endured some gruesome experiences (shipwrecked in Chile, it took him six years to get back to England).

Byron sailed in the *Dolphin* in 1764. His orders were to check the Falkland Islands as a possible base, which he did, and to sail up the west coast of North America to look for a strait from Hudson's Bay, a scheme pioneered by Drake. He decided not to bother with that, and instead set off west to look for the 'southern continent'. He put in to the island of Takaroa in the Tuamotus, dispersed hostile islanders by shooting over their heads, and amazingly found relics from a boat lost by Roggeveen. Having failed to find the Solomons, he touched on various other small islands, including one in the Gilberts (Kiribati) that still bears his name, and rounded the Philippines

to reach Batavia, by now a large but unhealthy city, whence he sailed home via the Cape. The voyage had taken less than two years, a record.

Before the year was out the *Dolphin*, refitted, was off again, this time commanded by the rather more reliable Samuel Wallis – the true forerunner of Cook. Like Cook, he took good care of his crews and was the first captain to keep scurvy at bay on such a voyage; ironically, as both Wallis and Cook found, the most dangerous place in terms of casualties was the 'European' city of Batavia. The *Dolphin* was accompanied by the sloop *Swallow*, commanded by Captain Carteret, a veteran of Byron's voyage. Unfortunately, the *Swallow* sailed like a barrel; the ships became separated after passing the Strait of Magellan (it took four months, a record of another sort) and completed the voyage independently.

Wallis followed the customary north-westerly route across the Pacific, but in the Tuamotus he was

THE NORTH PACIFIC

Peter the Great of Russia set in motion an ambitious plan to expand Russian territory to the east. The main task with which the Danish explorer, Vitus Bering (1680–1741), was charged, was to find where (or, as it turned out, if) Asia and North America were joined. Bering left St Petersburg in 1725 and took almost two years to reach Okhotsk, his forward base. Taking ship in 1728, he sailed as far north as 67°, far enough, one would think, to confirm the report of the local Chukchi that he had passed the eastern point of the land, but owing to fog he missed the American coast and was therefore uncertain.

The Russians were anxious lest they were forestalled commercially in the North Pacific by the French or the English, so Bering tried again. While his lieutenants made somewhat ineffectual voyages to the Kurils and Japan, Bering, with the more energetic Alexei Chirikov, at last set out for America in June 1741.

The two ships became separated and, after failing to find the fictional 'Gamaland', Bering made landfall on Kayak Island, off Alaska. Bering was not especially impressed; conditions on board were deteriorating, and many were down with scurvy, so they

prepared to return. In a grim state, they were forced to winter on Bering Island, heart-breakingly close to their base in Kamchatka. Bering himself was not among the survivors.

Meanwhile, Chirikov, whose competence, Professor Spate remarked, stands out 'in a milieu rife with inefficiency and irresolution', had sailed to a point beyond modern Sitka, farther east than Bering, and returned safely, though in poor condition. Not much had been learned about the

The death of Bering on the island named after him. Reality has been sacrificed to composition, but the scene is still an affecting one.

coast, but Alaska was, for the time being anyway, Russian.

Just as the Russian advance had been largely motivated by fear of preemption by others, the Spaniards made haste to make sure of California, one result being the foundation of San Francisco.

somewhat farther south than most previous travellers and thus encountered Tahiti. This moment may be regarded as a kind of crux in the exploration of the Pacific by Europeans. To the sailors who landed there, Tahiti seemed a kind of paradise, a land where, as J.C. Beaglehole put it, not even man was vile; reading their accounts, it still seems so today despite a few unacceptable customs (such as the occasional human sacrifice). But from the time Wallis's ship dropped anchor in Matavai Bay, the traditional society of Tahiti was, of course, doomed.

Wallis remained in Tahiti over a month, but the stern business of exploration had to continue (though he had to promise the local queen that he would return before she would willingly let him leave). He sailed west for a time, naming numerous islands after royal dukes and eminent admirals, before deciding that the condition of ship and crew dictated a course for Batavia.

Meanwhile, the little *Swallow*, against all odds, was making her own way around the world. Her tardy progress enforced a trans-Pacific voyage at the worst season, and, like everyone else, Carteret was compelled to sail in a more northerly latitude than he wished. He was, however, well to the south of Wallis, and discovered Pitcairn Island, soon to be made famous as a result of the mutiny in the *Bounty*. He rediscovered Quiros' Santa Cruz and sailed more or less through the Solomons, without recognizing them (he had already concluded they were wrongly located). Contrary currents prevented him entering Dampier Strait, but he found St George's Channel to the north, thus proving that New Ireland and New Britain are separate islands.

After spending five months in the small Dutch port of Bonthain in Sulawesi, he was able to sail to Batavia, where his ship, by now severely battered, was repaired. He was still forced to spend six weeks at the Cape (not entirely unwelcome) to revive his crew, before setting out on the final stage in January 1769. North of Ascension he was overhauled by a French ship, which hailed him and informed him that the *Dolphin* had already reached England and that his own ship had been assumed wrecked in the Strait of Magellan. Before Carteret could make further inquiries, the Frenchman 'shot by us as if we had been at anchor'.

The French ship was the frigate *Boudeuse*. She too had been around the world, though starting three months after the *Swallow* and delayed some time on business in the South Atlantic. Her captain was the dashing and gallant Comte de Bougainville (1729–1811).

BOUGAINVILLE

Though best known as a mariner, Bougainville had been a soldier before his voyage around the world, and was ADC to another gallant French commander, Montcalm, in Canada, 1756–7. At his own expense he established a French settlement in the Falklands, a useful base for South Pacific voyages, in 1764, a year before Byron claimed the islands for Britain (subsequently, the French ceded them to Spain).

After his circumnavigation (during which he lost only seven men) he was for a time a royal secretary, served again in North America and was disgraced after the French defeat at the Battle of the Saints in the Caribbean (1782). He

Bougainville, like Cook though in a different way, was the sort of man to whom anyone would have been pleased to offer a basket of fruit. Alas, formalities over, European culture had a disastrous effect on that of Tahiti.

narrowly escaped the Terror and sat out the Revolution on his Normandy estates until finding favour again under Napoleon. He died aged 82 in 1811.

A thorough gentleman and son of the Enlightenment, Bougainville was distinguished by personal charm as well as courage and high scientific intelligence – as a young army officer he had written a treatise on the calculus.

It was not until about a year after he had left France that Bougainville passed the Strait of Magellan, noting evidence of Wallis and Carteret ahead of him, at the real beginning of his exploratory voyage. Among the islands, he speculated on how such small, remote places had become populated, and gave vent to some critical considerations, with which many navigators would have agreed, on the tendency of home-bound geographers to record lands and continents on the most meagre evidence.

His course in the central Pacific was close to that of Wallis, and he too had the luck to strike Tahiti, though at a point some way to the east of the British. Tahitian hospitality survived even the murder of some of their countrymen by French sailors (the real 'savages' in the Pacific were Europeans, not Polynesians or Melanesians), and Bougainville's reactions were similar to those of Wallis, though phrased in a more scholarly manner.

Bougainville was no sluggard, and his two ships remained in Tahiti, in spite of its attractions, for little more than a week. He sailed due west and, unlike practically every navigator in the previous century and a half, he was willing to risk embayment on a lee shore of New Guinea/Australia. In the ensuing weeks, there were moments when he regretted his boldness. He touched the outer fringes of the Great Barrier Reef, surmised that much land, probably islands, lay beyond and, working his way north, sighted the coast of New Guinea.

He was on the verge of rediscovering Torres Strait, but his crew was in poor condition and he was intent on reaching a port as soon as possible. However, working his way out of the Gulf, in order to round New Guinea, was a nightmare – storms, poor visibility, shoals everywhere. He sailed through the Solomons, again without realizing their identity, and eventually found a haven off New Britain where there was wood and water, though not much food. By another extraordinary coincidence, he discovered the remains of Carteret's camp about 8 km (5 miles) away.

Unlike Carteret, Bougainville did not recognize St George's Channel as a strait (Dampier had recorded it as a bay), and therefore passed to the north of New Ireland. Within five weeks he reached a Dutch base in the Moluccas, where the men ate their first decent meal for many weeks. Batavia was reached twelve days after Carteret had left, and the *Boudeuse*, having left the store-ship behind, gradually closed the gap, until the *Swallow* was sighted in the Atlantic on 25 February. Carteret's ship, Bougainville recorded, 'was very small and went very ill, and

when we took leave of him, he remained as it were at anchor.'

COOK

In the 250 years since Magellan, much had been learned about the Pacific, yet from one point of view it is astonishing how much was still unknown. Exploration had been unplanned, unorganized and, excusably in the circumstances, often inefficient. The secrecy maintained by the various powers about their own discoveries had led to much unnecessary repetition. Some maps showed what was later found to be a single island in two or more places under different names. Roughly half the ocean had never seen a European ship, and some very long-standing problems had not been solved. Chief of these was the matter of the 'southern continent', and the relationship to it of Australia and New Zealand, regarded by some as a continental cape.

These questions were to be conclusively answered by James Cook (1728–79), son of a Yorkshire labourer who joined the Royal Navy at the age of 27 after an apprenticeship in a Whitby collier. Cook had risen fairly fast as a result of his natural abilities; he became known to the Admiralty through his meticulously accurate charting of Newfoundland waters and to the Royal Society through his observations of an eclipse of the sun. He was, however, a compromise choice to command the voyage of 1768, as the Admiralty, which was providing the ship, was unwilling to hand over command to a civilian, Alexander Dalrymple, a well-known scholar and proponent of the 'southern-continent' school and recommended as 'having a particular turn for discoveries' by the Royal Society.

The immediate motive of the voyage was impeccably scientific: to observe the transit of Venus across the sun, a rare phenomenon best to be observed in the southern hemisphere. On Wallis's recommendation, Tahiti had been selected. Besides this, however, Cook's voyage had strategic aims. After observations of Venus were completed, he was instructed to sail south as far as 40° to discover the supposed continent, 'unless it was sooner met with'. If it were not met with at all, he was to sail west until he reached the eastern coast of New Zealand. Having investigated that, he should return home by whatever direction he thought best.

Cook's ship was the *Endeavour*, built as a Whitby collier, the type of vessel Cook considered best for exploring the South Pacific as well as transporting

MEASURING LONGITUDE

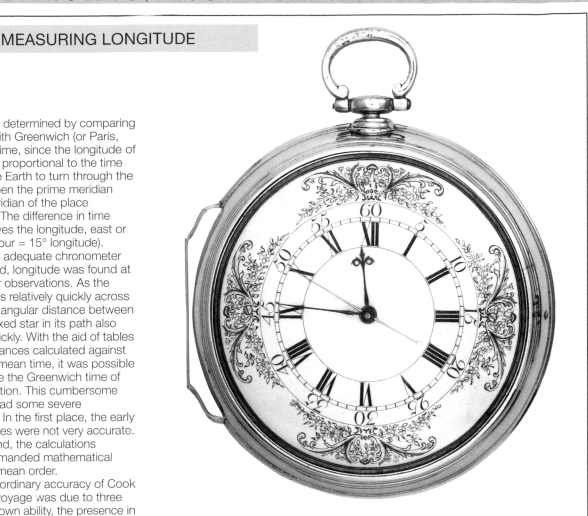

Longitude is determined by comparing local time with Greenwich (or Paris, etc.) mean time, since the longitude of any place is proportional to the time taken by the Earth to turn through the angle between the prime meridian and the meridian of the place concerned. The difference in time therefore gives the longitude, east or west (one hour = 15° longitude).

Before an adequate chronometer was invented, longitude was found at sea by lunar observations. As the Moon moves relatively quickly across the sky, the angular distance between it and any fixed star in its path also changes quickly. With the aid of tables of lunar distances calculated against Greenwich mean time, it was possible to determine the Greenwich time of the observation. This cumbersome technique had some severe drawbacks. In the first place, the early nautical tables were not very accurate. In the second, the calculations involved demanded mathematical skills of no mean order.

The extraordinary accuracy of Cook on his first voyage was due to three factors: his own ability, the presence in the *Endeavour* of Charles Green, from the Greenwich Observatory, and the existence of the *Nautical Almanac*, first published in 1767, with its very reliable tables. On his second voyage Cook carried a copy of the fourth chronometer of John Harrison, which recorded Greenwich time with great precision (it gave an error in longitude of less than eight miles at the end of the voyage).

Harrison was a Yorkshire carpenter, who set out to gain the prize of £20,000 offered by the Board of Longitude for an accurate marine timepiece. The four instruments he made between 1730 and 1760 can today be seen at the National Maritime Museum, Greenwich, and are an astonishing record of technological advance. Though Harrison's fourth chronometer passed all the Admiralty

Harrison's first three chronometers looked like machines devised by Heath Robinson, but his fourth, above, was a revelation, and as accurate as it was compact.

tests with flying colours, the Board of Longitude meanly withheld half the prize pending further experience, until, it is alleged, George III intervened ('I'll see you right, Harrison').

coal in the North Sea. She was strong and spacious, though not swift. She carried 94 people including a rich, bright young botanist, Joseph Banks, who was to become more famous than Cook himself. There was also a goat which had already sailed around the world with Wallis.

The *Endeavour* left Plymouth in August, called at Madeira and Rio, rounded the Horn in January and from a farthest south of over 60° sailed almost directly north-west towards Tahiti – farther south than previous voyagers and thus taking a further slice off the hypothetical continent. In Tahiti they spent three months, building an observatory and, to initial consternation, a fort, and enjoying the now expected hospitality of the people, thievish though they were (Cook failed to understand how someone

managed to steal a pair of stockings he was using as a headrest while he was, he said, fully awake).

Banks and his fellow naturalists found much to fascinate them, and for the sailors the beautiful Tahitian girls were very different from the raddled whores of Plymouth and Wapping. However, syphilis was already rife: Bougainville blamed Wallis and vice-versa. Cook, a clear-eyed man who in four visits to Tahiti learned to speak the language after a fashion, was troubled by feelings of guilt. He had no doubt of the 'fatal impact' of European civilization and suggested that anyone who disagreed should 'tell what the natives of the whole extent of America have gained by the commerce they had had with Europeans'. But, unlike the wilder devotees of the 'noble savage' cult, he knew there was no going back.

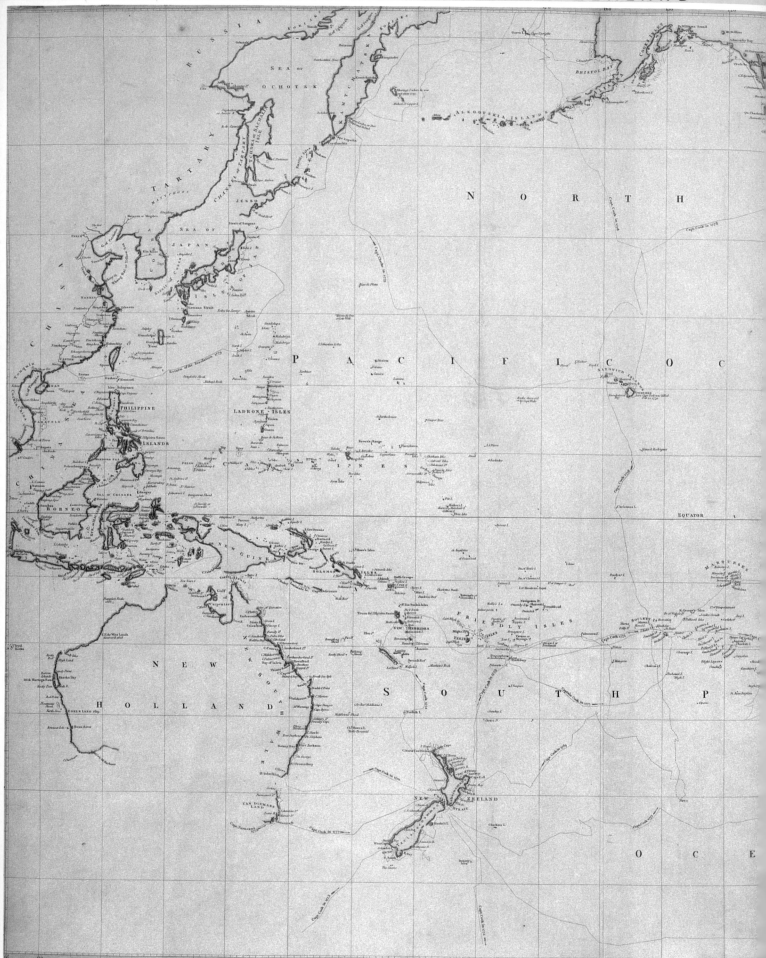

The Founding of Australia, *by Algernon Talmage RA. As the Union flag is raised in Sydney Cove on 28 January 1788, Phillip and his officers drink a toast to the new colony.*

Portrait of Cook by John Webber, 1776, who was best at topography. Cook's wife disliked the picture, on the grounds that it made her amiable husband look 'too severe'.

1787-9 Bligh of HMS *Bounty* survived an open boat journey from Fiji to Timor after being cast adrift by a mutinous crew. Christian reached Pitcairn.

1791-2 D'Entrecasteaux in search of survivors of the La Pérouse expedition re-established the position of the Solomon Islands.

1803-6 Krusenshtern commanded first Russian world circumnavigation. Published important maps of Japanese waters.
1838 United States Exploring Expedition

When the observations were completed and several islands had been carefully charted, the *Endeavour* sailed south, beyond 40°S, but without catching sight of the 'southern continent'. Cook turned to the west and in October reached the North Island of New Zealand. Early contacts with the Maoris, who considered all strangers hostile, were unhappy, though friendly relations were established later. Cook then embarked upon his masterly, six-month survey of the coasts of New Zealand, a classic of good seamanship. A French ship, on a private commercial voyage, was in New Zealand waters at the same time, but the two never met.

The main tasks with which Cook had been charged had been completed. Several alternatives now lay before him. The easiest option was to sail for home via the Cape. Another was to sail in the opposite direction, via Cape Horn, which, if they maintained a high latitude, ought to settle the existence of the 'southern continent' once and for all; but the season was dangerously far advanced for such a voyage and the *Endeavour*, after 18 months at sea, was hardly fit for it. After consultation, Cook opted for a third course: to return via the East Indies but, by sailing westward, to try to find the east coast of New Holland (Australia). As it happened, this was the most dangerous course of all.

Cook was aiming for Tasmania, to establish whether it were an island, but a gale drove the ship north and landfall was made near Botany Bay (the name signifying Banks's enthusiasm for the variety of flora), where they went ashore.

The culture of the Aborigines was beyond the understanding of Europeans. The Dutch had seen them as no more than 'poor and abject wretches'; Dampier as 'the miserablest people in the world'. Attitudes had changed somewhat during the Enlightenment; nevertheless, Banks regarded them as 'one degree removed from the brutes'. Cook, as usual, though understanding them no better, was more appreciative. 'They may appear . . . to be the most wretched people on earth but in reality they are far happier than we Europeans . . . They live in a tranquillity which is not disturbed by the inequality of condition . . .' (the nearest Cook, only just raised to the rank of lieutenant, came to criticizing the English social hierarchy).

Sailing north again, Cook noted and named Port Jackson (Sydney), though he did not investigate the splendid natural harbour. Bougainville had approached Australia farther north, and had been prevented from sighting the coast by the Great

Sketch of banded kangaroos by C. A. Lesueur, the French artist and naturalist who explored the coasts of Australia with François Péron in the early 19th century and collected over 100,000 zoological specimens.

Barrier Reef. Cook, coasting up from the south, was inside the Reef, which soon began to close in on him. He was in terrible trouble, and it was a miracle that the *Endeavour* did not sink after being stuck on the coral for 24 hours; they reached the shore by 'fothering' the hull – using a sail as a sling to cover the hole.

Patched up, the *Endeavour* resumed her nerve-racking progress: 'the most dangerous navigation that perhaps ever ship was in', dependent on the vagaries of the wind and currents within a perfect labyrinth of shoals and reefs. Still, Cook was determined to find out whether or not New Holland and New Guinea were joined, and in August 1770 he became the second captain to sail through the maze of Torres Strait, taking a more southerly passage than Torres himself. Thereafter the ship was in known waters, but already Cook had made by far the most fruitful voyage in the whole history of Pacific voyages of discovery.

Sadly, the worst was yet to come. Cook had not lost one man through sickness, but at Batavia, where a longish stay was necessary because of the state of the ship, the crew was decimated by fevers. Before he reached the Cape nearly 30 were dead, and scarcely a dozen were fully fit.

However, some questions remained unanswered. The devotees of the 'southern continent' theory were not discouraged by proof that New Zealand was an island. There was still a vast expanse of the southern ocean in which the continent might be lurking; also, the French were showing signs of unwelcome activity in the south Pacific.

Cook therefore was sent on his second voyage (1772–5), this time with two ships, *Resolution* and commanded by Wilkes produced over 220 charts on 280 Pacific islands.

1947 Heyerdahl sailed his raft *Kon Tiki* from Peru to Tuamoto Islands to demonstrate that pre-Inca civilizations may have reached the Pacific.

Adventure, again Whitby-built. On this voyage, in some ways even more remarkable than his first, Cook finally despatched the 'southern continent' theory by sailing around the world in a hitherto unheard-of latitude, twice crossing the Antarctic Circle (another 'first') and only missing a sight of the actual 'southern continent' by chance. Incidentally he rediscovered the Marquesas, unvisited since Mendaña's day, and discovered New Caledonia, South Georgia, the South Sandwich Islands and others.

Cook's third voyage (1776–80) aimed to solve another long-standing question: the possible existence of a North-West Passage around or through North America. Numerous mariners had sought the passage from the Atlantic; Cook was to search from the Pacific. From his favourite base in Tahiti, Cook sailed more or less due north, and in January 1778 made his last great discovery, Hawaii, named by him the Sandwich Islands. Friendly relations were established, and Cook was moved to ponder, not for the first time, how a single race of people came to be scattered so widely over the Pacific.

According to his instructions, Cook turned east about 40° and headed for the North American coast, Drake's 'New Albion'. Sighting what is now the coast of Oregon, he turned north and began his search for the elusive passage. In spite of Bering, the coasts of Canada and Alaska were virtually unknown; Cook was therefore drawing in the last major section of continental coastline on the world map, apart from those in polar regions. The promising inlets marked on what maps Cook had did not exist, and those he discovered, such as Cook Inlet, proved a disappointment.

He followed the line of the Aleutians, then turned north to Bering Strait, landing briefly on the Asian coast before continuing until the ice stopped him, in 70°44´N. He searched briefly for a passage farther, but the waning summer and a shortage of wood and water made him break off. Coasting the Asian shore, he crossed to the Aleutians, where he had an informative meeting with Russian traders.

He decided to winter in Hawaii, and found a suitable anchorage in Kealakekua Bay. Cook having been adjudged to possess divine status, relations with the Hawaiians were good, but they soon began to inquire when their guests were leaving, since supplies were growing short. Cook therefore sailed to find another anchorage, but was at once caught in a gale which sprung the foremast of the *Resolution* (she had performed magnificently on his second voyage but gave constant trouble on this one, partly no doubt the result of poor work in the naval dockyards), and the ships were forced to return.

They were not welcome, and in a fracas resulting from a stolen boat which Cook (whose occasional flashes of temper were more frequent on this voyage) was partly responsible for provoking, he was struck down and killed. The voyage continued, now under the command of Charles Clerke, a first-rate

Engraving, after Parkinson, of the Endeavour, *being careened after her near-fatal grounding on the Great Barrier Reef. She was laid up for six weeks, but opportunities for botanical research were not neglected.*

AUSTRALIA

1606 Jansz, a Dutch navigator, credited with discovery of Australia. Sailed into Gulf of Carpentaria while searching for gold in southern New Guinea.

1616 Australia's west coast discovered by the Dutchman Hartog.

1629 Dutch captains using trade winds from Cape of Good Hope mapped the shores of 'New Holland' and led to Dutch settlement in western Australia.

1642-3 Tasman discovered Van Diemen's

The Resolution *and* Adventure *in the Downs, before Cook's third expedition, for which he may have been physically unfit. From a painting by Francis Holman.*

captain but himself, at 31, already suffering from a lung disease which after another summer in the Arctic proved fatal. No advance was made on Cook's discoveries, and the ships returned to England in October 1780.

In the eleven years of Cook's voyages he virtually completed the discovery of the Pacific; it held no more great secrets. Although the motives for his work were largely political and strategic, the results were mainly scientific and geographical, which is a nice reversal of the usual result of European exploration. His greatness was universally recognized: the French government requested its commanders and officials abroad to give Cook free passage, even in time of war.

Of course, the exploration of the Pacific was not finished; it is not really finished yet. Of Cook's French contemporaries, probably the finest maritime explorer, besides Bougainville, was La Pérouse (1741–88), who sailed on a Pacific voyage, charged with establishing the position of the Solomons once and for all, in 1785. After carrying out various preliminary surveys with outstanding accuracy, La Pérouse put in at Port Jackson soon after the arrival of the First Fleet. His appearance caused some consternation, soon allayed by the great charm of the Frenchman, his obvious concern with scientific rather than political results, and not least his frank admiration for the work of Cook. He sailed for the Solomons in February 1788 and disappeared. Wreckage was found of his two frigates on a reef off the Santa Cruz Islands 30 years later.

The work which La Pérouse had begun was successfully completed by d'Entrecasteaux, sent to search for him in 1791. At last Mendaña, the subject of much angry grumbling by frustrated navigators over the centuries, was vindicated, as d'Entrecasteaux fitted physical features to the Spaniard's description. D'Entrecasteaux, among other minor advances, discovered the island named after him off New Guinea. Numbers of other Pacific islands bear the names of European discoverers, such as Marshall, a naval captain returning from Botany Bay.

Mutineers from the *Bounty*; fur traders from New England; an Italian, Malaspina, sailing (like Columbus) in Spanish service; former shipmates of Cook, like George Vancouver; all these made contributions to Pacific exploration before the end of the 18th century. Bass and, most notably, Flinders, had solved most of the remaining questions about Australia's coastline by 1803. But by that time, the main impetus of exploration was about to change. Geographers were beginning to wonder what would be found in the interior of that initially unprepossessing continent which, discounting Antarctica, was the true *Terra Australis*.

Land (Tasmania), west coasts of N and S Islands of New Zealand and the Friendly Islands (Tonga group).

1798 Bass sailed between Tasmania and Australia via the Bass Strait, and with Flinders explored Tasmanian coast, demarcating it as an island.

1801-2 Flinders made the first circumnavigation of Australia, accurately charting much of its coast.

1802 Baudin surveyed coast of New South Wales.

AUSTRALIA

THE SETTLEMENT OF AUSTRALIA

Cook's discovery of New South Wales was timely for the British because the success of the rebellious American colonists in 1781 meant that convicts, too numerous for British gaols and prison hulks, could no longer be dumped on North America. Botany Bay seemed an acceptable alternative, and in spite of the fact that nothing was known of the region other than what Cook had reported, New South Wales was settled less than 20 years after its discovery.

The First Fleet, consisting of 11 ships carrying nearly 800 convicts and a rather larger number of sailors and marines (plus families, in some cases, as unlike the sailors they were not due to return), not to mention the first governor, Captain Arthur Phillip, and stores for two years, sailed in May 1787 and arrived in January 1788 after a remarkably trouble-free voyage. Botany Bay proved a lot less attractive than Cook's report of it (where had all the good farming land vanished to?), and Phillip, who proved a much better leader than anyone had any right to expect, took the bold and sensible decision to move on to Port Jackson, after a reconnaissance expedition had reported favourably.

From a perspective of two centuries, there is a pronounced air of fantasy about the whole operation. How anyone could imagine such a venture would prosper is a mystery; yet prosper, after a while and after a fashion, it did. In the meantime, there was great misery and hardship, not only for the convicts and their guards but also for the Aborigines, in spite of Phillip's well-meant adjurations to treat them kindly.

Some fortuitous maritime discoveries were made. Norfolk Island (1600 km/1000 miles away, discovered by Cook) provided better fishing and timber than were readily available in the vicinity of Sydney; Howe Island (a new discovery) provided turtles and easily captured birds. Soon, Phillip was sending his ships as far as Tahiti and China, and whaling was begun. Otherwise, it was essential to establish the outlines of the island-continent and stake a claim which would keep the French out – the task painstakingly performed by Matthew Flinders in 1801–3. As for the vast interior, it remained a blank. Several years after the foundation of the settlement, no one had travelled as far as the Blue Mountains, 65 km (40 miles) away.

A sketch map of Sydney Cove and environs made by a convict soon after the arrival of the First Fleet, the ships of which are still moored in the bay.

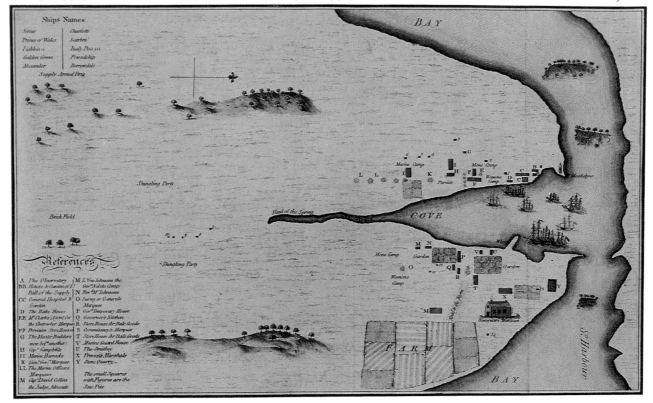

1813 Blaxland crossed the Blue Mountains in search of grazing.
1815 Evans pioneered route across the Great Dividing Range to the Bathurst plains, and

discovered mighty Lachlan River.
1817-8 Oxley investigated Macquarie and Lachlan rivers hoping to find a great inland sea.

1824 Hume and Hovell travelled from Port Jackson (Sydney) to Port Phillip (Melbourne).
1828-9 Sturt and Hume discovered the River Darling.

ACROSS THE BLUE MOUNTAINS

Naturally enough, the first efforts to penetrate the interior of Australia were made from Sydney and were motivated by the growing need to find more grazing land. The task was not easy, as the settlement was fenced in by mountains shrouded in a bluish haze, the effect of the oily eucalyptus trees, which to the unhappy convicts seemed to signify a paradisal land beyond (how wrong they were).

It was not until 1813 that the Blue Mountains were crossed, by Gregory Blaxland who, unlike earlier pioneers, elected to keep to the high ground instead of following the valleys. Even so, he and his companions made slow progress, sometimes covering only a mile or two all day, but after nearly three weeks they saw, from Mount York, the desirable prospect of lush green land stretching before them. The governor sent others to follow up Blaxland; there was a road to Bathurst by 1815 and in 1818 John Oxley, having failed to get far down the

John Batman, seen here negotiating with Aborigines, was born in Parramatta in 1801 of parents who had arrived in New South Wales in the convict ship Ganges. An enterprising character, his exploits included the capture of a notorious bushranger.

Macquarie River, turned east and discovered the Liverpool Plains.

By this time, restrictions on settlement having been removed, British emigrants were flooding in, increasing pressure for more land. Hamilton Hume, a native Australian, travelled from Sydney to near the modern Melbourne in 1824, though greatly harassed by insects and Aborigines. The botanist Allan Cunningham discovered the Darling Downs, pasture rich enough for anyone, in 1827 and went almost as far north as modern Brisbane, west of the Great Dividing Range.

Just as people nowadays speculate about conditions on other planets, formerly they evolved theories about unexplored lands on earth. The exploration of Australia's coastline had indicated a remarkable lack of outflowing rivers (partly because they were overlooked), and this gave rise to the theory that the island-continent contained a great inland sea, into which its rivers drained. The problem of New South Wales's drainage system was largely solved by the outstanding figure among the first generation of explorers of Australia, Charles Sturt, a 33-year-old soldier on the governor's staff when he was chosen for the task in 1828.

His first journey took him, with Hume, down the Macquarie River, beyond the swamps that had defeated Oxley. His account is full of the hazards that were to become familiar to explorers of Australia: intense heat, scarcity of water, aggressive insects and hostile Aborigines. In February 1829 he reached the Darling, but confessed he could not hazard a guess about its course.

On his second journey, Sturt took a more southerly route, along the Murrumbidgee and then the Murray. His chief companion this time was George Macley (or M'Leay), a young, red-headed naturalist who got on so well with the Aborigines that they were convinced he had once been one of their race. But as they proceeded west, the Aborigines became more hostile. In a famous incident, they were confronted by some 600 armed people, clearly on the point of launching an attack. Sturt was about to shoot one of the leaders, hoping to discourage the rest, when Macley stopped him, indicating the sudden appearance of four other men from another direction.

'Turning round, I observed four men at the top of their speed. The foremost of them, as soon as he got ahead of the boat, threw himself from a considerable height into the water. He struggled across . . . and in an incredibly short space of time stood in front of the savage against whom my aim had been directed.

1830 Sturt and Macley went by boat down the Murrumbidgee and Murray Rivers to the coast, proving they did not end in an inland sea.

1835-6 Mitchell confirmed drainage patterns of the Murrumbidgee, Murray–Darling river system, and opened fertile areas of western Victoria.

1836-48 Roe, first Surveyor General of Western Australia explored in the Perth, Albany and Bunbury districts and opened up Fitzgerald River area.

The dispersal of hostile tribes near the river named after the artist [Thomas] Baines, one of the foremost explorer-painters. Many early settlers drew no distinction between Aborigines and, say, kangaroos.

Seizing him by the throat, he pushed him backwards, and forcing all who were in the water upon the bank, he trod its margin with a vehemence and agitation that were exceedingly striking.' Violence having been averted by this fortuitous ally, the 600 became friendly. This was often the way: Aborigine hostility, though certainly sometimes fatal, was relative; they could often be distracted from imminent assault by something that amused them.

But the sensational events of this day were not over. Sturt and Macley had allowed their boat to drift on to a shoal and, having pushed her off, 'our attention was withdrawn to a new and beautiful stream coming apparently from the north'. They proceeded up the new river, accompanied by a noisy but now amiable multitude on the bank, for some way, and Sturt concluded, correctly, that it was the

Darling. He then turned back and followed the Murray for nearly 650 km (400 miles) to its mouth at Lake Alexandrina.

Sturt had opened up plenty of well-watered land to the colonists. His discoveries were followed up by (Sir) Thomas Mitchell, surveyor-general of New South Wales, who doubted Sturt's identification of the Darling. After two failures, due to attacks by Aborigines, his third expedition proved that Sturt was right. He then struck off on his own, south from the Murray, found the Glenelg River and sailed down to the sea at Discovery Bay.

His journey opened up another large and desirable stretch of land to European farmers, though this region was not entirely virgin territory. Whalers had established a small settlement on the coast and a few colonists from Tasmania were also in residence, unknown to the authorities in Sydney; in 1835 a Tasmanian settler had formally 'purchased' the site of Melbourne (remarking that it was 'the place for a village') from Aborigine chiefs. South Australia filled up rapidly.

223

1837-9 Grey explored north-western coast of Western Australia. Shipwrecked near Shark's Bay, he was forced to walk to Perth and noted major rivers.

1839-40 Journeys of Macmillan and Strzelecki explored rugged south-east and reported many large rivers, reviving interest in the inland sea.

1839-41 Eyre completed the first east-west crossing of the continent from Adelaide to Perth, 2000 km (1250 miles) across the Nullarbor Plain.

AUSTRALIA: KEY TO ROUTES

(1) Bass 1797–8. Was rowed in a whaleboat from Port Jackson (Sydney) to Western Port (near modern Melbourne).

(2) Flinders 1798. Sailed in a schooner to Flinders I., near Tasmania.

(3) Flinders and Bass 1798–9. Made an anti-clockwise circumnavigation of Tasmania.

(4) Flinders 1801–3. Sailed around the coast from SW anti-clockwise, passing through Great Barrier Reef to Torres Strait, and left from Arnhem Land.

(5) Blaxland 1813. From his farm near Sydney across the Blue Mountains to Mt Blaxland and back.

(6) Oxley 1818. From Sydney to Bathurst, followed Macquarie R., crossed Liverpool Plains and descended Hastings R. to Port Macquarie.

(7) Hume 1824–5. From near Goulburn to Port Phillip Bay, New South Wales, and back.

(8) Cunningham 1827. From an upper branch of the Hunter R. across Liverpool Plains to Darling Downs.

(9) Sturt and Hume 1828–9. From Sydney to Wellington down the Macquarie R., then to the Castlereagh and Darling rivers.

(10) Sturt 1829–30. From Sydney along the Murrumbidgee R. to the Murray R., across Lake Alexandrina to Encounter Bay.

(11) Mitchell 1836. From Parramatta, near Sydney, descended Lachlan R. to junction with Murrumbidgee. Continued to Darling R. Retraced steps, went up Murray R., crossed to the Glenelg R., to Discovery Bay, then returned to Sydney.

(12) Grey 1839. Taken by whaler from Fremantle to Bernier I., Shark Bay. Explored S part of Lake McLeod, then returned by sea and overland to Perth.

(13) Eyre 1840. From Adelaide to Lake Torrens, Lake Eyre (South), the Flinders Ranges and Port Lincoln.

(14) Eyre 1840–1. From Port Lincoln overland to Albany.

(15) Sturt 1844–5. From Adelaide to the Murray and Darling rivers, around Broken Hill, Barrier Range, Milparinka and Simpson Desert.

(16) Leichhardt 1844–5. From Brisbane went NW to Gulf of Carpentaria, then crossed Arnhem Land to Port Essington.

(17) Stuart 1860. From Chambers Creek, near Lake Eyre (South), across the Macdonnell Ranges to Attack Creek in Northern Territory.

(18) Burke and Wills 1860–1. From Melbourne N to Cooper Creek and the tidal water of the Flinders estuary at the Gulf of Carpentaria.

(19) Stuart 1861. From Chambers Creek followed general line of 1860 track and reached further N.

(20) Stuart 1862. Starting from Chambers Creek completed the crossing from his northernmost point in 1861 to Van Diemen Gulf.

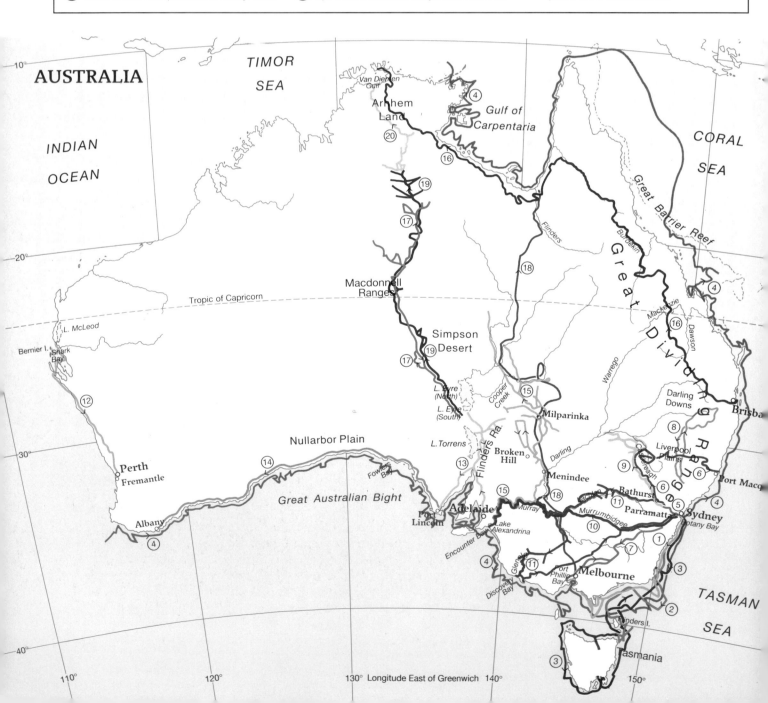

1844-5 Leichhardt travelled 4000 km (2500 miles) from Moreton Bay (Brisbane) to Port Essington (near Darwin) in 14 months, opening up grasslands in the north.

1844-5 Sturt and Stuart explored the extent of Lake Torrens. Travelled to edge of the Simpson Desert and stopped 250 km (150 miles) short of the centre of Australia.

1846 Mitchell investigated Victoria River, in present-day Queensland, convinced it would provide a north-west route to the sea and thus trade routes to India.

ACROSS THE CONTINENT

By the end of the 1830s the south-east of Australia was fairly well-known; indeed, much of it was settled. The bulk of the continent, not only the interior, was still a mystery. Future exploration was devoted to two main objectives. In the first place, it was desirable to establish overland routes to the settlements which had arisen around the coasts as a result of coastal exploration. In the second, it was necessary to learn the nature of the interior and to find a route across the continent.

The north-west coast was explored between 1837 and 1839 by (Sir) George Grey (later a notable colonial governor) partly from the sea, partly on land. Eventually he had to leave some of his party, ravenous and exhausted, 300 km (200 miles) behind while he made a successful last-ditch effort to reach Perth.

Early attempts to settle Western Australia encountered severe problems but by 1840 there was a substantial colony in the south-west corner of the country. But for the sea, however, the two colonies might just as well have been on opposite sides of the Earth rather than on opposite sides of the country, and pressure was naturally growing to establish a land connection. In 1840 the job was offered to Edward Eyre (later another colonial governor of some fame, or rather, in his case, notoriety).

Eyre had already knocked about the country, driving cattle from Sydney to remote settlements, and declared that the proposed route, along the Great Australian Bight, would be impossible for stock. (As Alan Moorehead remarked, even now no one in his right senses would attempt that journey, across the unforgiving Nullarbor Plain which even the Aborigines avoided, on foot.) Instead, Eyre undertook an expedition into the interior, discovering Lake Torrens and Lake Eyre (though he thought they were one) before his horse sank up to its belly through the salt crust and he gave up.

The following year, however, not put off by his experience, he decided to attempt the journey around the Bight, from Adelaide to Albany, if only

George Grey sketching Aboriginal rock paintings in the Kimberley Mountains, northern Western Australia; this engraving forms the frontispiece of his account (1841) of his travels.

THE PACIFIC, AUSTRALIA AND NEW ZEALAND

1847 Kennedy proved that the Barcoo river was Mitchell's Victoria River, and an upper tributary of Cooper Creek which flowed south west.

1848 Leichhardt disappeared in attempt to cross from Queensland to Western Australia. Search expeditions explore much new territory.

1848 Kennedy surveyed east coast of Cape York. All were killed except two who were saved by the brave exploits of guide Jacky Jacky.

to prove that it was useless. All went well as far as Fowler's Bay, because a boat accompanied them that far, carrying their stores. Thereafter there were no more anchorages, and the stores had to be carried on horseback. While at Fowler's Bay, Eyre made several trips westward but was always forced to return for lack of water. However, a message from the governor in Adelaide, urging him to give up the idea, probably served only to spur him on.

He reduced his party to four – one European, John Baxter, and three Aborigines – and, in the height of summer, set out. Eyre knew that food and, especially, water would be the main problems. He therefore adopted the technique of polar explorers, going ahead to lay down caches of supplies at intervals between the present camp and the next likely source of water. Sometimes they marched through the scrub, sometimes along the cliffs, sometimes on the beach. By the time they were half-way they were discarding coats, weapons, cooking pots and eating their horses. Baxter wanted to turn back before they had passed the point of no return; Eyre dissuaded him.

The two younger Aborigines disappeared for a couple of days but were driven back by starvation. A few days later, while Eyre was away from camp rounding up the horses, they shot Baxter – possibly by mistake or at least in panic at being caught stealing – and made off with his and Eyre's guns, as well as much of the food and water. Eyre and Wylie, the remaining Aborigine, continued, and soon the missing youths appeared in the distance, tracking them. After a while they disappeared, and were never heard of again.

Eyre still had a rifle, without which they could scarcely have survived because they were now largely forced to live off the land. One marvellous day he managed to shoot a kangaroo. Wylie, with his remarkable digestive powers, consumed innards, hind legs and even the hide. By the end of May the weather had changed; it became cold and wet, a welcome change, as thirst ceased to persecute them. The horses recovered sufficiently to be ridden, and they began to encounter green grass.

Early in June they spotted a boat, which they hailed, and within an hour, Eyre noted, 'I had the inexpressible pleasure of being again among civilized beings, and of shaking hands with a fellow-countryman in the person of Captain Rossiter, commanding the French whaler *Mississippi*.' That night he lay in a comfortable bunk but could not sleep. For nearly two weeks they remained in the *Mississippi*, living in what seemed like utter luxury. When they left, they carried as much food and supplies as they could possibly need, including a last-minute gift of six bottles of wine.

The weather was dreadful, wet and stormy, and they had to wade through seemingly endless swamps. Nevertheless, compared with what they had endured previously, the journey was child's play, and within three weeks they reached the little settlement of Albany on King George Sound. The expedition had discovered nothing of importance and had merely established what was known, certainly to Eyre, already: that the route was unviable as a trail for livestock. But that does not diminish Eyre's achievement. And it was, after all, the first overland link between east and west.

In his Australian phase, Eyre was known not only as a great traveller but also as a great defender of the Aborigines, whose culture he appreciated better than most Europeans and whose persecution, even when not deliberate, he deplored. 'It is a most lamentable thing to think that the progress and prosperity of one race should conduce to the downfall and decay of another,' he wrote, 'and still more so to observe the apathy and indifference with which this result is contemplated by mankind in general . . .' It is hard to believe that this is the same man who, as governor of Jamaica 24 years later, was removed from office by a government not particularly sensitive about such things for his ferocious suppression of the blacks.

Eyre's earlier expedition, into the centre of Australia, had been frustrated by the salt lakes in which he became, literally, bogged down. In 1844 another attempt was made by Sturt, at this time not far off 50 and perhaps past the age for such physical endurance tests. Hoping to avoid the problem encountered by Eyre, he went up the Darling River to Menindee, then walked north to Milparinka before turning north-west. It was unluckily a particularly hot summer, all the water holes were dry and therefore Sturt and his companions were compelled to remain near Milparinka (where there was a good supply) for six months, living part of the time in an underground chamber which they dug to escape the ferocious sun. Writing was extremely difficult because in the intense heat ink evaporated from a pen almost immediately.

It was July 1845 before enough rain fell to risk an advance. They covered about 650 km (400 miles) and were no more than 250 km (150 miles) from the centre of the continent when Sturt decided to turn back. He was in fact on the edge of the Simpson Desert and to have gone farther would probably

1855 Gregory's North Australian Expedition reversed Leichhardt's 1844 route in record time, and opened up new pastoral land.

1858 Gregory crossed from Brisbane to Adelaide. Reported Lake Torrens to be a series of lakes, not an impenetrable barrier, and discovered Lake Eyre with several rivers draining into it, so solving a long-standing geographical puzzle.

1858 Warburton established that Lake Torrens is not horseshoe-shaped.

LEICHHARDT'S WAY

Ludwig Leichhardt, a German whose portrait bears a marked resemblance to the Grossmiths' Mr Pooter, arrived in Australia at the age of 30 in 1843, and in little more than a year he was leading a remarkable expedition across the north-east.

The British government had recently established a small military outpost at Port Essington (then Port Victoria) on the Cobourg Peninsula, Arnhem Land; its main purpose was to succour the victims of shipwreck on the northern coast. The motive for Leichhardt's expedition was the desirability of establishing an overland link between that outpost and the northernmost settlement of New South Wales, on Moreton Bay (now Brisbane, Queensland).

Leichhardt's party of nine included two Aborigines and two youths. They started in September 1844, following the Dawson, Mackenzie and Burdekin rivers north to the Mitchell. They turned south-west to skirt the coast of the Gulf of Carpentaria, crossed Arnhem Land to the Alligator River and reached Port Essington in December 1845. It was a remarkable journey by anyone's standards, covering about 4000 km (2500 miles) and discovering much good pasture land. Yet the most extraordinary feature of the expedition is that it should have reached its goal at all.

Obviously, Leichhardt's abilities cannot be dismissed, since he achieved his objective in spite of severe difficulties. But he was a most inefficient explorer. He almost entirely lacked what are arguably the two most important qualities in an explorer, the gift of leadership and the ability to calculate his position. Some of his calculations would have placed him well out in the Coral Sea, and he went way off course after leaving the Burdekin.

Unlike Sturt, Eyre and other more capable explorers, Leichhardt had little sympathy with the Aborigines, for whom he expressed some contempt – an extraordinary attitude when travelling in the bush. As a result, not only did he get two teeth knocked out by one of his Aboriginal companions, whom he had insulted, he lost one man killed and several wounded in an Aborigine night attack, having posted no guard. He also failed to ration his supplies, so that his men were soon living largely on what wild life they could kill (more than half the stores were gone in the first 700 km/450 miles). Fortunately, it was not for the

Leichhardt: in the 19th century, half the world awaited any European of independent means and adventurous urges, and in some ways exploratory know-how had scarcely advanced since Columbus.

most part particularly difficult terrain.

In 1848 he set out to cross the continent from east to west. He crossed the Warrego but soon after disappeared. It is to be assumed that the 'sable gentlemen', as he called them, put an end to his career.

have been fatal. He made another attempt the following summer, taking a more easterly route. At Cooper Creek a thermometer which registered up to 53°C (127°F) was shattered.

Returning across the Stony Desert nearly killed the whole party. When Sturt eventually arrived in Adelaide he was almost blind, burnt black, sick with scurvy and unable to walk (he was carried on a cart). Nevertheless, he lived to the age of 74, dying at Cheltenham, England, in 1869.

In the late 1840s Australia was entering a period of rapid change. The principle of self-government was conceded, the colony of Victoria was founded and deportation to the eastern colonies was abolished. But no less important than these political advances was the discovery of gold. The population increased rapidly; so did roads and railways. Yet still no one had succeeded in crossing the continent.

After the fever of the gold rush had died down, this became an urgent ambition.

The first expedition to succeed was much the most elaborate and expensive ever mounted in Australia. It is also the most famous, not so much because of its success as of its dramatic failures. It was backed by the government of Victoria and the people of Melbourne, who together contributed about £10,000. Its leader was Robert O'Hara Burke, a former soldier, prospector and currently police superintendent at Castlemaine. He was by no means an obvious choice, being without any experience of real exploration, and critics have accused him of recklessness, though it should be remembered that with just a little more Irish luck, the expedition might have ended in triumph instead of disaster.

Temperamentally too, Burke was not the ideal leader. Early quarrels led to the withdrawal of his

The chief problem confronting the European explorers of Australia was aridity. The Mulga tree, supremely adapted to a desert environment, flourishes where mankind wilts.

second-in-command; Burke replaced him with William John Wills, a quiet young English surveyor who became a close and loyal comrade.

Another inauspicious portent: Burke was in a hurry. He knew that another expedition was setting off with the same objective from Adelaide (this was led by Stuart, who actually started first), and there was prize money as well as glory awaiting the first man to cross the continent. The expedition arrived at Menindee, the last outpost of European settlement, in October 1860. Summer was approaching, but Burke could not afford to wait until autumn, so he took a party of eight ahead to Cooper Creek (discovered by Sturt 30 years before), leaving William Wright to bring up stores later.

He set up camp in the shade of a coolibah tree and built a stockade to keep out animals and Aborigines. Here there were beautiful scenery, reeded waterholes, wild flowers and flocks of brilliant birds, but there were also flying armies of mosquitoes, scorpions and giant centipedes equipped with formidable nippers. Worst of all, there were rats, which made it necessary to hang food on strings from the trees and, by threading the ground

with their burrows, endangered the legs of camels and horses.

When Wright did not appear, Burke decided to press on with Wills, John King (a former British soldier) and Charlie Gray, a strong young fellow, though none too bright, whom he had picked up on the way. They took supplies for three months and each man had his gun and a sleeping roll. But they took little spare clothing and – a bad mistake – no tents. Crossing desert, plains, woods and rocky ridges in every kind of vicious weather from blistering heat to withering gales, in 57 days they were floundering through salt marshes near the mouth of the Flinders River. They knew by the tide that the sea was only a few miles away, but they turned back without actually seeing it.

Most of their food had gone and they had little luck as hunters, though they boiled the plant portulaca as a vegetable to keep scurvy at bay. Both

1860 Burke and Wills crossed from Melbourne to the north coast but died near Cooper Creek. Search expeditions explored much of north-eastern Australia.

1860-2 Stuart crossed Australia from Adelaide via Alice Springs to Darwin after several attempts. Pioneered route for the Central Overland telegraph ten years later.

1870 Forrest made the first inland crossing of Western Australia from Perth south-east to Esperance Bay, following Eyre's route in reverse.

the men and the animals were very tired, the result of malnutrition as much as physical effort, and it rained constantly so that they were never dry. Burke had an attack of dysentery but recovered in time to beat up Gray after Wills had reported him cheating on rations. A few days later Gray was found at dawn dead in his bed roll. The only horse had to be shot – there was no fat on his carcase – leaving two tottering camels.

The lure of the camp at Cooper Creek kept the three of them going day after day. So great was their eagerness that on the last day they marched 50 km (30 miles) to reach it. Unfortunately, it was not enough. William Brahe, left in charge, had waited four months fending off the rats (Burke had expected to be back in three). One of his men was ill

and needed medical attention, and Wright had never appeared with the supplies from Menindee. Brahe thought Burke and his party must be dead, or – not wholly improbable – had taken a ship from the Queensland coast. Just eight hours before the three exhausted transcontinental travellers staggered into the camp, Brahe and his company had ridden out. They left some food but little else, not even spare clothes.

Burke and Wills tried to follow Cooper Creek to the west, but it soon split up into small channels that disappeared among the rocks. Meanwhile Brahe and his party, having met Wright coming up belatedly with supplies, returned to the camp but, finding no sign of Burke, they rode away again. Burke dared not attempt a 250-km (150-mile) march across the desert

THE OVERLANDERS

Early exploring expeditions in Australia were largely motivated by the need for more farming – more particularly, grazing – land. Hot on the footsteps of the discoverers came a band of hard, bold men, driving their 'mobs' of sheep or cattle to new pastures, or to distant settlements where meat was scarce and prices accordingly high. The overlanders frequently undertook long treks through country which, if not totally unknown, was unmapped, and they played a significant part in 'opening up' Australia to white settlement.

Among the most notable feats was that of Patrick Leslie who, following Cunningham's advice, moved nearly 6000 sheep from a station in the Hunter Valley westward to the Darling Downs in 1840. Two years earlier, a couple of young Englishmen had earned undying fame by driving 300 cattle from a point east of Melbourne to what is now Adelaide, taking advantage of a shortage of meat among the early settlers of South Australia, who were paying a shilling a pound for kangaroo. News of the impending arrival of plentiful beef was passed from outlying homesteads, and when the enterprising drovers arrived, the entire population of the settlement was lined up to greet them.

The most famous of the overlanders were the Durack family, descendants

of a refugee from the Irish famine. They had made money in the gold rush and bought a cattle station in western Queensland. In 1879 they were troubled by drought when Alexander Forrest returned from his trek to report first-rate grazing land in the Kimberleys beyond the Fitzroy River in the far north-west. One of the sons went by boat to inspect the area, but it was too expensive to carry the stock by sea, so they set out in 1883 to drive about 8000 cattle a distance of 4000 km (2500 miles) through

Like most pioneer settlements, Australia at first survived by exploiting the sea. Its destiny, however, lay in stock-raising, especially sheep; early explorers were motivated by the need for pasture.

country much of which was little known. It took nearly two and a half years, and about half the stock were lost, through drought, flood, swamps, disease, Aborigine attack and crocodiles.

1872-6 Giles made four journeys into the western desert and became the first man to make the return trip across Western Australia.

1873 Warburton and Gosse set out to cross the continent from South Australia. Gosse returned after sighting Ayer's Rock.

1873 Warburton travelled from Alice Springs 3250 km (2000 miles) into Great Sandy Desert and on to the Oakover River, a ten-month journey of extreme hardship.

1874 Forrest's second crossing of Western Australia from west to east via Gibson Desert.
1875 Giles crossed from Port Augusta to Perth in 5 months using camels and returned by a more difficult northerly route.
1879 Alexander Forrest, younger brother to John, found 20 million acres of prime farmland on the Nicholson plains, after crossing the Kimberleys.
1883-5 The pioneering Durack family drove cattle 4000 km (2500 miles) overland from western Queensland to the Kimberleys.
1891-2 Elder Scientific Exploring Expedition traversed the South Australian deserts. Leader Lindsay returned, only Wells completed the journey.
1896 Wells travelled north from Lake Augusta in search of farmland for the southern goldfields and crossed Western Australia.
1896 Carnegie made a simultaneous north-south crossing of Western Australia from Doyle's Well to Sturt's Creek, a route parallel to that of Wells.
1896-1900 Hann travelled from the Gulf of Carpentaria through the Kimberleys to the north of the Fitzroy River.
1906-10 Canning established bore holes for the stock route linking the Kimberley Mountains with the gold districts of the south.
1931-5 Mackay carried out aerial surveys to east of the Darwin railway.
1939 Madigan using camels traversed Simpson Desert.

without water. The Aborigines offered some help; they gave them fish and showed them how to make *nardoo* (pounded seeds).

When Brahe reached Melbourne, a search party was organized. It made good time to Cooper Creek. The Aborigines seemed excited at the appearance of the white men, and the rescuers soon found out why. Among them was another white man, burned almost as black as they, fleshless, almost speechless. It was John King. Burke and Wills had been dead for two months.

John McDouall Stuart was six years older than Burke and less lavishly supported, but he was a more experienced traveller. He had been with Sturt on his last expedition and had since made several lesser trips on his own. Though he set out first, in March 1860, he took a route that was not only much longer but also tougher. He headed for the centre, found Chambers Pillar, a natural monolith he named after one of his patrons, and crossed the Macdonnell Ranges, named after the governor of South Australia. In April 1860, he reached the centre of the continent, and with one of his three companions climbed the hill now named after him (he named it after Sturt), where he planted the flag.

Soon afterwards the party was stopped by Aborigines, who set fire to the bush, and with stores low and scurvy appearing, Stuart turned back to

Burke and Wills, with King, sight Cooper Creek on their return from crossing the continent. Delight soon turned to dejection.

Adelaide. There he heard of the departure of Burke and Wills in August, which spurred him to renewed effort. He was off again in November, this time with the official backing of the South Australian government, but when he had gone 160 km (100 miles) or so beyond Attack Creek, he was again forced to turn back. By the time he reached Adelaide, the search party for Burke and Wills had already left Melbourne.

Less than a year after the start of his second attempt, Stuart was off again, with nine men this time and even more determined to achieve his goal. Once they had found a way through the rough country which had daunted him the previous year, the going became comparatively easy – 'extensive plains, well grassed, and of beautiful alluvial soil' – and in July they reached the sea near the mouth of the River Adelaide.

'I advanced a few yards on to the beach, and was gratified and delighted to behold the water of the Indian Ocean in Van Diemen Gulf, before the party with the horses knew anything of its proximity. Thring, who rode in advance of me, called out "The Sea!" which so took them all by surprise, and they were so astonished, that he had to repeat the call before they fully understood what was meant. Then they immediately gave three long and hearty cheers.'

Nineteenth-century explorers were great ones for giving three cheers, but the harsh facts remained that they then had to get back about 3250 km (2000 miles) to Adelaide and Stuart's health was already so poor he could not keep going a full day, even on horseback. Eventually his men had to make a sling between two horses in which he was carried. He did not expect to reach Adelaide alive, and it is something of a miracle that he did. They arrived on the same day that the bodies of Burke and Wills were being carried through the city on their way to burial in Melbourne.

Within ten years, a telegraph line was in existence between Adelaide and Darwin, following Stuart's route.

NEW ZEALAND
1624 Tasman sighted New Zealand's South Island.
1769 Cook landed at Poverty Bay, North Island. Circumnavigated and charted much of both North and South Islands.
1793 Hanson in *Daedalus* charted Bay Islands and befriends Tuki-tahua, a Maori chief who drew the first map of the interior of North Island.
1814-37 Marsden established mission at Bay of Islands, made many visits into the interior.

WHALING

Herman Melville, not an unbiased judge, remarked that Australia was more or less founded by the whalers. Certainly many coastal settlements began as the shore base and 'kitchen garden' of whalers, and although Australia's economic future lay with pastoralism, for a short period sealing, whaling and fishing were more important. Banks considered that sealing might prove a profitable basis for a colony in Tasmania, and in 1798 a brig from Sydney collected 9000 sealskins there. Yankee sealers did even better: a Nantucket ship unloaded 87,000 skins at Canton in 1807.

The first British whaler entered the Pacific in the same year as the First Fleet reached Botany Bay, but the British were hampered by the monopoly of the East India Company, and by the time that was ended (1801), the Yankees had secured the lion's share. The Australian industry at first concentrated on bay-whaling, operating close to the coast from a base on shore. Sydney and Tasmania were the main centres.

By 1830 local stocks were becoming exhausted, and Australian whalers took to the ocean. Over 200 whales were taken by ships and boats working from Hobart in 1837, and the value of whale products, chiefly oil, was almost as valuable to Tasmania

as exports of wool. Fisheries in general were vital to the Australian economy. Overall, in 1830, 'the value of fish and products derived from fish as exports was still nearly double the value of wool exports,' (Charles Wilson, *Australia 1788–1988*). By 1850 the Australian whaling industry was second only to the United States, with 35 pelagic whaling ships. Thereafter it declined though, unlike sealing, the main reason cannot have been, at that time, depletion of stocks.

Pioneer whalers, sealers and fishermen did not contribute significantly to geographical discovery (although they were the first men to see Antarctica), if only because their movements were not publicized. By

The decline of the whaling industry was probably due mainly to the falling price of oil, which made only the huge sperm whale, here hunted off New Zealand's North Cape, worth catching, for its ambergris.

and large an extremely rough crowd ('No law west of Cape Horn'), they committed many dreadful atrocities – many more, no doubt, than are recorded – while suffering a few themselves, especially in New Zealand (many Maoris were also employed on whaling ships). They considered the indigenous women anywhere fair game, and contributed to the increasing numbers of people of mixed race in the Pacific region.

NEW ZEALAND

The efficiency of Cook meant that New Zealand's coasts were remarkably well charted from the very beginning. There was, of course, much detail to fill in, and rough weather had prevented Cook surveying certain sections of the coast as closely as he would have wished. The east coast of South Island had proved particularly difficult, and what Cook had named Banks Island, for example, turned out to be a peninsula when investigated by Captain Chase in 1809. In the same year Captain Stewart carried out a close survey of the island now named after him; Cook had not spotted the strait dividing it from the mainland, though he seems to have suspected its existence.

A mission was established by Samuel Marsden at the Bay of Islands in 1814. From there he and other missionaries made several journeys into the interior of North Island. Within the next 30-odd years the missionaries, besides having considerable success in their primary task of conversion, penetrated to the

The mission post on the Bay of Islands, New Zealand, 1824, by Lejeune Chazal, an artist on the corvette Coquille, *of which Dumont d'Urville was then second-in-command (he later commanded her, renamed* Astrolabe).

EUROPEAN SETTLEMENT IN NEW ZEALAND

European interest in New Zealand after Cook's visits was desultory. After the settlement of Sydney it began to be more attractive, but mainly as an outpost of the more vigorous colonial growth in Australia. Potential settlers were deterred by the Maoris, a more formidable population than the Australian Aborigines. However, sealers and whalers found welcome bases on New Zealand's coasts where they could refit their vessels and replenish their stores. Many young Maoris served on European whalers, being skilful seamen and expert harpooners.

Pioneer traders sold goods, particularly (and disastrously) guns, to the Maoris, and set up timber and flax production in North Island for processing in New South Wales. In spite of occasional disasters, like the massacre of the crew of the *Boyd* (more than fully repaid) in 1809, relations between Europeans and Maoris were fairly good, as at that period there was no pressure on land.

In 1814 missionaries arrived, led by Samuel Marsden, a forceful character (with a claim to be the first explorer of North Island). He had some success in checking the tribal wars that, fought now with muskets, were decimating the Maoris. The British government wanted nothing to do with New

Zealand, but the keen imperialist, Edward Wakefield, formed a New Zealand company which, without government approval, sent settlers to New Zealand in 1839. At the same time, the French were making moves in the same direction, and in 1840 the British government bowed to the inevitable: Captain William Hobson, arriving just a week before the first large group of settlers, annexed New

Zealand to Australia, persuading the Maori chiefs to accept British sovereignty in exchange for a guarantee of their lands.

However, pressure on land from the growing number of settlers led to conflict. George Grey, former explorer of the Kimberleys and governor of South Australia, was sent as governor in an effort to restore order in 1845. He stood up for Maori rights and by the end of his second spell as governor, in 1868, the Maori War was drawing to an end. With the end of Maori resistance, the colonists, self-governing since 1855, introduced a 'free market' in land. The Maoris are still trying to regain their ancient homelands.

Samuel Marsden established the first Christian mission, staffed by three missionaries (one of whom subsequently 'went native'), at Christmas 1814, preaching the first sermon on the text, 'Behold I bring you glad tidings of great joy'.

via the Manawatu Gorge to Lake Wairarapa.
1844 Bishop Selwyn crossed North Island from Auckland to Wellington.
1844 Shortland made the first Maori census

on journey from Otago to Christchurch.
1846-8 Brunner and Ekehu explored the western coast of South Island, penetrated the fertile Buller valley, and traced the Grey River.

1847 Colenso reached Lake Taupo, North Island and crossed the Ruahine Range.
1847 Kettle was the first European to penetrate central Otago.

1850 Hamilton made first overland expedition from Invercargill to Dunedin and later examined the coast from Banks Peninsula to Cape Campbell.
1852 Lee and Jollie pioneered a stock route from Nelson to North Canterbury.

1857 Harper and Locke demonstrated that Europeans could travel from Canterbury to the west coast via Harper Pass.
1859 Rochfort surveyed Buller River area. Subsequently opened up a new route from the east coast to Westland.

1861-2 Hector surveyed mountain passes between Martin's Bay and Lake Wakatipu, West Coast Region.
1861-3 Haast carried out geological surveys in Canterbury province and Southern Alps. Excited European scientists with reports of glaciers.

centre of North Island. The most resolute traveller was William Colenso who, among other journeys, reached Lake Taupo in 1847.

European explorers did not, however, travel alone. As in other parts of the world they were accompanied by natives of the country concerned, in New Zealand almost exclusively so. Since the Maoris were naturally far more knowledgeable about the land of the long white cloud than were the Europeans, and a great deal more adept at living off the land, the achievements of the European explorers appear somewhat less remarkable than they would if the islands had been uninhabited.

Nevertheless, the rigours of travel in early 19th-century New Zealand, especially the larger, more rugged South Island, were considerable. Scarcity of water, the bane of Australian explorers, was seldom a problem, but New Zealand had obstacles of its own. The rivers, for example, are numerous and in

Ekehu, the famous Maori guide who accompanied Charles Heaphy and Thomas Brunner, from a drawing by Heaphy, who had trained as an artist as well as a surveyor.

NEW ZEALAND: KEY TO ROUTES

(1) **Heaphy, Brunner, Fox and Ekehu**, 1846. From Nelson to part-way down the Buller R.

(2) **Heaphy, Brunner and Ekehu**, March–Aug. 1846. From Nelson to Golden Bay, then overland along the coast to the Araura R., N of Hokitika.

(3) **Brunner and Ekehu** 1846–8. From Nelson descended the Buller R. to the coast, then SW to Tititira Head. Returned along Grey, Inangahua and Buller rivers.

(4) **Colenso** 1847. From Napier to Lake Taupo, then across the Kaimanawa Mts and the Ruahine Range.

(5) **Harper** 1857. From Christchurch to Lake Sumner, through Harper Pass, then along the NW coast to region of Okarito.

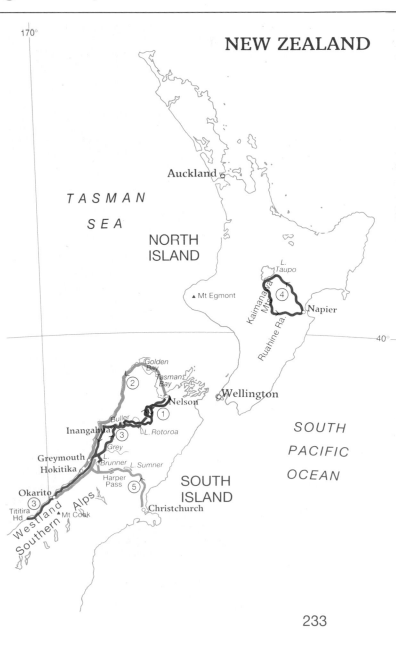

233

1861-3 M'Kerrow mapped vegetation of 12,750 sq km (4900 sq miles) of the Lake District.
1863 Barrington explored country between Hollyford and the Haast rivers. His reports led to a gold rush.
1885-96 Douglas recorded the chief ranges and glaciers of the Southern Alps.
1888 McKinnon and Mitchell crossed pass linking Milford Sound with Lake Te Anau to create the famous tourist route: the Milford Track.

general exceedingly fast: death by drowning was a notoriously common end for early travellers in New Zealand. As for the towering Southern Alps, they were scarcely penetrated until towards the end of the century. Mount Cook, the highest peak, was first scaled in 1894.

With the arrival of the first settlers at Port Nicholson at the beginning of 1840, the search began, as in Australia, for land. However, some of the settlers had other interests. Ernst Dieffenbach, a naturalist who had come out in the *Tory* with Wakefield, set out to climb Mount Egmont in the summer of 1839–40. He had great dificulty in persuading Maori guides to accompany him, as the mountain was taboo, and when he did get them they refused, after two unsuccessful attempts, to go farther than the snowline. Dieffenbach reached the top with a whaler named Heberly, but the summit was enveloped in fog and the spectacular view was hidden from them.

Sheep-farming expanded rapidly after 1842 when Charles Kettle and Alfred Wills, on behalf of Wakefield's company, discovered the Manawatu pass

PAKEHA

The Maoris were culturally closer to Europeans than, say, the Australian Aborigines, and from the earliest – friendly – contacts, some Maoris participated in the life of the Europeans, for instance on the whaling ships. Cultural intermingling was not entirely one-sided, however, and some Europeans – the odd refugee from a whaler, a few escaped convicts – took up permanent residence among the Maoris. They sometimes performed a useful office in negotiating on behalf of their tribe with European traders, and they were bound to their chief in a complicated, ritualistic association. The Maori name for a white man is a *pakeha*.

John Rutherford was an English sailor who was captured in about 1818 and spent ten years among the Maoris as a prisoner on parole.

GEYSERS

Early travellers in New Zealand were amazed to stumble upon the hot springs district, in what is now the south of Auckland province. In immense profusion, lakes and waterfalls, mud volcanoes, boiling pools (as well as cold ones), and high-spouting geysers (at the beginning of this century Waimangu was said to send its jet 500 metres /1640 ft into the air) are spread over an area of about 13,000 sq km (5000 square miles). The only regions comparable with this strangely beautiful, often unearthly landscape are Yellowstone National Park in the USA and Iceland.

Hot springs at Rotorua, North Island. Some of them reach boiling point, and were used for cooking as well as to supply crudely excavated baths.

through the mountains leading to excellent, and apparently uninhabited, grazing lands in the north.

In the same year Nelson was founded on Tasman Bay in the South Island. The Wairau Valley, beyond the Richmond Range, was soon discovered by a company man, but in this case the land was *not* unoccupied and European settlement there provoked the first serious clash with the Maoris over land.

The most demanding journeys in the early years were those of Charles Heaphy, Thomas Brunner and their Maori guide Ekehu. Heaphy and Brunner were surveyors employed by the New Zealand company; Heaphy was also quite an accomplished artist (and a

1888 Homer discovered pass linking the Upper Hollyford and Cleddau River. A tunnel was built 50 years later to provide access to Milford Sound.

1894-5 First crossing of the Central Alps by Fitzgerald.
1894 Fyfe, Clarke and Graham made first ascent of Mount Cook.

1948 Orbell discovered the rare bird, *Notornis hochstetteri*, thought to have been extinct for 50 years in the Takahe valley, Fiordland.

brave man – he won the Victoria Cross in the Maori Wars). In 1846 the three of them, in search of uncontested land, travelled south to a point beyond Lake Rotoroa, and later that year ventured down the coast, through very rough country which often demanded the skills of an experienced mountaineer, as far as the Arahura River. It was winter, and there rains and snow forced them to turn back, but in December Brunner set out on his most famous journey, accompanied by Ekehu and another Maori – *and their wives!*

Brunner's objective was the great tableland in the south which the Maoris spoke of, and the plan was to descend the Buller River and thence go south more or less parallel with the coast. Neither topography nor vegetation aided rapid progress, and in spite of Ekehu's hunting skills food soon became scarce, Brunner's dog being sacrificed to the pot. It took them about eight months to reach the mouth of the Grey River, where they overwintered because of Ekehu's sensible reluctance to press on during bad weather. On eventually reaching Tititira Head in November, Brunner was knocked over by a wave and damaged his right leg, which dissuaded him from continuing south.

In January 1848 they started on their return journey, first ascending the Grey River, but Brunner's condition began to deteriorate rapidly. One Maori couple went on alone; the faithful Ekehu remaining to coax him onward. As the southern winter approached, he became partly paralysed and his vision was badly affected. They found a commodious cave where they sheltered until Brunner's condition improved, and though he lost his sketches and notes in a fire, he was soon fit to travel again. They made good progress, overtaking the Maori couple who had left them, and, 18 months after they had begun, reached Nelson in June 1848.

Attempts to cross the mountainous spine of South Island were first made as early as 1850, and in 1852 an enterprising sheep farmer drove his flock from the vicinity of Nelson to Hanmer Plain on the east coast. The Harper Pass is named after Leonard Harper, who crossed from east to west by that route in 1857, descending the Taramakau River to the coast below Greymouth.

Farther south, the Southern Alps presented an insuperable obstacle. In 1863 a group of gold-miners, led A.J. Barrington, attempted to find an east-west route. In the high mountains, one man was lost and another slid two miles down a glacier on his back without serious injury. Food was practically non-existent at their altitude, and a rat was consumed with relish,

Mount Cook, known to the Maoris as Aorangi, is the highest peak in the spectacular Southern Alps; it was first climbed in 1894 following inducements by the government to conquer the last barriers of New Zealand.

yet, perhaps surprisingly, they eventually got back to Queenstown. They had proved, beyond much doubt, that no real pass existed.

Individual bushmen contributed odd bits of topographical information though, like Barrington, often without official recognition. One famous character in the 1880s and 1890s was Charles ('Mr Explorer') Douglas, who spent much of his adult life travelling through some of the toughest country in Westland Province, mapping hundreds of unknown valleys, sometimes employed by the government, sometimes following his own inclination. 'I have now been wandering about the uninhabited parts of New Zealand for over 5 and 30 years,' he wrote, 'always finding something in Nature new to me.' Perhaps that is the best sort of exploration.

THE
ARCTIC

FIRST REPORTS FROM THE FAR NORTH

'A land where the sun shines at midnight and the seas around it are curdled in winter,' said Pytheas, making the first report from the Arctic Circle. Pytheas was a Greek trader from Marseilles, who had come to Britain around 320 BC seeking tin ore. Hearing about this northern land, he sailed in search of it before returning home where nobody believed such unlikely travellers' tales.

Centuries later, around AD 870, Othere, a nobleman living in the north-west of Norway, became curious about the extent of the empty land beyond his home. He took ship along the coast, and discovered that it bore east, then south into the White Sea where he found so many walrus that his party killed 60 within three days. They went home well pleased with their cargo of fine ivory tusks.

By 1000, Vikings had settled in Greenland's fertile south-western valleys, supported by annual trading ships from Norway. These colonies died out in the 15th century, unable to survive the worsening climate, the loss of contact with Norway, and the hostility of the Eskimo people. Their very existence had been forgotten by the 16th century when Greenland voyages began once more.

In about 1360, a Franciscan friar, Nicholas of Lynn, sailed from Norway to a coast where he saw Eskimos and ruined stone houses, and where the sea froze in winter. This was probably Greenland. On his return Nicholas painted a fabulous picture of the Arctic, describing the Pole as a black and glistening magnetic rock in the midst of a whirlpool, surrounded

A glacier on Ellesmere Island in the Arctic Circle – early explorers were astonished to find the sun still shining at midnight in summer.

Scoresby's illustration of 'The Dangers of Whaling' from his Account of the Arctic Regions. *His critics thought it exaggerated.*

by a circle of mountainous lands divided by channels through which the sea was sucked in. Nicholas's magnetic rock may owe something to the mariner's compass which had reached Europe by the end of the 12th century and his whirlpool is reminiscent of the Maelstrom, which lay off the Norwegian coast north of the Arctic Circle and was rumoured to suck in passing ships.

In those early centuries European ships came to the Arctic only in summer. Navigation by sun and stars was difficult in these high latitudes, when fog obscured the sky or refraction and optical effects distorted the view. The magnetic compass in its primitive form was unreliable so far north and was in any case disturbed by the iron stoves, harpoons, stanchions and other gear in whaling vessels. Changeable weather alternated calm sunny days with icy gales, when men fought to handle frozen ropes and inflexible canvas. And while the indigenous people did not want for food, fuel and shelter, Europeans preferred to bring their own provisions and clothing from home, being slow to adopt the diet and skin garments of the Eskimo.

Any ship caught by the onset of winter risked being crushed by the ice, and would certainly run short of food. Yet the life of a Greenland whaler was probably no harder or more dangerous than the life of men in the remoter parts of Britain, whilst successful crews shared in the profits of their catch. In twenty years at sea in the early 19th century, the whaler captain William Scoresby lost only half a dozen men through accidents. He and other voyagers wrote with respect and admiration of the spectacular landscapes and awe-inspiring grandeur of this region, the clash and rumble of its ever-moving ice, and the mighty whales disporting in its waters.

THE EARLY ARCTIC VOYAGES

Britain and Holland, both active maritime trading nations during the 16th and 17th centuries, found

1527 Henry VIII sponsored first attempt to reach the North Pole.
1553 Willoughby and Chancellor searched for the North-East Passage.

1576-8 Frobisher on Baffin Island.
1585-7 Davis made three attempts to find a North-West Passage. Reached 72°12'N.
1594-7 Barents surveyed Spitsbergen and

Novaya Zemlya. Travelled 2575 km (1600 miles) in open boats back to Lapland.
1610 Hudson entered Hudson Bay searching for North-West Passage. Crew mutinied and

The Franciscan friar, Nicholas of Lynn pictured a magnetic North Pole rock emerging from a whirlpool surrounded by mountains.

the southern seaways to the Far East barred by the power and might of Spain and Portugal. Trading companies were obliged to seek another route into the Pacific Ocean – one which passed north of Russia or America, or even directly over the Pole – if they were to have safe access to the ports of China and south-east Asia. In 1553 three ships commanded by Sir Hugh Willoughby and including 18 merchants and a parson in their complements sailed on behalf of the Muscovy Company in search of a North-East Passage to the Pacific. The vessels became separated and Willoughby was 'frozen unto death' off Lapland, but Richard Chancellor reached the White Sea and travelled overland to Moscow where he established trade relations with Russia before returning to England in 1554. Chancellor went to Russia again in the following year but on the way home he and most of his crew were lost when his ship was wrecked off Scotland.

In 1556 Stephen Borough, a veteran of Chancellor's first voyage, took his small ship as far as the Kara Sea before ice and bad weather forced him to turn back and winter on the Russian coast. By this time trade with Moscow was prospering and the Company lost interest in a route to the Orient.

A little tract entitled *A Discourse of a Discoverie for a New Passage to Cataia*, written by Sir Humphrey Gilbert around 1566, may have prompted the voyages of Martin Frobisher (1535–94) into the Labrador region. Frobisher sailed in 1576, making for the southern tip of Greenland. Two of his three small ships were lost but he took *Gabriel* across to Baffin Island and into a bay which he believed to be the strait leading to Asia. Here some of his crew were killed in an encounter with hostile Eskimos and Frobisher returned to England, bringing with him one Eskimo captive and some rocks said to contain gold. This prospect of wealth encouraged his backers to send him out the following year. Frobisher simply sailed across to Baffin Island and returned with a cargo of ore, but on his third voyage, led astray by bad weather, Frobisher was pushed into Hudson Strait where he battled against unseasonally heavy ice and returned home empty-handed.

New patrons were found to support three voyages by John Davis (?–1622) who directed his search for the Passage from a more northerly latitude. On his first voyage of 1585 he sailed up the west coast of Greenland, crossed over Davis Strait to Baffin Island, discovering Cumberland Sound before bad weather forced his return. His second voyage followed much the same route but his third voyage in 1587 took him as far as 72°N before meeting the ice barrier which turned him across to Baffin Island and home.

If Davis has established a record northing, Henry Hudson (?–1611) penetrated further west than his predecessors when he sailed *Discovery* into Hudson Bay in 1610. He followed the coast south to James Bay where his ship was beset by ice. After enduring a hard winter, his crew mutinied. Hudson and his son were set adrift in a small boat and the crew sailed back to England. Several voyages were made to follow up these various early discoveries, the most rewarding being that of 1616 when Hudson's old ship *Discovery* sailed with William Baffin (1584–1622) as pilot to explore the northern portion of Davis Strait. They were able to reach 78°N and to coast the islands north of Baffin Island. These early voyages ceased after 1631, having brought their backers no wealth. Yet they put Davis Strait and Baffin Bay on to the chart together with the three great seaways of the Canadian Arctic: Smith Sound, Lancaster Sound and Jones Sound.

By the mid-17th century it was clear that neither the Gulf of St Lawrence nor Hudson Bay opened into the desired northern seaway. But if one was merely the mouth of a mighty river and the other a great bay, both were gateways to the vast forests of northern America. Denied the riches of the Orient, the traders bartered just as profitably with native trappers for the furs of beaver, bear, ermine, mink and lynx, and for copper and other local products. Several companies were formed to handle this trade, the most successful being the Hudson's Bay Company which is still in existence.

The Company did not announce its discoveries, lest other ship-owners should be attracted into the region. In 1741 the Admiralty, uncertain how far this exploration had progressed, sent Captain Christopher Middleton (d.1770), a former Company servant, into the Bay with HMS *Furnace* and HMS *Discovery*.

Middleton searched unsuccessfully for a north-western exit to the Bay, and returned the next year. There followed a bitter controversy between the expedition's promoter, Arthur Dobbs, who was certain that such a passage existed, and the Hudson's Bay Company and Middleton, who denied it.

In 1744 Parliament passed an Act offering 'a reward of £20,000 to any of His Majesty's subjects who should discover a North-West Passage through Hudson Strait to the western and northern ocean of America . . . to the benefit and advantage of the trade of this Kingdom'. Captain James Cook sailed through Bering Strait in 1778, confirming that Asia

ARCTIC SEA-ICE

Sea water freezes at −1.9°C, a temperature reached throughout the upper layers of the Arctic Ocean, most of which is permanently frozen. Semi-permanent ice forms on its margins, freezing every winter or continuously for several years, depending on climatic variations.

The surface water congeals in thin plates that winds and waves force together into rough pancake ice which eventually freezes into a thick unbroken floe. Strong winds or currents may break these floes apart, exposing temporary 'leads' of open water. The same forces may drive one floe against or over another, creating 'pressure ridges' up to 12 metres (40 ft) high and with deep roots extending to 46 metres (150 ft) into the sea.

All explorers speak of the incessant noise of the pack: the crash and grind of pressure ridges forming, and the ominous cracking that heralds the opening of a floe, perhaps the one on which they are standing. Detours round such unpredictable barriers usually double the mileage of any given route, and present constant hazards to man and dog alike.

Two circulation systems drive the Arctic surface water with its ice cover. The broad, clockwise Beaufort Gyre turns between the Canadian coast and the Pole while a steady drift from north of the Bering Strait moves over the Asian shelf to emerge into the Greenland Sea. Any ship which becomes fast in the pack, and any ice-station established on permanent

ice, will drift across the basin in one or other of these currents within the space of a few years.

Despite the ice cover, many explorers have been able to sound by wire through holes or leads in the ice. Echo-soundings from the ice or from ice-breakers, supplemented by sonar deployed from submarines passing beneath the ice, have now revealed

An ice 'pressure ridge' formed by ice floes being driven against one another. The ice pick in the foreground provides a clear indication of the scale.

the Arctic Ocean topography as a series of deep basins separated by the high Lomonosov Ridge, a lower spreading mid-ocean ridge, and other minor banks.

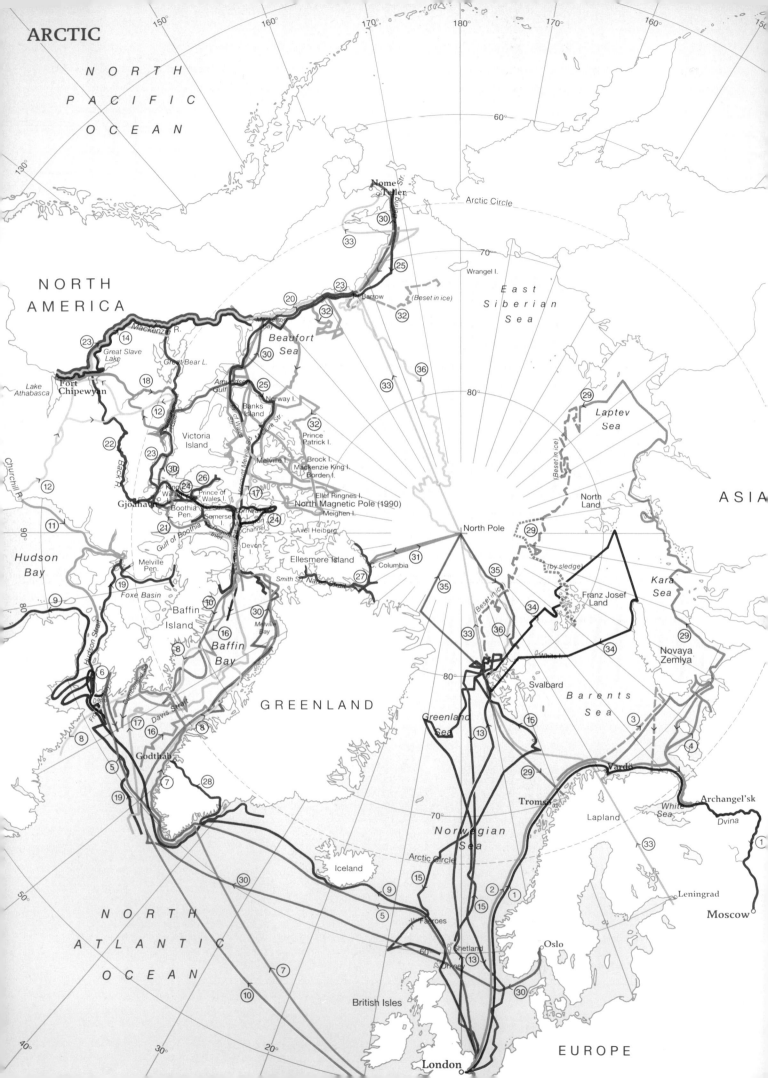

ARCTIC

N O R T H
P A C I F I C
O C E A N

NORTH
AMERICA

NORTH
ATLANTIC
OCEAN

GREENLAND

EUROPE

ASIA

East
Siberian
Sea

Laptev
Sea

Kara
Sea

Barents
Sea

Greenland
Sea

Norwegian
Sea

White
Sea

North Pole

North Magnetic Pole (1990)

Baffin
Bay

Hudson
Bay

Baffin
Island

Ellesmere Island

Franz Josef
Land

Novaya
Zemlya

North
Land

Svalbard

Iceland

British Isles

Faroes

Shetland

Orkney

London

Oslo

Moscow

Leningrad

Archangel'sk

Tromsø

Vardø

Nome
Teller

Pt. Barrow

Fort
Chipewyan

Gjoahaven

Godthåb

Lapland

Wrangel I.

Arctic Circle

Beaufort
Sea

Mackenzie R.

Great Slave
Lake

Great Bear L.

Lake
Athabasca

Churchill R.

Back R.

Victoria
Island

Banks
Island

Norway I.

Prince Patrick I.

Brock I.

Mackenzie King I.

Borden I.

Melville I.

Ellef Ringnes I.

Meighen I.

Axel Heiberg I.

Prince of
Wales I.

King
William I.

Boothia
Pen.

Somerset I.

Gulf of Boothia

Melville
Pen.

Foxe Basin

Devon I.

C. Columbia

Smith Sd. Nares Strait

Melville
Bay

Davis Strait

Hudson Strait

Amundsen
Gulf

Mackenzie
Bay

White I.

Dvina

Amundsen
Gulf

(Beset in ice)

(Beset in ice)

(Beset in ice)

(by sledge)

and America were separate continents. His brief survey was extended by Russian fur traders who established themselves in Alaska. But entry to the Passage defied discovery and interest then lapsed until the 19th century.

On land, Hudson's Bay Company posts were established further north and west although not, as yet, in the high latitudes which the ships had reached. In 1771–2 Samuel Hearne travelled down the Coppermine River to the Arctic Ocean and in 1789 Alexander Mackenzie of the North West Company took the more westerly route down the Mackenzie River to the same ocean. The Royal Navy was represented by Sir John Franklin's expeditions of 1819–22 and 1825–7 and by George Back who explored the Great Fish River (now the Back River) in 1833–4.

In 1837–9 Peter Warren Dease and Thomas Simpson, both Hudson's Bay Company servants, made extensive discoveries in the interior and on the coast between the Mackenzie and Great Fish rivers. They also discovered Victoria Land, now known to be a great island. By the mid-19th century the Arctic coast of mainland North America and parts of its adjacent islands were therefore fairly well explored.

George Back's painting of a tattooed Indian of northern Canada.

THE ARCTIC: KEY TO ROUTES

(1) **Chancellor** 1553–4. Sailed from London to White Sea. Ascended Dvina R. to Moscow.

(2) **Willoughby** 1553–5 (*approximate*). Accompanied Chancellor until separated by a storm.

(3) **Willoughby** may have seen part of Novaya Zemlya. Reached the coast of Lapland where he died.

(4) **Borough** 1556. Sailed from London to entrance to Kara Sea and wintered at Archangel'sk.

(5) **Frobisher** 1576. Sailed from London to Shetland and Frobisher Bay.

(6) **Frobisher** 1578. Sailed from Davis Strait to the entrance to Hudson Strait, then Frobisher Bay.

(7) **Davis** 1585. Sailed from Dartmouth to Greenland, Davis Strait and Cumberland Sound.

(8) **Davis** 1587. Sailed to 72°N in Davis Strait and Cumberland Sound.

(9) **Hudson** 1610–11. Sailed from R. Thames to Iceland, Greenland, Hudson Strait and Hudson Bay.

(10) **Baffin** 1616. Sailed from Gravesend to Davis Strait, Baffin Bay and Lancaster Sound.

(11) **Middleton** 1742. From Churchill R. estuary in Hudson Bay sailed along the W coast, then through Hudson Strait.

(12) **Hearne** 1771–2. From Churchill R. overland to Coppermine R. and the Atlantic Ocean.

(13) **Phipps** 1773. Sailed from Thames estuary to explore broken ice N of Svalbard.

(14) **Mackenzie** 1789. From L. Athabasca to Mackenzie R. and Arctic Ocean.

(15) **Buchan and Franklin** 1818. Sailed from Thames estuary to N of Svalbard and E of Greenland.

(16) **(John) Ross and Parry** 1818. Sailed through Davis Strait to Baffin Bay and Lancaster Sound.

(17) **Parry** 1819–20. Sailed through Lancaster Sound and wintered at Melville I.

(18) **Franklin** 1819–22. From Fort Chipewyan to Great Slave Lake, Coppermine R. and Coronation Gulf.

(19) **Parry** 1821–3. Sailed through Hudson Strait to Foxe Basin and along coast of Melville Peninsula.

(20) **Franklin** 1825–7. From Fort Chipewyan (L. Athabasca), to Great Slave Lake and Mackenzie Bay, then westward along coast.

(21) **Ross** 1829–33. Sailed to Lancaster Sound and Gulf of Boothia. James Clark Ross went W to explore northern King William I.

(22) **Back** 1833–4. From Great Slave Lake descended Back R. to its estuary.

(23) **Dease and Simpson** 1837–9. From Fort Chipewyan descended Mackenzie R. and followed coast to Point Barrow. Crossed Great Bear Lake, descended Coppermine R. and explored coast to E.

(24) **Franklin** 1845–7. From Lancaster Sound explored Wellington Channel, circumnavigated Cornwallis I., passed through Franklin Strait and became beset in ice near King William I.

(25) **M'Clure** 1850–4. Sailed through Bering Strait to Banks I. and Lancaster Sound.

(26) **M'Clintock** 1857–9. Sailed from Lancaster Sound to Prince Regent Inlet. Sledge parties explored around Prince of Wales I., Boothia Peninsula and King William I.

(27) **Nares** 1875–6. Sailed between Ellesmere I. and Greenland. Sledge parties explored nearby coasts.

(28) **Nansen** 1888. Sailed to Greenland and crossed from E coast to Godthåb.

(29) **Nansen** 1893–6. Sailed from Vardö, Norway, to Laptev Sea. While ship beset in ice made sledge journey towards Pole.

(30) **Amundsen** 1903–6. Sailed from Oslo, Norway, through Northwest Passage to Nome, Alaska.

(31) **Peary** 1909. From Cape Columbia, Ellesmere I., to the North Pole.

(32) **Stefansson** 1913–18. From Nome, Alaska, to Victoria, Banks, Melville and adjacent islands.

(33) **Nobile** 1926. From Gatchina, near Leningrad, over North Pole to Teller, Alaska.

(34) **Nobile** 1928. From Svalbard to Franz Josef Land and Novaya Zemlya.

(35) **Nobile** 1928. From Svalbard to N Greenland and North Pole. Crashed NE of Svalbard.

(36) **Herbert** 1968–9. From Point Barrow, Alaska, to North Pole and near Svalbard.

WILLIAM SCORESBY – 'THE ARCTIC SCIENTIST'

William Scoresby in later life.

Two of the Greenland whaling ships sailing out of Whitby in the early 19th century belonged to William Scoresby. His son, also named William (1789–1857), accompanied his father north each summer, returning to school during the winter. When he was 16, he attended natural history lectures at Edinburgh University, a combination of practical and theoretical learning which gave him an unrivalled knowledge of the Arctic.

Given his own command in the *Esk*, young Scoresby's lively curiosity, practical bent and artistic skill led him to investigate and report on all aspects of natural history. Encouraged by his teachers, who were delighted to have their own observer in these unknown latitudes, Scoresby studied the structure of snowflakes, measured the magnetic field, watched the aurora play overhead, and sketched the strange refractions so common in the Arctic where the layers of cold and warm air turn images of ships upside down.

He was fascinated by the sea and made many temperature measurements with a Six's thermometer let down in his 'Marine Diver', a valved brass container which collected sea water and plankton. He discovered that in polar regions warmer water lies under the cold fresh meltwater; he found that each drop of green water, where whales were feeding, seen under his microscope, held a myriad of tiny organisms. 'A whale requires a sea, an ocean to sport in:– about 150 million of these animalcules would have abundant room in a tumbler of water,' said Scoresby, marvelling that God had chosen to put the greatest of his creatures and the smallest in these remote seas.

Watching huge icebergs sail against the surface current made him aware of the deep counter-currents. He charted the coast and studied the plant and animal life of the land and sea. Whatever his crews' opinions of his strange hobby, they supported him because his ship was one of the most successful of the Whitby fleet, and this was in no small part due to his interest in marine science. Other whaling masters kept their knowledge secret; it was Scoresby, author of many learned papers, who first laid a truthful account of this magical region before the scientific community.

Before he abandoned the seafaring life to enter the Church, Scoresby wrote two books: *An Account of the Arctic Regions* (1820) and *Journal of a Voyage to the Northern Whale Fishery* (1822) which made him famous both in Britain and overseas.

Above *In the cold Arctic air, snow and ice flakes lasted long enough for Scoresby to sketch their delicate forms.*

Right *Arctic mirages: distorted and reversed images of distant ships, drawn by Scoresby.*

A ROUTE OVER THE POLE

An Eskimo artist recorded this arrival of Ross and Parry in full dress uniform.

Seen on a globe, the shortest route from Europe to the Pacific passes over the North Pole. In the 18th century there were a number of enthusiastic supporters of the theory that the Pole lay in an open temperate sea. This hoary myth was given substance by pointing to the wreckage and driftwood from Siberia that washed up in the Greenland Sea. One such supporter, the Hon. Daines Barrington, was able to persuade the Royal Society that it should propose to the Lords of the Admiralty the investigation of this 'interesting point in geography'.

Two sturdy bomb-vessels, HMS *Racehorse* and HMS *Carcass* were further strengthened to protect them in the ice. The Royal Society gave its support and advice; the Board of Longitude lent the necessary watches and instruments along with an astronomer, Israel Lyons, competent in their use. Commanded by Captain Constantine Phipps (1744–92) with Captain Lutwidge following in HMS *Carcass*, the expedition left the Nore in June 1773, with orders not to proceed beyond the Pole. In fact the ships got no further than 80°48'N.

After some weeks spent skirting or entering the sea-ice between Svalbard and Greenland the onset of bad weather forced Phipps to turn for home. However, on calm days during the passage he was able to investigate the depths of the sea for which he

had been issued with a rather primitive and ineffective thermometer and a water-bottle that failed to work. Phipps tried wrapping a wine-bottle in cloth, so that he could bring up the seawater with its temperature unchanged and take a reading on deck. He made some deep soundings, not always finding bottom.

The natural history observations were of greater value; indeed the polar bear is today known to zoologists as *Ursus maritimus* Phipps. Phipps's narrative of his voyage was of considerable scientific interest; it was widely read and influenced many of those who followed him into these northern waters. The Admiralty learned its geography lesson the hard way though lingering doubt would persuade their lordships to allow another attempt in 1818.

THE ADMIRALTY ARCTIC EXPEDITIONS

The 19th century was the great age of British naval expeditions. England had triumphed in the Napoleonic wars and when William Scoresby reported that the Arctic Ocean was less ice-bound than in former years, the Admiralty committed some of the ships and crews then available to another search for the North-West Passage.

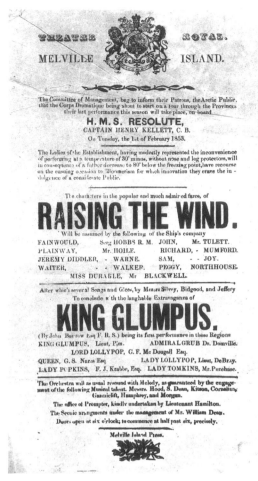

Winter entertainment on board HMS Resolute *in 1853. Most of the ship's company would have been involved in such winter revels.*

The first expeditions were purely exploratory but gradually their scope widened to include many new types of scientific observation. In its turn this requirement stimulated the invention and improved construction of scientific instruments and apparatus. In practice, the Admiralty viewed the Arctic expeditions as a training ground for future officers, and with good effect: from 1818 to 1844 W. Edward Parry, John Franklin, George Back, John Ross and his nephew James Clark Ross – all eventually to receive knighthoods – became famous for their bravery and endurance in the remote fastness of the polar seas.

In the spring of 1818 the Admiralty despatched four ships in an attempt to reach the Pacific. HMS *Dorothea* and HMS *Trent* under the command of David Buchan (b.1780) and John Franklin (1786–1847) were to keep a northerly course through the Greenland Sea in the hope of breaking through into the ice-free polar region. The other ships, HMS *Isabella* and HMS *Alexander*, under John Ross

(1777–1856) and W. Edward Parry (1790–1855), were to turn into the Davis Strait and seek a route north of the American continent.

A limited programme of scientific observations was imposed on these crews. Within Davis Strait, Ross mapped discoveries made by Baffin in 1616 but not charted and since forgotten. On entering Lancaster Sound he saw what appeared to him to be a range of mountains closing its far end. Some of his officers wondered if this were one more example of the mirages frequent in the region but Ross would not be contradicted. He dubbed the range 'Croker Mountains' in honour of the First Secretary of the Admiralty and resolutely set sail for home and the controversy over his eyesight and navigation skills that ensued.

Buchan and Franklin of course found no open polar sea. Their ships were battered by gales and continually beset by pack ice. They could do little scientific work and finally they too returned to England.

John Ross's report could only be checked by sending another expedition. Various official incentives were offered to crews willing to endure the harsh conditions and isolation of the high Arctic. The Act of 1744 had offered £20,000 for the discovery of a North-West Passage; that of 1776 offered £5000 for reaching 89°N by sea. The Act of 1818 confirmed these figures and authorized smaller rewards for partial successes: £5000 would be given to the officers and men of the first ship to cross the meridian of 110°W by sailing within the Arctic Circle, another £10,000 to those similarly crossing 130°W, and so on.

Edward Parry, who was one of those to challenge Ross's vision of the 'Croker Mountains', led the expedition of 1819. He took HMS *Hecla* and HMS *Griper*, provisioned for two years, into Lancaster Sound, and sailed over the supposed position of the 'Croker Mountains', and on into Viscount Melville Sound. Crossing 110°W, the ships' companies became eligible for the Parliamentary reward offered the previous year. They wintered in the ice – the first expedition to do so – but made little progress the following summer and returned home.

On his second voyage, 1821–3, Parry began his survey working northward from Hudson Bay. But he was unable to break through and connect the two regions then charted, and after two winters in the Arctic he returned home. A third voyage in 1824

The crews of HMS Hecla *and HMS* Griper *cutting into their winter harbour, September 1819.*

THE NORTH MAGNETIC POLE

Earth's magnetic field arises from eddy currents in the core, modified by the ever-changing solar wind that streams past the Earth as it orbits the Sun. Lines of magnetic force converge at the Magnetic Poles whose locations, which are not diametrically opposite, drift slowly in response to long-term changes deep within the Earth's core; they are presently over 1000 km (600 miles) from their respective Geographic Poles. High-energy solar particles entering the atmosphere are deflected by the magnetic field and give rise to the polar auroras.

A freely suspended magnetic needle aligns itself in the field, resting horizontally north-south at the Magnetic Equator and vertically at the Poles. The common navigator's compass therefore points some degrees away from Geographical North and when carried towards one of the Magnetic Poles, its response becomes increasingly sluggish and erratic. A dip needle, responding to vertical attraction at the Poles, gave interesting geographical results and such needles had been carried by enquiring travellers since the mid-18th century.

Terrestrial magnetism was for many centuries a mysterious force. There were arguments over the number and location of Poles, and whether the aurora influenced the magnetic needle. Until the mid-19th century it was so difficult to measure magnetism from a moving ship that it was not clear whether the Southern Hemisphere magnetic field mirrored that of the north. To illuminate the subject, and to assist navigation generally, observations of magnetic force and direction in the Arctic were particularly valuable.

John Ross, Parry, Franklin and others gradually narrowed down the area within which they hoped to find the Magnetic Pole itself. In 1829–33 John and James Clark Ross were on the Boothia Peninsula when they realized that the Pole was close at hand. James Ross set out with a sledge party of Eskimos to identify the

The aurora borealis, caused by charged solar particles entering the Earth's atmosphere near the North Magnetic Pole.

very spot, which he reached on 1 June 1831. An entire day spent making observations satisfied him, and he built a cairn where 'Nature had erected no monument to denote the spot which she had chosen as the centre of one of her great and dark powers'.

KEEPING HEALTHY IN THE ARCTIC

Adequate nutrition was essential for survival in the Arctic. Extreme cold and the tremendous exertions of sledging journeys demanded a high-calorie diet whilst the balance of that diet, especially its fat and vitamin content, had a direct effect on the men's health, strength and ultimately their sanity. By the 19th century lemon juice – found to be the only effective remedy for scurvy – was standard issue on long voyages. On Parry's first voyage of 1819–20 much of the juice was lost when it froze and burst its containers; in later years rum was sometimes mixed with the juice to lower its freezing point and reduce the chances of such disasters. But lemon juice was often left out of sledging party rations for the very reason that it was so difficult to distribute when frozen in bulk. Small chunks could not be broken off and melted, since the juice separated on freezing.

After 1860 West Indian limes were substituted for lemons, with potentially disastrous consequences, for lime juice has only half the ascorbic acid content, and the product was often erroneously referred to as 'lemon juice' so that ships' surgeons were unsure of its vitamin content.

Canned meat, soup and vegetables were available from the early 19th century, and were welcome additions to salted and dried provisions. Fortunate crews might, like the Indians and Eskimos, hunt large or small game, fish and marine mammals. On the margins of the high Arctic where the snow melted in summer, wild rice, scurvy grass and other edible plants grew. The Canadian guides who accompanied Franklin's small overland parties knew of these, and learned from the Indians how to make 'spruce beer' from a species of juniper tree, to prevent scurvy.

They introduced Franklin to pemmican, a mixture of dried pounded meat and melted fat. Eaten

The analysis of tinned meat issued to Franklin discounted suggestions that his expedition was supplied with poor-quality provisions.

without further cooking or preparation, it was the ideal food for such journeys. The large numbers of men taken to work sailing ships through the Arctic seaways could not find all the fresh food that they needed and suffered accordingly from their restricted diet.

---

made scarcely no advance. Parry had by then been appointed Hydrographer of the Navy and Franklin was left to pursue the search for the Passage, working overland and with small boats. In their years of Arctic travel, both men carried out valuable scientific work across a broad range of subjects, bringing back measurements and observations relating to astronomy, terrestrial magnetism, tides, gravity, meteorology and the developing marine sciences.

After Ross's expedition, the whalermen who had previously stayed in Davis Strait followed his track and found excellent fishing north of Melville Bay. Parry's third voyage led them into the equally lucrative Prince Regent Inlet. While Parry's reputation grew, John Ross's career prospects had been dashed by the episode of the 'Croker Mountains'. Hoping to regain favour, he persuaded a wealthy distiller, Felix Booth, to support an expedition. In 1829 he took ship in *Victory*, an erratic paddle-steamer whose machinery gave endless problems before she froze immovably into the ice at Felix Harbour. From this base the Rosses surveyed the area. James reached the North Magnetic Pole but food ran short in 1832 so they trekked north to find the stores that Parry had left after the wreck of his ship *Fury* in 1825. These provisions lasted through the winter; in 1833 they left Fury Bay in small boats and were fortunately picked up by a whaler.

Following the success of the Antarctic Expedition of 1839–42, the Admiralty decided to send another expedition to resolve the geographical problem of a North-West Passage. In 1845 Sir John Franklin, then aged 59, sailed with the screw steamers HMS *Erebus* and HMS *Terror*. His ships were last seen by a whaler in Baffin Bay in July of that year. In 1848, when no more news had reached England, official anxiety and public concern mounted. The first of a series of relief expeditions went out but no one even knew which route Franklin had followed, or where to begin to look for him.

1848-50 Rae surveyed Arctic coastline finding the key strait of the North-West Passage.
1850 Austin and M'Clintock sledge 11,500 km (7000 miles) in the Barrow Strait area.
1853-68 Rink travelled in south Greenland.
1854 Rae found Franklin's spoons at the mouth of the Back River.
1857-9 M'Clintock found remains of Franklin's expedition on King William Island.
1861-4 Nordenskjold examined islands of the Svalbard archipelago.

Sir John Franklin, and Lady Jane Franklin (1792–1875), his second wife.

The search parties were organized by both the Government and private individuals, especially by Franklin's widow, who was unremitting in her efforts. Six parties travelled overland and 34 expeditions used ships and sledges. They searched from the Bering Strait and from the eastern Arctic. Sledging techniques were developed and some thousands of miles of coastline were seen and mapped for the first time. Captain Robert M'Clure was only prevented from navigating the North-West Passage in HMS *Investigator* by a narrow sector of obstructing ice and his crew eventually received the £10,000 award for their achievement.

In 1850 three graves of the first men to die were found, pointing to where Franklin had spent his first winter. In 1854 Dr John Rae (1813–93) of the Hudson's Bay Company arrived home with personal belongings from the expedition. He had obtained these from some Boothia Eskimos who told him how some years previously they had passed a party of 40 starving white men dragging a sledge.

With this information, Lady Franklin sponsored the *Fox* expedition of 1857–9 under Captain Leopold M'Clintock, which found in a cairn on King William Island messages telling of Franklin's death and his companions' intention to march south. A sad trail of skeletons and relics along their route showed that the last man had perished by the mouth of the Back River. The flower of the Navy had volunteered for

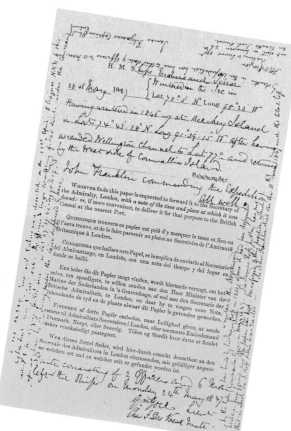

Document found in a cairn telling of Sir John Franklin's death on 11 June 1847.

'The critical position of HMS Investigator' *during the Franklin search, sketched by S. Gurney Cresswell.*

THE ARCTIC COUNCIL OF 1851

From 1851 an Arctic Council was responsible for co-ordinating the relief parties that went out to search for Franklin. The painting by Stephen Pearce shows the ten eminent members of the Council, all experienced explorers. The framed portraits show Franklin and Fitzjames, both members of the missing expedition, and Sir John Barrow, Second Secretary to the Admiralty from 1804–45 and responsible for its Arctic exploration programme, gazing down on the assembled officers.

the expedition and its loss was one of the greatest calamities to befall the nation. The search parties returned home, leaving the remaining blank spaces on the map to be filled in by various American, British, Norwegian and Canadian expeditions.

ON TO THE NORTH POLE

If the Arctic ice did not hide an open sea, it was debated whether the Pole could be reached on foot. Parry, who was still Hydrographer, believed that it could. In 1827 he sailed to Svalbard and headed north with two small boats which could be set on runners and towed as sledges. The labour of repeatedly manhandling the boats and loads from ice to water and back was made even more arduous by incessant rain. The ice surface was rougher than expected, and to make the conditions worse, the ice was drifting south nearly as fast as the men progressed northward. After struggling for 1100 km (680 miles), they had reached only 82°45'N. By 22 July the Pole was still 800 km (500 miles) distant, and Parry had to admit defeat.

Fifty years passed before the next assault on the Pole, the British Arctic Expedition of 1875–6 commanded by Captain (later Sir) George Nares

(1831–1915) in the steam sloop *Alert* and the steam whaler *Discovery*. The scientific community and old Arctic hands by then in high office all supported the idea of such an expedition and under the Royal Society's guidance a manual was compiled for the expedition's use. The attempt was to be made from the channel (now known as Nares Channel) between north-west Greenland and Ellesmere Island.

Nares sent out sledging parties to explore and survey the northern coast and one of his teams, led by A.H. Markham (1841–1918), *Alert's* commander, took its sledge *Marco Polo* across rough hummocky ice and deep powdery snow to reach 82°20′N off Cape Joseph Henry. At the end of the first year a serious outbreak of scurvy forced Nares to return. Stefansson later described the members of Franklin's last expedition as 'victims of the manners, customs, social outlook and medical views of their day'. Nares's men suffered for the same reasons: unsuitable clothing, insufficient snow-shoes, over-heavy sledges and, above all, inadequate diet. Although the expedition failed in its declared aim, valuable geological and natural history collections were brought back. Nares was unaware that he was battling through the

Commander Markham's painting of his party dragging their boat-sledge over rough ice, with one of the expedition ships in the background.

region with the heaviest and most ridged ice of the entire Arctic Ocean.

This was the last traditional naval exploring voyage into the Arctic. In 1882–3 the first International Polar Year opened the era of concerted scientific observations, with 15 manned stations in the Arctic and Antarctic. This was a prelude to the second IPY of 1932–3, and then the International Geophysical Year, 1957–8.

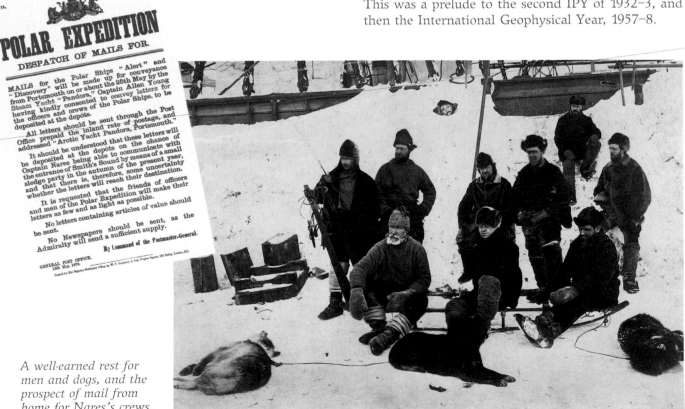

A well-earned rest for men and dogs, and the prospect of mail from home for Nares's crews.

1891-1909 Peary's six Greenland expeditions delimited its northern extent.

1893-6 Nansen in *Fram* drifted in pack-ice to 85°97'N, then set out on foot. Turned

back 370km (230 miles) from the Pole.

1895-7 First crossing of Spitsbergen by Conway.

1897 Andrée disappeared trying to fly a hot air balloon to the North Pole.

1903-6 Amundsen in *Gjøa* became the first to navigate the North-West Passage.

LIVING OFF THE LAND

John Rae's expert opinion had been that Franklin's and similar large expeditions were handicapped by their numbers and the huge loads of provisions that they carried. In Greenland, Nansen's small party had found game to supplement their diet. Vilhjalmur Stefansson (1879–1962), an anthropologist who lived for many years among the Eskimos, and one of Canada's most remarkable explorers, sought to make people aware of the economic value of the Arctic's vast grazing lands and tundras. Musk ox ranged as far north as Ellesmere Island. Elsewhere on land and even on the open ice, the variety of animals, birds, marine mammals and fish could supply the traveller with food, fuel, clothes and shelter.

Stefansson commanded the ill-starred Canadian Arctic Expedition of 1913–8, whose main objective was to explore the Beaufort Sea, the last blank space

The Eskimo family on Stefansson's expedition: Kuraluk, his wife Kiruk, and their two little daughters, Helen and Mugpi.

on the map. Two small vessels, the *North Star* and *Mary Sachs*, were to act as support for the parties of Europeans and Eskimos who would range over the area to be surveyed. Misfortune soon began. After the expedition's principal ship, the *Karluk*, disembarked one party at Point Barrow, Stefansson and a few men went off to hunt, and the ship became hemmed in by ice. A storm blew up and the *Karluk*, locked in the floes which grew daily thicker and more dangerous, began to drift along the coast of Alaska and then towards Wrangel Island, making about 65 km (40 miles) a day.

The dogs lived on the ice alongside, leaving 20 Europeans on board and a couple of Eskimo men, one of whom had his wife and two little girls with him. (The women on Stefansson's parties had the task of converting the animal skins into boots and clothing.) It was only a matter of time before the *Karluk* would be fatally crushed; supplies were got ready and when the inevitable happened, men, women and children set out in the dark and bitterly cold winter night across treacherous shifting and incredibly rough pack-ice. Only nine survived the 100-km (60-mile) trek to Wrangel Island.

Stefansson meanwhile, unaware of the *Karluk*'s fate, returned to Point Barrow and with two companions, a sledge and six dogs, and food for only 40 days, went to spend the summer on Norway Island hunting caribou and preparing meat and skins. When the *Karluk* failed to arrive, Stefansson took his men south and found the crew of the *Mary Sachs*, which had also suffered damage.

Over the succeeding years this party of 17 men travelled thousands of miles surveying and mapping, finding many cairns and stores left by previous explorers and sometimes grim testimony of their fates. The land and sea provided their food, clothing, fuel and shelter. On the final leg of their journey, Stefansson and a few companions hitched a 650-km (400-mile) lift by camping on a drifting floe, and they came at last over the pack-ice to reach solid ground in Alaska.

After studying medicine in his native Norway, Roald Amundsen (1872–1928) bought *Gjøa*, a small motorized sailing ship, determined to take her through the North-West Passage. In 1903 Amundsen and his six companions loaded her with petrol, equipment and supplies, and six dogs, and set sail. They passed serenely through Lancaster Sound, then in the James Ross Strait a storm drove *Gjøa* aground at high tide. After nerve-wracking days, jettisoning some of their precious stores to lighten ship, another high tide lifted her from the rocks.

FRIDTJOF NANSEN

The Norwegian Fridtjof Nansen (1861–1930), a zoologist by training, physically strong, good with his hands and delighting in winter's ice and snow, was well-qualified to lead the first crossing of the Greenland ice sheet. Nansen and his six companions reached Greenland's east coast in August 1888, their landing delayed by late pack-ice.

Travelling day and night, they hauled their sledges on a slow climb until they reached smoother ground where they lashed the sledges together and rigged a sail to speed them on their way. Still climbing, now on skis, they moved over the great dome of ice, 2500 metres (8200 ft) at its crest. The descent was easier until they reached deep and dangerous crevasses which they finally crossed, stepping on to the bare rock and earth of the west coast on 25 September.

Nansen's North Polar Expedition of 1893–6 was a bold attempt to demonstrate that a transpolar current moved across the Arctic from Siberia to the Norwegian Sea. The *Fram* was built to resist ice-pressure and Nansen sailed her into the pack where she drifted in a westerly direction, breaking free three years later north of Svalbard.

Ice and weather conditions were monitored throughout the voyage and the depth, temperature and salinity of the water measured, through holes in the ice, with painstaking accuracy. Nansen found the Arctic Basin far deeper than he had anticipated. The scientific reports from this expedition, which filled six large volumes, gave the first picture of circulation in a frozen ocean.

On his return, Nansen became Professor of Zoology at the Royal Frederick University. He played an active political role when the kingdoms of Norway and Sweden were separated in 1905 and he was appointed the Norwegian ambassador to Britain, 1906–7, returning to Oslo to become Professor of Oceanography at the Royal Frederick University in 1908. In the same period he served as unpaid Director of the Christiania (Oslo) Laboratory of the International Commission for the Exploration of the Sea, from its foundation in 1902 until 1908, setting standards of precision for instruments and method that became accepted practice in fisheries' hydrography. He was awarded a Nobel Peace Prize in 1922 for organizing relief work after the First World War among refugees and victims of the Russian famine.
Right *Nansen;* Below *Fram in the ice, her windmill generator visible on deck.*

The small ship Gjøa, *first through the North-West Passage, photographed by Amundsen.*

Winter found them close to the North Magnetic Pole, in their snug base Gjøahavn, where they built huts for themselves and the recording instruments, mapped the surrounding area, took game for the pot and enjoyed the company of Eskimos. After 19 profitable months, *Gjøa* was once more under way heading westwards and by August 1906 Amundsen brought her into the Pacific, the first vessel through the North-West Passage.

'THE POLE AT LAST'

Robert Peary (1856–1920) trained with the US Coast and Geodetic Survey before joining the Civil Engineering Corps of the US Navy. He organized and led six Arctic expeditions between 1891 and 1909, each time pushing further north, via Smith Sound and Nares Strait. His explorations settled the question of Greenland's northern limits, showing it to be an island.

Peary was driven by the desire to be the first man at the Pole, an ambition which he apparently achieved at his third attempt, on 6 April 1909. He believed in making the most efficient use of existing resources, relying mainly on Eskimos and their dogs, and using the best quality sledges, skin clothing and concentrated rations. Earlier in 1909 relaying support parties of 24 men, 19 sledges and 133 dogs advanced from a land base at Cape Columbia to clear trail, erect camps and lay stores. This enabled Peary and his Eskimo companions to have an easy march up to the forward point. They then sped over the 250 km (150 miles) to the Pole, 780 km (485 miles) back to base, allegedly covering the whole distance in 16 days.

Peary's jubilant remarks betray his obsession: 'The Pole at last. The prize of three centuries. My dream and goal for 20 years. Mine at last! I cannot bring myself to realise it. It seems all so simple and commonplace.' It was not, however, exploration. Nor

"STARS AND STRIPES

DR. FREDERICK A. COOK

APRIL 21
1908.

TWO DAUNTLESS AMERICA[
THOUSAND YEARS AND PL[
UPON THE AXIS OF THE

was he universally believed. Some doubted that he could have travelled so fast; others considered that his navigation had not allowed for ice-drift, while Frederick Cook claimed to have reached the Pole in 1908. Recent re-examination of the evidence, however, appears to support Peary's claim to have been at the Pole on the date shown in his log.

'The longest sustained journey in the history of polar exploration' was how Wally Herbert described his British Trans-Arctic Expedition (1968–9). Four men and their dog teams left Point Barrow in February 1968 and crossed 130 km (80 miles) of mush ice to the polar pack where they encamped for the summer, taking meteorological, geophysical and marine observations as their floe drifted north. When the sea froze once more, the men sledged towards the

This postcard would not have appealed to Peary, who claimed that the honour of being first man at the North Pole was his alone.

WINTERING IN THE ARCTIC

Wintering in the Arctic tested the qualities of officers and men to the full. The ships were secured, waggon cloth stretched over the deck for cover. In fine weather the men exercised on the floe, went off on hunting parties or cut ice for drinking water whilst the officers made their scientific observations. Afterwards there were talks and writing lessons for the men, lectures for the officers. A ships' newspaper was produced, and all hands joined in the theatricals which were the winter highlight.

HMS Hecla *and HMS* Griper *in Winter harbour, where they were frozen in from October 1819 to August 1820.*

Pole each day until the onset of darkness, when they received a scheduled air-drop of food, fuel and supplies including a prefabricated hut. Throughout the winter more scientific work, including accurate stellar position fixes to show their line of drift, kept them fully occupied. Their intention was to reach Svalbard by May 1969, but the threat of melting ice led to their being rescued by helicopter a few miles short of their destination.

The men were constantly aware of their insecure position; as Herbert wrote, 'The whole vast area was a confusion of currents, counter-currents and winds which moved the sea ice like brittle scum.' Even the pack was 'an area with a fantastic amount of pressure-ice movement – a lead would open up and come together again to form a pressure-ridge; then the floe would split in opposite directions and build another pressure-ridge at right-angles to it. By the time this had been going on all winter there would

DRIFTING ICE-STATIONS

The first manned ice-station was the Russian 'North Pole 1', assembled in May 1937. A team of scientists lived on this floe, recording the sea and weather conditions that it encountered on its way to the Greenland Sea where the crew and their precious data were rescued by an icebreaker. This was the first of many such stations, manned and automatic. Their work, with that of the fixed stations ashore, brought an entirely new understanding of the weather-making processes of the Arctic and of the Earth as a whole.

be an absolute chaos of ice.' Detours round these ice ridges and open leads meant that the expedition travelled 5820 km (3615 miles) to cover a point-to-point distance of 3090 km (1920 miles).

The Italia *leaving King's Bay for Nicholas II Land, 15 May 1928.*

AERIAL EXPLORATION

The record of aerial exploration of the Arctic begins with the ill-fated flight of the Swedish aeronaut Solomon Andrée in his drift balloon *Eagle* in 1897. The exact course of events was made clear when the remains of Andrée and his two companions were discovered in 1930 on White Island, a short distance from their departure point on Svalbard. According to their diary, the balloon had landed further to the north-west and the men had sledged to the island, where they later died.

An American journalist, Walter Wellman, made the first dirigible balloon flights in 1906 but never got far from his Svalbard base. In 1926 Umberto Nobile (1885–1980), an Italian engineer and aeronaut, brought his dirigible balloon *Norge* to the Arctic and in 1926 he flew from Svalbard to Alaska with Amundsen and 14 companions. Nobile was well-provided with instruments to make gravity, magnetic and weather observations. His route crossed unfamiliar regions and where the sky was clear of fog, he was able to take photographs.

In 1928 Nobile went back to the Arctic with the balloon *Italia*. Returning from his first mission towards the Siberian coast, Nobile took off again a few days later and flew over the North Pole. Then disaster struck and the balloon crashed in flames on the ice floe. Nobile and a few others were rescued by a Swedish aeroplane; seven more were picked up by Russian ice-breakers, the rest were lost at the time of the crash. The disaster was compounded by the tragic disappearance of Amundsen, who left Tromsø in a seaplane to go to their rescue and was never seen again.

During the Amundsen–Ellsworth Polar Flight of 1925 six men left Svalbard in two Dornier-Wal

1918-20 Amundsen's voyage in the *Maud* through the North-East Passage.
1924 Oxford University Exploration Club carried out first scientific survey of Svalbard.

1926 Nobile and Amundsen flew in a dirigible balloon over the North Pole.
1928 Byrd flew over the North Pole.
1930-1 Watkins led British Arctic Air Route

expedition to south Greenland.
1933-4 Lindsay completed the longest self-supported dog sledge journey across the Greenland ice-cap.

1934-5 Edward Shackleton's Oxford University north-west Greenland expedition.
1937-8 Wright and Hamilton surveyed east coast of Ellesmere Island.
1940-4 Voyage of the *St Roch* commanded by Larsen through the North-West Passage from west to east, and east to west.
1948-57 Victor's scientific exploration of Greenland ice-cap.
1953-72 Hattersley-Smith carried out scientific research at Tanquary Fiord,

Ellesmere Island.
1967-9 Herbert's British Trans-Arctic expedition made the first surface crossing of Arctic Ocean via the North Pole, a journey of 5820 km (3616 miles) using dogs.
1974 Uemura made solo dog-sledge journey 12,000 km (7450 miles) from Greenland to Alaska, and in 1978 reached the North Pole alone.
1981-2 Fiennes's Transglobe expedition circumnavigated the world via both Poles.

Fiennes subsequently (1984-90) made several attempts to man-haul to the North Pole unsupported. Raised £1 million for Multiple Sclerosis in 1990.
1986 Steger's dog sledge expedition was the first unsupported party to reach the North Pole since Peary.
1989 Swan's Icewalk expedition man-hauled to the North Pole but also carried out programme of pollution monitoring involving young people from many nations.

seaplanes. They flew for eight hours, by which time half their fuel had been consumed, before landing on the ice. They made two echo-soundings, confirming Nansen's earlier measurements, and then abandoned one plane, transferring the remaining fuel to the other, which carried both crews back to base. On the outward leg they had flown over 100,000 sq km (38,600 sq miles) without seeing land.

In the same summer, Richard Byrd (1888–1957) made a number of flights over Ellesmere Island and the Greenland ice cap. Flying from King's Bay in Svalbard, Byrd and Floyd Bennett covered the 1375 km (850 miles) to the Pole in about eight hours in the following year. Such was the accuracy of their navigation that the plane returned exactly to its point of departure. Subsequent Arctic flights were made for commercial reasons: establishing polar air routes, patrolling sea lanes and prospecting for minerals.

THE FUTURE

The Arctic Ocean remains the least known part of our planet, its vital strategic importance for military submarines having discouraged international co-operation and civilian investigation. Early in 1990 reports confirmed that the sea-ice is thinning. Faced by the threat of global climatic change, the nations with an interest in the Arctic formed a new International Arctic Sciences Committee to pool their research findings and to plan major new surveys. Individual groups will continue to measure the thickness and extent of sea-ice, changes in ice sheets, and the general atmospheric and ocean circulations. Ice-cores will be drilled, instrumented buoys will be tracked by ship's radar or satellite.

An international team of scientists has proposed a modern equivalent of Nansen's *Fram* expedition of 1893. A fully instrumented research ship with a hull designed to resist crushing would be allowed to freeze into the ice off Siberia. For the succeeding two or three years the ice would carry the ship from one side of the Arctic to the other, while her scientists made their measurements of the underlying water, the ice itself and the weather. At the same time, a robot submarine would map the underside topography of the ice sheet that in winter covers 52 million sq km (about 20 million sq miles) of the region.

THE
ANTARCTIC

At the bottom of the globe lies a frozen continent, which is separated from the rest of the world by the stormy Southern Ocean. It is encircled by pack-ice, ranked by huge tabular icebergs, and covered by an ice sheet, miles deep in places. Not surprisingly this so-called 'Seventh Continent' was the last to be explored. Even at the beginning of the 20th century, there was discussion as to whether the Antarctic really were a continent or only a great mass of ice resting on islands.

The sea defences of Antarctica were first penetrated by wooden sailing ships, and then by ice-strengthened ships and powerful ice-breakers. In the early years of the 20th century – the 'heroic age' of Antarctic exploration – the first sledging journeys were made by men, dogs and ponies into the interior of this great frozen land. Later on came tracked vehicles, such as the 'weasel' and 'sno-cat', and also the aeroplane, from which not only the surface of the continent has been mapped, but its shape under the ice. Later still came satellite imagery to provide further refinement to the maps.

The charts and globes of geographers in the 18th century and earlier had often outlined a vast and fruitful southern continent – *Terra Australis Incognita* – extending to quite temperate latitudes, where is now known to be nothing but sea. Sir Francis Drake, the Elizabethan sea dog and second circumnavigator of the world, was blown in the *Golden Hind* well to the south of Cape Horn, thus proving that no great southern land extended northward there.

It fell to two French mariners, J.-B.-C. Bouvet de Lozier, a Norman, and Yves Kerguelen de Trémarec,

Members of the British Commonwealth Trans-Antarctic Expedition, 1955–8, led by Dr (later Sir) Vivian Fuchs, frequently had to contend with severe blizzards such as the one shown in this photograph.

a Breton, to be the first to show the armchair geographers something of the reality of the sub-Antarctic islands of the Southern Ocean, which encircle the continent at great distances apart. During his voyage of 1738–9, Bouvet discovered a tiny ice-capped island, which now bears his name and whose Cape Circumcision he took to be the tip of *Terra Australis*. Forty years later, Kerguelen discovered the islands which bear his name and which Captain Cook later called the Islands of Desolation – cold, windswept, mountainous islands, not the fabled southern lands Kerguelen had first reported.

The great English navigator, Captain James Cook, RN (1728–79), made three outstanding voyages in the later 18th century, during the second of which in the *Resolution* and the *Adventure*, he sailed round the world in high southern latitudes, through icy and tempestuous seas. He encircled, but did not sight, the true Antarctic continent and appeared to disprove altogether the existence of *Terra Australis Incognita*. In words which have become famous in the history of polar exploration, he wrote in his journal on 21 February 1775:

I had now made the circuit of the Southern Ocean in a high Latitude and traversed it in such a manner as to leave not the least room for the Possibility of there being a continent, unless near the Pole and out of the reach of Navigation . . . thus I flater my self that the intention of the Voyage has in every respect been fully Answered, the Southern Hemisphere sufficiently explored and a final end put to searching after a Southern Continent, which has at times ingrossed the attention of some of the Maritime Powers for near two centuries past and the Geographers of all ages. That there may be a Continent or large tract of land near

1773 Cook became the first European to cross the Antarctic Circle, and circumnavigated the continent but never actually saw it.

1819-21 Bellingshausen crossed the Antarctic Circle and sighted Antarctica three days before Bransfield but failed to realize it.

1820 Bransfield discovered north-western coast of Graham Land on 30 January, and was the first person to chart part of the mainland.

A watercolour drawing by William Hodges showing Captain Cook's sailing ships, Resolution *and* Adventure *icing ship (to melt for water) in lat. 61°S, January 1773.*

the Pole, I will not deny, on the contrary I am of opinion there is, and it is probable that we have seen a part of it . . .

Captain Cook was the first to cross the Antarctic Circle. He also discovered the island of South Georgia and some of the South Sandwich Islands, which he called 'Lands doomed by nature to everlasting frigidness and never once to feel the warmth of the Suns rays, whose horrible and savage aspect I have no words to describe' (*Journal,* 21 February 1775).

SEALERS IN ANTARCTICA

Following the publication of Cook's *Voyage,* first British and then American sealers began the slaughter of thousands of fur seals (for their pelts) and of sea elephants (for their oil) on South Georgia and elsewhere in the Southern Ocean between 1778 and 1822, by which date the fur seals were almost extinct. The sealers were of course rivals and tended to keep their discoveries secret, but the number of vessels engaged in the work makes it certain that various islands and much of the north-western part of the Antarctic Peninsula became known to them.

Historians and geographers have argued about who first discovered the Antarctic Peninsula, the long 'tail' of Antarctica, which stretches north towards the tip of South America. It is quite certain, however, that Lt Edward Bransfield, RN, in the trading brig *Williams,* accompanied by her master William Smith, discovered part of the north-western coast of the peninsula, which he named 'Trinity Land' on 30 January 1820. The first chart of this area of the coast of Antarctica was a result of his survey. In November of the same year the American sealer, Nathaniel Brown Palmer in the shallop *Hero,* reported land, which was later called 'Palmer's Land', a name now transferred to the southern Antarctic Peninsula.

Leaving the port of Leith in Scotland in 1822, a British sealer, Captain James Weddell, in the brig *Jane* with the cutter *Beaufoy* in company, penetrated the sea which now bears his name, as far as 74°15′S, the furthest south yet attained. Weddell had been a Master in the Royal Navy during the Napoleonic Wars and his portrait hangs in the Royal Geographical Society. On a previous voyage he had visited the South Shetlands (north-west of the Antarctic Peninsula). His chart of those islands, of the South

Orkneys (also off the Antarctic Peninsula) and in particular of his tracks in the Weddell Sea can be found in his book, which went into two editions, and was entitled *A Voyage towards the South Pole, performed in the years 1822–24, containing an Examination of the Antarctic Sea, to the seventy fourth degree of latitude* . . .

Of a scientific and enquiring mind, Weddell made many interesting observations. Few, if any, other navigators have found the Weddell Sea so relatively free from ice and it is to his great credit that he made the most of his opportunity. Another British sealer, George Powell, also published a chart of the South Shetlands. He and the American sealer, N.B. Palmer first discovered and charted the South Orkneys during their joint voyages of 1821–2.

A GREAT RUSSIAN NAVIGATOR

A worthy successor to Captain Cook was the Russian naval officer, Captain Thaddeus Bellingshausen, who, with Captain M.P. Lazarev, circumnavigated the Antarctic continent in a high southern latitude in 1819–21. The tracks of their ships, *Vostok* and *Mirnyy*, complemented those of Cook 50 years before. They discovered the three northern islands of the South Sandwich Islands that had escaped Cook. Bellingshausen took special care to navigate in seas not sailed by Cook and in fact he much improved on Cook's record in distance covered within the Antarctic Circle.

An English translation of the narrative of the expedition was not published until 1945, so that for many years its achievements were little known. In the Introduction to this book, the editor, Frank Debenham, wrote of Cook and Bellingshausen:

Top *Portrait of Captain James Weddell (1787–1834).*

Below *Captain Weddell's ships,* Jane *and* Beaufoy, *in 74°15′S, February 1823.*

ANTARCTICA

1840 Wilkes commanding the US Exploring Expedition followed the coastline for 2500 km (1500 miles), and was the first to use the term Antarctic continent.

1892-4 Norwegian whaler Larsen penetrates Weddell Sea and discovered Oscar II Land.

1894 Borchgrevink with Norwegian

expedition made landing on Cape Adare, the first on Victoria Land.

1897-9 de Gerlache and Amundsen's vessel trapped in the ice for 12 months.

Between them the two great navigators therefore covered about 60° of longitude within the Circle, one sixth of its circumference, yet were unlucky enough to miss the mainland entirely, though one quarter to one third of its coast is very close to the Circle.

Nevertheless, it must be said that the Russians did in fact sight the ice edge of Greater Antarctica in January and February 1820. Opinion differs as to whether this constitutes the discovery of the continent or not.

Like Cook, Bellingshausen discovered and surveyed a number of islands in the Southern Ocean, in particular Peter I Island, the first land seen within the Antarctic Circle, and Alexander I Land (now Alexander Island). Both are to the west of the Antarctic Peninsula on the margins of what is now called the Bellingshausen Sea.

FIRST SIGHTING OF LAND

The first indisputable sighting of land in Greater (East) Antarctica was by Captain John Biscoe, in the brig *Tula* on 28 February 1831. In his journal he described his discovery of Enderby Land (named after the well-known London sealing and whaling firm which financed the voyage) as follows:

Captain Thaddeus Bellingshausen of the Imperial Russian Navy, second circumnavigator of the Antarctic.

THE ANTARCTIC: KEY TO ROUTES

(1) **Bouvet** 1738-9. During voyage of exploration sighted the NW cape of Bouvet I.

(2) **Cook** 1772-5. Circumnavigated Antarctica, discovering South Georgia and South Sandwich Is.

(3) **Bransfield** 1819-20. Discovered South Shetlands and part of NW coast of Antarctic Peninsula.

(4) **Bellingshausen** 1819-21. Circumnavigation in a high southern latitude. Called at South Sandwich Is, discovered Peter I I. and Alexander I., and surveyed South Shetlands.

(5) **Palmer** 1820-1. Sailed S from South Shetlands and reported land (part of NW coast of Antarctic Peninsula).*

(6) **Powell and Palmer** 1821-2. Sailed from South Shetlands to South Orkneys and return.*

(7) **Weddell** 1822-4. Sailed to South Orkneys, S part of Weddell Sea, South Georgia and Falklands.

(8) **Biscoe** 1830-3. Sailed from Falklands and circumnavigated Antarctica, discovering Enderby Land and Graham Land.

(9) **Kemp** 1833-4. Discovered Kemp Land.

(10) **Dumont d'Urville** 1837-40. Sailed to South Orkneys, South Shetlands and extreme NW coast of Antarctic Peninsula; discovered Terre Adélie.

(11) **Balleny** 1838-9. Discovered Balleny Is and may have seen Sabrina Coast.

(12) **Wilkes** 1838-42. Charted discoveries while sailing along the coast of Wilkes Land.

(13) **Ross** 1839-43. Circumnavigated Antarctica, discovering Victoria Land, Ross I. and Ross Ice Shelf. Visited Antarctic Peninsula.

(14) **Moore** 1845. Sailed near Wilhelm II Land.

(15) **Larsen** 1893-4. Sailed along Weddell Sea coast of the Antarctic Peninsula.

(16) **De Gerlache** 1897-99. Sailed to South Shetlands, along W coast of Graham Land and was beset in ice in Bellingshausen Sea.

(17) **Borchgrevink** 1898-1900. Sailed along coast of Victoria Land and Ross Ice Front.*

(18) **Von Drygalski** 1901-3. Discovered Wilhelm II Land and visited Gaussberg volcano.

(19) **Scott** 1901-4. Explored coast of Victoria Land and Ross Ice Shelf. Sledge journeys to S and W of McMurdo Sound.

(20) **Shackleton** 1907-9. From Ross Island base climbed Mt Erebus, sledged to within 1° 37' of the South Pole and reached the then vicinity of South Magnetic Pole.

(21) **Amundsen** 1910-12. From Ross Ice Shelf reached the South Pole and discovered Queen Maud Range.

(22) **Scott** 1910-13. From Ross Ice Shelf reached the South Pole; all five members of expedition died on return journey.

(23) **Filchner** 1911-12. Sailed from South Georgia, discovered Luitpold Coast and Filchner Ice Shelf.

(24) **Mawson** 1911-12. Discovered and explored George V land and Queen Mary Land.

(25) **Shackleton** 1914-16. Sailed from South Georgia, discovered S part of Caird Coast. *Endurance*, beset in ice, was crushed and sank.

(26) **Riiser-Larsen** 1929-30. Sailed from South Georgia to Dronning Maud Land, discovered and charted from the air Kronprins Olav Kyst and Kronprinsesse Märtha Kyst.

(27) **Mawson** 1929-30. Discovered Mac.Robertson Land, charted Kemp Land from the air and visited Enderby Land.

(28) **Mawson** 1930-31. Landed on George V Land, discovered Banzare Land and Princess Elizabeth Land. Charted Mackenzie Bay from the air. Landed on Mac.Robertson Land.

(29) **Rymill** 1935-7. Two sledge journeys made on Graham Land: first to E of Biscoe Is, second from Adelaide I. to George VI Sound and eastwards into Palmer Land.

(30) **Hillary** 1957-8. Pioneered overland route from Ross Sea to South Pole.

(31) **Fuchs** 1957-8. Crossed overland from Weddell Sea to Ross Sea.

*Routes not shown on map.

SAILING SHIPS IN ANTARCTIC WATERS

Much of the Southern Ocean and its islands and the coast of Antarctica was explored in wooden sailing ships, either powered by wind alone or, later, with small auxiliary steam engines. Approaching and recognizing the ice-bound coasts was difficult for their captains, as the editor of Bellingshausen's *Voyage* of 1819–21, Frank Debenham, explained:

It is interesting to note here two of the reasons why Bellingshausen and others after him had such difficulty in recognising the coast when they were near it. One is the effect of the winds and their weather, particularly upon sailing ships. When the wind comes from the north in those latitudes, while helping the ship to sail south it invariably brings thick and snowy weather, so that land cannot be seen. When, on the other hand, the south and east winds bring clear weather, they hinder the sailing ship in getting south, and bring out the loose ice from the coast, fending the ships off from a close approach.

The other reason, said Debenham, is the depth of the continental shelf round Antarctica. Scoured by huge icebergs, it measures nearer 200 fathoms (360 metres, 1200 ft) than the 100 fathoms (180 metres, 600 ft) off other continents.

Wooden sailing ships – sometimes naval 'bomb' vessels and sometimes whalers – were employed in these ice-infested waters, because of the

natural strength of their hulls and because their bows could be further strengthened for ice-breaking. Wooden ships like Byrd's *Bear of Oakland*, an old Scottish whaler, built in 1874, were in use as late as the 1930s. Largely powered by the wind, they had little need of coal depots. The *Discovery*, now berthed in Dundee, Scotland, is a fine surviving example of such a ship. She was built there in 1900, at a time when large wooden sailing vessels had become almost obsolete. Her first captain, Captain R.F. Scott, RN, described her construction as follows:

Most people who have voyaged in modern ships know that between them and the sea there has only interposed a steel plate the fraction of an inch in thickness; they may, therefore, be interested to know what the side of the "Discovery" was like. The frames, which were placed very close together, were eleven inches thick and of solid English oak; inside the frames came the inner lining, a solid planking four inches thick; whilst the outside was covered with two layers of planking, respectively six and five inches thick, so that, in most places, to bore a hole in the side one would have had to get through twenty-six inches of solid wood.

The hull of the *Discovery* was strengthened and stiffened by tiers of

crossbeams and by heavy wooden bulkheads. The bows or forward end of the ship were so fortified by oak stiffeners that they became almost solid. Nansen's *Fram*, preserved in Oslo, is another famous example of a wooden ship built for use in ice at about this time. Sadly, Drygalski's *Gauss* (later the *Arctic*), also specially built for polar exploration at Kiel, no longer survives.

The 'crow's nest' has long been a special feature of polar ships. Believed to have been invented some two hundred years ago by Captain William Scoresby, Sr, for use when whaling in the Arctic, it was a canvas or wooden structure, sometimes a large barrel, which was sent up and lashed to the fore or mainmast. Entry to the crow's nest was through a trap door in the bottom. Protected overhead by a canvas awning and relatively well sheltered by the barrel's sides, the mariner could survey the surrounding sea-ice with his telescope. From aloft he could make out promising 'leads' in the pack. He might be able to tell which of these water lanes between floes the ship might navigate to achieve the course laid down and reach her destination.

'The Erebus passing through the chain of bergs, 13 March 1842.' Sketch by J.E. Davis, Second Master of HMS Terror.

The Belgian expeditionary vessel Belgica *beset in the Bellingshausen Sea where she drifted for a year, involuntarily becoming the first ship to winter in the Antarctic.*

Blizzards, icebergs (some of them many square kilometres in extent) and the possibility of being 'nipped' or even beset in compacted sea-ice are some of the hazards of navigation in Antarctic waters. Another hazard can be the nearness of the South Magnetic Pole, which renders the magnetic compass quite erratic and unreliable.

In the 1930s, light aircraft began to extend the range of sight of the man in the crow's nest. More recently, helicopters have been used from the decks of extremely powerful icebreakers like the *Ob* and the *Glacier*. These vessels can force their way through sea-ice many metres in thickness, sometimes leading a small convoy of less strengthened vessels. Better charts, better navigational aids and better manoeuvrability are among the other advantages which modern navigators have over the old.

In tribute to his predecessors, Captain Edwin A. MacDonald, USN, a gold medallist of the Royal Geographical Society, dedicated his book, *Polar Operations* (1969) 'to those early captains who dared to pit their small, weak vessels against the dangers and unknowns of the polar ice fields'.

4 p.m. saw several hummocks to the southward, which much resembled tops of mountains, and at 6 p.m. clearly distinguished it to be land, and to considerable extent; to my great satisfaction what we had seen first being the black tops of mountains showing themselves through the snow on the lower land.

The mountains were what are now called 'nunataks' – peaks which stick up through land ice. Biscoe circumnavigated the Antarctic, accompanied by the cutter *Lively* commanded by Captain George Avery and a year later discovered Graham Land (part of the Antarctic Peninsula), Adelaide Island and the Biscoe Islands. Biscoe was 'firmly of the opinion' that he had found 'a large continent' off which he had coasted for 485 km (300 miles).

Another British sealer, Captain Peter Kemp in the *Magnet* may have discovered icy and desolate Heard Island as well as Kemp Land (Greater Antarctica) in November and December 1833. A few years later in February 1839, another Enderby sealing venture discovered the Balleny Islands, which guard the entrance to the Ross Sea. The expedition's captains, John Balleny in the *Eliza Scott* and Thomas Freeman in the *Sabrina*, also reported an 'appearance of land' near what was later called Sabrina Coast, Greater Antarctica.

CHARTING THE COASTLINE

Three national expeditions, French, American and British, between 1837 and 1843 took an important step forward in charting the Antarctic coastline. Both the French and the American expeditions did the greater part of their work in the warm waters of the Pacific. Captain J.-S.-C. Dumont d'Urville, commanding the *Astrolabe* with the *Zélée* (Captain C.-H. Jacquinot) in company, discovered and named Terre Adélie after his wife. The little Adélie penguins are reminders of her too. At least one egg of an Emperor penguin was collected by the French expedition and brought back home. A splendid atlas and other volumes were published afterwards in Paris, in the pages of which can be seen pictures of the French sailors and their officers on the rocky coast in January 1840. The French ships also visited and surveyed part of the Antarctic Peninsula and adjoining islands, notably Trinity Peninsula and the South Orkney Islands.

The United States Exploring Expedition of 1838–42 consisted of a squadron of five ships. They

1898 Borchgrevink established the first wintering camp on Antarctica at Cape Adare. Mapped coast of Victoria Land and Ross Sea areas.

1901-3 Drygalski discovered Kaiser Wilhelm II Land and the cone of Gaussberg, a source of valuable geological information.
1901-4 Scott led British National Antarctic

Expedition. Shackleton attempted to reach the South Pole but turned back at 82°17'S.
1901-3 Nordenskjold and Larsen by sledge along the Larsen Ice Shelf to 66°S.

too returned with a harvest of charts and collections, one of the indirect results of which was the founding of the great Smithsonian Institution in Washington DC. However, there was much controversy both about its leader, Lt Charles Wilkes, USN, who was court-martialled on his return, and about its charts on which some land was shown in positions that were later sailed over by other explorers. Wilkes's poorly equipped ships sailed westwards along the coast, discovering and charting what was later called Wilkes Land between 160°E and 98°E – a great arc of the Antarctic Circle.

Neither Dumont d'Urville nor Wilkes had earlier navigated in icy seas. The third and greatest of these three national expeditions was commanded by a man who had served a long Arctic apprenticeship as a midshipman and a lieutenant in the Royal Navy, Captain James Clark Ross, RN. His ships, the *Erebus* and *Terror*, were 'bomb vessels', stoutly built to withstand the recoil of heavy mortars on deck and additionally strengthened for work in sea-ice.

At the instigation of the British Association and the Royal Society, the Admiralty despatched Ross (who had already reached the North Magnetic Pole in the Arctic) to find the South Magnetic Pole, the location of these points being of great importance to science and navigation. His ships were the first to pass boldly through the belt of pack-ice bordering the Ross Sea and to sail that sea, discovering Victoria Land, Mount Erebus and Mount Terror (the former an active volcano amid the ice and snow) and the cliffs of the extraordinary 'Great Icy Barrier', now known as the Ross Ice Shelf.

Captain J.-S.-C. Dumont d'Urville, the commander of the Astrolabe.

Members of the French expedition charting the coastline while their ships lie at anchor in Antarctic waters.

Ross made two southern voyages from Hobart (Tasmania), the expedition's magnetic headquarters and from New Zealand and afterwards continued towards the area of the Antarctic Peninsula, making less dramatic discoveries there. Ross's second-in-command was Captain F.R.M. Crozier, RN, who was to perish in the Arctic with the lost Franklin expedition. The young assistant surgeon of HMS *Erebus* later became the eminent botanist and traveller, Sir Joseph Dalton Hooker.

NOTABLE SCIENTIFIC VOYAGES

Apart from many American sealing voyages to the sub-Antarctic islands, the south polar regions remained largely in peace for some 50 years after Ross. Two notable scientific voyages took place, however: that of Captain T.E.L. Moore, RN, in the *Pagoda*, making important magnetic observations, complementing those of Ross, in the South Atlantic and southern Indian Oceans, 1844–5, and that of HMS *Challenger*, the first steam vessel to cross the Antarctic Circle during her great oceanographic circumnavigation of the world, 1872–6.

While the *Challenger* was in these icy waters, rocks of continental type were dredged from the seabed. Scientists therefore conjectured that these had been scoured and transported by ice from lands far to the south. The voyage of the *Challenger* aroused the interest of scientists and geographers in the Antarctic regions and resulted in the revival of exploration there at the beginning of the 20th century.

At the very end of the 19th century, four vessels from the Dundee whaling fleet and the *Jason*, commanded by Captain C.A. Larsen, from the Norwegian port of Sandefjord, made unsuccessful whaling reconnaissances in the Antarctic Peninsula area, based on Ross's reports of whales observed years before. Some scientific and survey work was undertaken and Larsen collected fossils on Seymour Island, proving that the Antarctic climate had not always been frigid. He returned the following season (1893–4) and managed to sail the *Jason* down the Weddell Sea coast of the Antarctic Peninsula to 68°10'S, a latitude which remains the furthest south penetration by ship along that coast. This voyage was important geographically: when linked with Biscoe's in the west, it showed the narrowness of the land until well south of the Antarctic Circle.

At the opposite side of the continent, the first landing on Victoria Land was made in January 1895

Captain Sir James Clark Ross, RN (1800–62), whom Amundsen called 'a shining star'.

Adrien de Gerlache de Goméry, the leader of the Belgian Antarctic Expedition, 1897–9.

at Cape Adare from the *Antarctic* by other Norwegians engaged on a whaling reconnaissance, this time in the Ross Sea area. Three years later a British party financed by Sir George Newnes wintered at this spot under the leadership of C.E. Borchgrevink. They were the first scientists to do so intentionally. Their ship, the *Southern Cross*, sailed along the Ross Ice Front, which was found to have receded since Ross's day. A small group landed to reach a new high latitude, using dog teams in Antarctica for the first time.

Another privately financed expedition, a Belgian one, organized and led by Adrien de Gerlache de Goméry in 1897–9, explored the waters to the west of the Antarctic Peninsula, discovering Gerlache Strait and the Danco Coast. Their ship, the *Belgica*, was beset and drifted for a year in the Bellingshausen Sea, involuntarily becoming the first expeditionary vessel to winter in the Antarctic. The mate was the Norwegian Roald Amundsen, later to win fame as the first navigator of the North-West Passage and the first man to reach the South Pole.

The turn of the century saw a clutch of national exploring and scientific expeditions sent to the Antarctic. Much interest in the scientific and geographical questions to be solved there had been

1910-2 Scott with four companions reached the South Pole on 17 January 1912. All perished on the return journey.
1911-2 Filchner discovered Luitpold Coast

and Filchner Ice Shelf.
1911-2 Mawson's Australasian Antarctic expedition explored the area between Victoria Land and Kaiser Wilhelm II

Land.
1911-2 Japanese party led by Shirase sledged to 80°05´S in King Edward VII Land.

evinced by the voyage of the *Challenger*, one advocate of a further British venture remarking that more was known of the planet Mars than about a large part of our own globe.

As a result of the efforts of Professor Georg von Neumayer in Germany, of Sir John Murray, editor of the *Challenger*'s scientific results, and Sir Clements Markham, President of the Royal Geographical Society, in Britain, a German and a British expedition went south in a spirit of scientific co-operation. Led by Professor Erich von Drygalski in the *Gauss* (the second vessel to winter in the Antarctic pack ice), the Germans carried out a great deal of scientific work and discovered an extinct volcano, Gaussberg, on the coast of what they called Kaiser Wilhelm II Land (now Wilhelm II Coast).

The British expedition was sponsored partly by the Royal Society and the Royal Geographical Society, and partly by the British Government. Its ship, the *Discovery*, wintered for two seasons in a sheltered bay near what was named Hut Point, McMurdo Sound, at the head of the Ross Sea, under the shadow and smoke plume of Mount Erebus. The expedition had earlier discovered King Edward VII Land (now Edward VII Peninsula) at the far end of the Ross Ice Shelf.

It too did much scientific work, but is notable as making the first extensive land journeys on the Antarctic continent. Its leader was Captain R.F. Scott, RN, whose southern sledge party reached beyond 82°S, tracing a range of great mountains beside the Ross Ice Shelf. The following season, Scott and two companions sledged up the Ferrar Glacier through these mountains, on to the plateau of the immense ice sheet that covers the continent.

The expedition's relief ship, the little *Morning*, made two voyages to the Antarctic, under Captain William Colbeck, remarkable in their own right, on the first of which (1902–3), Scott Island was discovered near the entrance to the Ross Sea.

A Swedish, a Scottish and two French expeditions were also in the field at the beginning of the 20th century. All carried out comprehensive scientific programmes, as well as making geographical discoveries in their area of operation.

The Swedish Antarctic Expedition, 1901–4, led by Dr Otto Nordenskjöld made a major contribution to our knowledge of Graham Land (the northern part of the Antarctic Peninsula). Their ship, the *Antarctic* (Captain C.A. Larsen) was beset and sank in the pack-ice of Erebus and Terror Gulf. The three parties, into which the expedition had separated, eventually met at Snow Hill Island and were rescued by the Argentine sloop-of-war *Uruguay*.

The Scottish National Antarctic Expedition, 1902–4, in SY *Scotia* (Captain T. Robertson) was led by Dr W.S. Bruce. It made the first systematic oceanographical exploration of the Weddell Sea, discovering Coats Land. They wintered in the South Orkneys and there set up the first permanent station

Three famous explorers of the 'Heroic Age': Roald Amundsen, Robert Falcon Scott and Sir Douglas Mawson.

1916 The British Imperial Trans-Antarctic Expedition planned to cross Antarctica, but the *Endurance* sank in the Weddell Sea. Shackleton and five men made an heroic journey by boat from Elephant Island to South Georgia to get help.
1928-30 Wilkins failed to cross Antarctica by plane. Made aerial surveys of Graham Land, reported it to be an archipelago.
1928-30 Byrd from his base, Little America I, on the Ross Ice Shelf made the first flight over the South Pole on 29 November 1929.

in the Antarctic, which has been maintained since 1904 by the Argentine weather service.

The French expeditions were both led and commanded by Dr J.-B. Charcot in the *Français* (1903–5) and the *Pourquoi-Pas?* (1908–10), each a specially built three-masted wooden sailing vessel. They too made considerable contributions to the exploration of Graham Land and adjoining islands. The *Pourquoi-Pas?* discovered Marguerite Bay, the Fallières Coast and Charcot Island (to the west of Alexander Island).

These years also saw the rise of a Norwegian whaling industry in the Antarctic, regulated by the British Colonial Office in an effort to conserve stocks.

The Norwegians were also to make a number of geographical discoveries (as had the sealers a century before) in the course of their seaborne operations before and after the First World War. Particularly noteworthy were the explorations of Maj. Gen. Hjalmar Riiser-Larsen from the *Norvegia*, financed by the whaling magnate, Consul Lars Christensen. The Norwegian claim to a large sector of the Antarctic, Dronning Maud Land and to Bouvetøya, is largely based on these.

THE 'HEROIC AGE'

Exploration of the interior of the continent made great progress just before the First World War during what has been called the 'heroic age' of Antarctic exploration. E.H. Shackleton led a sledge party from Ross Island to within 160 km (100 miles) of the South Pole, greatly extending the work of Scott's party, of which he had been a member a few years before. The ranges of mountains were seen to continue alongside the Ross Ice Shelf and a second route to the polar plateau was found up the Beardmore Glacier. A scientific party sledged to the South Magnetic Pole, in Victoria Land; the crater of Mount Erebus, the active volcano, was also reached.

Much has been written about the 'race to the Pole' by Captain Scott and Roald Amundsen, 1910–2. Scott left from McMurdo Sound and Amundsen from winter quarters at the Bay of Whales, an indentation in the Ross Ice Shelf. Amundsen found a completely new route up the Axel Heiberg Glacier and arrived at the South Pole by dog team with four other Norwegians on 14 December 1911. Scott's man-hauling party of five reached it on 17 January 1912, but they all perished during the return journey. The manner of their deaths was to inspire the British

public and indeed the whole world.

During the winter of 1911 Amundsen's ship, the *Fram,* made oceanographical observations in the South Atlantic. Scott's parties investigated the biology, geology, glaciology, meteorology and geophysics of the region mainly from winter quarters on Ross Island, while Oates Land (to the west of Cape Adare) was discovered from the *Terra Nova.*

Contemporary with Scott and Amundsen were the German South Polar Expedition of 1911–2 in the *Deutschland*, led by Dr Wilhelm Filchner, and the Australasian Antarctic Expedition of 1911–4, led by [Sir] Douglas Mawson. The *Deutschland* was beset in the Weddell Sea for nine months. The German expedition's principal discoveries were the Filchner Ice Shelf at the head of the Weddell Sea and the Luitpold Coast.

A Japanese expedition in the *Kainan-Maru*, 1910–2, sledged some distance over the Ross Ice Shelf from the Bay of Whales, and also landed on King Edward VII Land.

Mawson's Australasian Antarctic Expedition in the *Aurora*, commanded by Captain J.K. Davis, accomplished much in the way of geographical exploration and scientific work in the area of the Antarctic to the south of Australia (later claimed as Australian Antarctic Territory). The main base was set up at Commonwealth Bay (where the hut still stands) and others on the Shackleton Ice Shelf and on Macquarie Island, half-way between Australia and the Antarctic. King George V Land and Queen Mary Land were discovered and explored, while a party sledged to the magnetic pole.

During a long sledge journey, Mawson's two companions perished and he was just able to struggle back to Cape Denison, dragging a sledge which he had made less of a burden by cutting it in half. He was later to give this to the Royal Geographical Society.

In 1914, when the First World War broke out, Sir Ernest Shackleton was about to depart for the south in the *Endurance* for an attempt to cross the Antarctic continent. The Admiralty did not detain him despite his offer of directing the Imperial Trans-Antarctic Expedition towards the war effort. The *Endurance* was beset and sank in the ice of the Weddell Sea and her company was eventually saved through Shackleton's leadership and the help of others.

Neither his Weddell Sea party, which discovered the southern part of the Caird Coast, first seen by the Scottish National Antarctic Expedition of 1902–4, nor the Ross Sea depot-laying party (in the

267

TRAVELLING OVERLAND IN ANTARCTICA

The first extensive journeys into the interior were made by the National Antarctic Expedition 1901–4, under the leadership of Captain R.F. Scott, RN. Both dogs and men were used in teams to pull the sledges, which were lightweight and flexible, made to the design of the Norwegian Arctic explorer and scientist, Dr Fridtjof Nansen. The clothing and equipment of this and subsequent expeditions were partly based on Nansen's experience and advice, which in its turn derived to an extent from the native people of the north.

Shackleton took ponies on the *Nimrod* expedition of 1907–9; Scott did likewise on the *Terra Nova* expedition of 1910–3. Mules used in the Himalayan snows by the Indian Army were brought south for the summer season 1912–3, as being better beasts of burden than the ponies. Scott pioneered the use of tracked vehicles, later to come into general use on snow and land-ice, while Shackleton had earlier tried an air-cooled Arrol-Johnston car. Neither of these early forms of mechanical transport was successful – nor was Rear Admiral Byrd's first Ford

snowmobile, which broke down 115 km (70 miles) from base.

However, Byrd's second expedition of 1933–5 showed that motorized vehicles could be used for long inland journeys. The conveyances included a Cletrac tractor, two Ford snowmobiles and three light Citroën trucks, specially adapted from desert to Antarctic use. In addition, 153 sledge dogs were taken, in case the vehicles proved unreliable.

Amundsen's achievement in reaching the South Pole in 1911 demonstrated how successful dogs could be, provided the party were willing to feed dog to dog. Speaking of the superiority of dogs over ponies, he wrote in *The South Pole* (1912):

Our dogs lived on dogs' flesh and pemmican the whole way, and this enabled them to do splendid work. And if we ourselves wanted a piece of fresh meat we could cut off a delicate little fillet; it tasted to us as good as the best beef. The dogs do not object at all; as long as they get their share they do not mind what part of their comrade's carcass it comes from. All that was left after one of these canine

meals was the teeth of the victim – and if it had been a really hard day, these also disappeared.

Gradually dogs have been replaced by machines such as skidoos or remote-controlled snow scooters for small parties – or the massive Kharkovchanka sledges, based on a tank chassis, whose trains since the IGY of 1957–8 have annually relieved the Russian station of 'Vostok' in the interior from the coastal one of 'Mirnyy'. Dogs were used by the British Antarctic Survey until 1974–5, having been fed on pemmican and vitamin pills on summer sledge journeys and on seal meat in the winter.

In his history of the BAS (1982), Sir Vivian Fuchs wrote:

Arguments raged between dog-men and tractor drivers, but no-one could deny that huskies inspired more love and entertainment in isolated groups of men than could be matched by machines. Nor were they ever felt to be expendable – men would go to any length to save a dog in trouble.

Left *'A quiet evening on the Barrier'* during the Nimrod *expedition, 1907-9. Plate from Shackleton's* The Heart of the Antarctic *(1909), probably by the expedition's artist, George Marston.*

Right *At the South Pole: Oscar Wisting, a member of the successful Norwegian expedition, 1910-2, led by Roald Amundsen.*

Two dog teams are still kept at the British station of Rothera for recreation or emergency use.

Not only dogs but men need feeding – and men have to be suitably clothed for the Antarctic climate and sheltered while asleep. Weight was a great consideration on early man-hauling or dog-driven sledge journeys, and because food – man's or dog's – took up three-quarters of the payload on a sledge, the daily food ration was cut to a minimum. Seals and penguins could often provide food on coastal journeys, but inland, there were no sources of nourishment for a party. For this reason, a system of depot-laying was developed. Food and fuel were left in these depots, which were usually laid in the autumn before the main sledging season. It was, of course, vitally important to be able to find them on the return journey. Captain Scott's Pole party died during a prolonged blizzard from scurvy and starvation, within a few miles of plenty – the depot which circumstances (or fate) had caused to be laid further to the north than originally intended.

The techniques of feeding and clothing a party in the field was continually evolving during the years an expedition spent in the Antarctic. The men of the 'Heroic Age' (1900–16) were unaware of vitamins (save at the very end with Shackleton's *Endurance* expedition), so that scurvy was likely to become a scourge on long journeys, where no fresh food was available. Vitamin pills overcame this terrible affliction. The reindeer-skin sleeping-bags of Scott's day – three-man, weighing 20 kg (40 lb) when dry – were later replaced by lighter eiderdown ones.

Pemmican (pounded dried meat) long remained a staple of the polar diet on lengthy sledge journeys. On the first of the expeditions of the 'Heroic Age' in 1901–4, the daily allowance per man was about 850 g (30 oz) *water-free* weight (ie, in concentrated form). Besides pemmican, the food included biscuit, oatmeal, Plasmon, pea flour, cheese, chocolate, cocoa, sugar, tea, onion powder, pepper and salt. Not being aware of the calorific content of different foodstuffs, Scott's men often added extra biscuits, mistakenly, instead of extra butter. The biscuit was packed in light 'Venesta' boxes and

the remainder weighed into handy bags for three men per week. Snow was melted for cooking in special lightweight stoves, economical of fuel, designed by Nansen and named after him. No wonder Shackleton dreamed of jam tarts flashing by!

For clothing and footwear, officers and men all wore 'a warm thick suit of underclothing, one or two flannel shirts, a jersey, a sweater, a pair of pilot cloth breeches, and a pyjama jacket' (Scott, 1905). Over these a Burberry outer suit of thin gaberdine (blouse, breeches and leggings) kept out wind and snow. Woollen balaclava helmets were worn – in early spring, under a gaberdine cover and in summer under broad-brimmed hats. Fur or felt mitts covered long woollen half-mitts. Reindeer fur boots *(finneskoes),* made in Norway and worn over two pairs of socks, proved the best cold weather footwear. Glass, leather or wooden snow-goggles were worn.

The man-hauling sledge harness was made of webbing passed round the waist and supported by braces over the shoulders. The two ends of the webbing band joined in an iron ring attached to a rope which was then secured to the sledge or trace. Weight was thus distributed evenly over the upper part of the body for

easier pulling. The Nansen sledges were made of ash, and ranged from 2.1 to 3.6 metres (7 to 12 ft) long.

The invention of nylon has been one of the most important factors in the production of light, warm and windproof clothing or sleeping bags. The design, manufacture and use of skis has also much changed since 1900. More suitable rations and tents have been developed too.

'Hoosh up': Captain Scott's Pole party, 1911. Left to right Seaman Evans, Bowers, Wilson and Scott. Photograph by H.G. Ponting.

Scott's last expedition, 1910–3.
Above *The* Terra Nova *at the ice foot.* Above right: *The ramparts of Mount Erebus.* Right: *At the South Pole, 18 January 1912.* Left to right (standing): *Oates, Scott, Wilson;* (seated): *Evans and Bowers.*

Aurora) contributed much to the exploration of Antarctica. However, the example of the 'Boss', as Shackleton was known, in extricating his men against all odds has never been forgotten.

So ended the 'heroic era' of Antarctic exploration. Sir Raymond Priestley's aphorism regarding the three principal figures has often been quoted:

> For swift and efficient travel, give me Amundsen; for scientific investigation, give me Scott; but when you are at your wits' end and all else fails, go down on your knees and pray for Shackleton.

It omits Sir Douglas Mawson, whom some would claim as explorer, leader and scientist, to be the greatest of them all.

AIRCRAFT IN ANTARCTICA

The 1920s and 1930s saw a number of expeditions using aircraft to explore the continent. One of these was Mawson's BANZARE expedition (British Australian and New Zealand Antarctic Research Expedition, 1929–31), which combined traditional transport in the form of Scott's old ship, the *Discovery,* with the new, a Gypsy Moth float plane. The latter would take off from pools in the pack-ice, thus extending the range of the expedition, as the 'eyes' of the ship and discovering the Banzare Coast, Mac.Robertson Land and Princess Elizabeth Land. A similar combination was used by the British Graham Land expedition of 1934–7, led by the Australian John Rymill, which in addition made some fine dog sledge journeys along and across the Antarctic Peninsula.

The same period also saw a revival of American interest in the Antarctic in the person of Richard Evelyn Byrd (later Rear Admiral, US Navy). Byrd established his base camps near the Bay of Whales, Ross Ice Shelf. They were called 'Little America I' (1928–30) and 'Little America II' (1933–5). The area to the east of King Edward VII Land was explored by sledge and plane, and called Marie Byrd Land.

A first flight by Byrd over the South Pole was made on 29 November 1929, piloted by Bernt

SIR DOUGLAS MAWSON, THE EXPLORERS' EXPLORER

Sir Douglas Mawson, the Australian explorer of the 'heroic age', was what would now be called a scientific leader, combining the ability to organize and explore with the discipline of scientific work. Like Sir Vivian Fuchs, leader of the first crossing of Antarctica, who resembles him in many ways, he was a Fellow of the Royal Society of London, a rare distinction. Mawson was born in Yorkshire in 1882 and emigrated to Australia with his parents two years later. A graduate of Sydney University, he was appointed lecturer in mineralogy and petrology by the University of Adelaide in 1905 and remained on its staff for the rest of his working life, becoming Professor of Geology and Mineralogy in 1921.

Professor T.W. Edgeworth David, of Sydney University, introduced Mawson to the Antarctic. They both became members of Shackleton's *Nimrod* expedition of 1907–9. Mawson's powers of leadership emerged during this expedition. He returned to Australia and initiated, organized and led the Australasian Antarctic Expedition of 1911-4, one which explored the hitherto unknown lands to the south of Australia. The idea for such an expedition came to him while 'tramping across the trackless snow-fields' towards the Magnetic Pole then situated in that great span of the Antarctic continent between Cape Adare and Drygalski's Gaussberg.

In 1928, the historian J. Gordon Hayes wrote of the expedition:

Sir Douglas Mawson's Expedition, judged by the magnitude both of its scale and of its achievements, was the greatest and most consummate that ever sailed for Antarctica. The expeditions of Scott and Shackleton were great, and Amundsen's venture

Right Sir Douglas Mawson's BANZARE expedition: three cheers for George V after the reading of the royal proclamation, Enderby Land, 13 January 1930. Photograph by Frank Hurley.

was the finest Polar reconnaissance ever made; but each of these must yield the premier position, when fairly compared with Mawson's magnificently conceived and executed scheme of exploration. Sir Douglas Mawson's expedition may be held up as a model for others to copy. Its excellence lay in its design, its scope and its executive success; and it owes its exalted position among the Antarctic expeditions mainly to the fact that it was originated and conducted by scientists of administrative ability, who are the fit and proper persons for such an undertaking. (Antarctica, p. 210).

The publication of *Mawson's Antarctic Diaries* (Sydney , Allen & Unwin, 1988) has provided a much clearer view, not only of Mawson's experiences in the Antarctic, but of the man himself. In the words of the editors, Fred and Eleanor Jacka, these show

the progressive stages in the development of a leader and scientist from a young man of 25, full of new impressions, eager to record the special qualities of existence in Antarctic conditions, often impatient, sometimes intolerant; then the more measured outlook of the man in

charge, conscious of his responsibility for the welfare of others and the requirements of the scientific objectives of the expedition; and finally the eminently experienced explorer and scientist still in his prime, confident in his ability to achieve much more than the limitations of lesser men will permit him . . . Saying that he was an outstanding scientist, a great explorer, a fearless yet responsible leader, a man passionately interested in the world around him – all this, it was felt, was not quite what was wanted. It could be added that he was a man of striking physique – tall, strong, endowed with great energy and stamina – of unquestionable integrity, that he could be obstinate and sentimental.

The Jackas quote the words of a former colleague to provide at least one answer as to Mawson's nature.

His personality was cast in the heroic mould. He had a comprehensive mind, which would have taken him to a foremost place in any profession he might have chosen.

That Mawson entered upon Antarctic exploration both geographical and scientific, for his life's work had enormous importance for the history of the continent. However, the *Diaries* have a universal appeal in showing how a true spirit of the 'heroic age' wrestled with the demonic forces to be found in the 'Home of the Blizzard'.

Balchen. Pioneering flights were also carried out at this time by the Australian, Sir Hubert Wilkins, piloted by A.H. Cheesman, and the American, Lincoln Ellsworth, piloted by C.B. Eielson and H. Hollick-Kenyon.

Meanwhile the *Discovery* (1925–7) and her successor *Discovery II* made a series of major oceanographic voyages (Discovery Investigations) with the aim of

Richard Evelyn Byrd (inset) and 'Little America', Ross Ice Shelf, 1928-30. The radio wires shine bright with hoar frost above the 'loneliest city in the world'.

establishing a scientific basis for the protection of the whale, which was being hunted in thousands by both Norwegian and British whaling companies. The new factory ships were able to operate on the high

THE BARRIER SILENCE

Mount Erebus from Hut Point, March 1911: a watercolour by Dr Edward Wilson.

The Silence was deep with a death like sleep.
  As our sledge runners slid on the snow,
And the fate full fall of our fur-clad feet
  Struck mute like a silent blow
On a questioning 'Hush', as the setting crust
  Shrank shivering over the floe;
And the sledge in its track sent a whisper back
  Which was lost in a white fog-bow.

And this was the thought that the Silence wrought,
  As it scorched and froze us through,
Though secrets hidden are all forbidden
  Till God means man to know,
We might be the men God meant should know
  The heart of the Barrier Snow
In the heat of the sun, and the glow
  And the glare from the glistening floe,
As it scorched and froze us through and through
  With the bite of the drifting snow.

Verses written by Dr Edward Wilson
during the *Terra Nova* expedition
1910–3 for the *South Polar Times*, the
expedition's newspaper or magazine.
The Great Ice Barrier is now known as
the Ross Ice Shelf.

THE FIRST PLANE TO LAND AT THE SOUTH POLE, 31 OCTOBER 1956

During United States 'Operation Deepfreeze II' the ski-equipped Skytrain (pilot, Lt Comdr Conrad S. Shinn, USN; co-pilot, Captain William M. Hawkes, USN) became the first plane to land at the South Pole on 31 October 1956. Rear Admiral Dufek described the outward flight:

We are over the northern rim of the South Polar Plateau. The exposed land beneath us looks like brown moraine. The vertical mountainsides show alternate horizontal layers of dark and light brown. Ahead to the horizon stretches the monotonous flat white of the polar plateau – elevation about 10,000 feet. A few wisps of white cloud appear before us. I hope it is clear at the Pole. Another two hours will give us the answer to our two

years of planning and work. (Diary, quoted on p. 197 of Operation Deepfreeze)

Of the actual landing at the South Pole, he wrote:

Shinn continued to circle, looking for the smoothest spot on which to land. "I'll make three passes," said Shinn, "one at four hundred feet, one at two hundred, and then drag the surface at one hundred feet. If it looks all right I'll come in for a landing." . . . At one hundred feet the surface looked reasonable . . . The plane came in smoothly, touched the surface, bumped a little – but I knew she was under control. She slowed to a stop, but Shinn kept his engines turning over. It was 8.34 p.m., October 31.

Strider opened the door and I stepped out onto the South Polar Plateau. It was like stepping out into a new world. We stood in the center of a sea of snow and ice that extended beyond our vision . . . Bleak and desolate, it was a dead world, devoid of every vestige of life except us. The bitter cold struck me in the face and chest as if I had walked into a heavy swinging door. The temperature was –58° Fahrenheit; 90° below freezing. The wind was just a little under ten knots. I looked at the surface. It was hard and rough, as Hawkes had predicted. The hard sastrugi *extended endlessly in a flat surface to the horizon in all directions . . . (Operation Deepfreeze p. 198–200)*

The plane, with its skis frozen to the surface, was only able to take off again after exploding and then jettisoning all 15 of its JATOs (jet assisted take-off bottles). Three hours later it landed at McMurdo Sound.

seas (out of range of British regulations) because they had stern slipways, up which the whales could be hauled and then rendered down into oil and meat. The first international efforts to regulate the slaughter were also made between the wars, but these measures were not nearly severe enough. Besides exploring the life of the Southern Ocean, Discovery Investigations carried out an immense amount of charting of these unknown waters.

The year 1939 witnessed the outbreak of the Second World War. From 1939 to 1941, the United States Antarctic Service Expedition, led by Rear Admiral Byrd operated from 'Little America III' on the Ross Ice Shelf and from Marguerite Bay, on the west side of the Antarctic Peninsula. Flights and sledge journeys extended Byrd's previous work and that of the British Graham Land Expedition.

In 1943–4, permanent British weather stations were established by the Royal Navy at Port Lockroy and Deception Island under the wartime code name 'Operation Tabarin' in Lesser (or West) Antarctica. From this after the War, the Falkland Islands Dependencies Survey (later the British Antarctic Survey) developed. Now based in Cambridge, this body has maintained a number of stations on or near the Peninsula, from which scientific work and surveys have been carried out ever since. Sir Vivian Fuchs FRS, a past President of the Royal Geographical

Society, was for many years Director of BAS and its predecessor.

The immediate post-war years saw the arrival of the massive United States naval 'Operation High-

Captain Riiser-Larsen in one of the early float-planes used to explore the Antarctic. These planes were carried aboard the Norvegia, *1927–9, shown in the background.*

1955-8 Soviet Antarctic Expedition established permanent bases on the Knox coast, at the Magnetic South Pole and Pole of Inaccessibility.

1956-7 Operation Deepfreeze I established US bases and an air-strip on Ross Ice Shelf.
1957 Operation Deepfreeze II landed supplies at South Pole to establish the

Scott–Amundsen base.
1957-8 International Geophysical Year. 12 nations co-operated to establish 55 scientific research stations on Antarctica.

The Kista Dan (J.L. Lauritzen, Denmark), one of a number of ice-strengthened vessels chartered by the post-war Australian National Antarctic Research Expeditions.

jump' in the southern summer of 1946–7. Rear Admiral Byrd was in overall command. Thirteen vessels (including a submarine) took part, divided into three groups from which numerous flights were made, including Byrd's second to the South Pole on 15 February 1947. 'Little America IV' was established near the Bay of Whales, from which overland journeys were made to the Rockefeller Mountains.

Many other, mainly national, expeditions were sent out to establish permanent stations on the continent and its surrounding islands after the Second World War. Particularly notable are the Australian National Antarctic Research Expeditions (from 1947 onwards) which have accomplished much exploratory and scientific work in the huge expanse of Australian Antarctic Territory. The French have done likewise in Terre Adélie, although, sadly, the construction of a runway for aircraft between the little islands off the coast seems likely to disrupt the penguins and other wild life studied assiduously over many years by French biologists.

Dr P.G. Law was the director of the Antarctic Division and voyage leader of the Australian expeditions from 1949 to 1966. During those years the red-painted, Danish ice-strengthened ships, *Nella Dan*, *Kista Dan*, *Magga Dan* and *Thala Dan*, chartered for the southern summer, became a familiar sight in the port of Melbourne as they docked and departed to relieve the Australian stations on Heard Island and Macquarie Island, and the stations 'Mawson', 'Casey' and 'Davis' on the mainland.

INTERNATIONAL GEOPHYSICAL YEAR

The Norwegian-British-Swedish Antarctic Expedition of 1949–52, led by the Norwegian, John Giaever, was the first international expedition to Antarctica. A base called 'Maudheim' was established on the ice shelf of Dronning Maud Land (the 'Norwegian sector'). Field parties operated from there and from an advance base situated to the south.

It could be said that this successful scientific and survey expedition was a forerunner of the International Geophysical Year of 1957–8, organized and co-ordinated by the International Council of Scientific Unions. The IGY (as it came to be known) was itself the successor to the International Polar Years of 1882–3 and 1932–3, the aim being for simultaneous or complementary scientific observations to be made from stations and by field parties during these special years. Inevitably, on a still relatively unknown continent, exploration and survey also continued and a number of stations have remained in being since the IGY.

Rear Admiral Byrd led his fifth Antarctic expedition in 1955–6 and saw the establishment of 'Little America V' on the Ross Ice Shelf, as part of a big United States IGY expedition known as 'Operation Deepfreeze I'. This task force consisted of seven naval vessels and included three icebreakers. One of these was the USS *Glacier* (8625 tons displacement) making her maiden voyage. Her ten diesel engines of 20,000 horsepower and her top cruising speed of 19 knots (about 35 km/22 miles per hour) were a far cry from the auxiliary sailing ships of less than 50 years before. With her well-strengthened hull, she was designed to break through ice 4.5 metres (15 ft) thick.

The first flights across the Southern Ocean to the Antarctic were made during 'Operation Deepfreeze I'. The aircraft were also used to make nine further long-range exploratory flights from McMurdo Sound across the continent, including one which reached the head of the Weddell Sea.

The following season saw a task force of eleven US naval vessels relieve the two wintering parties of 'Operation Deepfreeze I' and establish four further IGY stations, as part of 'Operation Deepfreeze II', led this time by Rear Admiral George J. Dufek.

The first landings were made at the South Pole where the 'Amundsen-Scott' station was established and supplied entirely from the air. Captain William M. ('Trigger') Hawkes played a leading part in these air operations. In Rear Admiral Dufek's words, he

MEN FOR ANTARCTIC EXPEDITIONS
(THEN AND NOW)

It is interesting to compare the advertisement said to have been placed by Sir Ernest Shackleton for personnel for the *Endurance* expedition, with the words of Sir Vivian Fuchs, past Director of the British Antarctic Survey.

Shackleton: *Men wanted for Hazardous Journey. Small wages, bitter cold, long months of complete darkness, constant danger, safe return doubtful. Honour and recognition in case of success. (Quoted by Roland Huntford,* Shackleton, *p. 365)*

Left *Shackleton's boat, the* James Caird *being hauled ashore on South Georgia, 10 May 1916.* Right *Shackleton and Hurley after the sinking of the* Endurance *in the Weddell Sea, 27 October 1915.*

Fuchs: *In this technological age men have to be chosen for the particular skills needed, but even so more than half the marks they are awarded at an interview are for their personal qualities. The most gifted and hard-working scientist in the country would still be turned down if the Selection Board felt dubious about his ability to live successfully with his companions . . . Despite every care in selection, in the end it is the quality of a man himself which makes him a success or failure . . . They are all ordinary chaps. We do not seek, or find, supermen. To be acceptable a man must behave naturally, without affectations, he must be helpful to others and capable of self-control, and of course it is essential that he is efficient at his particular job.*

(Of ice and men: the story of the British Antarctic Survey, pp. 319-20)

At the South Pole, 19 January 1958: Dr (later Sir) Vivian Fuchs being greeted by Sir Edmund Hillary and Rear Admiral Dufek, USN.

was 'undoubtedly the most experienced and best-qualified aircraft pilot in Antarctic flying in the history of this remote land'. Hawkes was command pilot on one of the two aircraft making the first flight from Christchurch, New Zealand to McMurdo Sound. The command pilot on the first landing at the Pole was Lt Comdr Conrad S. Shinn, USN, with Hawkes as co-pilot.

The IGY stimulated the Russians to return to the Antarctic for the first time since Bellingshausen's circumnavigation of 1819–21. The USSR's Northern Sea Route (the old North-East Passage) north of Siberia had been greatly developed during the 20th century, giving the Soviet Union the world's most numerous and powerful fleet of icebreakers and ice-strengthened ships as well as personnel used to working in the polar regions.

The 1955–6 Soviet IGY expedition, in the icebreakers *Ob* and *Lena* and under the overall command of Dr M.M. Somov, established 'Mirnyy'

station on the coast of Queen Mary Land and two others inland. The following season, under the leadership of Dr A.F. Treshnikov, progress was made towards the setting up of 'Vostok' and 'Sovetskaya' further inland, the first near to the magnetic pole and the second about 650 km (400 miles) short of the 'Pole of Inaccessibility', where 'Sovetskaya' should have been established. The two icebreakers continued their programme of oceanographic observations in the Southern Ocean, begun the previous year.

All the IGY nations (Argentina, Australia, Belgium, Chile, France, Japan, New Zealand, Norway, South Africa, United Kingdom, United States and the USSR) carried out meteorological and other scientific work during this specially designated period – and many were to continue for years, indeed even decades, after it.

This spirit of peaceful co-operation was to form the basis of the Antarctic Treaty, which came into

THE SCOTT POLAR RESEARCH INSTITUTE

The idea of establishing a polar institute is said to have occurred to two young members of Scott's Last Expedition when they were snowed up in a tent during a blizzard. The impetus for its founding came when these men, Debenham and Priestley, began writing the scientific reports of the expedition. They found that the experience and knowledge gained during earlier expeditions had been largely dissipated, because there was no repository for the records.

Since its foundation in 1925, the SPRI has become such a place of deposit for books, periodicals, diaries, other MSS, clothing, equipment, expedition reports, photographs, pictures, maps and charts. Now a department of Cambridge University, its staff over the years has not only published the journal *Polar Record*, but has produced sea ice atlases, historical studies, lists of expeditions, bibliographies, editions of explorers' diaries and scientific results thus making material available worldwide.

The building which houses the Institute was opened in 1934. Founded as a memorial to Captain Scott, the inscription on the outside of

the building reads QUAESIVIT ARCANA POLI VIDET DEI, which can be translated as 'He sought the secrets of the Pole and now sees those of God'. The Institute has always had an international character, assisting scholars, expedition members and enquirers from many lands. One of the most remarkable of its recent scientific

H.G. Ponting, whose photographs provide a fine visual record of Scott's last expedition. His work shows outstanding technical and artistic ability in extremely difficult conditions.

studies has been the topography of the land now covered by the immensely thick Antarctic ice sheet.

relief ship sank raised controversy over the role of private expeditions in the Antarctic. **1986-7** Monica Kristensen's 90° glacio-logical expedition used dogs to follow

Amundsen's route but had to turn back ten days short of the Pole to reach their support ship.

1990 International Trans-Antarctica

Expedition crossed Antarctica at its widest point from tip of the Antarctic Peninsula to the Soviet base at Mirnyy, a journey of 6500 km (4000 miles) using dogs.

force in June 1961, having been signed by all twelve nations in December 1959.

TRANS-ANTARCTIC EXPEDITION 1955-8

The first overland crossing of the continent was made by Dr (later Sir) Vivian Fuchs leading the British Commonwealth Trans-Antarctic Expedition of 1955–8. The crossing party started from the head of the Weddell Sea (Filchner Ice Shelf) on 24 November 1957 and continued via the Amundsen-Scott station at the South Pole to the Ross Sea. They arrived at New Zealand's 'Scott Base' on 2 March 1958 to a tremendous welcome and much public attention after travelling 3475 km (2150 miles), thus realizing Shackleton's dream of forty years earlier – the Imperial Trans-Antarctic Expedition of 1914–6.

The Fuchs expedition used light aircraft for reconnaissance and supply, but made the actual crossing, between 24 November 1957 and 2 March 1958, by large yellow tracked vehicles called 'sno-cats', plus one dog sledge team. Seismic and other observations were carried out *en route*. A single-engined Otter aircraft, piloted by Squadron Leader J.H. Lewis, RAF, flew across the continent from Weddell Sea to Ross Sea on 6 January 1958.

Meanwhile the New Zealand support party, led by Sir Edmund Hillary, the conqueror of Everest, pioneered the route from the Ross Sea to South Pole,

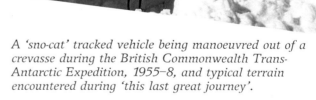

A 'sno-cat' tracked vehicle being manoeuvred out of a crevasse during the British Commonwealth Trans-Antarctic Expedition, 1955–8, and typical terrain encountered during 'this last great journey'.

driving Massey Ferguson tractors and arriving at the South Pole on 5 January 1958. The expedition's ships were the *Theron* (Captain H. Marø), the *Magga Dan* (Captain H.C. Petersen) and HMNZS *Endeavour* (Commander H. Kirkwood, RN).

Sir Edmund Hillary's book about this 'last great journey' was aptly named, *No Latitude for Error*.

OCEANOGRAPHY

BOUNDLESS OCEAN, UNFATHOMED SEAS

The ocean deeps never attracted explorers in the way that far-off lands did. Inaccessible to man, they held no wondrous kingdoms, no fabled mines of gold or gems. Neither warring tribes nor pagans ripe for conversion to the true faith inhabited their depths. The oceans certainly had a place in most early mythologies – Plato spoke of the city of Atlantis, submerged 9000 years previously for having made war against Athens – and they were home to a strange and wonderful range of monsters, but these, being generally considered hostile to mankind, were best left undisturbed. They were used emerging from the water, to decorate the empty spaces on early maps, where like Swift's 'elephants in places of towns' marching across the uncharted regions of the continents, they served to lead the eye towards the distant coastline.

In medieval and renaissance times, concepts of the oceans were shaped by two lines of philosophical thought. One drew largely on Old Testament writing, where a flat Earth, its continents separated by the Red Sea and Persian Gulf, and the Mediterranean, was bounded by the ever-flowing world ocean. The other, based on rational argument, favoured a spherical Earth with water filling the hollows, an idea held by many of the Classical Greek philosophers and never entirely lost during the Dark Ages.

When the Portuguese navigators ventured along the African coast, past the Equator and into the Southern Hemisphere, the flat Earth theory passed

The nature of coral mystified scientists until the 18th century when the 'flowers' were correctly identified as colonial animals living in a stony growth.

Sounding and dredging equipment on HMS Porcupine, *1868-70, was powered by a donkey engine below deck.*

into oblivion. Yet centuries more would pass before cartographers could be confident that they knew exactly how large the Earth was, and what proportion of its surface was covered by water.

Rational thinkers, from Classical Greece onwards, believed that nature obeyed certain laws. Wise men might therefore hope to discover how the oceans formed, what shape their basins were, why the water was salty, what caused the waves and tides and the currents that were seen to flow through the Bosphorus and Strait of Gibraltar. Many early ideas were subsequently attributed to Aristotle, whose works, together with those of Pliny, were required reading for scholars throughout the Middle Ages. Neither man had been outside the Mediterranean, beyond whose shores they relied on hearsay or imagination. Aristotle knew that oceans occupied depressions on the globe, but found it hard to account for their saltiness. He examined the marine creatures brought ashore by Greek fishermen and was the first to classify them into those with blood and those without – in modern terms, vertebrates and invertebrates.

In the 17th century new attitudes towards the natural world led to the formation of the Royal Society in London and similar academies in other European cities. Experiment and observation replaced speculation. When preparing his *Tracts* about the globe, published in 1671, the Hon. Robert Boyle (1627–91) tried to establish if the sea was frozen at the bottom, being so far from the Sun's rays, or hot, being so close to the subterranean fires that erupted through volcanoes. He wondered whether the sea became deeper the further one went out from the shore; if so, how could he account for mid-ocean islands? Boyle questioned men who dived on wrecks, but they knew nothing of the deep sea. This would have to be explored by means of apparatus, sent down on the seaman's hemp line. Indeed, for almost three centuries underwater exploration was carried out at the end of a very long line, the results dependent on what technical progress had been

In this map of 1539, monstrous creatures emerge from the uncharted depths of the Norwegian Sea to attack passing ships.

made. The scientists were often in doubt about the records brought back by their instruments and apparatus because they simply did not know what to expect.

Seamen regularly sounded to 50 fathoms (90 metres, 300 ft) with the ship under way, and greater depths were possible when the ship was stationary. The sounding was confirmed if sediments came up on the dab of tallow put on the base of the lead. The line was hauled in with great effort against the

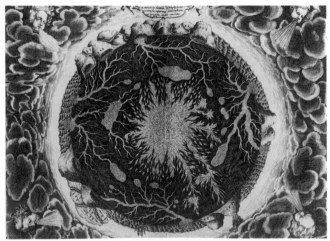

Athanasius Kircher, in his Mundus Subterraneus *of 1665, imagined the world's oceans to be interconnected by subterranean channels.*

friction of the water and if it broke, both lead and line were lost.

When the Royal Society turned its attention to the exploration of the sea, it had first to provide suitable apparatus, and the task of designing various instruments fell to its Curator of Experiments, Robert Hooke (1635–1703). He tested these in the Thames estuary. The Royal Society subsequently recommended their use in its *Directions for Seamen bound for Voyages*, published in 1662. Ships' captains were requested to investigate the deep sea and report their findings to the Society. But 17th-century technology was not equal to the demands of underwater work, and such random methods with unsuitable wooden apparatus were unproductive.

SUBMARINE EXPLORATION ANSWERS GEOGRAPHICAL QUESTIONS

The first planned underwater exploration was carried out along the Mediterranean coast of France by Count Louis-Ferdinand Marsigli (1658–1730) in 1706–8. Marsigli was an Italian nobleman who had been a military surveyor for Emperor Leopold of Austria, fighting the Turks in eastern Europe. Between campaigns he wrote a history and geography of the Danube region. He came to believe in the essential unity of geological structure and went to Montpellier in 1706 in order to confirm his ideas by looking at the geology of coasts and the adjacent seabed.

As Marsigli examined the offshore sediments he discovered curious growths, which are now known to be invertebrates: sponges, corals and bryozoa. For centuries sponges and coral had been gathered and sold dry, but Marsigli had never seen them in their natural habitat and at first he thought they were minerals that grew like the stalactites he had found in caverns.

Members of Montpellier's Académie des Sciences were also curious about the nature of coral, which was a valuable harvest for fishermen off the rocky Provençal coast, but disputed Marsigli's views. To resolve the matter, Marsigli undertook a comprehensive survey of the coast where he overcame the limitations of his simple apparatus by methodically working out from land. However, his examination of the invertebrates resulted in his thinking that they were marine plants, a view discarded later in the 18th century when the 'flowers' of coral were identified as colonial animals living in a stony growth of their own making.

MARSIGLI AND THE FIRST BOOK OF THE SEA

The first detailed study of the Mediterranean coasts of Provence and Languedoc was made by Louis-Ferdinand Marsigli in 1706–8. As he did not have his own ship, he went out with the local coral fishermen who manoeuvred their traditional scoops and nets into the underwater caverns and rocky ledges where the coral was believed to grow upside-down. Marsigli collected corals and whatever else came up in the nets, taking them home to dissect and examine under his microscope and analyse, by the primitive methods then available. One day he put a branch of coral in a bucket of water and saw its 'flowers' emerge, which led him into the error of believing that they were marine plants.

His soundings revealed the slope of the seabed, steep and rocky off the Provençal coast, flat and sandy off Languedoc. He plotted the distribution of rocks, sand and gravel; he collected samples of seawater, and discovered occasional underwater fresh springs. Curious to know if the deep water warmed in summer, Marsigli occasionally lowered his thermometer into the depths. But in 1707, thus engaged and far from land, his fishing boat was surprised by Algerian pirates and in the haste to haul up and make for home, Marsigli's thermometer was broken. In those days, no two thermometers were the same, so the project had to be abandoned.

Marsigli wrote up his findings in his *Histoire Physique de la Mer* which was the first book devoted entirely to the sea. Here he described the structure and sediments of the sea's basin, the nature of its water, its waves, tides and currents, and its 'marine plants'. The manuscript languished for years, until Marsigli went to Amsterdam where he arranged for its publication, with detailed maps and lavishly illustrated, in 1725.

Marsigli drew the coral structure, mapped the seabed where it grew, and sketched the nets used to fish it up.

Another century passed before the British Admiralty realized that marine science might benefit Arctic exploration. John Ross, sailing into Davis Strait in 1818 on his search for the North-West Passage, hoped to distinguish between rivers and seaways by measuring the temperature and salinity of the water beneath the surface ice meltwater. Estuarine deep water would be cold but fresh, that of marine channels would be slightly warmer and saline. Such measurements could be important aids to exploration where ice and snow masked the landscape, where visibility was hampered by fogs and the magnetic compass erratic. The Admiralty was optimistic of success, for the ships had been issued with Six's deep-sea thermometer and Massey's sounder, both invented some years previously.

Beyond home waters, ships' captains relied on their charts to indicate the way into unfamiliar harbours, to warn of dangerous submerged rocks and sandbanks, and to identify good 'holding ground' for safe anchorage. Soundings were noted on charts from the 16th century onwards. Chart-publishing was a private venture in Britain until the Hydrographic Office was established in 1795 to satisfy the Royal Navy's need for charts of every sea, thus beginning the continuous global charting which continues to the present day.

The best hydrographic charts offered a great deal of information about the ocean over the continental shelves. Near-shore underwater features were located by triangulation, and lines of closely spaced soundings gave a good picture of the nature of bottom

334-323 BC Aristotle wrote about the origin of the sea in his *Meteorologica*.
320 BC Alexander the Great reported tidal movements in the Indian Ocean. Used an underwater observation chamber.
c.310 BC Pytheas was the first to record the relationship between the tides and moon after circumnavigating Britain.
AD 23-79 Pliny the Elder's 37-volume *Historia Naturalis* included descriptions of the lunitidal interval.
AD 730 Venerable Bede improved on Pliny's

sediments. Further out to sea charting was far more arduous. Captain Robert Wauchope reported on a sounding that he had made in 1816 when he attached a water-sampler to 1435 fathoms (2624 metres/8610 ft) of rope, weighted by seven cannon-shot spaced down the line and with a 33 kg (72 lb) sinker. The rope itself was 6.3 cm (2½ inches) thick, increasing to 8.9 cm (3½ inches) near the surface. It took 22 minutes to veer this cumbersome assembly overboard and then the efforts of 100 men working the capstan for 1 hour 20 minutes to haul it in, due to the great friction between rope and water. Consequently such soundings were seldom made, and were judged worthy of report.

Soundings were made far apart and their location relied on the navigator's accurate observation of his position at the time. Charts also recorded isolated rocks and reefs that had been reported by ships' captains on earlier voyages but whose existence was doubtful. These 'vigias', as they were called, might be only icebergs or clumps of weed, glimpsed through fog or driving rain, but they remained on the charts, as a precaution, until modern sounding techniques confirmed their existence or they could finally be erased.

French and Russian expeditions were also active during the early 19th century. The Russian ships *Rurick* (1815-8) and *Predpriatie* (1823-6) left their Baltic home port and sailed round the world to Russia's Pacific settlements. Both captains sounded and investigated the deep water along their routes. French ships visited the Pacific and nosed down towards the Antarctic continent. Jules Dumont d'Urville explored and botanized on his two cruises in *Astrolabe* (1826-9 and 1837-42) but did not neglect the water beneath his keel; Abel Dupetit-Thouars in *Vénus* (1836-9) was on a political mission to help and protect French whalers in the Pacific but was also ordered to spend some time on hydrographic work as his route led through regions seldom visited by naval ships.

Apart from official reports, illustrated books were published about many of these expeditions, describing the excitements and achievements of the voyage for

Philippe Bauche's map of the Channel, 1752, an early example of the use of submarine contours (isobaths).

John Ross had this waterbottle and 'clamm', or grab, made on board his ship in 1818.

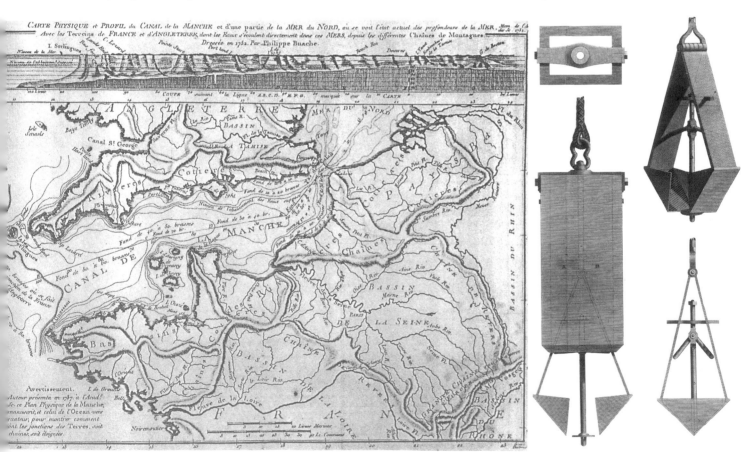

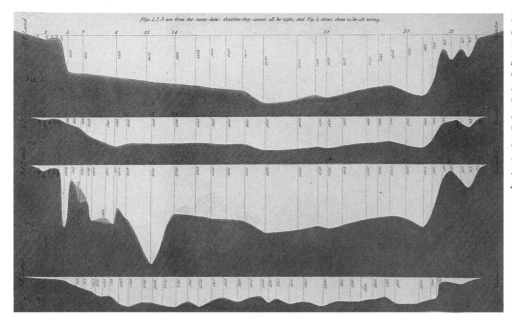

Four different profiles were obtained on the surveys for the first Atlantic cable, due in part to defective apparatus and poor position-finding. Fig 1, Arctic's soundings by Chart No. 1 Fig 2, Arctic's soundings by Chart No. 2 Fig 3, Arctic's soundings by her Abstract Log. Fig 4, Cyclops's soundings by Admiralty Chart.

popular readership. The underwater discoveries so confidently paraded, however, were still relying on instruments and techniques whose limitations were not always recognized.

Lt Matthew Fontaine Maury (1806–73), head of the US Depot of Charts and Instruments (later the US Naval Observatory) from 1842–61, enlisted the help of his ships' captains to compile his charts of surface currents and winds, and asked them to make deep soundings. Maury was suspicious of many of the great depths reported and hoped that the detaching-weight sounder invented by his assistant John Brooke would give more reliable results. The chart of the Atlantic which Maury published in his *Physical Geography of the Sea*, 1855, was based on relatively few soundings and made him say, 'There is at the bottom of this sea, between Cape Race in Newfoundland and Cape Clear in Ireland, a remarkable steppe which is already known as the telegraphic plateau . . . It is proposed to carry the wires along this plateau . . . the great-circle route is 1600 miles [2575 km] and the sea along the route probably nowhere more than 10,000 ft [3050 metres] deep.'

Maury's 'plateau' had a short life; some of his soundings were simply erroneous. None had registered the deeper basins while others had landed on the rocky mid-ocean ridge, a hazard rather than a haven for any cable. Maury's *Physical Geography* was influential but some of his statements owed more to his religious beliefs than to reality. The American Civil War (1861–5) delayed progress in

deep-sea exploration but US surveyors soon caught up and they had taken a leading position by the third quarter of the 19th century.

Other ancient concepts of the sea died hard. Professor Charles Wyville Thomson (1830–82), later to become one of the most famous marine biologists, recounted, 'There was a curious popular notion, in which I well remember sharing when a boy, that, in going down, the sea-water became gradually under the pressure heavier and heavier, and that all the loose things in the sea floated at different levels, according to their specific weight: skeletons of men, anchors and shot and cannon, and last of all broad gold pieces wrecked in the loss of many a galleon on the Spanish Main . . . beneath which there lay all the depth of clear still water, which was heavier than molten gold.'

EXPLORATION FOR COMMERCIAL NEEDS

A true three-dimensional underwater landscape took shape during the second half of the 19th century, following the invention of telegraphy. From modest beginnings in the 1840s, cable networks were extended until the American and European cable companies were talking about a transatlantic link. The advent of the steam-engine made this a feasible project. Steamships could hold to a predetermined course against wind and weather while their donkey-engines drove the heavy cable-handling gear. But the initial step was to obtain an accurate profile of the sea floor, so that sufficient cable could be manufactured, and

1725 Marsigli published *Histoire Physique de la Mer*, the first oceanographic treatise.
1775 Franklin used a thermometer to locate and chart the Gulf Stream, so speeding

future transatlantic voyages.
1795 Hydrographic Office established by Royal Navy to chart the world's oceans.
1798 Count Rumford's *Of the propagation*

of Heat in Fluids provided the basis for modern models of ocean circulation.
1803 Humboldt realized the effect of the Peru current on the climate of South

then paid out from the ship at a rate that allowed it to sink through several kilometres of water and come to rest evenly on the bottom.

The first sounding survey was made by Lt Berryman in USS *Arctic* in the summer of 1856, with the new Brooke sounders. Berryman worked across the

Atlantic and back but produced two very different profiles. The following year Lt Dayman repeated the exercise in HMS *Cyclops*. His instructions were to sound closely in water less than 100 fathoms (180 metres/600 ft), every 10 miles (16 km) until deep water was reached, then every 40 or 50 miles (65 or

EARLY INSTRUMENTS

HOOKE'S SOUNDER

Robert Hooke's sounder, invented in 1667, consisted of a wooden ball coupled by a wire spring to a stone or iron sinker. Dropped overboard, it sank to the bottom where the spring opened, the sinker fell off, and the ball returned to the surface. Hooke tested his sounder in water of known depth to find its rate of travel, and believed that this rate would hold for deeper soundings. In later years he proposed adding a pressure-measuring device, or a geared mechanism to register the distance travelled. Hooke's ideas were far ahead of the technology of his day.

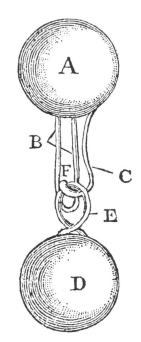

SIX'S DEEP-SEA THERMOMETER

James Six (1731–93) of Canterbury, Kent, was interested in scientific matters and he spent several years perfecting a self-registering thermometer for weather observations before modifying one for use under water, *c.* 1780. He wrote about the air thermometer in 1782, and described the marine thermometer in his book published posthumously in 1794. Both thermometers became popular; the first known use of Six's marine thermometer was in 1803–6, this and other instruments having been bought in London for the Russian circumnavigation in *Neva* and *Nadezhda*.

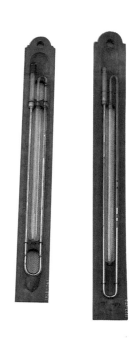

MASSEY'S WAYWISER SOUNDER

Edward Massey came from a family of Staffordshire watchmakers. First patented in 1802, his waywiser sounders owed their design to ships' logs but registered depth rather than horizontal distance travelled. Sinking through the water, the vanes turned a series of counting-wheels. The mechanism was slipped out of gear by the action of hauling it up, leaving the pointer to show what Massey claimed was a true vertical depth. Improved versions of these sounders were popular for the next fifty years.

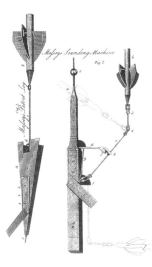

BROOKE'S DETACHING-WEIGHT SOUNDER

John Brooke made his first sounder, *c.* 1855, by hanging a pierced cannon-ball on a wire harness hooked to a rod. On impact with the seabed, the harness and ball were thrown off, leaving the light rod to be hauled up, with a little sediment in its hollow end. In later years Brooke's sounder was modified according to the depth and the nature of the bottom. A hollow tube worked best on fine sediments, whilst snapper-jaws were fitted for sounding over gravelly bottoms.

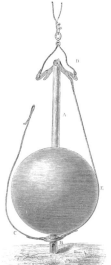

America's west coast.
1818 Ross used salinity measurements to distinguish between river and sea routes to search for the North-West Passage.

1823-6 Lenz on Kotzebue's Russian circumnavigation measured salinity changes and specific gravities at great depths.
1825 James adapted Deane's smoke helmet

to develop the SCUBA.
1831-6 Darwin on voyage of the *Beagle* studied structure of oceanic islands and the origins of coral reefs.

THE GULF STREAM

In the days of sail, the first ship home got the best price for her cargo. Captains of whalers and ships on regular Atlantic passage knew that a great current out of the Gulf of Florida shortened the journey time to Europe. On the return journey, captains who could avoid this current entered port days ahead of their less knowledgeable brethren. This trade secret was to be revealed by the enquiries of hydrographers such as de Brahm and scientifically minded passengers such as Franklin.

William Gerard de Brahm (1718–99), Surveyor General for the Florida region and its adjacent coastline, was the first to explore the Gulf Stream from Florida to beyond the Newfoundland Banks. He marked it on his chart of 1765, and publicized his findings on both sides of the Atlantic.

Benjamin Franklin (1706–90) noted the marked change in water colour and weed content when his ship entered the warm current. He persuaded his seafaring cousin Timothy Folger to mark the course, dimensions and velocity of the Gulf

Stream on a chart of the period, with advice to mariners.

Later editions of this chart, published in London and Paris under Franklin's name, became widely known, whilst Folger and de Brahm have been forgotten.

Like all rivers, the Gulf Stream has depth as well as breadth. Yet survey ships were borne along by the very current they sought to measure until 1876, when Lt John Pillsbury USN devised a method of anchoring in deep water, and lowered a heavy current meter into each level of the stream far below his keel.

Modern survey ships drop neutrally buoyant floats with transmitters attached into each level of the Gulf Stream, to rise and fall with changing temperature and salinity, and travel with the current, transmitting their position. Thermal imaging from satellites shows up the contrast between warm and cool surface water. Along its western flank, the stream flows at 100 km (60 miles) or more per day. Meanders develop on the ocean side, breaking off in eddies that spin out into the open water. Known about for many years, these eddies are now seen as vital elements of oceanic fronts: boundaries between

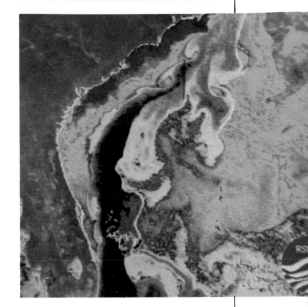

Warm water swirling north in the Gulf Stream, imaged by a heat-sensing radiometer on board a satellite.

water masses of differing qualities, similar to the atmospheric fronts of our daily weather systems. Changes in the spread of warm and cold water have direct if delayed effects on the fisheries and on Europe's climate.

80 km) until he approached the Newfoundland shore. Dayman took more care than Berryman over his own position fixes at the time of each sounding, since the laying ships would have to follow his track. He also used a variety of sounders, hoping in this way to reduce errors caused by defective apparatus.

After several false starts, the transatlantic cable was laid and functioning. Meanwhile the Admiralty was sounding other cable routes through the Mediterranean Sea and along the Red Sea to India. Cables linked Britain to its offshore islands and to Europe and Scandinavia; they crossed the Mediterranean from France to North Africa. In 1870 the British government nationalized the inland telegraph network, liberating a flood of capital which the commercial companies spent on purpose-built ships to survey and lay cables.

Time was money; fast yet reliable surveys were essential and new apparatus was therefore urgently needed. Sir William Thomson (1824–1907), better known as Lord Kelvin, Professor of Natural Philosophy at Glasgow University, telegraph engineer and

consultant, answered this need by inventing the wire sounding machine (among many other devices). Previous attempts to sound with wire had failed because it had been impossible to manufacture long runs of strong wire. Thomson succeeded, because recent progress in wire-drawing technology had given him the quality of wire that he wanted.

Cable engineers devised a range of sampling tubes for their own or Kelvin's sounding machines and, thus equipped, could complete each operation in minutes rather than hours, the ship being able to steam to the next position while the wire was reeled in since the friction between wire and water was negligible. If a cable broke or became faulty, repair ships searched for the cable by steaming back and forth over its position until they hooked it. As these 'grappling runs' were charted, wide areas of seabed topography were delineated, and the same process took place when cables were duplicated. The cables running along tropical coasts were laid beyond the continental shelf in cold water where they were undisturbed by fishermen or ships' anchors. Thus the continental slopes, and the canyons that scored through their flanks opposite the major river mouths, were added to the list of submarine topographical features.

The cable engineers sounded the approaches to volcanic islands carefully, seeking the safest place to bring the cables ashore. This work revealed, for the first time, the true structure of these rocky mid-ocean peaks. The cable ships also explored the deep-water shoals. Some of these had been known since the 18th century, by the sudden chill in the surface water caused by deep cold water rising up their flanks. They could then be mapped, one more element in an underwater landscape that was proving to be as diverse as any on dry land. The abyss was not a smooth basin carpeted with mud, but contained mountains and valleys, scarps and plains, volcanoes and freshwater springs, still water and swift-flowing currents, each unit with its distinctive ground cover of bare rock, gravel, shells or clay.

Before long it was apparent that the seabed was far more dynamic than had been supposed: cables were frayed by strong currents moving gravel across them, or broken by landslips on the continental rises. A great debate ensued as to whether the currents were driven by differences in the density of water-masses, or by surface winds or some other force. Much more information had to be gathered before a density-driven ocean circulation system was accepted. On the global scale, dense cold polar water sinks and drifts slowly towards the Equator, where it rises, warms, and returns towards the Pole. Regional circulation systems form where global currents are deflected, for example by a rise in the seabed. The resulting pattern is complex and is still being studied.

LIFE IN THE DEPTHS

The oceans contain the largest ecological regime on this planet. It is a truly three-dimensional world and presents few barriers to the individual ecosystems. Marine life ranges in size from microscopic bacteria to the giant whales and squid. There are some plants and animals closely related to those living on dry land; there are also free-floating plants and whole classes of animals that spend their life anchored to the seabed. The majority of fish, reptiles and mammals that inhabit the sea live close to the surface, sustained by a food chain that begins with green plants (phytoplankton) growing in the sunlit layer. Until recently, naturalists knew nothing of those species which spent their lives in the utter blackness of the abyss.

Marine plants and animals are collected as food, as objects of biological study, and for the sake of their rarity and value – pearls, red coral and murex shells have been prized since prehistoric times. The Mediterranean coral fishery had been regulated since the 16th century. The catch was limited and certain dredges which harmed the growing coral were banned. These curious stony growths had no parallel ashore and naturalists puzzled over their identity. Marsigli believed that they were plants; later in the 18th century two French naturalists, Jean-André Peyssonnel and Bernard de Jussieu, correctly transferred coral to the animal kingdom.

Likewise in cold northern waters zoologists brought ashore many new and interesting creatures for study. Dredging the open sea, however, was no weekend pastime for the amateur naturalist. A powerful ship was needed to tow a heavy dredge over the seabed and then haul it up. The few experiments made in the early 19th century were tantalizingly inconclusive – the creatures might have been captured anywhere between the surface and the seabed. It was not known how these organisms could thrive in perpetual darkness.

Edward Forbes (1815–54) joined HMS *Beacon* in the Aegean where he found that the number of species and their populations decreased between the surface and 300 fathoms (550 metres, 1800 ft) below which he supposed that life was absent. By this time many starfish and other bottom-dwelling creatures

Shells, sponges and bryozoa encrust this section of cable pulled up from the darkness of the deep Mediterranean.

enable compilation of navigational charts of the Atlantic and Pacific.
1854-5 Maury published first bathymetrical charts of the North Atlantic and his *Physical*

Geography of the Sea.
1854-6 Wallace described the Wallace line, biotic variations on what are now known to be on separate tectonic plates.

1856-7 Berryman and Dayman surveyed route of transatlantic telegraph cable.
1869-70 The Royal Society used naval vessels for scientific dredges of North Atlantic.

had been brought up clasped to the sounding line, but naturalists were reluctant to admit the evidence.

In 1860 some 65 km (40 miles) of a telegraph cable that had been laid across the Mediterranean three years previously was pulled up for repair. Parts of this cable had lain in the blackness of water up to 1200 fathoms (2200 metres, 7200 ft) deep, yet this had not prevented shells, corals and other organisms from growing to maturity on it. Between 1868 and 1870 HMS *Lightning* and HMS *Porcupine* were sent to dredge in the North Atlantic. Varied and abundant life was found throughout the expedition, and the dredge reached some 650 fathoms (1190 metres, 3900 ft) in regions of great pressure and complete darkness. Another important fact emerged: the deep-water temperature was not uniform. The scientists found distinct bodies of water in slow movement, each contributing to a grand oceanic circulation, and each with a characteristic fauna.

Other nations were also fitting out major expeditions to investigate the deep sea. The Austro-Hungarian *Novara* went round the world in 1857–9. *Novara*'s exploration programme was modest but, more importantly, the results were published in 24 volumes by 1862, thereby making all the data collected available to the scientific community. The success of the HMS *Lightning* and HMS *Porcupine* cruises encouraged British scientists to press for a comprehensive survey of the major oceans. The Admiralty agreed to refit HMS *Challenger* and she sailed in December 1872, Captain G.S. Nares in command, with five scientific staff under Professor Charles Wyville Thomson. She returned in May 1876 having passed through all except the Arctic regions, working in the open ocean, visiting coral reefs and volcanic islands, and skirting the permanent ice of Antarctica.

Challenger's findings established a range of values for the world's oceans. The collections were sent to specialists at home and abroad and their reports came out in a series of 50 volumes published between 1880 and 1895. The major scientific circumnavigations of the 1870s yielded vast quantities of data which took years to digest. With the growing interest in the oceans as a dynamic system, like the atmosphere, it made more sense to study its changes with time. Prince Albert I of Monaco (1848–1920) led the way, returning to survey particular areas every year, studying the variations in the warm Atlantic drift, and seeing how these factors affected the fish stock and their migrations. Then a network of shore biological stations backed by survey ships was established

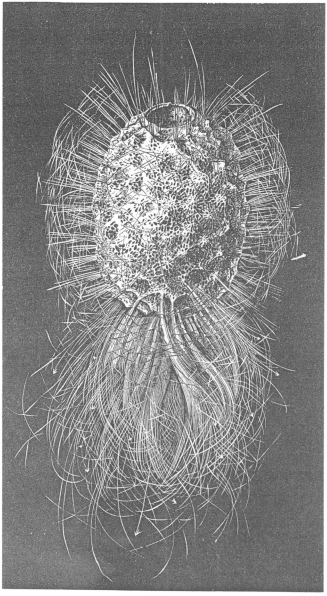

This delicate sponge, Rossella velata, *was dredged by* HMS Porcupine *from 650 fathoms (1190 metres/3900 ft) in the Strait of Gibraltar in August 1870.*

in Germany; Swedish biologists made long-term observations of the Baltic, and the famous Naples Zoological Station was founded and offered its facilities to visiting scientists of all nationalities.

Zoologists began to investigate the whole chain of life in the sea, beginning with the complex inorganic molecules that, with sunlight, sustained microscopic plant life – the 'grass of the sea' – on which minute herbivores grazed before they were in turn eaten. This stratum of floating marine life had no identity (Scoresby had spoken of the 'animalcules') until 1887 when Hensen coined the term 'plankton' to describe

HMS CHALLENGER

Navigating Sub-Lt Herbert Swire admirably introduced his ship and her programme in his letters home to his family:

The Challenger is a main deck corvette . . . fitted up with cabins, laboratories and every convenience for a scientific cruise on an extended scale. She is commanded by Captain Nares, a surveying officer of great experience, and besides her other regular officers she carries several naval surveyors and a civilian scientific staff consisting of Professor Thomson and five assistants, and a corporal of engineers who is a good photographer and is supplied with every appliance of his art. The Admiralty and Royal Society have fitted the ship with endless machines to further the objects for which this expedition has been set on foot, which consist mainly of important sounding and dredging operations to ascertain facts connected with organic life in the great depths of the oceans, and to thoroughly investigate matters connected with the oceanic drifts and currents; and we are to visit in succession almost every navigable part of the globe, making a complete circuit of the world and discovering no end of curious and scientific things.

The route taken by HMS Challenger on her voyage of scientific discovery 1872–76.

They set sail in December 1872 and after a rough passage into the Atlantic, began the routine of getting up steam every 300 km (200 miles) to sound and dredge, then banking down the fires and sailing another 300 km (200 miles) to repeat the operation. Sub-Lt Swire soon tired of this and filled his diary with the new and fascinating places and people that he met in the years before HMS *Challenger* dropped anchor once more in her home port in May 1876.

HMS *Challenger* sailed in all 110,870 km (68,890 miles); she obtained 492 soundings, and made 133 dredgings and 151 trawls. Not all the 'endless machines' gave good results, although the new reversing thermometer that was invented in 1874, of which some examples were sent out to the ship, heralded a new era in underwater temperature measurement. But shortage of time and the distance between stations often prevented suspect findings being checked, some of which were probably due to defective apparatus.

The scientists on board had not expected to find that globigerina ooze, debris of tiny shells of floating organisms, gave way in deeper parts to fine clays derived from land, and deposits made up of glassy radiolarian skeletons. Volcanic fragments were identifiable in all the sediments. In the Pacific strange manganese nodules

came up from the deep ocean floor south of Japan. After twice crossing the Atlantic, the naturalists realized that a central range of mountains divided it into an eastern and a western province, each with distinct water masses and fauna. It was another glimpse of the mid-ocean ridge. Marine biologists still consult the 'Challenger Reports' for their detailed information and beautiful illustrations.

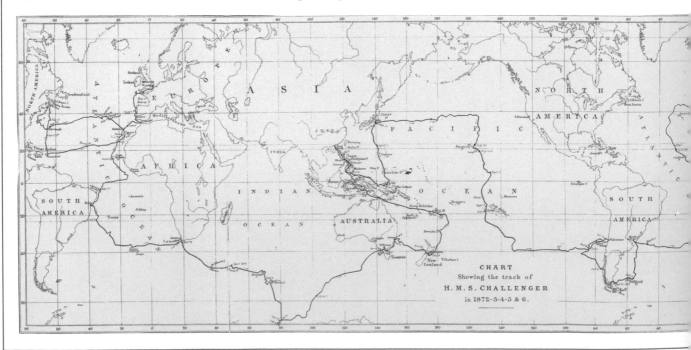

CHART
Showing the track of
H. M. S. CHALLENGER
in 1872-3-4-5 & 6.

HMS Challenger *in a watercolour from a personal diary.*

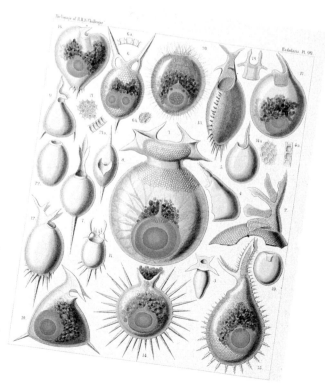

A series of radiolarians, named after Challenger *and her scientists, illustrated in the* Challenger Reports.

it. Fish depended ultimately on plankton and by the late 19th century the governments of Scandinavia, Germany and Britain were becoming worried about the declining catches of fish.

Even as *Challenger's* radiolaria (from the plankton) were sitting in Ernst Haeckel's laboratory in Jena awaiting his attention, that great zoologist was organizing the Plankton Expedition of 1889 which criss-crossed the Atlantic sampling and comparing plankton from tropical and temperate waters. But plankton and fish migrated across national boundaries. Many species of fish that fed in the waters of one country laid their eggs in another, and were caught when mature in the waters of a third. International cooperation was essential if stocks were to be managed and breeding grounds protected to the benefit of all.

The maritime nations of northern Europe came together and in 1902 set up the International Commission for the Exploration of the Sea (ICES). Each participating nation sent fisheries' research vessels to its designated areas four times a year. They employed standard apparatus, designed in ICES' laboratory, and their results were published rapidly and to an agreed format.

NEW EXPLORATION TECHNIQUES

Lord Kelvin sent one of his wire sounding machines to Washington DC where it was soon improved for use in US Navy surveying ships working in the Atlantic and Pacific Oceans during the last quarter of the 19th century. USS *Tuscarora* sounded for a cable between California and Japan in 1874. Meanwhile the German SS *Gazelle* made a circumnavigation which brought her into the Pacific in the same year, 1875, as HMS *Challenger*.

In 1895 HMS *Penguin* made several deep soundings by wire in excess of 5000 fathoms (9150 metres, 30,000 ft) during surveys for the planned British trans-Pacific cable. Taken with other great depths reported by HMS *Challenger* and USS *Tuscarora* some years earlier, these marked out a new feature: deep-sea trenches rifting the ocean floor in a series of arcs parallel to the coast. The early years of the 20th century saw cables laid from San Francisco to Honolulu and Guam, from where branches ran to Manila and Bonin. British interests were served by cables from Vancouver via Fanning Island, Suva and Norfolk Island to New Zealand.

Despite this increasing activity, prior to the First World War there was on average one sounding per

THE OCEANOGRAPHER PRINCE

Prince Albert I of Monaco acquired his schooner *Hirondelle* in 1873 and by 1875 had decided to devote his life to marine science, justifiably so, as many of his subjects were fishermen. For the next 40 years his summer cruises took him through the Mediterranean or out into the North Atlantic, even into the Arctic. His days were spent on the bridge and he supervised every net cast and deep dredging operation.

One stormy night near the Azores, the crash of breaking glass in the laboratory brought him and his officers from their bunks to find the bottled specimens from the day's catch washing round the deck as the ship pitched and water poured in through an open porthole. Another year, the ship ran on to a rock off the desolate coast of Svalbard, and the Prince, having put some of his men ashore, remained on board, joking with his officers about the cold bath they would surely be taking before long. However, a high tide saved them from this fate.

Hirondelle was without steam, the work toilsome. She was replaced by the steam yacht *Princesse Alice*, fitted with laboratories and deep dredging and sounding gear. During the Prince's 1901 cruise in the larger *Princesse Alice II* the dredge brought up from the record depth of 6035 metres (19,800 ft) a new species of fish, to be named in honour of the Prince's family, *Grimaldichthys profundissimus*.

In later years, Prince Albert reflected with pride on the new apparatus that he had developed, especially the closing nets for capturing fish in mid-water, and the photometers that measured the penetration of light within the sea. He could look back too on the series of lavishly illustrated volumes reporting the results of his and his colleagues' labours. Prince Albert also responded to the call for a world chart of ocean depths and supervised its production. The first edition of his *General Bathymetric Chart of the Oceans* was published in 1903. In 24 sheets, at a scale of 1:10 million, it was based on 18,400 soundings. A second edition followed in 1912.

Between 1910 and 1913 the famous aquarium, laboratories and museum, clinging to Monaco's rocky cliff, were built and opened for business. They still continue to attract marine biologists and the general public, as places where the results of exploration of the sea, and the history of that exploration, can be shared by all.

Prince Albert of Monaco, on board his ship Princesse Alice II.

The deep-sea fish Grimaldichthys profundissimus, *brought up from the record depth of 6035 metres (19,800 ft).*

14,000 sq km (5400 sq miles) in the Atlantic and one per 26,000 sq km (10,000 sq miles) in the Pacific and Indian Oceans. Even along cable routes, depth measurements obtained by lead and line were so far apart that they gave a misleading impression of a smooth basin occasionally interrupted by peaks or trenches. The first echo-sounders fitted to survey ships in the 1920s gave continuous traverses but their broad beams picked up only large-scale features. In the late 1950s narrow-beam sounders, stabilized against roll, sharpened the image of relief. Multiple narrow-beam sounders, at first restricted to military use, became commercially available from the 1970s.

The echo-sounder fitted on the *Mahabiss* for her expedition to the Red Sea and Indian Ocean in 1933–4 was one of the primitive audible type. Her crew had to endure 25 soundings per minute over most of her 35,400-km (22,000-mile) track through regions neglected by the major 19th-century expeditions. They were rewarded by traces showing systems of parallel ridges and gullies, and an extension to the Carlsberg Ridge – discoveries of major importance scarcely appreciated at the time. What *Mahabiss* had recorded was later seen to be a vital piece in the jigsaw of the Earth's crustal plates whose boundaries are the great ocean ridges and deep trenches. Acoustic sounding eventually revealed the global extent of these, Earth's mightiest physical features.

SEEING FOR OURSELVES

The human body is not adapted to life in the sea. Clumsy swimmers, our underwater vision is out of

1870 Jules Verne published *20,000 Leagues under the Sea*.
1872-6 The *Challenger* expedition covered 110,870 km (68,890 miles) and collected

thousands of samples.
1877-1910 Agassiz researched marine flora and fauna of the Pacific and Caribbean.
1882 US Fish Commission launched *Albatross*,

first dedicated oceanographic research vessel.
1889 Haeckel Plankton Expedition in the Atlantic looked at comparative distribution of this key organism.

Thomas Jones's 'Dry-Earth' globe showed the structural features of the ocean floor as understood at the end of the 19th century.

focus, and our bodies cannot withstand the sudden changes in pressure or the numbing cold. Over the centuries, therefore, numerous diving machines have been invented to enable men to repair underwater structures or to salvage material from wrecks. Such were the forerunners of today's free-ranging apparatus now venturing into the remotest regions of the underwater world.

The first practical diving apparatus consisted of a surface air-pump supplying an open helmet or full suit. Siebe's suits were issued around 1840 to divers working on HMS *Royal George*, wrecked in 1782, and in the 1850s Cabirol's suits were used in the eastern Mediterranean and elsewhere, to discover new sponge-fishing banks. Divers in such tethered suits, drawing their air from the surface, cannot walk far. The first Self-contained Underwater Breathing Apparatus, soon abbreviated to scuba, was invented by William James in 1825. James's diver still wore a full suit and helmet, but carried his air supply in a metal container strapped to his body.

In 1865 Benoît Rouquayrol and Auguste Denayrouze (while constructing breathing apparatus for use in poisonous atmospheres above ground) devised a pressure-regulating valve which delivered air at a balanced pressure and only when the wearer inhaled. Within two years a diving suit equipped

SEEING WITH SOUND

The factors that make it so hard for human beings to see under water – our blurred vision and the distortion of colour – do not affect sound waves. Sound travels through water at a known rate and is now used to image the seabed and objects within the water, such as shoals of fish or other underwater craft. Echo-sounders were developed in the First World War and came into civilian use in the 1920s.

Early models generated their sound pulses as hammer-blows on the ship's hull; these pulses travelled down to the seabed and the return echo was detected by a microphone in the ship. The speed of sound through water being known, the time taken for each pulse to make its double journey was an indication of the depth of water under the keel.

Echo-sounders became standard equipment after the Second World

War, silent ultrasound pulses replacing the tiresome hammer-blows. Beneath the main shipping routes a detailed picture of the sea floor was taking shape, accurate to within a few metres. By 1958 side-scan techniques were adding to the picture. Side-scan sonar transmits pulses sideways from a ship, or from a towed 'fish'. In the latter case, returning echoes are converted to electrical signals and sent up a cable to the usual inboard recorder where the trace builds up line by line into an image resembling a photograph.

At short range the system picks up small ripples in sand, or the texture of bare rock. Long-range systems can image objects 24 km (15 miles) distant and are used for rapid general surveys. Commercial models, available since the 1960s, are widely used for engineering and geological surveys.

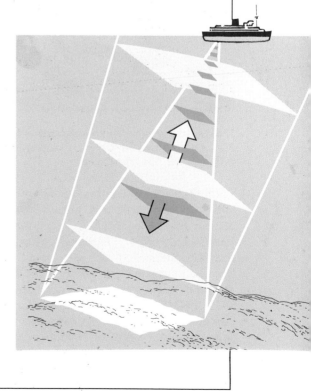

1893-5 Nansen's *Fram* Drift expedition in the Arctic pack-ice.
1895 HMS *Penguin* sounded depths of over 9150 metres (30,000 ft) in the Pacific whilst surveying route of the trans-Pacific cable.
1902 International Commission for the Exploration of the Sea established fishery research in the Atlantic and Baltic.
1903 Prince Albert I of Monaco published his 24-sheet General Bathymetric Chart of the Oceans based on 18,400 soundings.

Divers wearing the Cabirol apparatus were tethered to the surface by an air pipe and a control rope, which limited their freedom to explore.

with this apparatus was in commercial production. This was the outfit that Jules Verne gave his characters in his book *20,000 Leagues under the Sea*, published in 1870. Although Verne's underwater explorers travelled at will, most scuba diving is limited to around 30 metres (100 ft) where sunlight penetrates and the water is not too cold.

In 1943 Jacques-Yves Cousteau and Emile Gagnan fitted the Rouquayrol-Denayrouze demand-valve to high-pressure liquid-air cylinders and this is the scuba used today, along with the neoprene wet-suit which preserves body warmth. In exchange for his freedom, the scuba diver can wear a helmet with telephone, TV camera and lights, supplied by cable from his support ship.

In 1930 the American naturalist William Beebe (1877–1962) climbed into a pressurized steel 'bathysphere' and was lowered 900 metres (3000 ft) into the depths, the first man to look upon the living creatures of this dark and alien world. Just thirty years later USS *Trieste*, a free but non-powered craft, carried Jacques Piccard and Lt Don Walsh down through the icy water into the very bottom of the Marianas Trench. The two men sat in a tiny capsule beneath a huge buoyancy tank. Cast off at 0815 hours, they sank down, anxiously waiting for their echo-sounder to warn them as they neared bottom, which they reached at 1306 hours. Switching on their floodlight, Piccard was amazed to find a flat fish watching him – this creature, did it have eyes only to see phosphorescence? But biologists no longer needed to ask if life could exist in the greatest depth of the ocean; it could! Twenty minutes later, their ballast released, *Trieste* began her slow ascent, breaking the surface at 1656 hours. Their journey of 22 km (14 miles) had taken eight-and-a-half hours.

During the 1930s a US submarine named *Nautilus* failed in an attempt to penetrate below the floating Arctic ice. The first successful crossing was made in 1958 by a nuclear-powered submarine also called *Nautilus*. In the same year, USS *Skate* went under the ice and surfaced near the Pole where an American drift-station had been set up. Submarines from various navies now patrol regularly through the Arctic Ocean, using their sonar to map the basin floor and the undersurface of the ice. These surveys have shown the ocean bed to consist of a series of deep basins divided by ridges. Changes in the thickness of the floating ice cap are seen to reflect past climatic change, and to influence the weather of the northern hemisphere.

Divers working to 50 metres (165 ft) can breathe air; for deep dives oxygen is supplied with other gases. Under increasing pressure, nitrogen dissolves in the diver's blood. The longer and deeper his dive, the more decompression stops he must make during his ascent to allow this gas to leave his body; otherwise he will suffer a painful or possibly fatal attack of 'the bends'. Subject to such precautions, divers at ambient pressure can now work at 300 metres (1000 ft) and will soon be able to go much deeper. One-atmosphere armoured suits and submersibles are able to operate at 650 metres (2100 ft); cable-controlled manned vehicles reach deeper zones.

Trieste's buoyancy tank dwarfs the sphere in which Piccard and Walsh endured their 8½-hour return journey into the ocean's greatest deep.

In 1972–5 Project FAMOUS (French American Mid-Ocean Undersea Study) sent manned submersibles to examine the formation of ocean crust on the Mid-Atlantic Ridge where American and African plates are separating at a rate of 5–7.5 cm (2–3 inches) each year. A bathymetric map constructed from echo-soundings and underwater photographs disclosed promising dive sites and the French craft *Archimède* and *Cyane*, and the USS *Alvin* made 30 dives. FAMOUS demonstrated that

EXPLORING THE OCEAN FROM THE SKY

The analysis of altimeter data sent back by the dedicated ocean satellite SEASAT in 1978 was responsible for the production in 1982 of this fascinating computer image of the surface of the oceans of the world. The computer-generated colours of the surface of the sea show differences in surface elevation, which can be considerable, and also reflect the topography of the ocean floor to a high degree of accuracy.

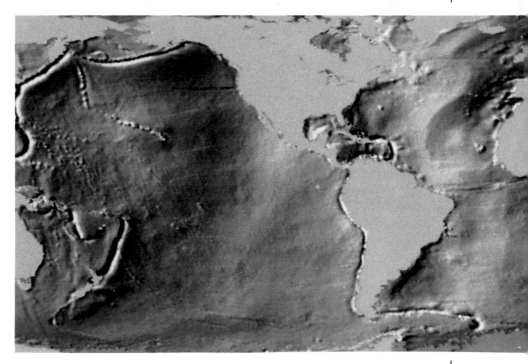

GLORIA EXPLORES THE OCEAN FLOOR

GLORIA is 8 metres (26 ft) long, and bright yellow. Her name is the acronym for Global Long Range Inclined Asdic. Her function is to map the deep sea floor using a unique side-scan sonar technique pioneered by the UK Institute of Oceanographic Sciences, where she was developed. Towed at a speed of 8 knots (nearly 15 km/9 miles per hour), the torpedo-shaped unit emits pulses of sound in a thin fan-shaped beam on either side and at right angles to the ship's track.

The echoes from the sea floor are recorded, and an acoustic image – or 'sonograph' – is built up by successive scans as the ship moves forward. At the same time, a secondary system penetrating the sea-floor sediments to a depth of 1000 metres (3280 ft) provides data on the underlying strata. GLORIA can survey over 20,000 sq km (7750 sq miles) a day and the recorded data are partly processed at sea and printed out on paper-strip charts.

The complete survey system assembles data from echo-sounders, side-scan sonar, seismic and magnetic recorders, performs a computer analysis, and presents it as a mosaic map, accurately located by radio and satellite navigation signals. From these charts, experienced geologists are able to pinpoint areas of specific interest which can then be studied in detail.

The 1982 Law of the Sea Treaty gave maritime nations the right to exploit an Exclusive Economic Zone, or EEZ, 200 nautical miles (370 km, 230 miles) wide, around their coasts. In the early 1990s, GLORIA was engaged on a six-year survey of the United States EEZ. The survey will help the US Government to identify locations of oil and economic minerals, suitable zones for fish or shellfish farming, sites for harnessing thermal energy or for disposing of toxic waste, and optimum routes for pipelines and cables. Here and elsewhere, GLORIA's surveys have revealed a surprising number of seamounts, volcanoes and earthquake zones previously unmarked on hydrographic charts.

valve to high-pressure liquid air cylinders to invent the aqua-lung.
1948 Trials of Piccard's bathyscaphe FNRS-2, a mobile underwater research and

exploration vessel at 1400 metres (4595 ft).
1958 The US nuclear submarine *Nautilus* cruised beneath the North Pole taking sonic readings used to produce the first contour

map of the Arctic Ocean floor.
1960 Piccard and Walsh in USS *Trieste* reached 10,924 metres (35,840 ft) whilst investigating the Marianas Trench.

1960 International Indian Ocean Expedition involved numerous ships from many nations.
1962-4 Cousteau's Conshelf projects established the first undersea work-stations off the French coast and in the Red Sea to enable divers to spend long periods without re-surfacing.
1969 Piccard in the six-man research submarine *Ben Franklin* 30-day investigation of the Gulf Stream.
1972 MacInnes established a manned research station (Sub Igloo) to explore under

the sea-ice of Resolute Bay, Arctic Canada.
1972-5 Project FAMOUS sent manned submersibles to investigate mid-Atlantic Ridge.
1978 NASA's dedicated ocean monitoring satellite SEASAT mapped 95% of ocean surface to a precision of 10 cm/4 inches.
1982 The treaty on the Law of the Sea.
1985-6 Ballard explored the *Titanic* in 3810 metres (12,500 ft) of water using a submersible *Alvin* and its remotely operated vehicle *Argo*.
1987 GLORIA, a compact long-range side-

scan imaging system to be towed behind a ship, came into use to examine the ocean floor.
1988 Sylvia Earle dived to 381 metres (1250 ft) off Hawaii to demonstrate the first open ocean use of a Jim-suit for scientific research.
1989 British oceanographic research vessel RRS *Charles Darwin* completed three-year voyage around the world.
1990-5 World Ocean Circulation Experiment uses data collected from ships and satellites to model climate change.

submersibles could undertake detailed geological mapping of rough deep-sea terrain, for the survey revealed the structure of the ridge, with its 1-km (1.6-mile) deep central rift valley, lava flows, and the transform faults that displaced the rift as the continental plates continued to move apart.

Submersibles diving on the Galápagos rift in 1977 discovered warm mineralized springs surrounded by colonies of filter-feeding bacteria. In 1978–9, near the Gulf of California, came the discovery of hot vents emitting dark plumes of sulphide-rich water at 350°C (662°F) through chimneys built up of silica and metal sulphides. Biologists were amazed to find these vents colonized by tube-worms, clams and other creatures, a veritable oasis of life which flourished despite the total absence of oxygen or sunlight.

Underwater archaeologists descend on ancient harbours and wrecked ships. They swim around the site, surveying and mapping underwater, before carefully excavating the area and recovering the finds. First to be explored were the wrecks of classical antiquity, lying in the clear waters of the Mediterranean, but techniques have advanced to the point where wrecks can now be excavated in the dark and turbid waters around northern shores. Submersibles on military missions have explored wrecked ships and submarines lying far beyond the reach of scuba divers and these are now available for civilian exploration.

Great publicity was given to the discovery of SS *Titanic*, sent to the bottom in 1912 after her hull was ripped open by an iceberg on her maiden voyage and found in 1985 by a Franco-American expedition under Jean-Louis Michel and Robert Ballard. US submersible *Argo*'s sonar first located the wreckage which was then inspected by the crew of USS *Alvin*, who photographed the remains of this great ship

USS Nautilus *returns home in 1958 after a successful crossing under the ice of the Arctic Ocean.*

now scattered some 24,000 metres (78,750 ft) below the surface.

Improbable as it might seem, the oceans can be explored from space. Although the dedicated ocean satellite SEASAT failed within a few months of its launch in 1978, it sent back altimeter data which, when mapped, showed that the surface accurately reflects the topography of the ocean floor. The increase in gravity over submarine ridges draws water away from regions over the trenches, and the resulting difference in sea surface elevation can be as much as 18 metres (60 ft). Meanwhile other satellites are sending back information: their sensors can measure surface temperature; their cameras show sea roughness, movements of icebergs, and the presence of fish and plankton.

A new ocean satellite is planned for the near future and multinational long-running projects continue to investigate the global ocean-atmosphere coupling that controls our climate, the effects of increasing pollution and changes to the ecological systems which include fisheries. Basic surveys continue; the ocean floor is still less well known than the face of the Moon.

Mineral prospectors are searching for oil and metal ores beyond the continental shelf. The so-called manganese nodules occur throughout the oceans and in deeper parts of the Pacific there are vast spreads of nodules containing in addition useful percentages of copper, nickel and cobalt. As yet, the cost of discovery and collection does not justify their exploitation – and the matter of who owns which parts of the seabed is unresolved – but it must only be a matter of time before these and other mineral sources are mined just like those ashore.

What of the future? A review of ocean science to the year 2000 concluded that it was impossible to predict the course of future research in a body as vast and complex as the world ocean, but to use it wisely, we must first understand it.

EXPLORATION TODAY

Many of the chapters in this book have touched on the exploits of modern-day explorers but there has been insufficient space to do justice to their quite significant endeavours and achievements. For those who have yet to receive wide public acclaim, only the passage of time will show how their expeditions have contributed to the exploration of our planet.

For over 30 centuries man has been exploring the earth, extending the limit of his physical horizons, and testing his courage and fortitude through the exploits of a particular breed of individual. Today one-third of the world's land is considered to be a wilderness area where few live and our knowledge of these regions remains scant. Exploration as Livingstone, Columbus or Cook would have defined it has all but ceased except in the ocean depths. We know what is over the horizon and what lies behind the next mountain. But because the map of the world has been constructed it does not mean that there are no new horizons and no new challenges to the explorer and geographer. It is the nature of the challenge that has changed. It is no longer to fill the blanks of wilderness areas; it is to understand how our earth functions and to determine man's role in the world he has now defined.

As we move into the fourth millennium this will be the overriding challenge of the new explorer. And because the task is so complex, it will no longer be the loner pitting his skills against the elements, though, of course, there are those who still aspire to such feats. It will be a multi-disciplinary team of scientists who, with new technological tools, seek to extend the boundaries of our knowledge and understanding, particularly in the oceans, tropical forests, deserts and polar regions.

Understanding the processes that influence the world's desert regions is a priority for field research today. An RGS team at work in the Wahiba Sand Sea, Oman.

The Oxford University Expedition to British Guiana in 1929 was one of the first to take a closer look at the rainforest canopy.

Throughout the world the scale of environmental problems, particularly for developing countries, is immense. Land degradation, deforestation and the loss of biodiversity, poor water quality and supply, rising urban populations and the build-up of hazardous toxic waste chemicals are considered major problems by the majority of leading international agencies including the Food and Agriculture Organization, the United Nations Environment Programme and the International Bank for Reconstruction and Development (World Bank). Many expedition teams now focus their attention on conservation and development issues, and those which collect baseline geographical data in order to monitor change are becoming more numerous. With a rapid increase in the proliferation of Non-Governmental Organizations (NGOs) dedicated to environmental research, conservation and development, there is an urgent need for collaboration between the various international agencies. Sustainable development is the ultimate goal.

THE ENVIRONMENTAL EVEREST

Surprisingly, we are discovering more about our world today than ever before. The new technologies have enabled us to make global observations and measurements which identify the processes that regulate the world and its four main components – the atmosphere, geosphere, biosphere and hydrosphere. The more we explore these processes, the more we learn that each is really one part of a complex whole. This emphasis on studies of the earth as an integrated system makes global environmental research the new age of discovery.

Until 200 years ago man's activities had little impact on the natural evolution of the world. However, today a global population of five billion people has considerable influence on the world's natural processes. Mankind has triggered change by burning coal, oil and gas, removing forests and

Exploring the rainforest by means of the 'field-university' in which international scientists participate. This particular base supported a Sarawak government and RGS expedition to the Gunung Mulu National Park, Sarawak.

damaging the ozone layer in the stratosphere 12 to 55 km (7 to 34 miles) above the earth. As a result carbon dioxide levels have increased by 30 per cent since the Industrial Revolution. Signals of change are being observed all over the world.

It is universally agreed that we need to understand what we are doing to the earth and how we can live in harmony with the environment. Greater knowledge of the intricate ecosystems and natural process is crucial. To speed up further the process of discovery and the collection of data from the field is now a top priority: there is an 'environmental Everest' to climb, but in comparative terms, scientists have yet to reach the 'hobnail boots and tweed jacket' stage of those trying to conquer mountains in the 1920s. There is much to be done and we need all the help possible.

THE FRONTIERS

Only a tiny fraction of the earth is densely inhabited. Tropical forests, the polar regions, hot deserts, underground cave systems and deep oceans are still comparatively unknown ecosystems, although those who have traditionally lived there understand them well. Scientist-explorers differ from their fellow researchers in the choice of localities in which they work: challenging environments with climatic or physical extremes.

Tropical Forests

Naturalists have played a major part in the history of exploration since the mid-19th century, collecting plants and animals from every corner of the globe, and stocking zoos, museums and herbaria with their specimens. But, despite the efforts of the taxonomists, only 1.5 million species have been described to date. No one knows how many species live on the planet but recent studies suggest that the figure may be as high as 50 million. This may mean that some 97 per cent of the world's flora and fauna remain to be described and named. The vast majority will be found either in tropical forests (and most of these are likely to be invertebrates) or in the world's coral reefs. Biodiversity is an important field of research, the scope of which is only just being understood. Some authorities claim that the greatest urgency is here in the forests, since they are being cut down faster than ever before. A United Nations study in the early 1980s suggested that 11–15 million hectares (roughly the size of England) are lost each year. More recent estimates, using satellite imagery, indicate that this figure may have doubled. These forests are home to many tribal peoples, some of them hunter-gatherers who demonstrate the enormous potential of forest products for economic or medicinal use. The study of ethno-biology offers hope for an economic alternative to logging.

Tropical forests exist in three major geographical blocks, lying either side of the equator in South America, South-East Asia and Africa. The Amazon accounts for a third of the world's remaining tropical forest, by far the largest undisturbed area. The heavily logged forests of South-East Asia account for about a quarter, the remainder being in West and Central Africa.

Few men are as respected in the field of tropical forest research as Professor Ghillean Prance, formerly of the New York Botanic Garden, who directed their Projeto Flora Amazonica, which undertook a floristic inventory of the Amazon lasting over ten years. More recently he has been appointed Director of the Royal Botanic Gardens, Kew. He has organized expeditions to Brazil every year since 1965 and has done much to promote the concept that, until it is demonstrated that the Brazilian forest has more to offer than the gold being mined beneath it, then it is unlikely that its destruction will be halted. Prance's hypothesis has met with scepticism in certain quarters but someone who shares his belief in the potential of the forest is Robin Hanbury-Tenison, who has spent 30 years defending tribal peoples in South America and South-East Asia. As one of the founders and president of Survival International, he is convinced that we have much to learn from the people of the forest. Orlando and Claudio Villas-Boas, who have worked with the tribes of the Xingu region since the 1940s, can truly be described as explorers in every sense of the word, penetrating and mapping unknown regions and championing the cause of the people among whom they lived. Similarly, their fellow-countryman, Candido Rondon, mapped vast areas of the region to which he gave his name. His explorations were so extensive that they appeared in a work of 130 volumes.

As the importance of biological diversity for the welfare of mankind is only just beginning to be understood, so too is the need for funds to be invested in better-designed facilities for rainforest field studies. The complexities of the rainforest and the number of specialist taxonomists who are needed to look at its diversity of species have encouraged a pro-liferation of observatories where scientists can base themselves for varying periods of time. These are often financed and administered by major international institutes. In Central America, for example, the Smithsonian Institution runs a station on Barro Colorado Island in Panama, while the Organization for Tropical Studies is responsible for the La Selva Biological Field Station in Costa Rica. The Royal Society has set up a five-year project based in Sabah's Danum Valley; and a site at Korup in Cameroon, originally funded by public subscription, is now run by the World Wide Fund for Nature. More recently the University of Brunei has created a 'University of the Rainforest' in its pristine forests in the Batu Apoi forest reserve of Temburong. These projects attract scientists of international standing and enable longer-term monitoring of the processes occurring within the forest itself rather than just its component parts. The Royal Geographical Society has probably been responsible for putting more scientists into the field to study tropical forest than any other NGO in the past two decades.

A number of countries with significant forest resources are now able to fund their own centres. In Brazil INPA, the Northern Amazon Research Centre, employing over 1000 people, must rank as the biggest. More modest is the Wau Institute of Ecology in Papua New Guinea, which attracts many undergraduate researchers who undertake their first projects there. However, the establishment of centres does not mean that the concept of the expedition has been superseded. Tropical forest expeditions are being organized by a large number of private and public institutes. Their scale and modus operandi vary enormously, from small teams of taxonomists visiting an area for one season, to on-going taxonom-ic research schemes such as the Flora Mesoamericana project, co-ordinated by the Missouri Botanic Garden and the Flora Amazonica project by the New York Botanic Garden. Many will need to raise money from charitable and commercial organizations and in so doing attract publicity for their work. The Royal Entomological Society of London celebrated its centenary by mounting Project Wallace, a year-long expedition to North Sulawesi, in conjunction with the Indonesian Institute of Science. The results focused attention on the need for taxonomy as the basic building block of forest research.

THE MARACÁ PROJECT

Since 1967 the Royal Geographical Society has organized a series of multi-disciplinary expeditions enabling international scientists from many nations to work together to contribute to our knowledge of the world's environment. These modern explorations are carried out by teams rather than by individuals, but the resulting discoveries are no less exciting and important than those of the great explorers of the past.

The Society's Maracá Rainforest Project, led by the Director, Dr John Hemming, carried out a survey of the rich forests of the riverine island of Maracá, an important tropical forest reserve in Brazilian Amazonia, and conducted four related programmes concerned with forest regeneration, soils and hydrology, medical entomology and land development. At the invitation of the Brazilian Environment Secretariat (SEMA) and in collaboration with the National Amazon Research Institute (INPA),

the RGS mounted the largest British project ever to work in Brazilian Amazonia. Maracá is a vast 100,000-hectare (250,000-acre) uninhabited island on the Uraricoera river, a tributary of the Amazon. Its forests, wetlands, patches of savanna and small hills are largely unexplored. The expedition, which was in the field for 13 months and had over 200 members, operated from the purpose-built SEMA research station on the eastern tip of the island. Much research was carried out in the interior of the island and this involved numerous arduous river trips up formidable rapids, mapping the myriad channels and waterfalls, cutting many new trails through the dense vegetation and often steep terrain. The success of this co-operative project led directly to the signing of an accord between British and Brazilian scientists for long-term research in Amazonia.

The Penan are hunter-gatherers whose traditional way of life is threatened by the felling of tropical forests. Yet it is such people who have the expertise to utilize these forests for their long-term sustainability.

In 1985–6 The Malaysian Nature Society organized an expedition to the Endau Rompin area of Peninsular Malaysia, which was a good example of how expeditions, by collecting field data, can contribute to the conservation of an area. Endau Rompin spans more than 80,000 hectares (190,000 acres) on the border between the states of Pahang Darul Makmur and Johor Darul Takzim, considered to be one of the few remaining expanses of lowland rainforest left in Peninsular Malaysia. Known as the Malaysian Heritage and Scientific Expedition, this project, with some 70 scientists and several hundred volunteers, made exciting discoveries and found many new plants that are endemic to the area. They included a beautiful fan palm with remarkable tree-climbing roots. Among new animals were a crab which lives in pitcher plants and a trapdoor spider. Two new flowers from the African violet family were also found. At the conclusion of the expedition the Malaysian state governments concerned proposed to designate Endau Rompin an area for conservation. This was a clear commitment that the region, the future of which had been hotly debated for many years, would be managed and conserved as a wilderness park. Further explorations have since taken place and future expeditions are being planned.

Until recent years the exploration of the forests was limited to the understorey, but reaching and working in the forest canopy is the ultimate frontier. Attempts to reach the canopy were pioneered by the 1929 Oxford University expedition to British Guiana (now Guyana), which first tried rocket-firers and line-throwers in an attempt to get a rope and pulley system erected in the branches of trees 30 metres (100 feet) high, but found the assistance of local climbers with spikes tied to their feet to be more effective. The team included Professor Paul Richards, who went on to write the seminal textbook on tropical forests. Little else was tried until the 1960s when a Dutchman, Adrian Kortlandt, with the help of Zairois pygmies, constructed a platform from which to observe chimpanzees. After that a few scaffolding towers, tree ladders and short walkways were built, but it was Andrew Mitchell, the scientific co-ordinator on Operation Drake and, later, Operation Raleigh, who pioneered lightweight portable walkways on rainforest expeditions, enabling scientists and the young people involved in the project to look out upon a new world.

Balloons and dirigibles have also been tried, but with limited success. New initiatives by the Smithsonian Tropical Research Institute included the erection of a huge tower crane which would raise and lower a module on an 80-m (260-ft) arm, enabling scientists to work anywhere in the canopy within five hectares (12 acres). It was planned to lower the crane into the Panamanian forest by helicopter. Scientists were confident that this would help to conquer tropical ecology's last frontier – the tree canopy where most of the photosynthesis takes place.

Hot Deserts

Many discoveries continue to be made today in the world's desert regions and with good reason. Explorations by teams looking for minerals and oil are joined by those searching for clues to help predict the changing shape of the world's arid regions. Although most arid areas have been visited, knowledge of desert processes remains scant. Today, well-equipped expeditions and work by scientists at permanent research centres all contribute to the understanding of the geography of deserts. There is some urgency in this. One-third of the earth's land surface is arid or semiarid and more than 600 million people make it their home. Furthermore, desertification is considered to be one of the most pressing environmental issues of the past two decades, with an estimated 200,000 sq km (77,000 sq miles) of agricultural land being lost every year.

Desert exploration has attracted many colourful characters, one of the better known being Brigadier Ralph Bagnold. Having developed a special interest in the Sahara long before the Second World War, he undertook a number of expeditions in the Libyan desert between 1926 and 1932, discovering traces of a 6000-year-old civilization depicted in magnificent rock art, which portrayed the Sahara at a time when it was both fertile and inhabited by warring groups. During the war Bagnold went on to head a special fighting unit, known as the Long Range Desert Group, which could carry out unsupported journeys of over 1000 km (600 miles) in this harsh terrain. Its operations resulted in decisive victories over the

Italian invading forces. He later researched sand movements and his text, *Physics of Blown Sand and Desert Dunes*, first published in 1941, remains an important work on the subject.

Wilfred Thesiger's great journeys in the Rub' al Khālī of Arabia and Theodore Monod's Saharan expeditions are two of the more recent significant examples of desert exploration. Both relied on traditional local knowledge and a train of sturdy camels. Michael Asher and Mariantonietta Peru followed this tradition in 1986 and made the first complete west–east crossing of the Sahara by camel. Henri Lhote's earliest French expeditions, in the 1950s, went in search of the Tassilli N'Ajjer rock art.

However, great exploratory desert expeditions are almost a thing of the past. Traditions do persist, mainly carried on by university-based teams under-

THE OMAN WAHIBA SANDS PROJECT

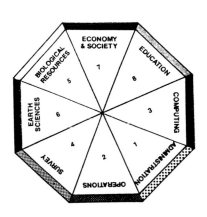

Understanding how plants survive extreme desert conditions will contribute to better management of the world's arid regions, currently home to some 600 million people.

Today, exploring the world is a high-tech team operation using all the technical paraphernalia of the late 20th century. The Oman Wahiba project shows just how exploration has changed in the last 50 years. The Wahiba Sands is a sand sea desert approximately the size of Wales lying in the eastern region of the Sultanate of Oman. An expedition organized by the Royal Geographical Society and the Oman government undertook to make a geographical statement of the Sands as a complete ecosystem, by examining the relationships between the people, the biological resources and the Sands themselves. To accomplish this in just four months a multi-disciplinary team of 43 was chosen. Three reconnaissance visits were arranged beforehand and a temporary 'field university' was built, including a laboratory, computer, medical and radio communication facilities.

The expedition was structured as follows.

1 Administration group (six people)

Responsible for the overall administration of the project.

2 Operations (two people)

An operations director and a transport/communications officer co-ordinated all field logistics, supplies, safety and casualty evacuation procedures. Navigation was assisted by satellite receivers in the Land Rovers. Considerable aerial and ground logistic support was provided by the Omani armed forces.

3 Computing (one person)

A computing officer designed and co-ordinated an IBM field-computing system, incorporating word-processing, database and Geographic Information System facilities.

4 Survey (six people)

A survey team mapped the routes in the Sands and specific areas for the geomorphologists who were studying sand movement and for the botanists who were preparing a vegetation survey.

5 Biological resources (eight people)

This team represented botany, plant physiology, entomology, herpetology, ornithology and mammalogy (large and small). A land use map and a vegetation map were drawn up.

6 Earth sciences (eight people)

A broad-based earth science team looked at the early development of the sands, the original source of the sand, the hydrology and current geomorphology.

7 Economy and society (eight people)

A team of Arabists spent time with the Bedu who live in the Sands to discuss changes taking place caused by increased oil wealth.

8 Education (four people)

Educational material about the Wahiba Sands was prepared for schools in Oman and also for an educational pack about sand deserts and desertification, and how animals and plants survive in this environment.

The above eight teams met regularly to discuss the progress of the project and to co-ordinate their findings, and a 600-page 'rapid assessment document' was presented to the government two weeks after completing the field work. A full international conference describing this pristine sand sea desert was held a year later at the Sultan Qaboos University. It was recommended that the Sands be designated a National Resource Reserve, indicating that they were worthy of special study, pending subsequent classification as either a National Nature Reserve or National Scenic Reserve.

EXPLORING THE PAST

The accounts of the early explorers are often interwoven with myth and legend. Separating fact from fantasy is a hard task for the historian, but two resourceful and accomplished researchers have achieved fame and rightful recognition for testing hypotheses about the practicalities of early exploration by reconstructing early voyages and journeys. In so doing they have explored the past and faced the very same dangers encountered by their predecessors.

The Norwegian anthropologist Thor Heyerdahl first formulated his theories on the origins of the Polynesian race while living on the Pacific island of Fatu Hiva in the Marquesas. He became

Tim Severin on Sohar. *Severin, like Heyerdahl, undertook epic voyages in specially constructed vessels.*

convinced that the Polynesian people had originated in the Americas and constructed a balsa-wood raft, *Kon-Tiki*, to demonstrate that such a journey was possible. He left Callao, the port of Lima in Peru, on 28 April 1947 and, after 101 days adrift, reached the Tuamoto Islands, a distance of 4300 nautical miles (7000km). Archaeological expeditions to the Galápagos Islands in 1953 and Easter Island in 1955 followed and led him to believe that Mediterranean peoples may have reached Central America before Columbus. In 1969 he constructed *Ra*, a papyrus reed boat which broke up just before reaching its destination. *Ra II* was more successful and crossed the Atlantic to Barbados in 57 days. Now convinced that mariners from the ancient world had been able to cross the Atlantic, he went on to build a reed-ship *Tigris* made from reeds collected from the banks of this river and using the skills of Bolivian Indians from Lake Titicaca. In 1977–78 he made the journey in both directions but was horrified by the pollution he saw and burned the boat in protest on landing at Djibouti in northeast Africa.

Tim Severin's major researches have also led him to make some remarkable sea voyages in reconstructed vessels. On his first voyage he and his crew of five sailed an 11-m (36-foot) leather boat in the wake of the 6th-century monk, St Brendan, across the North Atlantic. In *Sohar* he captained an Arab sailing ship retracing the seven voyages of Sinbad the Sailor from Muscat to China. To investigate the stories of Jason and the Argonauts and the search for the golden fleece, *Argo*, a 20-oar Bronze Age-style galley was built and rowed 18,500km (11,500 miles) from the Aegean Sea into the Black Sea, and was later used to follow

(Above) Thor Heyerdahl's Ra II *which crossed the Atlantic in 57 days in 1970 and (inset) Heyerdahl on board his papyrus reed vessel.*

Ulysses' *Odyssey*. He has since traced the route of the First Crusade from Belgium to Jerusalem by horse, and is currently following the courier routes established by the mounted riders of the medieval Mongol empire of Ghengis Khan and his heirs.

Both men share a passion for history and a love of reconstructing past journeys and voyages which through their attention to detail and prolific writings have demonstrated great feats performed by the earliest explorers.

taking earth and life science studies. Scientists like Dr Farouk El-Baz from Egypt use satellite imagery to help explore the geological zones of the Sahara. Expedition teams with efficient four-wheel drive vehicles, satellite navigation and good radios can drive to almost any corner of the great deserts. David Hall's expedition to Niger in 1970 used Land Rovers and camels to take scientists to remote areas in the Aïr Mountains. Tom Sheppard's west–east crossing of the Sahara from Mauritania to Egypt in 1975, using specially adapted Land Rovers, paved the way for others to follow. Today, unfortunately, political disputes are major obstacles.

Desert logistics still require careful planning. Expeditions to the further parts of the Arabian, Australian and Saharan deserts all need support facilities to enable them to operate there. New techniques continue to be pioneered and hot-air balloons, microlights and motor-bikes have all been used to facilitate access to difficult locations.

However, it is the small lightweight all-terrain vehicles (ATVs) that many consider to be the ultimate sand desert vehicle. These motorbike-like ATVs, with three to four balloon tyres at very low pressure, made the first crossing of the Grand Erg Occidental in the early 1980s, driven by a team of teenage riders.

Multi-national expeditions, backed up by satellite, radio and computer technologies, continue to collect information. Reliable vehicles with special sand tyres, balloon jacks, sand ladders and accurate satellite navigators now make it relatively easy to traverse the most difficult of desert terrains. The Royal Geographical Society undertook a multi-disciplinary expedition to the Wahiba Sands in the Sultanate of Oman in 1985–6 and to the Kimberley region in Western Australia, together with the Linnean Society of London, in 1988.

Growing scientific interest in deserts has led to the establishment of several centres of desert research, many of which welcome international scientists. These include the University of Arizona, the Hebrew University of Jerusalem, the Negev Institute of Desert Research in Israel, several universities in the Arabian Gulf such as the Sultan Qaboos University, Oman, and the Kuwait Institute of Science and Technology, the Universidad del Norte in Chile, the Desert Institute, the Turkmenistan Academy of Sciences (USSR), the Desert Department of Academia Sinica and the Central Arid Zone Research Institute, Jodhpur.

In 1977 the UN Conference on Desertification (UNCOD) called for urgent international action to assess the expansion of deserts, a matter of considerable concern since the 1960s and the tragic drought of the Sahel. Looking at specific scientific problems, such as erosion and over-grazing, or studying the potential resources of an area, is now high on the agenda of international desert research. Despite thorough investigations at a regional level, desertification is still little understood globally and effective long-term solutions remain elusive.

The Polar Regions

If you meet anyone within 1500 km (1000 miles) of either Pole, who, unlike the Inuit, Saami and Dene in the north, are visiting the region, there is a good chance they will be a scientist. In the past decades world attention has been focused increasingly on the polar regions as their political, economic, strategic and scientific importance has been recognized. It is now understood that the polar regions have a major influence on the life-support systems of planet earth.

The economic importance of the Arctic for the exploitation of oil, gas, other minerals and bio-resources has come to the attention of many nations, not just those on the Arctic rim. Being geographically situated between the superpowers, with the sea-ice providing cover for nuclear submarines, has given

the Arctic a unique strategic position. The short summer season and the severe climate impose exacting demands on those who wish to operate there. Arctic-rim nations including the United States, Canada and the USSR, as well as a number of non-Arctic countries, have increased significantly their scientific efforts in the Arctic, with a marked trend towards co-operative projects which enable nations with smaller budgets to participate.

Although Britain has no territorial claims in the Arctic, it is a signatory of the Spitsbergen Treaty of 1920. This brought Svalbard under Norwegian sovereignty, but gave right of access and the right to participate in commercial activities, such as mining and hunting, to its signatories, now numbering 40 countries. There are, nevertheless, floating stations which ring the Arctic – based chiefly on the mainland on icebergs and large sea-ice floats within the central Arctic basin. These research stations fulfil both operational (e.g., meteorological) as well as curiosity-driven science. Support is provided by logistic organizations, such as the Polar Continental Shelf project in Canada, and the various national programme operations (e.g., British Antarctic Survey, Australian Antarctic Division) in the South.

In the Antarctic the Scientific Committee on Antarctic Research (SCAR), a constituent body of the International Council of Scientific Unions (ICSU), enables the full international coordination of science programmes. It has been in existence since 1958, following the successful International Geophysical Year. August 1990 saw the founding of the International Arctic Sciences Committee (IASC), which hopes to act in a similar fashion, although it is not yet affiliated to the ICSU. There are other

Virtually all research in Antarctica is carried out from bases established by nations operating under the auspices of the Scientific Committee on Antarctic Research (SCAR).

303

organizations aiding Arctic research such as the Comité Arctique International and the Arctic Ocean Science Board.

A number of international multi-disciplinary projects have been developed in the last decade. YMER-80, for instance, originally planned to commemorate Nordenskiold's voyage through the North-East Passage, was eventually operated from the 8000-ton ice-breaker *Ymer* between northeast Greenland and Franz Josef Land, both to avoid the problems of international boundaries and to tailor the route to the needs of research. The team of 119 international scientists carried out oceanographic, glaciological, geological and biological work. Led by the late Professor Valter Schytt of Sweden, who was second-in-command on the Norwegian–British–Swedish Antarctic Expedition of 1949–52, it did much to renew Swedish interest in the polar sciences and contributed to the Swedish government's willingness to accede to the Antarctic Treaty in 1984.

The multinational Margin Ice Zone Experiment, 1980–87, the successor to AIDJEX, looked at the processes which occur at the margin between fully ice-covered waters and the open ocean of the Bering Sea in the fast Greenland current. The main summer expedition in June–July 1984 involved over 200 scientists from ten nations and included seven ships and eight aircraft. The Coordinated Eastern Arctic Experiment (CEAREX), 1978–89, studied the interactions of internal oceanic waves and eddies with Arctic sea ice. In addition, there are also Arctic components to many of the global monitoring

The global taskforce – international youth committed to contributing to environmental exploration – here supporting Robert Swan's successful walk to the North Pole in 1989.

programmes such as UNESCO's Man and the Biosphere Programme and (in the future) the World Ocean Circulation Experiment and International Geosphere–Biosphere Programme.

The Arctic has long been the training ground for polar work and the tradition of undergraduate adventure and research expeditions continues to the present day through universities and polytechnics, with destinations in Greenland, Iceland and Alaska. Brian Harland, who regularly organized expeditions to Svalbard, went on to establish the independently funded Cambridge Arctic Shelf Programme for geological investigation. Many expeditions put together by young people in their early twenties broke new ground in Greenland, particularly during the 1930s and 1950s. Gino Watkins pioneered the use of Eskimo (Inuit) kayaks for transport amongst the pack-ice but was unfortunately drowned at the age of 32. Paul Vander Molen, also a pioneer of new exploration techniques, used microlight aircraft and kayaks for aerial reconnaissance on his Iceland Breakthrough Expedition. Sadly, he was to die, of leukaemia, in 1985.

The British Schools Exploring Society has been organizing expeditions to the Arctic since its inception in 1932. It was founded by Commander Murray Levick, RN, the surgeon on Scott's last Antarctic expedition. He felt strongly that the dedication of

Scott's team in completing their scientific tasks, coupled with the loyalty and fellowship born of those endeavours, should be an essential experience for young people. He became convinced of the value of exploration in wild places in developing character, leadership and teamwork. This has been borne out by the number of young people participating in expeditions who have gone on to take up jobs in science, commerce and the community. Similar programmes involving students operate in North America and the USSR.

Robert Swan, who had already walked to the South Pole with Roger Mear and Gareth Wood (*In the Footsteps of Scott*), walked to the North Pole in 1989 with an eight-man team. Working in parallel with his 'Icewalk' was an international student expedition of 22 young people from 15 countries. With the support of Environment Canada the students experienced through lectures, scientific studies and outdoor activities the effects of pollution on the fragile Arctic environment. It was hoped that, by actually involving students in Arctic exploration, they would, on their return to their own countries, try to enlist support for Arctic conservation.

Attempts to reach the Poles, feats of human endurance, continue to the present day. The Cook–Peary controversy rages on in the pages of the *National Geographic* and in *Noose of Laurels*, a book by Wally Herbert, who made the first crossing of the Arctic Ocean using dogs in 1968–69. Many national and international groups have taken up the challenge of journeying to the North Pole. In 1990 two Norwegians, Borge Gusland and Erling Kagge, made their way, unsupported, to the Pole in 53 days, having evacuated an injured colleague by aircraft during the second week. Ranulph Fiennes and Mike Stroud got to within 145 km (90 miles) of the Pole. The Soviet Shapiro reached the Pole in 1979, then co-led the first 'manhaul' crossing of the Arctic Ocean via the North Pole in 1988 on the Polar Bridge Expedition. The American Will Steger led the first confirmed, unsupported dog sled expedition to the North Pole in 1986 and the 1990–1 International Trans-Antarctica Expedition which completed the first unmechanized crossing of Antarctica by dog sled. His colleague Richard Weber was to attempt a four-man unsupported manhaul to the North Pole and back in the spring of 1991.

Exploration does attract those who wish to 'live dangerously'. There is an accepted risk when climbing a mountain or trekking in polar regions. The rules can be chosen (and broken) by individuals who are prepared to explore under their own terms, with little regard for the concerns of established thinking, fellow explorers or even the media. This is not new. The journey is more important than the destination and, although there have been many 'last great challenges', usually to attract the media who then act as gatekeepers for the paymasters, there is no doubt that these feats will continue. Those who return inevitably become heroes to inspire and lead others to determine their own quests.

Unlike the Arctic where research is of a disparate nature, international scientific co-operation in the Antarctic is the norm. Although between 1775 and 1947 Antarctic explorers laid claim to various parts of the continent for their own nations, these claims were suspended after the Antarctic Treaty came into force on 23 June 1961. The provisions of the Treaty were intended to ensure that the Antarctic is used only for peaceful purposes, allowing freedom of scientific investigation and co-operation through the workings of SCAR. Twenty-four countries are currently active in Antarctic research, and some 70% of the world's population is represented through the signatories of the Antarctic Treaty.

Many ambitious programmes operate from a network of permanent research bases all over the continent (*see* map on p. 306), and field camps. These are manned by scientists, who stay mainly for a short summer season, and a smaller number who undertake work for a year or longer. The Antarctic is the highest, coldest, windiest, most remote place on earth. Operating in this, the world's last great wilderness, is not an easy task and scientists are making use of helicopters, fixed-wing ski-equipped aircraft, snow scooters and ice-strengthened research

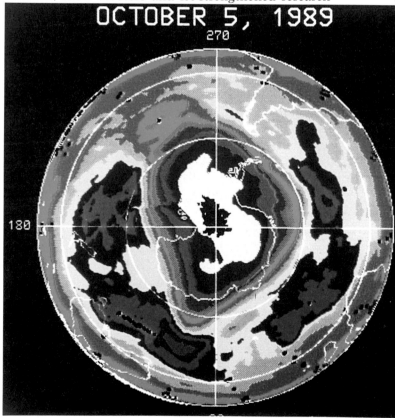

Patient and dedicated fieldwork in the Antarctic by Dr Joe Farman and his team from the British Antarctic Survey first warned the world that there was a severe depletion or 'hole' in the ozone layer, here shown on a satellite map taken in October 1989.

305

INTERNATIONAL TRANS-ANTARCTICA EXPEDITION

On 1 March 1990 an international team completed the first unmechanized crossing of Antarctica by dog sled from west to east. Co-led by the American Will Steger and the Frenchman Dr Jean-Louis Etienne, the six-man team included representatives from six countries (UK, France, Japan, China, the Soviet Union and USA) chosen to reflect peaceful co-operation in Antarctica – the international continent for science.

Enduring some of the harshest conditions on earth, the team and their 42 huskies made the first traverse of the mountainous Antarctic Peninsula in winter. After reaching the South Pole they went on to make the first crossing of the Area of Inaccessibility. Despite the arduous nature of their journey, a wide range of scientific investigations were conducted throughout the 6400-km (4000-mile) overland journey, including the first measurement of ground-level ozone across the continent, and pollutants such as aerosol deposits and DDT concentrations in mosses and lichens.

Their progress was monitored by radio linked to their base, the polar vessel *UAP*, and via Soviet satellite to the outside world. A live computer link with British schools enabled a complementary educational programme to take place. In this way the expedition was used as a means of increasing awareness about the importance of Antarctica and about the issues involved in the renegotiation of the Antarctic Treaty amongst a generation to whom Scott, Amundsen and Shackleton are names from the distant past.

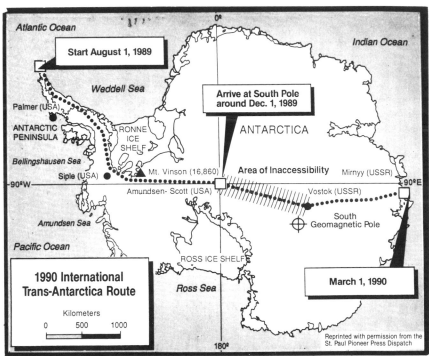

1990 International Trans-Antarctica Route

Kilometers
0   500   1000

Reprinted with permission from the St. Paul Pioneer Press Dispatch

vessels to aid their work, as and when the weather allows. Private expeditions of this nature are unusual in the Antarctic (unlike the Arctic), since there is no regular commercial means of transport.

Apart from its extraordinary natural beauty the frozen continent has many attractions for scientists, not least its influence on the global climate. As a result of the inclination of the earth's rotational axis and the high ice sheet the Antarctic is the main 'heat switch' for our planet, and the transfer of energy, mass and momentum from lower latitudes drives the global atmospheric system. Ice is, of course, a major feature of the region. Some 99% of the continent is buried by permanent ice up to 4.5 km (3 miles) thick. This flows outwards from a central dome and, where it reaches the sea, may form large floating ice shelves, from which massive tabular icebergs break off and float out into the Southern Ocean. Beyond lies the pack ice zone which may in winter cover some 20 million sq km (7 million sq miles).

Antarctic ice yields an archive of environmental information that goes back many hundreds of thousands of years. An analysis of core samples has given new definition to climatic change issues. At the Soviet Vostok Station French and Soviet scientists have recovered a 2000-m (6500-ft) thick core which provides a record extending back into the last ice age but one – 160,000 years ago. The results to date have enabled an intriguing correlation to be established between temperature and atmospheric pollution from man-made industrial processes, mainly in the northern hemisphere, such as heavy metals (lead, zinc, copper), pesticides (DDT) and PCBs. Work, mainly by British scientists, has established the levels and increase in these substances which act as the background and base levels for the way in which mankind is polluting the planet.

The 'hole' or thinning of the ozone layer was first discovered by the British Antarctic Survey and this discovery more than any other during the latter part of the 20th century drew attention to, and triggered a massive response in, the environmental issues of global concern.

A question currently being addressed by many groups in Antarctica stems from the effects of global warming (the 'greenhouse effect') on the stability of the ice sheet and its role in world sea-level change. Such studies form one of the six core programmes being established by SCAR for the Antarctic component of the International Geosphere–Biosphere programme.

The Southern Ocean, despite its extreme cold, is rich in nutrients and serves as a unique laboratory to help understand the biological productivity of the seas. On land, although only one per cent of the surface is not permanently covered by ice, it does support a unique flora and fauna. All who have visited Antarctica are drawn to return. Now tourists, too, are also being attracted to the frozen continent and there is pressure to establish better controls over the preservation of the Antarctic environment as well as continuing its role as a continent for science.

OCEANS AND THE MARINE ENVIRONMENT

The oceans cover two-thirds of the earth's surface, yet are the least-known environment on this planet. More people have been to the moon than have travelled 3000 metres (10,000 feet) beneath the sea. It requires sophisticated equipment and a great deal of money to explore the deep oceans. However, with increased international interest in underwater oil exploration, waste disposal, fisheries and climatic modelling, there is now considerable investment in the exploration of the seas. The possible application for military purposes (submarine and anti-submarine warfare) has also been a guiding factor in underwater research, especially those aspects concerned with acoustics and the nature of sediments. This means that modern-day ocean exploration and research are largely within the domain of national institutions, the universities and naval research establishments. Unlike space exploration there are a number of countries at the forefront of oceanic research including Japan, Canada, Australia, France, Germany and the United States, the last-named having the long-established Woods Hole and Scripps Institutes. In Britain it is the Institute of Oceanographic Sciences which takes the leading role, and plans have recently been announced to fund a new Centre for Deep Sea Oceanography at Southampton University.

US submersible Alvin's *three crewmen explore with the help of sonor apparatus. For close work,* Alvin *has lights and manipulators on the hull.*

At the end of the First World War knowledge of the ocean bottom was limited, with only one sounding per 14,000 sq km (5400 sq miles) for the Atlantic and one per 26,000 sq km (10,000 sq miles) for the Pacific. Then the sonic depth finder was invented by Harvey Hayes of the US Naval Experimental Station in Annapolis, Maryland. By 1923 the first bathymetric chart of the ocean floor was produced by this means from a continuously moving ship and the diverse topography of the ocean floor became apparent, showing undersea mountains, canyons and plains. The US submarine *Nautilus* made the first contour map of the Arctic Ocean floor on its voyage beneath the North Pole in 1958. In the 1960s the US Naval Oceanographic Office developed a multi-beam or swath echo sounder which vastly increased the area which could be covered in a single pass (in the region of one kilometre or half a mile). This, coupled with the development of GLORIA, a long-range sidescan sonar imaging system at the British Institute of Oceanographic Sciences (which can cover 60 km [35 miles] at one sweep), has transformed our ability to view the ocean floor.

Instruments mounted on satellites are capable of monitoring many aspects of the ocean. Radar, photographic and coastal zone colour scanners are all used. Radar altimetry and scatterometry and associated derived systems can measure wind speed and direction at the sea surface, wave height, mean sea level, sea temperature, and tides and currents. Today, much exploration of the sea is carried out from satellites. But, despite the huge advance in satellite technologies, survey ships are still useful for measuring the properties of the water column and providing ground-truth needed as a benchmark for satellite monitoring. Research vessels using increasingly sophisticated unmanned towed vehicles are now available to oceanographers. Existing towed instruments like GLORIA can survey an area the size of Wales in a day. GLORIA was used during the global voyage of the research vessel RRS *Charles Darwin*, 1986–9, to examine the tectonics of the area between Fiji and Tonga in the volcanic 'Ring of Fire' zone of the southwest Pacific.

However, surveys with ship-borne instrumentation are in themselves extremely expensive and, to date, satellites can see events only at the sea surface. Thus, priority is being given in Britain and elsewhere to the development of autosubs, free-ranging unmanned robotic vehicles. Soon there will be a new generation of autosub capable of navigating throughout the deep oceans using satellites both for navigation and for relaying routine data back to base. DOGGIE (Deep Ocean Geological and

Geophysical Instrumented Explorer) will gather data on the sea-bed close to the mother ship. The Deep Ocean Long Path Hydrographic Instrument (DOLPHIN) will use satellite navigation systems to cross oceans, taking physical, chemical and biological measurements.

Underwater vehicles which are devised for serious research have been used for spectacular purposes. Robert Ballard, himself a researcher at Woods Hole Oceanographic Institute, and his team, located and photographed the wreck of the *Titanic* which sank in 3810 m (12,500 feet) of water in the Atlantic. In 1989 *Jason* was used to recover delicate artefacts for marine archaeologists in their excavation of a Roman wreck 800 m (2620 feet) below the ancient sea trade route between Rome and Carthage. Deep-sea Remotely Operated Vehicles (ROVs), such as the French *Cyana* and the American *Alvin*, have been used to explore the hydrothermal vents known as 'Black Smokers' which occur along the mid-ocean ridge. Along the mid-ocean ridges new crust is

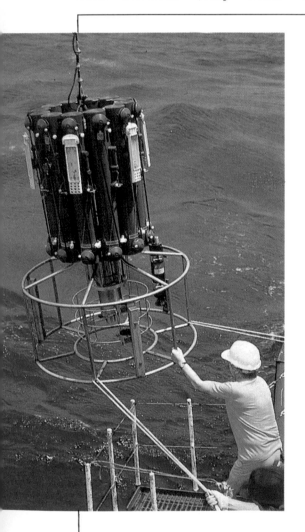

Lowering a CTD (conductivity, temperature, depth) instrument from the Charles Darwin. *The instrument also collects seawater for analysis.*

RRS *CHARLES DARWIN*

In 1831 the British naturalist Charles Darwin embarked on a world voyage on board HMS *Beagle*, which led to his controversial theory of the origin of species. (The Royal Geographical Society assisted Darwin with a small grant in much the same way as it supports university expeditions nowadays.)

More than 150 years later, scientists with the same thirst for adventure and knowledge completed a three-year global expedition in the Royal Research Ship (RRS) *Charles Darwin*. Their aim had been to discover some of the secrets of the world's deep oceans. Owned by the National Environmental Research Council, the *Charles Darwin* combines 20th-century satellite and computer technology with accommodation for 40 scientists and crew.

The seas cover nearly two-thirds of our planet. They have been described as the dynamo of climate and carry 50 per cent of the sun's heat between the tropics and the poles. During a 210,000-km (130,000-mile) circumnavigation of the world, which included visiting some 50 ports, the expedition collected a vast amount of data relating to global weather patterns and monsoon climates, the currents, the temperature and salinity of the oceans and their influence, tectonic plates and 'greenhouse' gases in the sea.

Both the Indian and Pacific Oceans

embrace some of the most geologically active regions in the world, characterized by earthquake zones and arcs of volcanic islands. The project produced unique 'pictures' of the seabed, using sound waves from a powerful device called GLORIA (Geological Long Range Inclined Asdic), developed by NERC's Institute of Oceanographic Sciences. GLORIA is an invaluable aid for scientists trying to piece together the complex jigsaw of plate tectonics. The sonar pictures give a tantalizing view of the rugged underwater terrain, with mountain ranges, volcanoes, deep trenches and meandering, river-like sediment channels. This includes the first image of a complete plate, the 400-km (250-mile) wide Easter Island microplate in the Pacific Ocean.

One of the many discoveries made by the expedition was that salinity was critical in determining changes in density and consequently the pattern of currents in the west equatorial Pacific Ocean. It was thought this might yield clues to one of the world's greatest climatic enigmas – the El Niño ('The Child') phenomenon. El Niño is the term used to describe the warming events that trigger catastrophic floods and storms in the equatorial Pacific. This kind of information is of global importance and underlines the urgency of the need for further exploration of the world's oceans.

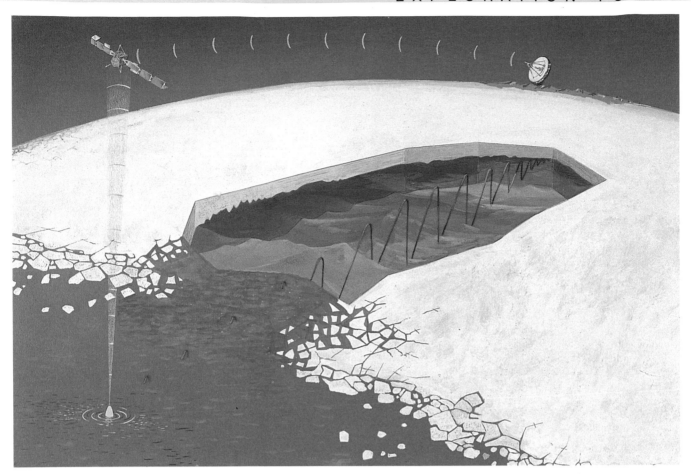

formed and water, which is heated up to 350°C (660°F), surges to the surface as underwater geysers. Manganese, iron, zinc, copper and sulphur are released into the water and deposited. Extraordinary life forms exist here and minerals with commercial potential are likely to be found. Jules Verne never offered a more exciting environment to his explorers.

In shallower waters most seafaring nations operate research ships along the continental shelf in support of fisheries and flood protection, and for oil prospecting, bathometric charting and coastal surveys. Diving is a relatively specialized operation. However, it is the work of Jacques-Yves Cousteau which has brought the fascinating world under the sea to the attention of millions of people. As a result of his practical achievements in the development of the aqualung and his underwater habitats Conshelf I, II and III, together with his inspiring film-making and writing, he more than probably any other individual has stimulated the imagination and encouraged popular and political support for the science of the sea.

The oil and gas industries worldwide have made advances both in civil engineering and in saturation diving techniques which have enabled professional divers to spend prolonged periods at high pressure without having to decompress. Dives under these circumstances at depths greater than 500–600 m (1640–1970 feet) are extremely rare and very carefully supervised. However, by using robots or

A diagram illustrating the work of the Deep Ocean Long Path Hydrographic Instrument (DOLPHIN), which is sending information back from beneath the ice cap.

ROVs oil is now being produced at depths of over 1000 m (3300 feet) and prospecting carried out at depths of 3000 m (9900 feet).

Among those who have attracted considerable media attention for diving feats are the American aquanaut, Sylvia Earle, who has led more than 50 expeditions involving more than 5000 hours underwater. Although she has used many conventional and saturation diving techniques and submersibles, she is best known for research using the Atmospheric Diving Suit (ADS) systems known as JIM, WASP and MANTIS. In 1970 she led the first team of women aquanauts during the Tektite Project in the US Virgin Islands. In 1986 she established the record for solo deep diving at 915 m (3000 feet) using Deep Rover.

The Canadian Joe MacInnes developed a portable diving station made of clear plastic. Using this, sub-igloo divers could rest and conserve air during their time underwater in the Arctic. In 1974 MacInnes became the first scientist to dive beneath the ice at the North Pole. His son, Jeff MacInnes, sailed through the North-East Passage in an 18-foot catamaran in three summer seasons from 1986 to 1988.

America's William Stone and Britain's Rob Palmer

COUSTEAU'S UNDERSEA WORLD

Jacques-Yves Cousteau invented the aqualung in 1943 in association with his colleague, Emile Gagnan, who designed the critical demand valve or regulator which enabled divers to breathe air from gas canisters attached to their backs. By enabling swimmers to move freely underwater his invention proved of considerable strategic importance in occupied France during the Second World War when used to plant submarine mines. However, it was Cousteau's films of sunken wrecks and later the natural history of the marine environment which brought the undersea world to the attention of millions of people. Now he has turned his efforts to campaigning for the conservation of Antarctica.

focused on the phytoplankton, but now it appears that the oceans support a much greater biomass than had previously been understood, with bacteria and fungi living in a massive chemical–bacterial soup. Attention is thus being focused on the organo-chemical properties and the circulation of the amino acids of the sea. Associated with this is the monitoring of contaminants and radioactivity: levels of DDT, tritium, mercury, caesium-137 and oil.

As is so often the case, those who are pushing forward the frontiers of the science of the seas are little known outside the scientific community, but exciting new work is being carried out on plate tectonics by America's Al Vine, Britain's Sir Edward Bullard and Drummond Matthews, and Xavier le Pichon in France. Ocean circulation experiments by Walter Monk, Sverdrup and Karl Wunsch, and the giant computer models established by Jim O'Brien of Florida State University, are adding greatly to the understanding both of the geography and the processes of that last great unknown on earth – the oceans.

THE CHALLENGE OF THE MOUNTAINS

In the pre-war era, mountaineering and exploration were often synonymous, since those wishing to reach high places in distant lands often moved through unknown country, charting new peaks, passes and glaciers. In the mountains of central Asia the surveyors of the Great Trigonometrical Survey needed to climb to gain vantage points from which to take their measurements. Today mountaineering is a major sport in its own right. Although mountaineers may still have to pass through relatively unknown terrain to reach their chosen objective, the emphasis is more often on the climb itself than on exploring the surrounding area. Despite satellite mapping techniques the heights of many mountains are still uncertain and, of the 400 or so peaks between 7000 and 8000 m (23,000 and 26,000 feet) in central Asia, approximately 170 are unclimbed. Eric Shipton and Bill Tilman are often cited as the archetypal explorer–mountaineers, and their maps and climbs in many parts of the world have taken on legendary proportions. Perhaps less well-known but equally remarkable is the partnership of Brad Washburn and his wife, Barbara, which spans more than 50 years. Washburn's combined skills as mountaineer, photographer and cartographer have resulted in some outstanding mapping, using aerial photography, first of Mount McKinley in Alaska and then of the heart of the Grand Canyon. This career has culminated in the remarkable production of a new map of the Mount Everest area at a scale of 1:50,000, which was published in the *National Geographic Magazine* in 1988 and is accurate to ten metres. Further maps at a scale of 1:10,000 will be prepared to help a major

are leading cave divers who have been responsible for pushing the limits of diving technologies while exploring the Blue Holes of the Bahamas. By experimenting with new mixtures of gases and re-breathers they have been able to extend their periods underground while exploring caverns and cave passages.

Scuba diving is now a major sporting activity around the world. REEFWATCH, a project based at the Tropical Marine Unit at the University of York, is harnessing the willingness of sports divers to protect the rich and fragile environment of the world's coral reefs by assisting in a monitoring programme. The publication in three volumes of the IUCN/UNEP Directory, *Coral Reefs of the World*, in 1988 gave clear indication of the areas which require further research.

The biology of the deep oceans has until recently

MOUNTAINEERING: THE CHALLENGES AHEAD

In 1990, when the immense South Face of Lhotse, the world's fourth highest mountain, was finally climbed solo by the Yugoslav Tomo Cesen, mountaineering's most celebrated 'last great problem' was solved. However, the giant 8000-m (26,000-ft) peaks will remain the ultimate testing ground, with untouched challenges like the North Face of Broad Peak or the East Face of Kanchenjunga still to be attempted, and the high-altitude ridge traverses, for instance the traverse of the four 8000-m summits of Kanchenjunga, awaiting oxygenless ascents.

Although most mountains have now been climbed, very little scientific fieldwork has been undertaken above 5000 m (16,500 feet). Measuring distances between mountain peaks to estimate rates of continental shift during the International Karakoram Project in 1980.

geological and glaciological survey of the region.

The geological and geophysical origins of mountains remained relatively unknown until the early 1960s when the theory of plate tectonics was recognized, not as a result of work in the mountain regions, but from evidence taken from the ocean floor. The 'clashing of continents' which formed the great mountain ranges of the world produced some outstanding and complex geological formations, which are now the focus of study. The rate of uplift requires minute measurement, which is being made possible by a range of sophisticated survey instruments from Global Positioning Satellites (GPS) to Electronic Distance Measurers (EDM). Both these techniques were used during the Royal Geographical Society's International Karakoram Project to re-survey Mason's 1913 triangulation in the hope of detecting movement. Mountain building is a very active process and the great mountain ranges cause major disturbances to roads and rivers through landslides, earthquakes and even glacier surges.

Mountains cover about a quarter of the earth's land surface, and about ten per cent of the world's population live in mountainous regions. A further 40 per cent can be said to rely on mountain resources such as water, timber, agricultural products and minerals. Man's impact is greatest in the vegetated zones and, from the Alps to the Andes, the pressures of population growth and, in some areas tourism, are having their effect. In the Hindu-Kush Himalayan region ICIMOD (the International Centre for Integrated Mountain Development), based in Kathmandu, is investigating long-term management strategies for a region which now supports a growing population of 50 million people, and the problems of soil erosion and deforestation are severe.

Brad and Barbara Washburn have spent their lives mapping mountain regions using aerial photography. This photograph was taken in 1940 on the summit of Mount Bertha, Alaska Coast Range.

A NEW PERSPECTIVE:
THE GLOBAL VIEW

Right up to the 1950s scientific exploration tended to be concerned with regionally based phenomena and was carried out by teams of nationally based scientists. To a certain extent this is still true, especially where data collected has a strategic or commercial importance. However, there is now an international realization of the need to monitor man's effect on his planet and never before have environmental issues been so high on the political agenda. Technological advances, especially in the use of satellites, have enabled massive amounts of data to be collected, while advances in computer technology allow this data to be analysed, either in order to identify trends or to develop models which will predict future change.

Global environmental research falls broadly into two categories. Firstly there are those processes which focus on regional phenomena that are repeated worldwide, such as deforestation, desertification, acid rain, soil erosion and changing land use. The second category is concerned with processes which are global in scale such as the water, energy and

At the frontiers of exploration the rainforest canopy and the world's oceans are both great unknowns. New technologies are required to investigate these areas. The Smithsonian Institution pioneered the use of a construction crane to reach the elusive canopy – an alternative to the inflatable 'raft' built by architect Gilles Ebersolt.

bio-geochemical cycles, and has led to the emphasis on studies of the earth as an integrated system. An ability to detect man-induced change in these natural systems is a key line of research, especially in tracking pollution.

Over the past 40 years the International Council of Scientific Unions (ICSU) has led the way by co-ordinating and supporting the efforts of scientists wishing to carry out international environmental research programmes, often in association with UNESCO and the United Nations Environment Programme (UNEP). Such programmes have included the International Geophysical Year, 1957–8, the International Biological Programme, 1964–74, and the programmes of the Scientific Committees on Problems of the Environment (SCOPE). UNESCO's Man and Biosphere Programme, International Hydrological Programme and the Inter-Governmental Oceanographic Commission have included elements concerned with research and education, and with the heightening of political awareness. UNEP's Global Environment Monitoring System (GEMS) has placed the emphasis on data gathering and has established GRID, the Global Resource Information Database, in Geneva.

One of the most significant programmes in terms of global processes is the World Climate Research Programme (WCRP), established in 1979 by the World Meteorological Organization. This incorporates four sub-programmes including the World Ocean Circulation Experiment (WOCE), which examines the role of the oceans as the dynamo of the earth's climate and the exchange of gases between the oceans and the atmosphere, including the ocean's ability to store carbon dioxide gas and drive the planet's winds. Other aspects of the Programme are the International Land Surface Climatology Project (ILSCP), designed to study the interactions between land and atmosphere, the Global Energy and Water Cycle Experiment (GEWEX), and the International Satellite Cloud Climatology Project (ISCCP), which examines the role of clouds in the climate system.

In recent years the lead in developing an integrated concept of research on the global environment has been taken by the United States, principally through NASA (the National Aeronautics and Space Administration) and the National Science Foundation which, through its Earth System Science, is now a key part of the ambitious and much-awaited International Geosphere–Biosphere Programme (IGBP), established in 1987 by ICSU. This will integrate a wide variety of disciplines in order to look at the interactive physical, biological and chemical processes of the earth system and see how they are influenced by mankind.

The IBRD (World Bank), FAO and other UN agencies, conservation bodies such as the International Union for the Conservation of Nature and Natural Resources (IUCN), the International Council for the Preservation of Birds (ICPB) and many individual

A diver hangs in front of a stalagmite grotto over 75,000 years old, deep in the underwater cave system of Lucayan Caverns, Grand Bahama.

countries have launched their own global research initiatives, and so there is need for closer co-operation in the future. These initial steps are paving the way for proper environmental monitoring of the globe and hence more accurate predictions of how we may limit man's harmful effects on his environment.

THE QUEST CONTINUES

However, such international activity should not lead to complacency. From ozone hole to climatic alteration, from deforestation to desertification, there is a wind of change influencing the priorities of explorers. There is an urgent need for new knowledge to help look after planet earth. The complexities of the world present new challenges every day. Fortunately, our innate curiosity about the unknown remains active. Explorers from all over the world are joining in the quest.

During the last decade, however, we have learnt one important lesson. Knowledge on its own is not enough. Putting the pieces of the geographical jigsaw together so that others can understand it is just as important, if we are to contribute to the changing map of mankind. It is the age of global thinking and a new agenda for earth knowledge is

being drawn up. All agree that the windows through which we view the splendours of the world and monitor its changes are far too small. It is no wonder that scientists are balking at having to provide predictions and solutions quickly and with authority. The holistic view of earth and its biosphere has identified huge gaps in our knowledge.

This gives explorers a purpose. There was never any great need to reach the Poles, climb the mountains or penetrate to the depths of the oceans except to satisfy individual curiosity. But today there is a real urgency. The acquisition of global knowledge about our planet's environments, people and places must be a platform for world understanding.

We have seen how busy explorers have been in the past. We owe our current inheritance and knowledge to their previous commitment, bravery and enthusiasm in sharing their discoveries. One feature of such discovery is that the more we explore, the more we learn there is to know – and so to explore. The quest continues. The challenges and opportunities are as great today as when Ulysses took the first explorer's step so long ago.

313

FURTHER READING

EARLY EXPLORATION

R. Carpenter, *Beyond the Pillars of Hercules* (New York, 1966).

M. Cary and E.H. Warmington, *The Ancient Explorers* (London, 1952).

E. Dunn, *The Adventures of Ibn Baṭṭūṭah* (London, 1986)

R. Latham (trans.), *Marco Polo: The Travels* (London, 1962).

O. and E. Lattimore, *Silks, Spices and Empire; Asia seen through the Eyes of its Discoverers* (New York, 1968).

C. Nadal, *l'Inventaire du Monde* (Paris, 1988).

J.H. Parry, *The Discovery of the Sea* (London, 1964).

B. Penrose, *Travel and Discovery in the Renaissance* (Harvard, 1952).

J.R.S. Phillips, *The Medieval Expansion of Europe* (Oxford, 1988).

D. Sinor, *Inner Asia and its Contacts with Medieval Europe* (London, 1977).

A. Stein, *On Ancient Central-Asian Tracks*, ed. by J. Mirsky (Chicago and London, 1964).

ASIA

W. Foster, *England's Quest of Eastern Trade* (London, 1933).

Z. Freeth and H.V.F. Winstone, *Explorers of Arabia* (London, 1978).

P. Hopkirk, *Trespassers on the Roof of the World* (London, 1982). *The Great Game* (London, 1990).

J. Keay, *When Men and Mountains Meet* (London, 1975). *The Gilgit Game* (London, 1977).

K. Mason, *Abode of Snow* (London, 1955).

J. McGregor, *Tibet: a Chronicle of Exploration* (London, 1970).

W. H. Murray, *The Story of Everest* (London, 1953)

Y. Semyonov, *Siberia; its Conquest and Development* (London, 1963).

T. Severin, *The Oriental Adventure: Explorers of the East* (New York and Boston, 1976).

R. Trench, *Arabian Travellers* (London, 1978).

D. Wright, *The English among the Persians* (London, 1977).

AFRICA

E. Axelson (ed.), *South African Explorers* (Oxford, 1964).

N. Broc, *Dictionnaire Illustré des Explorateurs et des Voyageurs Français du 19e siècle en Afrique* (Paris, 1988).

R. Forbath, *The River Congo* (London, 1978).

C. Lloyd, *The Search for the Niger* (London, 1973).

A. Moorhead, *The White Nile* (London, 1962). *The Blue Nile* (London, 1962).

D. Mountfield, *African Exploration* (London, 1976).

M. Perham and J. Simmons (eds.), *An Anthology of Exploration* (London, 1942).

T. Severin, *The African Adventure* (London, 1973).

D. Simpson, *Dark Companions* (London, 1976).

NORTH AMERICA

H.P. Biggar, *The Precursors of Jacques Cartier, 1494-1534* (Ottawa, 1911). *The Voyages of Jacques Cartier* (Ottawa, 1924).

G.W. Brown, *Dictionary of Canadian Biography*, vols 1-5, (Toronto, 1966).

The Champlain Society, *The Narrative of David Thompson* (Toronto, 1934). *The Works of Samuel de Champlain*, 6 vols (Toronto, 1922-34).

W.P. Cumming, R.A. Skelton and D.B. Quinn, *The Discovery of North America* (London, 1971).

R. Cole Harris, *Historical Atlas of Canada*, vol 1 (Toronto, 1987).

D.B. Quinn, *North American Discovery* (New York, 1971). *New American World: A Documentary History of North America to 1612*, 5 vols (New York, 1979).

J.B. Tyrrell, *Samuel Hearne, Journey to the Northern Ocean* (Toronto, 1911).

B. Willson, *The Great Company*. 1667-1871, 2 vols (London, 1900).

CENTRAL AND SOUTH AMERICA

C.R. Boxer, *The Portuguese Seaborne Empire* (London, 1969).

R. Furneaux, *The Amazon* (London, 1969).

E. Goodman, *The Explorers of South America* (New York, 1972). *The Exploration of South America: An Annotated Bibliography* (New York, 1983).

V.W. von Hagan, *South America Called Them* (London, 1949).

E.P. Hanson, *South from the Spanish Main* (New York, 1967).

J. Hemming, *The Conquest of the Incas* (London, 1970). *Red Gold* (London, 1978). *Amazon Frontier* (London, 1987).

A. Moorhead, *Darwin and the Beagle* (London, 1969).

J.H. Parry, *The Spanish Seaborne Empire* (London, 1966).

J. Ure, *Trespassers on the Amazon* (London, 1986).

THE PACIFIC, AUSTRALIA AND NEW ZEALAND

'Australia' in *Cambridge History of the British Empire*, vol 7, ed. by E. Scott (Cambridge, 1952).

G. Badger, *The Explorers of the Pacific* (Kenthurst, 1988).

P. Bellwood, *Man's Conquest of the Pacific* (Auckland, 1978).

J.C. Beaglehole, *The Discovery of New Zealand* (Oxford, 1961). *The Exploration of the Pacific* (London, 1966).

J.H.L. Cumpston, *The Inland Sea and the Great River* (Sydney, 1964). *Exploration of Australia* (New York, 1988).

E. and G. Feeken and O.H.K. Spate, *The Discovery and Exploration of Australia* (Melbourne, 1970).

J. Holland, *Lands of the Southern Cross* (London, 1971).

A. Moorhead, *Cooper's Creek* (London, 1965).

A.G.L. Shaw, *The Story of Australia* (London, 1983).

O.H.K. Spate, *The Spanish Lake* (London, 1979).

THE ARCTIC

R. Amundsen, *The Northwest Passage, being the Record of a Voyage of Exploration in the Ship Gjøa, 1903-7* (London, 1908).

W. Herbert, *The Noose of Laurels: the Discovery of the North Pole* (London, 1989).

A.L.P. Kirwan, *The White Road, a Survey of Polar Exploration* (London, 1959).

C.R. Markham, *The Voyages of William Baffin, 1612-22* (London, 1881).

J. Mirsky, *Northern Conquest: the Story of Arctic Exploration from Earliest Times to the Present* (London, 1949).

G.N. Nares, *Narrative of a Voyage to the Polar Sea during 1875-6 in HM Ships Alert and Discovery* (London, 1878).

U. Nobile, *My Polar Flights: an Account of the Voyages of the Airships Italia and Norge* (London, 1961).

C.J. Phipps, *A Voyage towards the North Pole undertaken by His Majesty's Command, 1773* (Whitby, 1978).

L. Rey (ed.), *Unveiling the Arctic* (Calgary, 1984).

J. Ross, *A Voyage of Discovery, made under the Orders of the Admiralty, in HM Ships Isabella and Alexander, for the purpose of exploring Baffin's Bay, and enquiring into the probability of a North-West Passage ...* (London, 1819).

W. Scoresby, *An Account of the Arctic Region*, 2 vols (Newton Abbott, 1969).

THE ANTARCTIC

J. Bertrand, *Americans in Antarctica, 1775-1948* (New York, 1971).

I. Cameron, *Antarctica, the last Continent* (London and Boston, 1974).

A. Cherry Garrard, *The Worst Journey in the World* (London, 1922).

Sir V. Fuchs, *Of Ice and Men: the Story of the British Antarctic Survey, 1943-73* (Oswestry, 1982).

R.K. Headland, *Chronological List of Antarctic Expeditions ...* (Cambridge, 1989).

F. and E. Jacka (eds.), *Mawson's Antarctic Diaries* (Sydney, 1988).

A.G.E. Jones, *Antarctica observed: who discovered the Antarctic Continent?* (Whitby, 1982)

L.P. Kirwan, *The White Road* (London, 1959).

H.R. Mill, *The Siege of the South Pole* (London, 1905).

L.B. Quartermain, *South to the Pole* (London and Wellington, 1967).

M.J. Ross, *Ross in the Antarctic* (Whitby, 1982).

S.A. Spence, *Antarctic Miscellany: Books, Periodicals and Maps relating to the Discovery and Exploration of Antarctica* (London, 1980).

R.A. Swan, *Australia in the Antarctic* (Melbourne and London, 1961).

P.E. Victor, *Man and the Conquest of the Poles* (London, 1964).

J. Tuzo Wilson, *I.G.Y.: the Year of the New Moons* (New York, 1962)

OCEANOGRAPHY

M. Bramwell (ed.), *The Mitchell Beazley Atlas of the Oceans* (London, 1977).

M. Deacon, *Scientists and the Sea, 1650-1900* (London and New York, 1971).

E. Linklater, *The Voyage of the Challenger* (London, 1972).

A. McConnell, *No Sea too Deep: the History of Oceanographic Instruments* (Bristol, 1982).

L.F. Marsigli, *Histoire Physique de la Mer* (Amsterdam, 1725).

M.F. Maury, *The Physical Geography of the Sea* (London, 1855; Cambridge, Massachussets, 1963).

E.L. Mills, *Biological Oceanography, an Early History, 1870-1960* (Ithaca, New York, 1989).

A.L. Rice (ed.), *Deep Sea Challenge: the John Murray/Mabahiss Expedition to the Indian Ocean, 1933-34* (Paris, 1986).

E.N. Shor, *Scripps Institution of Oceanography: Probing the Oceans, 1936-1976* (San Diego, 1978).

C. Sigsbee, *Deep Sea Sounding and Dredging* (Washington, 1880).

C.W. Thomson, *The Depths of the Sea* (London, 1873).

GENERAL

J.R.L. Anderson, *The Ulysses Factor: the Exploring Instinct in Man* (London, 1970).

J.N.L. Baker, *A History of Geographical Discovery and Exploration* (London, 1931).

C. Bonington, *Quest for Adventure* (London, 1981).

I. Cameron, *To the Farthest Ends of the Earth: the History of the Royal Geographical Society* (London, 1980).

I. Cranfield, *The Challengers: British and Commonwealth Adventure since 1945* (London, 1976).

F. Debenham, *Discovery and Exploration: an Atlas of Man's Journeys into the Unknown* (London, 1960).

H. Delpar (ed.), *The Discoverers: an Encyclopedia of Explorers and Exploration* (New York, 1980)

A History of Discovery and Exploration, 5 vols (London, 1970).

J. Hunt (ed.), *In Search of Adventure: a Study of Opportunities for Adventure and Challenge for Young People* (London, 1989).

D. Middleton, *Victorian Lady Travellers* (London, 1965).

E. Newby, *The Mitchell Beazley World Atlas of Exploration* (London, 1975).

A. Reid, *Discovery and Exploration: a Concise History* (London, 1980).

J. Riverain, *Concise Encyclopedia of Explorations* (London and Paris, 1969).

J. Robinson, *Wayward Women: a Guide to Women Travellers* (Oxford, 1990).

R.A. Skelton, *Explorers' Maps* (London, 1958).

P. Sykes (ed.), *The Story of Exploration and Adventure*, 3 vols (London, 1925).

INDEX

Figures in italics refer to captions.

INDEX